Confidence in Public Speaking

Telecourse Version

Eighth Edition

Paul E. Nelson
North Dakota State University

Judy C. Pearson
North Dakota State University

> **Instructor Manual/Testing Program and**
> **Student Study Guide Available**

Roxbury Publishing Company
Los Angeles, California

Library of Congress Cataloging-in-Publication Data

Nelson, Paul E. (Paul Edward), 1941–
Confidence in public speaking / Paul E. Nelson, Judy C. Pearson.—8th ed., telecourse version.
  p. cm.
Includes bibliographical references and index.
ISBN 1-931719-31-4
  1. Public speaking. I. Pearson, Judy C. II. Title.

PN4129.15.N45 2005
808.5'1—dc22   2004046693
                                                  CIP

Publisher: Claude Teweles
Managing Editor: Dawn VanDercreek
Project Editor: Nina M. Hickey
Copy Editor: Arlyne Lazerson
Proofreaders: Christy Graunke and Ginny Hoffman
Typography: SDS Design, info@sds-design.com
Cover Design: Marnie Kenney

Printed on acid-free paper in the United States of America. This book meets the standards for recycling of the Environmental Protection Agency.

ISBN 1-931719-31-4

The following chapters from the Sixth Edition are not included in the Eighth Edition of *Confidence in Public Speaking* (Telecourse Version): *First Speech, Conquering Speech Anxiety,* and *Group Leadership and Problem Solving.* Instead, these chapters are offered on the Roxbury website as free downloads for adopters of the GPN Telecourse and Roxbury's Eighth Edition of *Confidence in Public Speaking.*

ROXBURY PUBLISHING COMPANY
P.O. Box 491044
Los Angeles, California 90049-9044
Voice: (310) 473-3312 • Fax: (310) 473-4490
E-mail: roxbury@roxbury.net
Website: www.roxbury.net

Contents

Preface

This Eighth Edition of *Confidence in Public Speaking* is the Telecourse Edition that includes seventeen chapters. This book is meant to accompany the *Speaking with Confidence* videos, along with the *Student Study Guide*. The telecourse videos have been professionally produced to clarify concepts covered in these chapters.

Paul E. Nelson and Judy C. Pearson wrote the text along with five contributing authors: Jon A. Hess, University of Minnesota; Candice Thomas, Ohio University; Wendy H. Papa and Michael J. Papa, Ohio University; Gloria J. Galanes, Southwest Missouri State University; and Rita L. Rahoi and Lori A. Byers, who were doctoral students at Ohio University. Heidi Arnold, Rockingham Community College; Ellen R. Cohn, University of Pittsburg; Angela Grupas, St. Louis Community College–Meramec; Lawrence Hungenberg, Youngstown State University; Roxanne O'Connell, Roger Williams University; Mark Orbe, Western Michigan University; Jeanne Porter, De Paul University; and Ann Russell, Bladen Community College, reviewed and critiqued a preliminary draft.

The text recognizes that students today are of all ages, of many origins, and of many orientations. While diversity is a fact of life, the text transcends differences with its relentless focus on ethics in communication.

What Is in Each Chapter?

Chapter 1, Introduction, provides reasons for studying public speaking, reveals why most people fear it, and tells how to overcome the fear. Chapter 2, Listening and Ethics, reviews some misconceptions about listening, reveals some barriers to listening, and then tells how to become an ethical listener. Chapter 3, The Audience, tells why a speaker needs to analyze an audience and how to analyze an audience—including moral choices a speaker needs to make. Chapter 4, The Speaker, focuses on source credibility and the ethical choices facing the speaker. Chapter 5, Selecting a Topic and Purpose, reviews the general purposes of public speaking, some important specific purposes, and the choosing of a topic—including standards of evaluation.

Finding Information, the sixth chapter, gives you some ideas on how to find and how to evaluate information relevant to your speech. Chapter 7, Speech Organization and Outlining, adds structure and arrangement to your repertoire of speaking skills. Chapter 8, The Ethical and Effective Use of Evidence, Proof, and Argument, brings you some of the main ingredients of the body of your speech; it also shows how to avoid fallacies. Chapter 9, Introducing and Concluding Your Speech, unveils the functions of an introduction and the functions of a conclusion in public speaking. Chapter 10, Language in Public Speaking, tells you how to harness the power of words, how to choose them for your speech, and how to use them ethically.

Chapter 11, Delivering Your Speech, covers face, gesture, and movement—the reinforcing motions that accompany your words, thoughts, and emotions. Chapter 12, Presentational Aids, provides valuable insights about when and how to use visualization in your speech. Chapter 13, Informative Speaking, shows how to present information in ways that invite learning and understanding in your audience. Chapter 14, Persuasive and Presentational Speaking, moves into the sphere of influencing others to change, using ethical strategies. Chapter 15, Speeches for Special Occasions, introduces valuable guidelines for giving speeches on a variety of occasions. Chapter 16, Speech Criticism, provides guidelines for criticism of others' speeches and presentations. And finally, Chapter 17, Dynamics of Small Group Discussion, introduces small group communication, the types of small groups, and concepts such as norms, roles, and group culture.

The Eighth Edition of *Confidence in Public Speaking* incorporates updated chapters from both the Sixth and Seventh Editions of the text. Two new boxes have been added to each chapter: "Celebrating Diversity," which provides communication examples from diverse cultural groups, and "On the Web," which provides a list of informative websites. Coverage on the use of Internet search engines and Microsoft PowerPoint® has been added, as well as one or more of the relevant principles from the NCA Credo on Ethics. Also, additional quotes and questions have been added to the beginning of each chapter in order to encourage students to expand their perspective on the importance of effective public speaking.

Who Wrote This Book?

The two primary authors of this text are Paul E. Nelson and Judy C. Pearson, both of North Dakota State University. Paul is Chair of the Department of Communication, and Judy is Associate Dean of the College of Arts, Humanities, and Social Sciences. They co-authored six earlier editions of *Confidence in Public Speaking* and a number of other texts in communication.

Paul Nelson and Judy Pearson are a married couple whose first love was the basic public speaking course. They even met at a Basic Course Conference at Northern Illinois University. They have taught public speaking at Indiana University, the University of Minnesota, the University of Missouri, Michigan State University, Iowa State University, Bradley University, Ohio University, and North Dakota State University.

The following chapters from the Sixth Edition are not included in the Eighth Edition of *Confidence in Public Speaking* (Telecourse Version): *First Speech, Conquering Speech Anxiety,* and *Group Leadership and Problem Solving.* Instead, these chapters are offered on the Roxbury website as free downloads for adopters of the GPN Telecourse and Roxbury's Eighth Edition of *Confidence in Public Speaking.*

Chapter 1

Introduction

Aspire to decency; practice civility.
—Ted Koppel, June 14, 1998,
commencement address at Stanford

Question Outline

 I. Why should you develop public speaking skills?

 II. What are the seven components of the public speaking process?

 III. What is communication apprehension?

 IV. How can you overcome fear of public speaking?

 V. What are six keys to confidence?

 VI. What is the incremental method?

M*arcus Washington, a varsity football player, had seen it all, and he was not afraid of much of anything. Now he found himself required to take a public speaking course. His advisor said he had to take the course because it was required of all education majors. Marcus had faced guys almost twice his size in football, and he had been threatened more than once on the street, but—he thought to himself—he would rather do that all over again than give a speech in front of class.*

❖ ❖ ❖ ❖   ## Why Study Public Speaking?

As you sit in your first class in public speaking, you might wonder why you should bother to learn how to speak in public. After all, public speaking is frightening to many people and, generally, we try to avoid doing things that frighten us. You are not alone. To move you gently into communication studies, this chapter begins with the personal and professional benefits of developing your public speaking skills. You will learn some terms and concepts that will help you understand communication and be given an explanation of how public communication works. Finally, you will learn about the fear of public speaking and how to overcome that fear. You should begin by understanding why you should advance your skills in public speaking.

Two reasons emerge as most important for learning effective public speaking skills. The first is the feeling of satisfaction you will achieve when you become an effective public speaker. The second is the success that is possible when you are the manager, supervisor, or team leader who can inspire and motivate through communication. We believe that people should be able to say what they believe in meetings, in our judicial system, and in our form of government. We know that you may appreciate your public speaking course more after you complete the course: Alumni surveys consistently show that graduates particularly value their public speaking courses (McPherson 1998; Morreale, Osborn, and Pearson 2000).

Personal Advantages

Public speaking holds a number of personal advantages for you. First, you will gain a high degree of self-satisfaction. Second, you will become more confident. Finally, you will become more sensitive. Let us explore each of these personal advantages.

One reason you might want to learn how to speak in public is that this activity can give you a high degree of self-satisfaction. Many of the top public speakers of our time were once timid and afraid of other people. Thousands of people in business take the Dale Carnegie course in public speaking or join Toastmasters, an organization that provides practice in public speaking. A teacher in the Carnegie program once said that he decided to teach that course because he had spent so many years being afraid and inadequate in public situations. He found that conquering his fears and developing his skills were so self-satisfying that he ended up devoting his life to teaching other adults how to become effective public speakers.

We study public speaking for personal and professional gains. (Photo: Roxbury Publishing Co.)

You may also want to study public speaking because you will gain confidence. Indeed, the title of this book highlights this reason. Although people often come to a public speaking course with some fear, most people leave the course feeling very confident about public speaking opportunities. They feel higher in self-esteem and generally more secure in their speaking abilities than before they took the course.

Finally, public speaking will teach you to be more sensitive to other people. You will learn that public speaking is not a one-directional activity in which a speaker simply provides a message. Effective public speaking occurs only when the audience has been carefully considered in both the preparation and delivery of the speech. In the preparation phase, the speaker considers the audience's interest in the topic, their knowledge about it, and how they might be best informed or persuaded on the topic. In the delivery of the speech, the competent communicator responds to the audience's nonverbal and verbal feedback. Public speaking instruction also reminds us of the cultural diversity in our world and encourages us to consider the different ways that people come to know and experience that world.

Professional Gains

Professionally, you will benefit from your study of public speaking for three reasons. First, public speaking can immediately help you achieve your occupational goals by helping you earn higher grades in college. Second, public speaking skills will help you acquire employment. Third, public speaking will help you advance in your career. Let us explore each of these in more detail.

You know that graduating from college will help you attain higher-paying positions than those you would qualify for if you stopped your education at the high school level. According to the 1999 *World Almanac*, the median income of high school graduates was just under $25,000 per year; the median income for people with a college degree or more was over $53,000 (p. 386). You also know that people with higher grades in college are able to compete more favorably for professional occupations than are those with lower grades. Only students with high undergraduate grades are admitted to graduate school, law school, or medical school.

Public speaking can help you earn higher grades in college. A number of skills that are taught in public speaking courses can be applied in other courses. For example, active listening skills that you learn in your public speaking course can be applied in every class you take. Critical listening skills from your public speaking class should be applied to everything you are told. Similarly, you will learn how to organize ideas, a skill that is important in every paper you write. The public speaking class should make you keenly aware of your audience (your boss, your peers, your work team), an awareness that is highly useful in the classroom and in the workplace.

Public speaking skills can help you acquire part-time positions and full-time employment after college. One study in *Communication Education* (Curtis et al. 1989) showed that oral communication was the one factor "most important in helping graduating college students gain employment" (pp. 6–14). The same study listed another communication skill—listening—as second most valuable. Writing skills came in fourth. In public speaking class you will learn how to analyze an audience and respond to them appropriately, which will help you in job interviews. You will learn how to find information that will be useful as you are attempting to learn about employment opportunities. You will learn more about language, which will help you sound educated and aware of the world around you.

Public speaking will also help you advance in your career. According to Brilhart and Galanes (1998): "Numerous studies have found emergent leaders to be high in verbal participation. . ." (p. 172). People who are good at encouraging, explaining, motivating, and articulating goals tend to move up to more responsible positions. One of the authors once taught public speaking to union leaders, none of whom had finished college, and found that they needed no encouragement to learn, because they had already discovered that knowing something and being able to communicate their ideas to others made them more effective union leaders. In an article in the *Black Collegian* (1997), Bardwell argues that the way you "stand out in the crowd" is by being computer literate and by having strong verbal and written communication skills.

✔ Reality Check 1.1 ✔
Importance of Public Speaking Skills

Winsor, Curtis, and Stephens (1997) investigated the factors that help graduates obtain employment. They learned, from one thousand human resource managers, that public speaking, listening, and enthusiasm were among the most important skills.

The Seven Basic Elements of the Public Speaking Process

Some basic elements are present in all public speaking circumstances. They include the source of the message, or the speaker. The audience members, or receivers, must be present. A message—both verbal and nonverbal—is essential. A channel, or means of communication, must be available. Feedback, which includes verbal and nonverbal responses from the audience, must be demonstrated. Noise—any form of interference with the message—usually has a negative influence on the process. Finally, public speaking occurs in a context, or situation.

Source

The **source** is the person who originates the message. Who the sender is makes a difference in who, if anyone, will listen. Consider a person walking down a street in New York City. Blind people clink their cups for contributions, street corner evangelists shake their Bibles in the air, and vendors push everything from bagels to booties. Would you listen to the messages they are sending? Some of the talented singers, dancers, and instrumentalists might attract your attention, but few of the many contenders for your eye and ear would succeed. Sources send messages, but no communication occurs until the source and receiver are conjoined by the messages between them. Often we serve concurrently both as source and as receiver.

Similarly, in the lecture hall, you hear some professors who capture your attention and leave you wishing for more. Occasionally you hear others whose ideas put you to sleep. A source cannot exist without a receiver or a speaker without an audience because both are necessary components of effective communication.

Message

Verbal and nonverbal messages are an integral part of the communication process. What else links the source and the receiver? The **message** is sensed by both the source and the receiver: the facial expressions seen, the words heard, the visual aids illustrated, and the ideas or meanings conveyed simultaneously between source and receiver. **Verbal messages** are the words chosen for the speech. **Nonverbal messages** are the movements, gestures, facial expressions, and paralinguistic features that reinforce or contradict the words, such as pitch or tone of voice that can alter the meaning of the words.

Receiver

The **receiver,** listener, or audience is the individual or group that hears, and hopefully listens to, the message sent by the source. All individuals are unique. Receivers are individuals who have inherited certain characteristics and developed others as a result of their families, friends, and education.

The best speakers can "read" an audience; they can—through analysis or intuition—tell what an audience wants, needs, or responds to. This sort of group empathy allows some speakers to be seen as charismatic: They seem to exhibit what the audience feels.

Even a beginning speaker can learn to see the world through the audience's eyes. Nothing helps more in the classroom than to listen carefully to your classmates' speeches, because every speech will reveal as much about the speaker as it does about the issue being discussed. Few speakers outside the classroom are able to hear everyone in their audience reveal herself or himself through a speech.

Channel

The **channel** is the means of communication, whether it be coaxial cable, fiber optics, microwave, radio, video, or air. In the public speaking classroom, the channel is the air that carries the sound waves from the mouth of the source to the ear of the receiver. The channel might not seem to make very much difference, but messages have decidedly different impacts depending on whether they are heard as a rumor or observed on network news.

Some public speaking students discover the differences among channels when their teacher videotapes their speeches. Watching oneself electronically reproduced is not the same as watching a live performance, because channels are themselves part of the message. As Canadian professor Marshall McLuhan (1967) explained, "The medium is the message."

Feedback

Feedback includes verbal or nonverbal responses by the audience. During a public speech, most of the audience feedback is nonverbal: head nodding, smiling, frowning, giving complete attention, fiddling with a watch. All of this nonverbal feedback is data for the speaker to interpret.

The question-and-answer session is a good example of verbal feedback in which the audience has an opportunity to seek clarification, to verify speaker positions on issues, and to challenge the speaker's arguments. In any case, feedback, like the thermostat on a furnace or an air conditioner, is the speaker's monitoring device that continuously tells if the message is working.

Noise

Another component in the communication process is **noise,** the interference with, or obstacles to, communication. Noise is whatever keeps a source from gaining feedback, a receiver from hearing words or seeing facial expressions, and so on. Noise can be internal or external. During a speech, if you are distracted by the presence of another person whom you find attractive, then you are experiencing internal noise that keeps you from receiving the message. If you are unable to hear the speaker because the door is open and you cannot hear over the hall noise, you are experiencing external noise. "Noise" is a broad term used to classify anything that is an obstacle to communication, whether it be the wanderings of the mind or someone's radio music interfering with the speaker's words.

Situation

Communication occurs in a context called the **situation**—the time, place, and occasion in which the message sending and receiving occurs. The situation can determine what kind of message is appropriate. Only certain kinds of messages and speakers are acceptable at funerals, senate debates, bar mitzvahs, court hearings, and dedications.

In the classroom, the situation is a room of a certain size, containing a number of people who fill a specified number of seats. The physical setting can mean that you can talk almost conversationally or that you must shout to be heard.

The process of communication is the dynamic interrelationship of source, receiver, message, channel, feedback, noise, and situation. None of these components can be isolated, nor do any of them have any meaning without the others. They are what occurs in public speaking. Speakers and audiences influence each other.

For example, let's say that you are trying to convince fellow workers that they should unionize. You argue first that the union will result in higher pay. The audience appears unimpressed, so you argue that the union will bring such benefits as better working conditions. They doze. Finally you argue that the workers will get better medical and dental plans for their families, reducing their out-of-pocket health expenses. This argument gets attentive looks, some questions, and considerable interest. The audience has influenced what the speaker will say.

The speaker conveys a message through words and action, but the audience gives meaning to that message through its own thought processes. An example is the politician who wants to raise the drinking age. Audience members who are younger may hear the message as anti-youth, as having little to do with alcohol consumption. Mothers and fathers might see it as a way to protect their teenage children. Each audience member gives meaning to the message.

Audiences interpret messages; they construct messages of their own from the words they hear, and they carry with them their own rendition of the message and often others' analyses of the same message. A good example of the latter is the concept of "spin." Political campaigns these days are full of "spin doctors"—that is, media experts who try to tell an audience how to interpret a speaker's message. The experts decide for the audience who won a political debate, for example, by telling the audience what they were supposed to derive from the words. The idea of "spin" recognizes the notion that audiences construct their ideas of the message themselves, together with what others tell them the message meant. The process of communication is a transaction between source and receivers that includes mutual influence, the interpretation and construction of meaning, and the development of an individualized message that includes how others respond. What happens when people communicate? A transaction occurs in which speaker and listener simultaneously send, receive, and interpret messages. In public speaking, the temptation is to see the action as predominantly one-way communication: The speaker sends words and actions to the audience. However, in many public speaking situations, the audience influences the speaker through continuous feedback, sometimes with words and actions and sometimes almost subconsciously.

To demonstrate the powerful effect of the audience on the speaker, a teacher challenged his class to influence his behavior. One rule was that the moment he knew they were trying to influence him, the game was over. The class had to figure out what they could do to encourage the behavioral change. After ten weeks the teacher had not caught the class trying to influence him. They had documented, however, that, when the experiment began, the teacher stroked his chin once or twice each class period. They decided that the teacher would feel rewarded if they paid more attention, asked questions, and showed interest. Every time the teacher touched his chin, the class subtly rewarded him with their interest, attention, and questions. By the end of the ten-week course, they had the teacher touching his chin over twenty times each class session—and the teacher did not know it.

The point of this anecdote is that audiences influence speakers. In a political rally, they might do so with the words they yell, the movements and noises they make, or even with the signs they hold. In class, it could be the sight of heads nodding or eyes glazing over. The fact is that speakers influence audiences and audiences influence speakers, and they do so continuously in public speaking situations.

Confidence in Public Speaking

Although you have been speaking all of your life, and perhaps as much as one-third of your waking day, you may still have some apprehension about public speaking. Indeed, many people express some anxiety about public speaking. The *Bruskin Report* identified public speaking as Americans' number one fear (What Are Americans Afraid of?, 1973). Although 41 percent of those surveyed identified public speaking as their greatest fear, only 18 percent listed death. The contrast between these two numbers led comedian Jerry Seinfeld to conclude that if people go to a funeral, they would rather be the one in the casket than the one delivering the eulogy.

A later study that focused on social situations identified public speaking as the second most feared activity. The only situation more fearful was a party with strangers (Goleman 1984). In general, we appear to fear the unknown—the unknown person at a party or the unknown situation of presenting a public speech. Although we cannot help you learn about interacting with strangers at parties, our goal in this book is to help you conquer the unknowns of speaking in front of an audience. We will start by informing you about a commonly felt fear—the fear of public speaking.

Fear of Public Speaking

The fear of speaking in public goes by many different names. Once called "stage fright," a malady most often seen in beginning actors, the phenomenon is now called **communication apprehension.** The term covers many kinds of communication fears in diverse situations: fear of talking on the telephone, fear of face-to-face conversations, fear of talking to authority figures or high-status individuals, fear of speaking to another individual, fear of speaking in a small group, and fear of speaking to an audience.

Why should you learn about communication apprehension? Even the question is controversial. Some teachers of public speaking feel that discussing communication apprehension—even in a textbook—is questionable. Just as medical students think they have many of the diseases they study, students who read about the fear of public speaking may see themselves as more apprehensive than those who do not know about it. However, as more teachers learn about communication apprehension, they support discussion of the problem in textbooks.

You should know about communication apprehension for two reasons. The first is that you need to be able to see the difference between the normal fear most people experience before they give a speech and high communication apprehension, which is a more serious problem. The second reason is that people who are highly apprehensive about communication should receive special treatment for their problem, or they will spend a lifetime handicapped by their fear.

Let us look first at the scope, symptoms, and effects of high communication apprehension. Then we will examine some solutions to this problem (McCroskey 1996; McCroskey, Heisel, and Richmond 2001; Messman and Jones-Corley 2001).

High communication apprehension. About one out of every five persons is communication apprehensive, that is, 20 percent of all college students. Fortunately, that statistic means that four out of every five students, or 80 percent, are not apprehensive. Communication apprehensive people may not appear apprehensive unless they are engaging in a particular type of communication. High communication apprehension seems unrelated to general anxiety and intelligence. You may show no overt signs of anxiety in such activities as playing football, studying, eating, watching television, or walking to class. However, **the high communication apprehensive** (HCA) person has such strong negative feelings about communicating with other people that he or she typically avoids communication, or exhibits considerable fear when communicating. The scope of the communication apprehension problem may not appear large, but millions of people suffer from the fear of communicating.

A speech class can help you overcome normal communication apprehension. (Photo: Roxbury Publishing Co.)

One symptom of communication apprehension is that the HCA person tries to avoid communication situations. Two researchers conducted a study to find out what would happen if HCA students had a choice of an interpersonal communication course or a public speaking course. They found that HCA students overwhelmingly chose the interpersonal communication course. The researchers suspected that students perceived the public speaking course as much more threatening than the interpersonal communication course (Pearson and Yoder 1979). Similarly, in small group communication courses, HCA students tend to be nonparticipants or to repeatedly register for—and drop—the class. HCA students try to avoid participating in the kind of communication that arouses their fears.

What are some other characteristics of HCA people? They choose residence hall rooms at the ends of halls away from other people or housing away from busy streets and playgrounds. HCA people sit away from others or in places where leadership is not expected (near the corner of the table or far from the end where the leader might sit). When HCA people do find themselves in communication situations, they talk less, show less interest in the topic, take fewer risks, and say less about themselves than their classmates do. HCA people may be difficult to get to know. Even when they do find themselves in situations where communication is unavoidable, they discourage talk with signs of disinterest and silence.

The effects of high communication apprehension can be serious. HCA people are rarely perceived as leaders. They are seen as less extroverted, less sociable, less popular, and less competent than their peers (Feingold 1983). They are not perceived as desirable partners for courtship or marriage. They are viewed as less composed, less attractive socially, and less attractive as work partners. Because they communicate reluctantly and seem so uneasy when they do, others perceive HCA people negatively. Therefore, they tend to do poorly in interviews and tend not to get the same quality of jobs as non-apprehensive people do. However, they are not less intellectual, mentally healthy, or physically attractive (Feingold 1983). The consequences of being HCA seem serious enough to encourage us to look next at solutions.

One way to reduce high communication apprehension is to be aware of the malady and to understand that people with anxiety actually prepare differently, and less effectively, than do people without anxiety. Professor John Daly, of the University of Texas at Austin, and three doctoral students showed that anxious people are overly concerned with self and are negative in their assessments. They choose speech topics with which they are less familiar and have less sensitivity to public speaking situations (Daly et al. 1989). A **self-fulfilling prophecy**—behaving as others predict we will—is thus created. Anxious individuals are fearful, they prepare less effectively, and consequently they perform worse, reinforcing their fear of the public speaking situation. This cycle may be broken by more effective preparation.

A second way to resolve feelings of high apprehension is through relaxation. Two techniques are possible. First, you can practice muscle relaxation, which will assist you with the physical symptoms you may have. When you deliberately tense a muscle and then relax it, you experience physical relaxation. You can become less physically tense by consciously tensing and relaxing the muscles in the various parts of your body. You may wish to work systematically from head to toe or in another reasonable progression. You may want to sit in a comfortable position or lie down as you relax your muscles.

The other side of relaxation is stopping those thoughts that make you nervous. When you begin to have anxiety-producing thoughts, you may wish to consciously calm yourself.

Another remedy for high communication apprehension is professional help. The negative feelings about communication in the HCA person have often been developing since childhood. They do not disappear easily. Many schools and colleges have psychologists and counselors who have had professional training in reducing students' fears about speaking in public. Treatments that include training in the control of anxiety appear to be particularly helpful (Worthington et al. 1984). If you think you are among the small percentage of people who have an unusually high fear of public speaking situations, then you may want to talk to your public speaking teacher about the services available to you.

A final possibility for treating the fear of public speaking is called systematic desensitization. **Systematic desensitization** is the repeated exposure to small doses of whatever makes you apprehensive. A public speaking student might be asked over a number of weeks to think of what is frightening (e.g., going to the front of the room to speak) and then to immediately follow the frightening thought with thoughts that relax. This process repeated over time tends to diminish a person's anxiety about communicating.

So far, this section on the fear of public speaking has concentrated on the individual with extreme fear. What about the vast majority of persons who have a normal fear of public speaking? What are the signs of normal fear, and what can you do about reducing this normal fear—or even getting it to work *for* you instead of *against* you?

Normal communication apprehension. Most human beings feel fear when they speak in public. New teachers march into their classes armed with twelve hours' worth of material—just to be sure they will have plenty to say in their one-hour class. Experienced speakers feel anxiety when they face audiences that are new to them. Nearly all of the students in a public speaking class feel anxiety when they think about giving their speeches and when they deliver them.

What are the classic symptoms of communication apprehension for the public speaker? The authors of this book have given hundreds of speeches but still cannot sleep well the night before an important speech—one sign of anxiety or fear. Another common symptom is worry: you can't seem to get the speech out of your mind. You keep thinking about what giving the speech is going to be like, and you keep feeling inadequate for the task. When you actually give the speech, the common symptoms of fear are shaking—usually the hands, knees, and voice; dryness of the mouth—often called cottonmouth; and sweating—usually on the palms of the hands. One wit noted that public speakers suffer so often from dryness of the mouth and wetness of the palms that they should stick their hands in their mouth. For the public speaker, however, fear is no laughing matter. Let us turn from what the normal speaker *feels* to how the normal speaker *behaves* when afraid.

The speaker who is afraid—even with normal fear—tends to avoid eye contact, speak softly, utter vocalized pauses ("Well," "You know," "Mmmmm"), speak too slowly or too quickly, not know what to do with hands or feet, stand as far away from the audience as possible, and place as many obstacles as possible between the speaker and the audience (distance, lecterns, notes). The speaker who is overcoming fear looks at the audience; speaks so all can hear easily; avoids vocalized pauses; speaks at a normal rate; moves body, arms, and feet in ways that do not appear awkward; stands at the usual distance from the audience; and uses the lectern to hold notes instead of as a hiding place.

Now that you understand the fear of public speaking and the way a speaker acts when afraid, you need to understand how you can replace anxiety with confidence.

Celebrating Diversity

Martin Luther King, Jr., in one of his many speeches, affirmed, "Mankind must put an end to war or war will put an end to mankind." King's rhetoric of nonviolence would most likely cause him to be a critic of the current hostilities. Take a position on the situation in the Middle East and draft a short position statement, which you can share in class. How did King celebrate diversity in his statement?

❖ ❖ ❖ ❖   **Reducing Anxiety**

What can you do to reduce the anxiety that you are likely to feel before speaking? What thoughts can you think, what actions can you take, and what precautions can you observe to help you shift attention from yourself to your message and your audience? The following six keys to confidence can help you reduce your fear of public speaking.

Act confident. Actions often change before attitudes do. You may act as if you like others before you really do. You work with people (an action) as you get to know and like them (an attitude). Sometimes you may be more comfortable when you are acting. You dress up for a party and act in a certain way. You decide that you are going to have fun at a social event, and you act that way.

You can use the same strategy when you speak by thinking of public speaking as acting. You can say to yourself, "I am going to act confident when I speak," and then proceed to act confident even if you are not. It is not much different from acting cool on the street, playing the role of the intellectual in class, or pretending you are a sports hero in a game. You are simply acting as if standing in front of the class does not make you nervous.

Know your subject. Your first speech should be about something you know already. It should not require research. In fact, many communication professors ask you to talk about yourself. Whether you speak about some aspect of yourself or some other topic, you will be a better speaker if you choose a subject that you know something about.

When LaMarr Doston had to give his first speech, he could think of nothing about himself that he wanted to share with the class. He was glad that he did not have to do research for the speech, but he was unhappy that he did not know what to say about himself. After two days of worrying about it, LaMarr was in his office at work when he thought of what he was going to say: "I am LaMarr Doston, the Fast Food King."

LaMarr had worked for five different fast-food chains over the years. He worked his way from a mop jockey at one place, to counter server at another, to fry cook at a third, to night shift manager at a fourth, and now morning shift manager at the fifth food chain. LaMarr was good at his work, he was promoted frequently, commended often, and recommended highly. He seemed to know every job there was at a fast-food outlet. He was the Fast Food King.

Care about your subject. Amanda Carroll gave an introductory speech about herself, about being adopted and bi-ethnic. Amanda had one African American parent and one European American parent. As a baby, she was put up for adoption in a small Ohio town and raised by white parents. Amanda was very perceptive. She knew that people wondered about her origins because of her appearance. She satisfied the audience's curiosity and provided an added dimension by discussing the satisfaction of being chosen as a baby by parents who wanted and loved her.

If your teacher wants you to speak on a topic other than yourself, you should make sure that you select one that you know and care about. Do not talk about abortion, gun control, or other politically charged issues unless those are subjects in which you are passionately interested. The more you care about your subject, the more you are going to focus on the message and the audience instead of worrying about yourself.

See your classmates as friends. It would be difficult to think of an audience that is more concerned about your success than your classmates in a beginning public speaking course. Well, maybe your mother or your favorite uncle would care more, but the students in your speech class worry about you so much that if you should falter, they break into a sweat. They care how you do. See them as friends instead of uncaring strangers, and your perceptions will help you feel confident in front of the classroom.

See yourself as successful. If you are an inexperienced speaker, you may need to work at thinking positively about your prospects as a public speaker. You need to think about and then rehearse in your mind how you are going to give your speech. Some people might call this "worrying," but psychologists call it "mental imaging." Whatever you call it, you can use it to help you succeed.

One experiment had basketball players think about and then rehearse in their minds how they were going to improve their play. They were compared to players who actually practiced to improve their play. The players who rehearsed in their minds did as well as those who actually practiced. If it can work in basketball, perhaps it can work in public speaking as well. See yourself as successful and you are more likely to be successful.

Practice toward perfection. Everyone thinks that practicing your speech will be beneficial, especially if you do not practice it so often that it becomes a memorized speech. Practicing your speech under conditions that duplicate your classroom can also help.

Make sure that you take every opportunity to stand in front of the class before class begins and as your classmates leave the room. You need to see what the class looks like before you give your speech. Unless you have been a teacher, a business trainer, or have had other opportunities to speak in front of groups, you do not know what an audience looks like from the front of the room. The more you get accustomed to that sight before you give your speech, the better off you will be.

Most universities have classrooms that are empty some hours during the day or evening. Have some of your friends listen to your speech as you practice it in an empty classroom. The experience will be very close to what you will encounter when you actually give your speech. The practice will make you more confident.

Finally, you should consider some suggestions from students in a beginning speech communication class. When asked what they did to reduce anxiety, they mentioned the following ideas:

Move to the front of the room as if you owned it, and act as if the audience respects you and wants to hear your words.

Begin talking only when you feel comfortable. Look at the people in your audience before you start talking with them—just as you would in a conversation.

Focus on the friendly faces in the audience. Watch the people who smile, who look attentive, and who nod positively. Concentrate on the people who make you feel good about yourself and your speech.

Have your introduction, main points, and conclusion clear in your head. Practice them. The examples and supporting materials come easily when the important points are remembered.

Perhaps this information will come as no surprise to you, but one of the very best ways to overcome anxiety and to increase confidence is to take a course in public speaking. Your teacher will guide you, your classmates will support you, and the assignments will advance your knowledge and skill about public speaking. Teachers and classmates can help you discover your strengths and weaknesses. Repeated performances tend to reduce anxiety. Most of all, you will learn to focus your attention away from your anxiety and toward the message and the audience. You will be so busy communicating your message and monitoring the audience responses that your anxieties will be gone.

This book is called *Confidence in Public Speaking* because gaining confidence goes hand in hand with gaining competence in public speaking. At first you have to overcome fear, learn how to organize thoughts, learn how to best communicate those thoughts to an audience, and learn how to evaluate your effectiveness. Ordinarily, one course in public speaking will not be enough to make you a professional, but it is a necessary first step. This course will be your starting place, enough to give you the tools for future growth. The activities outlined in this book, with careful coaching by your teacher and the encouragement of your classmates, can launch you into a lifetime of increasing satisfaction and effectiveness as a public speaker.

You should be careful not to have unrealistic expectations. Not everyone starts from the same place. People of all ages, cultures, nationalities, and experiences today populate colleges. Some students have been active in the work world for years. Some have come to college with half a lifetime or more of experience; others have very little experience and may even be uncertain about their command of the English language.

This book works on building your confidence, so you can spend a lifetime working on your competence and your effectiveness with audiences in public speaking situations. With education and experience, you will learn more so that you can speak with authority on more subjects. During your lifetime, you will occasionally find issues at work, at home, in your neighborhood, and in social and professional organizations that make you want to speak out and influence other people.

Becoming Confident in Incremental Steps

Whatever your age, you have been speaking for many years. Your speaking may have been confined to talking to relatives, friends, classmates, or co-workers. You may not have had much experience talking to 20, 50, or 100 people at once. However, you can learn to speak to larger groups just as you have already learned to talk with those who are close to you.

The method of learning advocated in this book is the **incremental method,** or learning a complex act by learning in simpler, smaller pieces. An increment is a brief exposure to a larger whole. Taking a step is an increment in learning to walk. Learning to start a computer is a step in learning to use software. Learning to read a stock market report is a step in learning how to invest. In public speaking, the incremental method is based on the idea that a public speech is complex and can best be learned in increments, or small steps, that lead to mastery of a larger whole, the delivery of a complete speech in front of an audience.

This book encourages the notion of learning public speaking gradually in small, easy-to-master steps that give you encouragement as you learn. For example, learning to say a few words about yourself to an audience is easier than researching and speaking on a complex issue. Preparing a one-minute speech is easier than delivering a ten-minute speech. The idea of learning a complex activity gradually, in small steps, is the key to incremental learning.

Along with gradual learning, the incremental method depends heavily on cooperative support from your teacher and classmates. Teachers and fellow students who reinforce what you have done well are inviting you to do more of the same. Their constructive comments about what you could improve show support that is necessary for your development as a speaker.

The incremental method of gaining confidence in public speaking, then, is based on two ideas: gradual mastery of simple steps toward a complex goal and continued reinforcement and support as you learn the steps toward effective public communication.

✔ Reality Check 1.2 ✔
Why Study Communication?

According to Professor Rod Hart (1993), "Communication is the ultimate people-making discipline. . . . Those who teach public address and media studies teach that social power can be shifted and public visions exalted if people learn to think well and speak well." If freedom goes to the articulate, then communication teachers help the voiceless find their voice.

NCA Credo for Communication Ethics

The National Communication Association affirms nine principles of ethical communication. Two of those principles are:

- We advocate truthfulness, accuracy, honesty, and reason as essential to the integrity of communication.
- We endorse freedom of expression, diversity of perspective, and tolerance of dissent to achieve the informed and responsible decision-making fundamental to a civil society.

We will add additional principles in other chapters. For now, explain how these principles may affect your public speaking in this course.

Summary

The goal of this book is to help you become confident in your public speaking. Learning public speaking is important for you because it has personal advantages and allows professional gains. Personally, you may gain self-satisfaction, confidence, and sensitivity. Professionally, you may achieve better academic grades, you may have better chances to acquire employment, and you may have more opportunities to advance your career.

You have already practiced the elements of public speaking, even if you have never delivered a speech. The public speaking process incorporates seven basic elements: the source of a message, the receivers of a message, a message, a channel, feedback, noise, and a situation. Public speaking is a process and a transaction. You are at the beginning of a course that will probably have a positive and lasting effect on the rest of your life.

We encourage you to become a more confident public speaker. Most people fear public speaking, but this fear can be overcome. Speakers become increasingly confident as they become more competent in public speaking. Public speaking skills and competence are best learned in incremental steps. The ideas of incremental learning and positive reinforcement are two important aspects of learning confidence. Incremental learning is instruction in small bites that encourage you to feel good about yourself, your message, and your audience. The idea is to move from simple to complex speeches, shorter to longer time limits, and single to multiple ideas—and to do this gradually over the term.

Communication Narrative 1.1
Fear of Speaking and Speaking Out of Fear

Betty Homans is a thirty-three-year-old housewife who quit community college after her first year, married a guy she met at work, and bore two sons, now 2 and 4. She and her husband were devoting much of his paycheck to the mortgage on a not-very-fancy, aluminum siding house in a middle-class neighborhood. Mostly her life had been unruffled, but now something was happening that really made her mad: The zoning commission was having a public hearing about the possible sale of public land (actually the nice park right across the street from Betty's home) to a private developer. The developer was going to pay a generous price for the land, and the community government needed the money. But the homeowners were horrified at the prospect of losing their park to a developer who planned to build over fifty townhouses on the property. The new development was practically guaranteed to raise taxes, increase crowding, lower housing values, increase traffic, and invite a couple of hundred strangers into the community.

At the zoning commission hearing Betty was among twenty-five residents who had been selected to address the members of the decision-making group. She was the fifth speaker—after two young attorneys and two business owners. Betty was one of only three women in the lineup and appeared to be the youngest speaker as well. Betty had fire in her gut and passion in her heart. She knew that she had to persuade this group of ten older men to see the situation from the point of view of a young mother with children. At first she was so nervous that her tongue felt like a cotton rag; her hands were sweating; and she felt light headed as if she were going to faint. But the prospect of all those people, all those cars, a crowded school seemed like a threat to her two small sons. So she stood there at the microphone and told that commission how their decision would affect current residents and especially the children in the community. Her nervousness diminished sharply after the first minute or so, when she focused on getting her message across to the zoning commission. Out of fear of losing her happy home, Betty overcame, for the moment, her fear of public speaking.

Discuss the following questions with classmates inside or outside of class. How does a strong purpose diminish nervousness? Can you think of any instances when you were so determined that you spoke out fearlessly? Do you think that a young mother has any chance of persuading an official body like a zoning commission to accept her point of view? What arguments would you use if you were in Betty's situation? What perspectives and arguments would be most likely to work with a group like a zoning commission?

Vocabulary

channel The means by which a message is sent: air, paper, microwaves, wire, radio signals, video, and so on.

communication apprehension Communication anxiety in diverse situations: fear of talking on the telephone, fear of face-to-face conversations, fear of talking to authority figures or high-status individuals, fear of speaking to another individual, fear of speaking in a small group, and fear of speaking to an audience.

feedback Verbal and nonverbal messages from an audience to a speaker, who must interpret those messages.

high communication apprehensive (HCA) A person with strong negative feelings about communicating with others, a person who typically avoids communication, or a person who exhibits considerable fear when communicating.

incremental method Learning a complex act (like public speaking) in simple steps over time.

message Sensed by source and receiver, the message includes facial expression, words, visual aids, and meaning exchange.

noise Whatever interferes with the communication process by impeding the transmission or reception of messages.

nonverbal messages The gestures, movements, facial expressions, and nonword sounds (pitch and tone) that communicate meaning.

receiver The one to whom a message is sent.

self-fulfilling prophecy Behaving as others predict we will behave.

situation The context in which communication occurs.

source The originator of the message.

systematic desensitization The repeated exposure to small doses of whatever makes you apprehensive.

verbal messages The words that are chosen for a speech.

Application Exercises

1. Write as many reasons as you can why public speaking could be useful to you now or in the future.

2. Examine the characteristics of public speaking—improved language, organization, preparation, and delivery—and speculate about which of them you believe will cause you the fewest problems.

References

Bardwell, C. B. (1997). Standing out in the crowd. *Black Collegian*, 28, 71–79.

Brilhart, J. K., and Galanes, G. J. (1998). *Effective Group Discussion* (9th ed.). New York: McGraw-Hill.

Curtis, D. B., Winsor, J. L., and Stephens, R. D. (1989). National preferences in business and communication education. *Communication Education*, 58, 6–14.

Daly, J. A., Vangelisti, A. L., Neel, H. L., and Cavanaugh, P. D. (1989). Pre-performance concerns associated with public speaking anxiety. *Communication Quarterly*, 37, 39–53.

Feingold, A. (1983). Correlates of public speaking attitude. *The Journal of Social Psychology,* 120, 285–86.

Goleman, D. (1984, December 18). Social anxiety: New focus leads to insights and therapy. *New York Times,* p. C1.

Hart, R. P. (1993). Why communication? Why education? Toward a politics of teaching. *Communication Education,* 42, 97–105.

McCroskey, J. C. (1996). *An Introduction to Rhetorical Communication.* Englewood Cliffs, NJ: Prentice Hall.

McCroskey, J. C., Heisel, A D., and Richmond, V. P. (2001). Eysenck's Big Three and communication traits: Three correlational studies. *Communication Monographs,* 68, 360–366.

McLuhan, M., and Fiore, Q. (1967). *The Medium Is the Message.* New York: Bantam Books.

McPherson, B. (1998). Student perceptions about business communication in their careers. *Business Communication Quarterly,* 61, 68–79.

Messman, S. J., and Jones-Corley, J. (2001). Effects of communication environment, immediacy, and communication apprehension on cognitive and affective learning. *Communication Monographs,* 68, 184–200.

Morreale, S. P., Osborn, M. M., and Pearson, J. C. (2000). The centrality of the communication discipline. *Journal of the Association for Communication Administrators,* 29, 1–25.

Pearson, J. C., and Yoder, D. D. (1979). Public speaking or interpersonal communication: The perspective of the high communication apprehensive student. East Lansing, MI: National Center for Research on Teacher Learning. (ERIC Document Reproduction Service No. ED 173 870)

Peterson, M. S. (1997). Personnel interviewers' perceptions of the importance and adequacy of applicants' communication skills. *Communication Education,* 46, 287–291.

What are Americans afraid of? (July 1973). *The Bruskin Report,* 53.

Winsor, J. L., Curtis, D. B., and Stephens, R. D. (1997). National preferences in business and communication education. *Journal of the Association for Communication Administration,* 3, 170–179.

The World Almanac and Book of Facts 1999, 2004.

Worthington, E. L., Tipton, R. M., Comley, J. S., Richards, T., and Janke, R. H. (1984). Speech and coping skills: Training and paradox as treatment for college students anxious about public speaking. *Perceptual and Motor Skills,* 59, 394.

Chapter 2

Listening and Ethics

The one lesson I have learned is that there is no substitute for paying attention.

—Diane Sawyer (2004)

Question Outline

I. What are three false assumptions about listening?

II. What are four activities involved in the process of listening?

III. What are some barriers to effective listening?

IV. How can you improve your informative listening?

V. How can you improve your evaluative listening?

VI. How can you become an ethical listener?

Sarah Parker saw herself as more of a talker than a listener. After the first two brief presentations in class, she found herself enjoying the attention she received as a speaker. The difficult part for her was sitting through all the speeches by other people. For every speech she delivered, she listened to twenty-five. Instead of calling this class public speaking, she thought, they should have called it "public listening." She had to admit, though, that time went faster when she wrote down what the other speakers said and learned from what the other speakers did best. Also, she found that her friends noticed that she was better about listening to them instead of always dominating the conversation.

The Importance of Listening

Just as Sarah did, you will develop confidence as a speaker *and* improve your listening skills in this course. Both speaking and listening are essential components of public speaking, and both are seen as top skills necessary in gaining a job (Curtis, Winsor, and Stephens 1989). In the past, public speaking focused more on speakers and the creation and transmission of messages rather than on listeners and their active participation in the process (Fitch-Hauser and Hughes 1988). Recently, the role of listeners in communication has gained more importance (Morreale, Osborn, and Pearson 2000). Indeed, current experts believe that listening is essential to the development of citizenship and a civil society (Welton 2002).

You learn more by listening than by talking. Every speech you hear and every question asked and answered provides information about the people who will become your audience. Your serving as an audience member during your classmates' speeches provides you with an opportunity to analyze their choice of topics, the way they think, and the approaches they use. In short, being an audience member invites you to analyze your audience throughout the course. So you have a choice: You could be passive and distracted and learn little during other people's speeches or you could be active and attentive and learn much from other people's speeches.

You may not have thought of this fact when you enrolled in a public speaking class, but you will listen to many speeches for every speech you deliver. You will hear between 100 and 200 speeches in your public speaking course. You will learn ways to evaluate speeches, ways to improve your own speeches. You will learn methods of argument that you can employ.

Listening is also important beyond the classroom. Organizations frequently specify listening as a key communication skill for employees. Organizational leaders and personnel directors view good listening skills as a vital part of employee competence (Wolvin and Coakley 1996). In one study, business managers who were asked to rank the skills that were most important for them identified listening as most important (Gronbeck 1981).

✔ Reality Check 2.1 ✔
Communication Skills Valued by Employers

Winsor, Curtis, and Stephens (1997) surveyed 1000 human resource managers and found ". . . that the most frequent factors deemed important in aiding graduating college students obtain employment are basic oral and written communication skills." In addition, "Three of the top four—public speaking, listening, and enthusiasm—largely are oral communication skills."

On the Web

Go to *http://www.americanrhetoric.com/speechbank.htm* or a similar site where famous speeches are available in an audio format. Listen to one of the speeches with a classmate, roommate, or friend. Each of you should take notes on the speech and then compare your perceptions of the speaker's purpose and main points.

Three Myths About Listening ❖ ❖ ❖ ❖

Perhaps you think that you are already an effective listener. Most of us do. You might think that listening, unlike speaking, is something that cannot be taught. You might even think that, because nothing is wrong with your hearing, you are good at listening. If you think any of these things, you subscribe to some common myths about listening. Your effort to understand listening begins with disproving some myths that many people believe about listening.

Assuming That You Listen Well

If you ask a classmate if he or she listens well, the likely answer is yes. Virtually everyone from the kindergarten student to the college sophomore to the graduate professor believes that he or she listens effectively to other people. However, this assumption is not supported by research. Nichols and his associates conducted research at the University of Minnesota on thousands of students and hundreds of business and professional people. They found that people remember only half of what they hear immediately after a message, and only 25 percent of what they heard when tested two months later (Nichols and Stevens 1957). You may be comforted by these statistics the next time you do poorly on a final exam. After all, the average person remembers only 25 percent of what he or she heard earlier in the term. Nichols' research and your own experience in recalling information demonstrate that the assumption that you listen well is possibly inaccurate.

Assuming That You Cannot Be Taught to Listen Better

If you feel you are already an effective listener, you probably do not attempt to identify ways to improve your listening. On the other hand, if you feel you are not an effective listener, you may have resigned yourself to being inadequate in this area. One of the reasons you may fail to improve your listening is that there are few opportunities available. Today you can use the sources available on the Internet; unfortunately, most of them charge for their services (Eastment 2004).

Most of your communication time is spent listening, followed in order by speaking, reading, and writing (Markgraf 1957). Curiously, you probably spend an inverse proportion of time in required classes studying these subjects. You probably spent much of your time in grade school, junior high, and high school studying the two communication skills that we actually use the least: reading and writing. However, you have

Listen to learn from other speakers who become the audience for your speech. (Photo: Randall Reeder)

probably never taken a course at any grade level on the communication skill you use the most: listening. Because of the lack of course work and study in listening, we incorrectly assume that listening is a communication skill that cannot be learned.

Assuming That Listening and Hearing Are the Same Thing

How many times have you said, or has someone said to you, "What do you mean you don't know? I told you!"? People assume that if they say something to someone, the person is listening. For instance, you know how frequently you daydream while hearing a lecturer, how often you are distracted by the person next to you as you hear a student speaker, and how regularly you spend time planning your afternoon while sitting in morning classes. In each case, you can hear the speaker, but you may not do well on an examination of the material. Passing a hearing test is not a guarantee that you are listening effectively.

Hearing and listening are separate activities. Hearing is a physical function you are able to perform unless you suffer from physiological damage or cerebral dysfunction; **hearing** is the reception of sound waves picked up by the ear and sent to the brain. On the other hand, **listening** is a selective activity that involves the reception, selection, organization, and interpretation of aural stimuli. Listening is far more complex than hearing. Indeed, it involves our other senses as well. Phillip Emmert believes that listening is not complete unless individuals process nonverbal, as well as verbal, stimuli (Emmert 1991). Charles Roberts adds, "Listeners generally do not 'listen' with just their ears" (Roberts 1988).

✔ Reality Check 2.2 ✔
What Managers Expect

Maes, Weldy, and Icenogle (1997) tried to discover from a manager's point of view which communication competencies are most important. They report:

> Results of two studies show that oral communication is the most important competency for college graduates entering the workforce. Oral skills most important for entry level graduates are following instructions, listening, conversing, and giving feedback.

Handling customer complaints in small companies and using meeting skills in large companies were mentioned as special contexts in which communication skills were applied. Notice that listening, selecting, and interpreting all loom large as expected communication competencies in the workforce.

The Process of Listening

Listening involves a number of activities. Most of us are unaware of the different processes involved in listening because they occur quickly and almost simultaneously. The four activities that we will consider here are receiving, selecting, organizing, and interpreting. Listening and speaking are bound to each other like freedom and democracy: "Freedom is when the people can speak; democracy is when the government listens" (Farrugia 1999).

Receiving

Television broadcaster Diane Sawyer is reported to have said, "I think the one lesson I have learned is that there is no substitute for paying attention." Before the listening process can begin, we must receive sounds. Hearing is a requisite first step in listening. Sound waves travel through the air from speakers to listeners when we communicate in face-to-face situations. They are transmitted electronically when we are talking on the telephone, watching television, or listening to our favorite music tape or CD.

We may ready ourselves to receive sounds by going through any number of behaviors. You might turn the volume of your radio or television down low, close the door to your room, and even turn off the lights before making an important phone call, so you are not distracted by other sights and sounds. You might put your glasses on, or take your glasses off, in face-to-face interaction in order to receive sounds more efficiently. Some people rely on their other senses in order to adequately "hear" messages, while others tune their other senses out when they are trying to listen. As one person stated, "The time to stop talking is when the other person nods his head affirmatively—but says nothing."

Selecting

Once we have received sounds, we select those we will attend to and those we will ignore. None of us listens to all of the sounds in the environment. For example, if you walked to class, you were probably bombarded with a variety of sounds. You may have paid attention to the sound of your name being called behind you but ignored a construction worker who was noisily drilling a hole in the concrete.

Selection may be divided into two categories: selective attention and selective retention. **Selective attention** means we focus on certain cues and ignore others. In class, you may ignore what a man sitting in the front row has to say but listen carefully to the whispered comments made by your good friend seated next to you. You might not hear what someone is saying to you directly in a public speech because you are distracted by noisy water pipes.

Selective retention means that we categorize, store, and retrieve certain information, but we discard other information. If you played the car radio on your way to class, try to recall one of the songs, commercials, or public-service announcements you heard. Although your attention may have been drawn to a particular song or message this morning, you may find that you cannot remember anything you heard. Your mind has disposed of the sounds you heard on the radio. You may recall a criticism your date offered last night but have forgotten that your mother made a similar comment two days ago.

Organizing

Have you ever listened to a radio broadcast in another language? If you listened long enough, you may have begun to "understand" what the speaker was saying. You listened for common sounds and tried to arrange them into some meaningful message. Although the words were generally unknown, you attempted to place them into familiar patterns. We do the same thing in a variety of ways when we are listening to our own language. For example, we use the principle of **figure and ground,** which means that we identify some words, phrases, or sentences as more important and others as less important. The more important words become the figure, or focus, and the less important words become the ground or background. If a speaker rambles on, we try to identify what his most important points are and discard the rest.

We also use the principle of closure in our communicative experiences. **Closure** is an organizing method in which we fill in information that does not exist. Some people habitually omit the subject of the sentence, particularly when it is the words "I am" or "I was." So, for example, if a speaker says, "Wondering about another approach," we fill in "I am" at the beginning of the sentence. By supplying the missing pieces of the incomplete thought, we have clarified the speaker's message.

Proximity is another way that we organize the messages we hear. If a speaker tells you that a terrible disease looms on the horizon and then begins to speak about allergic reactions to drugs, you assume that the disease and the drugs are related in some way. **Proximity** means that we group two or more things that happen to be close to each other.

Similarity is a final method we use to organize messages. **Similarity** means that we group words or phrases together because they are similar in sound, beginning letter, or final syllable. Effective speakers will try to use alliteration—two or more words having the same initial sound—for their main points or for their subpoints. The textbook title *Interpersonal Communication: Concepts, Components, and Contexts* tells the reader that the book will be grouped in three sections that are alliterated with similarity in beginning sound. Another textbook, *Understanding and Sharing,* uses the common "ing" ending in its title. When listeners hear words that sound the same, they assume they are parallel in importance. They tend to view them as having some relationship to each other and they tend to remember them longer than words that do not have a common sound. Similarity can likewise be useful for the speaker when organizing and outlining a public speech.

Interpreting

Interpreting occurs when you receive, select, and organize a set of sounds and then blend them with your own understanding. For instance, if you are a staunch Democrat and you listen to a message by the Republican governor of your state, you may interpret her meaning differently than your roommate, who is a Young Republican. The message was identical, but your personal attitudes, values, and beliefs created a different mix of understanding. A simpler example occurs when someone uses a word out of context and you have great difficulty understanding what he or she is attempting to convey to you. For instance, if someone asks you for a "bib," you may interpret the word to mean a bibliography if you are in a classroom setting but as an item for a baby to wear if you are with a family in a restaurant. If one of your married friends who has children asks if he has left a bib at your apartment, you might have difficulty figuring out what he is specifically asking about.

The interpretative phase of listening is arduous. One person noted, "Easy listening exists only on the radio" (*http://www.listen.org*).

Barriers to Effective Listening

After reading the previous section, you may no longer believe that you naturally listen well, that you cannot learn listening skills, and that your hearing ability is the same as your listening ability. What are some of the factors that interfere with your ability to listen? Have you ever sat in a lecture and smiled when the lecturer made a joke, nodded when he or she sought affirmation, established eye contact with the lecturer, and still not remembered a single thing the lecturer said?

Our motivation to listen has not been widely studied, but we know that it is critical to our listening ability. Robert Bostrom (1990) observed that while researchers have spent a good deal of time trying to understand why people are motivated to talk, they have not shown the same interest in discovering why they are inspired to listen. Brian Spitzberg and Bill Cupach (1984) have argued that competence in communication is not possible without motivation. Motivation is equally important for the listener and the speaker.

Motivation is the key to effective listening. When we are not motivated to listen, we allow barriers to interfere. Here, we discuss four barriers to effective listening: faking attention, prejudging the speaker, prejudging the speech, and yielding to distractions. We begin by discussing a topic familiar to most college students: faking attention.

Listening requires receiving, selecting, organizing, and interpreting of information. (Photo: Charles Kuo/Daily Bruin)

Faking Attention

Adler and Towne (1999) tell an often-repeated story of Paul Cameron, a Wayne State University assistant professor, whose nine-week Introduction to Psychology class with 85 sophomores became part of an experiment. At random intervals during the course a gun was fired, often when Cameron was in mid-sentence. Immediately after the noise, the students were to write down what they were thinking at the moment. The results:

- 20 percent of the students were thinking about sex;

- 20 percent were remembering something;

- 20 percent were actually listening to the lecture, 12 percent actively;

- and the remainder were worrying, daydreaming, thinking about lunch, and other matters. (p. 289)

Students learn how to fake attention. They have had years of practice. You may use this strategy in situations in which the most acceptable social behavior is paying attention. This strategy is one you may use in classes, at social gatherings, and in "listening" to fellow students' speeches. You undoubtedly use this strategy when you are bombarded with more messages than you want to hear. Consequently, you may practice the appropriate nonverbal behavior—eye contact, attentive appearance, and apparent note taking—when you are actually wondering if the speaker is as tired as you are as you scribble pictures in your notebook. Faking attention is both a result and a cause of poor listening.

Three additional barriers to effective listening are prejudging the speaker, prejudging the speech, and yielding to distractions. Each of these barriers, in turn, has subtypes that may be of interest if you wish to improve your listening skills.

Prejudging the Speaker

We all make judgments about speakers before they say a word. You might dismiss a speaker because of attire, posture, stance, or unattractiveness.

Researchers have found that the speaker's gender appears to be an important variable in judgment. For instance, when male and female student speakers are given the same grade, the male speakers receive fewer positive comments than do the female speakers (Pearson 1979; Sprague 1971). Female evaluators give men higher evaluations than women (Pfister 1955), and male evaluators tend to grade women higher than men (Pfister 1955). In addition, one of the authors found that sexist teachers grade speeches differently than nonsexist teachers: they do not write as many comments (Pearson 1979).

A speaker's status is an additional preconceived judgment that affects our ability to listen to another person. If a speaker has high status, you may tend to accept the message more easily, without listening critically. You may not exercise careful judgment if the speaker is a visiting dignitary, a physician, an attorney, or a distinguished professor, for example. If you perceive the speaker to be low in status—a beginning student, a maintenance worker in the dormitory, or a student who flunked the midterm—you tend not to listen to his or her message at all, and you are unlikely to remember what the speaker said. Perceived status seems to determine whether you are likely to listen critically or at all.

Stereotypes also affect our ability to listen. If a speaker announces that she is a Republican, is opposed to women's rights, and believes a woman's place is in the home, you may prematurely judge her as a reactionary and ignore her speech. When speakers seem to belong to groups for whom you have little regard—rich people, poor people, jocks, brains, or flirts—you may reject their messages.

Do you dismiss seniors as too pretentious or people who slouch as uninteresting? If you draw such conclusions about speakers before they begin a speech, and then ignore the message as a result of this prejudgment, you are handicapped by a factor that interferes with your listening.

Prejudging the Speech

A third factor that may interfere with your ability to listen to a speaker is your tendency to prejudge the speech. The same human tendency that causes you to judge the speaker before a speech causes you to judge the speech before you understand it. The most common conclusions we draw prematurely about a speech are that it is boring, too difficult to understand, irrelevant, or inconsistent with our own beliefs.

You may judge a speech to be boring because you feel you already know the information the speaker is presenting, you have already experienced what the speaker is describing, or the speaker is trying to persuade you to do something you already do. In other words, your feelings of superiority—informational, experiential, or attitudinal—interfere with your ability to listen.

You may decide a speech is too difficult to understand and ignore it because you "wouldn't understand it anyway." You might tend to categorize many topics as too difficult or you may selectively identify topics that deal with certain subjects, such as thermonuclear power, quantum physics, or Keynesian economics, as too complex for your understanding, even though the speaker's purpose is to simplify the concept or to inform you of the basic terminology.

Occasionally you may decide that a speech is irrelevant. For some people, nearly all topics seem unimportant. Others dismiss some topics as soon as they are announced. For instance, a business major in the audience may feel that Native American literature does not affect him; a college sophomore may conclude that a speech on retirement is immaterial; an African American student may show no interest in a description of life in a European American community. One of the reasons people dismiss another person's topic as irrelevant is because of **egocentrism,** the tendency to view oneself as the center of any exchange or activity. People who are egocentric are concerned only with themselves and pay little or no attention to others. Whether you refuse to consider most speeches or ignore only certain topics, you are blocking your ability to become an effective listener. If you listen attentively to a speech beyond the statement of its topic or purpose, you may find information that clearly shows the speech's relevance for you.

Finally, you may dismiss a speech because you disagree with the topic or purpose. You may feel that a speaker should not inform you about how to smoke crack, provide information on birth control, show examples of pornography, or persuade you to limit salt or sugar consumption. Your opposition to smoking crack, practicing birth control, seeing nudity, or learning about nutritional findings may block your ability to listen to the speaker. You may conclude that the speaker is "on the other side" of the issue and that your seemingly different attitudes prohibit open communication.

Defensiveness, the feeling that you must defend yourself, commonly occurs when a speaker's topic or position on an issue is different from your own. You may be threatened by the speaker's position and feel that you must defend your own. You may believe you are being attacked because you champion a specific cause—such as women's rights, energy conservation, or the anti-tax movement—that the speaker opposes. You may be standing ready for anyone who dares provoke you on your favorite cause. You may be only too eager to find fault with another person's speech. In the speaking-listening process, try to recognize the blocks to effective listening caused by defensiveness and dismissal of the speech through disagreement.

Yielding to Distractions

The listener's four most common distractions are factual, semantic, mental, and physical. Yielding to **factual distractions** means listening only for the facts instead of the main ideas or general purpose of a speech. The formal educational experiences you have had in which you were required to listen to teachers in order to pass objective exams may have contributed to this tendency. Rather than looking at an entire speech, you may focus on isolated facts. You jeopardize your understanding of the speaker's main idea or purpose when you jump from fact to fact rather than attempting to weave the major points into an integrated pattern and regarding the facts as supporting information.

Semantic distractions are words or phrases that affect us emotionally. You may react this way if someone uses a word or phrase in an unusual manner, if you find a particular concept distasteful or inappropriate, or if you do not understand the meaning of a term. **Regionalisms**—words that are used in a way unique to a particular geographical area—provide one example of words used in an unusual manner. If a speaker talks about the harmful qualities of *pop,* and you refer to soft drinks as *soda,* you may react negatively to the word *pop.* If you feel that *girl* should not be used to designate a woman, then you may be distracted in listening to a speaker who does so.

Mental distractions include your engaging in daydreaming, counterarguments, recollections, or future planning while listening to a speaker. These mental distractions may originate from something the speaker has stated or from your own preoccupation with other thoughts. Perhaps mental distractions occur because of the difference between the speed at which we can listen and the speed at which we can speak. The average American talks at a rate of 125 words per minute but can receive about 425 words per minute. This discrepancy allows us to engage in many mental side trips that may be more relevant to us. Unfortunately, we may become lost on a side trip and fail to return to the original path.

Physical distractions include sensations and physical stimuli that interfere with our attention to a speaker. Stimuli that may affect our listening are sounds such as a speaker's lisp, a buzzing neon light, or an air hammer; sights such as a speaker's white socks, a message on the chalkboard, or bright sunlight; smells such as a familiar perfume, baking bread, or freshly popped corn.

In this section, we surveyed four sets of barriers to effective listening: faking attention; prejudging the speaker on the basis of gender, status, or stereotypes; prejudging the subject and dismissing it as boring, too complex, irrelevant, or opposed to our own point of view; and yielding to factual, semantic, mental, or physical distractions. Consider how you can overcome these barriers and become more effective as a listener.

We have considered three false assumptions about listening and some barriers to effective listening. We will now examine the two types of listening that occur most frequently in public speaking situations: informative listening and evaluative listening.

Informative Listening

Informative listening refers to the kind you engage in when you attend class and listen to an instructor, attend baseball practice and listen to the coach, or attend a lecture and listen to a visiting speaker. Your purpose in informative listening is to understand the information the speaker is presenting. You may try to understand relevant information about the speaker and factors that led to the speech, as well as the central idea of the speech itself.

Informative listening requires a high level of involvement in the communication process. Authors Wolvin and Coakley (1996) refer to informative listening as comprehensive listening and observe that it is especially important in employment settings. Without adequate information, they note, workers cannot do an effective job. What are some of the factors that contribute to effective informational or comprehensive listening? What can you do to overcome many of the barriers discussed in the previous section? Take a look at the practices listed in Figure 2.1, expanded on in the following paragraphs.

Figure 2.1
Ten Good Listening Practices

In order to be successful at informative listening, you can engage in at least ten practices:

1. Suspend judgments about the speaker,
2. Focus on the speaker as a source of information,
3. Concentrate your attention on the speaker,
4. Listen to the entire message,
5. Focus on the values or experiences you share with the speaker,
6. Focus on the main ideas the speaker is presenting,
7. Recall the arbitrary nature of words,
8. Focus on the intent as well as the content of the message,
9. Be aware of your listening intensity, and
10. Remove or ignore physical distractions.

Suspend Judgments About the Speaker

Suspend your premature judgments about the speaker so you can listen for information. Wait until you have heard a speaker before you conclude that he or she is, or is not, worthy of your attention. If you make decisions about people because of their membership in a particular group, you risk serious error. For example, beer drinkers may be thin, members of fraternities may not be conformists, and artists are often disciplined.

Focus on the Speaker As a Source of Information

You can dismiss people when you categorize them. When you focus on a speaker as a valuable human resource who can share information, ideas, thoughts, and feelings, you are better able to listen with interest and respect. Every speaker you hear is likely to have some information you do not already know. Try to focus on these opportunities to learn something new.

Concentrate Your Attention on the Speaker

If you find yourself dismissing many of the speeches you hear as boring, consider whether you are overly egocentric. Perhaps your inclination to find your classmates' speeches boring is due to your inability to focus on other people. Egocentrism is a trait that is difficult to overcome. The wisest suggestion, in this case, is to keep in mind one of the direct benefits of concentrating your attention on the speaker: if you focus on the other person while she is speaking, that person will probably focus on you when you are speaking. Even more important, you will come across better as a speaker if others perceive you to be a careful listener. Nothing else you can do—including dieting, using makeup, wearing new clothing, or making other improvements—will make you as attractive to others as learning to listen to someone else.

Listen to the Entire Message

Do not tune out a speech after you have heard the topic. More than likely, the speaker will add new information, insights, or experiences that will shed additional light on the subject. One professor teaches an upper-division argumentation course to twenty students each quarter. Four speeches are assigned, but every speech is given on the same topic. In a ten-week period, students hear eighty speeches on the same topic, but every speech contains some new information. The class would be dismal if the students dismissed the speeches after hearing they would all cover the same topic. Instead of considering the speeches boring, the students find them interesting, exciting, and highly creative.

Focus on the Values or Experiences You Share With the Speaker

We listen for information. (Photo: Mark C. Ide)

If you find you are responding emotionally to a speaker's position on a topic and you directly oppose what he or she is recommending, try to concentrate your attention on the attitudes, beliefs, or values you have in common. Try to identify with statements the speaker is making. The speaker might seem to be attacking one of your own beliefs or attitudes, but, if you listen carefully, you may find that the speaker is actually defending it from a different perspective. Maximizing our shared ideas and minimizing our differences result in improved listening and better communication.

Focus on the Main Ideas the Speaker Is Presenting

Keep in mind that you do not have to memorize the facts a speaker presents. Rarely will you be given an objective examination on the material in a student speech. If you want to learn more about the information being presented, ask the speaker after class for a copy of the outline, a bibliography, or other pertinent documentation. Asking the speaker for further information is flattering; however, stating in class that you can recall the figures cited but have no idea of the speaker's purpose may seem offensive.

Recall the Arbitrary Nature of Words

If you find that you sometimes react emotionally to four-letter words or to specific usage of some words, you may be forgetting that words are simply arbitrary symbols people have chosen to represent certain things. Words do not have inherent, intrinsic, "real" meanings. When a speaker uses a word in an unusual way, or when you are unfamiliar with a certain word, do not hesitate to ask how the word is being used. Asking for such information makes the speaker feel good because you are showing interest in the speech, and the inquiry will contribute to your own knowledge. If you cannot overcome a negative reaction to the speaker's choice of words, recognize that the emotional reaction is yours and not necessarily a feeling shared by the rest of the class or the speaker. Listeners need to be open-minded; speakers need to show responsibility in word choice.

Focus on the Intent As Well As the Content of the Message

Use the time between your listening to the speech and the speaker's delivery of the words to increase your understanding of the speech. Instead of embarking on mental excursions about other topics, focus on all aspects of the topic the speaker has selected. Consider the speaker's background and his or her motivation for selecting a particular topic. Try to relate the major points the speaker has made to his or her stated intentions. By refusing to consider other, unrelated matters, you will greatly increase your understanding of the speaker and the speech.

Be Aware of Your Listening Intensity

You listen with varying degrees of intensity. Sometimes when a parent or roommate gives you information, you barely listen. However, when your supervisor calls you in for an unexpected conference, your listening is very intense. Occasionally we trick ourselves into listening less intensely than we should. Everyone knows to take notes when the professor says, "This will be on the test," but only an intense listener captures the important content in an apparently boring lecture. You need to become a good judge of how intensely to listen and to learn ways to alter your listening intensity. Sitting on the front of the chair, acting very interested, and nodding affirmatively when you agree are some methods that people use to listen with appropriate intensity.

Remove or Ignore Physical Distractions

Frequently you can deal with physical distractions, such as an unusual odor, bright lights, or a distracting noise, by moving the stimulus or yourself. In other words, do not choose a seat near the doorway that allows you to observe people passing by in the hall, do not sit so that the sunlight is in your eyes, and do not sit so far away from the speaker that maintenance noises in the building drown out her voice. If you cannot avoid the distraction by changing your seat or removing the distracting object, try to ignore it. You probably can study with the radio or television on, sleep without having complete darkness, and eat while other people are milling around you. Similarly, you can focus your attention on the speaker when other physical stimuli are in your environment.

Consider whether you would be able to concentrate on the speech if it were, instead, a movie you have been wanting to see, a musical group you enjoy, or a play that has received a rave review. One man said that when he had difficulty staying up late to study in graduate school, he considered whether he would have the same difficulty if he were on a date. If the answer was no, he could then convince himself that the fatigue he felt was a function of the task, not of his sleepiness. The same principle can work for you. Consider whether the distractions are merely an excuse for your lack of desire to listen to the speaker. Generally you will find you can ignore the other physical stimuli in your environment if you wish to do so.

As we observed earlier, two kinds of listening are most common in public speaking situations. We have concluded our discussion of informative listening and will turn now to evaluative listening.

Celebrating Diversity

Choctaw Chief Pushmataha responded to Chief Tecumseh on the War Against the Americans. He began by stating, "Halt, Tecumseh! Listen to me. You have come here, as you have often gone elsewhere, with a purpose to involve peaceful people in unnecessary trouble with their neighbors. Our people have no undue friction with the whites. Why? Because we had no leaders stirring up strife to serve their selfish personal ambitions." (*http://www.americanrhetoric.com/speeches/nativeamericans/chiefpushmataha.htm*)

Why did the Chief feel he had to begin his speech by telling Tecumseh to halt and to listen to him? Is this a common device in public speeches? Imagine that you were Tecumseh. How would you respond to Pushmataha? Do you believe that Tecumseh would really listen to Pushmataha's commentary?

Evaluative Listening

Evaluative listening is the kind of listening you engage in when you listen to two opposing political speakers; judge the speaking ability of an author, attorney, or instructor; or listen to students in public speaking class. Your purpose in evaluative listening is to judge the speaker's ability to give an effective speech. Evaluative listening is an essential skill in and out of the classroom. What can you do to become a better evaluative listener?

You can be a more effective evaluative listener by following four guidelines. First, establish standards of appraisal. Second, consider the positive as well as the negative aspects of the speech. Third, view the speech as a whole entity rather than as a composite of isolated parts. Fourth, consider the speaker's **ethical standards,** the moral choices he or she has made in preparing and delivering the speech. Let us consider each of these guidelines in more depth.

✔ Reality Check 2.3 ✔
Communication Skills for Top Executives

Argenti and Forman (1998) say that "while most chief executive officers say that more than half of their daily work involves communications, little in their education prepares them for the task." Indeed, the authors add: "The level of training and skills can be dismal." The researchers conclude by stating that "executives who have invested time and effort in learning communication approaches clearly have what we call a communication advantage."

Establish Standards of Appraisal

In order to evaluate another person's public speaking ability, you must establish criteria by which you make your judgments. The criteria you establish should reflect your beliefs and attitudes about public speaking. Your instructor may suggest a set of criteria by which to judge your classmates' speeches. Many different sets of standards can be used to provide equally valid evaluations of public speaking; however, most include a consideration of the topic choice, purpose, arguments, organization, vocal and bodily aspects of delivery, audience analysis, and adaptation. The evaluation form shown in Figure 2.2 follows the suggestions offered in this text.

Consider the Positive As Well As the Negative Aspects of the Speech

Too often people use the word *evaluation* to mean negative criticism. In other words, if they are to evaluate a speech, a newspaper article, or a television program, they feel they must state every aspect of it that could be improved or did not meet their standards.

Evaluation should include both positive and negative judgments. As a matter of fact, many speech instructors feel you should begin and end your criticism of a speech with positive comments and "sandwich" your negative remarks in between. Research shows that students perceive positive comments to be more helpful than negative comments (Young 1974).

View the Speech As a Unit

It is very easy to focus on delivery aspects of the speech, to look only for a recognizable organizational plan, or to consider only whether the research is current. In viewing small bits of the speech in isolation, you may be able to justify a low evaluation you give to a classmate. However, considering all of the parts that went into the speech may not allow such a judgment.

Speeches are like the people who give them—composites of many complex, and sometimes conflicting, messages. In order to be evaluated completely and fairly, they must be examined within a variety of contexts. Do not be distracted by a topic that represents one of your pet peeves, allow language choices to overshadow the speaker's creativity, or accept the arguments of a speaker who demonstrates a smooth delivery. In short, consider the entire speech in your evaluation.

Figure 2.2
An Evaluation Form for a Public Speech

Speaker _____

Critic _____

Use this scale to evaluate each of the following:

1	2	3	4	5
Excellent	Good	Average	Fair	Weak

Introduction

____The introduction gained and maintained attention.

____The introduction related the topic to the audience.

____The introduction related the speaker to the topic.

____The introduction revealed the thesis and organization of the speech.

Topic selection and statement of purpose

____The topic selected was appropriate for the speaker.

____The topic selected was appropriate for the audience.

____The topic selected was appropriate for the occasion.

____The statement of purpose was clear and appropriate for the speaker, audience, and occasion.

____The stated purpose was achieved.

Content

____The speaker consulted available sources, including personal experience, interviews, and printed materials, for information.

____The speaker supplied a sufficient amount of evidence and supporting materials.

____The speech was organized in a manner that did not distract from the speech.

____The main points were clearly identified.

____Sufficient transitions were provided.

Source

____The speaker described his or her competence.

____The speaker demonstrated trustworthiness.

____The speaker exhibited dynamism.

____The speaker established co-orientation.

Delivery

____The vocal aspects of delivery—pitch, rate, pause, volume, enunciation, fluency, and vocal variety—added to the message and did not distract from it.

____The bodily aspects of delivery—gestures, facial expressions, eye contact, and movement—added to the message and did not distract from it.

____Visual aids were used appropriately to clarify the message.

Audience analysis

____The speaker demonstrated his or her sensitivity to the interests of the audience.

____The speaker adapted the message to the knowledge level of the audience on the topic.

____The speaker adapted the message to the demographic variables of the audience.

____The speaker adapted the message to the attitudes of the audience.

Conclusion

____The conclusion forewarned the audience that the speaker was about to stop.

____The conclusion reminded the audience of the central idea or the main points of the speech.

____The conclusion specified precisely what the audience was to think or do in response to the speech.

Ethical standards

____The speaker earned the audience's trust with an honest approach to the topic.

____The speaker cited sources of information and ideas.

____The speaker avoided distortion, exaggeration, and oversimplification of the issue.

____The speaker recognized other points of view on the issues.

✔ Reality Check 2.4 ✔
Even Psychiatrists Find Listening Challenging

Michael Nichols (1996) wrote a book entitled *The Lost Art of Listening: How Learning to Listen Can Improve Relationships*. He argues that listening is the fundamental psychotherapeutic skill and reminds readers that listening is difficult and should not be an assumed skill. As Erich Fromm (1998), a psychoanalyst, noted, the art of therapy is the art of listening.

Consider the Speaker's Ethical Standards

Speakers make moral choices about audiences when they choose a topic, when they decide what to say about the topic, and when they recommend a response to the speech. For example, a speaker can choose a topic that is appropriate or inappropriate for an audience; a speaker can unethically decide to withhold important information about the topic; or a speaker can recommend actions that are illegal or immoral.

Ethics and the Listener

Listeners need to distinguish between ethical and unethical speakers. Jon Hess (Nelson and Pearson 1996) wrote a chapter in an earlier edition of this text that provided relevant and important advice. Look carefully at Figure 2.3 before we cover each suggestion in more detail.

Figure 2.3
Advice for Giving Speeches With High Ethical Quality

1. Avoid unethical topics.
2. Present accurate information.
3. Avoid misleading the audience.
4. Use ethical emotional appeals.
5. Respect all cultural groups.
6. Do not hide your association with groups relevant to the topic.

Avoid Unethical Topics

Three students made poor judgments in choosing their speech topics, and they paid a high price when their listeners judged them. One skillfully delivered an informative speech on how to cheat by taking or buying speeches or term papers off the Net. Another told his audience all the reasons why they should despise immigrants. And a third speaker gave a demonstration speech on how to build a cheap but deadly bomb using chemicals readily available in commercial products. All three received zeros from different teachers for giving an unethical speech. Do you agree with the teachers' judgments?

If you are uncertain about the ethical quality of your speech topic, you should check your topic with your teacher before you waste time developing a speech that will yield a low grade and the possible disgust of your audience.

Present Accurate Information

You have a right, "a First Amendment Right," to speak on a topic even if you are not an expert. But your listeners have a responsibility to judge the accuracy of your words. Many people are pretty casual about their facts when they are in conversation, but the public speaker has to be more careful about the accuracy of claims made to a larger group. Do not just pass on information that you heard on the street; instead, verify information by checking more than one source and by striving to find the best sources of information.

Does a statistic that you hear in a speech sound inflated? Ask the speaker where the statistic originated. Find out if the source of information is reputable. Check the number against other known information on the topic. Is the speaker drawing an inference that goes well beyond the data? The ethical listener expects accurate information, and the ethical speaker provides accurate information. The ethical listener listens for the speaker's sources to help judge the accuracy of information.

Check what you hear against common sense. Check the speaker's sources of information to see if you agree that the speaker sought and found high-quality sources of information. Finally, check to see if you would draw the same inferences from the data that the speaker did. To be an expert on a subject is not required, but to be accurate about your topic and to say where you found your information is required.

Avoid Misleading the Audience

The competent speaker strives to be as honest with an audience as he or she would be with a friend. However, sometimes the strong focus on a single issue may encourage a speaker to mislead the audience. This situation is exactly what happened to Ibrahim Hassan when he gave a speech on gun control.

Ibrahim was not just another speaker on gun control. He had lost his best friend to a handgun, and he was very much in favor of limited access, strong punishments for possession, and even the death penalty for anyone who would use a handgun in the commission of a crime. Unfortunately, Ibrahim knew practically nothing about the other side of the issue—the right to bear arms and the controversial issue of government control of weapons—and so he never mentioned anything except the absolute necessity of getting rid of handguns.

The ethical listener tries to make sure that the speaker provides an honest accounting of the facts and opinions surrounding a controversial issue. Actually, a speaker can take a strong stand for one side of an issue as long as the speaker recognizes explicitly that other reasonable people can hold a different view. What does the ethical speaker do to appeal positively to the ethical listener? The ethical speaker tries to present all relevant information on an issue, cites sources, reveals when examples are hypothetical (made up), and insists that quotations reflect their originators' intent. This last issue is an important one because a speaker can change what the originator intended by leaving out a word here or there or by omitting part of a sentence that changes the meaning of the quotation.

Sometimes speakers' verbal messages are honest, but they lead the audience to different conclusions with suggestions or implications. This technique of "implicature" means that audiences tend to "read between the lines." Audience members conjecture about ideas that are not overtly stated. Ethical communicators must exercise care that they do not "tell more than the truth" (Riley 1993).

Use Ethical Emotional Appeals

Emotional appeals persuade an audience by using love, hate, prejudice, and other emotions to secure an audience response. Is your spouse reasonable when he is in a rage about the traffic on the way home? Is your roommate ready to discuss the rent when she just broke up with a guy she had dated for two years? The ethical listener believes that a speaker is being unethical when that speaker takes advantage of love, hate, or prejudice to persuade an audience to take a position or action that they otherwise would not have chosen.

The check against emotional appeals is that the listener should always perceive free choice, the listener should know that he or she does not have to do what the speaker says. Mobs, gang warfare, group attacks on individuals—all sorts of mayhem result when groups of people lose their common sense. The ethical speaker aims at change by appealing to humanity's higher motives. Gandhi drove out the British not with guns but with peaceful resistance; Martin Luther King, Jr., changed the laws and practices in America not with force but by pursuing a dream and demonstrations that shamed a nation; and Nelson Mandela rid his nation of white rule and immoral laws by envisioning a democracy with shared power and authority. In public speaking classrooms around the nation, speakers every day make choices about appealing to our worst or to our best motives. Just as destroying something is much easier than building something, to give a speech that appeals to our animal instincts is easier than working toward positive change.

Respect All Cultural Groups

The United States has people who were here first (Native Americans), people who came as conquerors and colonizers (British, French, and Spanish), people who were shipped here (indentured servants and Africans), people who were pushed out of their native lands by warfare and civil strife (Cubans, Africans, Central Americans, Haitians), people who were starved out of their countries of origin (Irish and Scandinavians), and people who sought a better quality of life (Mexicans, South Americans, and Caribbean Islanders). All of these cultures exist along with co-cultures such as gay and straight, young and old, rich and poor, black and white, the currently able bodied and people with disabilities, etc.

Civility among cultures and co-cultures begins with calling people what they wish to be called—even if that wish changes with some frequency. Usually people are quite open about whether they wish to be called Hispanic, Latino or Latina, homosexual, African American, blind, hearing impaired, or octogenarian. If a Korean wishes to be called Asian, then that is what you call her. Respect means that you care enough to call people what they wish to be called. The ethical listener is very aware of preferences and practices in various cultures and co-cultures and expects the ethical speaker to know and understand audience preferences.

Do Not Hide Your Association With a Group Whose Purpose or Work Is Relevant to the Topic

If you are a Palestinian who is seeking a homeland, then you are more ethical to reveal your association than to mask it. If you are a Roman Catholic who embraces a pro-life stance, then you are more ethical to reveal your religious affiliation because that affiliation is related to your cause. A National Rifle Association member who abhors gun control ought to reveal her association with that group. The principle is clear: If your membership in a group is relevant to the topic, then you are expected to reveal that membership.

Why should you reveal relevant memberships? The reason is that stating your association can possibly strengthen your cause, but hiding your association is likely to damage your cause—especially if your audience learns that you kept your association a secret from them. Also, if you are ashamed of the groups to which you belong, you perhaps ought to review your reasons for belonging to them.

NCA Credo for Communications Ethics

In the last chapter we introduced you to the NCA Ethics Credo. Here is a relevant principle for this chapter:

- We strive to understand and respect other communicators before evaluating and responding to their messages.

Summary

We have considered informative and evaluative listening in this chapter. You learned the role of listening in the public speaking classroom. You learned to identify three false assumptions about listening: most people assume that they listen well, that they cannot be taught how to be better listeners, and that hearing and listening are the same phenomenon. After we dispelled these misconceptions, you learned four sets of barriers to effective listening: faking attention; prejudging the speaker on the basis of gender, status, or stereotypes; prejudging the subject and dismissing it as boring, too complex, irrelevant, or opposed to your own point of view; and yielding to factual, semantic, mental, or physical distractions. You then considered fourteen practices in which you should engage when you listen for informative and evaluative purposes. You should:

1. suspend judgments about the speaker,

2. focus on the speaker as a source of information,

3. concentrate your attention on the speaker,

4. listen to the entire message,

5. focus on the values or experiences you share with the speaker,

6. focus on the main ideas the speaker is presenting,

7. recall the arbitrary nature of words,

8. focus on the intent as well as the content of the message,

9. be aware of your listening intensity,

10. remove or ignore physical distractions,

11. establish standards of appraisal,

12. consider the positive as well as the negative aspects of the speech,

13. view the speech as a unit, and

14. consider the speaker's ethical standards.

... have the right to think differently. (Photo: ...in Warren/Daily Bruin)

Advice for giving speeches with high ethical quality included avoiding unethical topics, presenting accurate information, avoiding misleading the audience, using ethical emotional appeals, respecting all cultural groups, and being open about belonging to groups relevant to the topic.

You will spend considerably more time listening than speaking in this course. Use that opportunity to advance yourself as a person who recognizes effective listening as the hard work that it is, who learns from the words and concerns of others, and who learns the responsibilities of being both a speaker and a listener. Effective listening can help you develop confidence as a communicator.

Vocabulary

closure The organizational method of filling in information that does not exist to clarify an incomplete message.

defensiveness The tendency to dismiss a speech because the speaker's topic or position on an issue is different from your own; a barrier to listening.

egocentrism The tendency to view oneself as the center of any exchange or activity; overconcern with the presentation of oneself to others; a barrier to listening.

emotional appeals These appeals persuade an audience using love, hate, prejudice, and other emotions.

ethical standards The moral choices made by a speaker in preparing and delivering a speech to an audience.

Communication Narrative 2.1
Sorry, I Wasn't Listening

Buford "Buba" Murdock worked on the loading dock of a huge book distributor. Every morning the dock supervisor had a 7 a.m. assembly with all the guys and the few women who loaded trucks for eight hours per day. The workers were all union, but they were expected to listen to the boss, Sandy Hegland, who was giving them the orders for the day while Buba was fiddling with his coffee cup and creamer. The meeting only lasted ten minutes, and mostly the purpose was to see if everyone would be in place for the loading to begin at 7:15. This morning nobody was missing, but Buba did miss most of what Hegland had said.

Around mid-morning, Buba Murdock was ready for his break. He had noticed that most of the other guys on the forklifts had moved considerably more boxes than he had. Hegland had even given him a puzzled frown at the end of his first hour of work because Buba had such a backlog of boxes that early in the morning. He never knew what was wrong until his buddy, Clarence "Whitey" Whitman, asked him why he was weighing every load when Hegland had told him that he didn't have to. Buba was mystified. He hadn't heard that nobody had to weigh loads this morning, but at least he understood why a very steamed Sandy Hegland was advancing on him during break. Hegland pointed out in front of the other workers that Buba was at least twenty loads behind everyone else. Hegland did not say Buba was stupid, but that certainly was the implication. A sheepish Buba Murdock, not wishing to be written up for an infraction, could only say, "I'm sorry, I wasn't listening."

If you were to analyze Buba Murdock's failure to listen, why would you say he did not receive the message when others did? Have you ever missed a message that nearly everyone else received? What was your reason? What could Sandy Hegland have done differently to ensure that his workers successfully received his message? What would you do to make sure such a mistake did not occur again?

evaluative listening Listening to a speaker for the purpose of evaluating his or her ability to present an effective speech.

factual distractions Factual information that detracts from our attention to primary ideas; a barrier to effective listening.

figure and ground The organizational method of identifying some words, phrases, or sentences as more important and others as less important.

hearing The physiological process by which sound is received by the ear.

informative listening Listening to a speaker in order to understand the information that he or she is presenting.

interpreting The process of receiving, selecting, and organizing a set of sounds and then blending them with your own understanding.

listening The process of receiving, selecting, organizing, and interpreting sounds.

mental distractions Communication with ourselves while we are engaged in communication with others; a barrier to effective listening.

physical distractions Environmental stimuli that interfere with our focus on another person's message; a barrier to effective listening.

proximity The organizational method of grouping two or more things that happen to be close to each other.

regionalisms Words that are used in a way unique to a particular geographical area.

selective attention The act of focusing on some cues while ignoring others.

selective retention The act of categorizing, storing, and retrieving certain information while discarding other information.

semantic distractions Words or phrases that affect the listener emotionally; a barrier to effective listening.

similarity The organizational method of grouping words or phrases together because they are similar in sound, beginning letter, or final syllable.

Application Exercises

1. State which of the barriers to effective listening will be the least, and the greatest, problem for you.

2. Are you an effective informative listener? After you have listened to a number of speeches in class, select one and complete the following:

   Speaker's name

   Topic

   Statement of purpose

   Main points:

   1.

   2.

   3.

   4.

   What are the speaker's qualifications for speaking on this topic?

   What response is the speaker seeking from the audience?

3. Establish standards of appraisal for evaluating speeches. In order to make judgments about your classmates' speeches, you need standards by which to evaluate them. Create a criticism form including all of the essential elements of effective public speaking. Note exactly what you would include and how you would weigh each aspect. (Does delivery count more for you than content? Is a great deal of evidence more important to you than adaptation to the audience?)

4. Write a speech criticism. Using the criticism form that you created in exercise 3, evaluate three speeches that other students

delivered in class. After you have completed your criticism, give each form to the speaker. Together discuss how accurately you have assessed the speech. Are you satisfied with the form? Do you believe your form would be useful for others? Does the speaker feel that the form included all the relevant factors? Can he or she suggest items that could or should be included? Is he or she satisfied with your use of the form? What differences of opinion exist between the two of you? Why? Can you resolve these differences? What has the experience demonstrated?

References

Adler, B. A., and Towne, N. (1999). *Looking out/Looking in* (9th ed.). Fort Worth, TX: Harcourt Brace.

Argenti, P. A., and Forman, J. (1998). Should business schools teach Aristotle? *Strategy and Business, http://www.strategy-business.com/press/article/18743?pg=0.*

Bostrom, R. (1990). *Listening Behavior: Measurement and Application.* New York: Guilford Press.

Curtis, D. B., Winsor, J. L., and Stephens, R. D. (1989). National preferences in business and communication education. *Communication Education,* 58, 6–14.

Eastment, D. (2004). Listening materials and how to find them. *ELT Journal,* 58, 97–101.

Emmert, P. (1991, March). *The reification of listening.* A paper presented at the International Listening Association's preconvention research conference, Jacksonville, FL.

Farrugia, A. (1999). "Freedom is when the people can speak; democracy is when the government listens." A quotation from *http://www.listen.org/quotations/morequotes.html.*

Fitch-Hauser, M., and Hughes, M. A. (1988). Defining the cognitive process of listening: A dream or a reality? *Journal of the International Listening Association,* 2, 75–88.

Fromm, E. (1998). *The Art of Listening.* New York: Continuum Publications Group.

Gronbeck, B. E. (1981). Oral communication skills in a technological age. *Vital Speeches,* 47, 431.

Kelly, C. M. (1967). Listening: Complex of activities—and a unitary skill? *Speech Monographs,* 34, 455–466.

Maes, J. D., Weldy, T. G., and Icenogle, M. L. (1997). A managerial perspective: Oral communication competency is most important for business students in the workplace. *Journal of Business Communication,* 34, 67–80.

Markgraf, B. (1957). An observational study determining the amount of time that students in the tenth and twelfth grades are expected to listen in the classroom. Unpublished master's thesis, University of Wisconsin.

Mead, N. A., and Rubin, D. L. (1999). Assessing listening and speaking skills—research. PENpages: College of Agricultural Sciences. *http://www.ericfacility.net/ericdigests/ed263626.html.*

Morreale, S. P., Osborn, M. M., and Pearson, J. C. (2000). The centrality of the communication discipline. *Journal of the Association for Communication Administrators,* 29, 1–25.

Nelson, P. E., and Pearson, J. C. (1996). *Confidence in Public Speaking* (6th ed.). Madison, WI: Brown & Benchmark.

Nichols, M. (1996). *The lost art of listening: How learning to listen can improve relationships.* New York: Guilford Press.

Nichols, R., and Stevens, L. (1957). Listening to people. *Harvard Business Review,* 35, 85–92.

Pearson, J. C. (1979, May). The influence of sex and sexism on the criticism of classroom speeches. Paper presented at the meeting of the International Communication Association, Philadelphia, PA.

Pfister, E. R. (1955). A study of the influence of certain selected factors on the ratings of speech performances. An unpublished doctoral dissertation, Michigan State University.

Phillips, R. (1996). Evaluate your own listening habits. *http://www.salesdog.com/newsletters/2004/n10186.asp.*

Riley, K. (1993). Telling more than the truth: Implicature, speech acts, and ethics in professional communication. *Journal of Business Ethics*, 12, 179–197.

Roberts, C. V. (1988). The validation of listening tests: Cutting of the Gordian knot. *Journal of the International Listening Association*, 2, 1–19.

Sawyer, D. (2004, February 24). Newsmaker: Diane Sawyer (compiled by Alicia Strand). *The Forum of Fargo-Moorhead*, A2.

Spitzberg, B. H., and Cupach, W. R. (1984). *Interpersonal Communication Competence*. Beverly Hills, CA: Sage.

Sprague, J. A. (1971). An investigation of the written critique behavior of college communication instructors. Unpublished doctoral dissertation, Purdue University.

Welton, M. (2002). Listening, conflict, and citizenship: Towards a pedagogy of civil society. *International Journal of Lifelong Education*, 21, 197–208.

Winsor, J. L., Curtis, D. B., and Stephens, R. D. (1997). National preferences in business and communication education. *Journal of the Association of Communication Administrators*, 3, 170–179.

Wolvin, A. D., and Coakley, G. C. (1996). *Listening* (5th ed.). New York: McGraw Hill.

Young, S. L. (1974). Student perceptions of helpfulness in classroom speech criticism. *Speech Teacher*, 23, 222–234.

❖ ❖ ❖ ❖

Chapter 3

The Audience

*Condense some daily experience into a glowing symbol, and
an audience is electrified.*

—Ralph Waldo Emerson

Question Outline

I. Why should a speaker analyze the audience?

II. How do audience characteristics affect your speech?

III. What are some of the demographic features of the audience
that you should consider in your audience analysis?

IV. What are the four methods of audience analysis?

V. Why consider the context in which you speak?

VI. What is unique about your classmates as an audience?

VII. How does a speaker adapt to an audience?

VIII. How are moral choices related to audience analysis?

Don London loved politics. When Professional Secretaries International (PSI)
invited him to talk to their group, he enthusiastically agreed. They did not give
him a topic for his speech, so he decided to promote his favorite candidate, conservative Republican Judge Sanford D. Hodson. On the night of the speech, Don
was startled to see as many men in the group as women. Nearly all the men were
employers who were there for "Boss's Night" as guests of their secretaries; nearly
all the women were secretaries.

As Don delivered his speech, he noticed he was getting very little reaction
from the members of PSI, but the men were showing unabashed enthusiasm for

his message of support for Judge Hodson. After a rather chilly farewell from his hostesses, Don returned home mystified because half of his audience seemed to dislike his speech, whereas the other half loved it.

The next day, a PSI member who had heard the speech told Don what had happened. The predominantly male guests were affluent middle- or upper-management people and owners of companies. They were mostly Republicans and supporters of Judge Hodson. The secretaries who had invited Don to speak were predominantly registered Democrats who strongly rejected Judge Hodson's political position on the issues. Few of them knew Don before the speech, but afterward they disliked him and his message.

The story of Don London emphasizes the importance of knowing your audience before you speak. As speakers we too often focus on ourselves. We speak on our favorite topics, without considering what the audience might want or need to hear. We use language that we understand without considering that the audience might not understand. Possibly our individualistic culture invites more attention to self and less to audience than might be the case in a more collectivist culture (Samovar, Porter, and Stefani 1998).

Don London should have known that the audience would consist of both men and women, that the men were predominantly Republican and the women predominantly Democrats. He should have known beforehand that a talk extolling Judge Hodson was inappropriate for the occasion, that it would offend the very people who had invited him to speak. Don could have given a speech with an important message for everyone if he had known about audience analysis.

Audience Analysis

What is audience analysis? **Audience analysis** is discovering as much as possible about an audience for the purpose of improving communication. Why should a speaker analyze an audience? Think of public speaking as another version of the kind of speaking you do every day. Nearly always, when you meet a stranger, you size up that person before you disclose your message. Similarly, public speaking requires that you meet and know the members of your audience so you are able to create a message for them. Public speaking is not talking to oneself in front of a group; instead, it is effective message transmission from one person to many people in a setting in which speaker and audience influence each other.

Let us consider the wide variety of audiences you might face in your lifetime:

Your classmates	Fellow parents	A religious group	A political group
Fellow workers	Retired people	A board of directors	A school board
Members of a union	A group of friends	A group of children	A social club
A civic organization			

Would you talk to all of these audiences about the same topic or in the same way? Of course not. Your choices of topic and your approach to that topic are both strongly influenced by the nature of your audience. We focus on the audience in a speech by learning the nature of that audience.

When we talk to individuals, we are relatively careful about what we say and how we say it. We speak differently to strangers than to intimates, differently to people we respect than to people we do not respect, and differently to children than to adults. Similarly, we need to be aware of audience characteristics when we choose a topic and when we decide how we are going to present that topic to the audience.

Imagine that you are about to speak to a new audience. How would you learn about the people in your audience? First, you could rely on conventional wisdom. Second, you could conduct a demographic analysis. Let us examine each of these increasingly specific ways of learning more about an audience.

On the Web

Examine three inaugural addresses of American Presidents. (A good site for these speeches is *http://www.bartleby.com/124/index.html.*) Consider how the three Presidents treated the audience differently. Or did they? Why might inaugural addresses be more alike than different?

Conventional Wisdom

Conventional wisdom is the popular opinions of the time about issues, styles, topics, trends, and social moves—the customary set of understandings of what is true or right. Conventional wisdom includes what most people are said to think. *Newsweek* devotes a few column inches each week to conventional wisdom about people and issues. Sometimes the President of the United States gets an arrow up (positive sign) one week and an arrow down (negative sign) the next week—on the same issue. Let us look at how conventional wisdom relates to audience analysis.

Keeping in mind that conventional wisdom is a gross oversimplification and that it is sometimes based more on the whim of the moment than on deep-seated convictions, we could still say that, at the beginning of 2004, first-year college students were less likely to choose a business major, slightly less concerned (but still extremely high overall) about getting rich, and more concerned about influencing social values than students 10 years earlier. Keeping track of trends helps the public speaker address concerns from a context that makes sense to the audience. A pro-military speech in 1970 would have been an act of courage; a pro-military speech in 2004 is commonplace.

By the end of 1990, youthful trust in authority figures had been undermined by a President who had sex with a intern; an almost continuous stream of public figures with feet of clay; and a Congress that talked tax cuts but sought increased spending. In a period of relative peace and prosperity, social order seemed to decay with road rage on the highways, racist and homophobic attacks on individuals, and even decreasing decorum in the classroom. Late in the decade, Peter Sacks (a pseudonym) wrote *Generation X Goes to College* (1996) about teaching apathetic students, and universities created task forces, "climate committees," and national forums to consider classroom incivility. As a Montana State University professor stated: "Television and politics have defrocked the social lives of adults and made everything look hypocritical. Kids develop a certain contempt for adults as a result. . . . They're suspicious of all the rules established by adults" (Schneider 1998). Stephen Carter (1999), a Yale Law School professor and author of *Civility: Manners, Morals, and the Etiquette of Democracy* believes that today's college students exhibit a diminished sense of decorum. On the other hand, politicians are increasingly focusing on good character and solid families; increasing numbers of Americans are going to church and in other ways becoming more spiritual; and teenage violence is on the decrease (Cooper 1999).

Conventional wisdom comes from keeping up with events, with knowing what is going on in our society and in our world. Conventional wisdom suggests broad patterns that people observe in behavior. Conventional wisdom also suggests topics that cry out for analysis and discussion. If, for example, the preceding statements about the way students behave is true of your university, then your suggestions in a speech for how to improve the situation would be welcome. If incivility is not a problem on your campus, then you can speak about how unjust conventional wisdom is about the situation at your school. In any case, conventional wisdom can be a starting point for further analysis and discussion.

✔ Reality Check 3.1 ✔
A Letter to the Editor About Communication Courses

Janet Maddox (1999, April 23), Director of the Office of Institutional Research at Oglethorpe University in Atlanta, wrote these words in a Letter to the Editor in *The Chronicle of Higher Education:*

"Many first impressions are formed when the mouth is first opened. Speech that is inappropriate to the audience and the occasion screams ignorance as loudly as a paper filled with spelling and grammatical errors. The question, then, is not whether oral communication is of vital importance to college graduates, but rather when and how it should be incorporated into the curriculum."

Demographics

What are some characteristics of the audience that can affect how they interpret your message? Some of the more obvious characteristics of an audience are called **demographics,** which literally means "characteristics of the people." They include gender, age, ethnicity, economic status, occupation, education, religion, organizational memberships, and physical characteristics.

Gender. What difference does it make to a speaker whether the audience is composed of men, women, or a mixture of the two? With some topics, the gender represented by the audience may make no difference at all. With others, gender representation may make all the difference in the world.

You may need to consider if your topic is sex-linked or sex-neutral, and to modify your treatment of it when speaking before generally male, generally female, or mixed-sex audiences. Given that the gender of the audience affects how you will plan and deliver your speech, you must consider the factors that may cause women and men to react differently to certain topics. You should be aware of the fact that some women (and some men) feel that women have been discriminated against, and will be watchful for signs of discrimination from speakers.

Throughout history, women have been treated as "less than men." While circumstances are better in some instances for women today, you should keep in mind that women and men are still not treated equally in most arenas. One speaker noted the discrimination that occurs in education:

- Three-fourths of all high schools still violate the federal law banning sex discrimination in education.

- Collegiate women undergraduates still receive only 70 percent of the aid that undergraduate males get in grants and work-study jobs.

- Women's college sports programs have never equaled men's in funding and doubtfully ever will.

- Only seven states have anti-discrimination regulations that cover all educational levels (Jones 1992).

Economically, women fare even worse. Julia Hughes Jones explained,

> Economically, women have the right to own property, inherit estates, and have a job; but American women face the worst gender-based pay gap in the developed world. We still earn seventy-one cents for every dollar earned by a man, and the average female college graduate earns less than the average male high school graduate. Even more telling is that the average female high school graduate earns less than the average male high school dropout (Jones 1992).

Gender considerations are linked to public speaking. Analyzing an audience on the basis of gender is not such an easy matter, however. While the average woman may earn less money than her male counterpart, many women make more money than the average man. A particular woman may be an executive, and a specific man may be a househusband. Similarly, even though women have had the right to vote for only about 75 years, 10 million more women of voting age reside in the United States today than men. Furthermore, women voters have been the deciding factor in many political races. Assumptions about an audience on the basis of biological sex may or may not be true.

Another gender issue is whether individuals in the audience are masculine or feminine. While most women are feminine and most men are masculine, this is not always the case. Some women have internalized masculine characteristics—they are aggressive, ambitious, and task-oriented. Some men have accepted feminine characteristics—they are nurturing, cooperative, and sensitive. Many women and men are **androgynous**—they combine masculine and feminine traits and exhibit them as they deem appropriate.

Celebrating Diversity

Given the information that is provided here, how might you begin to solve the problem? What could you do to begin to address the problem of different treatment of women and men? How could public speaking play a role in this effort? Are you motivated to make a difference in matters of discrimination against women?

Finally, you need to consider the sexual orientation of audience members. Gay and lesbian audience members might not respond to issues in the same ways as their heterosexual counterparts. You also need to be careful of the heterosexist assumptions that you make if you are discussing relationships or other salient topics. For example, if you are discussing couples in cohabiting relationships, you should not assume that these couples always

Know your audience well if you want your speech to succeed. (Photo: Jon Ferry/Daily Bruin)

include a male and a female. You should also avoid discussions of relational roles in which you identify "the woman's role" and "the man's role." Furthermore, do not assume that all people in relationships will eventually marry, since most states have laws prohibiting same-sex marriages.

You must also remember to be sensitive to language choices suggesting that people are married or are planning to get married. Do not use terms like "family," which conjures up images of traditional relationships, or "husband and wife," which implies heterosexuality. Instead, opt for more inclusive choices like "committed relationships" or "relational partners."

In general, you should exercise caution in making sweeping generalizations based on gender about your audience. Gender issues concern not only our biological sex, but also our internalized masculinity and femininity, and our sexual orientation. In your language choices, be inclusive rather than exclusive. Instead of "You and your wife," say "You and your partner." Do not call attention to biological sex as an exclusive descriptor such as "You men. . ." or "You women. . ."

✔ Reality Check 3.2 ✔
Audience Analysis in Advertising, TV, and With a Live Audience

Molly Bergstrom's (1998) master's thesis is entitled *The Advertisement, the Image, and the Audience: A Rhetorical Analysis of the Advertisements in Four 1996 Issues of Glamour Magazine.* The study shows the role of audience and gender.

David J. LeRoy's (1995) book, *Public Television: Techniques for Audience Analysis and Program Scheduling,* demonstrates how audience analysis is applied to public television.

Marya Holcombe and Todd Turrentine (1996) have an article entitled "'Herding Cats': How to Understand and Manage Your Audience" in *Competitive Intelligence Review,* 7(1), 29–35. The focus of the article is on addressing decision-making groups, meeting their criteria and concerns, and bringing audience analysis from the intuitive to the conscious level.

❖ ❖ ❖ ❖

Choose topics that are interesting to both women and men. Use examples that are free of stereotypes and that are interesting to people regardless of gender. Do not assume that the women are housewives or that the men work. Do not downgrade any sexual orientation in examples or illustrations of your main point or subpoints.

Age. The United States has a population of over 293 million people, including over 60 million under 15 and over 25 million 70 or older (*http://factfinder.census.gov*).

Advancing maturity changes people's preferences. Whereas small children seem to love loud noise, fast action, and a relatively high level of confusion and messiness, older people may be bothered by these same characteristics. Look at the following topics and decide which are more appropriate for youths, middle-aged people, or the elderly.

Placing your kids in college	Body piercing	Selecting a career
Choosing a major	Planning your estate	Managing your time
Health care in hostels	Saving dollars from taxes	Selecting a tattoo
Changing careers	Investment opportunities	Selecting new software
Dating	Social security reform	Traveling in Europe

The age of your audience members will affect the topic you choose and how you treat a particular topic. You might speak about powerful stereo speakers to a younger audience but reserve the topic of cashing in annuities for an older audience. On the other hand, you may discuss financial security with younger people or older people. However, your approach will be different if you know that your audience consists of traditional undergraduate sophomores or members of the American Association of Retired Persons.

The age of your audience will also partly determine what the audience knows from its experience. Some people will know about the Depression, World War II, and Civil Defense. Others will remember the Vietnam War, the Beatles, and the Civil Rights struggles. Today's youths will know the names of the latest music groups and the newest trends in clothing.

When you give your speech, consider the ages of the individuals in the audience and what you need to do to account for that demographic characteristic. How do the ages represented in your audience relate to the topic you selected and the approach you used to communicate it? Age is part of audience focus and it is a primary ingredient in audience analysis.

Ethnicity. One in ten persons in the United States is foreign born, the highest number since 1930 (*www.census.gov*). The states with the largest number of foreign-born immigrants are California, New York, Florida, New Jersey, and Texas. In California, for example,

Characteristics such as age, ethnicity, and gender can influence what interests an audience and how an audience receives a message.

❖ ❖ ❖ ❖   Hispanic or Latino and Asian numbers increased between 2000 and 2002. In 2000, 3,724,322 Asians were recorded while in 2002 that number jumped to 4,045,209. In 2000, Hispanic or Latino people numbered 10,773,996 while there were 11,647,327 in 2002. At the same time, the white population decreased from 22,432,751 to 21,705,267.

The ethnic makeup and identity of your audience members can make an important difference in your effectiveness. Ethnicity is defined "psychologically and historically through shared symbols, meanings, and norms. Ethnicity includes religious beliefs and practices, language, a sense of historical continuity, common ancestry, or place of origin" (Hecht, Collier, and Ribeau 1993). Ethnic groups have communication traditions that affect how members of that group speak and listen. Many ethnic groups have their own communication systems that are only partially shared with other groups.

Cultural rules, conversational patterns, and expectations may be different for people of different ethnic identities. For instance, African Americans and European Americans, while sharing aspects of American culture, each have unique styles of communicating. Sometimes dialects differ, sometimes conversational rules and expectations differ, and sometimes interactional styles like use of argument and discussion differ between the two groups (Hecht, Collier, and Ribeau 1993).

Carbaugh (in Martin, Nakayama, and Flores 1998) tells how difficult a course in public speaking was for members of the Blackfeet Indian Nation in Montana. The Blackfeet value public speaking skills but see them as reserved for those in leadership positions (mainly the tribal elders), as cautiously used because of the risks involved, and as exhibited often through silence. Yet white people see speakers acting on, influencing, and seeking change in an audience. Blackfeet see silence as a primary mode of expressing interconnectedness with a listener or active receiver. So a public speaking student from the Blackfeet Nation would feel presumptuous about speaking in front of a group of strangers and uncomfortable about communicating primarily with words. You can see that ethnic identity is a significant part of audience analysis; understanding and appreciating the ethnic makeup of your audience should be a factor in topic selection and approach.

As speakers, we also need to be sure that we do not accidentally or needlessly injure or insult audience members with ethnic backgrounds different from our own. Members of the dominant culture of the United States have had tumultuous relationships with members of smaller **co-cultures.** For example, Cuban Americans, Puerto Ricans, Vietnamese, and Appalachians are just a few of the groups that have been excluded from partaking in many of the privileges that members of the dominant culture enjoy. Members of various ethnic groups are sensitive to the discrimination that has limited their people.

Sometimes even well-known public speakers make errors that are outra-

Ethnic groups have communication traditions that affect how members of that group speak and listen.
(Photo: Claire Zugmeyer/*Daily Bruin*)

geous to members of ethnic co-cultures. Well-meaning people can accidentally use metaphors, language, or examples that members of other co-cultures find offensive. You can learn to be more sensitive to other groups by
practicing your speech with friends who have backgrounds different from
your own, or by interviewing and observing other people to determine the
kind of language they avoid and the types of examples, analogies, and metaphors that they employ.

✔ Reality Check 3.3 ✔
Attitudes of First-Year Students

Some facts and figures about students toward the end of the 1990s according to the 32nd annual survey of college freshmen (1997), as reported in the
1999 World Almanac and Book of Facts:

- More plan to earn master's degrees (39 percent) or doctoral degrees (15 percent);

- More expect to earn a B average or better (50 percent compared to 33 percent in 1972);

- More plan to spend less time on study and homework (3.8 hours/wk compared to almost 5 hours/wk in 1987);

- More—an all-time high—overslept and missed class or an appointment (35 percent);

- More describe themselves as "middle of the road" politically (55 percent);

- Fewer describe themselves as conservative or far-right (21 percent);

- Unchanged was the number who described themselves as liberal or far-left (24 percent);

- Fewer—a record low—felt that keeping up-to-date with political affairs was important (27 percent);

- Fewer felt that commitment to "influencing social values" was important (38 percent);

- Fewer supported legal abortion (53 percent compared to 65 percent in 1990);

- Half (50 percent) agreed that same-sex couples should be allowed legal marital status;

- Over one-third (34 percent) believe in the importance of laws prohibiting homosexual relationships;

- Fewer have a desire to "promote racial understanding" (32 percent compared to 42 percent in 1992);

- Fewer reported frequent or occasional beer drinking (53 percent compared to 75 percent in 1981);

- More—the highest in 30 years—reported smoking frequently (16 percent compared to 9 percent in 1987);

- More believe in legalizing marijuana (35 percent compared to 17 percent in 1989) (p. 271).

How do these national figures compare with your assessment of your campus or your public speaking class? Knowing an audience's attitudes and predis-
positions can be very helpful to a speaker, especially when you are seeking attitude change.

Economic status. According to the Census Bureau (1999), the median family income in the United States was just over $44,500 in the late 1990s. Twelve percent of all families had incomes over $100,000, and 10 percent fell below the poverty line—$16,000 for a family of four (*The World Almanac,* 1999). The median income for men was $35,000 and for women, $26,000. White men had a median salary of $36,000; black men, $27,000; and Hispanic, $22,000 (p. 386).

What is the economic status of your audience? Are they primarily wealthy individuals or are they from lower economic groups? People who are wealthier tend to be more conservative, are often older, may have more education, and have probably traveled more than less wealthy people. Wealthy people may be less open to new ideas because they are accustomed to being treated deferentially, with courteous submission to their wishes or judgments. They may be more difficult to persuade because they feel that they have already made good choices. On the other hand, less wealthy people may be more liberal, may be younger, may be less educated because of their age, and have probably lived in a relatively smaller geographical area. Less wealthy people may be open to new ideas and may be more easily persuaded because they have less to lose.

Some topics are appropriate for more affluent audiences, while other topics are right for less financially successful people. Tax cuts for the rich may be a fitting topic for residents of pricey retirement villages, while learning to survive on next to nothing might be the right topic for a support group of unmarried teenage mothers. The appropriateness of topics like ideas for vacations, plans for retirement, or suggestions for investments could vary greatly depending upon the overall economic status of your audience. Topics like these can be relevant to a wide spectrum of people, as long as you tailor your approach to fit the audience's needs and experiences.

Occupation. If you are speaking to a group of employed individuals, you will want to know what occupations are represented. Recently, one of the authors spoke to several hundred women in public service in Ohio. The audience included people in the governor's cabinet, state senators and representatives, mayors of many Ohio cities, and other women in elected office. The audience also included women in clerical, secretarial, and support staffs. The topic of the speech was the role of gender in the workplace. Needless to say, the task was difficult. Examples and illustrations had to be generic rather than specific. If an anecdote about a successful professional woman was used, it had to be balanced with an anecdote about the difficulties of minimal-wage jobs in order to include all audience members.

Your topic choice is affected by the occupations of the people in your audience. If your audience is comprised of physicians, you might not want to talk about increased health care costs. If you are speaking to attorneys, you may want to avoid discussions about settling issues out of court. Some teachers and professors like to hear about labor unions, but their supervisors and educational administrators are less fond of the topic.

The language you use in your speech is similarly affected by the audience members' occupations. You should avoid jargon that is unfamiliar to your audience, but you can use a few words that are unique to them in their work. Do your audience members come from professions in which people use concrete, specific language, or are they more likely to appreciate metaphors and poetic language?

Can you think of illustrations that come from the field of work represented by the people in your audience? Can you draw comparisons between your topic and what the audience members spend the majority of their day doing? Do you know some of the individuals whom they hold as expert or as trustworthy? Try to incorporate some of these illustrations, comparisons, and individuals in your speech.

Education. According to the *1999 World Almanac,* 18 percent of Americans 25 and over lacked a high school diploma, 24 percent, or about one-quarter, of the population over 25 held a bachelor's degree, and 8 percent had earned a graduate degree at the master's or doctoral level. Income correlated directly with educational attainment: high school graduates earned a median $31,000; males with some college earned a median $36,000; males with an associate degree (2-year) earned a median $38,000; and males with a bachelor's degree or more earned a median salary of over $53,000 (p. 386).

✔ Reality Check 3.4 ✔
How Engineers Use Audience Analysis

To demonstrate how many professions use audience analysis, look at this article by Bernadette Longo (1995, December) in *IEEE Transactions on Professional Communication.* Entitled "Corporate Culture and Its Effect on Audience Awareness," the article demonstrates that engineers have their own corporate culture whose values are expressed by their choice of strategies and the information they choose to include or exclude. Most importantly, the article addresses how engineers need to consider their audience when making their choices (pp. 239–244).

The same publication, in an article by M. Subbiah (1992, March) called "Adding a New Dimension to the Teaching of Audience Analysis: Cultural Awareness," tells technical professionals how to be sensitive to cultural differences when communicating with nonnative speakers in the classroom and in the marketplace (pp. 14–19).

Education is related to economic status and occupation. A person's level of education may tell you very little about his or her intelligence, ambition, sophistication, or status. However, people with more education tend to read and write more, are usually better acquainted with the news, are more likely to have traveled, and are more likely to have higher incomes. What are some of the implications of educational level for how the speaker approaches the audience?

1. People who read and write regularly tend to have more advanced vocabularies, so adjust your language choices to the educational level of your audience.

2. People who are receptive to new information need less background and explanation on current issues than those who are not.

3. People who have seen more of the world tend to be more sophisticated about differences between people and cultures.

Most important of all for your particular speech and topic, you need to take into account how much your audience already knows about your topic; whether the audience is likely to already have a position on your issue; and what their knowledge level will do to your attempt to increase what they know or to change their minds on an issue. Take your audience's educational level into account as part of your analysis, because it may be an important determinant of topics and approaches.

Physical characteristics. Imagine that you were going to speak to an audience of the National Federation of the Blind, to a group of individuals in wheelchairs, or to people who had another specific physical disability. How would you adjust your speech? Most of us do a poor job of adapting to these situations. Indeed, members of such audiences generally ask that they be treated like those without disabilities. Nonetheless, we tend to speak louder, enunciate more clearly, or make other changes. We also may become self-conscious about language usage that disparages specific people, or we may be insensitive to negative stereotypes that we use. Even if your audience does not include people with physical disabilities, it is important to try to rid yourself of negative stereotyping. A great deal of such negative categorizing is done so routinely by people that they do not even realize they are guilty of perpetuating myths about individuals with disabilities. For example, in his speech "Language and the Future of the Blind," Marc Maurer, President of the National Federation of the Blind, at their annual convention in 1989 discussed one of the stereotypes that he found particularly offensive: the idea that people who are not sighted are incompetent.

> Recently an advertisement appeared from the Carrollton Corporation, a manufacturer of mobile homes. Apparently the Carrollton Corporation was facing fierce competition from other mobile home builders, who were selling their products at a lower price. Consequently, the Carrollton Corporation wanted to show that its higher priced units were superior. In an attempt to convey this impression, the company depicted the blind as sloppy and incompetent. Its advertisement said in part: "Some manufacturers put out low-end products. But they are either as ugly as three miles of bad road, or they have so many defects—crumpled metal, dangling moldings, damaged carpet—that they look like they were built at some school for the blind." What a description! There is the ugliness of three miles of bad road, or crumpled metal, dangling moldings, and damaged carpet. The slipshod work is all attributed to the incompetence of the blind. It is not a portrayal calculated to inspire confidence or likely to assist blind people to find employment (Maurer 1989).

In this section we discussed the demographic characteristics of an audience. We discussed the importance of gender, age, ethnicity, economic status, occupation, education, and physical characteristics. In the next section, we turn to additional methods of analyzing audiences.

Methods of Audience Analysis

Some speakers seem to be able to analyze an audience intuitively, but most of us have to resort to formal and informal means of gathering such information. Individuals in advertising, marketing, and public relations have developed complex technological means of collecting information from audiences before, during, and after the sending of their message (Behnke, O'Hair, and Hardman 1990). However, for most of us, the ways we commonly collect information about audiences are through observation, informants, interviews, and questionnaires.

Technical Tip 3.1
An Online Tutorial on Audience Analysis

For a slightly different approach to the study of audience analysis that is consistent with the approach in this text, go to *http://www.hc-sc.gc.ca/english/ socialmarketing/social_marketing/tutorial/step2.html.* This website has six pages of good information on demographics, psychological profiles (psychographics), audience analysis, and audience segmentation. This brief lesson is also related to audience analysis for persuasive purposes. Best of all, this lesson is free and easy to access.

Observation

Watching and listening reveal the most about your audience during your **observation.** Looking at audience members might reveal their age, ethnic origin, and gender. More careful observation can reveal marital status by the presence or absence of rings; materialism by furs, expensive jewelry, or costly clothing; and even religious affiliation by such symbols as a cross or Star of David. Many people in an audience advertise their membership in a group by exhibiting the symbols of the group to which they belong.

In the classroom, you have the added advantage of listening to everyone in your audience. Your classmates' speeches—their topics, issues, arguments, and evidence—all reveal more about them than you could learn in a complex questionnaire.

Your eyes and ears become the most important tools of audience analysis as you train yourself to become a skilled observer.

Informants

When you are invited to give a speech outside the classroom, your best source of information may be the person who invites you. This person can be your inside **informant,** who can tell you the following:

1. What topics are appropriate

2. What the organization believes or does

3. How many people are likely to attend

4. What the setting or occasion will be

5. How long you should speak

6. What the characteristics of the audience are

A key question to ask is why you were invited to speak, since that information will help establish credibility in your introduction. If they want you because of your expertise on needlepoint, auto mechanics, or macramé, then you will want to stress that in your speech. If they invited you because you are a model citizen, then emphasize that area of your life. In any case, your informant should be able to help analyze your audience so there will be no surprises.

Within the classroom, all of your classmates serve as informants. Listen to their speeches. What do they value or believe? What topics interest them? With what groups or organizations are they affiliated? Your classmates' speeches can provide you with valuable information about the classroom audience that will listen to your own speeches.

Interviews

Discover information about your audience by interviewing a few members of the group. Many speakers gain some of their most relevant material during the cocktail hour, during the reception, and during the dinner before the speech. The competent speaker uses this time with the audience to learn more about them, their needs, and their interests. An **interview** for information on the audience should focus on the same questions listed in the preceding section on informants.

When you are conducting an audience analysis for a classroom speech, you can talk to a few people from class. Try to discover their opinion of your topic, how they think the class will respond to it, and any helpful suggestions for best communicating the topic.

The only problem with interviews is that they take time. Nonetheless, if the outcome is important, interviews are a way to discover more about your audience.

Questionnaires

Whereas interviews take more time to execute than to plan, **questionnaires** take more time to plan than to execute. The key to writing a good questionnaire is to be brief. Respondents tend to register their distaste for long questionnaires by not filling them out.

What should you include in your brief questionnaire? It depends, of course, on what you wish to know. Usually you will be trying to discover what an audience knows about a topic and the audience's predisposition toward that topic. You can ask open-ended questions, yes-or-no questions, degree questions, or a mixture of all three—as long as you do not ask too many questions.

Open-ended questions are like those on an essay test that asks an opinion—for example:

- What do you think should be done about teenage pregnancies?

- What policy should govern working men and women when their child is born?

- What punishments would be appropriate for white-collar crimes?

Yes-or-no questions force a decision—for example:

Should pregnant teenagers be allowed to complete their high school education?

_____ Yes _____ No

❖ ❖ ❖ ❖

Should a man be allowed paternity leave when his child is born?

_____ Yes _____ No

Degree questions ask to what extent a respondent agrees or disagrees with a question:

I believe that pregnant students should finish high school.

| Very strongly agree | Strongly agree | Agree | Strongly disagree | Very strongly disagree |

They may present a continuum of possible answers from which the respondent can choose:

Which of the following should punish embezzlement of $5,000?

| $5,000 fine | $4,000 fine | $3,000 fine | $2,000 fine | $1,000 fine |
| 1 yr. jail | 2 yrs. jail | 3 yrs. jail | 4 yrs. jail | 5 yrs. jail |

How much paternity leave do you think men should receive?

| None | Three days | One week | Two weeks | One month | Two months |

These three kinds of questions can be used in a questionnaire to determine audience attitudes about an issue. A questionnaire such as the one in Figure 3.1, administered before your speech, can provide you with useful information about your audience's feelings and positions on the issue you plan to discuss. All you have to do is keep it brief, pertinent, and clear. For detailed information on audience analysis through surveys see *http://www.audiencedialogue.org/kya5c.html* or *http://www.audiencedialogue.org/manual.html*.

**Figure 3.1
Sample Questionnaire**

Teenage Pregnancy
1. I think that pregnant teenagers should finish high school.
   ___Yes ___ No
2. I think that pregnant teenagers should complete high school with their class instead of in special sections or places.
   ___Yes ___ No
3. At what grade do you think pregnant teenagers should be allowed to continue their education with their class?
   7th   8th   9th   10th   11th   12th
4. To what extent do you agree that our society punishes pregnant teenagers too much?
   Very strongly agree   Strongly agree   Neutral   Strongly disagree   Very strongly disagree
5. What, if anything, do you think should be done about the males who are responsible for the pregnancies?

Situational Analysis

Four factors are important in analyzing the situation you face as a speaker: the size of the audience, the occasion, the time, and the importance.

Size of Audience

The **size of the audience** is an important situational factor because it can determine the level of formality, the amount of interaction with the audience, the need for amplification systems, and the need for special visual aids. The larger the audience, the more responsibility the speaker has to carry the message. Larger audiences usually call for formality in tone and language; smaller audiences allow for a more casual approach, a less formal tone, and informal language. Very large audiences reduce the speaker's ability to observe and respond to subtle cues, such as facial expressions, and they invite audience members to be more passive than they might be in a smaller group. Large audiences often require microphones and podiums that can limit the speaker's movement, and they may require slides or large posters for visual aids.

Speakers need to be flexible enough to adapt to audience size. One of the authors was supposed to give a speech on leadership to an audience of over 100 students in an auditorium that held 250 people. Only 25 students appeared at the conference. Instead of a formal speech to a large group, the author faced a relatively small group in one corner of a large auditorium. Two hours later, the author was supposed to speak to a small group of 12 or 15 that turned out to be 50. Do not depend on the planners to be correct about the size of your audience. Instead, be ready to adapt to the size of the audience that actually appears.

You must also be prepared to adapt to other environmental factors. Your presentation may be plagued with an unusual room arrangement, an unfortunate sound system, poor lighting, a room that is too warm or too cool, the absence of a podium or lectern, a microphone that is not movable, or a lack of access to audiovisual equipment. If you have specific audio, visual, or environmental needs, you should make your requests to the individual who has invited you to speak. At the very least, you will want to inquire about the room in which you are to speak. Even so, you may be surprised to find that equipment is not functioning properly or that the room that was assigned to you has been changed.

Occasion

The **occasion** is the second situational factor that makes a difference in how a speaker adapts to an audience. The occasion sets up a number of unstated constraints. The speaker is supposed to be upbeat and even funny at an after-dinner speech, sober and serious at a ribbon cutting, full of energy and enthusiasm at a pep rally, and prudent and factual in a court of law. Even in the classroom, there are a number of unstated assumptions about the occasion that you violate at your own peril: you are expected to follow the assignment, deliver the speech extemporaneously, maintain eye contact, keep to the time limit, dress appropriately, and so on.

Outside the classroom, the confident speaker finds out what the expecta-tions of the occasion are. Consider for a moment the unstated assumptions for these public speaking occasions:

- A high school commencement address
- A testimonial at a retirement party
- A talk with the team before a big game
- An awards ceremony for top employees
- A pep talk to your salespeople
- A keynote address at a conference
- A "shape up" talk to employees
- An announcement of layoffs at the plant

Each of these occasions calls for quite a different kind of speech, the parame-ters of which are not clearly stated but seem to be widely understood. Our so-ciety seems to dictate that you should not exhibit levity at funerals, nor should you be too intellectual at a ribbon cutting. One of the best ways to dis-cover what is expected is to find out from the individual or the organization inviting you to speak.

Time

The third aspect of any speaking situation that makes a difference to a speaker is when the speech is given—the **time.** Time can include the time of day, the time that you speak during the occasion, and the amount of time you are expected to fill. Early-morning speeches find an audience fresh but not quite ready for serious topics. After-lunch or after-dinner speeches invite the audience to sleep unless the speaker is particularly stimulating. The best situ-ation occurs when the audience has come only to hear the speaker and that is all it expects to do.

The time you give the speech during an occasion can make a big differ-ence in how receptive your audience happens to be. A speaker was asked to speak to an Alumni Academy, an audience consisting entirely of people who gave a thousand dollars or more per year to the university. Seven deans were supposed to tell the Academy about their colleges in a series of five-minute speeches—each of which lasted seven minutes or more. By the time the last speaker was scheduled to speak, the audience was tired. Instead of giving a five-to-seven-minute presentation about the university, the speaker told audi-ence members they would think more kindly of the university if they were simply allowed to go have dinner. The audience applauded and left, thinking good thoughts about the speaker who didn't speak because the audience was too exhausted to listen. Even when you are the last speaker in your class, how-ever, you will not be allowed to avoid giving the speech. Instead, when you know you will be one of the last speakers for the day, you should do your best to be stimulating, novel, and empathetic with an audience that has grown tired of hearing speeches.

The amount of time you are expected to fill is still another aspect of time. You will probably find that people are genuinely relieved when a speech is shorter than expected, because so many speeches are much longer than anyone wants. It is easy, as a speaker, to fall in love with the sound of your own voice and to overestimate how thrilled the audience is to hear you. However, audiences will be insulted if you give a speech that is far short of expectations—five minutes instead of 30—but they will often appreciate a 45-minute speech when they had expected an hour.

Time, then, refers to the time of day, the time when you speak during an occasion, and the amount of time you speak. Time is a situational factor that you should carefully consider as you plan your speech.

Importance

The fourth situational factor is the **importance** of the occasion, the significance attached to the situation that dictates the speaker's seriousness, content, and approach. Some occasions are relatively low in importance, but generally the presence of a speaker signals that an event is not routine. As a speaker, you need to take into account the importance of the occasion. An occasion of lesser importance must not be treated as if it were of great importance, and an occasion of greater importance should not be treated lightly.

Rituals and ceremonial events are usually perceived as high in importance. The speaker at a university commencement exercise, the speaker at the opening of a new plant, and the speaker for a lecture are seen as important players in a major event. Speakers at informal gatherings or local routine events are somewhat farther down the scale. Nonetheless, a speaker must carefully gauge the importance of an event lest the audience be insulted by his or her frivolous treatment of what the audience regards as serious business.

The Uniqueness of the Classroom Audience

Students sometimes think of the speeches they deliver in public speaking class as a mere classroom exercise, not a real speech. Nothing could be farther from the truth. Classroom speeches are delivered to people who are influenced by what they see and hear. In fact, your classmates as an audience might be even more susceptible to your influence because of their **uniqueness** as an audience.

1. The classroom audience, because of the educational setting in which the speech occurs, is exposed to messages it might otherwise avoid: the audience is "captive."

2. The size of the audience tends to be relatively small (usually 20 to 25 students) and constant, so that the class begins to take on some of the characteristics of an organization.

3. The classroom audience is more likely to include a wide range of positions on the issues, including opposition.

4. Classroom audiences include one person—the professor—who is responsible for evaluating and grading each speech.

5. Classroom speeches tend to be short, but must be informative or persuasive.

6. The classroom speech is nearly always one of a series of speeches in each class period.

7. The speaker has an opportunity to listen to every member of the audience.

8. The classroom speech audience may be invited to provide written and/or oral commentaries on the speech.

9. The classroom speaker has more than one opportunity to influence or inform the audience.

Your classmates, as the audience, do not stay the same during the quarter or semester during which you speak to them: they have their own positions on issues, but they change as they listen and learn; they have information about some subjects, but they are learning more in this class and others; and they are changing themselves as they prepare for speeches and learn more about the topics than they knew before. Next we will look at how you can adapt to this unique audience.

Adapting to Your Audience

This chapter has given you some tools—observation, informants, interviews, and questionnaires—to use in analyzing your audience. This chapter has also reviewed some audience characteristics that tend to make a difference in how an audience responds to a speaker: age, gender, ethnicity, economic status, occupation, education, and physical characteristics, as well as with conventional wisdom. However, the tools of analysis and audience demographics will do you no good unless you use them for the purpose of **audience adaptation.**

Technical Tip 3.2
Learn About Audience Analysis Via a Web Course

Do you want to learn more about audience analysis on your own? Universities offer web-based instruction through their distance learning courses. Online courses have become very popular in the last decade. To learn about online course offerings, go to *http://www.newsweekdistancelearning.com* and determine if any courses exist on communication, public speaking, or audience analysis.

In the case of an informative speech, adapting to the audience means **translating** ideas. Just as a translator at the United Nations explains an idea expressed in English to the representative from Brazil in Portuguese, a speaker who knows about baud rates, kilobytes, and megabytes must know how to translate those terms for an audience unfamiliar with them. Perhaps you have already met some apparently intelligent professors who know their subject matter well but are unable to translate it for students who do not. An important part of adapting an informative speech to an audience is the skill of translating ideas.

Your instructors—from kindergarten through college—are essentially informative speakers. You have heard people communicate informative material for thirteen years or more. Consider those experiences that were positive and those that were not. Use your better instructors as role models and try to avoid what the poorer instructors did. These experiences are valuable ones as you improve your own public speaking skills.

Consider some of your best instructors. Why are they effective in the classroom? Most likely it is because they "talk your language" and provide examples with which you can identify. They may use examples from current television programs, from sports events, or from local news. They probably avoid the highly specialized vocabulary that oftentimes accompanies a given subject matter. They probably do not use the style of presenting point after point with no examples; instead, they provide ample illustrations of each of the points they make.

Now consider those instructors you would deem as not so capable. What do they do that causes you to rate them lower? They may talk "over your head" and use sentence structure and language that you do not understand. They may use examples from events that occurred years before you were born and provide no context for them. They might use a great deal of jargon that confuses you. They may speak in a way that makes them seem unapproachable to you.

In the case of persuasive speeches, adaptation means adjusting your message both to the knowledge level of the listeners and to their present position on the issue. Use the tools introduced in this chapter and the audience characteristics to help discern where you should place your message for maximum effect. Too often speakers believe that the audience will simply adopt their point of view on an issue if they explain how they feel about it. Actually, the audience's position on the issue makes a greater difference than the speaker's position, so the speaker has to start by recognizing the audience's position on the issue.

Effective speakers adapt their message to the audience.

Two students in a public speaking class provided an excellent example of what happens when the speaker does and does not adapt to the audience. Both speakers selected topics that seemed to have little appeal for the audience because both appeared to be expensive hobbies. One of the students spoke about raising an exotic breed of dog that only the rich could afford. The entire speech was difficult for the listeners to identify with, since they could not see themselves in a position of raising dogs for the wealthy. The other student spoke about raising hackney ponies, an equally exclusive business. However, this student started by explaining that he grew up in a poor section of New Haven, Connecticut. His father was an immigrant who never earned much money, even though he spoke six languages. This student came from a large family, and he and his brothers pooled their earnings for many years before they had enough money to buy good breeding stock. They later earned money by selling colts and winning prize money in contests. By first explaining to the audience that he was an unlikely breeder of expensive horses, the speaker improved the chances that the audience could identify with him and his hobby. He adapted his message to the unique audience.

What kinds of messages influence you? Consider the variety of persuasive speakers you have heard—ministers, priests, rabbis, and other clergy; salespeople; teachers and parents; presidents of the United States and of other countries and elected officials; people lobbying for a special interest group; and people trying to convince you to change your long distance telephone service or to make another kind of purchase through a telephone call.

What kinds of appeals work for you—emotional appeals or logical ones? Do you need to believe in the ethical standards of the speaker before you will listen to what he or she has to say? Do you like to hear the most important arguments first or last? Do you believe authorities, statistics, or other kinds of sources? If you use your own experiences and thoughtfully reflect on them, you may be able to understand better how others might respond favorably to you as a persuasive speaker.

Ethics and the Audience

As you prepare to speak to a particular audience, remember ethical considerations, those moral choices you make as a speaker. Remember that audiences expect different levels of truthfulness in different situations. A comedian is expected to exaggerate, distort, and even fabricate stories. A salesperson is expected to highlight the virtues of a product and to think less of the competition. A priest, judge, and professor are expected to tell the truth. In the classroom, the audience expects the speaker to inform with honesty and to persuade with reason.

Most speakers have a position on an issue. The priest tries to articulate the church's position, the judge follows a body of precedents, and the professor tries to reveal what is known from her discipline's point of view. You, too, have reasons for your beliefs, your position on issues, and the values you espouse. The general guideline in your relationship with your audience is that you have that audience's best interests in mind. That is why classroom or community speeches encouraging child abuse, drug addiction, racial unrest, and cheating are viewed with alarm in our society. Making ethical choices begins when you consider your topic and how you will present it to a particular audience.

NCA Credo for Communication Ethics

One of the tenets of the NCA Credo is relevant to this chapter:

- We condemn communication that degrades individuals and humanity through distortion, intimidation, coercion, and violence, and through the expression of intolerance and hatred.

Summary

The best speakers focus their message and their attention on the audience. They know there is much more to giving a speech than familiarity with the topic. They realize that audience characteristics can be important in determining what an audience wants to know and do.

Your message must be aimed at your target audience. You can conduct your audience analysis through observation, informants, interviews, and questionnaires. Because the speech takes place in a particular situation, you must also be aware of such factors as the size of the audience, the occasion, the time, and the event's importance.

You have discovered that the classroom audience is unique, that it differs in many ways from other audiences. However, the classroom is a laboratory in which you can learn analysis and application through adaptation. It is also a place where you can learn to make moral choices, choices that apply to positive development in our society.

Communication Narrative 3.1
Audience Analysis Required

Ho Young-Don was very nervous about his presentation to the managers. After all, he was nothing more than a sales associate who had brought to his manager's attention a way to inspire sales associates to do more selling. His manager mentioned the plan to his boss, the corporate vice president, who invited Ho to address the monthly meeting of all the company managers from a dozen stores around the city. Now that the time had come to present his idea to the managers, his idea seemed less and less plausible.

What Ho saw when he entered the conference room shocked him. He had assumed that the managers would be like his own manager. After all, his manager was the only one he had ever met. What shocked him was that his manager was a middle-aged white male with a wife and three kids. But the room was mostly African American women who were younger than his boss. No Asians like himself were present, but that fact did not surprise him.

Ho had not moved much past his introduction when an African American woman about his age loudly asked him a question without even raising her hand. She wanted to know how much "floor time" he had with the company. He had forgotten to tell them that he had two years of part-time and two years of full-time employment with the company. Her question inspired another and yet another until Ho found himself answering questions instead of giving his presentation. Finally, his own manager suggested that Ho regain the floor and continue with his presentation.

Even though Ho had wavered on the quality of his idea before entering the room, he now became quite defensive about the idea in the face of the barrage of questions that the women asked him after his presentation. They were very skeptical about his idea and said so. At least one said she had tried the same idea two years ago and it failed dismally within a few months. By now Ho was crestfallen. He felt that his idea had been encouraged by his boss and shot down by his manager's colleagues. He felt that he had lost face in front of his own manager, who had expected him to gain acceptance from the other managers.

What could Ho have done before the speech to avoid some of the problems he faced in his presentation? What kinds of analysis explained in the chapter would have helped in this situation? What do you think Ho should have done differently? To what extent did cultural or co-cultural differences enter the picture? What would you do in a similar situation?

Vocabulary

androgynous Combining masculine and feminine traits.

audience adaptation Making the message appropriate for the particular audience by using analysis and applying its results to message creation.

audience analysis Discovering as much as possible about an audience to improve communication in a public speaking situation.

co-cultures Groups of people united by a common element who live in a culture operating within a dominant culture.

conventional wisdom The popular opinions of the time about issues, styles, topics, trends, and social mores; the customary set of understandings of what is true or right.

degree questions Questions used in interviews and in audience analysis questionnaires that invite an explanation, not just a yes or no response.

demographics Audience characteristics such as age, gender, education, and group membership.

importance The degree of significance attached to an occasion that dictates the speaker's seriousness, content, and approach.

informant The person or group inviting you to speak who informs you about the nature of your audience and its expectations for your speech.

interviews Situations in which information is sought by an interviewer from an interviewee in person or on the telephone.

observation A method of audience analysis based on what you can see or hear about the audience.

occasion A situational factor referring to the event at which a speech is given, and the kinds of speaking behavior appropriate for that event.

open-ended questions Like essay questions, questions that invite an explanation and discourage yes-or-no responses from the person being questioned.

questionnaires A method of audience analysis that asks written questions of individuals to discern their knowledge level or attitudes about a topic.

size of the audience A characteristic that can determine everything from the loudness of voice to the formality of language.

time The time of day, the specific time when you are scheduled to speak at an event, and the amount of time you are expected to speak.

translating The skill of rendering what you know into language and concepts the audience can understand.

uniqueness The particular characteristics of the classroom-speaking situation that make it different from other speaking events.

yes-or-no questions Questions used in interviews and in audience analysis questionnaires that invite only a yes or no response.

Application Exercises

1. Given the observations listed in this exercise, what do you think would be the audience's probable response to a speech on abortion, inflation, or gun control? Choose one of these topics or another topic suggested by your instructor. For each statement about the audience, state how you believe they would generally

feel about the topic. This exercise may be done individually or by the entire class.

The audience responded favorably to an earlier informative speech on race relations.

The audience consists mainly of inner-city people from ethnic neighborhoods.

The audience consists of many married persons with families.

The audience members attend night school on earnings from daytime jobs in factories and retail businesses.

The audience members come from large families.

References

Audience analysis. (1999). The online tutorial: Social marketing. *http://www.hc-sc.gc.ca/english/socialmarketing/social_marketing/tutorial/step2.html*.

Behnke, R. R., O'Hair, D., and Hardman, A. (1990). Audience analysis systems in advertising and marketing. In D. O'Hair and G. L. Kreps, *Applied Communication Theory and Research* (pp. 203–221). Hillsdale, NJ: Laurence Erlbaum Associates.

Bergstrom, M. E. (1998). The Advertisement, the Image, and the Audience: A Rhetorical Analysis of the Advertisements in Four 1996 Issues of Glamour Magazine. An unpublished master's thesis, North Dakota State University, 1998.

Carter, S. (1999). *Civility: Manners, Morals, and the Etiquette of Democracy.* New York: Basic Books.

Census Bureau. (1999). *http://www.census.gov/hhes/www/income99.html*.

Cooper, W. I. (1999, August 4). Youth violence declines: CDC's national study defies public perceptions. *The Washington Post. http://www.washingtonpost.com*.

Hecht, M. L., Collier, M. I., and Ribeau, S. A. (1993). *African American Communication.* Newbury Park, CA: Sage.

Holcombe, M. W., and Turrentine, T. (1996). Herding cats: How to understand and manage your audience. *Competitive Intelligence Review,* 7(1), 29–35.

Jones, J. H. (1992). A greater voice in action: Women and equality. *Vital Speeches of the Day,* 59, 109–111. Courtesy of Julia Hughes Jones, former State Auditor of Arkansas. From a speech she delivered at Charlotte, North Carolina, August 26, 1992.

Kaufman, H. (1990, December 20). Salt and Pepper. *The Wall Street Journal.*

Kelly, D. (1991, January 28). Students' concern for society rises. *USA Today,* p. 1.

LeRoy, D. J. (1995). *Public Television: Techniques for Audience Analysis and Program Scheduling.* Washington, D.C.: Corporation for Public Broadcasting.

Longo, B. (1995, December). Corporate culture and its effect on audience awareness. *IEEE Transactions on Professional Communication,* 38(4), 239–244.

Maddox, J. (1999, April 23). Letter to the editor. *The Chronicle of Higher Education. http://chronicle.com*.

Martin, J. K., Nakayama, T. K., and Flores, L. A. (1998). *Readings in Cultural Contexts.* Mountain View, CA: Mayfield.

Maurer, M. (1989, October 5). Language and the future of the blind: Independence and freedom. *Vital Speeches of the Day,* 56(1), 16–22. A speech delivered at the banquet of the annual convention, Denver, Colorado, July 8, 1989.

Michel, H. R. (1993). King—from Martin to Rodney: Changing white attitudes. *Vital Speeches of the Day,* 59(10). Reprinted with permission.

Porter, James E. (1992). *Audience and Rhetoric.* Englewood Cliffs, NJ: Prentice Hall.

Sacks, P. (1996). *Generation X Goes to College.* New York: Open Court.

Samovar, L. A., Porter, R. E., and Stefani, L. A. (1998). *Communication Between Cultures* (3rd ed.). Belmont, CA: Wadsworth Publishing Co.

Schneider, A. (1998, March 27). Insubordination and intimidation signal the end of decorum in many classrooms. *The Chronicle of Higher Education. http://chronicle.com.*

Subbiah, M. (1992, March). Adding a new dimension to the teaching of audience analysis: Cultural awareness. *IEEE Transactions on Professional Communication,* 35(1), 14–19.

The World Almanac and Book of Facts (1999). Mahwah, NJ: Primedia.

Zona, G. A. (1994). *The Soul Would Have No Rainbow If the Eyes Had No Tears and Other Native American Proverbs.* New York: Simon & Schuster.

Chapter 4

The Speaker

In words are seen the state of mind and character and disposition of the speaker.

—Plutarch

Question Outline

I. What is the relationship between the speaker and the audience?

II. What does "Credibility is in the eye of the beholder" mean?

III. How is the way you see yourself related to how audiences perceive you?

IV. What are four dimensions of speaker or source credibility in public speaking?

V. What considerations should you make in introducing another speaker?

VI. What are some of the ethical choices facing the speaker?

Sarah Lee strode up to the podium like a person about to announce a lotto winner. Her hands gripped the sides of the lectern as she leaned toward her audience, her eyes looking directly into theirs. Her words were penetrating, her manner confident, and her voice vigorous. For 10 minutes, her audience sat spellbound until she broke it off—leaving them wanting more.

The Speaker-Audience Relationship

Many public speaking students would like to experience Sarah Lee's confidence. The good part about this fantasy is that the story is very positive; the speaker is a hero. The bad part is that the story is deceptive: often communication between speaker and audience is less satisfying. Most of us when we begin public speaking are full of uncertainties about ourselves, our message, and our audiences. We need some experience to feel better about ourselves. We need to compose some messages until we get better at organizing our thoughts and ideas. And we need to develop a relationship with listeners until we feel more comfortable communicating with them. We need to grow in confidence by discovering more about ourselves as a speaker.

The communication process is a transaction. The seven components of the process are interrelated. They cannot be isolated. Speaker and audience cannot be separated: they are interdependent. Who the speaker is, what the speaker says, and what the speaker does make a difference, of course. What also makes a difference is how individuals in the audience—the receivers—respond to you and your speech. Speaker and audience are connected. This chapter explores the speaker-audience relationship. You will explore in turn the idea of *ethos,* or source credibility; the dimensions of credibility; how credibility can be improved in a speech; and how you can affect a speaker's credibility when you introduce the speaker.

Credibility Is in the Eye of the Beholder

Aristotle wrote 24 centuries ago that a speaker's "character may almost be called the most effective means of persuasion he possesses." That idea is as true today as it was then. Your character goes by many names: reputation, honesty, loyalty, sincerity, faithfulness, and responsibility. Aristotle called this idea *ethos;* today the term is source credibility. The idea focuses on the source's, or speaker's, contribution to the speaker-audience relationship. Source credibility is not something that a speaker possesses, like a suit of clothes used to dazzle an audience. Instead, credibility is created by the relationship between the speaker and the audience. **Source credibility** is the audience's judgment, or evaluation, of a speaker.

The audience rather than the speaker determines credibility. The audience perceives a speaker at a particular time, place, and occasion, talking about a particular topic. The implications for you as a public speaker are the following:

1. Credibility must be established with every audience you face. You might be fascinating to your classmates when you talk about binge drinking, but a room of electricians might be unimpressed with your qualifications on their issues.

2. You are more credible on some topics than on others: choose topics about which you can establish credibility with an audience. You might know plenty about environmental concerns but be relatively uninformed about political issues. Speak about the environment.

3. You may be more credible in some situations than in others. You might be perceived as highly credible at work but considerably less credible at leading public prayer, speaking at a ribbon cutting, or serving as master of ceremonies.

4. You may be more credible with one ethnic or cultural group than another. Would you be credible to an audience of African Americans, white business leaders, Latinos, or a gay and lesbian support group?

How Do You See Yourself?

How you see yourself can be how your audience sees you. Since source credibility depends on how your listeners perceive you, you should consider why self-perception is important to the public speaker.

Self-perception is how you view yourself, your competencies, your physical self, and your psychological self. Sarah Lee, the student portrayed in the fantasy at the beginning of the chapter, appeared to be high in self-confidence and self-assurance, devoid of anxiety, and determined to communicate. Her life history led her to that portrayal of herself.

Acting confident can make you feel confident. (Photo: Justin Warren/Daily Bruin)

What is your self-perception? If you were an animal, would you be an eagle or a mouse? Do you see yourself as master of the microphone, the pride of the podium, or the victim of a vicious audience? Your self-perception is communicated to the audience by your behavior.

A student consulted his instructor because his shyness showed every time he spoke. His voice was meek, his eyes focused on the floor, and the audience felt sorry for him. Fellow students tried to be supportive: "Don't be afraid of us; we're your friends," said one. "Look at us," said another, "so we can hear what you say. The little that I heard sounded good to me." The student said that his classmates were seeing him exactly as he felt. The student decided to try a new approach. He decided to act confident. To bolster his courage, he practiced his speech over and over in the empty classroom. He sometimes pretended the audience did not believe him. At other times, he pretended that they agreed with every word. Acting confident made him feel confident (Bem 1970). He behaved more boldly than his self-perception would ordinarily permit. More than ever before, his actions depicted his true feelings about the issue.

The way you see yourself is often the way your audience will see you. Maybe you will have to behave confidently before you feel confident, but working on your self-perception is the first step toward being confident. One important way to improve your self-perception is to succeed at every classroom speech.

On the Web

The way you feel about yourself is often communicated to the audience in unconscious ways. To determine your self-esteem, you might want to take a self-esteem test. The website "queendom" has a variety of personality and relationship tests. Go to *http://www.queendom.com/tests/minitests/fx/self_esteem.html* for a test on self-esteem.

Are You Afraid of Your Audience?

Many speakers fear their audience. According to a cluster of articles in *U.S. News and World Report* (1999, June 21), shyness now has a new label: Shyness is now called "social anxiety." The authors, Schrof and Schultz, describe the malady: "The heart races, palms sweat, mouth goes dry, words vanish, thoughts become cluttered, and an urge to escape takes over" (p. 50).

Unfortunately, this "source of overwhelming dread" describes almost exactly the way beginning speakers feel when they are giving their first speeches. The authors claim that shyness is the third most common phobia—after depression and alcoholism—and they add that it affects "roughly 1 out of every 8 people" (p. 50). Schrof (1999) writes: "The fear of public speaking is by far the most prevalent social anxiety . . ." (p. 57). However, before you diagnose yourself as a victim of "debilitating shyness," you should also consider these words from the same authors:

> Shyness is a nearly universal human trait. Most everyone has bouts of it, and half of those surveyed describe themselves as very shy. Perhaps because it is so widespread, and because it suggests vulnerability, shyness is often an endearing trait. . . . The human species might not even exist if not for an instinctive wariness of other creatures. In fact, the ability to sense a threat and a desire to flee are lodged in the most primitive regions of the brain. (p. 50)

Commercial interest in shyness should not be overlooked. Unnamed in psychiatry manuals until 1980, the shyness that half the population says they experience is now the target of SmithKline Beecham, a pharmaceutical company whose antidepressant, Paxil, may be destined to be the Prozac of the future (Koerner 1999). Schrof (1999) suggests that ordinary people, petrified at the thought of giving a public speech, overcome that anxiety through practice (p. 57). Public speaking teachers have for years successfully helped students overcome shyness without psychiatry or expensive drugs.

How Does Your Audience See You?

An audience will judge you as credible depending on what you show and tell them. Why do you dress up when you go for a job interview? Are you trying to deceive the interviewer into thinking you always look this good? No, but you are trying to make a good impression for the purpose of securing a job. Similarly, audiences judge a speaker even before the speaker talks. Your perceptions of your fellow students are based on everything you sense about them: the way they look, the way they act, the way they sound. When you speak in front of them, you are trying to make a good impression, to communicate a message.

You can help determine **audience perceptions** with your own choices. The kind of language you use can tell a great deal about your education. Your vocabulary can reveal how much or how little you know about a subject. Your use of arguments and evidence can demonstrate how logical or reasonable you are. How you dress tells the audience what kind of relationship you want with them. A smooth performance can show that you cared enough to prepare and practice a speech for them.

You earn the right to speak about particular topics. As one petite female student said in the beginning of her speech:

> I am a woman. I am five feet tall. I have spent 25 years in a world that seems to be designed for six-foot-tall men. Today I am going to talk about that problem so you can empathize with small people.

You earn the right to talk about children by raising them, about various jobs by doing them, and about your neighborhood by living there. You can also earn the right to talk by interviewing others, reading about an issue, and studying a topic. Ultimately the audience decides whether you have earned the right to tell them about an issue.

What Do Audiences Want?

On the premise that good theory breeds good practice, we are going to look at four dimensions of source credibility that seem to affect how audiences perceive speakers. The four components are common ground, dynamism, trustworthiness, and competence (Tuppen 1974).

✔ Reality Check 4.1 ✔
Your Comfort Level as a Source

The National Communication Association (1998) commissioned Roper Starch Worldwide to interview over 1000 people in a survey. One question aimed to discover people's comfort level in various communication situations. Each person was asked whether they felt very comfortable, somewhat comfortable, or not at all comfortable communicating in each of the situations listed. Here is part of one table showing the results:

Situation	Very Comfortable	Somewhat Comfortable	Not Too Comfortable	Not At All Comfortable
On the telephone	60%	33%	4%	2%
Face-to-face	65%	32%	3%	1%
Speaking at a meeting	34%	36%	17%	9%
Giving a presentation or speech	24%	34%	22%	17%

Clearly few people feel "very comfortable" giving a speech and more than a third feel uncomfortable.

Common Ground

Before the class began, the speaker, Jack Thomas, "drew" a floor plan on the classroom floor with masking tape. The floor plan filled the room, so most of the classroom chairs were within the tape boundaries. The speaker pointed out that he lived in married student housing. This housing was a joke on campus because it consisted of World War II-vintage Quonset huts, tin buildings that looked like half-buried coffee cans. The student walked around his floor plan, telling his audience the square footage in the kitchen, the bedroom, the living room, and the bathroom. Did the people in class have that much space? He pointed out that his housing cost two hundred dollars per month. How much were classmates paying for housing? By the time Jack Thomas finished explaining the facts about married student housing, his audience no longer thought of it as a joke.

Common ground is what a speaker shares "in common" with the audience.

Jack Thomas used a dimension of speaker credibility called **common ground,** a term, like communion, communism, and communication, that denotes "sharedness." You can share physical space, ideas, political positions, race, religion, organizational membership, gender, age, or ideology with an audience. Introduced early in a speech, common ground becomes a catalyst for other dimensions of source credibility. Why? Because we like familiarity, because we like to be affirmed ("I agree with you"), and because agreement and affirmation build rapport with an audience.

Common ground is a very relational dimension of source credibility. Common ground is like a verbal handshake; it tells the audience members that you want to have a relationship with them. You may want to consider features about yourself that you have in common with your audience. What aspects of your past or present experiences may be shared by them?

Dynamism

Have you ever watched the Sunday morning ministers on television? A few are dressed in Ph.D. gowns, with velvet strips on their arms. They speak with big words and little movement, much like many college lecturers. Others are human dynamos who pace the stage, cry over touching passages from the Bible, bang out songs about Jesus on their piano, yell, sweat, whisper, and shake their fists.

The ministers who stand so stiffly, gesture little, and seem lifeless are lacking in **dynamism;** the preachers who exhibit energy, action, and expression are high in dynamism. You do not have to imitate the Sunday morning orators, but you should learn how to deliver your messages with energy and concern. You should learn how to move, how to gesture, and how to vary your pitch; using these elements of dynamism helps you hold your audience's attention. When you go to the zoo, for example, you spend little time watching the lions sleep in their cage, but everybody likes to watch the monkeys because they swing, groom, and entertain. Effective speakers don't have to be monkeys, but neither do they want to come across as sleepy lions—looking good but boring. Here are some ways that you can add dynamism to your speech delivery.

1. *Purposeful movement.* Get some emotion in your motion. Animation can be seen as a sign of the speaker's warmth and affection for the audience. The speaker's genuine enthusiasm for the topic can be contagious. The audience may appreciate some motion and emotion about the topic.

2. *Facial expression.* Use your eyes, eyebrows, and mouth to denote surprise, pleasure, annoyance, disapproval, or skepticism. Your face does not have to be a composite of emotions, but your expressions should relate positively to your message.

3. *Lively language.* Use action verbs and concrete, specific nouns to liven your speech. "He flew through the house like a hornet on fire" is more exciting than "He hurried through the house."

Speakers exhibit dynamism through energy, action, and expression. (Photo: Dave Hill/*Daily Bruin*)

4. *Gestures.* Use your arms, hands, head, and neck to help convey your message. Gestures that reinforce the message result in high-fidelity communication.

All of these are methods of encouraging the audience to see you as dynamic. However, remember that source credibility is an audience perception, so you must be very careful to exhibit dynamism in ways that are appropriate to the audience, the situation, and the topic. Do not act on this section on dynamism, however, by standing up in front of an audience exuding energy without saying anything. Dynamism may or may not be your strength. Do not worry. Other dimensions of source credibility may play to your strengths.

Trustworthiness

In class one day, David Gold gave what appeared to be an outstanding speech against the censorship of music videos by church groups seeking to limit the raw lyrics and images on late-night television. After David's speech a fellow student, Emily Wentworth, asked for David's sources. Since the professor had stated the policy of revealing sources when requested, David gave Emily his list of references. The next week, Emily gave a speech revealing that David had modified many of the quotes the class heard in his speech. He had paraphrased the words of the church officials to make them sound more extreme than they actually were. Also the position he took on the issue was not supported by some of the groups he cited in his speech. Embarrassed, David decided to drop the course because Emily had shown him to be unethical. Would the class who heard David's speech and Emily's rejoinder ever trust anything David said? The consequences for violating trust can be severe.

This dramatic event stunned the class and was a vivid demonstration of the importance of trustworthiness. **Trustworthiness** is a dimension of source credibility that refers to the speaker's integrity, honesty, fairness, and sincerity.

Trust, like most virtues, is difficult to build but easy to destroy. A person who has been faithful in a relationship for years can falter once and find that trust destroyed. A friend who deceives, betrays a confidence, or lies is usually no longer a friend. The worst of family disputes, terrible working relationships, and long-term feuds are based on a loss of trust.

In public speaking, the audience has expectations that, if violated, lead to a speaker's loss of trustworthiness. The audience has the right to expect that you followed the rules in preparing your speech. Their expectations may include the following:

1. The speaker has actually spoken to the people interviewed and is quoting or paraphrasing them accurately.

2. The speaker has actually gathered evidence from the sources claimed and is quoting or paraphrasing that information accurately.

3. The speaker reveals which parts of the speech are taken directly or indirectly from other sources with oral footnotes (see later in this chapter).

4. The speaker has the best interests of the audience members in mind and does not encourage them to do things the speaker knows will be psychologically or physically harmful to them.

5. The speaker is expressing personal beliefs and ideas and is not just pretending in order to impress the audience.

Lest we become too dismal in this discussion of trustworthiness as a dimension of source credibility, we must point out that violations of trust are rare. Nearly all students prepare and deliver their speeches by following the rules. They do not try to trick or deceive their audience, lie, fabricate, exaggerate, or threaten the listeners' welfare. They follow the ten recommendations for public speakers, observe the Golden Rule, and make the moral choices that characterize ethical speakers.

Competence

An African American professor from an Ivy League school gave a lecture at a midwestern university, a university that had once gone to the Supreme Court to keep an African American student out of its law school. The white listeners were highly skeptical of an African American professor, since they had never seen a black Ph.D. before. The professor spoke for fifty minutes without notes. His speech included long quotes from books, which he cited by title, year of publication, and page number. His speech on racism was interesting

❖ ❖ ❖ ❖

and novel to the audience, and his address overflowed with arguments, evidence, and powerful reasoning. When the speech was completed, the questioning began. The audience seemed ready to take him on, but the professor was as adept at debate as he was at public speaking. By the time his lecture was over, most members of the audience were highly impressed by his competence.

Competence is the audience's perception of the speaker's expertise, knowledge, and experience. (Photo: Mark C. Ide)

Competence is the audience's perception of the speaker's expertise, knowledge, and experience on the topic or issue at hand. Competence is the proof that you know what you are talking about, that you can talk the talk and walk the walk.

How do you demonstrate your competence? You might have a résumé that shows your age, education, experience, and goals. A résumé is your statement of competence on paper. Another way to show your competence is by your ability to do things. A lab technician shows competence by fixing the computers every time they fail. A security person shows competence by achieving a zero property and cash loss in the company served. A financial advisor shows competence by lowering taxes, increasing profit, and decreasing losses.

How do you exhibit competence in a public speech? The professor cited in the preceding true story did it by flashing his photographic mind. You can do it by:

1. Disclosing your relationship to the topic: "Since I am the only Mormon in this class, I would like to explain some of my beliefs so you will understand me and my religion better."

2. Using sources that are not used by everyone else: "According to *Daedalus*, a publication of the National Academy of Arts and Sciences . . ."

3. Wearing clothing or objects to signal your relationship to the topic: "As this lab coat might indicate, I am a biochemistry major. My topic? The safety of sugar substitutes."

4. Using live models to illustrate your point: "To help me with my speech on violence in football, I want you to meet my 280-pound, six-foot-six friend, Rocky Scaradelli."

5. Revealing experiences related to the topic: "I

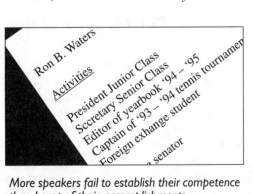

More speakers fail to establish their competence than boast of their accomplishments.

worked at the bottom of city government for over fifteen years, so I have a few stories to tell about inefficiency in government."

6. Demonstrating talent: "These ten watercolors of Wisconsin wildlife are some of the pictures I completed when I was stationed there."

7. Avoiding disorganization: a speech that the audience perceives as sloppily organized reduces the speaker's credibility.

8. Using appropriate facial expressiveness and greater vocal and facial pleasantness (Burgoon, Birk, and Pfau 1990).

You will think of creative ways to signal your own competence without being blatant. You always tread the fine line between arrogance about your competence and simple openness about your knowledge or ability. More speakers fail to establish their competence than overplay their credibility by boasting arrogantly about their accomplishments.

Now that you know the four dimensions of source credibility, you might think that a credible speaker has to be equally strong on common ground, dynamism, trustworthiness, and competence. Actually, for a speaker to function positively in all four dimensions at once may be impossible. For example, the more a speaker emphasizes competence or expertise, the less the listeners may see the speaker as being like them. The more a speaker emphasizes common ground, or similarity, the less the audience may see the speaker as being expert. What you do is emphasize your own strongest dimensions for the audience. If you are not very dynamic, then emphasize your expertise; if you are not very competent, then emphasize your common ground with the audience.

Celebrating Diversity

Haiti has been unstable for decades. In the past Haiti has asked the United States for help. Sometimes the United States has offered assistance and military power. Probably because of this support, war has been deterred and political chaos has been avoided. Should the United States continue to respond to the requests of Haiti? What arguments would you use if you were supportive of this notion? What arguments would you use if you opposed providing support? Learn more about Haiti at *http://www.haiti.org/* and *http://www. infoplease.com.*

How Do You Introduce Another Speaker?

One of the ways you can learn to apply the theory behind common ground, trustworthiness, dynamism, and competence is to introduce another speaker. This is an optional application assignment explained at the end of the chapter, but it is shown here to demonstrate how you can use the ideas presented.

The assignment, in this case, was to interview another student outside class, have both the introducer and the person being introduced stand in front of the room, and have the introducer try to reveal specific details and a general theme about the person. This particular public speaking class was almost half varsity and club athletes. Notice how Bree uses this fact to establish common ground between the speaker and the audience. In this speech, Bree Speidel (1999), a member of the varsity swim team, introduces another kind of athlete, Kate Haffey. Bree's purpose was to positively affect Kate's source credibility immediately before Kate gave a speech on ultimate Frisbee.

Bree Introduces Kate

If you have ever walked through the grassy area outside the residence halls, you have probably passed Kate Haffey playing Frisbee with a few friends. In fact, whether the time is 4 p.m. or 3 a.m., the chances are fifty-fifty of seeing Kate at practice.

Since Kate came to college and joined the ultimate Frisbee club team, the sport has become a major part of her life. She spends an average of eight hours a week practicing and goes to about three tournaments per quarter. Kate met most of her friends through sports. Dedicating so much time to athletics is not a new experience for Kate, however, because sports have always been a major part of her life.

Kate grew up in Mayfield Village, an eastside suburb of Cleveland, with her mother, father, and two brothers. Because she was the youngest child and the only girl, her brothers motivated her to participate in sports. She started playing softball when she was five and soon after learned tennis, soccer, and basketball. Her competitive nature caused her to always strive to be the best in a variety of sports. By her sophomore year in high school, Kate had decided that she excelled at tennis much more than any other sport; therefore, she began to focus all her attention on this discipline. Her efforts paid off her senior year when her tennis team won its division for the first time in history. Also, Kate was named to the all-conference first team along with her doubles partner. This accomplishment was Kate's greatest achievement as a high school athlete.

Today, however, Kate is here to explain to us her new love, ultimate Frisbee, and she is, as you can see, armed with her Frisbee. I present you with Kate Haffey.

Bree focused her attention on Kate's athletic experience and ability in order to elevate her credibility in a public speaking class with an unusually large number of accomplished athletes. Her strategies were to show Kate's dedication to ultimate Frisbee, to state that she plays on the club team, and to bolster Kate's renown as an athlete by mentioning her being named to the all-conference first team in tennis. You can decide if Bree, the varsity swimmer, did a good job of introducing Kate, the ultimate Frisbee player.

What Is the Right Thing to Say?

How would you feel if a friend introduced you to an audience? Your friend mentions that you have been pals for years, that you have gotten drunk together more than a few times, and that you were almost arrested once. Whether you are introducing another speaker or delivering a speech, you are always making **ethical choices** about what to say. Remember that you are trying to help the person you introduce build credibility and that you are trying to support the best interests of the audience when you speak. Thus, saying negative things about a speaker or playing to the baser motives of an audience (hate, violence, coercion) are regarded as negative ethical choices. You do not want to exaggerate the speaker's positive qualities, either. Your goal is to present the speaker in a positive light.

✔ Reality Check 4.2 ✔
Source Credibility and Leadership in the Business World

Two books are mentioned here to show how business is interested in the subject of source credibility.

Pearce, T. (1995). *Leading Out Loud: The Authentic Speaker, the Credible Leader.* San Francisco: Jossey-Bass. This book, intended for the lay reader, links source credibility to public speaking and leadership. 174 pages.

Kouzes, J. S., Posner, B. Z., Kouzes, J. M., and Peters, T. (1995). *Credibility: How Leaders Gain and Lose It, Why People Demand It.* San Francisco: Jossey-Bass. Part of the Jossey-Bass management series, this book explores the concept of source credibility from a business perspective. Based on surveys of 15,000, 400 case studies, and 40 interviews, the authors reveal six disciplines and related practices for developing and sustaining source credibility. 334 pages in the paperback edition.

As an ethical speaker, you will want to say what you sincerely believe, not just what the audience wishes to hear. While you can strive for audience satisfaction, you should only do so if you are sincere in the message you present. In addition, you do not want to be too "in your face." Although your perspective may vary from those of some of your audience members, you must seek to maintain a positive rapport with the audience.

Remember also that the public speaker in a democratic society behaves responsibly by trying to improve or develop that which is good and by trying to eradicate that which is bad. Naturally, opinions differ on what is good or bad, but reasoned debate, valid argument, and uses of evidence are all part of learning to be an effective and ethical speaker.

Finally, you need to be aware of how others see you. Do you come across as opinionated, too stuck on your own point of view to see alternatives? Are you seen by your audience as too slick to trust, as too naive to believe, or as too uncertain to have a position of your own? What you choose to say and how you choose to say your message affect the audience's perceptions of you as a speaker.

How to Avoid Plagiarism

One of the worst offenses that a speaker can commit is called **plagiarism.** This offense means that you used someone else's work as if it were your own. Blatant examples of plagiarism are such practices as using a speech or outline on which another student received a top grade, using a speech or outline downloaded off the Net, or using a speech or outline from some text other than your own. Unfortunately, some students are so unaware of this form of cheating that they do not realize that what they are doing is an offense. Depending on the severity of measures at your school, the consequences for plagiarism can vary from failure on the assignment to failure in the course to dismissal for academic dishonesty.

Students are not the only ones who commit plagiarism. Joseph Biden (D-Delaware) was a promising candidate for president of the United States when he lifted parts of a speech from a British politician. Once exposed, he was no longer a viable candidate. Ironically, plagiarism is exceedingly easy to avoid. All you have to do is attribute ideas or quotations from others by using an oral footnote. As long as you say "According to Graca Machel. . ." or "This week's *Newsweek* provides the following information about. . . ," then you have revealed that you are using someone else's information and you are giving them credit for that information.

Jon Hess (1996), who wrote a chapter on ethics for an earlier edition of this text, provides us with some examples of how plagiarism looks. He used an article in *Redbook* (1994) on why spouses argue over money to illustrate plagiarism. Start by reading the next three paragraphs.

> Whether your rows are over peppers or Porsches, there's barely a married couple that hasn't occasionally battled over money.
>
> And while money has always been a touchy topic, signs show that it's probably standing in the way of marital bliss now more than ever. With Americans marrying later, we tend to wed with more possessions and more debt. Responsibilities from previous marriages—child support and alimony—may turn up the tension even more.
>
> Some fights are just about dollars and cents. But others are really about emotional hot spots. "Money is so symbolically loaded," says Olivia Mellan, a psychotherapist and author. "It picks up other issues—love, power, security, control, independence, need. When you argue about money, you're arguing about all those feelings" (Barrett 1994, in Hess 1996).

Now examine a speech based on the *Redbook* article. Worded as follows, the speech contains plagiarism. Can you find the infraction?

> Many husbands and wives fight over money. Often it's because they don't like how their spouse is spending the money. Since Americans tend to marry later in life than they used to, their financial situations can be more difficult. People tend to have more possessions and more debt when they get married than they used to. And carry-overs from earlier marriages, like alimony or child-related expenses can complicate life even more.
>
> But there can be more to it. Money is so symbolically loaded. It picks up other issues—love, power, security, control, independence, need. When you argue about money, you're arguing about all those feelings.

This example illustrates two forms of plagiarism. In the first paragraph, the speaker paraphrases the *Redbook* author by taking the idea and putting the idea in his own words. The paraphrase includes no oral footnote. In the second paragraph, the speaker directly quotes the *Redbook* author but without using quotation marks or oral footnotes to indicate someone else's idea or words. Here is how the passage could be used in a speech without plagiarism.

> Many people fight with their husband or wife over money. An article by Katherine Barrett in the November 1994 issue of *Redbook* reports some of the reasons that might be the cause. She notes that often it is because they don't like how their spouse is spending the money. Since Americans tend to marry later in life than they used to, their financial lives can be more difficult. People tend to have more possessions and more debt when they get married than they used to. And carry-overs from earlier marriages, like alimony or child-related expenses can complicate life even more, says Barrett.

> But there can be more to it. The same article I just mentioned quotes Olivia Mellan, a psychotherapist, as saying, "Money is so symbolically loaded. It picks up other issues—love, power, security, control, independence, need. When you argue about money, you're arguing about all those feelings."

In this last sample, the speaker mentions the *Redbook* magazine and the name of the author with an oral footnote. The speaker carefully states which ideas come from Katherine Barrett. In the second paragraph the *Redbook* article is mentioned again but this time with the introduction of a person quoted in that article. Correctly citing sources is easy to do; neglecting or forgetting to cite sources is a serious offense called plagiarism.

Summary

Source credibility is a product of the source-audience transaction. Your view of yourself—whether you are confident or not—can be transmitted to an audience, so an upbeat, positive attitude is vital in a speaker. Most important, though, is how the audience evaluates you and your message, since the listeners determine your effectiveness as a speaker.

Source credibility is also the audience's perception of the speaker's competence, dynamism, trustworthiness, and common ground. Common ground is whatever you have in common with your listeners; trustworthiness is how honest they feel you are; dynamism is determined by how energetic they find you; and competence is how qualified they judge you to be. In all cases, the speaker has to display these characteristics if he or she desires the maximum positive response from listeners. You can apply the theory behind source credibility and its four components when you introduce another speaker.

Communication Narrative 4.1
Speaker Superior

Karl Krinos was a business executive, a person of impeccable manners and excellent education. He was Vice President for finance at Zoline Inc., a company with large holdings in international industries. Because he was often asked to speak to business groups, he had learned through bitter experience not to leave his introduction to chance.

In the past the PR Division of any company that invited him to speak would ask for his statement of credentials; that currently consisted of nearly 15 pages of facts about his education, his contributions to business and community groups, and awards for his participation. The PR people would assign some low-paid employee to convert the facts into an introduction. Some were pretty good; some were pretty bad—and almost all were too long and too boring.

On one occasion in the past Karl spoke at a firm where he was introduced by a fellow Eastern University alumnus and a member of his same fraternity. In front of an audience of two hundred fellow business executives, this person embarrassed Karl beyond belief. He told the audience that Karl rarely went to class and had been very popular with the ladies when he was an undergraduate. In a vain attempt to make himself seem more of a buddy than Karl remembered, the fellow implied that more than once he and Karl had gotten high together. In this crowd, the revelations undermined Karl's credibility in a manner that his entire speech could not overcome.

From that point on, Karl provided his own introduction, devised by his own PR Division and himself, that he provided well in advance with the request that his host use the prepared introduction. The introduction that he provided was adapted by mentioning the name of the group, the place and the occasion. But it was brief and relevant to the topic. These days, Karl did not worry about the possible embarrassment that can occur when you leave your introduction mostly up to chance.

Your ethical standards as a speaker are reflected in what you talk about (topic), whom you talk to (audience), and how you present your information (full disclosure or partial revelation). The content and delivery of your speech tell the audience what kind of ethical standards you embrace.

Knowing about source credibility can help you grow in confidence as a public speaker, especially if you begin by recognizing that speakers earn credibility through their knowledge, ideas, relationship to the audience, and adherence to high ethical standards.

Vocabulary

audience perceptions The way the audience assesses the speaker and the message.

common ground Similarities between the speaker and the audience; used in introductions of others and early in a speech to help establish source credibility.

competence The audience's perception of the speaker's expertise, knowledge, and experience.

dynamism The audience's perception of the speaker's boldness, activity, strength, assertiveness, and energy.

ethical choices The speaker's choices of topic, argument, evidence, and reasoning that appeal to the audience's higher motives.

plagiarism This offense means that you used someone else's work as if it were your own.

self-perception How you view your physical and psychological self, an important consideration in how others perceive you.

source credibility Called ethos by the ancients, the term refers to the audience's perceptions of a speaker.

trustworthiness The extent to which the audience finds a speaker honest, fair, and sincere—high in integrity.

Application Exercises

1. The way in which others see you is often influenced by how you see yourself. This exercise should be completed both early and late in the term to see if your public speaking class has altered your self-perception. Circle the adjectives that best describe the way you perceive yourself. Underline the adjectives that best

describe the way you think the audience will perceive you as a speaker. Complete the exercise in pencil the first time so that you can repeat it at the end of the term.

Assertive	Reserved
Fast	Thorough
Effective	Scientific
Formal	Conservative
Bold	Analytical
Shy	Poised
Daring	Friendly
Slow	Talented
Anxious	Exciting
Attractive	Humorous
Colorful	Cautious
Extreme	Caring
Good-looking	Bright
Energetic	Gracious
Experienced	Polite
Bashful	Open-minded
Casual	

2. Write down a topic and list three things you could do to signal your competence on that topic. For example, under the topic "Teenage Pregnancies," you might state (a) I know a number of single mothers who started with a teenage pregnancy; (b) I can tell you what has happened to them in the years since they were teenage mothers; and (c) I can tell you what I have read, heard, and experienced about the issue over the past three years.

3. List all the common ground you share with most people in your audience. Use this list for suggestions when you try to establish common ground with your audience.

4. Write an introduction of yourself that could be used by a classmate introducing you as a speaker.

References

Bem, D. (1970). *Beliefs, Attitudes and Human Affairs.* Belmont, CA: Brooks/Cole.

Burgoon, J. K., Birk, T., and Pfau, M. (1990). Nonverbal behaviors, persuasion, and credibility. *Human Communication Research*, 17, 140–170.

Hess, J. (1996) in Nelson, P., and Pearson, J. *Confidence in Public Speaking.* Madison, WI: Brown & Benchmark.

Hurley, A. E. (1997). The effects of self-esteem and source credibility on self-denying prophecies. *The Journal of Psychology,* 131(6), 581ff.

Koerner, B. I. (1999, June 21). Coming to you direct: Public service ads—or just a sales pitch? *U.S. News and World Report,* 126(24), 54–55. *http://www.usnews.com.*

Kouzes, J. S., Posner, B. Z., Kouzes, J. M., and Peters, T. (1995). *Credibility: How Leaders Gain and Lose It, Why People Demand It.* San Francisco: Jossey-Bass.

National Communication Association/Roper Starch (1998). How Americans Communicate. Annandale, VA: National Communication Association. *http://www.natcom.org/research/Poll/how_americans_communicate.htm.*

Pearce, T. (1995). *Leading Out Loud: The Authentic Speaker, the Credible Leader.* San Francisco: Jossey-Bass.

Rosnow, R. L., and Robinson, E. J. (Eds.). (1967). *Experiments in Persuasion.* New York: Academic Press.

Schrof, J. M. (1999, June 21). Panic on the podium: Why everyone gets stage fright. *U.S. News and World Report,* 126(24), 50–57. *http://www.usnews.com.*

Schrof, J. M., and Schultz, S. (1999, June 21). Social anxiety: For millions of Americans, every day is a struggle with debilitating shyness. *U.S. News and World Report,* 126(24), 50–57. *http://www.usnews.com.*

Seiter, J. S., Larsen, J., and Skinner, J. (1998). "Handicapped" or "Handi-capable?": The effects of language about persons with disabilities on perceptions of source credibility and persuasiveness. *Communication Reports,* 11(1), 21ff.

Slater, M. D., and Rouner, D. (1996). How message evaluation and source attributes may influence credibility assessment and belief change. *Journalism & Mass Communication Quarterly,* 73(4), 974ff.

Speidel, B. A. (1999). An introduction of Kate Haffey. From a speech of introduction in Interpersonal Communication 103, Public Speaking, Ohio University, Spring Quarter 1999. Used with permission.

Tuppen, C. J. (1974). Dimensions of communicator credibility: An oblique solution. *Speech Monographs,* 41, 253–260.

Wall, K. M. (1998, June 1). Enhancing your credibility: Does your audience believe you? *Employee Benefits Journal,* 23(2), 34ff.

❖ ❖ ❖ ❖

Chapter 5

Selecting a Topic and Purpose

Do not, for one repulse, forego the purpose that you resolved to effect.

—William Shakespeare

Question Outline

    I. What are the general purposes of public speaking?

    II. What three elements are included in a specific purpose?

    III. What is a thesis statement?

    IV. How can you use three different methods of topic discovery?

    V. What are the six suggestions for selecting a topic?

    VI. What standards can you use to evaluate your topic?

Fernando Sanchez had sharpened his pencil three times, had changed the music on his radio twice, and had been thinking for fifteen minutes about speech topics. His teacher told him to come to public speaking class with three possible speech topics. In spite of his best efforts, he could think of nothing to say. Finally—after half an hour of fruitless thinking—he decided to try personal brainstorming, a method suggested in the textbook. He filled a third of a page in five minutes with topics that were in his head. Then he circled three that he cared about the most. He chose the one that he felt had the most information available in periodicals and on the Net. Fernando had just taken the first step in speech preparation—topic selection.

❖ ❖ ❖ ❖   ## Purposes of Speeches

Without a plan, you do not know where you are going. Without a blueprint, you don't know what you are building. And in public speaking, without a purpose, you do not know what you should say. In this chapter we will consider how to prepare your speech. You will learn

a. how to identify your general purpose,

b. how to develop a specific purpose statement,

c. how to write a thesis statement (a one-sentence summary of your speech), and

d. how to identify and evaluate topics for a speech.

Speeches have both general purposes and specific purposes. We will consider both purposes in this section of the chapter.

General Purposes

In the broadest sense, the **general purpose** of any speech is to inform, to persuade, or to entertain an audience. In class, the general purpose of your speech may be determined by your teacher. When you are invited to give a speech to a particular group, the person who invites you may suggest a purpose. If you are not given a general purpose, you should consider the speech occasion, the audience, and your own motivations as you determine the general purpose of your speech.

The three general purposes of speaking can sometimes overlap. You often have to inform your audience before you can persuade them. Sometimes a speech to entertain also serves to inform. Or, you may choose a speech to entertain that unintentionally persuades an audience. Most speeches, however, can be distinguished as mainly informative, persuasive, or entertaining.

The speech to inform. The **speech to inform** seeks to increase the audience's level of understanding or knowledge about a topic. Generally, the speaker provides new information or shows how existing information can be applied in new ways. The speaker does not attempt to persuade or convince the audience to change attitudes or behaviors. The informative speech should be devoid of persuasive tactics. The following topics would lend themselves to a speech to inform:

Why are some drugs illegal?	What are sexually transmitted diseases?
What does alcohol do to the brain?	What are the effects of our immigration laws?
What is sickle cell anemia?	What are alternative medicines?
What do job interviewers expect?	What do interviewers want in a cover letter?

Remember, the main idea behind an informative speech is to increase the audience's knowledge about a topic.

The speech to persuade. The **speech to persuade** seeks to influence, reinforce, or modify the audience members' feelings, attitudes, beliefs, or behaviors. Persuasive speakers attempt to change what the audience members already know, but go on to alter how the audience feels about what they know, and ultimately how they behave. The following topics would lend themselves to a speech to persuade.

Give to charity	Try aerobic exercise
How to reduce poverty in the United States	Change our gun laws
Why the census should cease asking about race	Improve low-cost housing
Why young adults should worry about heart disease ·	Lower tuition

Remember, the purpose of a persuasive speech is change: change feelings, change attitudes, change beliefs, and change values. In other words, the persuasive speech seeks an altered state in the future.

The speech to entertain. The **speech to entertain** seeks to amuse an audience with imaginative and organized humorous, droll, or witty supporting materials. When you listen to a comic's routine on television, when you attend to a storyteller recounting humorous stories, or when you are in the audience of an after-dinner speaker, you are provided with a speech to entertain. Speeches to entertain, like speeches to inform or persuade, have a specific purpose and a central idea. The following topics would lend themselves to a speech to entertain.

How to make your marriage amusing	The problems with roommates
How much should you love your neighbor?	Why politicians are funny
Why women are better football fans than are men	Excuses for missing class
New discoveries: The first year of marriage	Men are like dogs; women, like cats

Remember, the purpose of a speech to entertain is to amuse others with your wit and humor. The effect you seek is more immediate than long lasting. Your purpose, if fulfilled, is that the audience is entertained during your presentation.

Specific Purposes

The general purpose involves nothing more than stating that your goal is to inform, to persuade, or to entertain. The specific purpose goes a step further. Here *you identify your purpose more precisely as an outcome or behavioral objective.* You also include the audience in your specific purpose. For example, a specific purpose statement might be, "My audience will be able to list the five signs of skin cancer." A **specific purpose statement** thus includes your general purpose, your intended audience, and your precise goal. Some additional examples of specific purpose statements follow.

The speech to entertain seeks to amuse or divert the attention of an audience. (Photo: Peggy Harrison/Courtesy of Elaine Lundberg)

- My audience will be able to explain how hate crimes are legally determined.

- My audience will be able to state some causes of date rape.

- My audience will state the benefits of regular exercise.
- My audience will be able to identify helpful herbs.
- My audience will stop drinking alcoholic beverages.
- My audience will join a sorority or fraternity.
- My audience will donate organs after their death.

Statements of specific purpose guide the entire speech like a map or blueprint. When you are developing your specific purpose, you should consider the following four characteristics of good purpose statements.

1. They are declarative statements rather than imperative (expressing a command, request, or plea) or interrogative (questioning) statements. They make a statement; they do not command behavior, nor do they ask a question.

   YES My audience will be able to state some reasons for academic failure.

   NO Why do students flunk out of college?

2. Strong specific purpose statements are complete statements; they are not phrases, clauses, or fragments of sentences.

   YES My audience will be able to defend our university's policies on liquor.

   NO The importance of liquor policies.

3. They are descriptive and specific, rather than figurative and vague or general.

   YES My audience will learn how to save a choking victim using the Heimlich Maneuver.

   NO My goal will be to demonstrate the value of human life through the judicious use of a proven maneuver for helping victims.

4. They focus on one idea rather than on a combination of ideas.

   YES My audience will be able to distinguish between a dessert and a table wine.

   NO I want my classmates to develop better taste in wine products and to know the difference between straight and blended whiskeys.

If your statement of purpose meets these standards, then you are ready to proceed to creating a thesis statement for your speech.

Thesis Statement

The general purpose and the specific purpose may be developed early in the speech preparation process. You may decide the general kind of speech

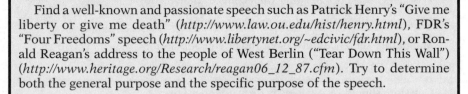

On the Web

Find a well-known and passionate speech such as Patrick Henry's "Give me liberty or give me death" (*http://www.law.ou.edu/hist/henry.html*), FDR's "Four Freedoms" speech (*http://www.libertynet.org/~edcivic/fdr.html*), or Ronald Reagan's address to the people of West Berlin ("Tear Down This Wall") (*http://www.heritage.org/Research/reagan06_12_87.cfm*). Try to determine both the general purpose and the specific purpose of the speech.

you will give and the specific goal you have before you conduct your research. However, until you have become informed on your topic, you will probably not be able to develop the thesis statement.

The **thesis statement** is a one-sentence summary of the speech. The thesis statement is similar to the topic sentence or central idea of a written composition: a complete sentence that reveals the content of your speech. Some examples of thesis statements follow.

College campuses need to campaign against bigotry on and off campus.

Elective cosmetic surgery may result in higher self-esteem, improved personal relationships, and better occupational opportunities.

Student misbehavior on campus and in the classroom is a problem.

A college education no longer guarantees a living wage.

Friendships with the opposite sex may lead to greater understanding and increased empathy for other people.

Now that we have considered general purposes, specific purposes, and thesis statements, we turn our attention to topic selection. In the next part of the chapter, we will consider how to search for, select, and evaluate a topic.

Topic Selection

Many people have difficulty getting started with the speech preparation process because they cannot think of topics for their speeches. Like Fernando, they spend time sharpening their pencils, pacing the floor, and doing whatever they can to avoid getting started. After you have read this section of the chapter, you should have an easier time finding a topic for your speech. What are some methods you can use to find a topic that is appropriate for your speech?

Searching for a Topic

When you need to find a topic, you can help yourself by using a method for finding a topic. Among the systematic methods are listing topics, monitoring your behavior, engaging in personal brainstorming, identifying current topics, and clustering topics.

Listing topics. **Listing topics,** a systematic method of finding a topic, can be done in two ways. The first is to narrow down a broad category to specifics—for example:

The USA has more prisoners than most nations on earth

U.S. prisons are a major taxpayer expense

Prisoners cost more per year than college students do

Drug convictions account for much of the increase

Mandatory sentences also bloat the prison population

Dealers and users alike fill the prison cells

Our state should reconsider its drug offender laws

Our city should reconsider its drug offender ordinances

The second way to use listing is to *start with a broad category and then list related ideas*—for example:

Overpopulation

Historical overpopulation

Sociological effects of overpopulation

Control of overpopulation

Gridlock on our city streets

Birth control and overpopulation

Overpopulation predictions for the next decade

Mass transit: A solution to gridlock

Housing in overpopulated areas

The single term that interests you is used to stimulate thought about a large number of related topics that would make good speech topics.

Monitoring behavior. Another method of topic selection is **monitoring your behavior,** examining what you do to unmask what you really like. What do you do each day? How do you spend your time? Monitor your behavior for a few days. How much time do you spend browsing on the Internet? How much time do you spend watching TV? What sports do you play? Keeping a diary or log of your behavior may help you identify a topic for your speech.

You may not be fully aware of some of your own interests, so study yourself to discover them. You might not realize you are more interested than most people in biology until you become aware that you have taken more courses in that subject than any other. You might not realize your expertise on foreign films until you note that you go to more foreign films than most people do. Whether the behavior is taking biology courses or watching films, your actions often indicate your main interests. Those interests can suggest topics you will enjoy exploring as you prepare for a speech.

After you have monitored your behavior, examine your interests more closely. If you observe that you spend at least an hour each day on the computer, then analyze more closely what interests you. How much time do you spend on e-mail, in chat rooms, or looking for entertainment? How much time do you spend seeking news, sports, or features? The same kind of analysis works for the newspapers you read, the magazines you read, and the hobbies and recreation you most enjoy. Examining your choices helps you pinpoint your areas of interest and suggests topics on which you might already have expertise.

Engaging in personal brainstorming. A third way to discover your own ❖ ❖ ❖ ❖
interests is to try **personal brainstorming,** thinking of topics that already
reside in your mind. **Brain-
storming** is usually a small-
group activity in which the members of the group think of a number of ideas. After gathering a
large number of ideas, the group
reduces the number to a few by
assessing their quality. Personal
brainstorming is sitting down
and giving yourself five minutes,
or another prescribed time, to
think of as many ideas as you can
for speeches. The items do not
need to be titles, just ideas.

Brainstorming may be easier
for you if you identify some categories that can be used to get you
started. For example, you may

*A closer look at a category you like can produce a topic
for your speech.*

want to think of people, places, or things. Or, you may want to consider
events, issues, or concepts. After you have identified some general categories,
you can think of items that would fit in each. For example, if we use people,
places, or things, we might come up with some of the following ideas:

People	Places	Things
George W. Bush	Kosovo	salsa
Bill Gates	Australia	rodents
Keenen Wayans	The Grand Canyon	pornography
Bill Cosby	Hollywood	vests
Madonna	Lake Mille Lacs	soda
Steven Spielberg	Napa Valley	cigarettes
Tom Cruise	Bangkok, Thailand	geography
Al Gore	Central LA	religion
Whoopi Goldberg	South Chicago	fishing gear
Jennifer Lopez	Miami	cocaine
Sandra Day O'Connor	Mount Rushmore	anchovies
Ricky Martin	Central Park	red beans and rice
Chris Rock	Nepal	conventional wisdom

Naturally, the words listed during personal brainstorming need to be evaluated for audience interest and the speaker's ability to gather information. We
will consider some general guidelines for selecting topics and how to evaluate
topics in a later section of this chapter. We should also note that the chosen
topic needs to be narrowed. However, this personal brainstorming method
generates a large number of topics, and this method may be useful for you.

Identifying current topics. Identifying **current topics**—topics of interest today because they are in the news or on the minds of people in your audience—is another method of finding a topic. Among the best sources of ideas
on current topics are newspapers, magazines, TV news/discussions/docu-
mentaries, radio talk shows, and the Internet. Specialized magazines of political opinion and editorials from major newspapers are especially good at provoking ideas for speeches.

> ### Technical Tip 5.1
> ### Finding Topics on the Net
>
> Although using speeches found on the Net is unethical, you may get some ideas for speeches by looking at some of the following URLs.
>
> *http://faculty.cinstate.cc.oh.us/gesellsc/publicspeaking.* Carla Gesell-Streeter's "Public Speaking" site comes to you from Cincinnati State Technical and Community College. The site includes help with speech topics: international topics (Rowley 1991) and domestic topics. Designed to be helpful to beginning public speaking students.
>
> *http://web.sau.edu/WastynRonaldO/topics.html.* This site has a relatively long list of general topics for speeches. The list contains some topics that are informative and some that are persuasive. All topics on the list need to be narrowed for use in the classroom speech.

Still another way to find a topic is to consider some issues covered in recent student speeches. Here is a brief list of topics from student speeches:

- The case for nuclear power
- The power of poetry
- Are professional athletes overpaid?
- Why junk food is good for you
- High profits for drug companies
- Why increase defense spending?
- Rising healthcare costs
- Are college athletics too big?
- Women in politics
- Avoiding AIDS
- What you should know about financial aid
- Choosing fabrics for wear
- Nursing—a noble calling
- Children who have children
- The problem with required courses
- What does a mechanical engineer do?
- Why banks fail
- Securing a loan
- Should students invest?
- Our child-support laws
- Finding entry-level jobs

If you do not find a topic by listing topics, monitoring your behavior, engaging in personal brainstorming, or identifying current topics, then you might want to try an approach to discovering a topic called "clustering."

Clustering topics. **Clustering** topics, linking related ideas in a nonlinear fashion, is a method originally devised for helping students with written composition (Rico 1983). Clustering can work equally well in helping discover speech topics. The method works like this: think of a concept or an idea you

Celebrating Diversity

Do you believe that a person's country of origin, race, gender, or other features determines her or his interest in some topics? After you have used one of the methods for determining a topic that is suggested here, compare your list with that of another person who is different from you in place of origin, race, or gender. Would they be interested in hearing a talk on these topics? Why or why not? What would be more appealing to them?

know something about. Write that topic in the middle of a sheet of paper and circle it. Then, for ten minutes, let your mind free associate as you write down any other subjects related to the first or subsequent ideas. Circle them and attach them to the concept from which they originated. If you wish, use capital letters to indicate a particularly good idea for a speech.

Clustering topics is different from listing topics because in clustering you are relating ideas to each other; when you list topics, they may share no logical connections. Figure 5.1 shows what a student produced after three minutes of instruction on clustering (Peters 1990). He came up with eighteen topics related to genetic engineering in ten minutes. Many of his ideas could be developed into speech topics by narrowing them, selecting them for appropriateness for the audience, and choosing topics of interest.

Selecting a Topic

Here are some general guidelines for topic selection used successfully by public speaking students:

1. *Speak about topics you already know.* What subjects do you know about—science, cosmetics, mechanics, or childcare? Speak about something you already know, and save a lot of research time.

2. *Speak about topics that interest you.* What subjects arouse your interest? What do you like to read about? What elective courses do you choose? Selecting a topic that interests you will make your exploration worth the effort.

3. *Speak about topics that are uniquely your own.* Have you had unusual jobs or travel experiences? Look at your background for ideas to share with your audience.

4. *Speak about current topics.* What are the Internet, newspapers, magazines, radio, and TV news covering at the moment? Which of those news items would you like to discuss with a campus expert? Usually people have little background about current news, so items that interest you could be examined more thoroughly in a speech.

5. *Speak about topics your audience finds interesting.* What do people in your class enjoy talking and hearing about? Which of their favorite topics could you discuss with some authority? If people tend to talk with you about certain subjects, then you might want to consider a speech about one of those topics.

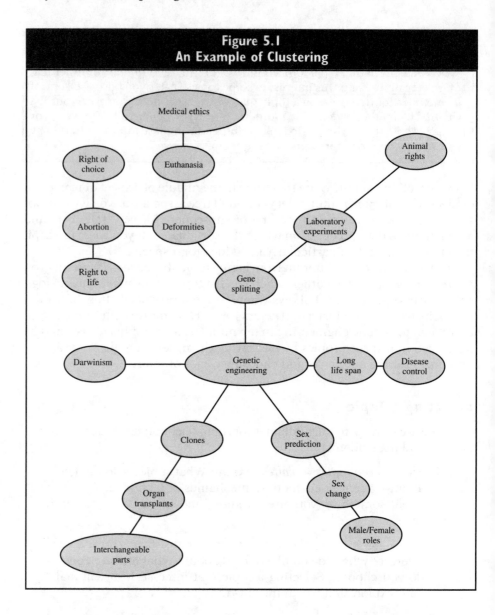

Figure 5.1
An Example of Clustering

6. *Speak about a topic that the audience embraces but you do not*. Are there any ideas that seem to be accepted without question by your audience but that you think could be challenged? Try to convince members of the audience to join your way of thinking on such a topic.

Evaluating Topics

Once you have arrived at a general topic, the next step is evaluation, deciding if the topic meets the standards of **appropriateness** for the speaker, audience, ethical standards, and occasion.

Appropriate for You

❖ ❖ ❖ ❖

Although you must always remember to remain focused on the audience, the first step in evaluating a topic is to consider whether the topic is of interest to you. A speech is appropriate for you as a speaker if you can generate interest in the topic. Your ability to deliver an interesting speech depends in part on your own interest in the topic. If you are enthusiastic, then the audience is likely to share your feelings. If you are not, the audience will probably sense your passivity. Avoid audience disinterest by selecting a topic that interests you.

Research is every speaker's obligation. You should either know something about your topic, or you should have a sincere interest in learning more about it. Choose topics about which you know a great deal. A topic is appropriate for you if you know—or can learn—more about it than most of the people in the audience. Most of us possess only superficial knowledge on most topics. A speaker can generally learn more about a specific subject than is generally known to an audience. When you have such knowledge, you are said to have subject matter competence.

Appropriate for the Audience

The audience is of central concern to the speaker as she or he considers speech topics. A speech is appropriate for an audience if the content is both interesting and worthwhile to the audience.

One of the primary functions of audience analysis is to discern what will interest the audience. The speaker is responsible for generating audience interest. Let us say that you are very interested in coin collecting, but you realize that practically nobody else in the class is. You have both interest in, and knowledge of, the topic. You do not have to give up that topic as long as you can get class members interested. One way to arouse audience interest might be to show how easy and profitable coin collecting can be.

Also consider whether your topic is worthwhile for the audience. If the audience is already familiar with the topic, be careful about the information you are presenting. Try to present new information about familiar topics; do not repeat what the audience is already likely to know. A speech about a topic too familiar to the audience

Sometimes a particular topic is just right for you. (Photo: Mark C. Ide)

will be highly uninformative. A speech about a topic that is too trivial will not be worth the audience's time. A proper analysis of your audience should reveal both how interesting and how worthwhile your topic would be.

Appropriate Ethical Standards

Your topic should meet ethical standards—that is, the standards of appropriateness in speaking about topics that improve our society. Perhaps the easiest way to illustrate appropriateness is to consider briefly some ideas that are inappropriate: a speech on how to make money through prostitution, drug pushing, and child pornography; a speech encouraging anti-Semitism, sexism, and homophobia; or a speech that fosters negative stereotypes, misogyny, and prejudice. More subtle examples of speeches that are unethical include speeches that provide an audience with information on how to avoid getting a speeding ticket or how to cheat on income taxes. You can avoid violating ethical standards if you remember that, as a public speaker, you strive to improve society, not to undermine or destroy our culture. Also remember the difference between effectiveness and ethics—someone who sells unneeded insurance to an elderly person for an unwarranted profit may be effective in sales but is deficient in ethical standards.

Appropriate for the Occasion

Finally, consider the topic's appropriateness for the occasion: is the subject significant, timely, and tailored? A speech topic is **significant** if the content meets the audience's expectations of what should occur on that occasion. In a classroom speech, for example, a common expectation is that the speech should be on a topic of importance to the class, the campus, the community, or the world. A speech on your breakfast preferences, your date Saturday night, or your most recent fight with your mate may not warrant publicity.

A speech topic is **timely** if it can be linked to the audience's current concerns. A student who gave a speech about a revolution in Liberia did a fine job on the speech, but the revolution had occurred several years before, and the student failed to demonstrate how the topic related to the present. Ancient history can be timely if the speaker can show how that history speaks to the present.

A speech is **tailored** if the topic is narrowed to fit the time allotted for the speech. To cover the rise and fall of the Roman Empire in a five-minute speech is difficult, but to talk about three ways to avoid osteoporosis through your diet is possible. Most speakers err in selecting too large rather than too small a topic. A narrow topic allows you to use research time more effectively: researching too large a topic will result in cutting much of your material to meet the time requirement of the speech. Refer to the criteria in Figure 5.2 as guidelines for evaluating your topic for appropriateness.

Figure 5.2
Checklist for Topic Appropriateness

1. Do you, as the speaker, have *involvement* with the topic?
2. Do you, as the speaker, have *competence* in the topic area?
3. Based on audience analyses, does this topic hold *interest* for your audience?
4. Based on audience analyses, is the topic *worthwhile* to your audience?
5. Is the topic *significant* in terms of the speech occasion?
6. Is the topic *timely* or appropriate for the speech occasion?
7. Have you appropriately *narrowed and limited* the topic for the occasion?

NCA Credo for Communication Ethics

One of the principles of ethical communication applies to this chapter:

* We promote communication climates of caring and mutual understanding that respect the unique needs and characteristics of individual communicators.

Summary

Speeches have both a general purpose—to inform, to persuade, or to entertain—and a specific purpose, which includes your general purpose, your intended audience, and your precise goal. The thesis statement, similar to a central idea in a written composition, is a one-sentence summary of the speech.

In this chapter, we examined methods of searching for a topic. They included two kinds of listing: using a broad category to suggest a series of more specific, related topics, and using a broad category to suggest a series of other broad but related topics that could be narrowed for public speaking topics. Other methods of searching for a topic include: monitoring your own behavior to see what interests you; engaging in personal brainstorming to generate a large quantity of topics that can be critically analyzed later; consulting a list of current topics; and using clustering, or a free association of ideas related to one main concept, to discover topics.

Once chosen, topics need to be evaluated for their appropriateness for you as speaker (interest and knowledge), their appropriateness for your audience (interest and value), their appropriateness to ethical standards (positive ethical choices), and their appropriateness for the occasion (significant, timely, and tailored). Narrowing the topic appropriately for your time constraints is important if everyone wants an opportunity to speak.

Communication Narrative 5.1
The Right Purpose

George Makharadze, district sales manager for TeleWorldCom, Inc., was not terribly worried about giving his presentation to the ten regional sales managers. He was an accomplished speaker who had taken public speaking from a demanding instructor at the community college before he transferred to the university for his undergraduate degree. In addition, his MBA program in business school was an experientially-based curriculum with no classes but with a one-year project in which he had given a dozen speeches to influential groups. So George was not a nervous beginner, but he was a little worried nonetheless.

George's boss, the Vice President for Sales and Product Development, had passed to George a message from the president of the company that every region had to increase sales by 15 percent in the next six months. Regional sales managers who could not keep up with the new pace would be replaced at the end of the fiscal year. George's mission was to meet with the regional sales managers and inspire them to meet the new target in an unusually brief time. Neither the president nor the vice president cared much how George accomplished this task. After all, George, not the top officers, would be firing the unsuccessful managers.

George knew that all of his regional managers were competent. He also knew that threatening them with job termination would not inspire them to greater productivity. In fact, some of his best regional managers would find new and better jobs quickly if George placed their current jobs in jeopardy. He decided not to tell them about the threat. His backup position was that if any of the regional managers did not rise to the challenge, he could still fire one of them with six months to spare.

Besides not telling his regional sales managers about the threat, George decided not to make the 15 percent goal an individual one but a group goal for all of the regional managers. His reasoning was that some managers had regions that were much more difficult to develop, while other managers had regions where increased sales were much more likely. George decided that if one manager doing her very best could only achieve 10 percent, another manager in a stronger region might make up for that shortfall with a 20 percent increase in sales. All he had to do was to get all of them to work together to make this plan work.

When George gave his presentation to the assembled regional sales managers, he was very enthusiastic. He knew that he had a short-range and long-range purpose. His short-range purpose was to convince the managers to cooperate in achieving an overall goal by working with each other instead of competing with each other. His long-range goal was to increase the sales by 15 percent for the next six months. The job threat would remain unstated for six months and would be used then only if necessary. George's strategy for unifying the regional managers was to minimize competition among them and increase their cooperation by introducing an outside threat. The outside threat and the reason for the concern of upper management was the increasing incursion of at least three emerging competitors. These competitors were selling the same services for about the same cost. George's company had the advantage of a positive reputation and a longer history in the business. As George stated the goal to the sales mangers: "We want TeleWorldCom to be not only the biggest Internet service provider but the best."

How does topic selection in a business context differ from topic selection in the classroom? What do you think was George's theme for his speech? How would you have planned this speech differently if you were the district sales manager? How are purpose, theme, and plan related to the corporate culture of the audience? What does George assume about his audience?

Vocabulary

appropriateness A standard for judging whether the content is both interesting and worthwhile to the audience.

brainstorming Usually a small-group activity in which the members think of a number of ideas.

clustering A method of topic selection in which you start with a broad topic area and then visually free associate by linking and circling your ideas on a sheet of paper.

current topics Topics of interest today because they are in the news or on the minds of people in your audience.

general purpose To inform, persuade, or entertain are the general purposes.

listing topics A systematic method of discovering a topic by either narrowing down a broad topic or starting with a broad category and listing related ideas.

monitoring your behavior To examine what you do to unmask what you really like.

personal brainstorming Thinking of topics that already reside in your mind.

significant A standard for judging whether the content meets the audience's expectations of what should occur on that occasion.

specific purpose statement A statement that identifies your purpose more precisely as an outcome or behavioral objective; the statement includes your general purpose, your intended audience, and your precise goal.

speech to entertain A speech that seeks to amuse an audience with imaginative and organized humorous, droll, or witty supporting materials.

speech to inform A speech that seeks to increase audience understanding or knowledge about a topic.

speech to persuade A speech that seeks to influence, reinforce, or modify the audience members' feelings, attitudes, beliefs, or behaviors.

tailored Narrowing a topic to fit the time allotted for the presentation.

thesis statement A one-sentence summary of the speech.

timely Linking of the topic to the audience's current concerns.

Application Exercises

1. Examine the following specific purpose statements. Identify those that are good examples, and explain why the others are bad examples.

    1. The charms of Venus.
    2. My audience will be able to explain the plans for the United States space program in the next decade.
    3. What do women want in their personal relationships?
    4. My audience will be able to identify five kinds of love.
    5. To persuade my audience to live and let live.
    6. To entertain my audience about sex.
    7. To identify the primary causes of lung cancer.
    8. To explain early baldness in men.
    9. To inform my audience about getting drunk on weekends.
    10. My audience will go to graduate school.

2. To gain experience in formulating general purposes, specific purpose statements, and thesis statements, complete the following exercise. For each of the topics, specify the missing information.

Topic	General Purpose	Specific Purpose Statement	Thesis Statement
Edible plants	To persuade	_____	_____
Waterbeds	_____	_____	_____
Crack	To persuade	_____	_____
Shoplifting	To inform	_____	_____

❖ ❖ ❖ ❖

| Selection of the Pope | _____ | My audience will be able to explain the process the Vatican uses to select the Pope | _____ |
| Animal abuse | _____ | _____ | Incidents of animal abuse are becoming a common occurrence throughout the United States |

3. To discover the usefulness of brainstorming and to generate a number of possible topics, try this exercise. Take out a pen and paper, check the time, and allow yourself exactly five minutes to write down as many topics as come to mind. The topics do not have to be stated as specific speech topics; they can be individual words, phrases, or sentences. The range in number of ideas written in this exercise varies from five or six to as many as thirty possible topics.

After you have written down all the topics you can generate in five minutes, write three more topics in the next three minutes. To write down any more ideas is difficult for most people, but some find their best ideas come after they have brainstormed for a period of time and believe they have exhausted all of their ideas.

After you have completed your list of topics, select five that are particularly interesting to you. Finally, from these five, select the one that has the best potential for a public speech. Keep in mind that you should already have, or be able to find, information about this topic and that you will have to adapt the topic to a specific audience.

4. Take out paper and pencil and divide the paper into four or six sections. Write down one of the following topic areas at the top of each section.
   - Job experiences you have had
   - Places you have traveled
   - City, state, or area you are from
   - People who make you angry
   - Happy experiences you have had
   - Unusual experiences you have had
   - Personal experiences with crime involvement in marriage, divorce, or other family matters
   - Experiences with members of other groups—the old, the young, other racial or ethnic groups
   - The effect of the drug culture on your life
   - Your relationship to local, state, or federal government
   - Your background in painting, music, sculpture, theater, dance, or other arts

- Your feelings about grades, college education, sororities and fraternities, college requirements, student government, or alternatives to a college education
- Your reactions to current radio, television, or film practices, policies, or programming
- Recent Supreme Court decisions that affect you
- Your personal and career goals

Spend approximately three to five minutes jotting down specific topics for each of the four to six topic areas you chose. Underline one topic in each area that is especially interesting to you. From these four to six underlined topics, select the one for which you have the most information or best access to information and which you can adapt to your specific audience.

References

Peters, B. (1990). This cluster was created by this student at Ohio University, Athens, Ohio.

Rico, G. L. (1983). *Writing the Natural Way.* Los Angeles: J. P. Tarcher, Inc.

Rowley, E. N. (1991). *Speech Manual for Communication 101.* Terre Haute, IN: Indiana State University.

Chapter 6

Finding Information

As a general rule the most successful person in life is the person who has the best information.[1]

—Benjamin Disraeli

Question Outline

    I. What are the steps in effective research?

    II. What is the role of your personal experience in providing information for your speech?

    III. What should you do before, during, and after an interview?

    IV. What are some sources of information in the library, and how do you find them?

    V. How should you find sources and record information from them?

    VI. How can the Internet be used to find information?

    VII. What is a correct way to cite information from written and interviewed sources?

    VIII. What are oral footnotes?

Janet Levy had been diagnosed with respiratory allergies, and they created considerable discomfort for her. She suffered from a stuffy nose, frequent sneezing, and a cough. Her eyes, nose, and throat were constantly itchy. Her physician told her that the most effective way to control her symptoms was to avoid allergens. However, she learned through allergy tests that she was allergic to molds, dust, and pollen. She had tried nonprescription antihistamines and decongestant tablets, but they didn't seem to work. Nasal sprays and drops worked for a while, but they seemed to be less helpful after a week or two of regular use.

Janet had heard on the Discovery Health Channel ("How America Measures Up," 1999) that an increasing number of people were complaining of allergy symptoms. She thought maybe she could deliver an informative speech about the condition and reveal treatments.

Janet's problem was finding information. She could have used the Health Channel program if she had remembered the date, but she did not. She could look in the library for magazine articles, but she knew that the topic was fairly specialized, so maybe not much had been written—at least for the layperson. Then she remembered that the Health Channel also advertised a website. She went to her computer and looked at http://www.Discoveryhealth.com. *There she found the information that would get her started. Before she completed her task, she had discovered half a dozen great websites and two authoritative periodicals that included the latest information about allergy control.*

Researching Effectively

People like to know more about a subject. Ben Stein's TV program "Win Ben Stein's Money" has been novel entertainment for several years on Comedy Central. The game is based on Stein's wide knowledge of many disciplines. Contestants challenge Stein, who bets his own money, and the winner is the one who knows the most about the most subjects. The show is popular because people love to watch some individual beat the very intelligent Ben Stein at his own game. The amazing part is how much some people, like Stein, really know. He knows so much because he knows how to find information and how to remember that information.

You will find that doing research can also be very interesting. At first, you may find it frustrating because you have to learn how to find information, record it, and adapt it for your speech, but you will also find that research can be distracting. As you look for the things you need for your speech, other items attract your attention. This section is designed to help you become an effective researcher by providing helpful hints about finding material for your speech.

Begin the Research Process

In order to research effectively, you must get started. It is important to find a topic without delay. Too often people waste most of their time finding a topic, and then spend very little time researching it. A more effective strategy is to choose a topic early and leave yourself maximum time for research.

Start early and narrow the topic. In addition to finding a topic early, you should narrow it to fit the time allowed. The body of a five-minute speech is rarely more than three or four minutes long because the introduction and conclusion take about one to two minutes. The body includes transitions and organizational moves that take time. Thus, you actually have a limited amount of time to present the supporting material of your speech. Let us follow two students who are starting their research for their public speaking course.

Researching a specific topic. Richard "Rich" Hoce wanted to learn about college sports. A controversy over the firing of a basketball coach at his campus stirred his interest. Rich Hoce chose the Sports Sciences and Sports Administration category on the SearchNet. He found that he had several interface possibilities, including ABI/Inform, which indexes articles from about 800 business publications, and the *Business Periodicals Index,* which Rich knew was good for basic literature searches within the business area. He also found ERIC (Educational Resources Information Center), which consists of the Resources in Education (RIE) file of document citations and the Current Index to Journals in Education (CIJE) file of journal article citations from over 750 professional journals. Other choices ranged from a sports discussion group to a medical express line.

Since Rich was interested in college sports, he selected ERIC. ERIC then offered the option of searching through journals from 1966 through 1981, journals from 1982 through 1994, or journals from 1995 to 2004. Because he wanted the most current information, he chose the more recent journals. Rich then entered a multiple subject search using "college" and "sports" for his two key words. This search yielded 61 entries, which Rich knew was too broad. He added the word "scholarships" as a third key word but found that no entries included a combination of the terms "college," "sports," and "scholarships." He had narrowed his topic too far.

Rich thought about his topic for a while and decided that he really did not select key words that reflected his interests. He actually wanted to focus on basketball. He went back to ERIC and typed "college" and "basketball." His efforts were rewarded, as he found nine entries for this combination.

The bibliographic entries were varied. One article featured the star of the Arizona State women's basketball team, who discussed how she balanced the demands of college basketball with her academic work. Another article provided information on how Cam Henderson invented the zone defense. Rich also found a highly technical article that considered reinforcement, adversity, and responses to adversity in the videotape play of fourteen college basketball teams. Rich's search also uncovered articles about the broadcasting of basketball games in rural areas, loyalty, alumni giving, and college basketball programs. After he had reviewed the nine articles, he identified six that he wanted to examine in more depth. Rich went to the library's computerized library catalog system to find the call numbers and locations of the articles.

Researching for a topic. Teresa Rojas-Gomez was not in the same situation as her classmate. When she went to the library, she did not have a particular speech in mind. She had no strong feelings about a topic, but she knew that she wanted to talk about something of current interest. As an international student, she was not sure what issues were of contemporary interest in the United States. She spoke to a member of the library staff, who told her about a periodical known as the *CQ Researcher,* which was published by Congressional Quarterly Inc. She learned that this weekly publication had begun in 1990 and that it had formerly been known as *Editorial Research Reports.* Each week, the periodical featured a different issue of current interest. In examining a few of the back issues, Teresa found the following topics:

Racial tensions in schools
Prozac controversy
Religion in America
Electing minorities
Blood supply safety
Genetically engineered foods
Economic sanctions
Birth control choices
Arts funding
Crime victims' rights
Religion and politics
Foreign policy and public opinion
Regulating tobacco
Dietary supplements
The courts and the media
Nuclear arms cleanup
Welfare experiments
Public land policy
Home schooling

Teresa observed that each issue was divided into sections identifying the problem; the background of the problem; the chronology of events surrounding the problem; the current status of the problem; the future outlook of the problem; current bibliographical sources including books, reports, and studies; and a section entitled "The Next Step," which included additional information from a newspaper and periodical abstracts database of current research divided according to relevant topics.

Teresa found the issue on Prozac to be particularly interesting and decided to do her speech on this topic. She went directly from the *CQ Researcher* to the library's computerized library catalog system to look up books and articles that were included in the *CQ Researcher* and to find additional books. She had eight excellent sources for her speech about the harmful side effects of Prozac and related antidepressant drugs. Her audience seemed especially interested in learning about the negative effect such drugs have on sexual functioning and behavior.

How many sources do you need for a speech? The guideline that most successful speakers use is the "three per minute" rule, which suggests that they examine at least three sources for every minute they are speaking. For example, if you are to give a five-minute speech, you should examine at least 15 different sources. You generally end up using about one source per minute from this larger bibliography. Most speech teachers would probably approve of using five sources for a five-minute speech, or eight sources for an eight-minute speech; however, you should discuss the number of sources expected with your instructor.

Record Potential Sources

Your next step in research is to make a bibliography card for each book, magazine article, or newspaper article that appears to relate closely to your topic. A **bibliography card for a book** should list the author, title, place of publication, publisher, date of publication, call number (to locate the book in the library), and any notes you might want to make about the specific information in the book or its importance. A bibliography card for a book would look like Figure 6.1. Notice that the name of the author is written in normal order and that the title of the book is underlined. Underlining with a typewriter or in handwritten copy is a way of indicating that it appears in italics when printed.

Figure 6.1
A Bibliography Card for a Book

Sandra Lipsitz Bem. <u>An Unconventional Family.</u> New Haven: Yale University Press, 1998.

Sandra Bem provides this autobiographical account of why she and her husband, Daryl Bem, became pioneers on gender studies. The well-known psychology professor and author describes a childhood and young adulthood of gender nonconformity. She provides a description of an egalitarian relationship and a feminist set of child-rearing practices. The final chapters of the book analyze her partnering and parenting practices with in-depth interviews of her two adult children.

A **bibliography card for a periodical** has slightly different information (see Figure 6.2). It should include the name of the author, the title of the article, the name of the periodical (underlined), the volume if indicated, the date of publication in parentheses, and the pages on which the article appears in the periodical.

Figure 6.2
A Bibliography Card for a Professional Journal (Magazine or Periodical)

J. R. Hocker, and T. S. Frentz. "The Gods Must be Crazy: The Denial of Descent in Academic Scholarship." <u>Quarterly Journal of Speech</u> 85 (1999), 229–246.

Hocker and Frentz creatively trace the metaphors of "up" and "down" to demonstrate that we uncritically celebrate the former and vilify the latter. Through the examination of Greek poetry and philosophy, the authors provide a historical frame in which to make their distinctions clear. They conclude by suggesting some general ways that we can expand our current academic situation by living these ancient truths more fully.

Figure 6.3
A Bibliography Card for a Newspaper

Leonard A. Cole. "A Plague of Publicity." <u>The Washington Post</u>, August 16, 1999, A15.

This editorial considers the increased concerns about biological and chemical terrorism. He begins the editorial by discussing Secretary of Defense William S. Cohen's warnings about a biological weapons attack in the United States. The author concludes, "While the risk of bioterrorism may have increased in recent years, insisting that a real attack is imminent or inevitable is gratuitous. Indeed, continuing a stream of alarmist statements is likely to provoke only more anxiety and more hoaxes." (p. A15)

A **bibliography card for a newspaper** includes the name of the reporter (if available), the headline, the name of the newspaper (underlined), the exact date, the section, and the page number. See Figure 6.3.

A final suggestion concerns the survey of sources and the gathering of a potential bibliography for your speech. You should have more sources in your potential bibliography than you can use, but not so many that you have wasted time writing them. With a potential bibliography of 10 sources, only about half are likely to yield material that you can use in your speech. In short, survey with your eyes a large number of potential sources, record on note cards the bibliographic information for those you think will be relevant for your speech topic, and record information only from the ones that prove related to your ultimate goal and the immediate response you seek from your audience.

Make Index Cards or an Electronic File

Your first temptation might be to take a notebook to the library, start writing down the bibliographic information, and enter all the information from that source in your notebook. Similarly, you might be tempted to electronically record too much of the information from that source in your notebook. Similarly, you might be tempted to electronically record too much of the information available on websites. Overrecording information is a serious mistake. Writing your sources and information in a book will make the information difficult to retrieve. Writing information on index cards or on electronic files makes them easy to rearrange, organize, and retrieve.

One method of recording ideas, quotations, and information from both interviewed and written sources is to use index cards. Buy 3"x5" or 4"x6" index cards without lines. Use them to record the potential sources and to record the information you find in them. Better yet, record your information electronically. Following are some hints about writing notes on index cards or recording your sources electronically.

1. Exercise extreme care to record your sources and write your notes legibly. Nothing is more irritating than being unable to decipher your own notes when you need them for the speech.

2. Write one idea, quotation, or bit of information on each card. Do not try to write as much as possible on each card because you will have difficulty retrieving and reorganizing the information.

3. Get in the habit of recording the subject, author, title, and page on the top of each card so you do not forget where you found your information (see Figure 6.4).

4. Take more notes than you need but not so many that you have wasted time. If some information looks relevant and interesting, write it on a card. However, do not try to write down everything you see, or you will have to discard much of what you wrote.

Notice that the index card in Figure 6.4 is a direct quotation limited to a single idea: faculty ambivalence about the use of technology in the classroom. Notice also that the direct quotation has three spaced dots, called an ellipsis, indicating that words were edited out to save space on the card and time in the speech.

Figure 6.4
A Source Card From an Interview With Direct Quotation

O'Banion, *A Learning College for the 21st Century,* p. 65

"Technology does not always hit the mark with educators . . . and while many see technology as a magic bullet, just as many view technology as a broken arrow. In spite of claims that technology can transform teaching and learning, that transformation is not likely to take place unless faculty actually use technology."

An index card from a telephone interview might resemble Figure 6.5. The lack of quotation marks indicates that this index card contains a paraphrase rather than a direct quotation from the source.

Figure 6.5
A Source Card From a Telephone Interview With Paraphrase

Topic: Home Security
Mr. Gurd Hazelstein
President
Craine Security, Inc.
Fairfax, VA

Mr. Hazelstein told me that approximately 17 percent of the homes in the metro area contract for home security. For between $300–400 per year, a home security company will monitor a home for both fire and breach of security. A fire brings an immediate response from the nearest fire station; a breach of security brings a call from the security company. If the party who answers the phone *does not* say the pre-arranged code word, then the security company immediately notifies the nearest police or sheriff's department.

1/5/2001

❖ ❖ ❖ ❖

You are very likely to use electronic means of gathering information for your speech. You may want to consider the most efficient, yet accurate, way of recording this information. Index cards remain the recommended method, but how can you put the information from the computer in index card form? If you can download information on your own disks, you can format the information for note card size. You can also cut out the data from the computer printouts and paste it on note cards, or you may be able to print it from a computer word processor. You will find that the index cards facilitate the alphabetization and creation of bibliographic materials.

Learn as You Look

Every person who prepares a speech by doing research learns that it is good to keep an open mind about the topic. Your early notions about the topic may change as you learn more about the subject. It is appropriate to do the following:

1. Narrow your topic as you discover its true scope.

2. Modify your own position on an issue consistent with what you now know about the topic.

3. Pursue new directions on the topic that you did not know when you began your research.

Doing research is learning; let it make you more intelligent, more informed, and more confident.

Personal Experience as a Source of Information

At the beginning of this chapter, Janet Levy began the research process by drawing upon her own personal experiences. For many speeches, this is a good place to start. One of the richest sources of information is you. You have gone to school for a dozen years or more. You have worked at part-time and full-time jobs. You have gone places and met people who taught you lessons in living. You may have married and returned to school after serving in the armed forces or after raising a family. Whatever your story, it is not exactly like anyone else's. In your own personal experience, you can find information that will provide ideas, supporting materials, and arguments for your speeches.

Unfortunately, many students do not see themselves as unique. Sometimes, on the first day of class, instructors ask students to identify themselves

Celebrating Diversity

We often do not reflect on our own diversity. Consider that your classmates, family members, or neighbors do not share characteristics or experiences that you have had. Where have you traveled that is unique? What experiences have been turning points for you? When we think about diversity we think about others rather than ourselves. Each of us is distinctive from every other human being. Our celebration of diversity should also include a celebration of ourselves.

by name, major, hometown, year in school, age, and any other demographic characteristics they may wish to share. Then each student is asked to state in what way he or she is unique, different from others in the class. If any characteristic is repeated, then that person has to think of another unique feature. The class decides if the characteristic or experience is unique.

How to Find Information

1. Use your personal experience as a source.
2. Interview for information.
3. Use the library for information.
4. Search electronic sources for information.

How is this exercise related to discovering information for your speech? Your unique experience with a topic should be part of your speech. Sharing your experience demonstrates your interest and involvement with the topic. A speaker is doing more than simply fulfilling an assignment when he or she talks about alcoholism and its effects on his or her own family. A person who talks about gene transplants is higher in credibility when he reveals his work in the biological sciences.

Your talent can make you unique.

People are often unaware of their own uniqueness, tending to think that many others have done or experienced what they have. One of the authors spent two years as the chief pre-law advisor for a large university. The biggest difficulty in writing the "Dean's Recommendation" for the prospective law students was getting them to think of how they differed from hundreds of other applicants. Even a twenty-minute interview with each student failed to reveal uniqueness. Often students came back later with second thoughts. One student came back two days after the interview to ask if it made any difference that she was a concert pianist. "How was that related to law school?" she inquired. A concert pianist has practiced most of her life. That kind of discipline is exactly what law schools demand. Another student remembered that he had learned the Russian language—in Russia. Still another saw nothing unusual about finishing college in three years with a 4.0 average. Your uniqueness may not be as dramatic as these examples, but the point is that people have difficulty seeing uniqueness in themselves even when it clearly exists.

Although personal experience should be the first consideration in looking for speech material, it should be used critically. Your personal experience should do the following:

1. Enhance your credibility as a speaker on your topic.

2. Provide examples or supporting material.

3. Demonstrate your relationship to the topic.

Some examples of speeches based on personal experiences and interests include a speech on St. Patrick's Day by a woman who was Irish and had celebrated the holiday every year with her family (Kovatch 1994). Another woman talked about body piercing. She herself had several body piercings, had friends who had had body piercings done on everything from "their noses to their foreskins," and she had interviewed a number of professional body piercers (Campbell 1994). A woman who had collected Walt Disney films all of her life gave a speech on the changes she perceived in Disney's animated films (Smith 1994).

Another woman had a long interest in Native Americans. She attended several powwows as she grew up in her native state of Ohio. She was also a member of the Native American Center in Columbus, Ohio, and regularly volunteered there. She gave most of her speeches in her public speaking class on Native Americans—one on the warrior Tecumseh, another on the Native Americans of the Eastern Woodlands, and a third on Native American religious freedom rights (Planisek 1993). One effective way of incorporating personal experience into your speech is to use your credentials to establish credibility in the introduction of the speech. One student (Bailey 1994) began his speech like this:

> I have been a sign interpreter for over six years. I have been active in the deaf community and its causes. I taught sign language classes at Youngstown State University for two years, and I also lectured on how to best incorporate a deaf student into a mainstream class for all education majors at YSU. I have enjoyed working in the summers as a counselor at camps designed for deaf children and teens, and I am currently working part-time as an interpreter at East Elementary School here in Athens for a profoundly deaf first-grader. I enjoy my work, and I am glad to be part of this exciting community.

Needless to say, the students were fascinated by this speech on signing. They gave the speaker high marks on credibility.

Before the Interview

1. Determine your purpose.

2. Write out your questions.

3. Select an interviewee.

4. Arrange an appointment.

Consider your own experiences first as you gather information for your speech. Do not assume that any experience you have had will be appropriate, however. Ask yourself if the experience you wish to relate in the speech is typical. Is it so typical that it is boring, or so unusual that it was probably a chance occurrence? Will the audience learn from your experience? Does your experience constitute proof or evidence of anything? If your personal experience meets some of these expectations and does not violate the sensibilities of your audience, then it will probably be an asset in your speech.

Interviewing for Information

A second important source of ideas and information for your speech is other people. Full of faculty and staff, your campus has many experts on particular subjects. Your community, likewise, is populated with people who have expertise on many issues: government workers on politics; clergy on religion; physicians, psychologists, and nurses on health care; engineers on highways and buildings; and owners and managers on industry and business. The following story illustrates how a speech can be based on an interview.

> Yolanda Jefferson went to her speech professor's office in despair. She was supposed to give her speech in two days. She had selected a topic but could find nothing on the subject because someone had cut out all of the information from the magazines, newspapers, and books in the library. Yolanda was frustrated and angry. Her speech professor recommended that she give her speech on a topic that was of highest interest to her at the moment: the destruction of library resources.
>
> Yolanda made an appointment to see the associate director of the library. She hit a gold mine. The associate director was part of a national study team investigating the destruction of library resources. He was gratified to find a student interested in this issue who would tell other students how serious the problem was.
>
> After two hours with the associate director, Yolanda knew the average number of pages destroyed in the magazines, the cost of repairing or replacing the damaged books, and the amount of damage at her own college. She had more information than she could have found in many days of research. When Yolanda gave her speech, she supplemented her personal experience with facts and figures that made her more of an authority on library barbarity than anyone in the room.

Find out who can best answer your questions. (Photo: Mark C. Ide)

You may not find all of the information you need in a single interview, but you may discover that interviewing is an efficient way to gather information on your topic. The person you interview can furnish ideas, quotations, and valuable leads to other sources. First, however, learn when and how to conduct an interview, and how to use the results.

Before the Interview

If you can find the information as quickly and easily by looking it up yourself, then do not seek it through an interview. Instead, interview when:

1. The information is not readily available. Maybe the issue is so current that it is not covered in the papers. Perhaps the issue affects such a narrow band of people that it has been overlooked. Interviewing can unearth information that is not in books, magazines, newspapers, or on the Internet.

2. The authority on the subject is available. If you have people on your campus or in your community who have expertise on your topic, then their opinions should be sought.

3. Quotations and specific ideas are necessary for your speech. Often you can elicit higher-impact quotes from experts for your speech than the press gets because experts learn to be very prudent around reporters. These quotations and ideas can give your speech the sizzle it needs to gain audience interest.

Before your interview, determine your purpose, write out your questions, select a person to interview, and arrange an appointment.

Your *purpose* for the interview should be related to the immediate response you seek from the audience and your ultimate goal. For example, your immediate response might be "to learn the Heimlich Maneuver," and your ultimate goal might be for your audience "to save lives by using life-saving techniques on victims." What purpose would be served in having an interview about a maneuver to save victims of choking? Persons in medicine or public health can provide you with authoritative quotations, real-life stories, and reasons for your audience to listen. All of this is possible if you ask the right questions.

Your *questions* should be carefully designed to produce the information you need. Make them specific, clear, and necessary. Some can be "yes or no" questions, but most should call for an opinion, a judgment, or an explanation. All questions should be queries that cannot be easily answered by simply looking them up. As much as possible, the questions should be stated without bias, without suggesting an answer, and without threat, anger, or hostility.

Following are some sample questions appropriate for a speech on the Heimlich Maneuver.

How many choking victims are there per year in the United States?

What age groups are most likely to be affected?

Where (in the home, restaurants) do such incidents usually occur?

How effective is the maneuver in helping victims?

Are there any dangers in having laypersons use the maneuver?

Do you think more people should learn the maneuver?

Have you ever used the maneuver to help a victim?

Is there anything related to the Heimlich Maneuver that you think I should tell my audience that has not already been mentioned?

Perhaps you can think of still more questions that an expert might answer better than could other sources, but the point is that experts are usually accessible and willing to talk—even to a student who is preparing a speech for a class.

Selecting your interviewee is the next important step. Your first consideration is "Who can best answer my questions?" You might want to ask your teacher for an opinion on this issue. Among your criteria for selecting a person for an interview are availability, accessibility, and affability. A person might be on campus or in your community but may not grant interviews, or a person may be available and accessible but unfriendly to interviewers.

The big surprise for many public speaking students is finding out that many important people are willing to submit to an interview for a campus speech. Most people are flattered that others want to know their opinion. If your interview is well planned and well implemented, then other students are likely to be welcomed by this same interviewee.

Making an appointment usually involves talking to a secretary or administrative assistant. This person is correctly called a "gatekeeper" because he or she controls the gate, or door, to the employer's office. The way you treat the secretary can determine whether or not you get an appointment, so be polite, clear about your mission, and reasonable about the amount of time that you want and when you want it.

Some guidelines for securing an interview include the following:

1. Look professional when you ask for the interview. This can help you in gaining an appointment.

2. State your purpose clearly and succinctly. It is best if you can tell the secretary what your mission is, but another alternative is to type a brief note that can be passed to the interviewee.

3. Ask for an appointment early. Some people will be too heavily scheduled to see you on short notice. The earlier you ask for an appointment, the better your chances of securing an interview.

4. Ask for a brief amount of time. Usually a 10- to 20-minute appointment is sufficient. It is better to ask for a brief appointment and let the interviewee extend it than to ask for a large amount of time that you do not use.

5. Show up for your appointment at least five or ten minutes early in case your interviewee wants to meet you early. If you are going to be late, call ahead and ask the secretary if you should cancel.

These guidelines will serve you well as you prepare for the interview itself.

During the Interview

1. Record if permissible.

2. Keep your tone positive.

3. Be flexible.

4. Practice active listening.

5. Cite information accurately.

6. Leave as scheduled.

❖ ❖ ❖ ❖   **During the Interview**

One decision you will have to make concerning your interview is whether to *record the meeting*. The advantages of a tape recording are accuracy and completeness. The disadvantages are that some interviewees do not like to be recorded, the presence of a recorder can inhibit disclosures, and sometimes the machine fails, leaving you with a useless tape and no notes. Always ask the person you are interviewing if you can use the tape recorder, and take notes anyway in case technology fails.

Interviews rarely start with the first question. Instead, expect the interviewee to express curiosity about you and your project. Be perfectly frank about your purpose, the assignment, and the audience. The interviewee is doing the verbal equivalent of a handshake with the questioning.

During the interview, be very careful about the *tone* of your questions and comments. You are not in the role of an investigative reporter performing an interrogation. Instead, you are a speaker seeking information and cooperation from someone who can help you. Your tone should be friendly and your comments constructive.

During the interview, be *flexible*. Even though you have prepared questions, you may find that the responses answer more than one question and your preplanned order isn't working as well as you thought it would. Relax. Check off questions as you ask them or as they are answered. Take a minute at the conclusion of the interview to see if you have covered all of your questions.

Practice active listening during your interview. Show an interest in the person's answers. If you hear something that you want to get verbatim, write it down, or ask the interviewee to repeat it if necessary. Do not try to copy every word but do get an accurate rendition of direct quotations.

Make sure that you have accurate *citation information*, your interviewee's name, title, and the name of the company, agency, or department. You will be citing this person's words and using oral footnotes to credit them, so you need correct source information. If the interviewee has time, you may want to read back your direct quotes for verification.

Finally, remember to *depart*. Give your interviewee an opportunity to stop the interview at the designated time. The interviewee—not you—should extend the interview beyond the designated time. The interviewee will appreciate your gracious goodbye and gratitude for granting the interview. As a parting gesture of good will, thank the secretary as well.

After the Interview

1. Review your notes.

2. Listen to your tape.

3. Make note cards.

After the Interview

As soon as you can after the interview, *review your notes*, write down items that were discussed without complete notes, and make sure you can read your own direct quotes. If you taped the interview, *listen to your tape* as soon as possible. If you wait even a few hours, you may have difficulty remembering exactly what was said. Although the words are preserved on the recording, the nonverbal cues are not.

The best way to ensure that your interview can be used in your speech is to write the most important material, especially the direct quotations, *on note cards,* each carefully marked with the name of the source and the sequence of cards (see Figure 6.6). With careful preparation before the interview, attentive listening and accurate note taking during the interview, and quick review and note card composition after the interview, you will increase your confidence as a speaker.

Figure 6.6
A Sample Interview Notecard

Dr. Carson B. Axelrod (M.D. from Stanford U.)
Chair, Dept. of Internal Medicine
Pomeroy Community Hospital

"Laypersons using the Heimlich Maneuver should be wary about employing the maneuver on infants. An adult can take a firm, rapid squeeze without fear of fracture, but a small child could become a dual victim of choking and broken ribs."

Interviewed 2/24/01

Using the Library for Information

The library is the focal point of most colleges and universities. Your public speaking course gives you an opportunity to use this very useful resource. It will be one of your important sources of information. Unfortunately, most of us do not know how to use the library wisely or well. In addition, we feel foolish asking others for help because we feel that understanding how a library is organized and functions is basic information that we should have learned when we were younger.

One undergraduate woman who had worked in a university library for over two years gave one of her informative speeches on the library. She was wise in selecting this speech topic because many of her classmates had experienced difficulty in using the library. After she established her relationship to the topic, she introduced her topic by saying:

> Was doing the research for this speech a hassle? Have you ever gone to the library to do research for a paper and not been able to find anything on your topic? Have you ever had trouble finding a restroom?

> Everybody here will have to use the library at some time or another, and I intend to give you a few hints that will make the experience less painful for you and also for those people who work there.

> In the next few minutes I would like to discuss the setup of our library, the many resources available to us, and I would like to give you a few helpful hints and shortcuts that will help you with assignments such as speeches and papers. (Tyre 1994)

This speech was highly valued by the student's classmates. Many of them reported that they used the information from the speech throughout the academic term.

The Library Staff

We have been looking at people who can help with your speeches. One of the most important partners for success in your public speaking class is the library staff. These individuals know the library well, and part of their job is to help you use it to your advantage.

If you have not actively used your library, consider a library tour with a member of the library staff. In addition, many college and university libraries have video programs that describe the various resources they include. Finally, do not be afraid to ask questions when you are frustrated by a problem. Librarians and their assistants are professionals whose jobs are to serve the patrons. Be sure you have specific questions in mind when you approach them, be courteous in your interactions, and show your gratitude for their assistance. The library should not be a mystery to you; instead, it should be a place that can help you succeed. The more you know about the library, the better you can use it.

In the next section of this chapter, you will learn some preliminary information that will help you even before you go to the library. The primary sources that you will use in your speeches include books, which can be found in the computerized catalog system or in the card catalog; magazines and journals, which can be found in general and specific computerized and noncomputerized indexes; newspapers, which can be found in computerized and noncomputerized indexes; and reference works such as dictionaries, encyclopedias, yearbooks and almanacs, and books of quotations.

Books

Very few speeches will be prepared without the assistance of non-reference books. Where do you find books in the library? The answer seems both obvious and trite—books are everywhere in the library.

Where do you find exactly the *right* books for your speech? Most likely you will use a computerized library catalog system. Each library refers to this electronic aid with a different name, but most computerized catalog systems work the same way. You will be able to search for sources if you know the author, title, or subject of your search. You should check at your own library

---

Technical Tip 6.1
Finding Books on the Internet

Books on the Internet: *http://www.lib.utexas.edu/Libs/PCL/Etext.html* links to McGraw-Hill and other online book sources, Great Books Home Page; American literature plus history, political, and legal texts.

Books Online: Titles *http://digitallibrary.upenn.edu*. Looking for books online? This site offers a way to find them.

The EServer: *http://eserver.org*. This site has over 10,000 humanities texts in many disciplines. The site also has links to academic journals and libraries.

to determine exactly how you can access information. Most computerized library systems can be accessed within the library, as well as from remote locations with the assistance of a modem and a telephone line.

Magazines and Journals

Magazines and journals are also staple sources for speechwriters. How can you easily find information in popular magazines such as *Newsweek, Sports Illustrated, Consumer's Guide, Vital Speeches, Glamour, Car and Driver, Time, Psychology Today, Runner's Magazine, Cosmopolitan, U.S. News and World Report, Details, Modern Maturity, TV Guide,* or *Ebony*? How about journals such as *Sex Roles, Communication Education, Journal of Marriage and the Family, Deviant Behavior, Journal of Social and Personal Relationships, Public Health Reports, American Behavioral Scientist, Communication Quarterly, American Journal of Sociology, Philosophical Quarterly, Journal of Personality and Social Psychology, Family Issues, Human Relations, Violence Victims, American Psychologist, Journal of Sex Research, Adolescence,* or *Family Relations*? Obviously, thumbing through the various magazines and journals would take too much time. Even examining the index within a specific journal or magazine would take far more time than most people have to complete the research for their speech.

To effectively and efficiently find material in magazines and journals, you should use general and specific indexes. The most familiar general index is the *Reader's Guide to Periodical Literature,* which includes a current listing of between 180 and 190 of the most frequently read magazines published in the United States. The *Reader's Guide* dates back to 1900, and most libraries carry all of the volumes back to this date.

The *Reader's Guide to Periodical Literature* is now also available in an electronic form. All of the issues of the index published since January of 1983 are now available on the Internet and on CD-ROM. In either form, the *Reader's Guide* provides author, title, and subject indexes. You may look up material if you know the author or title of the article, or just the subject matter.

You may also need to use a more specialized index for your topic. A properly narrowed topic often requires specialized information. For example, if you decide to attack the grading system, you might find some information in the *Reader's Guide,* but you would find more in the many periodicals and journals that specialize in education. The *Education Index,* for instance, can lead you to articles in 150 magazines and journals. Remember that specific indexes lead you to specialized periodicals written for professionals and experts. You may find that you have to simplify the articles for your audience's understanding.

Some of the special indexes to periodicals are:

- *Applied Science and Technology Index* (author, title, subject)
- *Art Index* (author, subject)
- *Bibliographic Index* (subject)
- *Biography Index* (subject)
- *Biological and Agricultural Index* (subject)
- *Book Review Index* (author, title, subject)

- *Business Periodicals Index* (subject)
- *Catholic Periodical Index* (subject)
- *Education Index* (author, subject)
- *Engineering Index* (subject)
- *Index to Book Reviews in the Humanities* (author, subject)
- *Index to Legal Periodicals* (author, subject)
- *Music Index* (author, subject)
- *Public Affairs Information Service* (subject)
- *Quarterly Cumulative Index Medicus* (author, subject)
- *Social Sciences and Humanities Index* (author, subject)
- *Technical Book Review Index* (author, subject)

Some of these general and specific indexes have been computerized. We already mentioned that the *Reader's Guide to Periodical Literature* has been computerized since 1983. In addition, a variety of others are available.

None of these electronic indexes is difficult to use. In some cases, you need to type a key word, the author's name, the title of the article, or the subject matter of interest, and press "search" or "enter." In other cases, the procedure is only slightly more complicated. Ask a library staff member to help you during your first attempts to use these electronic resources. You will find that they save you valuable time, and they oftentimes provide more complete information.

Most college and university libraries are updating their indexes with information retrieval services available in an electronic format. These services are sometimes referred to as SearchNets or databases. They are known by several different product names. Some examples are InfoTrac Database, Expanded Academic Index, and Find Articles. Within these systems, you may find smaller indexes. For example, within InfoTrac Database, you will find InfoTrac OneFile and Expanded Academic ASAP. Within Expanded Academic ASAP, you will find specialized indexes such as the Computer Database and the Health Reference Center. You will want to learn if your library has such services and how to use them. In most colleges and universities you will be able to access information from your home computer.

Another way to search for information is through general search engines such as Yahoo, Google, and Dogpile. A more recent development is the blog, or web log. The blog is an online personal website where individuals can share their ideas with others. Some blogs appear to be like a diary or journal; others are filled with late-breaking news; and still others provide in-depth analyses of the issues of the day. People interested in politics seem to be particularly apt to create blogs. The blog may be a useful site of information for you.

Newspapers

Finally, you will want to examine newspapers, particularly if you are speaking on a current event. Just as you cannot look at all magazines or journals, you will not have time to examine all issues of a newspaper, or all issues of several newspapers for the same day. Instead, you can begin your newspaper search with a newspaper index. The following newspapers are indexed:

- *Chicago Tribune* (1972–present)
- *Los Angeles Times* (1972–present)
- *The New York Times* (1851–present)
- *Wall Street Journal* (1958–present)
- *Washington Post* (1972–present)

You can also use the electronic retrieval system called the *National Newspaper Index* to find a source in *The New York Times,* the *Wall Street Journal,* or the *Christian Science Monitor* from 1970 to the present; or the *Los Angeles Times* or the *Washington Post* from 1982 to the present. Ask a library staff person if your library has this electronic index. Again, it could save you valuable time. Current issues of the *Christian Science Monitor* are available at *http://www.csmonitor.com,* and current issues of the Wall Street Journal are available at *http://www.wsj.com.*

Technical Tip 6.2
News, Newspaper, Radio, and Magazine Websites

News Media Websites

MSNBC http://www.msnbc.com. Microsoft Corp. and NBC spawned this Information Age website which brings you online news that is reliable and timely.

Reuters News Room http://www.reuters.com. A world-wide wire service whose news is available to you with both stories and photos.

Newspaper Websites

Los Angeles Times http://www.latimes.com
New York Times http://www.nytimes.com
Washington Post http://www.washingtonpost.com
Rocky Mountain News http://www.rockymountainnews.com
Seattle Times http://www.seattletimes.com
USA Today http://www.usatoday.com
HeraldLink—Miami Herald http://www.miami.com/mld/miamiherald/
Dallas Morning News http://www.dallasnews.com

Radio News Websites

All Things Considered—NPR http://www.npr.org/programs/atc. National Public Radio's news show.

BBC World Service—London http://www.bbc.co.uk/worldservice. World's largest radio network.

Timecast—the ReadAudio Guide http://www.timecast.com. Live and pre-recorded newscasts from a variety of top news media. Links to many other talk radio stations and sports and music programs.

News Magazines

Asiaweek Online http://www.pathfinder.com/Asiaweek
Knight Ridder http://www.kri.com/
U.S. News and World Report http://www.usnews.com
Time http://www.time.com/time/

> **Pathfinder** *http://pathfinder.com.* A host to online versions of news from online versions of *People, Fortune, Time, Life, Sports Illustrated,* and many others. Some sites require free online registration.
>
> **TV News**
>
> **Online NewsHour** *http://www.pbs.org/newshour.* Public Television's news hour along with sound clips and cross-referenced transcripts linked to stories and to speeches.
>
> **World News—CNN** *http://www.cnn.com/WORLD/.* Continually updated international news.

If you become confused about these available reference works, then remember only one thing: Members of the library staff can help you find the information you need.

Reference Works

Most libraries have a reference room or reference area that includes several different kinds of materials. We cannot describe every reference source, but some of those that you are most likely to use are dictionaries, encyclopedias, yearbooks and almanacs, and books of quotations. We will consider the usefulness of each of these.

Dictionaries

Need help pronouncing a word? Wonder what a technical term means? Want to know where a word came from? Dictionaries—desktop, comprehensive, and specialized—are the resource to use.

For most of your speeches, the collegiate dictionary is sufficient to find spelling, meaning, and pronunciation, but sometimes you may need more. A comprehensive dictionary, such as the *Oxford English Dictionary,* can tell you most of the known meanings and origins of a word. A related reference work, the thesaurus, can provide you with lists of words with the same (synonyms) or opposite (antonyms) meanings. Still another kind of dictionary, a dictionary of usage, can tell you how words are used in actual practice. Do you know when to use *affect* and *effect?* A dictionary of usage can tell you. Some examples of these references are:

In Print

- *Black's Law Dictionary*
- *Black's Medical Dictionary*
- Fowler, H. W., *A Dictionary of Modern English Usage*
- Partridge, Eric, *Dictionary of Slang and Unconventional English*
- *Roget's International Thesaurus*
- *Webster's New Dictionary of Synonyms*

Online

- Acronym List *http://www.ucc.ie/info/net/acronyms/index.html*

- Dictionaries *http://www.math.uni-paderborn.de/dictionaries/Dictionaries. html*
- Roget's Thesaurus of English Words and Phrases *http://thesaurus.reference.com.*

Encyclopedias

Encyclopedias are great for finding background information. If you want to give an informative speech about any subject except the most current, you can find some information in a general encyclopedia, such as *Encyclopaedia Britannica,* or a specialized encyclopedia, such as the following:

In Print

- Buttrick, George A., and Keith R. Crim, (Eds.), *Interpreter's Dictionary of the Bible*
- *Dictionary of American History*
- *Encyclopedia of Philosophy*
- *Encyclopedia of World Art*
- Illing, Robert, *Dictionary of Musicians and Music*
- Mitzel, Harold, ed., *Encyclopedia of Educational Research*
- Munn, Glenn G., *Encyclopedia of Banking and Finance*
- Turner, John, ed., *Encyclopedia of Social Work*

Online

- Britannica Online *http://www.eb.com*
- Biographical Dictionary *http://www.s9.com/biography/*
- Free Internet Encyclopedia *http://cam-info.net/enc.html*

Facts and Figures: Yearbooks, Almanacs, and Websites

Yearbooks and almanacs provide facts and figures on a large range of subjects. What songs were popular in the 1960s? Who owns the Minnesota Twins? When did the last earthquake rock Los Angeles? Who is the leader of Japan? How many Native American tribes reside in the United States? How much iron ore was produced in 1990? How many CEOs of Fortune 500 companies are women? Who are some of the famous living women in America today? Topics as different from each other as these can all be found in yearbooks and almanacs. The following list of books of facts, statistics, and details may be helpful to you as you prepare your speech.

In Print

- *Americana Annual*
- *The Annual Register of World Events*
- *Current Biography*
- *Dictionary of American Biography*
- *Dictionary of National Biography*

- *Economic Almanac*
- *Facts on File*
- *Information Please Almanac*
- *New International Year Book*
- *Rand McNally Cosmopolitan World Atlas*
- *Statesman's Yearbook*
- *Statistical Abstract of the United States*
- *Who's Who of American Women*
- *Who's Who in America*
- *World Almanac and Book of Facts*

Online

- FindLaw—Internet Legal Resources *http://www.findlaw.com*
- Government Information Locator Service *http://www.access.gpo.gov/ su_docs/gils/*
- Government Resources on the Web *http://www.lib.umich.edu/ govdocs/govweb.html*
- Household Economic Statistics *http://www.census.gov/hhes/www/*
- Library of Congress *http://www.loc.gov/*
- Statistical Abstract of the United States *http://www.census.gov/ prod/www/statistical-abstract-us.html*
- 4000 Years of Women in Science *http://crux.astr.ua.edu/4000WS/ 4000WS.html*
- USSC-U.S. Supreme Court on the Web *http://www.usscplus.com*
- Police Officer's Internet Directory *http://www.officer.com*
- Lectric Law Library *http://www.lectlaw.com*
- Government Statistics *http://www.fedstats.gov/*
- Law Library of Congress *http://www.loc.gov/rr/law/*
- Science Learning Network *http://www.sln.org*
- LawInfo *http://LawInfo.com*
- West Legal Directory *http://www.wld.com*

Books of Quotations

Have you ever noticed how excellent speakers often have just the right quotation to begin or end their speeches? Individuals who speak frequently seem to be particularly adept at summarizing their ideas with the pithy words of famous people. Do these people have good memories or private collections of quotations? Maybe so, but they might also rely on the many different kinds of books of quotations that are available for speakers and writers.

What are some of the possible sources of quotations? Probably the best-known collection is *Bartlett's Familiar Quotations*. This mainstay in the market contains well over 20,000 quotations from both contemporary and historical figures. Similarly, *Respectfully Quoted: A Dictionary of Quotations Requested from the Congressional Research Service* features over 2,000 quotations that are routinely requested or asked to be verified by the Congressional Research Service of the Library of Congress. The *Oxford Dictionary of Quotations* and the *Home Book of Quotations* are also large collections of quotations that have existed for nearly sixty years.

Paperback books of quotations are also available. *The Pocket Book of Quotations* is printed regularly. Specialized paperback books such as *The Quotable Woman* might also be useful to you.

Similarly, books of anecdotes might be helpful to you. These books include longer stories told by famous people or about famous people. Some of these include the large volume *The Little Brown Book of Anecdotes,* and smaller books like *The Oxford Book of American Literary Anecdotes* and *Presidential Anecdotes.* Most of the quotation and anecdote books are indexed so you can find a quotation or anecdote by topic or author.

Most libraries now offer dictionaries, encyclopedias, yearbooks, almanacs, and books of quotations in an electronic form. You may be able to request an actual CD-ROM, which you can insert in a computer. Or, you may be able to request encyclopedia, dictionary, thesaurus, or quotation materials within an existing program that has already been installed on a computer. The second edition of the *Oxford English Dictionary* is available on CD-ROM and can be searched in a variety of ways. A common encyclopedia database is the *New Grolier Multimedia Encyclopedia,* which includes the text of the *Academic American Encyclopedia* and adds to it pictures, sounds, movies, and other visuals. *Time Almanac: 2004* contains the complete text of all issues of *Time* magazine since 1989, and also includes an almanac of facts and figures. The library staff can assist you in finding these and other such materials electronically.

Searching the Internet for Information

Four computers comprised the entire Internet in 1969. Since that time, the **Internet,** or the matrix of networks that connects computers around the world (*http://www.dictionary.com*) has grown exponentially. Most of us know the Internet through the **World Wide Web,** which is simply a collection of Internet sites that offer text and graphics and sound and animation resources (*http://www.dictionary.com*).

The World Wide Web consists of websites and web pages. Each of these is accessible through its own address, also known as a URL (uniform resource locator). If you have a browser on your computer (such as Netscape Navigator or Microsoft Internet Explorer), you can reach a particular website by simply typing its URL. If you do not know the URL of the source you are seeking, you can use a search engine to find it. Some search engines are listed below. Simply type the URL and then follow the straightforward directions provided to find information.

- Yahoo!: *http://www.yahoo.com* Started by two Stanford students organizing their bookmarks, this index is popular and comprehensive.

- Google: *http://www.google.com* A comprehensive and flexible search engine.
- About: *http://www.about.com* This search engine features a person who acts as a guide and can be e-mailed with questions.
- AltaVista: *http://www.altavista.com* A powerful and flexible search tool that includes more than 30 million web pages.
- Aliweb: *http://www.aliweb.com* Use key words, URLs, etc., in this index to databases and sites.
- Excite: *http://www.excite.com* Full of information about the Internet and the parent of NetSearch, a web navigator.
- Lycos: *http://www.lycos.com* A great starting point which contains a brief abstract of each site's text.
- HotBot: *http://www.hotbot.com* HotWired's search engine that indexes over 90 percent of the known Web.

On the Web

Some search tools provide complete full-text articles. FindArticles.com, available at *www.findarticles.com,* has over 5.5 million articles that are gathered from more than 900 publications—both magazines and journals. Do a search on this source to find new information about your speech topic.

Internet Vocabulary

BOOKMARK is a feature of most web browsers in which important links can be saved in a file without having to look up the URL.

HOME PAGE is the first page on a website to which supporting materials are linked.

HYPERLINK means a link in a WWW document that leads to another website or to another place in the same document.

INTERNET means a network of interconnected computer networks.

SEARCH ENGINE is a program on the Internet that allows you to search quickly and efficiently for information.

URL stands for uniform resource locator or the address of a website, such as *http://brou.com.*

WEB BROWSER is a tool for viewing pages on the WWW.

WWW stands for World Wide Web, which links all the individual websites.

Searching the World Wide Web for Information

You can easily research your entire speech without leaving your computer as long as you know how to navigate the World Wide Web. Five warnings are necessary before you investigate your topic.

1. *Information overload.* The World Wide Web currently has over 300 million sites and will be closer to half a billion by the time you read this book. The problem is information glut: so much information is available that the untrained eye has difficulty discerning a real diamond in the pile of costume jewelry.

2. *Distractions galore.* Researchers used to be distracted by the books they were not looking for; now researchers are distracted by the websites they discover by accident, the ones that have nothing to do with the topic they are researching. A web researcher has to learn how to keep focused to save time.

3. *Uneven quality.* Nobody regulates the quality of websites. A hate group or a psychopath can have a website that is as attractive as the one provided by the most reputable news organization. Figuring out which information is accurate or true is a continuing challenge to the web researcher.

4. *Limited history.* Websites include much current information but limited older information. If you are looking for information more than five years old, you may have to do your research the old-fashioned way in periodicals, books, and newspapers.

5. *Commercial interests.* The Internet moved rapidly from a domain dominated by government, military, and education to one dominated by business. Today, nine out of every ten sites added are from businesses, selling everything from baby carriages to cigar holders. Many of these newly added commercial sites are of limited value to the speech researcher.

Evaluating Sources on the Web

The beauty of the Internet is that information is available immediately. We truly have "just in time" education when learners can access information at any time they desire. The "beast" of this development is that the information on the Internet is not equal in value or accuracy. In addition, those creating websites are sometimes motivated by commercial interests rather than educational ones.

In order to evaluate the diversity of information that is available on the web, we offer a model created by Robert Harris, an English professor at the Vanguard University of Southern California (*http://www.virtualsalt.com/ evalu8it.htm*). Harris created the CARS (an acronym for Credibility, Accuracy, Reasonableness, and Support) checklist, which is a useful set of criteria for those seeking high-quality information. Harris notes that in addition to the four criteria listed below, the person seeking quality sources should note whether the site includes the author's name, title, and organizational affiliation; the date that the site was created or revised; and the author's contact information. Information such as this helps the reader evaluate the site. Let us consider the four criteria.

Technical Tip 6.3
Finding Information on the Net

The Internet can overwhelm you with information. Rather than suffocate yourself with coal dust in your search for diamonds, you should learn how to find the information you need as directly as possible. Here are some written and Internet sources that can lead you to information on the Internet:

Want, R. S. (1999). *How to Search the Web: A Quick-Reference Guide to Finding Things on the World Wide Web* (2nd ed.). New York: Want Publications. This book explains in non-technical terms how to use search engines to find the millions of websites in cyberspace. The book discusses both simple and advanced search procedures.

Barrett, D. J. (1997). *Netresearch: Finding Information Online* (Songline Guides). Cambridge, MA: O'Reilly & Associates. This book offers techniques for locating information on America Online, CompuServe, GNN, Microsoft Network, Prodigy, and dialup and direct Internet connections. This book teaches you how to fish instead of giving you the fish.

Luckman's World Wide Web Yellow Pages (3rd ed). New York: Barnes and Noble. This source and its CD have over 1000 pages of web addresses, along with ratings for content, design, organization, and load speed. Among the most interesting sections for speech research are the ones on news, science and technology, business, government and politics, health and medical, humanities, arts, and music.

---

1. *Credibility*. The source should be authentic and reliable. The author's credentials and the evidence of quality control may determine credibility. Is the author appropriately educated or trained? Does she or he have sufficient experience with the topic? Has the information been reviewed by experts or endorsed by appropriate organizations?

2. *Accuracy*. The information should be up to date and comprehensive. While some work is timeless, other information changes rapidly. The information should also be complete and detailed.

3. *Reasonableness*. The source should be fair, objective, moderate, and consistent. Is the information balanced, free of obvious bias, and does it seem probable? Does it avoid intemperate tone or language, overclaims, and sweeping statements of excessive significance?

4. *Support*. The information should be consistent within and with other known material. Does the source provide internal and external consistency? Do the claims have identified sources? Is documentation of secondary information provided? Do other sources provide the same information or corroborate the author's claims?

Creating the Bibliography

After you have completed your interviews, used the library, searched the Internet, and narrowed down your sources, it is time to create a bibliography. If you have done a good job recording complete information on your bibliography cards, this task will be simple. If you have only captured partial information, you may have to go back to your original sources to find volume numbers, page numbers, the years of publication, the first names or initials of the authors, and so on.

The bibliography of your speech includes a list of the sources consulted or the sources actually used in the speech. Your instructor will tell you whether you should include all of your sources or only those you actually cite in your speech. In any case, you will want to provide them in correct bibliographic form.

Two common bibliographic forms are those provided by the American Psychological Association (APA 2001) and the Modern Language Association (MLA 2003). In order to become familiar with the differences in these two style guides, you should consult the original sources. Alternatively, you may wish to purchase a reference book that includes both of these styles or the style preferred by your instructor (Ebest, Brusaw, Alred, and Oliu 2004).

Three basic bibliographic formats are the entries for a book, a periodical, and a newspaper article. We provide examples of these three for both APA and MLA styles. For other types of bibliographic entries, you are again encouraged to seek a reference book.

APA Style

Books:

Loeb, P. R. (1999). *Soul of a citizen: Living with conviction in a cynical time.* New York: St. Martin's Griffin.

Sotile, W. M., and Sotile, M. O. (1998). *Supercouple syndrome: How overworked couples can beat stress together.* New York: John Wiley & Sons.

Periodicals:

Michaels, L. (2001, March). Seattle's second coming. *Conde Nast Traveler,* pp. 186–195, 209–213.

Cohn, J. (2001, February 19). The jungle. *The New Republic,* pp. 23–27.

Ono, K. A., and Buescher, D. T. (2001, March). Deciphering Pocahontas: Unpackaging the commodification of a Native American woman. *Critical Studies in Media Communication,* 18, 23–43.

Newspaper articles:

Phillips, D. (2000, November 20). The coming threat to air traffic. *The Washington Post National Weekly Edition,* pp. 18–19.

Oldenburg, D. (2001, February 25). A 'mindful' way to better listening. *The Forum,* p. B3.

MLA Style

Books:

Loeb, Paul Rogat. *Soul of a Citizen: Living With Conviction in a Cynical Time.* New York: St. Martin's Griffin, 1999.

Sotile, Wayne M., and Mary O. Sotile. *Supercouple Syndrome: How Overworked Couples Can Beat Stress Together.* New York: John Wiley & Sons, 1998.

Periodicals:

Michaels, Lisa. "Seattle's Second Coming." *Conde Nast Traveler* (March 2001): 186–95, 209–13.

Cohn, J. (2001, February 19). "The Jungle." *The New Republic*, pp. 23–27.

Ono, K. A., and D. T. Buescher. (2001, March) "Deciphering Pocahontas: Unpackaging the Commodification of a Native American Woman." *Critical Studies in Media Communication*, 18, 23–43.

Newspaper articles:

Phillips, Don. "The Coming Threat to Air Traffic." *The Washington Post National Weekly Edition*, 20 November 2000: 18–19.

Oldenburg, Don. "A 'Mindful' Way to Better Listening." *The Forum*, 25 February 2001: B3.

You have probably noticed that the sources are listed in alphabetical order by the last name of the first author or by the name of the article if no author is given. Generally, you also place all of your sources together rather than dividing them up into books, periodicals, and newspaper articles. The following bibliography (Haffey 1999) would be typical. Can you determine if the style is APA or MLA?

Bibliography

American Cancer Society 16 May 1999: Homepage. Online document. Available: *http://www.cancer.org/.* 1 June 1999.

"Cancer Scope: Statistical Games Garner Great Glee," *International Council for Health Freedom Newsletter* 30 June 1999: 19–20.

Hudson, Tori. Women's Health Update: Resources in Women's Health, Organizations, Foundations, Associations, Research. *Townsend Letter for Doctors and Patients* 178 (1998), 126–128.

Havlick, H. D. "D-Day for Cancer? Natural Ammunition for the Battle." *Healthy and Natural Journal* 6 (1998): 88–91.

Serwach, Joseph. "Non-Profit Mergers Muddy Accountability." *Cain's Detroit Business* (1999): 23.

The advice on citations above is appropriate for written work—outlines, manuscripts, term papers. Next, you will learn how to cite the source in an oral presentation, a public speech.

Ethics in Research: Oral Footnotes

When you deliver your speech, you will not read your bibliography to the audience. Instead, you will indicate to them with oral footnotes where you found your information. These oral footnotes will be placed throughout the speech, not at the end of your talk. They only appear at the end of the speech in the formal outline.

The following incident illustrates clearly the importance of oral footnotes. On the front page of the *Boston Globe* appeared an article with a picture of the dean of the College of Communication at Boston University. The headline read: "BU Dean Used the Words of Another: Source Not Given During Speech." The lead paragraph explained that "In his May 12 commencement address before a crowd of future journalists and filmmakers . . . the dean of the College of Communication at Boston University repeated nearly word for word portions of an article by a nationally known film critic but never acknowledged the source" (Flint and Cohen 1991). Nearly word for word? The article exhibited six paragraphs that were either direct quotations or closely paraphrased sections. The article reported fourteen passages repeated nearly word for word.

This speaker, who had joined the faculty as a professor of international relations and journalism, should have known better. His own college provided students with guidelines about plagiarism and the penalties for it. All he would have had to do to avoid this serious breach of ethics is to say that the words and ideas were first printed in Michael Medved's article, "Popular Culture and the War Against Standards," in the February 1991 edition of *Imprimis,* a scholarly journal published by Hillsdale College. He probably would have been safe if he had used an abbreviated oral footnote crediting Medved with the words and ideas. Instead, he was dismissed as dean for his indiscretion and his violation of ethical standards.

A few years ago, a candidate for president of the United States had to drop out of the race for using portions of a British politician's speech, and a candidate for president of a major university dropped out of the race for using portions of another person's publication in a speech without attribution. The moral of these true and tragic stories is clear: you must credit the words and ideas of others with oral footnotes.

What is an oral footnote, and when should you use one? A footnote is used in written works to indicate where information was found. Usually it includes the name of the author, the name of the article, the name of the magazine or paper, the date of publication, and the page on which the quotation or idea was found. In public speaking, an oral footnote is much briefer but equally important. It may be just the name of the person or the publication or speech that is being quoted or paraphrased, or it might include the year or date of publication or the place where the speech was delivered. However brief the citation, the important thing is that the audience understands that the words or ideas came from a source other than the speaker.

What needs to be cited by an oral footnote? Anything that is taken from a source should be cited. It could be a direct quotation, in which you state the exact words of another person from print or a speech. It could be a paraphrase—that is, the words of a source not directly quoted but put in your words. The dean used an author's exact words, and he followed the same idea so closely that he practically filled in the blanks with his own information. That he took the idea from someone else was indisputable. What do oral footnotes look like? In Figure 6.7, you will find the proper form for oral footnotes.

Before leaving the subject of oral footnotes, you should be aware of the connection between oral footnotes and the ethics of public speaking. Following the Golden Rule—"Do unto others as you would have them do unto you"—is an ethical guide for public speakers. Would you want others to use something you wrote or said as if it were their own? In our society, using the words of another person, whether those words were in a speech or a newspaper article, is regarded as a serious offense, so serious that people's careers and opportunities have floundered on that single charge of plagiarism. In citing sources, it is much better to be too careful than to be careless, because the consequences are rough and avoidance is easy. Part of gaining confidence as a public speaker is the certainty that you have avoided plagiarism by using oral footnotes.

Figure 6.7
Oral Footnotes for Public Speaking

Citing a source for paraphrased information:

"According to the 1999 *Consumer Reports Buying Guide,* Michelin's Alpine snow tire is one of the very best."

Citing a source for a direct quotation:

John Daly in *Communication: At the Helm* cites a national survey indicating that ". . . Upwards of 25 percent [of the participants] were incapable of giving clear and accurate directions to a fire department about how to get to their homes."

Citing a magazine, a reference work, and a speech:

Last week's *U.S. News and World Report* said that . . .

According to the 2000 *Information Please Almanac* . . .

A month ago, Jesse Jackson said in a campus speech . . .

Summary

As you have learned, effective research requires careful planning. Start your research as soon as you select and narrow a topic, leave time for interviews and for surveying library sources, record your sources and the information in them, and modify your plan as you learn more about your chosen subject.

Communication Narrative 6.1
Seeking Information

Andrea Aronson was a successful executive in a bank in Minnesota. Married to an attorney, with whom she shared three children, she also was a supermom. The Aronsons were admired by others in their community for the way they balanced work and home responsibilities. The couple was active in several community groups and regularly attended meetings at the middle school and elementary school where their children attended school.

When the school system found itself at the crossroads of some difficult decisions created by diminishing enrollments, increasing costs, decreasing state support, and increasing federal and state mandates, Andrea ran for the school board. A popular candidate, she won the race easily and was selected to chair the nine members of the local school board. Andrea's responsibilities on the board became arduous as the problems that propelled her to run for office worsened.

Some of the members of the community encouraged the board to hire a consultant firm to review the problems they faced. Andrea, and a majority of the board, felt that doing so was an unnecessary cost and that they could research the problems themselves.

If you were Andrea or other members of the local Minnesota school board, how would you begin the process of research? Where would you find information? Would you interview others? Would you use library resources? How would the Internet be helpful?

This chapter on finding information stressed the importance of using your personal experience as a resource—as long as it is directly related to the topic or shows your relationship to the topic. The interview is a valuable means of securing information for your speeches, especially if the interview is well-planned, well-executed, and followed up with accurate notes and quotes.

A third place to find information—besides yourself and other people—is the library. The library staff should be a partner in your plan to produce superior speeches. The library section surveyed the resources available in computerized catalog systems, card catalogs, indexes, dictionaries, encyclopedias, yearbooks and almanacs, and newspapers. You will find that electronic research possibilities will continue to enhance your ability to find pertinent information. The Internet is a wonderful resource, but information found on websites must be evaluated carefully.

❖ ❖ ❖ ❖

NCA Credo for Communication Ethics

One of the principles of ethical communication applies to this chapter:
- We promote access to communication resources and opportunities as necessary to fulfill human potential and contribute to the well-being of families, communities, and society.

This chapter concluded by revealing the importance of citing your sources with oral footnotes. Some colleges and universities expel students who use the words of others without citation. Others give a failing mark in the course or on the assignment. All educational institutions require, as a rule of scholarship, that the words and ideas of another person be attributed to the original author. Anything less is regarded as a breach of ethics.

Vocabulary

bibliography card for a book Lists the author, title, place of publication, publisher, date of publication, call number (to locate the book in the library), and any notes you might want to make about the specific information in the book or its importance.

bibliography card for a periodical Includes the name of the author, the title of the article, the name of the periodical (underlined), the volume if indicated, the date of publication in parentheses, and the pages on which the article appears in the periodical.

bibliography card for a newspaper Includes the name of the reporter (if available), the headline, the name of the newspaper (underlined), the exact date, the section, and the page number.

Internet The matrix of networks that connects computers around the world.

World Wide Web A collection of Internet sites that offer text and graphics and sound and animation resources.

Application Exercises

Evaluating Personal Experience

1. Write the name of your topic in the top blank and list below it three aspects of your personal life or experience that could be used to enhance your credibility or to provide supporting materials for your speech.

    Topic

    Personal Experience

    a.

    b.

    c.

    Evaluate your personal experience by checking off each item as you use it to examine the experience.

    Was your experience typical?

    Was your experience so typical that it will be boring or so unusual that it was a chance occurrence?

    Was your experience one that this audience will appreciate or from which the audience can learn?

    Does your experience constitute proof or evidence of anything?

Library Scavenger Hunt

2. You are much more likely to use reference works if you know where they are in the library and if you know what kind of information is in them. The following exercise is designed to better acquaint you with the library and its reference works.

    a. From the computerized catalog system or the card catalog, find the author and title of one book that deals with your topic.

    Author   **Title**

    b. Using an electronic periodical index, find the name and author of an article that deals with your topic.

    Author   **Title**

    c. From the *Reader's Guide to Periodical Literature*, find the title and author of one article on your topic.

    Author   **Title**

    d. Using the *Education Index* or other specialized index, give the author, title, and name of publication for an article on the topic you have selected.

    Author   **Title**

    Publication

    e. Using an encyclopedia, yearbook, or almanac, find specific information about your topic. In one sentence, explain what kind of information you found.

    Source

f.   Using an almanac or a government publication, state some information about a topic in correct form on an index card.

g.   Using an electronic newspaper index, look for a current article that is related to your topic.
     Author (if provided)
     Title
     Newspaper
     Bibliographic Form

To check your answers, compare them to the examples in the chapter.

3.   See if you can state your sources accurately by placing these sources in proper form for a bibliographical entry.

Source A: The name of the book is *What Employers Want.* The book was published in 1999. The author is Harry Holzer. The place of publication is _____. The publisher is Russell S. Foundation.

Source B: The name of the periodical is *Communication Theory.* The date of publication is August 1999. The article runs from page 229 through 264. The author is Leonard C. Hawes. The name of the article is "The Dialogics of Conversation: Power Control, Vulnerability." The volume number is 9.

Source C: The name of the reporter is John M. Berry. The name of the newspaper is *The Washington Post.* The article appears on page E1. The title of the article is "Fed's Relationship to Markets Growing More Complicated." The date of the newspaper is August 17, 1999.

Source D: This article is entitled "9/11 Report to Cite 10 Missed Opportunities: Panel Faults Two Administrations but Doesn't Call Attacks Preventable." It was published in the *Washington Post* on Wednesday, July 21, 2004. The authors of the article are Dan Eggen and Mike Allen. The article was on page A01. The article was accessed at *http://www.washingtonpost.com/wp-dyn/articles/A127-2004Jul20.html* on July 21, 2004.

──**Note**──

1. "Man" was changed to "person" in this quotation.

References

Bailey, S. M. (1994). An unnamed speech delivered in Interpersonal Communication 103, Public Speaking, Ohio University, Spring Quarter, in a section taught by Dan Shapiro.

Campbell, R. D. (1994). An unnamed speech delivered in Interpersonal Communication 103, Public Speaking, Ohio University, Spring Quarter, in a section taught by Dan Shapiro.

Ebest, S. B., Brusaw, C. T., Alred, G. J., and Oliu, W. E. (2004). *Writing From A to Z: The Easy-To-Use Reference Handbook* (4th ed.). Mountain View, CA: Mayfield Publishing Company.

Flint, A., and Cohen, M. (1991, July 2). BU dean used the words of another: Source not given during speech. *The Boston Globe.*

Haffey, K. (1999). A Smart Investment. A speech delivered in Interpersonal Communication 103, Public Speaking, Ohio University, Spring Quarter, in a section taught by Paul E. Nelson.

How America Measures Up. (1999). Discovery Channel.

Kovatch, L. (1994). An unnamed speech delivered in Interpersonal Communication 101, Public Speaking, Ohio University, Spring Quarter, in a section taught by Kim Varey.

Luckman's World Wide Web Yellow Pages (3rd ed.). (1999). New York: Barnes & Noble.

Mates, B. T., Wakefield, D., and Dixon, J. M. (1999). *Adaptive Technology for the Internet: Making Electronic Resources Accessible.* Washington, DC: American Library Association.

MLA Handbook for Writers of Research Papers, 6th ed. (2003). New York: The Modern Language Association of America.

Planisek, R. (1993). Unnamed speeches delivered in Interpersonal Communication 101, Public Speaking, Ohio University, Fall Quarter, in a section taught by Marsha Clowers.

Publication Manual of the American Psychological Association, 5th ed. (2001). Washington, DC: American Psychological Association.

Smith, J. (1994). An unnamed speech delivered in Interpersonal Communication 101, Public Speaking, Ohio University, Spring Quarter, in a section taught by Kim Varey.

Tyre, E. (1994). An unnamed speech delivered in Interpersonal Communication 103, Public Speaking, Ohio University, Spring Quarter, in a section taught by Kim Varey.

Wilson, D. L. (1993). Array of new tools is designed to make it easier to find and retrieve information on the Internet. *The Chronicle of Higher Education,* 39, A17–A19.

Chapter 7

Speech Organization
and Outlining

Science is organized knowledge. Wisdom is organized life.
—Immanuel Kant

Question Outline

I. Why is speech organization important to the speaker and to the audience?

II. What are the three steps involved in organizing the body of the speech?

III. What are some suggestions that a speaker should use in identifying and writing the main points of a speech?

IV. What are some of the patterns that can be used in organizing your main points?

V. How can the speaker connect main points and subpoints during the speech?

VI. What are the three principles of outlining?

VII. What are the three types of outlines speakers use most often?

VIII. What should you include in a formal outline?

Nagora Wynkoop was not in trouble for lack of a topic. He knew only one subject more than other people knew, and that subject was emergency medicine. Nagora had worked for more than twenty years as a paramedic on an *ambulance. Technically, he worked for the fire department, but his work had always been rescue. Because his unit was located by some very large highway systems as well as some highly used local roads, he and the ambulance driver spent most of their time hauling accident victims to the hospital.*

Nagora knew how to stop arterial bleeding, how to bind compound fractures, where pressure points were located, what to do about a large open wound, and how to strap a person to a backboard to avoid further injury. What he did not know was how to organize twenty years' worth of information about emergency first aid. Which of the many areas should he cover? What information should come first? How many things should he try to talk about? Nagora decided that he needed to read the chapter on organization and outlining to find out the answers to his questions.

To help you increase your confidence in public speaking, this chapter will focus on how to organize and outline a speech. You have already found information on your topic; now you need to understand how best to organize that material. In this chapter we will begin by discussing the importance of speech organization.

The bulk of this chapter will discuss how to organize and outline the body of a speech. We will consider how to divide the body into main points, how to determine the order of the main points, and how to incorporate supporting materials.

We will also consider how speakers can show the connections between their main points and subpoints by exploring the role of transitions, signposts, internal previews, and internal reviews.

Finally, we will turn our attention to outlining, where we will discuss the three principles of outlining—subordination, division, and parallelism, and the three types of outlines—the preparation outline, the formal outline, and the key word outline.

The Importance of Organization

Imagine that you have spent a great deal of time writing a carefully organized speech. After you have finished, you try an experiment. You deliver your speech as you have planned it to one group of people. For another group of people, you organize the speech randomly, moving sentences and ideas around haphazardly. Although you used all of the same words and, indeed, all of the same sentences, your speech has no structure to it. How do you think the two audiences would respond? Do you think both audiences would see you as a competent speaker? Do you think the two audiences would be able to recall a similar amount of information from your speeches?

Researchers have conducted experiments similar to the one we are describing. Speakers who gave well-organized speeches—compared to those who were not well organized—found a number of benefits. First, audience members could understand the organized speeches better (Thompson 1960). Second, audience members perceived speakers who delivered organized speeches as more competent and trustworthy than speakers who delivered disorganized speeches (Sharp and McClung 1966). Clearly, audiences appreciate well-organized speeches.

Speakers also benefit from taking the time to carefully organize their speeches. First, speakers state that they are more confident when their messages are more (rather than less) organized (Greene 1984). Second, they believe that they deliver their speeches more smoothly (Greene 1984). Third, Paul Fritz and Richard Weaver (1986) found that to the extent that students can learn and master the ability to organize ideas, they will be better analytical thinkers. Organizational skills probably generalize in positive ways beyond the speaking situation. In short, learning how to organize ideas for a speech will help you as a speaker and in a variety of other future endeavors.

Organizing the Body of the Speech

The introduction, body, and conclusion are the three main components of any speech. In this chapter we consider the organization of the body of the speech. Generally, the body of the speech is organized and created before the introduction and conclusion.

Technical Tip 7.1
More on Outlines and Outlining

Price, J. (1999). *Outlining Goes Electronic.* Westport, CT: Ablex Publishing Corp. This book uses an historical approach but promotes the use of an electronic outliner, software that "accelerates and transforms the process of outlining," according to the author, Jonathan Price *(JonPrice@aol.com).*

http://www.powa.org. This site has an entirely different approach to organization for students seeking ideas beyond or around outlining. The site tells about informational and argumentative writings that are very close to informative and persuasive speaking.

Divide the Body Into Main Points

The first task in organizing the body of the speech is to identify the main points that you will discuss. Examine the material that you have gathered and consider the key issues you want to address. If you have written your specific purpose, you may be able to identify your main points easily. For example, one journalism student gave a speech on writing books (Planisek 1993). Her specific purpose was to have her audience learn the steps involved in writing a book. Her main points included the following:

I. How to get started writing your book.

II. How to do research.

III. How to do the actual writing of the book.

IV. How to publish your book.

These sets of main points divide the topic into main ideas that can be explained and discussed further. The main points, as we see here, provide the skeleton for the body of the speech. They will be fleshed out with supporting materials, examples, evidence, and further divisions of subpoints and sub-subpoints.

As you are considering your speech topic, your specific purpose, and the main points that you will develop from them, you should keep in mind some other advice about main points. First, you should consider having between two and five main points. Second, you should word your main points in a parallel manner. Third, your main ideas should be approximately equal in importance. Let us consider each of these suggestions in more depth.

Limit your main points to between two and five points. The number of points in a speech is limited by the number an audience can easily remember. An audience might remember none of the main ideas in a fourteen point speech, but they can usually remember a smaller number. Most speeches have three main points, but any number between two and five is fine. Some topics are difficult to divide, and you may come up with only two main points. For example, imagine that you are going to speak on the way husbands and wives view marriage. A topic like this one has only two obvious main points:

I. Husbands' views of a traditional marriage are often more positive than wives' views of marriage.

II. Wives' views of a traditional marriage are often less positive than husbands' views of marriage.

Other topics are more easily divisible into a greater number of points. For instance, if you are talking about some process, you could divide your talk up into the five main steps of the process. Imagine that you are giving a speech on growing your own vegetables. You could organize your speech with these five main points:

I. Prepare the soil with surface tilling.

II. Plant the seeds or starter plants in measured rows.

III. Protect the plants from chemicals, insects, and drought.

IV. Harvest the crops by picking or cutting at the correct time.

V. Prepare your garden for the next year by clearing weeds, turning the soil, and covering it with mulch.

You might be tempted to divide your topic into more than five main points. For example, if you are going to talk about breeds of dogs that are good house pets, you may have a dozen or more breeds that could each be a main point. When this occurs, you want to examine your list of several main points and determine if there are ways to group these points under broader, more generic categories. For instance, the long list of dogs may be able to be subsumed under the main points of small dogs, medium-sized dogs, and large dogs. Or, you might be able to divide them into short-haired, medium-haired, and long-haired dogs.

Word your main points in a parallel manner. A second suggestion is to word your main points in a manner that is as parallel as possible. Parallel construction in speaking and writing increases clarity, sounds more engaging, and lingers longer in memory. Parallel construction means that you repeat words, phrases, and sentences. Which of the following would be easier to hear and easier to remember?

No Parallel Construction
We cannot do much more to honor this place than has already been done by those who died here. What we say today will be quickly forgotten. What will be remembered is the many who died here.

Parallel Construction
We cannot dedicate—we cannot consecrate—we cannot hallow this ground. The brave men, *living and dead,* who struggled here have consecrated it far above our poor power to *add or detract. The world will little note nor long remember what we say here,* but *it can never forget what they did here.*

The italics in the second example has repeated independent clauses (We cannot . . .), followed by parallel and balanced pairs (living and dead, add or detract), followed by parallel and balanced independent clauses in the form of an antithesis. The words are from Abraham Lincoln's *Gettysburg Address.*

Let us re-examine the main points on the speech about how to write a book (Planisek 1993).

I. Get started on writing your book.

II. How to do research.

III. The actual writing of the book.

IV. Publishing your book.

While these main points clearly define four steps in the writing of a book, they are not parallel. They might be rewritten as follows:

I. Getting started on the book.

II. Doing research for the book.

III. Writing the book.

IV. Publishing the book.

They could also be written this way:

I. How to get started on writing your book.

II. How to do research on your book.

III. How to write your actual book.

IV. How to publish your book.

While these changes in wording may appear to be subtle, they affect the way subsequent subpoints and sub-subpoints will be written. In general, using parallel construction in your main points encourages more parallel development of supporting ideas. When your main points are organized similarly, the audience is more likely to remember them.

Ensure that your main points are all relatively equal in importance. Another important consideration to keep in mind is whether your points are relatively equal to each other in importance. Your main points should be approximately the same in magnitude. One way that you can check this aspect as you develop the main points is to consider how much subdividing you are doing for each point. If one main point has several subdivisions but the others have almost no subdivisions, that point must be more important than the others.

Similarly, when you practice your speech later on, you may find that you do not spend equal time on each main point. Each main point need not be granted exactly the same amount of time, but the time you spend discussing each point should be relatively similar. If you have three main points, you should probably spend between 20 and 50 percent of your total time allotted for the body of the speech on each one. If you have five main points, you might spend between 10 and 25 percent of your total time allotted for the body of the speech on each one. In the speech about writing a book, the speaker spent about 20 percent of her time on how to get started, nearly 50 percent of her time on how to do research, and about 15 percent of her time on the last two main points (doing the actual writing of the book and publishing the book). Her time allotments for each main point were not identical, but the timing was not extremely different. Further, her allotments might reflect the actual proportion of time involved in each of these activities when one writes a book.

On the Web

As a beginning public speaker, outlining may seem a bit arduous. The Internet has many helpful sites to introduce you to the concepts and importance of outlining. One such site is *http://www.speakingsolutions.com/resources/outline.html*.

Patterns of Organization

Usually Informative	Either Informative or Persuasive	Usually Persuasive
Time-Sequence	Cause-Effect	Problem-Solution
Spatial Relations	Topical Sequence	Monroe's Motivated
	Climactic	Sequence
	Anticlimactic	

Determine the Order of the Main Points

Sometimes the order of your main points seems obvious. For example, in the speech on writing a book, the speaker arranged the main points in chronological order. In other words, she talked about what occurs first in the writing of a book, what occurs next, and so on. The speech would have seemed bizarre if the publication of the book preceded how to get started on writing a book.

At other times, the organizational pattern is less clear. In this section we provide you with some alternatives you can consider for the organization of your main points. As you will see, you actually have several options for organizing your main points.

The general purpose of your speech will suggest potential organizational patterns. Among the possible organizational patterns for your speech are:

1. The time-sequence and spatial relations patterns, which are often used in informative speaking;

2. The cause-effect and topical sequence patterns, which are used both in informative and persuasive speaking;

3. The problem-solution and Monroe Motivated Sequence patterns, which are often used in persuasive speaking; and

4. The climactic or anticlimactic pattern, which describes a way to order arguments, ideas, or supporting materials so they can be superimposed over other patterns.

The topic of your speech and the specific purpose will also affect your organizational pattern. For example, if you are giving a speech on a step-by-step process, you will probably rely on the time-sequence pattern. If you are attempting to persuade an audience to sign a petition, you might use a climactic pattern. The effective and ethical public speaker develops a large repertoire of organizational possibilities that can be applied appropriately to the general purpose, specific purpose, and topic.

Time-sequence pattern. The **time-sequence pattern** states the order of events over time. This pattern reveals when something occurred. You should use this pattern when your primary purpose is to tell your audience how something came about over a period of time. Examples would be stating the steps in constructing a cedar chest, in making French bread, in growing an eastern white pine from seed to maturity, or in recounting the watershed events leading to the Civil War. This pattern is commonly used in "how to do it" speeches because the audience will be unable to "do it" unless steps are followed in the correct order. A speech outline using the time-sequence pattern is shown in Figure 7.1.

Figure 7.1
An Example of the Time-Sequence Pattern of Organization

Immediate purpose: To instruct the class on the steps for refinishing an outside wooden door.

Introduction

Attention Getter   I. Many homes, condos, and apartments have natural finish front doors that have become weathered from sun, wind, snow, or rain.

             II. Today I am going to show you some easy steps to refinish that entrance to your home.

Body

Steps to   III. Preparation of the exterior door is essential.
Improvement

A. Use commercial stripper, sometimes twice, to completely remove the old finish.

B. Use a plastic scraper to remove old finish and to avoid damaging the wood.

C. Carefully remove all traces of the chemical with low-suds detergent and a light wipe with steel wool.

IV. Application of exterior varnish takes time and patience.

A. Without thinning the product, brush one light layer on the wood.

B. After allowing ample time for drying, lightly steel wool the surface so the next coat will adhere.

C. Wipe off all residue with a dry cloth before applying a second light layer of product to the surface.

D. The last coat needs no further attention—the job is done.

Conclusion

Action Step V. A brush, a small can of varnish, a clean rag, and light sandpaper or steelwool are all you need to do this simple project that will make you happy every time you enter your home.

Spatial relations pattern. The **spatial relations pattern** demonstrates how things are related in space. You would use this pattern when you have to show an audience where places are located on a map; where the tachometer, odometer, and speedometer are located on a dashboard; or how to select choices on a menu-driven computer screen with a mouse. Your purpose, not the topic, determines your choice of organizational pattern. So if your purpose is to show the audience how to arrange lighting for fashion photography, you would use a spatial relations pattern to show them the lighting design and location of the subject. The example of spatial relations in Figure 7.2 shows how a speaker could use a detailed map to show location of historical sites.

Figure 7.2
An Example of the Spatial Relations Pattern of Organization

Immediate purpose: To show the audience how to locate historically important sites in our area.

Introduction

I. Unknown to many students, this area has a number of historically important sites.

Thesis sentence II. Knowing how to find these sites will increase your appreciation for this area of the country.

Body

Main points III. As indicated on the map, there are three historically significant sites within walking distance of the university.

A. The Broadheart Log Cabin was discovered under clapboard siding on West State Avenue.

B. The President's Mansion was built by a coal baron in the 1800s.

C. The Pendleton Building on Main Street was the scene of the area's most dramatic murder.

Conclusion

Review   IV. All three buildings are open year-round and admission is free.

V. I encourage all of you to learn more about the local area by visiting these historic sites.

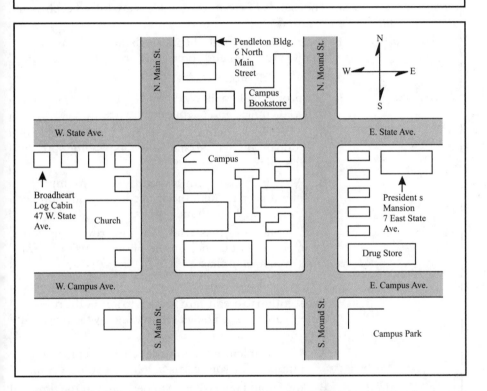

Problem-solution pattern. The **problem-solution pattern,** depicting an issue and how to solve it, tends to be used more often in persuasive than in informative speeches. The statement of the problem is difficult to describe without framing the issue in some way that indicates your own perspective, which you want the audience to adopt. For example, let us say you describe the problem of pickpockets and muggings. That problem is your perspective on crime. One could just as easily define crime economically as the millions of dollars lost in white-collar crimes like fraud, embezzlement, and scams. That angle is a different perspective on crime. The point is that to describe a problem reflects a point of view that you want your audience to adopt.

The solution is even more likely to be perceived as persuasive because your solutions to problems ordinarily advocate some policy or action that you want your audience to embrace. In the case of person-on-person crimes, you might, for example, advocate closer control over who has weapons or stronger penalties for using them. In the case of white-collar crime, you might advocate closer surveillance by the Attorney General, more wide-spread warnings about scam artists, or jail time for so-called victimless crimes. In both cases, you select a particular solution that you end up persuading your audience to adopt.

Figure 7.3
An Example of the Problem-Solution Pattern of Organization

Immediate purpose: To convince my audience to discontinue practices that invite credit card fraud.

	Introduction
Statement to gain audience's favorable attention	I. Thousands of credit card holders are bilked each year by thieves.
Thesis sentence	II. Today, you will find out more about the problem of credit card fraud and some solutions to the problem.

Problem

Main points	III. The problem of credit card fraud is stolen cards, unauthorized copies, and telephone phonies.
	A. When your credit card is taken by a pickpocket or robber, you may be charged for a spending spree by the thief.
	B. When you pay with a credit card, an employee might keep an unauthorized copy so your number can be used for phone purchases.
	C. Telephone crooks trick you into revealing your credit card number on the phone to use it themselves for purchases.

Solution

IV. The solution to credit card fraud is to follow the rules on stolen cards, keep copies secure, and avoid revealing your number to strangers.

    A. Report stolen cards immediately by keeping phone numbers for your cards in a list off your person.

    B. You should take your customer's copy at the time of purchase.

    C. Never tell someone your credit card number on the phone unless you placed the call for a purchase.

Conclusion

Review   V. You can avoid credit card fraud by being a cautious customer.

    A. Treat your plastic as if it were worth your line of credit because that is what you can lose—and more.

    B. Watch, guard, and protect your credit card with vigilance and maybe even insurance.

VI. Your credit card may be worth a fortune to you and those who would prey on you: use it defensively.

The problem-solution pattern raises one serious question for the speaker: how much should you say about the problem or the solution? Usually you can work out a proper ratio based on what the audience knows about the issue. If the listeners are unaware that a problem exists, you may have to spend time telling them about it. On the other hand, if the problem is well known to all, you can spend most of your time on the solution. This pattern lends itself nicely to outlining, with the problem being one main head and the solution the other. An example of the problem-solution pattern of organization is shown in Figure 7.3.

Cause-effect pattern. The **cause-effect pattern** of organization describes or explains a problem and its ramifications. Some examples include the cause of Parkinson's Disease and its effects on the body; the causes of urban blight and one local government's solution; and the causes of low- and high-pressure weather systems and their effect on ground temperature. As with the problem-solution pattern, this one lets you decide how much time you should spend on the cause(s) and how much on the effect(s). A cause-effect pattern of organization is shown in Figure 7.4. This outline suggests that the speaker will spend about two-thirds of the allotted time talking about the causes of social drinking and about one-third talking about the effect of those factors.

Figure 7.4
An Example of the Cause-Effect Pattern of Organization

Immediate purpose: To persuade the class that social drinking leads to alcoholism.

	Introduction
Statement to gain audience's favorable attention	I. Jobs, school, and families bring stress, which many of us try to reduce with alcohol.
Thesis sentence	II. For some the social drinking will become problem drinking, which can become alcoholism.
	Body
Main points	III. Why an individual becomes chemically dependent on alcohol remains a mystery, but the reasons seem rooted in nature and nurture.
	A. Children of the chemically dependent have a much greater chance of becoming chemically dependent themselves.
	B. Persons who drink risk becoming chemically dependent.
	IV. Social drinking can become problem drinking.
	A. The person who cannot seem to stop drinking is already a problem drinker.
	B. The person who passes out, blacks out, or cannot remember what occurred has a serious drinking problem.
	C. The person whose relationships with others begin to fail with regularity has turned from people to alcohol.

❖ ❖ ❖ ❖

V. The problem drinker becomes an alcoholic.

A. The person who is unable to stop drinking has become chemically dependent.

B. The person who is alcoholic must usually be helped by others to stop.

C. The most common way to avoid recurrence is to never drink again.

Conclusion

Review

VI. The best illustration that social drinking leads to alcoholism is that a nondrinker will never become an alcoholic.

A. Persons with a family history of chemical dependence can protect themselves by abstinence.

B. Persons whose families see a person becoming dependent might want to encourage nondrinking before the problem becomes worse.

Climactic and anticlimactic patterns. The **climactic** and **anticlimactic** patterns can be seen as a way to organize an entire speech, or as an overlay—a pattern that can "go over" or be superimposed over other organizational patterns. For example, you could organize a problem-solution speech in which you use a climactic pattern to describe the problems and an anticlimactic pattern to describe the solution. Or you could have a time-sequence pattern in which your entire speech builds toward a climactic ending about how you survived a traumatic event, what brought a big dispute to an end, or where your journey will end. The climactic speech, like a good story, builds toward some exciting conclusion. The anticlimactic speech starts with the excitement and then proceeds to unravel the story behind the excitement. An example of a climactic pattern is shown in Figure 7.5. For further information on the climactic and anticlimactic patterns, see Figure 7.6.

Figure 7.5
An Example of the Climactic Pattern of Organization

Immediate purpose: To have classmates recognize that teachers who emphasize learning need to be evaluated differently than teachers who emphasize teaching.

Statement to gain audience's favorable attention

Introduction

I. The stereotypical view of the college professor is a highly educated person who lectures to an audience of relatively passive students who take notes, ask a few questions, and show that they know the material on exams.

A. In most college classrooms, all but a very small amount of time is spent listening to the professor.

B. In most college classrooms, the amount of interplay between teacher and student is minimal to none.

C. In most college classrooms, the grade depends

heavily on playing back lecture or text as portrayed by the teacher.

Thesis sentence   II. A newly emerging movement in higher education takes the focus off "the sage on the stage" (the traditional lecturing professor) to "the guide on the side" (the professor whose focus is student understanding of the issues and problems).

Body

Examples to support thesis   III. Students will notice the difference between traditional teaching and the new mode of instruction because they will be doing, thinking, and solving, not just passively listening.

    A. In medical schools, passive instruction on anatomy, physiology, and hematology have been replaced by problem-based learning, starting with a patient whose medical problem needs a solution from the students.

    B. In business schools, MBA students spend two years starting a business by developing a business plan, going through zoning, financing, hiring, etc.

    C. In science, students learn by working on real problems such as managing toxic waste, killing mosquitoes without using DDT, and genetically altering food crops.

Need for change   IV. Students need to evaluate teachers who use active learning differently than they evaluate traditional teachers.

    A. Most college evaluation forms favor "the sage on the stage" by addressing the teacher's knowledge, accessibility, and understandability.

    B. Teachers who promote active learning need to be evaluated by questions like, "Did you learn from your group project?" "Did your team work well in solving the problem?" or "Did your teacher assist your group in resolving the issue?"

Conclusion

Review and challenge   V. Teacher-centered classes are highly satisfying to the teacher, less so for the learner.

  VI. Learner-centered classes are highly satisfying to both the teacher and the learner.

 VII. Learner-centered classes need to be evaluated by how much the student learned, how much the student enjoyed the learning, and whether the learning persists.

Topical sequence pattern. The **topical sequence pattern** is a highly versatile organizational pattern. Seen by some as the pattern of last resort and by others as the most important form of organization, the topical sequence pattern simply means that you divide up your topic. For instance, the following

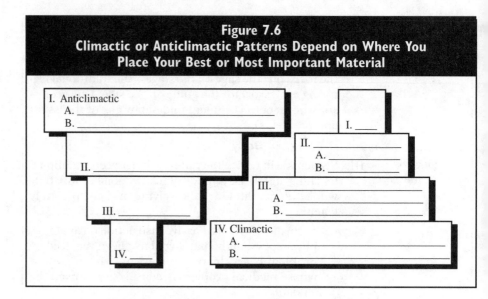

Figure 7.6
Climactic or Anticlimactic Patterns Depend on Where You Place Your Best or Most Important Material

organizational patterns are all topical: a speech showing advantages and disadvantages, a speech citing different qualities of some object or thing, a speech on the pros and cons of an issue, four qualities of a leader, or three types of local transportation. Figure 7.7 shows an example of the topical sequence pattern.

Figure 7.7
An Example of the Topical Sequence Pattern of Organization

Title: *Grade Inflation Is Bad for You*

Immediate Purpose: To invite students to measure their grade point average against national norms in a persuasive speech against grade inflation.

Introduction

Attention Getter　I. Your hard-earned GPA may be worth much less than you think.

    A. Over the last 25 years, grades have moved upward.

    B. Improved grades are not reflected in improved standardized test scores.

Thesis　II. We had better stop grade erosion to maintain the value of our own grades.

Body

Evidence　III. National increases in grades are eroding your grade point average.

    A. College students today study approximately half as much as their parents' generation but expect higher grades.

    B. Because of college and honors courses in high school, students often graduate with a score above the top (e.g., a 4.5 in a 4.0 scale).

    C. The average GPA at most universities hovers around 2.8 or higher.

❖ ❖ ❖ ❖

Examples	IV. Escalating grades have confounded admissions and honors.
	A. University of California–Berkeley could fill its first year class with applicants having a 4.0 or higher.
	B. Many universities have had to raise the GPA levels for graduating with honors.
Effects	V. The effects of grade inflation affect you and your future.
	A. Employers will no longer be impressed with a B average since a 3.0 is almost normative at many colleges and universities.
	B. Admission to graduate, medical, and law schools will be increasingly difficult to achieve through grades.
	C. If GPAs keep rising, your current GPA will appear less and less impressive in the future.

Conclusion

Action Step	VI. Grades inflate because of pressure from parents and students.
	A. You should not encourage your parents to complain about your grades.
	B. You should not complain your own way to a higher grade.

Another example of the topical sequence pattern that can be used in persuasive, legal, or logic-based speeches is the "speech of reasons." In the speech of reasons, the body is divided into a series of arguments for or against some proposition. The speech is persuasive because the main points, the reasons or arguments, move the audience toward acceptance. Such a speech could also have an overlay of climactic organization, with each argument increasing in strength, relevance, or potency.

Monroe's Motivated Sequence. **Monroe's Motivated Sequence** (Gronbeck et al. 1997) was developed by Alan Monroe, who applied John Dewey's work on reflective thinking to persuasion. This organizational pattern includes five specific components: attention, need, satisfaction, visualization, and action. Following this sequence, you would first attempt to capture the attention of your audience. You want your audience to decide that it is important to listen to you.

Second, you establish the need for your proposal. You want to describe a problem or show why some need exists. You want your audience to believe that something must be done.

Third, you present the solution to the problem or show how the need can be satisfied. You want your audience to understand how your proposal will satisfy the need.

Fourth, you go beyond simply presenting the solution by visualizing it for the audience. You want the audience to envision enjoying the benefits of your proposal.

Last, you state the behavior that you expect of your audience. In this step, you request action or approval. You want your audience to respond by saying that they will do what you have asked. Your speech should have a strong conclusion that asks for specific, but reasonable, action.

One student (Reindel 1994) was upset by the second-hand smoke that he was forced to breathe each day. His speech, which followed the steps of Monroe's Motivated Sequence, is shown in Figure 7.8.

**Figure 7.8
An Example of Monroe's Motivated Sequence**

A Law Against Smoking in Public

I. **Introduction**

   A. Twice a day I walk to Bentley Hall for class and, just as I get to the doors, I am engulfed by a cloud of smoke from a group of people who insist on smoking before class. Something must be done about this.

   B. In the book entitled *Passive Smoking* by Susan Neumister[1], second-hand smoking is defined as the phrase associated with the inhalation by nonsmokers of tobacco smoke produced by smokers.

   C. A study in *Current Science* by Ingrid Wickelgren reports that cigarette smoking kills 419,000 Americans every year.[2]

   D. There are three reasons why I am credible on this subject.

     1. I have lived with smokers and asthma sufferers for much of my life.

     2. I have been locked on the 6th floor of the library studying smoking for the past week.

     3. I take classes in Bentley Hall.

   E. Today I'll begin speaking about the problem of smoking in public places. Secondly, I will present my solution and prove that it must be enacted. Finally, I'll speak about what will happen if my solution is not enacted and what will occur if it is enacted.

II. **Need**

   A. First of all, the problem is that 40 million Americans smoke.[3]

   B. Germs and poison live in second-hand smoke, and this smoke is everywhere.

     1. It lurks in front of Bentley Hall and every other hall across campus.

     2. You can't go out for a night of boot scootin' country dancing at a club uptown without coming home saturated with the stench of smoke.

     3. Even restaurants are filled with smoke.

   C. Smokers poison themselves, and when they smoke in public, they poison everyone else as well. Second-hand smoke kills.

   D. The World Health Organization says that unless people are encouraged to quit smoking, the number of deaths due to smoking will reach half a billion.[4]

III. **Satisfaction**

   A. My solution is to enact a law forbidding cigarette or any other drug smoking in public.

B. Smokers can have as many cigarettes as they want in the privacy of their own homes. However, in public places, smoking would be prohibited.

C. My proposal would bring many benefits.

  1. It would decrease the number of hospitalized asthma victims.

  2. It would promote purer air.

  3. It would greatly diminish deaths due to passive smoking.

  4. It would take away the odor on clothes and the watery eyes caused by smoke.

D. Veronica Johannesen was awarded workers' compensation benefits for asthma developed on the job in New York City from second-hand smoke.[5]

E. Even corporate giants like GM and Texas Instruments are tightening policies on smoking or banning it entirely to save money.

F. Smokers object to this proposed law.

  1. Smokers claim that this is America and the government may make no law to abridge their freedom to smoke.

      a. It is true that it is their right to smoke, but they do not have the right to put the health of nonsmokers at risk.

      b. According to a 1994 *Wall Street Journal* report, the EPA used studies on the risk of second-hand smoke to ban smoking from all office buildings.[6]

  2. Another argument by smokers' rights advocates claims that second-hand smoke in no way jeopardizes the health of nonsmokers.

      a. The *Journal of the American Medical Association* reports that active and passive smoking causes immediate physiological changes and illnesses in children.[7]

      b. According to a 1994 *Wall Street Journal* report, the EPA used studies on the risk of second-hand smoke to ban smoking from all office buildings.[6]

      c. The American Heart Association recommends reducing children's exposure to tobacco hazards.[8]

IV. **Visualization**

  A. Let's imagine what will happen if my proposal is not accepted.

    1. If it is not enacted, we will continue to unnecessarily suffer from burning eyes, coughing attacks, and smoke-stained skin.

    2. *U.S. News and World Report* says children are getting hooked on nicotine in alarming numbers.[9]

  B. Finally, let's flip the coin and imagine a cigarette smoke free environment.

    1. Unsuspecting victims of second-hand smoke will no longer perish.

    2. Smokers' children will no longer be as prone to suffering.

    3. We can once again feel free to breathe in public.

V. **Action**

  A. Today we looked at the problem of smoking in public places. Secondly, I proposed the solution that smoking be outlawed in public

> places. Finally, we imagined two scenarios: one in which my proposal is not accepted and nonsmokers serve as targets for death, and the other scenario in which the law is enforced and living conditions improve.
>
> B. On a personal level, I do not hesitate to ask someone to put a cigarette out. I refuse to silently wait as I become a statistic.
>
> C. Remember, smoking is a colorful habit. Your teeth turn yellow, and your lungs turn black. Though you may not smoke, this could happen to you just because you go country dancing, out to eat, or even to Bentley Hall.
>
> ---
>
> This speech was given by John R. Reindel during Fall Quarter 1994 at Ohio University in Interpersonal Communication 103: Public Speaking, taught by Kim Varey. The outline is based on Reindel's outline and is reprinted with permission from the student. The speech contained the following endnotes: 1. Susan Neumister, *Passive Smoking* (Monticello, IL: Vance Bibliographies, 1985); 2. Ingrid Wickelgren, "Are Smokers Addicts?" *Current Science* (September 9, 1994): 10–12; 3. Walecia Konrad, "Smoking Out the Elusive Smoker," *Business Week* (March 16, 1992): 62–63; 4. From a World Health Organization report on *ABC World News Tonight* (number 4186) September 19, 1994; 5. "Is Secondhand Smoke Illness Compensable?" *Occupational Hazards* 56 (no. 8) (August 1994): 67; 6. "Secondhand Cancer?" from a television program entitled *Wall Street Journal Report* (number 628) October 8, 1994; 7. Andrew A. Skolnik, "First AHA Statement on Tobacco and Children," *Journal of the American Medical Association* 272 (no. 11) (September 21, 1994): 841; 8. Skolnik, 1994; 9. "Kids are Getting Hooked," *U.S. News and World Report* 117 (no. 12) (September 26,1994): 24.

We have surveyed seven organizational patterns you can use in your public speeches. The one you select for your own speech should be determined largely by the topic you select, the purpose of your speech, how much the audience knows about the topic, and which arguments or evidence the audience will perceive as strongest or best.

Do not conclude from this discussion that these are the only ways to organize a speech. Storytelling, for example, has been shown to be effective in criminal trials by lawyers who need to convince jurors to make sophisticated judgments about complex information (Bennet 1978). In another case, a student delivered a highly effective speech by telling a series of five stories about himself, interspersed with a refrain that was his main point. His organization was effective, but the speech defied the principles of outlining. The number of ways in which you can organize your speech is limited only by your imagination.

Incorporate Supporting Materials

As we stated, the main points create the skeleton of the body of the speech. The speaker must flesh out this skeleton with subpoints and sub-subpoints. These subordinate materials include examples, illustrations, proof, and other supporting materials.

In this section we draw your attention to the idea that speakers do not stop the organizing process once they have identified their main headings. Let us take, for an example, the speech on the Native Americans of the Eastern Woodlands. This informative speech was very straightforward. The speaker supported the main points by including the following subpoints, as well as some presentational aids that are not shown here (Planisek 1993).

I. The Native Americans inhabited an area of North America known as the Eastern Woodlands.

   A. The geographic region where these Native Americans lived can be seen on a map of the United States.

   B. The principal tribes inhabiting the area are listed on my poster.

II. Eastern Woodland Native Americans lived in wigwams and longhouses.

   A. Tribes or bands that preferred individual or family living quarters chose the wigwam.

   B. Tribes or bands that preferred a more communal arrangement chose the longhouse.

III. The Eastern Woodland Native Americans were distinctive in appearance because of their attire and ornaments.

   A. The accompanying pictures of males show them in everyday and battle dress.

   B. The accompanying pictures of females show them in informal and ceremonial attire.

Developing the supporting materials may not be quite so straightforward. Persuasive speeches are often more complicated than are brief informative speeches like the one just outlined.

You may be an expert researcher who is able to find far more information on your topic than you can possibly use in your speech. Which information do you use and which do you discard? Two authors state that in an ideal situation, the speaker chooses "the most important facts and figures," "the most authoritative judgments about a situation, made by sources the audience will respect," and "at least one interesting story or example that helps humanize and clarify the situation" (Osborn and Osborn 2003).

For the speech on second-hand smoke, the speaker found facts and figures that showed the harm caused by second-hand smoke. He could have found facts and figures on the harm caused by first-hand smoke, but that would have been less relevant to his thesis. He cited the authors of books and magazine articles who were experts on second-hand smoke. He also began and ended his speech with circumstances with which his audience was familiar—walking to classroom buildings, eating at restaurants, and going to bars. He personalized it further by observing that everyone in his audience was a second-hand smoker. This speaker probably received high marks for highly appropriate supporting materials.

Before we conclude this section, we need to look at the ways that speakers manage to hold their speeches together. If you identify and organize two to five main points and appropriate supporting materials, your job is still not completed. You also need to devise methods of moving from one point to another, of telling the audience where you are in the overall speech, where you are going next, and where you have been. This "glue" is critical in a speech because audience members cannot "reread" a speech as they can reread an essay if they get lost in the organization.

Celebrating Diversity

The outlining strategies we describe here are linear. Our culture encourages us to engage in linear organization. People in this culture tend to see items in a progression. We understand beginnings and endings. Other cultures are not linear and these methods of outlining and organizing may literally seem "foreign" to them.

Configural cultures are not linear and people within them tend to see how the array of the parts creates a whole. They are thus more interested in patterns rather than in the sequential development of ideas. People in these cultures are less rigid about time. They tend to think in images. They value relationships between and among people and things as more important than the individual people or items.

Consider the Connections

Transitions, signposts, internal previews, and internal reviews are the mortar between the bricks. Together they allow the audience easy access to the information you are presenting. Audience members appreciate being informed that you are finished with one point and moving on to another. They show high regard for the speaker who lets them know where he or she is within the organization of the speech. They value previews, which tell them what lies ahead, as well as reviews, which tell them what they have just heard. Let us consider each of these four devices.

Transitions

Transitions are statements throughout the speech that relate back to what has already been said and forward to what will be said. For instance, a transition might sound like this:

> Now that you have seen the consequences of smoking, consider some methods of kicking that habit.

This particular transition points back to the consequences of smoking already covered and forward to methods of kicking the smoking habit.

Transitions also move the speech and the speaker toward, then away from, visual aids.

> We know that cancer is a vicious consequence of smoking; just how vicious cancer is can be seen on this graph, which indicates how likely you are to contract the disease if you smoke.

After explaining the figures on the visual aid, another transition moves you back into the speech:

The graphs are grim evidence of how smoking is correlated with cancer, but cancer is not the only terrible consequence: pulmonary emphysema affects smokers more than any other group.

As with all transitions, the statement reflects back to what was said and forward to what will be said. Such transitional statements appear throughout the speech as you move from main point to main point and into and out of support material.

Signposts

Signposts, like road signs on a highway, reveal where the speaker is going. Signposts are often briefer than transitions because they do not have to point backward and forward; they have only to tell the listener where the speaker is in the speech. Some examples include the following:

My first point is that . . .

Another reason you should . . .

One of the best examples is . . .

To illustrate this point, I will . . .

Let us look at this picture . . .

A second, and even more convincing, argument is . . .

One last illustration will show . . .

Signposts are the guides that help the audience follow your movement through the speech. Skillful use of signposts and transitions will clarify your organization and help you become a confident speaker.

Internal Previews

Internal previews inform listeners of your next point or points, and are more detailed than transitions. They are similar to the statements a speaker makes in the introduction of his or her speech, but they occur within the body of the speech. Examples of internal previews include the following:

I will tell you next about how you can prevent skin cancer in four different ways.

My next point is that depression can be prevented, and I will tell you how you can prevent this condition in your own life.

Share an image with me as we explore the beauty of the Canadian Rockies next.

The speaker who discussed the Eastern Woodland Native Americans might say, "I would like to tell you next about the types of homes that were built and inhabited by people living in the Eastern Woodlands. As you will determine, two distinctive types of homes predominated." She would be introducing her second main point and suggesting how she was going to subdivide that point.

Suppose the speaker said, "We have just discussed the geography of the Eastern Woodlands, and we will now turn our attention to the types of homes that predominated in the Eastern Woodlands." In this instance, she would be offering a transition. If she added to this transition, "As you will determine, two distinctive types of homes predominated," she would be providing both a transition and an internal preview.

Internal Reviews

Internal reviews remind listeners of your last point or points and are more detailed than transitions. They are similar to what a speaker does in the conclusion of his or her speech, but they occur within the body of the speech. Examples of internal reviews include the following:

> I have just told you about three reasons you should not drink and drive.

> My four main points concerning suicide among children were . . .

> Let me remind you of what I just told you . . .

We have considered the importance of speech organization and discussed the three steps that are involved in organizing the body of a speech. We also discussed some suggestions for identifying the main points of a speech, and offered seven patterns you can use to arrange your main points. Finally, we discussed ways that the speaker can connect main points. We turn now to the second major topic of this chapter: outlining the speech.

Principles of Outlining

The organization of a speech is generally shown in an outline form. Outlining is relatively easy to learn. There are three principles that govern the writing of an outline—subordination, division, and parallelism. The following sections are devoted to helping you understand these three principles so you can learn how to compose an outline.

Subordination

If you follow the **principle of subordination,** your outline will indicate which material is more important and which is less important. More important materials usually consist of generalizations, arguments, or conclusions. Less important materials consist of the supporting evidence for your generalizations, arguments, or conclusions. In the outline, Roman numerals indicate the main points, capital letters indicate the subpoints under the Roman numeral statements, and Arabic numbers indicate sub-subpoints under the subpoints. Figure 7.9 shows a typical outline format. Notice, too, that the less important the material, the greater the indentation from the left-hand margin.

The principle of subordination is based not only on the symbols (numbers and letters) and indentations, but also on the content of the statements. The subpoints are subordinate to the main points, the sub-subpoints are subordinate to the subpoints, and so on. Therefore, you need to evaluate the content of each statement to determine if it is broader or narrower, more important or less important, than the statements above and below it. The student outline in Figure 7.10 illustrates how the content of the statements indicates levels of importance.

❖ ❖ ❖ ❖

Figure 7.9
Symbols and Margins Indicating Subordination

I. Generalization, conclusion, or argument is a main point.

   A. The first subpoint consists of illustration, evidence, or other supporting material.

   B. The second subpoint consists of similar supporting material for the main point.

      1. The first sub-subpoint provides additional support for the subpoint stated in "B."

      2. The second sub-subpoint also supports subpoint "B."

II. The second generalization, conclusion, or argument is another main point in the speech.

Division

The second principle of outlining is the **principle of division,** which states that if a point is to be divided, it must have at least two subpoints. For example, the outline illustrated in Figure 7.10 contains two main points (I, II), two subpoints (A, B) under main point I, and three sub-subpoints (1, 2, 3) under subpoint A. All items are either undivided (II) or divided into two or more parts. The principle of division can, however, be applied too rigidly: sometimes a main point will be followed by a single example, a solo clarification, or an amplification. Such cases can be regarded as exceptions to the general rule: points, if divided, must be separated into two or more items of approximately equal importance.

Figure 7.10
Content Should Show Division Into Two or More Categories

I. Jumping rope is a cardiovascular (CV) activity.

   A. A cardiovascular activity is defined by three main requirements.

      1. Large muscles must be used in rhythmic, continuous motions.

      2. The heart beat per minute must be elevated to an intensity that is approximately 85 percent of a person's maximum rate.

      3. The elevated heart rate must be maintained for twenty to thirty minutes to achieve a CV "training effect."

   B. Other CV activities include running, swimming, and handball.

II. Jumping rope requires simple, inexpensive equipment.

Parallelism

The third principle of outlining is the **principle of parallelism,** which states that main points, subpoints, and sub-subpoints must use the same grammatical and syntactical forms. That means that in a sentence outline you would use all sentences, not a mixture of sentences, dependent clauses, and phrases and that the sentences would tend to appear the same in structure, with subject followed by verb followed by object, for instance. Figure 7.11 illustrates a sentence outline using parallel form (Grable 1991).

An outline can use parallel construction without consisting entirely of sentences. For example, a key word outline on note cards might consist of single words used to remind you of the content as you deliver your speech.

To review the information on the principles of outlining, you should examine Figure 7.12, which briefly explains each of the three principles.

Figure 7.11
Form and Content Unite Through Subordination, Division, and Parallelism

An Informative Speech on Automobile Tires

Specific purpose: My audience will be able to decode the information printed on their tires.

Understanding Your Tire Symbols

I. "Original equipment" tires tend to be generally good for ride, endurance, traction, and noise, but they are not outstanding in any of these features.

II. Upgrading your tires requires that you understand the new system of symbols printed on tires: 205/60R13 85H, for example.

  A. The 205 stands for "section width," or 205 millimeters wide.

  B. The 60R is 60 percent aspect ratio with radial construction.

    1. A "low aspect" tire has a smaller diameter.

    2. A radial tire rides soft and looks underinflated.

  C. The 13 means that the tire fits on a 13-inch diameter wheel, which is what you had better have on your car if you expect to use this tire.

  D. The 85 is "load index," which means the tire can handle 1135 pounds.

  E. H is a speed rating that means the tire can handle a speed of up to 130 miles per hour.

III. Before you upgrade your original equipment, you should decide if you want to have a wider tread, to increase the aspect, to buy larger or smaller wheels, to increase or decrease the amount of weight the tire can carry, or to buy a tire that can handle more speed.

Types of Outlines

In the preparation and delivery of a speech, you will generally make three different kinds of outlines. First, you will create a preparation, or working, outline. Next, you will probably be required to provide your instructor with a formal outline. Finally, you may want to create a key word outline on notecards, which you can use when you actually deliver your speech. Although these three outlines are related, their functions and formats are different.

Figure 7.12
Outlining Principles of Subordination, Division, and Parallelism

I._____.	Every "I" must have a "II."	Each entry must be a
A._____.	Every "A" must have	complete sentence, a
B._____.	at least a "B."	phrase, or a single
1._____.	Every "1" must have	word; entries may not
2._____.	at least a "2."	be a mixture of
a._____.	Every "a" must have	sentences, phrases,
b._____.	at least a "b."	and words.
i._____.	Every "i" must have	
ii._____.	at least an "ii."	
II._____.		

The Preparation Outline

After you have selected the topic for your speech and have gathered information for it, you will begin to sketch out the basic ideas you wish to convey to your audience. The **preparation outline** is your initial or tentative conception of your speech. It is your original plan showing what you intend to say in the speech.

For example, imagine that you want to speak on Native American religious beliefs and their implications in current American issues. You might start out by identifying some of the Native American religious beliefs and some of the current issues that involve those beliefs. Your preparation outline might look something like this (Planisek 1993):

Native American religious beliefs

Belief in a Supreme Being

Belief in guardian spirits

Belief in afterlife

Belief that the earth and nature are sacred

Current issues that infringe upon Native American religious beliefs

Use of peyote

Destruction of shrines

Destruction of burial sites

As you conduct more research, you might add to this working outline, or you may delete subpoints for which you can find no proof or examples. You may also rearrange it or add additional main points. Since this is a preparation, or working, outline, it is always in process. After you have spent some time researching your topic and trying a variety of ways to organize your information, you will create a formal outline.

❖ ❖ ❖ ❖   **The Formal Outline**

A **formal outline** is a final outline in complete sentence form. The formal outline includes the following elements:

1. The title

2. The specific purpose

3. The thesis statement

4. The introduction of the speech, which may be outlined or written out in full

5. The body of the speech in outline form

6. The conclusion of the speech, which may be outlined or written out in full

7. A bibliography of sources or references consulted

An example of a formal outline from a student speech about Native American religious freedom rights can be found in Figure 7.13 (Planisek 1993).

Now that you have seen an example of a formal outline, let us consider briefly each of its seven parts.

Title. The title of the speech may be optional within the classroom setting, but a title is necessary if you are going to speak in most other situations. In formal speaking situations, another person will introduce you. Usually he or she will tell the audience about your credentials and will conclude by stating the title of your speech.

A speech title should be relatively short. The title may contain a clever play on words, alliteration, or other stylistic features. The name of your speech may also be a simple set of words that describe your speech. For example, one student gave a speech on pet care with the title "Dog Care." Other examples of titles from student speeches follow Figure 7.13.

Figure 7.13
An Example of a Formal Outline With
Scripted Introduction and Conclusion

Title: The Religious Freedom Rights of Native Americans

Specific purpose: To inform my audience of the beliefs of the religions of the Native Americans and how those beliefs have been violated in current American decisions.

Thesis statement: Native Americans have specific religious beliefs that have been violated in several recent decisions.

Introduction

I will begin with a short passage from the First Amendment of the U.S. Constitution: "Congress shall make no law respecting an establishment of religion, or prohibiting the free exercise thereof . . ."

Our forefathers, many of them, originally came to America in search of religious freedom. Yet still today, the first inhabitants of this land, the Native Americans, are fighting for this religious freedom that most of us take for granted. States Oliver Thomas, an attorney at Georgetown University, "The Native Americans... are unique because they predate the Constitution. There's something troubling about our government's coming in and telling Native Americans who have carried on for centuries with their faiths that you can't do this or you can't do that." If the government suppresses religious freedom, what other rights that affect us and that we hold dear might the government endanger? Just how secure are our religious beliefs and practices from governmental tyranny? It is a question few of us have considered and few can answer, including myself. I have long been interested in Native American culture and I have done research into their lives and beliefs. Thus, today I would first like to speak to you on various Native American beliefs and then to discuss current religious issues surrounding Native practices. By doing so, I hope to increase your awareness of the problems that Native Americans have in securing the same religious rights we so ignorantly enjoy.

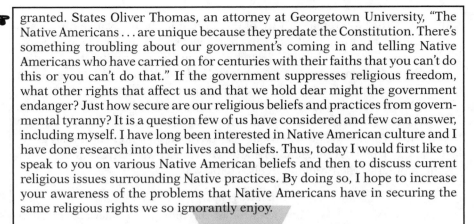

Transition

Body

I. There are many rich beliefs in the religion of the Native Americans.

   A. Most Native American tribes believed in a Supreme Being.

   B. Many native tribes believed guardian spirits manifested themselves in animals.

   C. All tribes believed in an afterlife.

   D. All tribes believed the earth and nature were sacred.

   E. Native American beliefs are not entirely different than those of the other religions of the world.

Transition

II. Many current issues involve Native American religious practices.

   A. Peyote use by Native Americans has come under fire.

      1. I will define the word peyote.

      2. I will define a typical peyote service and its goals.

      3. The 1965 Drug Control Act hampers the legal use of peyote.

   B. Also threatened is the Native American belief that holds the land as sacred.

      1. The Forest Service wants to build a ski lift through an Indian shrine.

      2. A burial site may be leveled so motorists can see a Wal-Mart.

      3. The Supreme Court's ruling in 1988 threatens Native American sacred sites.

      4. Walter Echohawk urges support of Native American religious rights.

Conclusion

Today, we have briefly looked at various Native American beliefs and current issues involving their religious practices. We all must realize that we take our religious freedom for granted while others are still fighting for their rights.

All I ask is that you remain aware of the difficulties facing Native Americans today in their battle for religious freedom. Please continue to educate yourselves; read books; and attend lectures here at the university about Native Americans. November is Native American Heritage Month, and I suggest you visit Follette's Bookstore, which has dedicated an entire window and book section to Native Americans in honor of the month. I would like to close on a note from Native American Pat Lefthand: "We are in a battle for survival of our very way of life. We've had 500 years of attacks on our way of life. The land is gone. All we have left is our religion." I believe we at least owe Native Americans the right to practice their religion freely. Thank you.

Bibliography

Axtel, J. (1987). Colonial America without the Indians: Counterfactual reflections. *Journal of American History, 73,* 995.

Eckert, A. (1992). *A sorrow in our heart: The life of Tecumseh.* New York: Bantam Books.

Hagen, W. (1985, Winter). Full blood, mixed blood, generic and ersatz: The problem of Indian identity. *Arizona and the West, 27,* 310.

Meier, P. (1986). *The American people: A history.* Lexington, MA: D. C. Heath and Company.

Native Americans battle to save sacred lands. (1993, July 11). *The Columbus Dispatch,* p. 5F.

Nichols, R. (1988). Indians in the post-termination era. *Storia Northamericana, 5,* 74–77.

Oswalt, W. (1988). *This land was theirs: A study of North American Indians.* Mountain View, CA: Mayfield Publishing Company.

Svingen, O. (1987, Fall). Jim Crow, Indian style. *American Indian Quarterly, 11,* 277.

Welager, C. A. (1972). *The Delaware Indians: A History.* New Brunswick, NJ: Rutgers University Press.

Sample titles:

- The Benefits of Compact Discs
- Remembering the Holocaust
- Preventing Child Abuse
- How to Meet Someone New
- Save for Retirement
- Reducing your Taxes

Titles do not have to be clever, but they must be an accurate portrayal of the speech. If they go beyond the scope of the talk, the audience will be disappointed. If they are misleading, people may be frustrated with the speech. If you spend more time working on a provocative and interesting title than you do on creating an engaging speech, your audience's high expectations will not be realized.

Specific purpose. The general purpose of a speech simply states whether your intention is to inform, to persuade, or to entertain. The specific purpose is more precise because it also includes the audience. For example, a specific purpose might be "To inform my audience of methods to stop smoking." A **specific purpose** thus includes your general purpose, your intended audience, and your precise goal. Some additional examples of specific purpose statements follow.

> My audience will be able to explain the religious importance of the Jewish celebration of Passover.

> My audience will be able to identify common herbs that can be used to remedy minor medical problems.

> My audience will be able to recite the different "benefits" offered to employees who work by the hour, month, and year.

> My audience will be able to state three arguments that show why more women should major in chemistry.

Thesis statement. The **thesis statement** is a one-sentence summary of the speech. The thesis statement is similar to the topic statement or central idea of a written composition. It is a complete sentence that tells exactly what your speech is about. Some examples of thesis statements follow.

> Compact discs are superior to other audio recordings in at least three major ways.

> The United States Holocaust Memorial Museum is a dramatic tribute to the testimony "Never forget, never again."

> Tobacco should be declared an addictive drug like cocaine because of the health problems it creates for this country.

Introduction. The introduction of a speech should comprise about 15 percent of the total speech time. It should fulfill four functions: gaining and maintaining attention, relating the topic to the audience, relating the speaker to the topic, and previewing the message by stating the purpose and forecasting the organization of the speech. Many speakers write out their introductions and virtually memorize them so they feel secure in how they will begin their talk. Others outline their introductions and deliver them extemporaneously. You will learn much more about introductions later in this text.

Body. The body of the speech comprises the bulk of the speech. This main portion generally consists of about 75 to 80 percent of the entire talk. The body should be outlined using the principles of subordination, division, and parallelism discussed in this chapter.

Conclusion. The conclusion is even shorter than the introduction. If the introduction to the speech is about 15 percent of the entire speech, then the conclusion should be about 5 percent of the speech, and certainly no longer than 10 percent. The functions of the conclusion include forewarning the audience of the end of the speech, reminding your audience of the main points, and specifying what the audience should do as a result of the speech. Conclusions also will be discussed in detail later in this text.

Bibliography or References. The formal outline includes a list of the sources consulted and the sources actually used in the speech. Your instructor will tell you whether you should include all of your sources or only those you actually cite in your speech. In any case, you will want to provide them in correct bibliographic form.

The communication discipline uses a style popularized by the American Psychological Association, called "APA style." For that style and others you can consult Bourhis, Adams, Titsworth, and Harter's *Style Manual for Communication Studies*, (2002).

Three basic bibliographic formats are the entries for a book, a periodical, and a newspaper article. We provide examples of these three for APA style.

APA Style

Book:
Deutschman, A. (2000). *The second coming of Steve Jobs*. New York: Broadway Books.

Magazine:
Perez, S. (2004, March). State of the onion. *Gourmet*, pp. 76–85.

Newspaper Article:
Froslie, E. H. (2004, February 26). Church leaders cry, speechless. *The Forum of Fargo-Moorhead*, p. 1.

The Key Word Outline

Finally, you will want to make a key word outline on note cards. The **key word outline** is a brief outline that you can use during the delivery of your speech. The outline may include words that will prompt your memory, sources that you are citing within the speech, or even the complete quotations of material you are repeating. The key word outline may look very messy or unclear to someone other than the speaker. See Figure 7.14 for an example of a key word outline.

Figure 7.14
An Example of a Key Word Outline

Working Off Fat

Introduction

Do you have a body by Jake, a slinky torso by Susan, or a video-shaped profile by Jane? Well, I don't. I know it. And I show it. But I'm doing something about it, and so should you. Here is what I learned about weight control through exercise—and 25 years of trying.

Transition

Body

I. Why exercise?
   A. Beauty
   B. Everyday health
   C. Long life
II. How to exercise
   A. Motivation
   B. Routine
   C. Invest in self

III. How to keep going
   A. Self-rewards
   B. Good habits
   C. Fun

Conclusion

Don't buy expensive equipment and don't hurt yourself trying. Instead, do as I told you: improve your looks, your heart, and your lungs by investing in yourself. Get in the good health habit by exercising often. And don't forget to reward yourself—with something other than fattening food.

Summary

This chapter on speech organization and outlining began with a discussion of the importance of speech organization. Speakers who present organized speeches are perceived as more competent than are speakers who present less organized speeches. Further, their messages are more memorable. In general, audiences give higher marks to well-organized speakers.

When you organize the body of a speech, you should first divide the body into main points. You should probably have between two and five main points. These main points should be worded in a parallel manner and should be approximately equal in importance.

After you have identified the main points for your speech, you need to determine the order in which you will present them. Some typical ways to order or pattern your speech include the time-sequence, spatial relations, problem-solution, cause-effect, climactic, anticlimactic, topical sequence patterns, and Monroe's Motivated Sequence. Finally, you need to incorporate the supporting material into your organizational plan.

The effective and ethical public speaker also considers the connections between ideas. Among the connecting devices available are transitions, which are brief linkages in the speech; signposts, which tell the audience briefly where the speaker is within the speech; internal previews, which forewarn the audience of that which is to come; and internal reviews, which remind the audience of what has already been covered.

Next we turned to outlining the speech. Outlining includes three important principles. The principle of subordination means that the symbols and indentation of your outline should show which material is more important and which material is less important. The principle of division states that when points are divided, they must have at least two subpoints. The principle of parallelism states that main points, subpoints, and sub-subpoints should use the same grammatical and syntactical forms.

During the speech preparation process, you will probably create three types of outlines. The preparation outline is your initial or tentative conception of your speech. A formal outline is a final outline in complete sentence form. It includes the title, specific purpose, thesis statement, introduction of the speech, body of the speech, conclusion of the speech, and a bibliography of sources consulted. The key word outline is a brief outline—often on notecards—created for you to use during the delivery of your speech.

Communication Narrative 7.1
Get Organized!

Peter Carpenter had a messy room, a cluttered car, wrinkled clothes, a dump-like work area, and a mind that could best be described as "an unorganized figure." He often missed appointments because he did not write them down, frequently missed classes because he forgot what day it was, and twice he had forgotten Betsey's birthday even though she was the woman he had been dating for three years. No wonder Peter was worried about his public speaking course. He had just over one week to prepare a five-minute speech. He was not worried about stage fright; he was worried about how he would ever get organized enough to produce a five-minute speech.

Betsey saved him—again! She sat down with Peter one night over a burger and made him focus on what he knew. Admittedly, Peter did not know a lot about anything, but he did know a little about a lot. Betsey seemed to know better than he did that cars were something Peter knew about—at least more than most people. Not only did Peter work at a service station, but his uncle owned a local Toyota dealership, and his own dad had once sold auto parts. Peter showed more affection for his car than he did for Betsey. After all, the car was his constant companion, and even though the car was cluttered, the outside was always clean.

Next, Betsey got Peter on the Internet surfing for information about cars. Every time a list of information appeared, Betsey had Peter say what interested him the most on the list. Before ten minutes was up, Peter had agreed that "used car sales" was going to be his topic, and his speech would be an informative speech about "how to buy a used car without getting cheated."

He would use his own expertise to tell the class how to spot an auto that might be more worn than its odometer indicated, how to determine if the car had been in an accident, and how to discover if parts had been replaced with inferior products. He had a three-part organization, which would take about five minutes to explain. No wonder Peter called Betsey "his organizer." Without her, he never would have figured out how to find a topic and organize it for delivery.

Vocabulary

anticlimactic pattern   An organizational arrangement in which the strongest arguments and supporting materials are presented first and then descend in order of importance.

cause-effect pattern   An organizational arrangement in which part of the speech deals with the cause(s) of a problem or issue, and part of it deals with the effect(s) of the problem or issue.

climactic pattern   An organizational arrangement in which the arguments and supporting materials are presented in increasing order of importance, with the strongest arguments and evidence presented last.

formal outline   A final outline in complete sentence form which includes the title, specific purpose, thesis statement, introduction of the speech, body of the speech, conclusion of the speech, and a bibliography of sources consulted.

internal previews   Statements that inform listeners of your next point or points and are more detailed than transitions.

internal reviews Statements that remind listeners of your last point or points and are more detailed than transitions.

key word outline A brief outline created for you to use during the delivery of your speech.

Monroe's Motivated Sequence An organizational arrangement based on reflective thinking that includes five specific steps: attention, need, satisfaction, visualization, and action.

preparation outline The initial or tentative conception of a speech in rough outline form.

principle of division An outlining principle that states that every point divided into subordinate parts must be divided into two or more parts.

principle of parallelism An outlining principle that states that all points must be stated in the same grammatical form.

principle of subordination An outlining principle that states that importance is signaled by symbols and indentation.

problem-solution pattern An organizational arrangement in which part of the speech is concerned with the problem(s) and part with the solution(s) to problem(s).

signposts Direct indicators of the speaker's progress; usually an enumeration of the main points: "A second cause is . . ."

spatial relations pattern An organizational arrangement in which events or steps are presented according to how they are related in space.

specific purpose The purpose of your speech, which includes your general purpose, your intended audience, and your precise goal.

thesis statement A one-sentence summary of the speech that is similar to the topic statement or central idea of a written composition.

time-sequence pattern An organizational arrangement in which events or steps are presented in the order in which they occur.

topical sequence pattern An organizational arrangement in which the topic is divided into reasonable parts, such as advantages and disadvantages, or various qualities or types.

transitions The links in a speech that connect the introduction, body, and conclusion, as well as main points and subpoints; they provide previews and reviews, and lead into and away from visual aids.

Application Exercises

1. Think of a speech topic not mentioned in this chapter that would be best organized into each of the following patterns. Write the topic in the appropriate blank.

   Time-sequence

   Topic:

   Spatial relations

   Topic:

   Problem-solution

   Topic:

Cause-effect

Topic:

Climactic and anticlimactic

Topic:

Topical sequence

Topic:

Monroe's Motivated Sequence

Topic:

Can you explain why each pattern is most appropriate for each topic?

2. Go to the library and find the publication called *Vital Speeches of the Day,* which is a collection of current speeches. Make a copy of a speech and highlight the transitions, signposts, internal previews, and internal reviews.

References

Bennet, W. L. (1978). Storytelling in criminal trials: A model of social judgment. *Quarterly Journal of Speech,* 64, 1–22.

Bourhis, J., Adams, C., Titsworth, S., and Harter, L. (2002). *Style Manual for Communication Studies.* New York: McGraw-Hill.

Ebest, S. B., Brusaw, C. T., Alred, G. J., and Oliu, W. E. (2000). *Writing from A to Z: The Easy-To-Use Reference Handbook* (3rd ed.). Mountain View, CA: Mayfield Publishing Co.

Fritz, P. A., and Weaver, R. L., II. (1986). Teaching critical thinking skills in the basic speaking course: A liberal arts perspective. *Communication Education,* 35, 177.

Grable, R. (1991, July). The do's and don'ts of upgrading tires. *Motor Trend,* 112–115.

Greene, J. O. (1984). Speech preparation processes and verbal fluency. *Human Communication Research,* 11, 61–84.

Gronbeck, B. E. (Ed.), German, K. (contributor), Ehninger, D., and Monroe, A. (1997). *Principles of Speech Communication.* New York: Addison-Wesley Publishing Co.

Osborn, M., and Osborn, S. (2003). *Public Speaking* (6th ed.). Boston: Houghton Mifflin Co.

Planisek, R. (1993). An unpublished speech delivered in Interpersonal Communication 103, Public Speaking, Ohio University, Fall Quarter, in a section taught by Marsha Clowers. Printed with the student's permission.

Price, J. (1999). *Outlining Goes Electronic.* Westport, CT: Ablex Publishing Corp.

Publication Manual of the American Psychological Association (4th ed.). (1996). Washington, D.C.: American Psychological Association.

Reindel, J. R. (1994). An unpublished speech delivered in Interpersonal Communication 103, Public Speaking, Ohio University, Fall Quarter, in a section taught by Kim Varey. Reprinted with the student's permission.

Sharp, H., Jr., and McClung, T. (1966). Effect of organization on the speaker's ethos. *Speech Monographs,* 33, 182–183.

Thompson, E. C. (1960). An experimental investigation of the relative effectiveness of organizational structure in oral communication. *Southern Speech Journal,* 26, 59–69.

Chapter 8

The Ethical and Effective Use of Evidence, Proof, and Argument

The most savage controversies are those about matters as to which there is no good evidence either way.

—Bertrand Russell

Question Outline

I. Can you use four kinds of evidence effectively and ethically in persuasive speeches?

II. Can you decide which of the four kinds of proof to use in persuasive speeches?

III. What are the components of an argument?

IV. What are three types of claims?

V. How can you construct an effective argument?

VI. How should the ethical and effective persuader use four kinds of argument?

VII. What are some common fallacies or faulty arguments?

Svetlana Matveev worked for the Russian International Trade Association as an attorney, a negotiator, and a translator. Her job was to increase the amount of international trade between the United States and Russia. Today, her mission was to meet with C. Hershel Hamfrey, the person in charge of international trade for Targill Inc., one of the world's largest agribusiness corporations. She would be expected to prove to this top executive and his team that her country would be a worthy partner in a multibillion dollar agreement. She did not know what would convince this tough audience.

She had plenty of information, was very intelligent, and was fully prepared. She did not know what these listeners would accept as proof that her country was financially ready to pay for their food products, what these listeners would accept as proof that her government's leadership was stable for a long-term agreement, and what arguments these listeners would accept as credible. Should she use facts and figures? How about stories of peasants and children badly in need of food? Should she use the words of the prime minister for assurance? She had to determine how to shape her information into an instrument of persuasion. She had to fashion her knowledge in a way that Targill executives would find the information convincing. Billions of dollars in agreements rode on her success or failure.

In this chapter you will learn how to use evidence, proof, and argument in an effective and ethical way. You will learn about a variety of forms of evidence, which will be defined and explained. You will learn how to apply the four kinds of proof—personal proof, emotional proof, logical proof, and mythic proof—to the persuasive speech. The chapter includes information on how to structure arguments, including the components of an argument, the types of claims, the types of argument, and common fallacies or faulty arguments. Finally, you will learn more about ethical issues that are essential to the speaker who wishes to alter the feelings, attitudes, or behaviors of others.

How Can Evidence Be Used Ethically and Effectively in the Persuasive Speech?

Evidence consists of supporting materials used in a persuasive speech. **Supporting materials** include information that "backs up" or reinforces your arguments. They include—but are not limited to—statistics, facts, opinions, examples, illustrations, tests (e.g., DNA or blood tests), objects (e.g., a weapon with fingerprints), and analogies. When supporting materials are used to argue for a position, they become evidence.

Evidence may be viewed as the building blocks or basic elements of the persuasive process. If the evidence you use is viewed as irrelevant or insufficient, then your entire persuasive effort can fail. For example, imagine that you are going to give a persuasive speech forewarning your classmates about the dangers of Hepatitis C. Here is a brief speech by Emily Pawlosky (1999) which you should examine for its use of evidence.

A Silent Killer

"You are going to die. I am going to die. We all are going to die." This quote from my favorite movie, *What About Bob,* may sound exaggerated, but the statement is true. What we do not know is how we are going to die. The world today provides many ways to die, but the silent killer I am going to discuss in the next few minutes can be prevented.

Each year more and more men and women like us become infected with a virus as deadly as AIDS. Called Hepatitis C, this virus can be transmitted in ways as varied as sex or sharing a toothbrush. You need to listen carefully because this speech can save your life.

You may be curious how I am qualified to speak on this topic. Well, I was reading *Cosmopolitan* recently when I saw an article about Hepatitis C. After reading the article, I realized the dangers of this disease and how our everyday activities can spread the disease. The topic seemed ideal for this audience. While I have no experience with Hepatitis C, I have thoroughly researched the topic and I am prepared to tell you what this silent killer is, how you can become infected, and ways you can prevent infection.

According to Julia Califano's article in *Cosmopolitan*, hepatitis is a disease that affects the liver. Without treatment, the liver deteriorates until the organ functions no longer. Eventually the malfunctioning liver poisons the affected person's body. In 1989, scientists discovered a new strain of hepatitis. The danger of this new strain, the C-strain, is that people can carry the infection for 10-20 years without symptoms. Experts believe that as many as 70 percent of women and men in their 20s and 30s carry the virus but have no clue they are infected and are possibly spreading the disease to others. If true, this statistic means that approximately 19 of the 27 people in this room could be infected.

Califano adds that people contract Hepatitis C in various ways, but most people are infected by the disease through blood to blood contact. Perhaps you think you are safe because you have not had blood to blood contact with your best friends? Well, you are wrong. The killer can live in a drop of blood for days, meaning that you can be infected by someone else's razor or tweezers. Still think you are safe? Well, you can become infected with Hepatitis C when you are pierced or tattooed. Even a person who uses a condom every time, washes his hands constantly, and never shares personal items can become infected. What is even scarier? This deadly disease has no cure. Hepatitis C is not just a disease of drug users; this disease affects "It cannot happen to me" people.

Because you can get this disease, I will tell you how NOT to become infected, according to the Hepatitis Information Network. First, don't share needles. While you might laugh and tell me you are not an addict, I would point out that needles are used both for piercing and for tattooing. If you are doing anything with needles, you need to check out the reputation of the parlor, ask about their sterilization methods, and make sure that the needles used on you have been thoroughly sterilized. Second, avoid using anyone else's personal items: toothbrushes, razors, and tweezers. Even someone you trust—your boyfriend or spouse—can be a carrier. Third, Hepatitis C can be contracted through sexual intercourse—unless you use protection. As you have been told time and time again: "use protection."

Now that you know the dangers, I would like to remind you that Hepatitis C is not just a disease of drug users. The disease can affect you and me. Personal hygiene and common sense are good preventative measures. "You are going to die. I am going to die. We all are going to die." But, hey, at least we won't die from Hepatitis C!

Before reading further, you should decide what you think of the evidence, the sources, and the arguments in this speech. Then you should read the analysis by this text's authors in the following paragraph.

Emily is a journalism major with good writing skills. The example appears here because the speech was one of the best in a class of good students. However, the speech is not flawless. For example, to use *Cosmopolitan* magazine as a source on a health or medical issue is not the most credible source. A source like *The New England Journal of Medicine* or *Lancet* would be much more credible. The claim that "as many as 70 percent of women and men in their 20s and 30s carry the virus" appears exaggerated. Such a claim needs to be based on something before a speaker tells an audience that 19 of them could be infected. Some cautions such as sharing your toothbrush seem farfetched. Another flaw is that only two sources appear in the speech, *Cosmopolitan* and a website on hepatitis. The latter—a website—can be anything from highly unreliable to highly reliable. We would need to know more about the source. To clarify how evidence is used both ethically and effectively, we will consider each of the four forms of supporting material: facts and figures, examples, narratives, and testimony.

Facts and Figures

Facts and figures are statements or numbers about which people agree because they are verifiable. In the informative speech, facts and figures are used to illustrate and clarify the points you wish to make. In the persuasive speech, they provide a foundation from which you argue your case. Speakers usually provide facts and figures early in a persuasive speech, and they frequently serve to forewarn the listeners about the speaker's position on an issue.

An example of facts and figures that could be used early in a speech encouraging men to participate to a greater extent in household chores follows.

> Surveys indicate that women do most of the household chores, although more women are working outside the home.
>
> Nearly three times as many women as men do most of the household cleaning, according to surveys.
>
> At the same time, more women are working outside the home; the number of full-time working women has increased by 1 million each year since 1960.
>
> In Ohio, 82 percent of women surveyed did most of the cleaning and the housekeeping, according to an October survey commissioned by Merry Maids Inc., a cleaning service. Twenty-six percent of the men in the survey said household chores were their primary responsibility.
>
> In addition to the 30 to 40 hours a week spent working outside the home, women spent 40 to 44 hours a week on housework, said a study done in July at the University of Missouri. Their husbands or male partners spent about 13 hours a week on household chores, the survey said. ("Surveys . . . Chores," 1994)

Facts and figures are verifiable statements or numbers from reliable sources that can be used to support your arguments in a persuasive speech.

Examples

An **example** is a specimen, an instance that represents a larger group. Nancy L. McGrath provided an example in the information about women doing more household chores than men. McGrath wrote, "Yes, I do all the housework at home—from the bathrooms to laundry to kitchen and every-

---

On the Web

Find a speech on the web which has a persuasive purpose. For example, you might select Jimmy Carter's speech on human rights and foreign policy (*http://usinfo.state.gov/usa/infousa/facts/democrac/55.htm*) or you might select George W. Bush's speech on September 11, 2001 (*http://www.whitehouse.gov/news/releases/2001/09/20010911-16.html*). Identify the facts and the figures that are included in the speech. Conduct research to determine if you can prove, or verify, these facts and figures. What can you conclude?

---

thing in between. Granted, my husband does clean the gutters, mow the lawn, and maintain the cars, but these are seasonal; my job is every day." ("Surveys . . . Chores," 1994). Examples come in a variety of forms. A brief example, like the one above, is a mere sentence or two. **Extended examples** are longer, generally three sentences or more. Examples may also be categorized as actual examples or hypothetical examples. **Actual examples** are based on reality, like the two examples above. **Hypothetical examples,** by contrast, are plausible, but they are created by the speaker to make a point. An ethical persuader reveals to the audience which examples are reality-based and which are hypothetical.

Narratives

Narratives are stories told to illustrate a point. In the informative speech, narratives serve to illustrate or to make obvious the major point or subpoints the speaker is providing. In the persuasive speech, narratives serve a variety of functions. They encourage a positive relationship between the speaker and the listeners, they make abstract ideas concrete, and they help to create memorable messages.

David Archambault (1992), former President of the American Indian College Fund, provides an example of a narrative in a speech to the Rotary Club in Murray, Utah. The speech was entitled, "Columbus Plus 500 Years: Whither the American Indian." Archambault reminded the audience of the Massacre of Wounded Knee.

Madeleine Albright's opinions of world events were based on her position as Secretary of State.

More than 100 years ago, our great Chief Sitting Bull was murdered. His people—frightened that they too would be killed—set out on foot across South Dakota along with Chief Big Foot. Carrying their children, they fled across the frozen prairie through the bitter sub-zero cold 200 miles to seek refuge on the Pine Ridge reservation in southwestern South Dakota.

On December 29, 1890, near a creek now known to all the world as Wounded Knee, Chief Big Foot and his followers were massacred. No one knows who fired first, but when the shooting was over, nearly 300 Indians—men, women, and children—lay dead and dying across the valley. Their bodies were dumped into a mass grave. The survivors were unable to hold a burial ceremony, a ceremony we call the wiping away of tears. It meant the living could never be free.

Archambault's description in this narrative gave non-Native Americans a glimpse of the pain felt in his culture over an event more than 100 years earlier. A narrative or story has the advantage of being more memorable and of conveying passions more convincingly than can facts and figures (p. 491).

Testimony

Testimony consists of opinions that support the speaker's claims. You can use your own opinions, but audiences are frequently more impressed with the words of an expert. Testimony can also be used in an informative speech, but its role is more crucial in the development of a persuasive speech.

An example of testimony was provided by Marc Maurer (1989), then President of the National Federation of the Blind, in the banquet speech he delivered in Denver, Colorado. Maurer was explaining to the audience that thought and speech are one. He said, "Thoughts cannot occur without being verbalized (either physically or in the mind), and words cannot be spoken or imagined without expressing thought. The words and the thoughts are the same." He then provided testimony from a wide range of characters. (pp. 16–22):

> The historian and essayist Thomas Carlyle once noted that language is not the garment of thought but the body of it. Modern anthropologists have advanced the Whorf-Sapir hypothesis, which declares that all of human culture is fabricated by language. The poet Percy Bysshe Shelley said that man was given speech, "and speech created thought." Samuel Taylor Coleridge observed that "language is the armory of the human mind, and at once contains the trophies of its past and the weapons of its future conquests." Socrates asserted that language is the guiding spirit of all human endeavors. "Such as thy words are," he said, "such will thine affections be; and such as thine affections will be thy deeds; and such as thy deeds will be thy life." If the language is modified, the thought is also altered. If the thought is shifted, the deed cannot remain the same. Therefore, to change a pattern of behavior, we must change the habit of speech (pp. 16–22).

Maurer's words about the power of language and the link between language and thought are testimonial evidence. Within his speech are more testimonials from Carlyle, modern anthropologists, Shelley, Coleridge, and Socrates. His speech illustrates the power of testimonial evidence.

Evaluating Evidence

If you have done your research properly, you will have an abundance of evidence to use in your speech. How will you decide which materials to use and which to discard? You will need to apply some criteria of effectiveness and ethical standards.

What are some of the characteristics of effective evidence? First, **effective evidence** *is always relevant to your argument*. You will find considerable evidence for most arguments, but the evidence will vary considerably in its relevance to your argument. For example, you might argue that grocers close to campus are taking advantage of students by charging higher prices. You chose the topic because the same grocery chain has a store in your hometown, and you believe that they overcharge there as well. Your opinion about the hometown grocery store is less relevant than more substantial proof, such as a comparison of prices in the city where your campus is located with prices of groceries in an off-campus area. Another more relevant piece of evidence would be a quotation, testimonial evidence, by the manager of the campus grocery, who admits that she charges more to make up for shoplifting, bad checks, and breakage. Always choose the evidence that is most relevant to your argument.

Second, *effective evidence is easily understood by the audience.* DNA tests, blood tests, and fingerprints may be evidence that lawyers can use in a jury trial where the lawyers have as much time as they need to educate the jurors, but in a one-shot public speech you will not have time to educate the audience about such complicated forms of evidence. Instead, choose evidence your audience will understand. An educated audience is likely to understand statistics if you put them in context and explain their importance. An audience of small children might be partial to stories that illustrate your point. All evidence may not be useful in your persuasive speech, but evidence that the audience can understand will be more persuasive.

Third, *effective evidence is striking or remarkable.* This quality will make your evidence more memorable. You might say, for instance, that "More Americans die by car than by warfare" and that "It is safer to fly on any commercial airline—including commuter flights—than it is to drive to the airport." Striking or remarkable facts capture audience attention and provide impressive support for your argument.

Fourth, *effective evidence is novel.* The speaker who uses ordinary or well-known evidence will be less persuasive. The speaker who uses evidence the audience has never heard before will be more effective. A student speaking on the National Rifle Association (NRA) made a novel point. He said that the NRA argues that everyone needs weapons for protection against potential enemies, an armed citizen militia. But, he added, a list of members of the NRA in enemy hands would provide the names and addresses of most gun owners in this country. Novel evidence attracts audience attention and supports the persuader's argument.

Fifth, *effective evidence makes your case without losing your audience.* In other words, you should present the evidence in enough detail to enhance clarity, but you should not make your evidence so extensive that the audience loses both interest and understanding. At a trial dependent on DNA, the defense lawyer's exhaustive efforts to get ordinary people to understand genetic markers and testing could result in a jury overcome by complex detail.

Sixth, *effective evidence is significant, and thus more persuasive.* Significance means importance. Your evidence can be relevant but insignificant. Discovering that a can of mushroom soup costs more at the campus grocery than at the grocery store elsewhere is relevant, but not significant. Finding that all soups, crackers, canned goods, bread products, meats, and produce cost more at the campus grocery is significant because the evidence is larger in importance.

Seventh, *effective evidence is highly credible.* "Who said it?" is an important question about testimonial opinions, because the audience might find their union president much more credible than the president of the company. "Who found the evidence?" may be an important question to ask about surveys, alleged facts, and other information gleaned from research. If the survey of customers' preferred clothing styles was done by a textile manufacturer, then it is less credible than if it was done by a more neutral party like a university or professional polling service. Finally, "What did they find?" can be an important question because the findings could be an aberration, an accidental blip in statistics. Findings that are inconsistent with other known evidence invite questions about accuracy. The credibility of your sources is always important when you consider evidence for a persuasive speech.

What are some of the characteristics of ethical evidence?

1. **Ethical evidence** (if it consists of facts and figures, actual examples, true narratives, or testimony) *is true.* If you are using hypothetical examples or narratives, you should clearly indicate that to your audience, probably both before and after you provide the evidence.

2. *Ethical evidence is recent.* If you are providing evidence from long ago, you should carefully qualify your evidence. Circumstances from another era or century may have less application for current events than do more recent findings.

3. *Ethical evidence is provable.* If your evidence is known only to you—and no interviewee, printed source, or video supports you—then your audience cannot assess accuracy or credibility. Your truthfulness could be called into question.

4. *Ethical evidence is understandable to an audience.* Explain statistics so the audience can put them in context and understand them. Always clarify your arguments and evidence, because your case is proven only if the audience understands your point.

5. *Ethical evidence provides complete information to the audience.* Do not omit evidence that casts doubt on your position. Instead, you should admit to contrary evidence but try to explain that evidence. If you give your audience statistics on how many people get killed with handguns each year and you are only using the states of North and South Dakota but fail to reveal that, you are behaving unethically.

6. *Do not overdramatize evidence for effect.* Ethical persuaders do not "inflame the passions." Do not treat the audience as pawns in a chess game. The student who faked a pulsating wound with animal blood in front of the class to emphasize the need for first aid training upset the students so much that the teacher gave the speech a failing grade.

Analyze this brief excerpt with the information you have gained by reading this chapter. What evidence does Pomeroy have? Does he present facts and figures? Can they be verified? What claims does he make? Has he constructed an effective argument?

Celebrating Diversity

Diversity is also evident in our politics. Belonging to a particular political party or purposefully not joining a party suggests difference. Representative

Earl Pomeroy wrote an editorial while he was running for his seventh term as a congressperson from North Dakota. In the editorial, he wrote:

> I flew home with a soldier the other day. It struck me how different our journeys were. I was on my way to Washington, D.C., while he was heading half a world away. "Back to Iraq," he said without complaint.

> . . . A few hours later, in the congressional office, I thought again about this soldier. I had just learned that the administration's budget for veteran's services would force cuts in the health care programs provided to those who have previously served our nation's military. . . .

> I've seen some very bad ideas during the years I have represented North Dakota, but cutting veterans services while sending our soldiers to Iraq is one of the worst. . . .

> By now, the soldier I traveled with is back on patrol in a dangerous sector of Baghdad. He represents the selfless service of all who have served our country in military service, and he will be in my thoughts as we fight in Washington to restore the cuts to veterans' services. Our country simply must keep its commitment to those who have sacrificed so much on our behalf (Pomeroy 2004).

Using Proof Ethically and Effectively

Proofs are the means by which speakers support their claims. Proofs were originally proposed in the Golden Age of Greece, which began in approximately 500 B.C. Although earlier rhetoricians had discussed proof, Aristotle was the first to systematically examine and discuss the nature of proof.

Aristotle (1931) distinguished some proofs as being **extrinsic proofs,** which support claims by referring to objective evidence such as confessions, contracts, and existing laws (p. 10). The residence hall director who says you are being removed from the hall for possessing illegal drugs in your room can use your dormitory contract and the university policies on illegal drugs as extrinsic proofs for her claim that you should be removed. The lawyer can say your confession of guilt is grounds for conviction. And the traffic cop can fine you by imposing the extrinsic proof of local law. An extrinsic proof, then, is something that lies outside the speech itself that can be used to prove the merit of a case. If the law says "55 mph" and you were going 65 mph, then an extrinsic proof (the moving violation laws) can be used to convict you.

Intrinsic proofs (Aristotle 1931, pp. 10–12) consist of the evidence in a communicative message that "authorizes, sanctions or justifies belief, attitude, or action" (Fisher 1978). Also called "artistic proof" or "modes of persuasion, these intrinsic proofs use the moral character of the speaker, the emotionality of the issue or audience, and the logic of the arguments to persuade an audience" (Thonssen and Baird 1948). These artistic proofs lie within the speaker and the speech itself, not outside the speech like laws, confessions, and contracts. The listener must understand and agree that the evidence is compelling and requires a change in his or her feelings, beliefs, attitudes, or behavior. Aristotle further categorized intrinsic proofs into ethos (personal), pathos (emotional), logos (logical), and mythos (mythic). These proofs are important to you as a persuasive communicator who wants listeners to believe your propositions and to be influenced by your message. We will consider each of these types of intrinsic proof in depth.

Personal Proof

Ethos, or personal proof, is the perception of the character of the speaker by an audience. Aristotle (Cooper 1997) saw ethos as a combination of the speaker's knowledge, good will, and moral character. He said: "The instrument of proof is the moral character . . . when the delivery of the speech is such as to produce an impression of the speaker's credibility; for we yield a more complete and ready credence to persons of high character . . ." (pp. 10–11). Today this aspect of intrinsic proof is called **source credibility,** and contemporary communication research suggests that it includes five aspects: competence, character, sociability, composure, and extroversion (McCroskey 1966).

Technical Tip 8.1
More on Source Credibility

In addition to McCroskey's 1966 study of source credibility, you can expand your knowledge of source credibility by consulting the following sources, some online.

McCroskey, J. C. (2000). *An Introduction to Rhetorical Communication.* (8th Ed.). Boston: Allyn & Bacon.

McCroskey, J. C. and Young, T. J. (1997). *Ethos and Credibility: The Construct and Its Measurement After Three Decades.* URL: *http://www.jamescroskey.com/publications/96.htm.*

Wheeless, L. R. and McCroskey, J. C. (1997). *The Effects of Selected Syntactical Choices of Source Credibility.* URL: *http://www.jamescroskey.com/publications/53.htm.*

Competence refers to the degree to which listeners perceive you as knowledgeable and informed about your topic. Robert Lutz (1998) was such a person. Passed over for chair and CEO of Chrysler Corporation in 1992, Lutz survived "by accepting his fate and making the most of it" (in Graham 1998). In 1991, before Lutz's reorganization of Chrysler, the company lost $795 million; after Lutz's reorganization, in 1994, the company reported record profitability with a net income of $3.7 billion! According to the *Investor's Business Daily* reporter, "Lutz won the chairman [Lee Iacocca] over with persistence, forcefulness and the soundness of his logic" (Graham A6). According to Lutz himself: "Maybe it wasn't so much what I said as how I said it. . . ." (in Graham A6). In the rarefied atmosphere of Fortune 500 companies, Lutz was seen as extremely competent.

To be viewed as competent, you will need to read and learn as much about your topic as you can. You should learn about the arguments of both proponents and opponents to your proposition. When you are finished conducting your research, you should have far more information than you are able to present in your persuasive speech. You should be able to answer questions after your speech in an informed and reasoned way. You should also be able to meet the objections of those who hold contrary beliefs. Professors are an example of a category of people who signal competence by knowing more than others do about a subject—so are attorneys, physicians, engineers, and fashion designers, to name a few (see Figure 8.1).

Figure 8.1
Speaker Credibility

As you prepare your speech, consider the following qualities of a credible speaker. To be effective, consider how you can encourage your audience to see you in these ways. To be critical, be sure you are not misrepresenting yourself.

1. **Competence**: Will your listeners perceive you as knowledgeable and informed about your topic?
2. **Character**: Will your listeners see you as trustworthy, honest, and sincere?
3. **Sociability**: Will your listeners see you as being friendly, pleasant, and like-able?
4. **Composure**: Will your listeners see you as being controlled, poised, and re-laxed?
5. **Extroversion**: Will your listeners see you as outgoing, energetic, and talk-ative?

Character means that listeners see you as trustworthy, honest, and sincere. H. Jackson Brown, Jr., observed in *Life's Little Instruction Book* that "Character is what we do when we think no one is looking" (in Shields 1998). After President Clinton suffered a loss of character for his often-denied affair with a White House intern, the Republican candidate for governor of California tried to smear the Democratic candidate by linking him by association with Clinton. But San Francisco mayor, Willie Brown, defended the Democrat, Gray Davis, by saying: "There is nobody in the world who would ever believe Gray Davis ever slept with anyone other than Sharon [his wife of 15 years] or would ever sanction it" (in Shields 1998). Davis' character saved him from the smear; voters did not believe that his behavior mirrored Clinton's just because both men were Democrats. How can you be viewed as a person of high character? You should show that you follow ethical practices in the communicative process. You can be honest in your dealings with others. In general, you can show that you are a person of integrity. Religious leaders are an example of a category of people whose character is a mainstay of their credibility.

Sociability refers to the idea that your audience sees you as friendly, pleasant, and likeable. T. D. Jakes is such a person. A Pentecostal bishop from Dallas, Jakes' church attracts 16,000 members. He plays up his links with popular figures like Deion Sanders of the Dallas Cowboys and Natalie Cole, but he also sends his bus downtown to gather up homeless people, who get showers, clean clothes—and for the women: hair-styling and makeup (Miller 1998). Even the *Wall Street Journal* reporter who profiled Jakes said:

> . . . He in person conveys an authenticity and a sincerity that fans say is the key to his success. "People open up to him, confide in him," says Mr. [Jesse] Jackson. "He can be in a crowd of thousands, and everyone thinks he's talking directly to them." (p. A9)

T. D. Jakes, originally a country preacher from West Virginia, has carried sociability to new heights.

In the classroom setting, you can encourage others to see you as sociable by coming to class early to talk with others, by initiating interactions, and by being warm in your interpersonal encounters with other students. Your speeches can "do something" for your classmates, just as T. D. Jakes' sermons do something for his parishioners. You can also be cordial during the presentation of your persuasive speech. People in sales and nearly all service-oriented businesses depend to some degree on their sociability for their credibility.

Composure means that the listeners view you as being in control, poised, and relaxed. Although you can be overly controlled, you may need to control your tension and anxiety in the public speaking setting. In your interpersonal interactions with audience members, show that you are confident. Broadcasters, public relations spokespersons, and beauty contestants are among the groups in American society whose composure is an important feature of their credibility.

Extroversion refers to the audience's perception that you are outgoing, energetic, and talkative. Television evangelist Jimmy Swaggart of Baton Rouge, Louisiana, is an example of a speaker who exudes extroversion: he paces about, he sings, he plays the piano and electric organ, and he preaches with so much energy that he sweats, cries, and shakes during his religious services.

Clearly, extroversion is a dimension of credibility that is culturally determined. Extroversion is probably exhibited more on the streets of New York City than in small towns in the Midwest. African Americans, Italians, and Puerto Ricans seem to value extroversion more than people who came from England, Finland, and Vietnam. In other words, the value of extroversion varies by co-culture, region of the world, and ethnic origin—to name a few of the possibilities.

To better understand credibility, read the introduction of a speech presented by David Archambault (1992), a member of the Native American tribe Lakota, to a Rotary Club. As you read this excerpt, consider how Archambault established his credibility.

> Haul Kola. That is how we Lakota say "Greeting, Friends." I am happy to be here today to represent Native American people. I am an Ikea Wicaska—an ordinary man. We think of an ordinary man as not superior to anyone else or, for that matter, to anything else. We—all people and all things—are related to each other.
>
> We begin our spiritual ceremonies with the phrase "Oni takuya Oyasi," which means all my relations. We believe that all people are ultimately part of one nation—the nation of mankind, but that this nation is only one of many nations that inhabit the Mother Earth. To us all living things are nations—the deer, the horses, things that crawl, things that fly, things that grow in and on the ground. All of these nations were created by the same Power, and none is superior to another. All are necessary for life. We are expected to live and work in harmony. (p. 491)

How did David Archambault establish his credibility? First, Archambault is a Lakota speaking to a Rotary Club, so his own ethnicity is a visible sign of his competence on this topic. Second, Archambault speaks Lakota, so he is rooted in his ethnicity by language, which adds to his competence. Third, he says he represents Native American people, so he sees himself as a spokesperson, a sociability characteristic. Fourth, he levels the relationship between himself and his audience by calling himself at the outset "an ordinary man" related to all living things and linked to all nations. This statement speaks to his character, the audience's perception of honesty, trustworthiness, and sincerity. In very few words, David Archambault establishes a number of credibility factors that encourage his audience to heed his words.

If you wish to establish positive credibility with your audiences, you, too, will wish to demonstrate these five characteristics as well as you can. Also, remember the ethical dimension of ethos: the ethical communicator does not represent himself or herself falsely. You do not pretend to be sociable while disliking the audience; you do not act as though you know more about the topic than you actually do.

Emotional Proof

A scholar once noted that the "normal human mind is not content merely to be logical and realistic; . . . it craves food for its emotions also" (Rogers 1929). **Pathos,** or emotional proof, involves attempts to persuade an audience with emotional appeals. If you attempt to evoke pity, sympathy, or other such strong emotions, you are using pathos. Your audience has both emotions and reasoning abilities. If you ignore the emotions of your audience, you will probably be unable to persuade them. As Karlins and Abelson (1970) stated the idea:

> The creature man is best persuaded
> When heart, not mind, is inundated;
> Affect is what drives the will;
> Rationality keeps it still. (p. 35)

Some of the emotional appeals you might use include idealism, transcendence, determination, conviction, and the dramatic example. **Idealism** is communicating the highest expectations of humanity, however rare their practice in reality. Mother Teresa is an example of an idealist whose work among the poor in India made her famous throughout the world. Maggie Kuhn, leader of the Gray Panthers, was an idealist who sought a better life for America's aging population. Jesse Jackson exhibits idealism through his "rainbow coalition," and former President Jimmy Carter promotes idealism through Habitat for Humanity. The persuasive appeal using idealism argues for peace among nations, harmony among races, and elimination of poverty. An appeal to idealism projects people and the world as they should be.

Transcendence is another positive emotional appeal, similar to idealism, which attempts to rise above or transcend people's differences in search of bonding similarities. Malcolm X, in the time before his assassination, saw in Islam a religion that appealed to people of all colors, a unifying force that he missed in the Black Muslim movement. Nelson Mandela believed that South Africa could transcend its racial, economic, and tribal differences to achieve a democratic government. In a persuasive speech using transcendence, the speaker picks a perspective that rises above conflict to find unifying similarities.

Determination is a positive emotional appeal characteristic of long-term movements. Republicans exhibited determination in their twenty-year struggle to gain control of the Senate and the House of Representatives in 1995. Cesar Chavez spent years in a determined effort to organize low-paid laborers. A persuasive speaker can show determination by arguing in favor of causes thought to be lost, by joining minority voices in movements against the dominant position on issues, and by trying in speech after speech to gain ground on an issue that most others oppose.

Conviction is a positive emotional appeal characterized by a deep feeling of certainty in the righteousness, truth, and virtue of your cause. Union leaders have strong convictions about the right to organize for better pay, better benefits, and better working conditions. Corporate leaders have strong convictions about capitalism, the virtue of profits, and the vice of government intervention. The Pope proclaims the convictions of the Roman Catholic faith for 900 million believers around the world. In a persuasive speech, you use the positive emotional appeal of conviction when you speak about the importance of your education in securing a living wage, the need for an economy that welcomes entry-level workers, and the right to have health benefits even for employees who earn low wages.

One final type of positive emotional appeal is the **dramatic example,** a narrative or story that illustrates a message in a manner that stirs the emotions. Aristotle (in Clark 1957) relates how Aesop defended a person with the fable of a fox caught in the rocks:

> The fox was infested with dog ticks which sucked his blood. A benevolent hedgehog offered to remove the ticks, but the fox declined the kind offer on the ground that his ticks were already full of blood and had ceased to annoy him much, whereas if they were removed, a new colony of ticks would establish themselves and thus entirely drain him of blood. "So . . .," said Aesop, "my client will do you no further harm; he is wealthy already. If you put him to death, others will come along who are not rich, and their peculations will empty your treasury completely." (p. 127)

In the Bible such stories are called parables, in children's stories they are called fables, and in speeches they are called dramatic examples. Most TV programs about police or emergency rooms are built around dramatic examples. Religious leaders often use them to illustrate their point about adopting their faith. Students tell stories about car accidents, drug abuse, family conflict, and athletic prowess to persuade their audiences about their topic. To demonstrate that such stories are used in modern times, a candidate for president used this one, which the columnist called a "Tax Parable" (Dionne 1999):

> You see, I come from this little town called McKees Rocks, where if the wind blew the wrong way, you find yourself out of work. But you know, there's one thing I found out there. The only people who hate rich people are guilty rich people. You see, the people who are struggling every day in America, they realize that if a rich guy takes his money, invests it, creates a job—that I get the job. Then I go to college and I get smart, then I buy him out and he works for me. That's the way we see it in Middle America. (p. A23)

This parable for modern times is a dramatic example intended by the speaker to capture the Republican perspective on taxes.

An example of emotional appeals is provided in a speech written by Solomon Moore (1989). Solomon was then a high school senior at Wooster High School in Ohio. He began his speech, entitled "The Elusive Peace":

❖ ❖ ❖ ❖

> In the Middle East, as the war between Iran and Iraq supposedly dies down
> the world begins to see that whatever they were fighting for has been drowned
> by the blood of people. In Central America, thousands upon thousands perish
> as communist and democratic puppet masters cry, "Freedom!" and fill their
> lands with guns instead of education, soldiers instead of teachers. In South
> Africa, the government sits high upon the scarred backs of the Bantus, who
> see nothing but the dusty road to fascism beneath them.

He concluded with another set of powerful emotional appeals.

> In order to grasp peace the world must want it. The nations and the peoples of
> the world must have some reason to embrace peace. Perhaps the whole world
> will have to squirm under a tyrannical government, not just Haiti or Libya.
> Perhaps the whole world will have to feel hunger's bite, not just Ethiopia or
> Sudan. Perhaps then peace will be craved. But never will it be too late for
> peace. Nothing people can do can thwart peace. Peace is inevitable. . . . When
> the peoples of the world realize this, the earth will be but one nation, and hu-
> mankind, its citizens.

Moore appeals largely to the audience's idealism as he discusses the possibility of peace for the world. He shows determination as he notes that "Nothing
we can do can thwart peace. Peace is inevitable." Moore's conviction is obvious throughout the introduction and conclusion. Finally, he provides dramatic examples in discussion of the Middle East, Central America, and South
Africa. Moore's speech is a fine example of the powerful role of emotional
proof within a persuasive speech.

For centuries people have been concerned about the ethical use of emotional appeals. Thonssen and Baird (1948) note the concern:

> Much of the adverse criticism of public speaking as an art, from before Aris-
> totle's time up to the present day,
> has grown out of people's fears of
> the orator's exercising demagogic
> influence. Critics have viewed ap-
> prehensively the control which an
> orator can exercise over audiences
> by appealing to their feelings. It
> has been held, and with justifica-
> tion, that an irresponsible orator
> can, through emotional manipula-
> tion, induce belief or action—all
> without the support of factual data
> or with the data distorted and
> warped to suit his sinister design.
> (p. 359)

The law attempts to wrap cases in logic and evidence, but juries often decide cases on other grounds.

What should you do if you want
to use emotional proof effectively
and ethically? You will want to
ensure that your audience understands the relationship of the emotional
appeal to your proposition or main point. You will also want to choose an
emotional appeal that is vivid and memorable. Ethically, you need to be sure
that the feeling, attitude, or behavior that you want to change in your audience warrants an emotional appeal. You do not want to incite your audience
to riot or leave them all in tears for no compelling reason.

❖ ❖ ❖ ❖   ## Logical Proof

Logos, or logical proof, occurs when you try to persuade an audience with logical appeals, reasoning, and arguments. In other words, logical appeals tend to be rational evidence. Logical appeals are not the opposite of emotional appeals but another distinctive mode of proof.

Logical appeals include the "finding of arguments necessary to prove the validity of a proposition" (DeVito 1986, 186). This fairly technical definition suggests that three elements are necessary in logical appeals. First, we have a statement or proposition that must be proven. Second, we have evidence that suggests the statement is true. Finally, we have a conclusion that binds the proposition and the evidence.

Julia Hughes Jones (1992), then auditor of the state of Arkansas, delivered a speech on the anniversary of women's suffrage in the United States. Her speech, entitled "A Greater Voice in Action: Women and Equality," included the following section:

> Why is a vote important? Many times, a single vote has changed the course of history. More than a thousand years ago in Greece, an entire meeting of the Church Synod was devoted to one question: Is a woman a human being or an animal? It was finally settled by vote, and the consensus was that we do indeed belong to the human race. It passed, however, by just one vote.

> Other situations where one vote has made a difference:

> In 1776, one vote gave America the English language instead of German.

> In 1845, one vote brought Texas and California into the Union.

> In 1868, one vote saved President Andrew Johnson from impeachment.

> In 1923, one vote determined the leader of a new political party in Munich. His name was Adolph Hitler.

> In 1960, one vote change in each precinct in Illinois would have defeated John F. Kennedy.

> History has proven the enormous power of one single vote. (pp. 109–111)

In this excerpt, Jones asserts—and then must prove—her statement that a single vote is important, indeed, that "a single vote has changed the course of history." Then she provides factual evidence that illustrates the importance of one vote. She finally concludes, tying her evidence to her initial statement by repeating, "History has proven the enormous power of *one single vote.*"

If you want to use logical proof effectively, be sure that your evidence demonstrates your statement or proposition. You also need to be sure that the audience understands the conclusion that ties the evidence to the statement. In order to be ethical, you will not provide untrue pieces of evidence, nor will you use evidence that does not prove your statement. Finally, you will not go beyond your evidence in your conclusion.

Mythic Proof

You probably know what a myth is: a tale or legend of unknown origin that reveals how or why something occurred in the past. You might not know the word **mythos,** a related but somewhat different concept that summarizes attitudes and beliefs that characterize a group or society. For example, Manifest Destiny was part of American mythos that guided our behavior for a century and justified taking lands from Mexicans and Native Americans. Mythos said the dominant American culture had the God-given right to take land from the Atlantic to the Pacific, and from Canada in the north to the Rio Grande River in the south. Slavery was justified by the mythos that the Bible justified dominance over the sons of Ham; Hitler's aggressive military and genocide against the Jews was justified by the mythos of a pure Aryan race; and several American wars have been justified by the American mythos that says: "We are the police force for the world."

The reason that mythos has been added to our repertoire of persuasive proofs is that America includes cultures from many lands, each of which has its own mythos. America has co-cultures with their own mythos. These co-cultures range from the fundamentalist Christian mythos that everyone needs to be Christian to be saved, to the Black Muslim idea that African Americans should be united in self-protection and faith, to the White Supremacist idea that America should be for white people only. To illustrate the concept further, let us turn to a less divisive mythos concerning our concept of time.

An African American expatriate from Paris lectured at Harvard to university administrators about time. Time, he said, has a different meaning to European Americans than it does to African Americans, largely because of their countries of origin. Europeans lived for centuries in harsh climates where timing of planting, cultivation, and harvest was a matter of life and death. Doing things "on time" was of crucial importance to survival. Africans lived for thousands of years in places where food was simply picked, not planted or harvested, and where time was not crucial to survival. One of the results is a different mythos about time. At the Frankfurt, Germany, international airport, the large flight schedule for world-wide flights says over and over: Lufthansa (the German airline) "on time." Nearly every African flight said "delayed" or had a sign on the airline desk saying "tomorrow." Is this explanation an oversimplified theory about differences in ideas about time? Perhaps, but such ideas about time are not unheard of among German Americans and African Americans who have been away from their countries of origin for generations.

The persuasive power of mythos is important in a diverse society. Some Native Americans see time as renewable seasons with no real beginning and no real end (Lake 1991). The Hopis have no words to designate time but view time as "a smooth flowing continuum in which everything in the universe proceeds at an equal rate, out of a future, through a present, into a past" (Whort 1975). Some Christian groups believe that every word in the Bible is literally true, while other Christian groups see stories like the one in Genesis as being a metaphorical explanation about the origins of humans. Mythos may not be what is taught as logical reasoning, but who would deny that mythos about races and marriage between races was somehow confounded in the famous O. J. Simpson case? In a country like America, where hundreds of cultures converge in one larger society, our respect for, and knowledge of, the mythos that guides people's thoughts becomes one of the ways we influence each other.

Mythic proof—traditional ideas and stories—is conveyed mainly through the use of metaphors and narratives. When Bill Clinton (1993) became president, he used the metaphor of the seasons to portray both his program and that of his predecessor. Read carefully these excerpts from his inaugural address:

> This ceremony is held in the depth of winter. But, by the words we speak and the faces we show the world, we force the spring.
>
> A spring reborn in the world's oldest democracy, that brings forth the vision and courage to reinvent America . . .
>
> So today, we pledge an end to the era of deadlock and drift—and a new season of American renewal has begun . . .
>
> Yes, you my fellow Americans, have forced the spring. Now, we must do the work the season demands . . .
>
> And so my fellow Americans, as we stand at the edge of the 21st century, let us begin with energy and hope, with faith and discipline, and let us work until our work is done. The scripture says, "And let us not be weary in well-doing, for in due season, we shall reap, if we faint not." (p. A12)

The speech is replete with references to a European American mythos about time, work, progress, seasons, planting, and harvest. Unstated is the idea that the Bush administration must have represented winter, while the new president represents the renewal of spring. Scripture is invoked to resonate with the large number of Americans who believe in the Bible. He suggests that Americans will reap a great harvest if they plant and work hard in the spring. The use of mythos to persuade is the best explanation for what is happening in these passages. The discourse is not a string of arguments with evidence; instead, the piece is a systematic appeal to age-old mythos resident in American culture.

Mythos is difficult to manage for the ethical communicator in our contemporary diverse society. Americans from Mexico, Cuba, Puerto Rico, Vietnam, Columbia, Canada, China, Japan, India, and hundreds of different countries of origin bring to us their own mythos. So do Baptists, lesbian women and gay men, musicians, veterans, union members, and Republicans. The ethical persuader must consider the particular audience members in order to know which mythos might appeal. Certainly one group's mythos might be less ethical than another's. The ideas that Americans must speak English, that all conceptions should result in children, and that one religion is better than another are based in different mythos that invite ethical evaluation in our national discussions.

You learned earlier that evidence consists of supporting materials used for a persuasive purpose. These basic elements of the persuasive process are used to support your propositions or positions. Certain rules guide the way we combine evidence and propositions to create conclusions. **Argument** consists of the presentation of a claim or conclusion and the evidence that supports it (DeVito 1986). Certain inferences or assumptions often go unstated in arguments.

If you want to convince an audience that your idea meets their needs, you will be interested in learning about arguing. If you wish to demonstrate the benefits of your plan, you will need to understand the information in this section. If you want to show that your idea is consistent with the audience's present beliefs, attitudes, and values, this information will be helpful to you.

Components of an Argument   ❖ ❖ ❖ ❖

As you have been reading about evidence and proofs, you may have already discerned the components that form an argument. Essentially, the components are only two in number: a claim and evidence. The **claim** is the conclusion you wish your audience to accept. **Evidence** consists of supporting materials used in a persuasive context. When you make an argument, you need to provide a claim and evidence for that argument. Sometimes the relationship between the two is fairly obvious; at other times, you may have to explain to your audience how claim and evidence are related.

Before we consider the nature and types of argument, we need to consider in more depth the notions of claims. In the next section, we will distinguish between claims of fact, claims of value, and claims of policy.

Types of Claims

Public speeches, especially speeches intended to persuade others, are full of claims that the advocate wants the audience to accept. This section provides you with terms to describe those claims: claims of fact, value, and policy. Why should you know, understand, and use these terms? First, the terms provide you with language to describe what you use in your own speeches and hear in those of others. Second, the terms allow you to think critically about their use. When you hear a speaker claiming a fact, you know that you have a right to know where the speaker found that fact and if the source is credible. Third, the terms help you to know what kinds of evidence or proof are necessary for the different claims. For example, no one can absolutely demonstrate that a policy will work as claimed because a claim attempts to predict how something will work in the future. Predictions are frequently foiled by unintended results. To understand claims, we will consider each of the three types in more detail.

Claims of fact. **Claims of fact** deal with truth and falsity. They are concerned with the occurrence, the existence, or the particular properties of something. Examples of claims of fact include:

The United States does not have enough water to meet normal needs.

The most likely way for a child in the United States to die is at the hands of another child.

The most likely suspect in a homicide is someone known to the victim.

Women do not have equal opportunities for employment in the United States.

California has suffered more natural disasters in the last decade than any other state.

Claims of value. **Claims of value** require judgments of good and bad. Such claims are grounded in the participant's motives, beliefs, and cultural standards. Desirability and satisfaction are often central to claims of value. Examples of claims in this category include:

A college education is desirable for everyone.

The USA needs fewer lawyers and more computer experts.

The most important issue facing America is that of increased violence in our neighborhoods, businesses, and homes.

Society would be better off with fewer business majors and more science majors.

Claims of policy. **Claims of policy** concern future action. The purpose of a policy claim is to argue that a course of action should be taken or supported in a specific situation. The word *should* is generally included in a claim of policy. Examples of claims of policy include the following:

Rules against nepotism should be dropped.

People over the age of seventy should not be allowed to work.

Husbands who rape their wives should face the same penalties strangers face when they are found guilty of rape.

College students should have no required courses.

The age for drinking alcohol legally should be raised to twenty-five.

The Construction of a Sound Argument

The components of an argument are few in number, which may suggest to you that constructing an argument is fairly easy to do. On the contrary, the construction of an effective and ethical argument is complex. Here is an example of an argument provided by a student speaker from a speech entitled "Keep the Elderly at Home." In this speech, Julie L. Cook (1994) argues that nursing homes have inherent problems. She said, in part,

> This country has 20,000 nursing homes but over half of them are substandard. According to *Nursing Home Life: What It Is and What It Could Be*, nursing homes focus on the physical and medical aspects of geriatric care. Little is being done to satisfy any non-medical needs, to make patients' lives meaningful, livable, or natural. Even though all nursing homes have to balance care and costs, our elderly should not be required to live an existence that is not worthwhile.

Would you accept the speaker's argument? She has made a claim and she has offered in evidence some paraphrased testimony. Some people might conclude that her evidence is sufficient and that she has made the link between the claim and the evidence. Other people might find her support inadequate.

In his speech on world peace, Solomon Moore (1989) provided a claim and evidence. Moore said:

> The biggest problem caused by the building up of armaments is not their destructive power, but instead the drain of available resources, which many nations could put to better use. For instance: the amount of money spent on researching new forms of death is seven times what is spent on new ways to prolong life. The training of military personnel in the United States costs twice as much as the budget for the education of 300 million South Asian children. At present levels, everyone during his or her lifetime will sacrifice three to four years of income to the arms race. With less than one percent of the world's military budget, almost twenty-five million lives could be saved by vaccinating all children against polio, measles, tetanus, and by draining swamps and providing medicine to rid the world of malaria. The present nuclear arsenal contains the explosive power of over 6000 World War IIs. Every two days the world spends $4 billion on military expenditures, and every two seconds four people starve to death. And when the world does finally put the money into the 930 million people who are hungry all of the time, it's like a grimace of kindness on a murderer's face.

In this argument, Moore links his claim to both logical and emotional evidence. He uses facts and figures and examples. He also uses simile ("a grimace of kindness on a murder's face") to make his evidence more striking. Do you find this argument stronger or weaker than the one provided by Cook? Why?

When Julie Cook gave her speech, she was a sophomore in college, majoring in business administration. Julie is a middle-class European American female. When Solomon Moore gave his speech, he was a 17-year-old high school senior. A native of Ohio, Solomon is African American. Does this information change the way you see their arguments? How does this small amount of personal information contribute to the speaker's ethos, or personal proof?

Aristotle (1931) observed that, "A speech has two parts. Necessarily, you state your case, and you prove it" (p. 220). Both speakers used the two components of an argument: a claim and evidence. As we have seen, however, these two elements can be put together in a variety of ways. To be an effective persuasive speaker, you will need to consider all of the elements in public argument, including the kinds of evidence and the types of proof available to you.

Types of Argument

Although all arguments make a claim and provide evidence, arguments can be made on different bases. Let us consider the four most common types of argument: the argument by analogy, the argument from cause, the argument by deduction, and the argument by example or induction.

Argument by analogy. An **argument by analogy** points out similarities between two things, comparing something that the audience knows well to something the audience does not know well. To say that our society is analogous to a stew or a salad suggests that all of the ethnic groups in our pot retain their original flavors but are enhanced by being mixed together. To say that our society is a melting pot suggests that ethnic groups lose their individual identities to become something else—Americans. To clarify the concept of argument by analogy further, you should know that some analogies are figurative and others are literal.

A **figurative analogy** *takes two fundamentally different things and compares their common properties.* For example, this is how one student (Pearson 1993) described her family:

> My family is a football team. My father's position is the quarterback who calls his own plays. He decides what strategy to take and then implements it. My mother could be considered my dad's right arm and, therefore, is placed in the position of running back, the star running back. She is the consistent one who will always get at least four yards. My "little" brother resembles the entire front line. Not only by his physical size but also by his concern for our family. He would never let anyone penetrate through the line to get to any of us. My sister holds the position of second string quarterback. She's a lot like my father as far as attitudes and values. She is very independent and believes "her way" is always best. My position on the team would be on the sidelines. I am the biggest fan, the loudest cheerleader and, at times, the head referee. I am not as involved in the play by play because of geographical barriers. However, when I am able to be with my family I play an active role. Regardless of victory or defeat my family remains strong and united, our spirit never faltering. Together we are definitely a winning team!

This analogy comparing the student's family to a football team clarified the relationships and roles of her family members. Audience members with some knowledge of American football understood reasonably well what her family was like.

A **literal analogy** is a comparison of two similar things instead of two fundamentally different things. The city of Columbus solved its traffic flow problems by creating a grid of one-way streets. Should the city of Cleveland do the same thing? A speech favoring the plan of one city for another would use a literal analogy.

A real-life example of a literal analogy occurred when National Public Radio correspondent Nina Totenberg was summoned before the Senate Special Independent Counsel for reading portions of Anita Hill's affidavit to the Senate Judiciary Committee to nine million listeners. Republican supporters of Clarence Thomas, a nominee for the Supreme Court, were angry about leaks to the press. The purpose of the hearing was to force Totenberg (1994) to reveal her sources, which she regarded as a violation of journalistic ethics. Here is part of her response:

> At the beginning of our Republic, in 1798, one party, the Federalists, sought to silence its critics in the upcoming election by making it a crime punishable by up to two years in prison and a fine of $2000 to "write, print, utter or publish" any material that would bring government officials into "contempt or disrepute." (See A. Lewis, Make No Law, 1991.) Under the Sedition Act, editors and publishers of opposing Republican Party papers were jailed and fined. But many of our most famous Founding Fathers were outraged by the Act—James Madison and Thomas Jefferson called it a blatant violation of the First Amendment. Jefferson, after being elected President, pardoned those convicted under the act and within less than half a century the law (which lasted only three years) was in such disrepute that Congress paid back many of the fines that had been imposed under it. In 1964, the Sedition Act was, at long last, held unconstitutional. I suspect that Congress may one day look back on these press subpoenas with equal disdain. (pp. 202–203)

Totenberg's defense is a literal analogy comparing the hated and ineffective Sedition Act of 1798 with the legal subpoenas of 1992. Incidentally, she never did reveal her sources, but Clarence Thomas did, of course, become an Associate Justice of the United States Supreme Court.

The key to determining just how ethical an analogy is depends on how parallel the compared cases are. By definition, both figurative and literal analogies compare different things, but the appropriateness and ethical value of an analogy depends on the similarities. If the Sedition Act of 1798 and the forced appearances of journalists at hearings in 1992 are sufficiently similar in comparison, then the analogy can be said to be appropriate and ethical. If the Sedition Act and the subpoenas are sufficiently different in comparison, then the analogy can be attacked as "apples and oranges" and found ethically suspect. Always, the speaker and listeners as critical thinkers need to analyze, compare, and decide.

Argument from cause. An **argument from cause** occurs when you reason from a cause to an unknown, but likely, effect. You are arguing that one event caused, or was responsible for, a second event. Some common examples of argument from cause include the following:

Smoking causes cancer.

Alcohol and drug consumption while you are pregnant causes birth defects.

Excessive exposure to the sun causes skin cancer.

Unsafe sex causes the spread of disease or pregnancy.

Skipping classes causes lower grades.

Yo-yo dieting causes heart problems.

Achieving high grades in undergraduate schools causes easier admission to graduate school.

An example of an argument from cause is provided in a speech by Cheng Imm Tan (1994), a Buddhist Unitarian Universalist minister, who works with Cambodian, Vietnamese, and Chinese women in the Asian American Task Force Against Domestic Violence. Her speech is about the plight of Asian women who find themselves alone in American cities when they leave the men who abuse them. See if you can find the arguments from cause in her speech.

> Since 1970, the Asian American population has doubled each decade. It is the fastest growing group in the United States. Today, 60 percent of the Asian American population are immigrants.
>
> . . . Although much has been done in the last fifteen years since the battered women's movement began to address domestic violence in the United States, for most Asian women, the gains made have not been accessible.
>
> . . . The relative isolation of the Asian communities . . . has meant marginalization and invisibility. Violence in the home continues to be seen as a private family matter. Most Asian women are not aware of available resources or of their legal rights. Many also fear reporting abuse because of their fear and distrust of governments and authorities. Like other people of color, they also fear discrimination and unfair treatment.
>
> . . . Asian refugee and immigrant women are particularly isolated. Many do not speak or understand English. Even those who do speak English are not confident in using the language. Since shelters and hotlines do not have staff who speak Asian languages, this language barrier ensures isolation. In fact, few battered women's shelters serve Asian women. Many battered women who have fled to a shelter have returned because the unfamiliarity of the shelter environment, language difficulties, and cultural differences make separation from their community unbearable. . . . (pp. 224–225)

Cheng Imm Tan's speech cites numerous causes—isolation, language and cultural barriers, and ignorance—for the effect: battered Asian women do not receive help in American society.

How does the ethical and effective persuader assess arguments from cause? First, you must consider whether the cause and effect presented are linked at all; in other words, are the cause and effect related? Second, you need to determine whether the cause and effect are strongly or only weakly related. Third, you need to determine if the effect may be related to a different cause.

For example, you might decide to give a persuasive speech in which you encourage people not to drink alcohol and drive an automobile. You argue, in your speech, that people who drink and drive are far more likely to have accidents than are those who do not drink. In this instance, the cause is drinking and the effect is an automobile accident.

If your argument is to be successful, you will have to convince your audience that the cause and effect you are describing are related to each other. Your audience will have to agree that drinking and accidents are related.

Second, you will have to show that the link between drinking and automobile accidents is an important one. If someone can demonstrate that only 5 percent of people who drink and drive have automobile accidents, your argument may be defeated. People may agree that drinking causes accidents, but the percentage of this incidence within the total number of accidents is too low to be of much concern.

Third, you need to determine if the effect may be related to a different cause. For example, if multiple causes for automobile accidents—age, sex, personality characteristics, distance from home, speed of vehicle, etc.—can be shown to be just as relevant as drinking, the audience may see the cause-effect link but dismiss the link because the effect is related to other causes.

Similarly, someone might argue that drinking is actually the effect of another phenomenon—say, age or personality or predisposition to alcoholism. They could argue that one's age, personality, or predisposition is the cause of automobile accidents and that drinking and accidents are both effects. Here again, your ability to think critically needs to be applied.

Argument by deduction. An **argument by deduction** occurs when you reason from a general proposition, or from a generally accepted truth, to a specific instance or example (DeVito 1986). In deductive argument you have a **conclusion** deduced from a major and a minor premise. Instead of resulting in a probability, as inductive reasoning does, a deductive argument results in a conclusion that necessarily follows from the two premises. A deductive argument looks like this:

Major premise: All insects have six legs.

Minor premise: Ants are insects.

Conclusion: Therefore, ants have six legs.

Notice that if the premises are true, then the conclusion must necessarily be true also, because in a sense the two premises are the same as the conclusion.

In conversation and even in most speeches, a deductive argument usually does not sound or look quite as formal as the argument appears in our example. In fact, the argument cited would more likely appear in a speech like this: "Since all insects have six legs, ants must too." The reasoning is still deductive, except that the minor premise is implied rather than openly stated. At other times, the conclusion is implied and the major and minor premises are provided in words. An **enthymeme** is a deductive argument in which either the minor premise or the conclusion is implied rather than stated. Since deductive arguments most often appear as enthymemes in speeches, they are difficult to detect and even more difficult to analyze. For this reason, to listen closely to the reasoning in speeches is necessary to determine what has been implied—or *seemed* to be implied, but actually wasn't—in addition to what has been stated openly.

Here are some examples of enthymemes. If you say "Henry Wong is Republican because he is Chinese," then you have a conclusion with these premises: All Chinese are Republicans; Henry Wong is Chinese; therefore, Henry Wong is Republican. In other words, part of the deductive argument is omitted. If you say "All fraternity men are drunks," then you have a major premise for a deductive argument that can say: All fraternity men are drunks; Fred is a fraternity man; therefore, Fred is a drunk. The key to recognizing an enthymeme is to know that the reasoning is incomplete, that some of the deductive argument is omitted.

If you feel you have particularly strong arguments by deduction in your own speech, you might consider taking the time to state the premises and conclusion clearly and completely rather than providing them less completely as enthymemes. Well-reasoned deductive arguments can have great persuasive power, because once the audience has accepted the validity of the premises, the conclusion is inescapable. Mathematical proofs commonly take the form of deductive arguments, and the reasoning in your own speech can have all the clarity and impact of such proofs: if A equals B, and if B equals C, then A equals C.

How does the ethical and effective persuasive communicator test deductive arguments? The tests are straightforward. First, you ensure that both the major premise and the minor premise are true. Second, you ascertain that the premises are actually related to each other.

An example of an argument by deduction occurs in this speech by Nannerl O. Keohane (1991), president of Wellesley College, entitled "Educating Women for Leadership: Drawing on the Full Human Race." Examining Keohane's deductive argument will allow us to illustrate the tests for the effective and ethical persuader. Keohane states,

> We know that a society cannot flourish, indeed cannot survive, without at least a minimal sense of shared ethical standards and goals. To renew this sense among our own people we need students educated on our campuses who are familiar with the great moral examples provided by men and women in the past who have wrestled with their own ethical dilemmas. We need to be sure they have read deeply in philosophy and literature, religion and biography, to understand how human beings develop a sense of truthfulness and compassion and how such attributes advance our common goals. (p. 19)

Keohane's major premise is that a society cannot flourish without a minimal sense of shared ethical standards and goals. Her minor premise, unstated, is that people will have a sense of shared ethical standards and goals if undergraduate students become familiar with moral examples and read in the areas of philosophy, literature, religion, and biography. Her conclusion is that undergraduate students should become familiar with such examples and read in these areas.

If Keohane's major and minor premises are related to each other and are true, then the conclusion must also be true. In most speeches, matters of truth are not so easily ascertained, however. Someone might disagree with the major premise. They could point to societies that flourished without a sense of shared ethical standards. They could also disagree that the minor premise is true. They might argue that people who are familiar with moral examples and well read in philosophy, literature, religion, and biography do not necessarily have a sense of shared ethical standards. The truth of her conclusion is based on the truth of her premises. Again, if the premises are agreed upon as true, then the conclusion is inevitably true.

Argument by induction. An **argument by induction,** or example, is an argument from specific instances to a general conclusion. The conclusion is not necessarily true, but it is highly probable. An argument by example was provided in the section on logos in the excerpt of a speech by Julia Hughes

❖ ❖ ❖ ❖

Jones. Jones argued that one vote has changed the course of history. She proved her proposition by providing example after example of instances when one vote decided major issues.

Another example is provided in the following speech excerpt by Nannerl O. Keohane (1991). In this excerpt Keohane argues that women are holding an increasing number of leadership positions around the world. She stated:

> There are women generals and women judges, women neurosurgeons and opera conductors and newspaper editors, and even, occasionally, a woman CEO.

> Such new leaders join the legions of strong women who have traditionally been leaders in more familiar fields: in early childhood education, on the boards of symphonies and art museums, in the soup kitchens and in the peace movement, in all kinds of non-profit organizations that so enrich our lives.

> There are more women in politics, as well, more women governors, mayors, even presidential and vice-presidential candidates these days. If someone had said ten years ago that the mayors of several of America's largest cities in 1990 would be women, or that one-half the cabinet, one-half the legislature, and the prime minister of Norway would be female, they would have been laughed out of court. (p. 19)

Keohane's list of examples is extensive. She cites women in leadership in a variety of careers. These examples allow her to conclude that women have a greater number of leadership positions today than in the past. She begins with specific examples and ends with a generalization.

In Keohane's case, as in all cases of argument by example, the conclusion is not necessarily true. This argument provides evidence that allows an "inferential leap" to the generalization. Since the argument requires an inference, the generalization that is drawn may be false, but it is viewed as generally, or probably, true.

How can we determine the likelihood that the generalization is true? Some specific tests can be applied to the inductive argument to test its validity:

1. We need to ensure that the examples are true.

2. We need to be sure that the examples are recent.

3. We consider whether the examples are relevant.

4. We need to determine if the examples are adequate in number.

5. We consider whether the examples are typical.

The "adequate in number" criterion is a judgment call since the audience members, not the speaker, decide whether they have heard enough instances to prove the case. In Keohane's speech, the generalization that women have attained more leadership roles remains only a probability, even with the large number of examples that she presented.

Are her examples true? We might have to cite her sources or cite independent sources of our own. In our search we can also determine the recency of Keohane's examples. We need to consider if her examples are relevant. What if women held other leadership roles in the past that have now been taken over by men? What if these leadership positions are not very important ones? Next we need to consider if she has provided an adequate number of examples. Finally, we need to decide if the examples that Keohane has presented are representative of all, or most, leadership positions. Similar questions allow us to see that the generalization, while probably true, can always be questioned by a reinterpretation of other evidence or by the introduction of contrary evidence.

You now know about four types of argument and the specific tests that the ethical and effective communicator uses to examine each. In addition, you need to ask four general questions to ensure that your reasoning and evidence are generally sound.

1. *Is your evidence consistent with other known evidence?* An example is the end-of-the-century downturn in U.S. students going to graduate school. The most commonly heard argument is proclaimed in a *Washington Post* (Layton 1999) headline: "With Booming Economy, Graduate School Enrollment Declines" (B4) and "More People Choosing Jobs Over Grad School, Educators Say" (B1). That contention—that graduate school enrollment declines with economic booms—appears to be true when you look at the issue only in its broadest terms. For instance, the Council of Graduate Schools says graduate enrollment declined 1 to 2 percent between 1996 and 1999. But a closer look reveals that the declines are relatively major-specific: the declines fall mainly in biological sciences, engineering, and the physical sciences—especially among American-born students (B1). During the same time period, international students fueled an increase in graduate enrollments, and enrollments gathered steam in fields like health care and business (B4). So the declining enrollments argument is true at one level but questionable at another level. The critical thinker explores the details.

2. *Is there any evidence to the contrary?* When you try to reason with evidence, you must always be aware of any evidence that does not support your cause. An opponent can do much damage to your arguments and your credibility if she can find contrary evidence that you did not mention. Usually you are better off mentioning any conflicting evidence, especially if you can argue against the conflicting evidence in your presentation.

3. *Does your generalization go beyond your evidence?* Speakers always face the danger of overstating what their evidence shows. A small study that shows grade inflation is treated like a university-wide problem. Evidence of a local problem becomes a national problem in the speech. Always be careful that you do not go beyond what your evidence demonstrates.

4. *Is your evidence believable to the audience?* In persuasive speaking, you need to provide only enough evidence to have the audience believe and act as you wish. More than that is too much; less than that is too little. A large amount of evidence that the listeners find unacceptable will not persuade them; a small amount that the audience finds acceptable will be sufficient to persuade.

❖ ❖ ❖ ❖

Fallacies of Argument

In addition to the tests that should be considered if you want your arguments to be effective and ethical, a number of standard fallacies or faulty arguments have been identified. These fallacies are based on plausible but invalid reasoning. We will consider some of the most common fallacies. If you wish to consider additional fallacies, you may wish to consult resources on argumentation and discussion.

Hasty generalization violates the rules of inference by coming to a conclusion with too little evidence. Some examples would include the following: The last woman I hired was calling her kids on the phone all the time, so I stopped hiring women; I'll never trust college students because several of them have taken items from my store without paying; My last ride with an Iranian taxi driver convinced me never to ride with an Iranian taxi driver again. In all cases, a conclusion was drawn based on a sample of one, which was generalized to all women, college students, and Iranian cab drivers. Coming to a conclusion with very little evidence is regarded as faulty reasoning.

Technical Tip 8.2
More About Fallacies

This book and two Internet sources can provide you with more information about fallacies:

Rybacki, K. C. and Rybacki, D. J. (1999). *Advocacy and Opposition: An Introduction to Argumentation.* Boston: Allyn & Bacon.

Common Argument Fallacies (1997). URL: *http://www.midnightbeach.com/hs/fallacys.htm.*

Argument Fallacies (1997). URL: *http://www.brimstone.com/~jasona/hobbies/ranting/logic.html.*

Post hoc, ergo prompter hoc fallacy literally means "after this; therefore, because of this." The faulty reasoning involved is that of false cause: just because one thing occurs after another does not mean that it was caused by the first thing. Here are some examples: I had a car accident immediately after I saw a black cat, which everyone knows is bad luck. I got a headache after eating at an Italian restaurant, so I am going to avoid headaches by avoiding Italian restaurants. I get sick at work a lot because the structure is a "sick building." Just because two events correlate does not mean they necessarily cause each other. The car accident was not caused by a black cat, the headache was a hangover, and the illness at work was from a chronic condition in the person that had nothing to do with the workplace. The lesson of the post hoc fallacy is to not confuse correlation with causation.

Equivocation fallacy means that the same word is used in different ways to result in an incorrect interpretation. Some examples of equivocation in action are the following: The Constitution says that "All men are created equal," so women must not be equal to men. We say that "America is the land of the free," so we must be free to do anything we like. I have an "open door" policy, but you will have to wait two weeks for an appointment. The words "men," "free," and "open door" are words that are used in two different ways resulting in an incorrect interpretation. Sometimes equivocation is used intentionally to confuse others. Iowa State University (and perhaps others as well) had a bar called "The Library" so students could tell others that they spent the entire evening in the library—a deliberate equivocation.

Faulty analogy fallacy means that the analogy has gone too far. An analogy compares two fundamentally different things, and the comparison can be carried over to some—but not all—characteristics. Here are some examples: most English police do not carry weapons, and that country has substantially fewer murders, so we should disarm our police to achieve a lower murder rate. America is like ancient Rome in its fascination with violence, nudity, and drinking, so our society is about to meet the same fate as Rome. Many animals kill each other to establish territoriality just as humans do; that is why we will never have peace. English society and American society are similar in some respects, but not all, so disarming the police may or may not work in American society. America and Rome are centuries apart and fundamentally different, so our current behavior is not destined to have the same ending as did ancient Rome. Animals and people are different enough so that there is no guarantee that we will be unable to settle territorial disputes peacefully. The faulty analogy carries the comparison too far.

Red herring fallacy occurs when extraneous issues are introduced to distract attention away from the argument. Examples of the red herring fallacy come from the political arena. When George W. Bush was regarded as the most likely person to become the Republican nominee for president of the United States in 1999, the press was mainly interested in whether he had ever taken illegal drugs even as a youth (Novak 1999; Cohen 1999). When the U.S. government was embarrassed to discover that some of China's advances in weaponry were based on plans purloined from the United States, the government pounced on Wen Ho Lee, a nuclear scientist from Los Alamos National Laboratory. Lee is a U.S. citizen who is ethnic Chinese. The former counter-intelligence chief at Los Alamos said that the case against Lee was "built on thin air" and that Lee "was suspected largely for ethnic reasons" (Espionage Scandal 1999). To draw attention away from a presidential candidate who was fleecing his opponents, the press drew attention to possible indiscretions in the distant past. A government under pressure to find someone guilty of espionage chose a Chinese scientist against whom no compelling case had been made. The red herring fallacy, a claim irrelevant to the main issues, is a common ploy in American politics.

Slippery slope fallacy is erroneous reasoning that suggests that if one event occurs, then a chain of other events will follow. Similar to the "domino theory," the slippery slope fallacy suggests that if the first event happens (the first domino falls), that event will create a second event (the second domino falling), and then another (the next domino will fall), until a series of events has occurred (all of the dominos will eventually be knocked down).

The slippery slope fallacy often occurs around the issue of gun control. People argue that if large automatic weapons such as AK-47s and Uzis are controlled, then handguns will be controlled next. After handguns, they believe that all types of shotguns and rifles will be banned, and soon people will be defenseless in their own homes. They thus argue that people should have the right to own powerful automatic weapons originally designed for wartime.

❖ ❖ ❖ ❖

Argumentum ad hominem fallacy occurs when you attack the other person rather than the issue. Similar to the tactic of name-calling, ad hominem occurs when people who espouse the right to life and oppose abortion call people who espouse the right to choice "murderers" and "criminals." Similarly, when Rush Limbaugh labels women who want equal rights as "femi-Nazis," he is using an ad hominem fallacy rather than considering the validity of their arguments.

False dilemma fallacy exists when listeners are provided with only two choices even though a variety of options are available. For instance, if you support a particular political candidate and tell your audience that the choice is simple—either your candidate or four more years of despair, depression, and downsizing, you are committing this fallacy.

Bandwagon, or appeal to popular opinion fallacy is present when a phenomenon is viewed as true or right because a majority of people believe that thing to be right or true. The clichéd parental remark to teenage children, "If your friends jumped off a bridge, would you jump off it, too?" is parents' way of letting their children know that they have committed this fallacy. Although the parental response is tired from overuse, the expression does suggest that none of us should engage in a behavior simply because a majority of other people do.

Begging the question is a fallacy that occurs when someone uses language to make claims that they have not proven. One way this may be done is if someone argues in a circular fashion. For instance, if you argue that education is important because well-educated people are generally better off than are people who are not well-educated, you have not really proven your claim either that education is important or that well-educated people are better off. Another way you can beg the question is by using "devil terms" or "angel terms" in association with a concept that you oppose or propose. When Dr. Jack Kevorkian discussed "issues of human dignity" when he considered the right to die, he was essentially begging the question. If you believe in human dignity (and who would say that they do not), then you are obligated to agree with Kevorkian's circular reasoning.

You have learned to recognize and explain ten fallacies: hasty generalization, post hoc, equivocation, faulty analogy, red herring, slippery slope, ad hominem, false dilemma, bandwagon, and begging the question. Knowing these fallacies and learning how to apply them to everyday discourse and speeches will help you to become a better critical thinker.

Additional Ethical Concerns

Persuasive speaking offers ample opportunities for ethical mischief. Certainly persuasive speaking can be used for positive purposes: stop smoking, start exercising, do not overuse your credit card, and avoid AIDS. However, persuasive speaking can also be used to sell unwanted insurance, unneeded repairs, overpriced products, and ineffective diets. Distinguishing between ethical and unethical persuasive appeals is a challenging task for which there are some general guidelines:

1. Be careful whom you trust. The smooth-talking individual can be a pathological deceiver, whereas an unattractive, inarticulate person can have your best interests in mind. When buying or sell-

ing, dating or mating, you should look at past behavior and the testimony of others who have had more experience with the person with whom you are dealing. In short, source credibility should always be an issue.

2. Analyze and evaluate messages for reasonableness, truth, and benefit to you or humankind. Our social norms discourage acceptance of messages for purely emotional reasons ("I bought the $3000 ring because I wanted it"; "I married him because of his cute little nose"). Instead, our society encourages us to accept messages because they meet our standards of reason, because we find them to be true, or because the message seems to benefit others or us more than the message will harm us.

✔ Reality Check 8.1 ✔
Nicotine Is Not Addictive?

Toward the end of the 20th century, tobacco executives made themselves famous for publicly arguing that cigarettes are non-addictive. The CEO of Philip Morris USA said: "I believe nicotine is not addictive." The Chair of RJR Tobacco Co. said: "Cigarettes and nicotine clearly do not meet the classic definitions of addiction" (in Schwartz 1999). Others testified in the same vein at the public hearing on C-SPAN.

Many observers assumed they were lying. What do you think? Does the argument depend on how they define *addiction?* Can the executives argue that cancer and pulmonary emphysema only correlate with illness and death but do not cause them? What evidence exists concerning this issue? What position do you take, and how do you defend that position with arguments and evidence?

---

3. You and your messages will be more persuasive if you have a long, positive history ("The thing you only get to lose once is your reputation"); if your past invites others to trust you and your word; and if others tend to benefit from your messages as much or more than you do (that is, you don't seek compliance for selfish purposes). A nationally known evangelist was caught for the second time in the company of a prostitute. Will the money keep flowing to a person who cannot be trusted to stay on the straight and narrow himself? Are you building a history that will help or harm you when you attempt to persuade others?

Summary

In this chapter you learned how to use evidence, proof, and argument in an effective and ethical way. You first learned that four kinds of evidence can be used in an ethical and effective way in persuasion. They include facts and figures, examples, narratives, and testimony. After considering some ethical and effectiveness criteria for evidence, we turned our attention to proof. The modes of proof include personal proof, emotional proof, logical proof, and mythic proof.

We then shifted to a discussion of effective argument. To understand argument, we need the foundation of understanding evidence and proof. In addition, we need to know that claims are of three types: claims of fact, claims of value, and claims of policy. Although arguments consist only of evidence and claims, the construction of a sound argument is complex.

What types of argument are most common? We considered the argument by analogy, the argument from cause, the argument by deduction, and the argument by induction or example.

If we consider public discourse today, we know that many people use argument inappropriately. We thus devoted some attention to understanding the fallacies associated with argument. We considered the hasty generalization; post hoc, ergo prompter hoc; equivocation; faulty analogy; red herring; slippery slope; argumentum ad hominem; false dilemma; bandwagon or appeal to popular opinion; and begging the question fallacies. The chapter concluded with some additional ethical considerations.

Communication Narrative 8.1
The Death Penalty

Anthony Porter ("Illinois . . . Freed" 1999) was charged in the shooting deaths of two teenagers. He received the death penalty at his Illinois trial. He spent 17 years waiting for execution as his appeals failed one after another. Then just 48 hours before he was to be executed by lethal injection, he was saved by a group of students. A journalism class used its research skills to uncover an unjust conviction. A Milwaukee man confessed to the murder for which Anthony Porter, 43, was charged and convicted. If Porter is cleared of all charges, he will be the tenth Illinois death row inmate to be exonerated. Nor was he the first convict cleared by the students in a journalism class.

Can you think of any reasons why our judicial system—based on the right to an attorney, on legal argument, and on the use of evidence—should convict innocent persons on death penalty charges? How would you explain how these mistakes could occur? What are some examples of jury and prosecutor concerns that might override their attention to argument and evidence? Should argument and evidence reign supreme in the courtroom and on the streets?

Vocabulary

actual examples Instances based on reality.

argument The presentation of a claim or conclusion and the evidence which supports it.

argument by analogy The argument that occurs when you argue that if two cases are alike in known ways they are similarly alike in unknown ways.

argument by deduction The argument that occurs when you reason from a general proposition, or from a generally accepted truth, to a specific instance or example.

argument by induction An argument from specific instances to a general conclusion.

argument from cause The argument that occurs when you reason from a cause to an unknown, but likely, effect.

argumentum ad hominem A fallacy which occurs when you attack the other person rather than the issue.

bandwagon or appeal to popular opinion A fallacy which is present when a phenomenon is viewed as true or right because a majority of people believe it to be.

begging the question A fallacy which occurs when someone uses language to make claims that they have not proven.

character A dimension of speaker credibility meaning that listeners see you as trustworthy, honest, and sincere.

claim The conclusion you wish your audience to accept.

claims of fact Claims that deal with truth and falsity.

claims of policy Claims that concern future action.

claims of value Claims that require judgments of good and bad.

competence Refers to the degree to which listeners perceive you as knowledgeable and informed about your topic.

composure A dimension of speaker credibility meaning that listeners view you as being in control, poised, and relaxed.

conclusion The result of deductive reasoning, which is valid if it is correctly arranged.

conviction A positive emotional appeal based on a deep feeling of certainty in the righteousness, truth, and virtue of your cause.

determination A positive emotional appeal based on single-minded will power to achieve a purpose.

dramatic example A positive emotional appeal based on a story or narrative that illustrates a message in a manner that stirs the emotions.

effective evidence Evidence that is relevant to your argument.

enthymeme A deductive argument in which either the minor premise or the conclusion is implied rather than stated.

equivocation Faulty reasoning based on shifting one meaning of a word to another meaning.

ethical evidence Consists of facts and figures, actual examples, true narratives or testimony that is true.

ethos A mode of proof also known as personal proof that refers to the audience's perceptions of the character of the speaker.

evidence Supporting materials used in a persuasive context.

example A specimen, an instance, that represents a larger group.

extended example Three or more sentences of an instance representing a larger group.

extrinsic proofs Proofs that support claims by referring to objective evidence such as confessions, contracts, and existing laws.

extroversion A dimension of speaker credibility that refers to the audience's perception that you are outgoing, energetic, and talkative.

facts and figures Statements or numbers about which people agree because they are verifiable.

false dilemma A fallacy which exists when listeners are provided with only two choices when a variety of options are available.

faulty analogy A generalization based on insufficient evidence.

figurative analogy A comparison of the common properties between two fundamentally different things.

hasty generalization A generalization based on insufficient evidence.

hypothetical examples Instances created by the speaker to make a point.

idealism A positive emotional appeal based on communicating the highest expectations of humanity, however rare their practice in reality.

intrinsic proofs Proofs that consist of the evidence in communicative messages that justifies belief, attitude, or behavior.

literal analogy A comparison of the common properties between two similar things.

logos A mode of proof also known as logical proof that occurs when you try to persuade an audience with logical appeals, reasoning, and arguments.

mythos A mode of proof also known as mythic proof that occurs when you try to persuade an audience with stories and statements that depict the values, beliefs, and feelings of a group of people.

narratives Stories told to illustrate a point.

pathos A mode of proof also known as emotional proof that involves attempts to persuade an audience with emotional appeals.

post hoc, ergo prompter hoc A fallacy based on mistaking correlation for causation: just because one thing happens after another does not mean that the second event was caused by the first.

proofs The means by which speakers support their claims.

red herring A fallacy which occurs when extraneous issues are introduced to distract attention away from the argument.

slippery slope A fallacy which suggests that if one event occurs, then a chain of other events will follow.

sociability A dimension of speaker credibility referring to the idea that your audience sees you as friendly, pleasant, and likeable.

source credibility Includes five aspects: competence, character, sociability, composure, and extroversion.

supporting materials Information that "backs up" or reinforces arguments.

testimony Opinions that support the speaker's claims.

transcendence A positive emotional appeal based on rising above differences in search of bonding similarities.

Application Exercises

Can you distinguish between the varieties of claims that a persuasive speaker can make? Mark each claim with F for fact, V for value, P for policy, and O for opinion. Some items may fit in more than one category.

1. The best place to live in America is Miami, Florida.

2. Everyone should fight the death penalty.

3. You cannot live without oxygen.

4. The country should zone out trailer houses.

5. You should have some fruit every day.

6. Concealed weapons should be outlawed.

7. Schools should not be allowed to teach Darwinism.

8. We should raise taxes to improve roads and bridges.

9. I think chewing tobacco is good for me.

10. We should all follow the Golden Rule.

References

Americans challenged to embrace change and sacrifice. (1993, January 21). *The San Francisco Chronicle*, A12.

Archambault, D. (1992). Columbus Plus 500 Years: Whither the American Indian. A speech delivered to the Rotary Club, Murray, Utah, April 6, 1992. Reprinted in *Vital Speeches*, 58(16), 491–493.

Aristotle. (1931). *Outlines of the History of Greek Philosophy*. London: Oxford.

Clark, D. L. (1957). *Rhetoric in Greco-Roman Education*. Morningside Heights, NY: Columbia University Press.

Cohen, R. (1999, August 19). And confessing everything but. *The Washington Post*, A21.

Clinton, W. (1993, January 20). *Inaugural Speech*. Available online: *http://www.bartleby.com/124/pres64.html*.

Cook, J. L. (1994). An unpublished speech delivered in Interpersonal Communication 101, Public Speaking, School of Interpersonal Communication, Ohio University.

Cooper, L. (1997). *The Rhetoric of Aristotle*. Englewood Cliffs, NJ: Prentice Hall.

DeVito, J. A. (1986). *The Communication Handbook: A Dictionary*. New York: Harper & Row.

Dionne, E. J., Jr. (1999, February 19). Tax parables. *The Washington Post*, A23.

Espionage scandal. (1999, August 19). *The Washington Post*, A20.

Fisher, W. R. (1978). Toward a logic of good reasons. *The Quarterly Journal of Speech*, 64, 378.

Freeley, A. J. (1997). *Argumentation and debate: Critical thinking for reasoned decision making*. Belmont, CA: Wadsworth Publishing Co.

Graham, J. (1998, October 8). Auto executive Robert Lutz: Ramming through change got the job done, but the cost was high. *Investor's Business Daily*, A6.

Illinois Leaders study death penalty as 10th inmate is freed. (1999, February 14). *The Washington Post*, A21.

Jones, J. H. (1992). A greater voice in action: Women and equality. *Vital Speeches*, 59, 109–111.

Karlins, M., and Abelson, H. (1970). *Persuasion: How opinions and attitudes are changed*. New York: Springer Publishing Co.

Keohane, N. O. (1991, April 26). Educating women for leadership: Drawing on the full human race. *Vital Speeches*, 57(19), 605–608.

Lake, R. A. (1991). Between myth and history: Enacting time in Native American protest rhetoric. *Quarterly Journal of Speech*, 77, 123–151.

Layton, L. (1999, May 17). More people choosing jobs over grad school, educators say. *The Washington Post*, B1, B4.

Lutz, R. (1998). *Guts: The seven laws of business that made Chrysler the world's hottest car company*. New York: John Wiley & Sons.

Maurer, M. (1989). Language and the Future of the Blind: Independence and Freedom. A speech delivered at the annual convention of the Federation of the Blind, Denver, CO, July 8, 1989. In *Vital Speeches*, 56(1), 16–22.

McCroskey, J. C. (1966). Scales for the measurement of ethos. *Speech Monographs*, 33, 65–72.

McCroskey, J. C. (2000). *An introduction to rhetorical communication*. (8th Ed.). Boston: Allyn & Bacon.

Miller, L. (1998, August 21). Grammy nomination, book deal, TV spots—A holy empire is born. *The Wall Street Journal*, A1, A9.

Moore, S. (1989). The elusive peace. An unpublished speech delivered as original oratory at a forensic tournament, Wooster High School, Wooster, Ohio.

Morehead, A. (1990). An unpublished speech delivered in Interpersonal Communication 103, Public Speaking, School of Interpersonal Communication, Ohio University.

Novak, R. D. (1999, August 19). The cocaine question: Riding it out. . . . *The Washington Post*, A21.

Pawlosky, E. (1999). A silent killer. An unpublished speech delivered in Interpersonal Communication 101, Public Speaking, Ohio University, Spring Quarter, in Paul Nelson's class.

Pearson, J. C. (1993). *Communication in the family: Seeking satisfaction in changing times*. New York: HarperCollins.

Pomeroy, E. (2004, February 26). Veterans deserve better from Bush administration. *The Forum of Fargo-Moorhead*, p. A9.

Rogers, A. K. (1929). Prolegomena to a political ethics. In *Essays in honor of John Dewey on the occasion of his seventieth birthday*. New York: Henry Holt & Company.

Rybacki, K. C., and Rybacki, D. J. (1999). *Advocacy and opposition: An introduction to argumentation*. Boston: Allyn & Bacon.

Schwartz, J. (1999, January 31). Reengineering the cigarette. *The Washington Post Magazine*, pp. 9–13, 21–24.

Shields, M. (1998, September 19). California continuity. *The Washington Post*, A45.

Surveys say women still do most of household chores (1994, January 16). *The Athens Messenger*, B8. Reprinted with permission of the editor.

Tan, C. I. (1994). Women's fund talk. In V. L. DeFrancisco and M. D. Jensen (eds.), *Women's voices in our time: Statements by American leaders* (pp. 224–225). Prospect Heights, Ill: Waveland Press, Inc.

Thonssen, L., and Baird, A. C. (1948). *Speech criticism: The development of standards for rhetorical appraisal*. New York: The Ronald Press Company.

Totenberg, N. (1994). Statement before the Senate Special Independent counsel. In V. L. DeFrancisco, and M. D. Jensen (eds.), *Women's voices in our time: Statements by American leaders* (pp. 202–203). Prospect Heights, IL: Waveland Press, Inc.

Whort, B. L. (1975). An American Indian model of the universe. In D. Tedlock and B. Tedlock (eds.), *Teachings from the American earth: Indian religion and philosophy* (p. 121). New York: Liveright.

Chapter 9

Introducing and Concluding Your Speech

*There is nothing more difficult to take in hand, more peril-
ous to conduct, or more uncertain in its success than to take
the lead in the introduction of a new order of things.*
                                    —Niccolo Machiavelli, *The Prince*

Question Outline

   I. What are four functions of an introduction?

  II. How can you gain and maintain audience attention?

 III. How can you relate the topic to the audience?

  IV. Why should you relate the speaker to the topic?

   V. What are the ingredients of a first-rate introduction?

  VI. How can you prevent mid-speech sag?

 VII. What are three functions of the conclusion?

I *am sitting on the edge of my bed, glued to the television, and at this moment
nothing else exists. Mississippi is up by two on Valparaiso with 2.7 seconds left.
The tension in the air is intolerable. Both teams come to the floor. The Valpo forward takes the ball out of bounds, and the Mississippi coach has elected to guard
the man taking the ball out of bounds. He throws a strike to the cutting center at
the opposite foul line. For some unconscionable reason, two Mississippi defend-
ers go to the ball. The center passes the ball to Bryce Drew, Valpo's main offensive
weapon. One second remains. He lets off a feathery three point shot. The horn*

sounds. YES! The basket is good. With one shot, Bryce and Valpo have gone down in college basketball history! Welcome to March Madness. (Wood 1999)

These were the opening lines in Matt Wood's (1999) speech about the annual NCAA College Basketball Tournament. His idea was to grab the audience's attention with a minute of peak excitement at an actual game. This introduction grabbed the audience's attention. In this chapter, you will learn how to begin and end your speech. We will begin with the introduction. Why is your introduction so crucial to an effective speech? The answer is that much of the audience's impression of you is determined in the first fifteen seconds of the speech (Harms 1961). To learn how to develop an introduction, we will examine the four functions of an introduction, review some strategies that you can use in your introduction, and see some examples of introductions from student speeches. Later in the chapter, we will look at some of the same aspects in the conclusion of your speech.

The beginning of a speech is where most speakers feel the most stress, and the ending often determines whether or not the audience responds as you wish. This chapter will help you learn how to start and finish your speeches with confidence and competence.

The Functions of an Introduction

Outside the classroom, someone else is likely to introduce you. In the classroom, you will probably introduce yourself and your topic to the audience in that part of the speech called the introduction. An introduction serves four functions. You will examine these functions along with examples from student speeches. The four functions are:

1. to gain and maintain favorable attention,

2. to relate your topic to your audience,

3. to relate yourself to the topic, and

4. to preview the message by stating the purpose and forecasting the organization of the speech.

Gaining and Maintaining Favorable Attention

The first function of an introduction is gaining and maintaining attention. Have you ever watched a teacher try to teach a group of very small children? As the teacher talks, the children turn around and look at each other. Sometimes they start talking to each other. Occasionally they touch someone. Encouraging children to pay attention is difficult.

Adults are not very different. True, adults have learned to look as if they are listening. Their eyes are correctly directed, and their bodies may not move as much as children's bodies do, but the adults have replaced their overt physical activities with mental activities. When you speak to your classmates, their minds may be flitting from your speech to plans for the weekend, to the test the next hour, or to the attractive person in the next seat. You need to gain and maintain their attention. You have to direct their focus to you and your speech.

Spend time planning your introduction. Because you are most likely to be nervous at the very beginning of your speech, you should both plan and practice the opening minutes. Your introduction often determines whether the audience listens to your message. The introduction and conclusion are the bookends of your speech: If either should fall, the entire middle may fall as well.

In this chapter you will learn ten of the many ways you can gain and maintain attention. Which method should you select? How will you determine a way to gain and maintain the attention of your audience? The principles of audience analysis and adaptation are crucial at this point. Matt Wood, whose introduction starts this chapter, learned that most of his classmates were going to deliver speeches on very serious, heavy subjects, so he decided to give a light-hearted, humorous speech about basketball tournaments. The audience was so relieved that they graded his speech as the best of the day. You, too, need to select a topic and decide how you are going to present that topic—with special attention on the beginning of the speech.

Present a person or object. Presenting a person or object is used more often for informative speeches than for persuasive ones, but the method can be used for both. A student speaking on health food may give everyone a granola bar to eat while listening to the speech. A student who works at a bank may begin a speech about the dangers of a checking account by distributing one blank counter check to each member of the audience. A student who informs the audience about classical ballet may bring a ballerina to class to demonstrate a few turns on point during the speech. All of these can be effective ways to gain and maintain attention.

Invite audience participation. Inviting audience participation early in your speech attracts their attention and interest in your topic. One student who was speaking about some of the problems of poverty asked his audience to sit crowded elbow-to-elbow during his presentation. Another asked the audience three questions about energy and requested they indicate by a show of hands whether they knew the answers. Because most members of the audience were unable to answer the questions, they listened carefully for the answers. One energetic student wrote an Internal Revenue Service notice for every person in class, which summoned each one to an audit. As the student began his speech, each person in the audience opened up a plain white envelope with the unwanted message inside. Such audience participation gained and maintained their attention.

Imagine a situation. You might have the audience imagine that they are standing on a ski slope, flying through the air, burrowing underground, and so on. As one student wrote in her plan for an introduction: "In order to gain audience attention, I will ask them to picture in their minds a hospital scene in which each of them is the patient on the operating table. They must watch their own death and subsequent resuscitation. This picture will prepare them for my topic on a second existence and raise the question in their minds of what actually happens in the interim." Inviting the audience to imagine a hypothetical situation is an effective method of gaining and maintaining attention.

Use audio and video equipment. A student's speech on alternative music began with a one-minute excerpt from a song. A deputy sheriff showed a videotape of a drunken driver being arrested in a speech on driving while intoxicated. A theater major specializing in costuming used videotape of the actors in costume—a silent videotape for which she provided the commentary in her speech—in an informative speech about technical theater. For a focus on sounds and words, audiotapes are ideal. For more total involvement and visualization, videotapes are the answer. Remember when using audio and video that they are support for your speech, not the speech itself.

Arouse audience suspense. One student began his speech by saying, "A new sport has hit this state, yet it is a national tradition. It is held in the spring of the year in some of our most beautiful timbered areas. It is open to men and women alike, with women having the same chance of success as men. It is for responsible adults only and requires common sense and patience. This sport of our ancestors is . . . ." Arousing curiosity captures the audience's attention.

Use slides or film. A student who was speaking on big city slums began with a rapid series of twelve slides, showing trash heaps, crowded rooms, rundown buildings, and rats. An international student from the Philippines showed attractive photographs of her native land. A varsity football player, who was speaking on intentional violence in the sport, showed a film of two kickoff returns in which he and others were deliberately trying to maim their opponents with their face guards. The audiences—seeing the slums, the tropical beaches, and football violence—were attentive.

Technical Tip 9.1
Quotations on the Web

http://www.motivateus.com: The quotes at this site are motivational, inspirational, and positive.

http://cyber-nation.com/victory/quotations: Quotes here are listed by subject and author; a search option is also available. You can even sign up to receive a quote by e-mail every day.

http://www.quotationspage.com: This site lists quotes by subject and author.

Read a quotation. The quotation can be hypothetical, literary, poetic, dramatic, or real. The reading can even be an inspirational passage from a speech delivered by a famous person. One student who was giving a speech about some of the delights of being middle-aged quoted President Reagan's speech to the Washington Press Club dinner when he turned seventy. "Middle age," Reagan told the Press Club, "is when you're faced with two temptations and you choose the one that will get you home at 9 o'clock" (Reagan 1981).

You can find quotations in newspapers, news magazines, and collections of speeches such as *Vital Speeches of the Day.* You can find collections of quotations in resource books such as *Bartlett's Quotations* or *Respectfully Quoted,* a dictionary of the quotations most often requested by Congress and high government officials for their speeches. You can consult specialized books of quotes by women, African Americans, and other ethnic groups. You can also find quotations on the Internet (see On the Web below).

Although you can find quotations by using all of the shortcuts mentioned above, nothing really replaces wide and deep reading, watching, and listening about an issue. Always be sure to cite your sources when you use a quotation.

State striking facts or figures. Facts and figures can bore your audience to tears or rouse them out of a stupor. A student speaking in favor of gun control found this statement:

> For at least a century and probably longer we have been the most murderous "developed" society on earth. Since 1980 nearly 400,000 Americans have died at the hands of fellow citizens—more than the number of Americans who died on the battlefields of World War I and World War II combined (Harwood 1997).

Another student found figures related to her pro-life stance on abortion:

> Of the estimated 210 million pregnancies that occur around the globe each year, 46 million or 22 percent end in abortion, according to a report by the Alan Guttmacher Institute, which promotes reproductive health (Smith 1999).

And a third student had these facts and figures on her speech about prisons:

> According to the director of The Sentencing Project in Washington, D.C., at the end of the century the USA had an all-time high of 1.8 million people in prisons. We have a lockup rate ten times higher than other industrialized democracies. And "the nation's already overcrowded prison systems had to add more than 1,000 extra beds every week last year to accommodate almost 60,000 extra prisoners." (Gainsborough 1999, A16)

These speakers were counting on the large number of Americans killed by fellow citizens, the large number of abortions, and the extraordinary growth in the prison population to capture the audience's attention.

Tell a story. Telling a story to gain the audience's attention is one of the oldest and most commonly used methods. Your story can be actual or created, as long as you tell your audience which kind of story you are using. The following is an actual story:

One method of gaining and maintaining attention is with a story. (Photo: Justin Warren/Daily Bruin)

> When I was sixteen years old, a group of friends and I were showing off for some girls our age at a swimming pool. I went off the dive as I had done hundreds of times before, but this time I screwed up and smashed my nose with

my knee. I had to have re-constructive surgery. After the surgery I remember sitting in the recovery room and spitting up fluids into my hands. I fell back and woke up two days later in a dimly lit room. I realized that I was tied down. With my right hand I located a tube running down my leg and another running up my leg. I had reacted to the anesthetic. My lungs had filled with fluids, and I had begun to drown. Revived with CPR and with lungs drained, I was now on life support with a "swan" running into my heart. On the third day, after two more drowning sensations, I began to recover and was removed from life support. I left the hospital on the fourth day. I was just glad to feel the sun again. (Burch 1999)

Douglas Burch used his own story in his speech, but you can use other people's stories as long as you reveal your source to your audience.

Use humor. Although often overused, jokes or humor to gain and maintain attention can be effective, especially if the humor is related to the topic. Too often jokes are told for their own sake, whether they have anything to do with the subject of the speech or not. Another word of caution: if you are not good at telling jokes, then you ought to practice your humor before your speech in front of the class. On the other hand, if you are quite good at telling jokes or using humor in conversation, then humor related to your topic might be a good option for you. Finally, be careful that your humorous story is not so long or so compelling that the audience focuses only on the funny story and not on your speech.

Some speakers are not good at telling jokes, but they are witty. When you think of humor in public speaking, you should think of the term humor in its broadest sense to include wit and cleverness. Test your humor on friends before trying to tickle an audience—this testing reduces anxiety and increases the chance that the humor will work.

An example of a speaker who shocked her audience with her wit is Dr. Johnetta Cole, President of Atlanta's Spelman College. She was invited to address the National Press Club, a group that probably had never heard from a black female college president. Dr. Cole won over her audience by proposing a toast in black English: "We bees fur'lowin difrunce an' 'spectin difrunce til difrunce don make no mo difrunce," a toast that she translated for the crowd: "We are for allowing difference and expecting difference until difference doesn't make any more difference" (Wallisch 1988). That toast was a clever way for Dr. Cole to say "I am black and I can speak the language of the streets. I am also a woman who is a college president. I would like African American women to become so common in high positions that seeing a person like me as president would not be unusual."

One word of warning: always make sure your attention-getter is related to the topic. Jokes told for their own sake are a weak way to begin a speech. Another undesirable way to start is to write a provoking word on the board and then say, "I just wanted to get your attention." All of the examples in the ten methods of gaining attention are from student speeches. They show that students can be creative in order to gain and maintain audience attention.

These ten methods of gaining and maintaining attention in the introductory portion of a speech are not the only ones. There are dozens of other ways. Just think of imaginative ways to involve the audience. You can start by stating a problem for which your speech is the solution. You can create dramatic conflict between seemingly irreconcilable forces: business and government, teachers and students, parents and children, or grading systems and learning. You can inform the listeners about everyday items they do not understand: stock market reports, weather symbols, sales taxes, savings accounts, and automobiles.

Relating the Topic to the Audience

The second function of an introduction is relating the topic to the audience. You can relate almost any topic to an audience, preferably in the introduction of a speech. This introductory move assures the audience of a connection between them and the topic. You should find many helpful examples in the previous section on audience attention. A student gave a speech on women's rights, a topic the audience cared little about. However, in her introduction she depicted the plight of married women who have fewer job opportunities and receive less pay than their male co-workers. She asked the audience how they would feel under such circumstances. How would the men like their wives and girlfriends to earn less than male co-workers in the same jobs? Most of the men wanted their girlfriends and wives to be able to earn as much money as men in the same circumstances. The audience listened to the speech with more interest because the speaker took pains to relate the topic to both the men and the women in class.

To relate your audience to your topic, you can introduce your speech with a brief case study for which your speech is an analysis and your conclusion is a solution. Cheng Imm Tan (1992), who used the case study opening, began her speech like this:

> I would like to start by telling you a story. This is the story of Sothi, a Cambodian refugee woman. Sothi is a Cambodian refugee woman who survived the disruption of war as well as violence in the home.
>
> Sothi did not come from a rich or well-known family, but life was good. She was married to a man who treated her well, and they had a son together. They lived near her parents who had a plot of land on which her husband worked. Then the war broke out. Her husband was drafted into the army, and she was moved to another province to work on a communal farm. Before too long news came that he had been killed in action. Life became increasingly hard. There was not enough food to eat, her son became sick, and medical care was not readily available. Separated from her parents and unsure of what the future might bring, she decided to escape to Thailand to get medical care for her son.
>
> One day while she was getting her daily ration of water at the refugee camp in Thailand, she noticed a man staring at her. She had caught his fancy. He pursued her. He came to the house, brought her little gifts, and tried to get her attention. When she refused his advances, he became increasingly violent and threatened to blow the family up with a grenade if she refused to marry him. She married him, and together they had three more children, but the violence did not stop. In 1982 they were resettled in Boston, Massachusetts. Under the pressure of adjusting to a new environment, his drinking and gambling increased and so did the threats and the beatings. He would beat her because he could not find a job, because he lost in gambling, because he felt humiliated at the unemployment office. Isolated in a foreign city, Sothi bore the abuse in silence. . . . (p. 223)

This case study of what happens to immigrant women who are victims of spouse abuse became an analysis of the issue, and concluded with recommendations for reforms. A case study that poses a problem that captures the audience's attention gets the audience involved in the issue, and encourages the audience to get involved in the solution.

Relating the Topic to the Speaker

The third function of an introduction is relating the topic to the speaker. In the previous section, you related the topic to the audience. In this section, you will look at three strategies for relating the topic to you, the speaker.

Dress for the topic and occasion. You can wear clothing that will signal your credibility on a topic, that shows your relationship to the topic and the occasion. One student aroused the audience's interest in the topic and the speaker by showing up with a hardhat on his head, a sweat rag around his neck, and a flashlight in his hand. He was encouraging his classmates to take up the questionable activity of exploring the university's steam tunnels.

Other ideas for using appropriate clothing to signal your relationship to the topic are to wear a warm-up suit for a speech on exercise, a white laboratory coat for a speech on chemistry experiments, or a dress or suit for a speech on how to interview for a job. In all of these cases, the speaker's attire reminds the audience of the topic and makes the speaker look like an authority.

Invite the audience to participate. **Audience participation** means that the speaker makes the audience active participants in the speech. A student at Iowa State University figured out a clever way to get his audience to understand how cramped he was in the university's married student housing. Before class he had outlined the floor space of his apartment with masking tape. Before his speech began, he had everyone move his or her chair inside the tape boundaries. The twenty-two chairs barely fit. During the five-minute speech, the audience felt the cramped conditions the speaker described. They were participants in his main message. Being uncomfortably stuffed together reinforced the message and made his presentation memorable as well. Having the audience try the life-saving maneuver, try the dance step, or try the dormitory food are examples of audience participation.

Use self-disclosure. A third strategy for relating yourself as a speaker to your topic requires no special clothing and no audience participation. Instead, all you have to do is reveal yourself, especially how you have knowledge about the topic. Sometimes **self-disclosure,** revealing something about yourself that others cannot see, is confessional: "I had malaria," "I am an alcoholic," or "I was the victim of a mugger."

Tips on Self-Disclosing

1. Your self-disclosure must be honest information about yourself and your experience. A student who "tricked" his listeners by making up a story about his army experiences was quickly exposed by an army veteran in the class. The audience never trusted him again.

2. Your self-disclosure needs to be carefully considered. Revealing private information to your friend is quite different from revealing thoughts, feelings, and experiences to an audience. You should carefully consider the consequences of revealing to a class some information that you would not tell your own mother.

3. You need to be able to handle emotionally your own disclosures. A student who lost her father to leukemia found that all she could do was cry when she tried to talk about the subject. You need to be in control when addressing emotionally charged subjects.

Self-disclosure has considerable impact on the audience, mainly because personal revelations violate the audience's expectations. A daring disclosure in a public speaking class occurred when a mild-mannered young man revealed that he had been in a Louisiana prison on a drug offense—for six years. He spoke with great feeling about the effects of our penal system on an individual. Since nobody else in class had served a day in prison, the students regarded this six-year veteran of our penal system as an expert. Not all self-disclosures have to be so dramatic. Indeed, some of the best examples pose a common problem, such as this speech about forgiveness.

> I remember the first big fight between my parents. Late one weeknight, I was lying in bed trying not to hear the things they yelled at each other. The words and the screams seemed to last forever. Finally, the fight ended with a slam of the door and a shattering of porcelain. I slowly crept out of my bed and walked out to see what had brought the silence. My father stood in the living room staring at the wall. On the carpet were pieces of a present my father had given my mother many years earlier: a statue of an old woman walking beside a shaggy donkey. Now this once cherished gift lay in pieces on the shag rug. I could think of only one thing to do. As my dad left to sit at the kitchen table, I went into the pantry and found our Superglue. Then I went into the living room and carefully found each piece of porcelain. I sat on the couch and tried to fix this broken artwork the same way I wanted to be able to fix whatever was wrong between my parents. My mother walked in with a new pack of cigarettes, saw what I was doing, and began to cry. She sat down beside me and watched. Moments later, we were joined by my father. In the time we sat there no words were spoken. I worked quietly, tears flowing down my cheeks. My parents stared off on opposite sides of the room. Later, they were side by side. Without a word, forgiveness had taken place. My work was done, the statue fixed, and my parents fixed for now. (Stegemoller 1998)

Another student spoke on structural barriers to people with physical disabilities and revealed that she knew about the subject because of a hip operation that forced her to learn how to walk all over again. Both of these students disclosed information that the audience had not known; it enhanced their credibility and captured the audience's attention.

Self-disclosure must be used carefully in public speech. Most self-disclosure occurs in interpersonal communication, when only two or three people are engaged in conversation. Be sure that you can handle the disclosure. One woman decided to tell a class about her sister's recent death from leukemia, but she found she could do nothing but cry. The speaking situation is one that is already filled with a certain amount of tension, and you do not want to overload yourself with more emotion than you can handle. To avoid this problem, you may wish to check your emotions by practicing your speech in front of close friends. Practicing the emotional portions over and over may help you control your feelings when you deliver the speech in front of an audience.

Self-disclosure must be considered carefully for a second reason. As stated, self-disclosure generally occurs when one person provides personal information to one or two others. In general, we do not tell highly personal information to a large number of people. Perhaps the story of your unwanted pregnancy will gain the attention of the audience, but do you want twenty of your peers knowing such information? Do not self-disclose information that is potentially embarrassing to yourself or to people who care about you.

Previewing the Message by Stating the Purpose and Forecasting the Organization

The fourth function of an introduction is stating the purpose and forecasting the organization and development of your speech. This step should be taken late in the introduction because your forecast reveals for the audience the length and direction of your speech.

The *specific purpose statement* tells the audience of the informative or persuasive intent of your speech. It is optional in persuasive speeches where the purpose is not revealed until the end of the speech. **Forecasting** tells the audience how you are going to cover the topic. Here is an example that clearly indicates both the specific purpose and the organization:

> You should start buying your books at the student co-op bookstore because the textbooks are less expensive, the used books receive a higher price, and the profits go for student scholarships.

The type of speech is persuasive. The specific purpose is to have the listeners stop their book trade at the commercial bookstore and start buying and selling books at the student co-op. The speech will have three main points.

Here are some additional examples of statements of purpose and forecasting from student speeches. The specific purpose statement is italicized in each for emphasis:

> Follow my advice this evening and *you can earn 10 dollars an hour* painting houses, barns, and warehouses. First, I will show you how to locate this kind of work. Next, I will teach you how to bid on a project. And, last, I will give you some tips on how to paint well enough to get invited back.

> *You can understand your own checking account.* I will help you "read" your check by explaining the numbers and stamps that appear on the face; I will help you manage your checking account by showing you how to avoid overdraft charges; and I will demonstrate how you can prove your check cleared.

Forecasts and statements of specific purpose can take many forms. They do not have to state blatantly that you wish "to inform" or "to persuade," but your intentions should be clear to you and to your audience.

Demonstrating the Functions in a Speech

To see how the four functions operate together in a single introduction, examine the student introduction in Figure 9.1. The side notes indicate which function is being fulfilled. Notice that the speaker gains and maintains attention, relates the topic to himself and to the audience, and forecasts the development of the speech. Remember that using a story is just one strategy that can be used in an introduction. There are many more equally effective types of introductions. Let us turn next to some suggestions for introducing your speech.

Suggestions for Introducing Your Speech

Even though you now know the four functions of a speech introduction, some additional tips will help you deliver an appropriate and effective speech introduction. You need to recognize time constraints, capitalize on your own abilities, create an appropriate mood, prepare the body of the speech before you prepare the introduction, experiment with your introduction, and prepare your introduction precisely, but deliver it casually. In this section, we will explain each of these suggestions further.

Figure 9.1
An Example of an Introduction

Death Race

Begins with a narrative, a story to gain attention

Role plays a veteran checking out his gear to maintain attention

Story is a subtle means of relating himself to the topic: he has had the experience

Arouses curiosity about the topic to maintain attention

Story employs drama, adventure, and conflict

Begins to announce the topic

Relates topic to audience. Announces topic, forecasts development, and states specific purpose

With sweat beading on my forehead and adrenalin gushing through my body, I solemnly survey my mission. Gusting winds cut through my jeans as a cloudy sky casts shadowy figures on the surroundings. I check through my gear one final time, for a failure of any item can spell certain death for me. Let's see. Good tread on tennis shoes. Check. Fluorescent vest turned on. Check. I take time to reflect on my previous missions. Yes, you could say that I am a veteran. I've been there and back many times. Two hundred or so successful assignments without a serious injury. A good record. A couple of close calls, but never anything more than a sprained ankle or a hurt ego. But today is a new day. I must not let my record lull me into carelessness. I'm ready. The time is now, for, if I wait one minute longer, I'll be late for class!

The thoroughfare is crowded and I can barely see my destination. Cautiously I look both ways, up and down the street, once, twice, three times before I venture out. An opening breaks and I begin to hurry. Wait! A Mack truck just pulled out and is rushing toward me. Will he see the flashing warning lights? Will he read the big yellow sign proclaiming my right of way? As he rumbles recklessly toward me, I realize that the answer is no. I cover the remaining twenty feet in a couple of leaps and bounds. Exhausted, my mission is complete. I have successfully crossed a campus street.

Does this story sound familiar to you? How many times a day do you have to risk life and limb to cross a campus street? How often have you been angered by the drivers who ignore the pedestrians, the crosswalks, and the warning lights? We have all had the experience.

Today I want to discuss with you what can be done to end this terror for the innocent pedestrian on campus. I want to talk about three suggestions that I have for alleviating the problem of crosswalk warfare: closing certain streets, increasing off-campus parking, and installing lights and crosswalks in strategic areas.

1. *Recognize time constraints.* In any speech, the introduction should comprise about 15 percent of the total speech time. In a classroom situation, you are asked to deliver relatively short speeches. Therefore, the introduction to your speech should be relatively brief, as well. For example, if you are giving a 10-minute speech, the introduction should last between one and two minutes.

   If you advance to longer speeches, your introduction may be extended. Speakers who talk for an hour may have introductions that are five minutes in length, for example. In all cases, the speaker needs to consider the amount of time to spend on the introduction in relation to the length of the entire speech.

2. *Capitalize on your own abilities.* As you have observed in this section of the chapter, many techniques can be used to capture and maintain audience attention. You need to consider the techniques that work best for you. You may excel at telling stories but not be very good at using audio or visual equipment. You may be an expert at arousing suspense but uncomfortable when telling a joke. Consider your own strengths and play to those strengths in the introduction of your speech.

3. *Create an appropriate mood.* If you are going to attempt to persuade the audience to be more sensitive in their use of language, you should not antagonize them first by showing them how clumsily they use language now. If you are an after-dinner speaker and humor is expected, you do not want to provide a speech filled with facts and figures and devoid of amusing material. You cannot expect an audience to be crying one moment and laughing the next. Consider the mood of your audience and the tone you want to set. Begin to set that tone in your introduction.

4. *Prepare the body before planning the introduction.* When you begin preparing your speech, do not start with the introduction. If you begin your speech by looking for appropriate introductory materials, you may have difficulty. Instead, do the research necessary for the body of your speech first. As you read materials and interview people, consider the stories, facts, figures, quotations, and humor that you find. Determine if any of your gathered materials might contribute to your introduction as you continue to gather and file information.

5. *Experiment with your introduction.* Within the first few seconds of your speech, your audience will decide if they should pay close attention to your message or if they are going to merely tolerate you. Your introduction, therefore, is critical. Rehearse more than one possible introduction. Consider whether each attempt is appropriate for your audience, your purpose, your topic, and you. Which introduction sets the mood you want to establish? Do not adopt the first introduction you think up. Experiment with different possibilities and be open to alternatives.

6. *Prepare your introduction precisely; deliver it casually.* Your instructor may ask you to script your introduction or to provide an outline of your introduction. In either case, you want to be confident about the first words that you will say to an audience without reading them. Many speakers feel more confident if they have planned their introduction exactly as they will deliver it. They also feel less anxious if they deliver the introduction from relatively few notes. The more familiar your introduction is to you without memorizing it, the more poised you will appear to the audience. In the first few seconds of your speech, the audience will see you as a credible speaker who is worthy of their complete attention.

Mid-Speech Sag

At this transition point in the chapter—between information on introductions and information on conclusions—let us pause for a moment and think about what comes between the introduction and the conclusion.

The chief justice of the state supreme court gave a luncheon address (Moyer 1988). He started with a story of a young lawyer who was out in the countryside on a call when he ran low on gas and had to stop at a one-pump "station" that looked more like a shack. Outside the shack was an old man sitting on a chair with a large junkyard dog at his feet. "Does your dog bite?" asked the lawyer cautiously as he slowly opened his car door. "Nope," said the old man. The lawyer jumped from the car and stepped to the pump when the dog snarled and growled so loud that the lawyer leaped into his car and slammed the door. "I thought you told me that your dog doesn't bite," said the lawyer with undisguised anger in his voice. "He don't," said the old man, "but this dog does." The speech started off strong and ended with an upbeat conclusion, but the rest of the speech—like so many—suffered from **mid-speech sag.** The latter occurs when the speaker places too little emphasis on the body of the speech. That is, all the energy, humor, and excitement were built into the beginning and the ending. The middle was like a tape recording of legal cases and decisions that mainly inspired sleep. In the middle of the speech, the body became largely a collection of evidence delivered with a minimum of enthusiasm.

At this midpoint in the chapter, remember that most of the time in a speech is spent in the middle, the body. Keeping the audience interested in that part of the speech is a continuing challenge. You can regain audience attention sometimes by repeatedly revealing how the speech is related to the audience, because, if it is not related, then you shouldn't be talking. You can try many of the attention-gaining-and-maintaining techniques that are mentioned earlier in this chapter; they are not for exclusive use at the beginning of a speech. Finally, you can keep in mind that it is easier to get an audience's attention than it is to keep it, easier to arouse the audience at the beginning and end than in the body of the speech, and simplest to keep the listeners' attention throughout a speech if the content speaks to them.

You should talk to audience members about what is vital to them—their jobs, their kids, their neighborhood, the threats to their existence, the opportunities that meet their aspirations—and they will listen to you. They will not

❖ ❖ ❖ ❖   fall asleep. The content should be the most captivating aspect of a speech. The humor, the gestures and movement, and the attention-gaining techniques are simply allies in the speaker's attempt to impart information and influence behavior.

The Functions of a Conclusion

A dramatic conclusion can make a speech memorable. (Photo: Mark C. Ide)

We have discussed the introduction of the speech very thoroughly. Let us now consider the ending, or conclusion, of the speech. Just like the introduction, the conclusion of a speech fulfills certain functions: (1) to forewarn the audience that you are about to stop; (2) to remind the audience of your central idea or the main points in your message; and (3) to specify what the audience should think or do in response to your speech. Let us examine each of the functions of a conclusion in greater detail.

Forewarning the Audience of the End

The **forewarning function** warns the audience that you are about to stop. Can you tell when a song is about to end? Do you know when someone in a conversation is about to complete a story? Can you tell in a TV drama that the narrative is drawing to a close? The answer to these questions is usually yes, because we receive verbal and nonverbal signals that songs, stories, and dramas are about to end. How do you use this brake-light function in a speech?

The most blatant, though trite, method of signaling the end of a speech is to say, "In conclusion. . ." or "To summarize. . ." or "In review. . ." Another way is to physically move back from the lectern. Also, you can change your tone of voice to have the sound of finality. There are hundreds of ways to say, "I'm coming to the end." For instance, as soon as you say, "Now let us take my four main arguments and bring them together into one strong statement: you should not vote unless you know your candidates," you have indicated an impending conclusion.

Reminding the Audience of Your Main Points

The second function of a conclusion—*to remind the audience of the thesis of your message*—is the **instant-replay function.** You could synthesize a number of major arguments or ideas into a single memorable statement. A student giving a speech on rock music concluded it by distributing to each classmate a sheet of paper that had the names of local rock stations and their locations on the radio dial. You could also simply repeat the main steps or points in the speech. For instance, a student who spoke on the Heimlich Maneuver for saving a choking person concluded his speech by repeating and demonstrating the moves for saving a person's life.

Specifying What the Audience Should Do   ❖ ❖ ❖ ❖

The third function of a conclusion is to clearly *state the response you seek from the audience,* the **anticipated response.** If your speech was informative, what do you want the audience to remember? *You* tell them. If your speech was persuasive, how can the audience show its acceptance? A student who delivered a speech on periodontal disease concluded by letting her classmates turn in their candy for a package of sugarless gum. Other students conclude by asking individuals in the audience to answer questions about the content of the speech: "Sonya, what is the second greatest cause of lung cancer?" Whether your speech is informative or persuasive, you should be able to decide which audience behavior satisfies your goals.

Methods of Concluding Your Speech

We have considered the functions of a conclusion. You know that you need to forewarn the audience that you are about to end your speech, that you should remind them of your main points, and that you should specify what they should do in response to your speech. How do you accomplish these functions? In this section we will consider four conclusionary techniques: ending with a quotation, asking a question, telling a story, and closing with a striking statement.

Ending With a Quotation

Quotations provide an effective end to your talk. Most speeches that you will present in the classroom will be less than fifteen minutes in duration. You should confine yourself to a brief quotation or two. A good example of concluding a speech with a quotation follows.

Benjamin E. Mays, an important individual in the Civil Rights Movement and a mentor to the late Dr. Martin Luther King, Jr., gave the eulogy at King's funeral. After a moving speech, Mays (in Smith 1971) concluded:

> I close by saying to you what Martin Luther King, Jr. believed: "If physical death was the price he had to pay to rid America of prejudice and injustice nothing could be more redemptive." And to paraphrase the words of the immortal John Fitzgerald Kennedy, permit me to say that Martin Luther King, Jr.'s unfinished work on earth must truly be our own.

Mays' quotations—from the man he eulogized and from the president of the United States who was assassinated only four and a half years earlier—were powerful. He soothed the audience by suggesting that King's death was not in vain, and he urged listeners to action.

In longer speeches, extended quotations can be used. In an inspirational speech on how older couples managed to have long and happy marriages, one of the co-authors used a quotation from a children's book. Since the speech was one hour in length, the introduction, as well as the conclusion, were longer than they would be in most classroom speeches.

Margery Williams, in *The Velveteen Rabbit,* has the last word:

> "It doesn't happen all at once," said the Skin Horse. "You become. It takes a long time. That's why it doesn't often happen to people who break easily, or who have sharp edges, or who have to be carefully kept. Generally, by the time

you are Real, most of your hair has been loved off, and your eyes drop out and you get loose in the joints and very shabby. But these things don't matter at all, because once you are Real you can't be ugly, except to people who don't understand." (Williams 1983)

This conclusion was especially effective because the introduction of the speech used the same book and a slightly longer excerpt. The parallelism between the introduction and the conclusion gave the speech a sense of closure.

Asking a Question

Speakers use questions to invite listeners into their topics; they use questions to close their talks to encourage them to learn more about the topic or to take action. Katie Haas (1994), a college sophomore of German heritage, gave a speech on the Holocaust. She concluded her informative speech with a question and an answer to the question.

> In conclusion, the Holocaust can only be understood when one understands the history behind the horror, the actions taken, and the aftermath. You might ask, "But why study it?" A large part of the world seems to want to forget it, which can be seen in last April's *USA Today* survey in which 22 percent of adults and 20 percent of high school students say it seems possible that the Holocaust never happened. Another 38 percent of adults and 53 percent of students did not know what the term "Holocaust" referred to. As members of the human race we must not forget, because only in learning about the past can we free ourselves of repeating our errors.

You may conclude your speech with a question and an answer or you may leave your question unanswered. Evangelists and politicians sometimes use the technique of the unanswered question in order to motivate congregations or voters to answer the question for themselves and to act upon their answer.

Telling a Story

Audience members enjoy hearing stories. Stories are especially apt in a conclusion when they serve to remind the audience of the purpose of a speech. Bree Speidel, a varsity swimmer, concluded with a story about a day in the life of an athlete.

> Imagine yourself curled up and snug in bed when the phone rings. It is 5:30 in the morning, twenty degrees outside, and once again you "conveniently" forgot to set your alarm for morning practice. Believe me, at this hour the last thing you want to hear is your coach's voice telling you to get out of bed and to put on a swimming suit.
>
> So, you climb out of bed and think evil thoughts all the way over to the pool. If you are lucky, and it is a Friday morning, you will see a few die-hard partygoers coming home from their long night out. But sadly, even this sight is one you cannot enjoy because you know that, while they were out having a good time, you were in bed having nightmares about yardage and butterfly strokes. (1999)

The stories that you tell may be real or hypothetical. The ethical speaker is careful to distinguish between actual events and those that are created for the speech.

Closing With a Striking Statement

Do you remember the student quoted earlier about her fighting parents and the shattered porcelain? She created a conclusion for her speech that was striking in its use of metaphor:

> Forgiveness came to my parents in slivers. They started off forgiving each other for the little things; the shortcomings and downfalls of everyday life. Day by day, my mom and dad grew closer together as they learned to let go of everything that pushed them farther apart. Alone, the slivers of forgiveness were like the slivers of porcelain, scattered around randomly. After the working and the gluing, the tears and the pain, these slivers came together to form a masterpiece of a marriage. (Stegemoller 1998)

This "forgiveness in slivers" ending brings the speech full circle from the scene in which the porcelain figure is shattered on the living room carpet. The fact that the parents mended their relationship after such tumult made a satisfying conclusion to the speech.

A student gave a speech with a clever ending that summarized his arguments and gave the speech a memorable ending. His speech was on car accidents, the wearing of seat belts, and the disproportionately large number of college-aged people who die on the highways. He talked about how concerned we are that an accident not be our fault. His conclusion: "It is not who is right that counts in an accident; it is who is left." The statement formed a grim conclusion that made the main point memorable.

Suggestions for Concluding Your Speech

Even though you have learned about the functions of a speech conclusion, some additional tips will help you deliver an appropriate and effective conclusion. You need to recognize time constraints, conclude with strength, and experiment with your conclusion. Let us consider each of these suggestions in more detail.

1. *Recognize time constraints.* Earlier you learned that the introduction to the speech should be brief; we observe now that the conclusion should be even shorter. Nothing is more frustrating to an audience than to listen to a long speech and hear the words, "And, in conclusion. . .," and then listen to you talk for four more minutes.

2. *Conclude with strength.* You might be tempted to pay little attention to your conclusion because the ending is brief. Although the conclusion should be short on time, the ending should be long on impact. If you have begun with a strong introduction and have avoided mid-speech sag, you have created a favorable impression in the minds of your listeners. Do not lose their respect in the last few moments of your speech.

   The conclusion is the last message you provide to your audience. You want their last impression of you to be as powerful as their first impression. Just as in the introduction, you want to prepare a precise message. You want them to know what your main points were. You may want to practice your conclusion without memorizing the words until you feel comfortable delivering the message with minimal notes, but do not read the conclusion.

3. *Experiment with your conclusion.* As you research your topic, consider whether any of the materials you come across are appropriate for your conclusion. Can you offer a conclusion that is parallel to your introduction, as the student did in the porcelain figure speech? Can you create parallelism with an introductory and concluding quotation? Can you start and end with a question? A humorous anecdote in the beginning of the speech might be matched with another witty story at the end. Do not automatically use the first conclusion you considered. Try several different approaches. Just as in the introduction, consider your audience, the purpose of your speech, the mood you are attempting to create, and your own strengths. Feel free to experiment. Your goal is to create a last, and a lasting, impression with the audience.

Celebrating Diversity

The Creek Chief Red Eagle addressed General Andrew Jackson and his soldiers. The Chief concluded,

There was a time when I had a choice and could have answered you; I have none now. Even hope has ended. Once I could animate my warriors to battle, but I cannot animate the dead. My warriors can no longer hear my voice. Their bones are at Talladega, Tallashatchie, Emunckfow and Tohopeka. If I had been left to contend with the Georgia Army, I would have raised corn on one bank of the river and fought them on the other. But your people have destroyed my Nation. I rely on your generosity (*http://www.americanrhetoric.com/speeches/nativeamericans/ chiefredeagle.htm*).

Do you believe this conclusion was effective? Re-read the section on conclusions and explain how it meets (or fails to meet) the advice that is provided.

Summary

This chapter has concentrated on beginnings and endings, the skills necessary for developing the introduction and the conclusion of a public speech.

In the first section, you learned four functions of an introduction: to gain and maintain attention, to relate the topic to the audience, to relate the speaker to the topic, and to preview the message by stating the purpose and forecasting the organization. You previewed ten strategies for gaining and maintaining attention, you gained some ideas for relating the topic to the audience, and you learned three strategies for relating the speaker to the topic. You also viewed some suggestions on how to prepare an effective introduction for your speeches.

Before we turned to conclusions, we considered mid-speech sag, which may occur when the introduction and conclusion are very strong and the body of the speech sags and drags in the middle of the speech. You were encouraged to pay as much attention to the body of the speech as you do to beginning and ending the speech.

In the last section of this chapter, you learned three functions of a conclusion: forewarning the audience of the end, reminding the audience of your main points, and specifying what the audience should do. You also learned about four methods of concluding a speech: ending with a quotation, asking a question, telling a story, and closing with a striking statement. Finally, you learned some suggestions that might improve your public speeches.

Communication Narrative 9.1
Getting Started

Gerald Fitzpatrick was a successful banker. He started as a teller right out of high school, kept working for a bank while he completed his community college degree, and worked part-time as a loan officer while he finished at the university. Now he was an assistant vice president of a relatively large bank.

Gerald was the resident expert on bankruptcy, especially the ones that occurred under Chapter 7 of the Bankruptcy Code. The bank was concerned about personal bankruptcy because too many people were reneging on their personal loans and then avoiding payment entirely by declaring personal bankruptcy. The home mortgages and auto loans were not a big problem because the bank could always repossess a house or a car. Personal loans for other purposes—to renovate a kitchen, build a garage, landscape the yard, etc.—had to be written off as a loss when a person declared bankruptcy.

Because Gerald was so current in his knowledge about Chapter 7 bankruptcy, the bank president had asked him to address the entire loan officer group for the main bank and seven branches. He knew the information but did not know how he was going to get the loan officers very excited about a potentially dry subject. Then he found an article by Robert J. Samuelson (1999) that provided him with information that he blended into his introduction that he scripted like this:

Fellow loan officers, I am speaking to you today as a person who spends most of his time sorting out this bank's losses at the hands of people who declare personal bankruptcy. To give you some idea of the scope of this problem, I turn to Robert J. Samuelson, the economist and syndicated columnist, who provides the following striking facts:

- twice as many people declared personal bankruptcy in 1998 as in 1988;

- in 1988, 1.4 million people declared personal bankruptcy;

- single women filed about 40 percent of the bankruptcy cases;

- the median income of bankruptcy petitioners is $23,000.

What I am going to show today is that our own bank's easy credit promotions, especially on our credit cards, are one of the most important contributors to the bankruptcy problem. Another aspect is the legal profession's advertising to litigate bankruptcies. And a third aspect of the issue is the liberalized bankruptcy law that has been in effect since 1978. I will suggest in the next fifteen minutes how we ourselves have contributed to the problem of personal bankruptcies, how we can discourage debtors from turning to attorneys, and what we can do about the current bankruptcy laws.

> Gerald used striking facts and figures to create a context in which he could analyze the issue of personal bankruptcy and its relationship to the bank. What other strategies could he have chosen to open his remarks? What is your opinion of his choice to use facts and figures? What would you do if you faced his audience on this issue?

Vocabulary

anticipated response To clearly state the response you seek from the audience.

audience participation Means that the speaker makes the audience active participants in the speech.

forecasting Tells the audience how you are going to cover the topic.

forewarning function Warns the audience that you are about to stop.

instant-replay function Reminds the audience of the thesis of your message.

mid-speech sag Occurs when the speaker places too little emphasis on making the body of the speech as captivating as the introduction and the conclusion.

self-disclosure Revealing something about yourself that others cannot see.

Application Exercises

1. *Gaining and Maintaining Attention.* Think of a speech topic. Then use any three of the ten methods of gaining and maintaining attention listed in the text to introduce your topic.

2. *Signaling the Conclusion.* Watch your professors for a few days. How do they indicate that classes are over? How many of them use ordinary ways to signal the end, such as saying, "For tomorrow read pp. 229–257"? What are some more imaginative ways that your teachers conclude their classes and lectures? Do any of them use methods that you could imitate in a public speech?

3. *Concluding a Speech.* Between class sessions, develop a conclusion that can be tried on a small group of classmates. See if you can fulfill the four functions given in the text. Try especially to develop skill in summarizing, synthesizing, and stating the main point of your message in language that will be striking and memorable. State the topic of the speech and its relationship to the immediate audience. Describe your qualifications for delivering a speech on this topic (i.e., the relationship between you and the topic). Preview the message by stating the purpose and forecasting the organization of the speech.

References

Burch, D. (1999). If I could just have yesterday. An unpublished speech delivered in Interpersonal Communication 103, Public Speaking, Ohio University, Athens, Ohio, in Paul Nelson's class.

Fadiman, C. (ed.). (1985). *The Little, Brown Book of Anecdotes.* Boston: Little, Brown and Co.

Gainsborough, J. (1999, August 25). What happens after prison. *The Washington Post,* A16.

Haas, K. (1994). An unpublished speech delivered in Interpersonal Communication 103, Public Speaking, Ohio University, Winter Quarter, Athens, Ohio, in a class taught by Marsha Clowers.

Harms, L. S. (1961). Listener judgments of status cues in speech. *Quarterly Journal of Speech,* 47, 168.

Harwood, R. (1997, December 1). America's unchecked epidemic. *The Washington Post,* A25.

Moyer, T. (1988, December 13). An unpublished speech delivered to Rotary International in Athens, Ohio.

Reagan, R. (1981, February 6). Reagan's one-liners. *New York Times,* A13.

Samuelson, R. J. (1999, August 25). Bankruptcy for profit. *The Washington Post,* A17.

Smith, A. L. (1971). *The Voice of Black Rhetoric: Selections.* Needham Heights, MA: Allyn & Bacon.

Smith, D. (1999, January 30). What on earth? A weekly look at trends, people and events around the world. *The Washington Post,* B1.

Speidel, B. (1999, April 27). A year in the life of an athlete. An unpublished speech delivered in Interpersonal Communication 103, Public Speaking, Spring Quarter, Ohio University, Athens, Ohio, in Paul Nelson's class.

Stegemoller, K. (1998). Fixing my parents: Forgiveness every day. An unpublished speech delivered in Interpersonal Communication 206, Ohio University, Athens, Ohio, in Paul Nelson's class.

Tan, C. I. (1992, April 25). Women's fund talk. A speech delivered at a workshop titled "Women's Organizing for Freedom and Justice" on April 25, 1992. The speech is included in *Women's Voices in Our Time,* edited by Victoria L. DeFrancisco and Marvin D. Jensen. Prospect Heights, IL: Waveland Press. Courtesy of Cheng Imm Tan, 1994.

Wallisch, B. (1988, Spring). Twenty seconds to profundity: How to handle the broadcast media. *Educational Record: The Magazine of Higher Education,* 16.

Williams, M. (1983). *The Velveteen Rabbit.* New York: Simon & Schuster.

Wood, M. (1999). NCAA college basketball. An unpublished speech delivered in Interpersonal Communication 103, Public Speaking, Ohio University, Athens, Ohio, in Paul Nelson's class.

Chapter 10

Language in Public Speaking

The limits of my language mean the limits of my world.
—Ludwig Wittgenstein

Question Outline

I. How do words provide power?

II. Does spoken differ from written language?

III. How can you avoid problems with your words?

IV. What words should you use in public speaking?

V. How can you use words ethically?

Douglas Burch appeared to be a traditional undergraduate in his twenties, but he was an eight-year veteran of the U.S. Army, a soldier so skillful that he was assigned to work at the most secret levels in military intelligence in the National Security Administration. He was brawny as well as bright. An engineering major, he had been honored with medals, and had been wounded more than once. He was the father of an infant daughter. Here is part of a speech he delivered to his public speaking class, an audience that consisted mostly of 20-year-olds:

I want to relate a little story to you. Growing up I had this one teacher who always had to be the hardest, never made it easy, never gave me a break. To make matters worse, she always gave me the test before she gave the lesson. How was this fair? I did learn, and I grew to love this teacher regardless of how cruel she was to me. Can you guess her name? Her name is life. She is hard and she is dirty, sometimes scary, and sometimes mean. Somehow, she is always beautiful. That is life, and we have no choice but to accept it. We do, however, have a choice to learn from it and to make the most of it. Life, you see, is comprised of a series of little tests and challenges that you learn from after the fact. When you stand back and look at life, it is one big test. When the test is complete, what will you have learned; what will you have accomplished? . . . You have to start living your dream today. You have to start making it happen today. You can't have yesterday back, and tomorrow is not guaranteed. (1999, p. 1)

Doug had a way with words. He turned an abstraction, life, into his teacher. His words communicated his experience with life in a vivid manner because he chose a method—**personification** or turning an abstraction into a living being—that did not come across as a mature adult talking to kids.

Moments later in his speech, Doug Burch (1999) said to his classmates: "I wish I knew the right words to make you understand; unfortunately, your teacher is also my teacher." Composing your speech always ends up being a quest to find the right words. This chapter is devoted to helping you find the right words. How do you compose your speech so you employ word power, so you choose the right words, and so you avoid offending others?

How Do Words Provide Power?

Speakers and writers love words. You will learn to love them too as you learn more about how words work. But first you may need to be convinced that words are powerful. Look, for example, at the old saying, "Sticks and stones will break my bones, but words can never hurt me." The statement suggests that sticks and stones can be harmful, but words cannot. Actually, you might agree more with the statement that "bones heal, but word wounds can last forever." After all, often the words before a physical fight were the provocation for the body blows. Whether you actually hit someone or not, you probably do remember the words of someone who insulted you, treated you with disrespect, or commented negatively in front of others about you.

Words can cause fights, but they can mend relationships as well. Words like "I'm sorry," "You were right," "I was wrong," and "I did not mean what I said" are mending words. Words like "You did a great job," "I'd hire you any time," and "You have a fine future with this company" are words that most people would like to hear. Words can start or stop a battle. They can make you feel wonderful—or awful. Words are powerful. Let us see what else words can do.

Words Organize and Classify

Words allow us to organize and classify, to group and cluster individual things into larger, more manageable units. Instead of having to identify every individual thing with a specific word, we cast them into a larger group. So we refer to cars, tables, chairs, houses, cities, states, and countries. That is how we use words to organize our world.

We also use words to classify our world. Imagine you are trying to get your friend to locate someone in a crowd. The conversation might go something like this:

"I just saw a guy from my public speaking class."

"Which one is he?"

"The tall one."

"The fat one with the red cap?"

"No, the one with a shaved head and sunglasses."

Words quickly allowed you to limit your friend's search for your fellow student by gender, height, weight, hair length, and accessories. Words allow you to organize and classify your reality.

Your speeches allow you to organize and classify your reality. Examine this excerpt from a speech by varsity basketball player Jason Crawford:

> My uncle Johnny grew up in a well-educated family. He moved on to college where he earned a degree in engineering, a profession he pursued to the fullest. This man was alcohol-free the first 23 years of his life. Then one day he decided to pick up a drink. Little did he know that first drink would lead to many episodes down the line.
>
> After a time, he became more addicted and became an alcoholic. Johnny found himself driving home from a local bar one night and was pulled over by the police. Unable to function, Johnny decided that he was going to play a little game of cat and mouse. As the police officer approached the car, Johnny sped off. While trying to get away, he crashed into another car, killing two innocent victims. Johnny was also hurt, not physically but mentally. This episode would scar Johnny for the rest of his life. Uncle Johnny is now looking at life from behind bars. (1999, p. 1)

Our words allow us to organize and classify our reality.

Jason's speech begins with broad organizational categories—well-educated families, alcoholics, police, and victims—but Uncle Johnny moves through classifications: an engineer, a non-drinker, a drinker, an alcoholic, an arrest resister, a killer, and a criminal. Your speeches, too, will use words to organize and classify your reality for an audience.

Words Shape Thought

Have you ever thought about how words affect the way you think? We tend to think in words and images, but most of us have not considered that the words we use can affect the way we think. Do these facts about language make any difference in how we think?

- We have many more words about war than about peace.

- We have many more words that negatively describe women, immigrants, and minorities than we have positive ones.

- We have more words because our variable climate and seasonal food production encourage language development (Nettle 1998).

- We have many more words describing violence than describing cooperation.

Concerning words about war, the *Bulletin of the Atomic Scientists* (Rothstein 1999) has an article forewarning atomic scientists about "the language police" who want to strip speech of "linguistic violence." Mainly what the article discusses is the prevalence of war words and metaphors in our language. Years ago, Lakoff and Johnson (1981) wrote a book, *Metaphors We Live By*, which demonstrated the large number of words that emerged from the military only to become part of our everyday discourse. Smith (1997) lists some examples: "to beat a hasty retreat," "to get off on the wrong foot," and "to mark time." Perhaps you can think of others like "fight your own battles," "he bombed that exam," "he lived to fight another day," "he went down in flames," and "we destroyed the opposition." We are left to ponder whether our warlike language shapes us into thinking in warlike terms that may lead to more warlike behavior.

Edward Sapir and Benjamin Lee Whorf (1956) believed that language and perception were linked. Their **Sapir-Whorf Hypothesis** states that our perception of reality is determined by our thought processes, and our thought processes are limited by our language; therefore, language shapes reality. Similarly, European scholars like Derrida (1974), Foucault (1980), Habermas (1984), and Lucan (1981) assume that language creates reality: that "our knowledge of the world, ourselves, and others is determined by language" (Wood 1997, 366). The implication is that your language does reflect how you think and does create your reality upon which you act. A person with no good words about people from other lands probably has a "reality" that does not allow for much positive thought about immigrants. Likewise, a person whose reality is replete with good words about foreigners probably thinks positive thoughts about them.

The words in your speech describe your worldview, and your words shape the way others perceive their reality. Andrew Robinson, an exercise physiology major and a veteran runner, began his speech like this:

> You and your friends decide to play a late night game of basketball. You throw on an old pair of tennis shoes and eight of you head to the recreation center. After you have been playing for forty-five minutes or so, sweat is dripping down your face and back, and you are huffing and puffing from running up and down the court. You get stuck guarding this quick kid who moves instantly from one spot to the next before you can react. He drives toward the baseline with you right on him. As he nears the bottom of the key, he crosses over to his left to get around you. You try to stop, but as you plant your left foot, you feel your ankle roll as pain shoots up your leg, and you fall to the ground. (1999, p. 1)

Andrew was warming up to a speech not about basketball, but about selecting the correct shoes for your sport. By the time Andrew finished his speech, with more agonizing stories about painful hips, sprained ankles, and sore toes, he had shaped his audience into discarding their "old pair of tennis shoes" and buying shoes dedicated to their sport.

Words Are Representational and Presentational

Your name is a mere representation of you. Words are **representational** in representing concrete and objective reality of objects and things. Thus the word *computer* conjures up a CPU, monitor, and keyboard; the word *cellular phone* evokes a small handset and tiny screen; and the words *Wall Street* represents an actual street in Manhattan where a frenzied-looking crowd of people make financial decisions. Your name represents you but represents you differently to different people. Think of what different meanings are evoked by your name in the professor who calls your name in roll call, your roommate, and your spouse or mother. Your name represents you for all of these people, but the meanings evoked are not the same. What is the same is that your name represents you in their minds.

Words are also **presentational.** That is, words present images, ideas, and perspectives (Stewart 1991; Wood and Duck 1995). For instance, if someone describes you to someone else by mentioning your approximate age, your hair color, your body shape, and your disposition, then the words are presenting or asserting the way that person sees you. Words both represent and present our perceived reality.

In a speech, you can use words to represent or to present. For example, imagine that you are buying a new car and you have a choice of seat covers variously described as:

A. An animal hide

B. A steer's skin

C. Leather

D. Hand-selected, butter-soft, glove-leather seat covers

Which would you choose? All four descriptions represent the same thing—leather seats—but the words in D present an image of seat covers that are seductively soft, not just cow hide. Different descriptors have different **nuances,** or small degrees of difference in the meanings they are intended to evoke. A home, a mansion, a townhouse, a shack, a log cabin, a tenement, and a duplex are forms of permanent lodging, but no one would say that the words all mean the same thing.

Doug Burch, the army veteran, had these words to say about his eight years in the armed forces. The lines come from part of a speech in which he had to explain to his classmates why he is unique.

> I have traveled to and from different countries and have seen the most glorious sunsets. I have watched the sun rise one too many times after being up all night. I have sailed around the Spanish Isles and snorkeled among its reefs. I have shared stories and drink with dockhands along the way. I have sat in pubs and bars with strangers who do not speak English and have tried to carry on a conversation. I have learned about many cultures, and that just because ours is one of the most advanced does not mean it is the best. I am starting to feel unique because I have learned about life, and I can still smile. (1999, p. 2)

Some of Doug's words represent things (mostly nouns), while many others are presentational because they evoke images (mostly verbs and adjectives). You too will use words both to represent and to present in your speeches.

Words Are Abstract or Concrete

Your name is an abstraction; the groupings of letters that constitute your name are an **abstraction** or simplification of what a person or thing stands for. In the same way that the word *building* cannot capture the complexity of engineering, design, elevators, facing, plumbing, electrical, glass, and steel that comprise "a building," your name is an abstraction, a simplification, of what you are.

Scholars called **semanticists,** people who study words and meaning, thought of a clever way to encourage students to envision **levels of abstraction,** the degree to which words become separated from concrete or sensed reality. Professors like S. I. Hayakawa (1978), a Canadian scholar who served as president of San Francisco State, introduced the "ladder of abstraction" to demonstrate that words are not binary, but can have degrees of abstractness and concreteness. The authors think the ladder of abstraction should look like a step ladder standing on its head (see Figure 10.1). At the top of the V-shaped ladder, at the most abstract level, is "living being," followed by "mammal," "omnivore," "human," "female," "teenager," and "Rebekah." Does referring to our daughter Rebekah as an omnivore seem the same to you as calling her by her own particular name, "Rebekah"? The level of abstraction you choose makes a difference in how people are likely to attribute meaning.

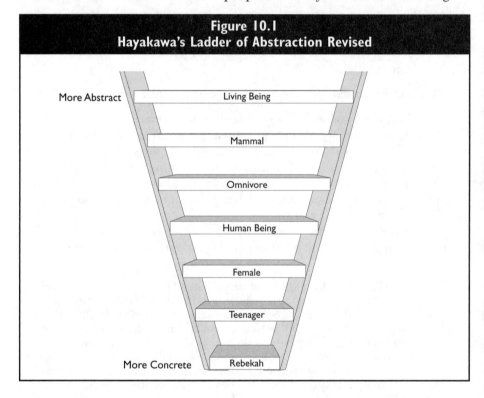

Figure 10.1
Hayakawa's Ladder of Abstraction Revised

More Abstract — Living Being

Mammal

Omnivore

Human Being

Female

Teenager

More Concrete — Rebekah

Why should a speaker be concerned about **abstract and concrete language?** The reason you should be concerned is because people respond quite differently to words at different levels of abstraction. Words fall somewhere on a continuum from highly abstract to highly concrete. While abstract words tend to be general, broad, amorphous, and separated from sense data, concrete words tend to be specific, narrow, particular, and based on sense data. At a recent class reunion, a classmate described his current occupation by saying "I'm in transportation." That term "transportation" turned out to be abstract language for "city bus driver." By using the word *transportation,* the classmate was encouraging people in the audience to perceive him as anything from a pilot to a train engineer to a ship captain—all of whom are "in transportation"—but the more specific and concrete term, *city bus driver,* provided a more accurate representation.

The public speaker needs to know about abstract and concrete language because audiences seem to respond more predictably to concrete than to abstract language. Consider these possibilities with abstract words followed by concrete words.

Abstract	Concrete
I love sports	I'm a soccer player
I drive a late-model vehicle	I drive an Audi TT roadster
Some foods make me ill	I'm allergic to milk products
I'm a drug user	I take an aspirin each day
I'm a homemaker	I have a husband and six kids

As you can see, the more abstract terminology leaves much more to chance. The concrete terms are more likely to evoke the intended meanings in the listeners.

Notice the concrete words in this statement by Emily Pawlosky (1999), who was asked how she felt about taking a class in public speaking:

> I love public speaking. I have taken a public speaking class in high school. I was on the forensics team in high school. I was a morning news anchor with KOTV. This class does not frighten me.

She states her feeling and follows the feeling with three specific, concrete details in a few sentences. You too can learn to use concrete language to evoke more predictable meanings than you can evoke with abstract words.

On the Web

Have you ever noticed that some people have huge vocabularies and seem to be able to express ideas clearly as a result? Language skills are not an acquisition, but are learned each day. In order to build your language skills, write down new words that you hear in class, in speeches, and in conversations. Spend some time each week going to sources such as *http://thesaurus.reference.com, http://www.m-w.com,* or *http://encarta.msn.com/encnet/features/dictionary/dictionaryhome.aspx* to learn the definition of these terms as well as synonyms for them. You will be surprised that small efforts will pay large dividends.

Words Are Denotative and Connotative

Public speakers need to be aware of the varied meanings evoked by their words. One means of understanding varied meanings is to distinguish between denotative and connotative meanings. **Denotative meaning** can be thought of as the agreed-upon, or dictionary, meaning of a word. Keep in mind that dictionary meanings are really an historical listing of how words are used, not necessarily the current meanings. Our everyday use of words can be well ahead of the dictionary meanings.

The denotative meaning of the words *anorexia nervosa* might be "the pursuit of thinness through self-starvation," but to victims, their family, and friends, the term has emotive connotations. The **connotative meaning** of a term, the emotionally laden, personalized meaning, portrays "a relentless pursuit of thinness, a striving for a certain look over good health, and a kind of 'addiction' that can lead to the death of a practitioner." In other words, the denotative meaning is more of a generic description, while the connotative meaning is the feelings, the fears, and the fatalism that the word carries. Denotatively you could call *Roe v. Wade* "a Supreme Court case," but anyone who knows what that case did to political, moral, and emotional debate in this country would realize that the connotative meaning swirling around that case is what made the decision controversial.

You can observe the effects of denotative and connotative meaning in these few words introducing Katie Bigler's speech about a local bar known by many names but apparently known by all.

> I have five words for you: sticky, puke, cheap beer, hook-ups. That's right, I am talking about the Greenery, better known as "The Cheese." This fine institution acquired its nickname because of the charming reputation and standards this bar has lived up to quarter after quarter.
>
> Chances are only a select few of you have not ventured into the Greenery, so here is a little background for those who have missed out. Once you have peeled off your shoes on the entrance tiles, you push and shove your way toward the sticky bar which is filled with minors and overage cradle-robbers. The muggy back draft hits you like a brick wall. Your new cashmere sweater clings to you from the combination of sweat and spilled beer, and your fresh cigarette holes that can never be fixed. (1999, p. 1)

Katie's word choices emphasize the connotative meanings, the appearance, the smell, the characters, and the feelings evoked in the bar. In your speeches, you need to consider the connotative power of words on your audience.

In this section on "word power" you have learned that you can use words to organize and classify, to shape thought, to represent and to present, to speak abstractly or concretely, and to reflect denotative and connotative meanings. The main point you need to remember is that words have the power to inflict pain, to start a battle, to make you feel wonderful, and to start a relationship or end one. The public speaker needs to treat words with care so they convey the speaker's intended meaning.

Does Spoken Language Differ From Written Language?

The man was president of the university. He gave dreadful speeches. His audiences usually consisted of people expected to be there: vice presidents, deans, department heads, and some retirees with time on their hands. He read every word, mostly without looking up. His sentences were highly complex, his ideas abstract, and his words long. He thought he spoke for posterity, not for the audience in front of him, and he published all of his speeches in a book that was little read and quickly forgotten.

The speaker had a problem. He did not know the difference between written and spoken style. He was a brilliant person who truly thought that a well-composed essay made a fine speech. He was wrong. His audiences did not understand what he was talking about, they could not follow his organization, and they ended up fighting sleep as he read his speech from a script.

What is the difference between written style and spoken style? Speaking requires short sentences so you can take a breath, while written sentences can be long and complex because they can be read more than once. Speaking is immediate. If the audience didn't get it, it is gone and it must be repeated if they look mystified. Speaking is personal: it uses personal pronouns and personal stories to make a point. Written work has only the words to convey the message. The speech has gestures, facial expressions, vocal intonation, and body movement. Written work lies flat on the page and has no voice, while the spoken word can be shouted, whispered, or spoken slowly for dramatic effect.

The author of a written work does not know how you react to the words. The speaker who observes the audience while speaking knows your reaction to every word, phrase, and sentence. The writer cannot adapt to your inattention or misunderstanding, but the speaker can see when your attention wanes and rephrase when you misunderstand. You are a passive receiver of the written word and an active receiver of the spoken word. The reader does not know the writer, but the speaker becomes part of the message received by the listener. As the reader, you can give life to the written word, but you largely rely on the speaker to give life to the words of a speech.

You can avoid speaking like the university president by watching how effective speakers speak, by choosing to deliver an extemporaneous speech from an outline or a few notes rather than reading from a script, and by practicing your words with an ear to how they will sound to an audience. You can be a much better speaker just by recognizing the differences between written and oral style. See Figure 10.2 for a comparison of the two styles.

Your words are a reflection of your mind. If you can't think it, you can't say it. If you do not have a concept in mind and understand the concept, you cannot express that concept with words. In fact, most first- and second-year college classes teach you the language of biology, sociology, political science, history, and philosophy. The lower-level courses are loaded with vocabulary, with words that represent concepts that you must understand to know the field of study.

Avoiding Problems With Your Words

Language is powerful and uniquely human. Some animals can communicate, but none can talk about what they did yesterday and plan for tomorrow. Language is also something that people argue about. In the 1980s, an entire movement sprang up regarding **politically correct language.** That movement centered on language used to describe nondominant individuals and groups in American society. The politically correct movement grew, then grew excessive, then became the butt of jokes, and now lingers more in the halls of academe than in the world of commerce. However, you need to know about the movement both because professors still care about this issue and because the controversy grew out of a need to respect other people. Communication teachers believe that respect for others is a value that ought to be exhibited in student speeches.

Figure 10.2
A Comparison of Speaking and Writing

The Language of Speaking	The Language of Writing
Uses short sentences with action verbs and one idea per sentence	Uses longer, complex, compound, and compound complex sentences
Uses contractions, sentence fragments, short words, slang	Uses few contractions, no fragments, few difficult words
Tends to use personal stories, experiences	Tends to use an impersonal voice
Uses concrete, specific, picture-producing words	Often uses abstract words, difficult to picture
Uses personal pronouns: *I, me, we, us, you, they*	Uses *one, a person, he or she*
Receives immediate feedback	Receives delayed or no feedback
Tends to say the same thing several ways—repetitive	Tends to be concise, with little or no repetition
Reinforces words with facial expression, voice, gesture	Reinforces words by bold type, pictures, punctuation
Reinforces transitions by gesture and movement	Restricts transitions to words
Vocalized pauses distract	Does not use vocalized pauses
Uses pauses and silence for dramatic effect or emphasis	Dashes, dots, and empty space indicate pause or silence

From *Speak With Confidence*, 5th Edition, by Albert J. Vasile and Harold K. Mintz. Copyright © 1989, 1986. Albert J. Vasile and Associates, Inc. and Harold K. Mintz. Reprinted by permission of HarperCollins Publishers, Inc.

The Politically Correct Movement

Whatever the origins of the PC movement, one of its outcomes was that many Americans became highly conscious of the language they employed to address women, people of color, lesbian women, gay men, people in wheelchairs, immigrants, physically challenged people, and even individuals who were unusually tall, short, or wide. The concern was a good one because until this movement began, "might made right"; that is, the majority of people labeled others without regard for the feelings of the individuals being labeled.

The power and flexibility of language was especially apparent in how women and African Americans were treated. "Girls" was out, "women" was in. "Negro" was ancient, black was O. K., "people of color" was fashionable, and "African American" was preferred by most Americans of African origin. An important change was taking place: until now the dominant culture decided which name was correct. The PC movement changed that by declaring that people had the right to decide what they should be called. For example, men who loved men decided whether they should be called gay, homosexual, or queer. What words should you choose in your speeches? If you are uncertain what people prefer to be called, then you should ask them, to avoid offense. The notion that people themselves should decide how speakers should label them seems like an idea rooted in respect.

Sexist Language

One part of the politically correct movement that continues to make sense is to avoid **sexist language,** to honor mothers, sisters, and daughters by recognizing their presence in our language and by avoiding derogatory, demeaning, or offensive utterances toward and about women.

Public speakers should strive to avoid sexist language. According to Pearson, West, and Turner (1995), a speaker can use three strategies. The first strategy is to change the subject of the sentence from singular to plural. To say "A plumber should know his tools," you change the subject to plumbers: "Plumbers should know their tools." Using plural subjects usually avoids the use of either "him" or "her" (p. 79).

A second strategy for avoiding sexist language is to substitute words as shown below:

Sexist	**Nonsexist**
all men	all people
mankind	citizens
manmade	handmade
fireman	firefighter
mailman	mail carrier
chairman	chair (p. 79)

Nearly always, a speaker can find a nonsexist substitute for a sexist term, but you should be wary about saying something ludicrous like "person hole cover" for "man hole cover." Sometimes even a good idea can be carried to an extreme that can make you appear lacking in intelligence instead of nonsexist (Safire 1999).

A third strategy is to alternate the use of "he" and "she" in your speech so that sometimes you are using one pronoun and sometimes you are using the other. You should try especially hard not to always refer to physicians, attorneys, and professors as "he" and serving people, child-care workers, and nurses as "she."

Stereotypes and Differences

A **stereotype** is a hasty generalization about an individual based on an alleged characteristic of a group. Walter Lippman first used the word stereotype many years ago in his book *Public Opinion* in the 1930s. Lippman borrowed the term from the new machine at the time that printed the same sheet of print over and over, a machine called "a stereotype." Today the term has come to mean the misjudging of an individual by assuming that he or she has the characteristic of some group—that every single individual is just exactly like the others as in the case of the stereotype machine.

Our society is full of stereotypes, especially about nondominant groups. Republicans are wealthy, Asians are brainy, Italians are lusty, business owners are greedy, and jocks are dumb. The problem is that stereotypes are often incorrect, even as generalizations, and even more often they are incorrect when applied to an individual. Public speakers should be careful not to perpetuate stereotypes because their use is likely to be offensive.

Similarly, you should avoid calling attention to irrelevant differences. When you describe someone as a *female* judge, an *Hispanic* professor, a *woman* doctor, or the city council member *in a wheelchair,* you are emphasizing irrelevant qualifiers about them. The implication might be that people who are female are rarely judges or doctors, that people of Hispanic origin are generally not professors, and that individuals in wheelchairs are typically not elected to city council. Or, even worse, a listener might assume that you do not believe that people from such groups ought to be in such positions.

You should also *avoid humor that is sexist or racist.* A great deal of humor is based on in-group, out-group relationships. For example, people in one state of the United States will construct elaborate sets of jokes about people in an adjacent state. People in Minnesota tell stories about people in Iowa. In Ohio, West Virginia is the target of choice. Similarly, men tell jokes about women, or European Americans may create stories about African Americans. Such "joke-telling" is taboo for the public speaker. The potential humor is more than offset by the probable harm. Privileged persons in the dominant culture must exercise care in how they label less powerful groups, and members of marginalized groups need to exercise care in how they label persons in the dominant culture.

Racist Language

Public speakers can avoid considerable difficulty if they simply follow this principle: Call people by the labels they choose for themselves. Straight people should not determine what gay people should be called. White people should not determine what African Americans, Hispanics, and Haitians should be called. Also, you need to be careful because some language that is regarded as acceptable within a given group is not regarded as acceptable when used by outsiders. African Americans, for example, may use language with each other that is inappropriate for other people to use.

Racist language, stereotypes, and sexist language continue to be features of the Political Correctness movement that deserve a speaker's attention and observance. Avoiding these features and humor against marginalized groups is the right thing to do.

What Words Should You Use?

You already know that you can use words to organize and classify, that words shape thought, that words both represent and present, that words are more or less concrete or abstract, and that they can be denotative or connotative. You also know to avoid sexist, racist, and stereotypical words in your speeches. With all of these features in mind, you may be wondering what moves you can make with the words in your speeches.

Use Words That Simplify

You will often know more about your subject than the people in your audience. However, you must be careful not to use language that reduces understanding. This writer, for example, is describing Senator John McCain:

. . . He would see the heavens fall rather than court Iowa by supporting etha-nol subsidies; who, ever an oak, never a willow, insouciantly goes his own way.

. . . The media call McCain a "maverick," even though he seems to be, oxymoronically, a predictable maverick. (Will 1999, A17)

George F. Will, an excellent writer and a Ph.D. from Princeton, is a syndicated columnist who writes from right of center but scars many a Republican. His "ever an oak, never a willow" is a clever way to describe the unshakeable McCain, but many readers may have floundered on "insouciantly" and "oxymoronically," which are designed more to highlight Will's high I.Q. than to enlighten the reader. The effective public speaker tries to simplify, to ren-der the words understandable to the audience.

Use Substitutions and Definitions

George Will could have substituted simpler words for *insouciantly* and *oxymoronically*. He could have said "indifferently" or "uncaringly" instead of *insouciantly*, and he simply could have left out the word *oxymoronically*, which means contradictory, or two words with opposing meanings, as in "predictable maverick." Substitution of simpler for more complex words is common in public speaking if you are seeking wide-based understanding.

Another positive move is to define any terms that may seem potentially confusing to an audience. One student speaker explained that "blood wings" is a term from the military in an unauthorized ritual during which the wings you earned as a medal of honor are pinned and punched into your chest (Burch 1999). Another student said:

> . . . I am talking about a CD filled with MP3s. For those of you who have not heard of this breakthrough, MP3 stands for Movie Picture Expert Group Layer 3. MP3 files offer CD quality music that can be downloaded off the Internet for free and has a compression rate of a regular music file of about 10:1. In other words, the MP3 can hold 10 times more music. (Resnik 1999, p. 1)

This speaker correctly defined his terms as he moved through his speech be-cause he knew that most people in his audience at that time had little knowl-edge of the subject. You too should be sensitive to the terms that need substitution or definition.

Use Comparison and Contrast

Speakers often use comparisons and contrasts to clarify their messages. This student, asked to distinguish himself from others in a "I Am Unique" speech early in the course first compared and then contrasted his appearance to that of others in the class:

> *Comparison:* I then looked at my physical make-up. I am 5'7" tall, weigh roughly 155 lbs., and have short brown hair. I think I just described 90 percent of the male population at the university.

> *Contrast:* I thought distinguishable marks might help separate me a little. I have over 70 stitches that have left scars, along with two scars from stab

wounds. The most distinguishable mark on me is a tribal tattoo on my back which I had done in England. (Burch 1999, p. 1)

A **comparison** shows how much one thing is like another; a **contrast** shows how unlike one thing is from another. You can use both for clarification for your audience.

Use Synonyms and Antonyms

Another method of clarifying a word or concept for an audience is to use **synonyms,** or words that mean more or less the same thing, or to use **antonyms,** or words that are the opposite in meaning. A **thesaurus** is a source for synonyms; *Roget's International Thesaurus,* for example, has around a quarter of a million synonyms, including 36 for the word *thief.* The source is accessible on the Internet at *http://www.thesaurus.com.* Students who want an inexpensive thesaurus with around 5,000 words should try Anne Bertram's (1997) *In Other Words: Making Better Word Choices in American English.*

Use the Origin of the Word

Technically, the origin of a word is called its **etymology.** Often a word's etymology will help an audience remember the term. For instance, the term *hypothesis* breaks down into two parts, *hypo* and *thesis.* Hypo means "less than" so when you receive an inoculation called "a hypo" you are receiving "less than" a deadly dose so you will build antibodies. The word *thesis* means "a defensible argument," so a hypothesis is "less than a defensible argument." That is why researchers at the outset must explain their hypothesis, that which they will set about to prove.

Telling a more complete story about a word is more likely to make the word and the concept more memorable. Here is how one author expressed his disdain for people who misuse language:

> Being sensitive to the language and scornful of its misuse is nothing new. Long ago, the Latin word *balbus* meant someone who stammered or spoke haltingly. That word passed into Spanish as *bobo* and in turn spawned *booby* or *boob.* And just as we mimic incomprehensible language with the words *blah blah,* the Greeks made fun of what they considered gibberish with the words *bar-bar.* The Greeks were proud of their language, as we all are, and were scornful of those who did not know it. Eventually *bar-bar* came to mean "foreign" or "savage" and in time transmuted to *barbaros* and the related *barbarous, barbarism* and *barbarian.* (LaRocque 1999)

Every dictionary has a brief etymology of the words, but some sources tell a more complete and compelling story. Examples are William Safire's (1972) old but classic work, *The New Language of Politics* and Anne H. Soukhanov's *Word Watch: The Stories Behind the Words of Our Lives* (1995). Safire (1998) is a columnist for *The New York Times Magazine* who frequently writes about language, especially the origin of words and expressions. Language lovers will know his work. These sources and others reveal the stories behind the words, stories that help an audience remember the meaning and the significance of the words in your speech.

Use Words That Evoke Images

An effective speaker uses creativity to paint word pictures in audience minds (Sheard 1996). Dr. Ronald Applbaum, president of Kean University in New Jersey, used this illustration to help his audience understand how the world population looks:

> I recently read that if we could shrink the earth's population to a village of 100 people and maintain the existing human ratios, the village would look like this:
>
> 57 Asians,
> 21 Europeans,
> 14 from the Western Hemisphere, and
> 8 Africans.

He added:

> 51 would be female,
> 70 would be non-white,
> 70 would be non-Christian,
> 80 would live in substandard housing,
> 70 would be illiterate,
> 50 would suffer from malnutrition, and
> 1 would have a college education. (1997, p. 38)

Dr. Applbaum's words created a picture in people's minds that made the concept of "world population" more concrete, specific, and easy to understand. You use your own creativity and audience sensitivity to help explain difficult or complex subjects.

Use Correct Grammar

The way you talk affects your credibility with an audience. Paula LaRocque (1999), writing for *The Quill*, says:

> Language misuse ranks high in terms of the negative reaction and irritation it can elicit from people. Most people give considerable value to their native language and their perceptions of its proper use. Thus, people who mis-utilize language are often accused of either maiming, massacring, brutalizing or butchering it. Society's inherent understanding of being civilized apparently means, in part, the ability to communicate well with grace, accuracy, and without offense. (p. 31)

Even one grammatical error can signal to the audience that you are not ready for prime time. One mistake to an audience outside the classroom signals that you are not well educated.

Bad grammar is much like having a bit of spinach in your front teeth: Everyone sees that spinach, but nobody bothers to tell you it is there. Similarly, outside your speech class you are unlikely to encounter anyone, including your boss, who will say "We are holding you back from responsible management positions because you constantly misuse your language." The truth is that consistent correct use of language gives a speaker credibility because other people assume that he or she is educated and sophisticated. Grammatical errors, even a few of them, invite others to perceive you as uneducated and unsophisticated. See Figure 10.3 for some common grammatical errors.

Figure 10.3 Common Grammatical Errors	
Incorrect	**Correct**
He (or she) don't	He (or she) doesn't
You was	You were
I done it	I did it
Between you and I	Between you and me
I been thinking	I've been thinking
I've already took algebra	I've already taken algebra
We seen it	We saw it
Him and me went	He and I went
Give me them apples	Give me those apples

Adapted from H. Gregory, *Public Speaking for College and Career*, 4th ed. New York: McGraw-Hill. Reprinted by permission of the McGraw-Hill Companies.

Celebrating Diversity

Denzel Washington plays Coach Herman Boone in the movie, *Remember the Titans.* View the audio clip of his speech to the men at Gettysburg at *http://www.americanrhetoric.com/MovieSpeeches/moviespeechrememberthetitans.html.*

What lesson is Boone trying to teach his audience? How does Boone use language to communicate his message? Does the fact that Boone is an African American influence his persuasive skills?

Use Vivid Words

Kyle Messaros (1999) started his persuasive speech, "A Better Vacation," with these words:

> How many of you are sick of the same boring vacation every year? A vacation in which mom, dad, and the kids pile into the family minivan and drive countless hours to the beach, only to get sunburned, get sand in their shoes, and pay outrageous amounts of money for just about anything. Well, if this story sounds like your family—and it probably does—then I may have a solution for you. How about instead of driving south for your next vacation, you head north for something a little different. I'm talking about a vacation spot most of you have never considered, and that is Minnesota. (p. 1)

Kyle's speech was successful in part because he selected words that produced images and evoked feelings (sunburns and sand in the shoes). His words—sick, boring, pile, countless, outrageous—are designed to stimulate. A less inventive speaker might have said: "Want to try a new vacation spot? Try Minnesota," but those words would not have evoked the same kind of response that Kyle received with his word choice.

Use Parallelism and Repetition

Parallelism is the repetition of syntax or structure, the repeating of certain words, phrases, or sentences. Parallelism has striking effects in speaking because the audience gets caught up in the cadences, or rhythms, of linguistic structure. Usually, parallelism is accompanied by increased volume, increased energy, and increased forcefulness as the repeated forms build toward some climactic ending.

Observe how parallelism works in this speech by Chris Meek (1999), an engineering student who was co-owner of Cobat Creek Paintball:

> Do you want to get involved in America's fastest growing sport?
>
> Do you want to get involved in a sport in which size, age, and even sex make no difference?
>
> Do you want an ultimate stress reliever in which communication and quick wits make the difference between winning and losing?
>
> Then I have the sport for you, an adult version of capture-the-flag—paintball. (p. 1)

Chris Meek's introduction also illustrates the use of **repetition,** repeated words, which are an inherent part of parallel form. You will find that using parallel form and using repetition make your speech easier to remember, make your speech more energetic, and make your speech more memorable.

Using Words Ethically

You already know that one of the central ethical issues in the use of language is to acknowledge through oral footnotes the use of another person's words. Violating that rule can result in failing the class or even expulsion in most colleges and universities. You might be less aware that words can be used unethically. Two examples here will illustrate the point: (1) exaggeration and oversimplification and (2) perspective taking.

Exaggeration and Oversimplification

Another word for exaggeration in language is **hyperbole** (hi-PURR-bull-ee), which is a kind of overstatement or use of a word or words that exaggerate the actual situation. To call a relatively normal fire "the biggest conflagration this city has ever seen" is an example. The ethical speaker exercises care in describing events, people, and situations. You should use vivid, concrete language as long as the words do not overstate or exaggerate. The warning appears here because in the heat of a persuasive speech, you might be tempted to state your side of the issue with exaggerated or overstated importance.

A second error in language is **oversimplification,** describing a complex issue as if that issue were a simple one. Political campaign speeches are full of examples. The candidate for senate says, "We'll whip this crime problem with more prisons." The candidate for the state house of representatives says, "No new taxes." And the candidate for governor says "Welfare reform." Bumper sticker slogans rarely solve problems and neither do sound bites. Most social issues are highly complex and most solutions have unintended consequences. The candidate who says "Get rid of welfare" practically never means cutting the billions of dollars that big businesses save with tax loopholes or the millions that go to farmers in the form of crop subsidies. Instead, their slogan tends to mean "take money from those who have the least" and "leave those with the most alone." The ethical speaker tries to examine issues thoroughly, states them as descriptively as possible, and provides sound reasons for why the audience should adopt a certain position on the issue without exaggeration or oversimplification.

Language and Perspective

Your words reflect your **perspective,** your point of view or perception. The words you choose in public speaking indicate to others how you see the world, whether you intend them to or not.

Imagine you are giving a speech about taxation. If you choose to talk about "rich people," "poor people," and "middle class people," you are using language that divides America into economic classes. That is a particular perspective. If you talk about the "struggling young people" and "the social security set," you are dividing Americans by age—another perspective. Talk of the "marriage penalty" and high taxes on single wage earners divides the adult population into those who are married and those who are not. No matter how you discuss the issue, you use language that indicates your perspective.

How is this concept related to ethical speaking? Consider the connotations of the words that you can use to describe individuals who earn over $100,000 annually: "top 10 percent in income," "rich people," "wealthy individuals," "fat cats," or "privileged class." Each description indicates a perspective, but some of them—like the last two—indicate a medium-to-strong negative connotation that may or may not be fair to high-earning individuals. In other words, the words you choose can indicate prejudice, bias, or unfairness toward individuals or groups.

Unless you are careful with your language, you can make serious errors in your depictions of people. Consider the word *Hispanic.* That word can be used to describe millions of people. Some of them are European Americans (Spanish), some of them are people of color (e.g., South Americans of African or Indian origin), some of them are Cuban Americans, some of them are Mexican Americans, and some of them are Puerto Rican. Here again, the ethical speaker uses the description preferred by the people described.

Suggestions for Language in Public Speaking

While we have discussed some of the more theoretical aspects of language, we turn now to some practical suggestions. In this section, we will offer four suggestions. First, you should choose language that is at a level appropriate for your audience. Second, you should choose language that the audience can understand. Third, you should choose language that is consistent with who you are, the topic, and the situation. Finally, you should choose language that meets high ethical standards. Let us consider each of these suggestions in more detail.

1. *Choose language at a level appropriate for the specific audience.* The public speaker must choose to speak with relatively formal or relatively casual words. Nearly always, the language of public speaking is elevated above that which you would use on the street or in conversation with close friends. But the language

choices need to be at the correct level of formality for the audience.

2. *Choose language that the audience will understand.* Using words the audience cannot comprehend might impress the audience with your vocabulary, but language that is not understood by the audience neither informs nor persuades them. If you do use words that the audience is unlikely to understand, you are expected to define, explain, or provide examples.

3. *Choose language consistent with yourself, the topic, and the situation.* If you do not normally use legal or medical terms, you will feel and look uncomfortable using them in a public speech. Your language needs to be consistent with your level of knowledge and experience. The language needs to fit the topic: using overly dramatic words unwarranted by the topic constitutes exaggeration, and understating complex problems indicates a lack of analysis. The situation or occasion may dictate a certain kind of language—you don't speak the same way in a mosque, synagogue, or church as you do at a toxic dump site. The words need to fit the situation.

4. *Choose language that meets high ethical standards.* Your language needs to avoid exaggeration and oversimplification. Your language needs to recognize that words reflect a perspective. Avoid language that offends others because of their race, sex, sexual orientation, or physical or mental disability. Your task is to inform, persuade, or entertain, not to offend.

NCA Credo for Communication Ethics

One of the ethical principles provided by NCA is relevant in this chapter:
* We are committed to the courageous expression of personal convictions in pursuit of fairness and justice.

Summary

This chapter began by answering the question: Why do words have power? You learned that words organize and classify reality, shape thought, represent and present reality, vary in degrees of abstractness and concreteness, and exhibit denotative and connotative meaning.

The second section answered the question: How does spoken language differ from written language? That section included how to avoid problems with your words, how to avoid sexist language, how to avoid stereotypes, and how to avoid racist language.

The third section answered the question: What words should you use? The answers were to use words that simplify, use substitutions and definitions, use comparison and contrast, use synonyms and antonyms, use the origins of a word, use words that evoke images, use correct grammar, use vivid words, and use parallelism and repetition.

The fourth section answered the question: How do you use words ethically? This section warned against exaggeration and oversimplification and sensitized you to your own perspectives.

The chapter ended with the suggestions that you speak at a level appropriate for your audience, use language that your audience can understand, use language consistent with your self, your topic, and the situation, and use language that meets high ethical standards.

Communication Narrative 10.1
What's in a Name?

This chapter argues that words have power, that words evoke meanings in people, and that those meanings have serious consequences. Nonetheless, few observers predicted the furor that has emerged over the naming of athletic teams. Abe Pollin, owner of the Washington Bullets, determined that the team name was sending the wrong message in a city with an unfortunate reputation for flying bullets. He renamed the team The Wizards, which practically nobody likes but which does not, at least, honor violence. The more controversial name changes have involved teams whose names or practices denigrate Native Americans.

Eugene Robinson (1999, August 22) argued that the new owner of the Washington Redskins should change the team's name. "Maybe there was a day when sports teams could call themselves Redskins or Braves and imagine that nobody minded; when the 'tomahawk chop' was nothing but good clean ballpark fun," Robinson submits, "but that day belongs to the distant past." Stanford University changed the team name from the Indians to the Cardinals. Why, then, do other teams keep names like the Redskins, the Braves, and the Indians?

One reason, cited by Robinson, is tradition. These teams have had Indian names for many decades, the teams are identified by the names, and the people who pay for the tickets mostly like those names. The Indian-related names, said the proponents somewhat defensively, were actually a way to honor Native American culture.

Another reason the Indian names persisted is that most people did not think the names were racist. Although no surveys were offered in evidence, the claim may very well be true that most people do not see the Indian names as racist.

The controversy is not yet over, however, because the Native Americans did not see the team names as a manner of honoring them, and the "most people" who saw the names as non-racist were non-Indian. The Native American organizations, as well as Indian individuals, have complained for many years about the names of teams, their logos, and their mascots. As Robinson stated in his article:

Names matter. Names define an identity, announce an intention, set a tone. Names can be bouquets or weapons. Anyone who's ever been called 'Fatso' knows this is true. (p. 5)

Actually, he stated the argument even more forcefully by pointing out that only two million Native Americans are included in a total U.S. population of over 270 million—far less than 1 percent. In other words, team owners can rationalize that the Indian names may be offensive but not to very many people, so basically the casual racism is O. K. He adds:

Is that too cynical? Well, can you imagine a team called the Washington Darkies? Would any college field a team called the Fightin'

Yoruba? What about the Houston Hispanics for a new soccer franchise? What is it, except numbers, that makes those names unacceptable but Indian-derived names just fine? (p. 5)

A more recent dispute over Indian names in the world of college sports comes from the University of North Dakota, where a big benefactor threatened to withdraw his millions in promised support if the athletic team did not keep the name "Fighting Sioux" (Brownstein 2001). Words have power. Words make a difference. And words are what you have to choose for your speeches. Make intelligent choices, understand the effects of your selections, and learn to be both effective and ethically upright with your words.

Vocabulary

abstraction A simplification of what a person or place stands for.

abstract language Words that are very broad and wide in their meaning, making the speaker less certain of the response they will evoke.

antonyms Words that are the opposite in meaning from another word.

comparison Shows how much one thing is like another by highlighting similarities.

concrete language Words that are specific, narrow, particular, and based on sense data.

connotative meaning The emotionally laden, personalized meaning of words.

contrast Shows how unlike one thing is from another by highlighting differences.

denotative meaning Can be thought of as the agreed-upon or dictionary meaning of a word.

etymology The origin of a word.

hyperbole Using a word or words to exaggerate or overstate a situation.

levels of abstraction The degree to which words become separated from concrete and sensed reality.

nuances Words with small but meaningful differences.

oversimplification Describing a complex issue as if it were a simple one.

parallelism The repetition of syntax or structure; the repetition of certain words, phrases, or sentences.

personification Turning an abstraction into a living being.

perspective Your point of view; the way you perceive the world, reflected in the words you choose.

politically correct language A movement which included improving the language used to describe nondominant groups and individuals in U.S. society.

presentational A characteristic of words as presenters of images, ideas, and perspectives.

repetition Words repeated exactly or with slight variation.

representational A characteristic of words as standing for concrete and objective reality, for objects and things.

Sapir-Whorf hypothesis A language theory suggesting that our thought processes determine our perception of reality, and our language limits our thought processes; therefore, our language shapes our reality.

semanticists People who study words and meanings.
sexist language Derogatory, demeaning, or offensive utterances toward and about women.
stereotype A hasty generalization about an individual based on an alleged characteristic of a group.
synonyms Words that mean more or less the same thing.
thesaurus A source for synonyms.

Application Exercises

1. Translate the abstract terms in the column on the left into more concrete terms in the blanks on the right.

   a. A recent article._____

   b. An ethnic neighborhood._____

   c. A good professor._____

   d. A big profit._____

   e. A distant land._____

   f. A tough course._____

   g. A tall building._____

   h. He departed rapidly._____

   i. She dresses poorly._____

   j. They are religious._____

   Now examine carefully each of the words you have placed in the blanks and place a check after each one that may be a poor moral choice because it skews the audience's response in a negative or unduly positive direction. In other words, it lacks honesty and accuracy.

2. Examine the words in the column on the left. Write in the blank after each word (a) its denotative meaning and (b) its connotative meaning. Remember that the denotative meaning is a descriptive definition; the connotative meaning is the feeling or emotion evoked by the term.

   Girl   a._____

                       b._____

   Terrorist   a._____

                       b._____

   Environmentalist   a._____

                       b._____

   Developer   a._____

                       b._____

Senator   a._____   ❖ ❖ ❖ ❖

                 b._____

References

Applbaum, R. L. (1997). World communication association 1997 biennial convention, San Jose, Costa Rica. *World Communication*, 26(3–4), 38–39.

Bertram, A. (Ed.). (1997). *In Other Words: Making Better Word Choices in American English.* Lincolnwood, IL: NTC Publishing Group.

Bigler, K. (1999). The cheese. An unpublished speech delivered in Interpersonal Communication 103, Public Speaking, Ohio University, Athens, Ohio, in Paul Nelson's class.

Brownstein, A. (2001, February 23). A battle over a name in the land of the Sioux. *The Chronicle of Higher Education*, 47(24), A46–A49.

Burch, D. (1999). You can't have yesterday. An unpublished speech delivered in Interpersonal Communication 103, Public Speaking, Ohio University, Athens, Ohio, in Paul Nelson's class.

———. (1999). I am unique. An unpublished speech delivered in Interpersonal Communication 103, Public Speaking, Ohio University, Athens, Ohio, in Paul Nelson's class.

Crawford, J. (1999). Killing us one by one. An unpublished speech delivered in Interpersonal Communication 103, Public Speaking, Ohio University, Athens, Ohio, in Paul Nelson's class.

Derrida, J. (1974). *Of Grammatology* (G. Spivak, Trans.). Baltimore: Johns Hopkins Press.

Foucault, M. (1980). *Power/Knowledge: Selected Interviews and Other Writings: 1972–1977* (C. Gordon, Ed.). Brighton, UK: Harvester.

Habermas, J. (1984). *The Theory of Communicative Action. Vol. 1: Reason and the Rationalization of Society* (T. McCarthy, Trans.). Boston: Beacon.

Hayakawa, S. I. (1978). *Language in Thought and Action.* Orlando, FL: Harcourt Brace Jovanovich.

Lakoff, G., and Johnson, M. (1981). *Metaphors We Live By.* Chicago: University of Chicago Press.

LaRocque, P. (1999, May). Between you and I, misutilizing words ranks high pet-peevewise. *The Quill*, 87(3), 31.

Lippman, W. (1922). *Public Opinion.* New York: Macmillan.

Lucan, J. (1981). *The Four Fundamental Concepts of Psychoanalysis.* London: Penguin.

Meek, C. (1999). Aspects of paintball. An unpublished speech delivered in Interpersonal Communication 101, Public Speaking, Ohio University, Athens, Ohio, in Paul Nelson's class.

Messaros, K. (1999). A better vacation. An unpublished speech delivered in Interpersonal Communication 101, Public Speaking, Ohio University, Athens, Ohio, in Paul Nelson's class.

Nettle, D. (1998, December). Explaining global patterns of language diversity. *Journal of Anthropological Archaeology*, 17(4), 354–375.

Pawlosky, E. E. (1999). An unpublished paper written in Interpersonal Communication 103, Public Speaking, Ohio University, Athens, Ohio, in Paul Nelson's class.

Pearson, J. C., West, R. L., and Turner, L. H. (1995). *Gender & Communication.* Madison, WI: Brown & Benchmark.

Resnik, N. (1999). MP3 World. An unpublished speech delivered in Interpersonal Communication 101, Public Speaking, Ohio University, Athens, Ohio, in Paul Nelson's class.

Robinson, A. (1999). If the shoe fits. An unpublished speech delivered in Interpersonal Communication 103, Public Speaking, Ohio University, Athens, Ohio, in Paul Nelson's class.

Robinson, E. (1999, August 22). Images, antics and insults. *The Washington Post Magazine,* 5.

Rothstein, L. (1999, May). The war on speech. *Bulletin of the Atomic Scientists,* 55(3), 7.

Safire, W. (1972). *The New Language of Politics.* New York: Collier Books.

———. (1998, November 15). Up the down ladder: Getting over the rhetoric of getting ahead—and putting all this behind us. *The New York Times Magazine,* 34.

———. (1999, May 16). Genderese. *The New York Times Magazine,* 30.

Sapir, E., and Whorf, B. L. (1956). Science and linguistics. In J. B. Carroll (Ed.), *Language, Thought and Reality* (pp. 207–219). Cambridge, MA: M.I.T. Press.

Sheard, C. M. (1996). The public value of epideitic rhetoric. *College English,* 58, 765–795.

Smith, D. C. (1997, July/August). Is the use of metaphors innocuous or cause for concern? *Peace Magazine, http://www.peacemagazine.org.*

Soukhanov, A. H. (1995). *Word Watch: The Stories Behind the Words of Our Lives.* New York: Henry Holt and Company.

Spender, D. (1980). *Man Made Language.* London: Routledge and Kegan Paul.

Stewart, J. (1991). A postmodern look at traditional communication postulates. *Western Journal of Speech Communication,* 55, 354–379.

Will, G. F. (1999, August 25). Giddy over McCain. *The Washington Post,* A17.

Wood, J. T. (1997). *Communication Theories in Action.* Belmont, CA: Wadsworth.

Wood, J. T., and Duck, S. (1995). Off the beaten track: New shores for relationship research. In J. T. Wood and S. Duck (Eds.), *Understanding Relationship Processes: Vol. 6. Understanding Relationships: Off the Beaten Track* (1–21). Thousand Oaks, CA: Sage.

Chapter 11

Delivering Your Speech

Discretion is being able to raise your eyebrow instead of your voice.

—Unknown

Question Outline

I. What kind of delivery should you choose?

II. What does "effective delivery" mean?

III. What are four modes of delivery?

IV. How does the situation influence the type of delivery you should choose?

V. What is the function of vocal aspects of delivery in your public speaking?

VI. How do nonverbal aspects of delivery function in your public speaking?

VII. What steps can you take to improve your delivery?

Rhonda Strauss was cool and confident when she went to the front of the room to deliver her speech. She had practiced her speech one time in front of a full-length mirror and two times in front of two friends. Her speech was on note cards, but in her first rehearsal in front of the mirror she found herself looking at the cards too much. Also, her voice sounded boring. During her second rehearsal, Rhonda's friends suggested some minor changes and encouraged her to put down the note cards so she could move and gesture. During her second rehearsal, her delivery was noticeably better. For a few seconds she felt a little *nervous, but once she started her introduction she was so focused on her audience and their reactions that her anxiety disappeared. She was surprised to discover that time seemed to fly as she delivered her speech.*

Rhonda Strauss knew her topic and her audience, and she knew what she was expected to do when delivering her speech. The best speakers make delivery look easy. They do so by practicing their speeches until they feel confident, look poised, and sound conversational. This chapter is committed to helping you learn how you can be as skillful as Rhonda.

You will learn what makes delivery effective, when to use the various modes of delivery, how to use movement and gesture effectively, how to use your voice correctly, and how to improve your delivery. You will find that speech delivery is not as difficult as you might think. You should also find good delivery easier to achieve with practice and experience.

Most politicians, preachers, and teachers make delivery look easy because they know their subject matter well, they know their audience well, and they get considerable practice giving the same or similar messages repeatedly. Similarly, you can learn to deliver your speech smoothly if you understand what your audience needs or wants, familiarize yourself with your subject matter before you give the speech, and practice your speech to gain poise and confidence. The classroom is an ideal place to learn delivery because your teacher and classmates can give you suggestions and encouragement to improve with every speech. To paraphrase a statement in *PR Reporter* (Lesly 1988): The difference between a merely competent speaker and a really good speaker is the difference between a hamburger cook at McDonald's and the head chef at Lutece: both will provide you with a meal, but only one will make a memorable impression on you (p. 1). Your goal is to use this chapter to learn effective delivery and to make a memorable impression.

What Is Effective Delivery?

Effective delivery is a way of presenting a speech that does not call attention to itself. Ray Grigg (1988) writes, "Too loud and we are not heard. Too bright and we are not seen. Too fancy and we are hidden. Too much and we are obscured" (p. 15). His advice is well taken for the public speaker. If your audience is watching your gestures, your body movements, and your pronunciation rather than the content of your speech, you should reconsider what you are doing. Delivery should enhance the message, not distract listeners from the message.

Effective delivery appears conversational, natural, and spontaneous. Your delivery should be comfortable for you and your audience. When you speak in this manner, your audience will believe that you are speaking with them, not at them.

How can you focus on your ideas rather than your delivery? How can you draw your audience's attention to your message rather than to your delivery? How can you sound conversational and natural? The answers to all three of these questions are the same. Develop your message first, and then revise your words for delivery.

To keep the focus on your message, select a topic about which you have keen interest or deep convictions. Your involvement in your topic will allow you to speak about an issue with an appropriate amount of vocal and bodily enthusiasm. If you are committed to the ideas you present, your delivery will come naturally. An upset parent defending his or her child at a PTA meeting needs no notes. The delivery naturally follows from the message.

To begin practicing your speech, concentrate only on the basics—speaking intelligibly, maintaining eye contact, and avoiding mannerisms that will distract listeners. Be sure you are pronouncing words correctly. Avoid nervous habits such as playing with a strand of your hair, rubbing your face, tapping a pencil, or pulling on an article of your clothing. If you are practicing in front of friends, use their feedback to help you discover problems, and correct them in subsequent performances.

As you continue to grow in experience and knowledge as a public speaker, you should observe how highly experienced public speakers deliver their messages. How do they appear conversational and yet inviting to their audiences through voice inflection and body movements? What do they do to enhance the impact of their ideas? Which of these techniques can you adapt to your own speeches? Which aspect of other people's speaking styles do you want to avoid? Both positive and negative examples will help you become more effective.

What Are Four Modes of Delivery?

The four modes of delivering a speech are (1) extemporaneous, (2) memorized, (3) manuscript, and (4) impromptu. While each mode is appropriate for different topics, audiences, speakers, and situations, your instructor will identify which mode is appropriate for your assignments.

Extemporaneous Mode

The **extemporaneous mode** occurs when a speaker delivers a speech from an outline or from brief notes. This mode of delivery is most commonly taught in the public speaking classroom. As we shall determine, the advantages of extemporaneous delivery far outweigh the disadvantages for the beginning public speaker. Indeed, for most speakers, this mode is the top choice.

Extemporaneous speaking sounds conversational, looks spontaneous, and appears effortless. However, extemporaneous speaking requires considerable effort. A speaker selects a topic appropriate for the audience, completes research on the topic, organizes the main points and supporting materials, practices the speech with a working or key word outline, and finally delivers the speech with maximum eye contact, appropriate gestures, and motivated movement. The speaker may occasionally glance at notes, but the emphasis is on communicating a message to an audience.

You may have experienced extemporaneous speaking without realization. Have you ever prepared for a class by reading the assignment, caught the drift of the professor's questions, jotted a few words on your notes, and given an answer in class? Your answer was a brief, extemporaneous speech. Have you ever sat in a meeting about an issue you knew something about, written a few phrases to remind you of your line of argument, and then addressed the group with your point of view? Your "speech" was extemporaneous because it included your background preparation, an organization of your ideas, brief reminders, and a conversational delivery.

An extemporaneous speech is not practiced to the point of memorization. In fact, the speaker never repeats the message in exactly the same words even in practice. The idea is to keep the content flexible enough to adapt to the audience. If the audience appears puzzled by something you say, then you can include a definition, a description, or an example to clarify your position. Audience members like to be talked with, not lectured at, read to, or talked down to.

The extemporaneous mode is also different from the manuscript mode of delivery. The individual who uses a manuscript has every word written down in a text that looks much like a written report. The person who uses the extemporaneous mode has only brief notes, sometimes including little more than key words or phrases that remind the speaker of a story, a concept, or some historical information.

What are the advantages of the extemporaneous mode of delivery? First, this mode is the most versatile: The speaker, free from notes, can engage in excellent eye contact. This eye contact allows careful audience analysis and immediate audience adaptation. Second, and unlike the impromptu speech, extemporaneous speaking demands attention to all aspects of public speaking preparation. The speaker has an opportunity to consider the important dimensions of selecting a topic, determining a purpose, doing careful research, identifying supporting materials, organizing the speech appropriately, and using language in a spoken style that best communicates the message. In short, the extemporaneous speech allows high-quality communication.

The extemporaneous method of speaking appears spontaneous in spite of all the speaker's preparation. (Photo: Peggy Harrison/Courtesy of Elaine Lundberg)

Third, extemporaneous speaking invites bodily movement, gestures, and rapid response to audience feedback. The speaker can add or delete information based on the audience's responses.

Fourth, the extemporaneous speech is more likely to sound conversational because the speaker is not reciting scripted words. The language, then, is more inviting because the speaker who is talking with the audience, not at the audience, creates the words. Fifth, in case you get lost and lose your place in the speech, an outline is easier to manage than is a manuscript of a speech.

What are the disadvantages of the extemporaneous speech? If the speaker must be careful that every word needs to be exact, the speaker might more appropriately use the memorized or manuscript mode. If the speaker has no time to prepare, then the impromptu speech may be necessary. Under most circumstances, however, the extemporaneous mode is the speech method of choice.

Memorized Mode

The **memorized mode** of delivery is one in which a speaker has committed a speech to memory. This mode entails more than just knowing all of the words; instead, the mode usually involves the speaker's rehearsal of gestures, eye contact, and movement. The speaker achieves this mastery of words and movement by practicing a speech over and over in much the same way that an actor masters a dramatic script.

Oratory contests, the lecture circuit, and banquet speeches are common places for witnessing the memorized mode. Ceremonial occasions, where little audience or topic adaptation is expected or needed, invite memorization. Campus lecturers can earn $5,000 to $20,000 or more a night for merely filling in the name of a different college in their standard speech. Politicians usually have a stock speech that they have delivered so many times that they have every word memorized. Some speakers have delivered the same speech so many times that they even know when and how long the audience is going to applaud, laugh, or respond.

What are the advantages of the memorized method of presenting a speech? The main advantage is that this mode permits maximum use of delivery skills: every variation in the voice can be mastered, every oral paragraph stated in correct cadence, every word correctly pronounced at the right volume. With a memorized speech, you have continuous eye contact and you eliminate a search for words. Because no notes are used, bodily movements and gestures are freer.

However, the memorized mode has three disadvantages.

1. Memorization permits little or no adaptation during delivery. The speaker is likely to focus more on the internalized manuscript than on the listeners. If the audience appears to have missed a point, the speaker has difficulty explaining the point in greater detail.

2. A second disadvantage is that recovery is more difficult if you make a mistake: if you forget a line, you have to search for the exact place where you dropped your line.

3. A third disadvantage, especially for beginning speakers, is that a speech sometimes *sounds* memorized: the wording is too smooth, the pacing too contrived, and the speech is too much of a performance instead of a communicative experience. The beginning speaker is more likely to be disadvantaged than advantaged by using the memorized method. However, later on you may find a place for the memorized speech in your public speaking repertoire. In some formal situations later in your speaking career, you may turn to the memorized speech. Some formal situations, such as commencement addresses, routine political campaign speeches, and repeated rituals and ceremonies call for little adaptation, making memorization a good choice.

Manuscript Mode

The **manuscript mode** of delivering a speech occurs when a speaker writes out the complete speech in advance and then uses that manuscript to deliver the speech. The manuscript method is most useful when a speaker is to be precise, must avoid error, and must defend every word. A president who delivers a foreign policy speech in which the slip of a word could start a war, a minister who carefully documents a sermon with biblical quotations, and a politician who releases information to the press are examples of speakers who might adopt this mode.

Many professors lecture from a manuscript. At some point they have written out their lecture. Sometimes professors transform their lectures into textbooks. In any case, as a student you have seen many manuscript speeches.

What are the advantages of the manuscript speech? Generally, the complete manuscript prevents slips of the tongue, poor wording, and distortion. Manuscripts often boost the confidence of beginning speakers because they need the security of their manuscript.

The disadvantages outweigh the advantages, however. While using a manuscript might make the beginning speaker feel more confident, the delivery often suffers. Among the problems engendered by manuscripts are these:

1. Manuscripts frequently reduce eye contact because the speaker is reading the script rather than observing the audience.

2. The speaker may also use fewer gestures. Being bonded to the podium and the script prevents the speaker from gesturing to emphasize or illustrate points.

3. Vocal variety may be lacking as well, because much of the speech is being read.

4. The pacing of the speech may be too rapid or too slow for the audience. The speaker will sound inappropriate because written style is markedly different from a spoken style. Instead of sounding conversational, the speech will sound like an essay being read.

5. The manuscript method also hinders audience adaptation. The speaker is not watching the audience; to observe and respond to audience feedback is difficult. In general, the manuscript method is not recommended for most public speaking situations.

When you answer a question in class, you are giving a brief impromptu speech. (Photo: Justin Warren/*Daily Bruin*)

Impromptu Mode

The word *impromptu* means "in readiness." When you give an impromptu speech, you are speaking "on the spur of the moment." The **impromptu mode** entails giving a speech without advance preparation. Unlike the extemporaneous mode, the impromptu method involves no planning, preparation, or practice. You may be ready for an impromptu speech because of your reading, experience, and background, but you do not have any other aids to help you know what to say.

You have already delivered impromptu speeches. When your teacher calls on you to answer a question, your answer—if you have one—is impromptu. You were ready because you had read the assignment or had prepared for class, but you probably had not written out an answer or certain key words. When someone asks you to introduce yourself, explain something at a meeting, reveal what you know about a particular subject, or give directions, you are delivering your answer in an impromptu fashion.

What are the advantages of the impromptu method? One advantage is that this mode reveals your skill in unplanned circumstances. In a job interview, you might be asked to answer some questions for which you had not specifically prepared. Your impromptu answers may tell a potential employer more about you than if you were given the questions ahead of time and had prepared your answers. Similarly the student who can give an accurate, complete answer to a difficult question in class shows a mastery of the subject matter that is, in some ways, more impressive than in an exam or another situation in which the student may give partially planned answers.

Another advantage of the impromptu mode is that the method provides you with opportunities to think on your feet, to be spontaneous. As you engage in impromptu speaking situations, you learn how to quickly identify the important points in the information you wish to share or the major arguments in the persuasive appeals you offer. People in our culture need to be able to give impromptu speeches at everything from fraternity, sorority, or residence hall meetings to social clubs and business meetings.

The impromptu speech also has disadvantages. The primary problem is that spontaneity discourages audience analysis, planned research, and detailed preparation. Most people who are seeking to gain employment, trying to sell a product, or aspiring to academic honors should not risk delivering an impromptu speech. Such circumstances require greater preparation. An impromptu speech can consist of a poor answer as easily as a good one. The lack of planning makes the outcome of the impromptu method of speaking uncertain.

Your mode of delivery must be appropriate for you, your topic, the audience, and the situation. Memorizing five pages of print may not be your style. A manuscript speech is out of place in a dormitory meeting, a discussion among class members, or any informal gathering. Ultimately the method of delivery is not the crucial feature of your speech. In a study to determine whether the extemporaneous or the manuscript method is more effective, two researchers concluded that the method of delivery does not determine effectiveness. The speaker's ability is more important. Some speakers are more effective with extemporaneous speeches than with manuscript speeches, but others use both methods with equal effectiveness (Hildebrandt and Stevens 1963).

Mode of Delivery, Amount of Preparation, and Need for Notes

Mode of Delivery	Need for Notes	Amount of Preparation
Extemporaneous	Low	High
Memorized	None	Very High
Manuscript	High	High
Impromptu	None	None

❖ ❖ ❖ ❖   ## How Can You Use Your Voice Effectively?

How you use your voice is more of a concern in public speaking than in conversation. For example, when you converse with your friends on campus, do you focus on how loud you are talking, on whether or not you are looking directly at your listeners, on your hand and body movements, and on the rate and pitch of your voice? Probably not, for most people. These delivery features are all a natural part of conversing. You don't even think about them. Effective public speakers learn to speak in front of an audience as if they are having a conversation. The voice and movements are a natural accompaniment for the words. In fact, some teachers believe that the best way to improve delivery is not to emphasize it directly (Walter and Scott 1969). Instead, these teachers encourage students to let effective delivery flow from the message, the audience, and the situation.

As you study delivery, you will examine this skill in parts, but remember that delivery and the message comprise an organic whole. Message and delivery are interrelated parts of a system. If the "what you say" is important to you and to your audience, the "how you say it" will not demand your attention. Like Rhonda Strauss in the introduction to this chapter, you will be so busy trying to communicate your message that you will gesture, move, look, and sound like a very competent speaker.

We will examine eight vocal aspects of delivery, but the first four—rate, pause, duration, and rhythm—can all be subsumed under the aegis of time because they are related to the speed, tempo, and punctuation of a speech.

Celebrating Diversity

One of the most publicized hate crimes in the last decade was the murder of Matthew Shepard. Because he was gay, Matthew was brutally murdered while a student at the University of Montana. Since Matthew's death on October 12, 1998, his mother has traveled the world speaking to audiences about hate crimes. Judy Shepard was not a public speaker before Matthew's death, but is now an experienced and powerful speaker. Because of the passion that she feels about the topic, she uses her body and voice to communicate clearly with audiences. Do you hold passion about a particular cause? Consider your strong feelings as you determine a speech topic. You will find that your delivery will improve because of your stance on the topic.

Adjust Your Rate to Content, Audience, and Situation

Rate, the first vocal characteristic of delivery, is the speed of delivery. Normally American speakers speak at a rate between 125 and 190 words per minute, but audiences can comprehend spoken language much faster. Speech rate improves the speaker's credibility and rapid speech improves persuasion (Miller 1976). In another study, students shortened their pauses and increased their speaking rates from 126 to 172 words per minute. The increased rate affected neither the audience's comprehension nor evaluation of the speakers' delivery (Diehl, White, and Burk 1959). Thus, faster speaking can be better speaking.

Instructors often caution beginning speakers to slow down. The reason for caution is that beginning speakers frequently vent their anxiety by speaking very rapidly. A nervous speaker makes the audience nervous as well. On the other hand, fluency comes from confidence. A speaker who is accustomed to audiences and knows the subject matter well may speak at a brisk rate without appearing to be nervous. Effective speakers sound natural, conversational, and flexible. They can speak rapidly or slowly, depending on the message, the audience, and the situation.

The essential point, not revealed by the studies, is that speaking rate needs to be adapted to the speaker, audience, situation, and content of the speech. First, become comfortable with your rate of speaking. If you normally speak rather slowly, you might feel awkward talking like a competitive debater. If you normally speak at a rapid pace, you might feel uncomfortable speaking more slowly. As you learn to speak publicly, you will probably find a rate that is appropriate for you. Second, adapt your rate to the audience and situation. A grade-school teacher does not rip through a fairy tale; the audience is just learning how to comprehend words. A public speaker addressing a large audience without a microphone might speak more distinctly and cautiously to make sure the audience comprehends her words. Martin Luther King, Jr., in his famous "I have a dream" speech, began his address at a slow rate, under 100 words per minute, but as he became more passionately involved in his topic and as his audience responded, he finished at almost 150 words per minute.

The content of your speech may determine your rate of delivery. A story to illustrate a point can be understood at a faster rate than can a string of statistics or a complicated argument. The rate should depend on the effect you seek. Telling a story of suspense and intrigue would be difficult at a high rate of speed. Rarely does speaking "too fast" refer to words per minute; instead, "too fast" usually means the rate at which new information is presented without being understood. Effective public speakers adjust their rate according to their own comfort, the audience, the situation, and the content of their speeches.

Use Pause for Effect

A second vocal characteristic is the **pause**—a brief silence for effect. Speeches are often stereotyped as a steady stream of verbiage, yet a public speaker can use pauses and silences for dramatic effect and to interest the audience in content. You might begin a speech with rhetorical questions: "Have you had a cigarette today? (Pause) Have you had two or three? Ten or eleven? (Pause) Do you know what your habit is costing you a year? (Brief pause) A decade? (Brief pause) A lifetime? (Longer pause)" After each question, a pause allows each member of the audience to answer the question in his or her own mind. Questions like these queries are called **rhetorical questions,** or questions for which you do not really expect an oral answer.

Another kind of pause—the **vocalized pause**—is really not silent at all. Instead, this kind of pause is a way of delaying with sound. The vocalized pause can negatively affect an audience's perception of the speaker's competence and dynamism. The "ahhhs," "nows," "you knows," and "whatevers" of a novice speaker are annoying and distracting to most audiences. Unfortunately, even some highly experienced speakers have the habit of filling silences with vocalized pauses.

One organization teaches public speaking by having members of the audience drop a marble into a can every time a speaker uses a vocalized pause. The resulting punishment—the clanging of the cans during the speech—is designed to break the habit. A more humane method might be to rehearse your speech for a friend who can signal you gently every time you vocalize a pause. One speech teacher helps her students eliminate vocalized pauses by rigging a small red light on the lectern. Every time a student speaker uses a vocalized pause, the instructor hits the light for a moment. Do not be afraid of silence; most audiences would prefer a little silence to a vocalized pause.

Use Duration for Attention

Duration refers to how long something lasts, and, in a speech, on the microlevel it can refer to how long the sounds last and on the macrolevel to how long various parts of the speech last. Whereas rate refers to speed of speaking, duration refers to how long you dwell on your words. An anchorperson who says, "Tonight, I am speaking to you from London" is likely to say it by caressing every word but might deliver other parts of the newscast in rapid-fire fashion. Dwelling on the sound of your words can have dramatic impact; the duration gives the words a sense of importance.

Similarly, duration can refer to the parts of a speech: how long you spend on the introduction, the main points, the examples, and the presentational aids. The duration of most introductions is usually relatively short, the body relatively longer, and the conclusion shortest of all. The duration should be related to importance; you want to stay longest on the main parts of your message and their support material and only briefly on the least important parts.

Use Rhythm to Establish Tempo

Rhythm refers to the tempo of a speech. All of the linear arts seem to have this characteristic. A novel or play starts slowly as the author introduces the characters, establishes the plot, and describes the scene. Then the emphasis shifts to the development of the plot and typically accelerates toward a conclusion, which brings the novel to a close. A musical piece also has some of these characteristics, though music could be said to consist entirely of rhythm.

In a speech, the rhythm usually starts off slowly as the speaker gives clues about who he is, what he is going to speak about, and how he is going to cover the topic. During the body of the speech, the tempo accelerates, with verbal punctuation indicating what is most important. The conclusion typically slows in review as the speech draws to a close. You can practically hear the drum rolls and trumpets on the important parts as the speech marches through time.

The rhythm of a speech includes not only its overall rhythm—the tempo of the major parts—but also the words, sentences, and paragraphs. One example of rhythm is the use of repetitious sounds as in the case of alliteration, the repetition of the initial sounds of words. For instance, it is more memorable to say "color, clarity, and carats characterize a good diamond" than to say "brightness, transparency, and weight give a diamond value."

Another example of rhythm occurs in sentences when initial words are repeated: "I served my country because I am a patriot; I served my country because I saw it as my duty; and I served my country because its protection is my first concern." Similarly you can achieve rhythm with rhetorical devices, such as antithesis: "Not because I loved Octavius less, but because I loved Rome more."

Use Pitch for Expression

Pitch is the highness or lowness of a speaker's voice, its upward and downward inflection, the melody produced by the voice. Pitch is what makes the difference between the "Ohhh" that you utter when you earn a poor grade on an exam and the "Ohhh" that you say when you see someone really attractive. The "Ohhh" looks the same in print, but when the notes become music, the difference in the two expressions is vast. The pitch of your voice can make you sound animated, lively, and vivacious, or it can make you sound dull, listless, and monotonous. As a speaker, you can learn to avoid the two extremes: you can avoid the lack of pitch changes that results in a monotone and the repetitious pitch changes that result in a singsong delivery. The best public speakers use the full range of their normal pitch. They know when to purr and when to roar, and when to vary their pitch between.

Pitch control does more than make a speech aesthetically pleasing. One of the more important features of pitch control is that it can be used to alter the way an audience responds to words. Many subtle changes in meaning are accomplished by pitch changes. Your pitch tells an audience whether the words are a statement or question, whether they are sarcastic or ironic, and whether you are expressing doubt, determination, or surprise.

You learn pitch control by constant practice. An actor who is learning to say a line has to practice it many times, in many ways, before he can be assured that most people in the audience will understand the words as he intends them. A public speaker rehearses a speech in front of a sympathetic audience to receive feedback on whether the words are being understood as she intends them. Perhaps you sound angry or brusque when you do not intend to. Maybe you sound cynical when you intend to sound doubtful. Possibly you sound frightened when you are only surprised. You may not be the best judge of how you sound to others. Therefore, trust other people's evaluations of how you sound. Practicing pitch is a way of achieving control over this important aspect of delivery.

Use Volume for Emphasis

A sixth vocal characteristic of delivery is **volume,** the relative loudness or softness of your voice. In conversation you are accustomed to speaking at an arm's length. When you stand in front of an audience, some of the listeners may be quite close to you, but others may be some distance away. Beginning speakers are often told to **project,** to increase their volume so that all may hear the speech. Interestingly, students who only hours or minutes before were speaking loudly enough for taxi drivers, roommates, and family members to hear become quiet in front of their classmates. Projection means adjusting your volume appropriately for the subject, the audience, and the situation.

Volume is more than just projection, however. Variations in volume can convey emotion, importance, suspense, and subtle nuances of meaning. You whisper a secret in conversation, and you stage whisper in front of an audience to signal conspiratorial intent. You speak loudly and strongly on important points and let your voice carry your conviction. An orchestra never plays so quietly that the patrons cannot hear the music, but musicians vary their volume for emphasis. Similarly, public speakers who consider the voice an instrument learn how to speak softly, loudly—and at every volume in between—to convey their intended meaning.

Use Enunciation for Clarity

Enunciation, the seventh vocal aspect of delivery, is the pronunciation and articulation of words. **Pronunciation** is the production of the sounds of a word. **Articulation** is the physiological process of creating the sounds. Because your reading vocabulary is larger than your speaking vocabulary, you may use words in your speeches that you have never heard spoken before. To deliver unfamiliar words is risky. Rather than erring in public, practice your speech with a friend, roommate, or spouse who can tell you when you make a mistake in pronunciation or articulation or check pronunciation in a dictionary. Every dictionary has a pronunciation key. For instance, the entry for the word *deification* in *Webster's New World Dictionary of the American Language* follows:

de-i-fi-ca-tion, (dē-ə fi kā shən) *n.* [ME.; OFr.],

1. act of deifying. 2. deified person or embodiment.

The entry indicates that the word has five syllables that carry distinct sounds. The pronunciation key says that the *e* should be pronounced like the *e* in elate, the *i* like the *a* in ago, and the *a* like the *a* in ape. The accent mark indicates which syllable should receive heaviest emphasis. You should learn how to use the pronunciation key in a dictionary, but if you still have some misgivings about how to pronounce a word, ask your speech teacher for assistance.

Another way to improve your enunciation is to prolong syllables. Such prolonging makes your pronunciation easier to understand, especially if you are addressing a large audience assembled outside or in an auditorium with no microphone. The drawing out of syllables can be overdone, however. Some radio and TV news announcers hang onto the final syllable in a sentence so long that the device is disconcertingly noticeable.

Articulation errors are so common that humorous stories are often based on them. Many **malapropisms,** or mistaking one word for another, are based on articulation errors. A newspaper article on malapropisms mentioned these:

A copulation explosion *for* A population explosion

Making an obstacle of themselves *for* Making a spectacle of themselves

Go for the juggler *for* Go for the jugular

He took milk of amnesia *for* He took milk of magnesia (Harden 1999, 1D)

Medical terms seem to be a special problem. One man came to the hospital information desk seeking his wife who was there "to get a monogram" as he motioned to his right breast. You are likely to hear an occasional malapropism in your public speaking class when speakers venture into the unfamiliar without practicing their speech in front of a caring audience.

Articulation problems are less amusing when they occur in your speech. Four common articulation problems are addition, deletion, substitution, and transposition. **Addition** occurs when an extra sound is added. For example, if a person says "pic-a-nic" instead of "pic-nic," "ath-a-lete" instead of "athlete," or "real-ah-toor" instead of "real-tor," he or she is making an error of addition. A very common variation of addition is saying "em-pah-thet-ic" for the word "em-path-ic."

Deletion occurs when a sound is dropped or left out of a word. Examples of deletion are "rassberry" for "raspberry," or "libary" for "library." Deletion also commonly occurs when people drop the final sounds of words such as "reveren'" for "reverend," "goin'" for "going," or "comin'" for "coming." Finally, deletion occurs when individuals drop the initial sounds of words such as "'possum" for "opossum."

Substitution occurs when one sound is replaced with another. When speakers use the word "ant" for "aunt," "git" for "get," "ruff" for "roof," "crick" for "creek," "tomata" for "tomato," or "axe" for "ask," they are making substitution errors.

Transposition occurs when two sounds are reversed. College students who call their teachers "perfessor" instead of "professor" or persons who say one "hunderd" instead of one "hundred" are making an error of transposition.

Use Fluency for Fluidity

The eighth vocal characteristic of delivery is **fluency**—the smoothness of delivery, the flow of the words, and the absence of vocalized pauses. Fluency cannot be achieved by looking up words in a dictionary or by any other simple solution. Fluency is not necessarily very noticeable. Listeners are more likely to notice errors than to notice the seemingly effortless flow of words and intentional pauses in a well-delivered speech. The importance of fluency is emphasized in a study that showed that audiences tend to perceive a speaker's fluency, the smoothness of presentation, as a main ingredient of effectiveness (Hayworth 1942). You can, however, be too fluent. A speaker who seems too fluent is perceived as "a fast talker," or "slick."

To achieve fluency, you must be confident of the content of your speech. If you know what you are going to say, and if you have practiced the words, then

On the Web

William Jefferson Clinton was considered an excellent orator during his presidency. His physical stature, and his use of gestures, bodily movement, eye contact, and vocal variety were used to his advantage. Go to *http://usinfo.state.gov/usa/infousa/facts/speeches/clinton/clinton.htm* to view some of his speeches. What can you learn from Clinton and from other well-known orators concerning delivery?

disruptive repetition and vocalized pauses are unlikely to occur. If you master what you are going to say and concentrate on the overall rhythm of the speech, your fluency will improve. Pace, build, and time various parts of your speech so that delivery and content unite into a coherent whole.

How Can You Use Your Body to Communicate Effectively?

We have considered the vocal aspects of delivery. Let us now examine the bodily aspects. Eye contact, facial expression, gestures, movement, and physical appearance are five bodily aspects of speech delivery—nonverbal indicators of meaning—that are important to the public speaker. In any communication, you indicate how you relate to the material and to other people by your gestures, facial expression, and bodily movements. When you observe two people busily engaged in conversation, you can judge their interest in the conversation without hearing their words. Similarly, in public speaking, the nonverbal aspects of delivery reinforce what the speaker is saying. Researchers have found that audiences who can see the speaker, and his or her behavior, comprehend more of the speech than audiences who cannot (Kramer and Lewis 1951).

Some persons are more sensitive to nonverbal cues than are others. Research conducted on a "Profile of Nonverbal Sensitivity" found that females as early as the third grade are more sensitive to nonverbal communication than males. However, men in artistic or expressive jobs scored as well as the women. The findings suggest that such sensitivity is learned. A second finding on nonverbal communication is that, until college age, young people are not as sensitive to nonverbal communication as older persons are (Rosenthal 1974). This study, too, supports the notion that we can and do learn sensitivity to respond to nonverbal cues, such as eye contact, facial expression, gestures, and movement.

Use Eye Contact to Hold Audience Attention

The first nonverbal aspect of delivery that is important to the public speaker is **eye contact.** This term refers to the way a speaker observes the audience while speaking. Studies and experience indicate that audiences prefer maintenance of good eye contact (Cobin 1962; Napieralski, Brooks, and Droney 1995) that improves source credibility (Beebe 1974). Eye contact is one way you indicate to others how you feel about them. You may be wary of a person who will not look at you in conversation. Similarly, in public speaking, eye contact conveys our relationship with the audience. If you rarely or never look at audience members, they may be resentful of your seeming disinterest. If you look over the heads of your audience or scan them so quickly that you do not really look at anyone, you may appear to be afraid. The proper relationship between you and your audience should be one of purposeful communication. You signal that sense of purpose by treating the audience members as individuals to whom you wish to communicate a message, and by looking at them for responses to your message.

Eye contact—the frequency and duration of looking at the person to whom you are speaking—varies with gender, personality, and culture (Richmond, McCroskey, and Payne 1987). Americans of European descent tend to use more eye contact than do Americans of African descent. Such differences in behavior can lead to misunderstanding. The African American's averted eyes can lead the European American to interpret disinterest. The European American's more intent eye contact could be perceived by an African American as staring or as aggressiveness. Some cultural groups such as some Latin Americans, Southern Europeans, and Arabs tend to stand close and look directly into the other person's face. Many people from India, Pakistan, and Scandinavia, on the other hand, turn their bodies toward the person to whom they are speaking but avoid steady focus on the other person's face.

How can you learn to maintain eye contact with your audience? One way is to know your speech so well and to feel so strongly about it that you have to make few references to your notes. A speaker who does not know a speech well tends to be manuscript-bound. You can encourage yourself to keep an eye on the audience by delivering an extemporaneous speech from an outline or key words. One of the purposes of extemporaneous delivery is to help you adapt to your audience. Adaptation is not possible unless you are continually monitoring the audience's reactions to see if your listeners understand your message.

Other ways of learning eye contact include scanning or continually looking over your entire audience, addressing various sections of the audience as you progress through your speech, and concentrating on the head **nodders.** In almost every audience, some individuals overtly indicate whether your message is coming across or not. These individuals usually nod "yes" or "no" with their heads. You may find that you can enhance your delivery by finding the friendly faces and positive nodders who signal when the message is getting through to them.

✔ Reality Check 11.1 ✔
More on Eye Contact

Taylor, L. (1996, August 30). Next time you don't get the job, grab a mirror and practise [sic] eye contact, and do stay rooted to the spot. *New Statesman, 125,* 55. An amusing article about the possible excesses of stressing nonverbal communication.

Napieralski, L. P., Brooks, C. I., and Droney, J. M. (1995, June). The effect of duration of eye contact on American college students' attributions of state, trait, and test anxiety. *The Journal of Social Psychology, 135,* 273–80. A scholarly article indicating that as eye contact increased, a videotaped model was judged to have less anxiety of all three types and that the effects were stronger for the female than for the male model. This study adds to the research that shows individuals being judged positively for increased eye contact.

Use Facial Expression to Communicate

Another nonverbal aspect of delivery is **facial expression,** using the eyes, eyebrows, forehead, and mouth for expression. Socrates, one of humanity's greatest thinkers, noted over two thousand years ago that, "Nobility and dignity, self-abasement and servility, prudence and understanding, insolence and vulgarity, are reflected in the face and in the attitudes of the body . . ." (cited in Weitz 1974). Studies of children between five and ten years of age show that they learn to interpret facial expressions early and that interpretation improves with age (Gosselin and Simard 1999). Researchers found that there are male/female differences in expressivity and self-regulation even at six months of age, with males having more difficulty than females (Weinberg, Tronick, and Cohn 1999). Some experts believe that the brain connects emotions and facial expressions and that culture determines what activates an emotion and the rules for displaying an emotion (Ekman 1969). Speakers who vary their facial expression are viewed as more credible than those who do not (Burgoon, Birk, and Pfau 1990).

Ekman and Friesen (1967) believe that facial expression shows how we feel and that body orientation (leaning, withdrawing, turning) expresses the intensity of our emotion. Pearson, West, and Turner (1995), in their book *Gender and Communication,* cite studies showing differences between male and female facial expressions. For instance, women use more facial expressions and are more expressive than men; women smile more than men; women are more apt to return smiles; and women are more attracted to others who smile.

Because facial expressions communicate, public speakers need to be aware of what they are communicating. A good example is that smiling can indicate both goodwill and submissiveness. Animals, such as chimpanzees, smile when they want to avoid a clash with a higher-status chimpanzee. First-year students smile more than upper-class students (Pearson, West, and Turner 1995). Constant smiling may communicate submissiveness or nervousness instead of friendliness, especially if the smiling seems unrelated to the content of the speech.

As a public speaker, you may or may not know how your face looks when you speak. You can practice in front of a mirror, videotape your practice session, or speak in front of friends who will help you. The goal is to have facial expressions consistent with your intent and your message.

Use Gestures to Reinforce Message

Gestures are "any visible bodily action by which meaning is given voluntary expression" (Kendon 1983). Although you probably are unaware of your arms and hands when you converse with someone, you may find that they become bothersome appendages when you stand in front of an audience. You may feel awkward because standing in front of an audience is not, for most of us, a natural situation. You have to work to make public speaking look easy, just as a skillful golfer, a graceful dancer, and a talented painter make their performances look effortless. Beginners make golfing, dancing, painting, and public speaking look difficult. Professionals make physical or artistic feats—like public speaking—look easy.

What can you do to help yourself gesture naturally when you are delivering your speech? The answer lies in your involvement with the issues and with practice. Angry farmers and irate miners appear on television to protest low prices and poor working conditions. Untutored in public speaking, these passionate people deliver their speeches with gusto and determined gestures. The gestures look very natural. These speakers have a natural delivery because they are much more concerned about their message than about when they should raise their clenched fists. They are upset, and they show it in their words and actions. You can deliver a speech more naturally if your attention is focused on your message. Self-conscious attention to your own gestures may be self-defeating: the gestures look studied, rehearsed, or slightly out of synchronization with your message. Selecting a topic that you really care about can result in the side effect of improving your gestures, especially if you concentrate on your audience and message.

Gestures differ with the size of the audience and the formality of the occasion. With a small audience in an informal setting, gestures are more like those you would use in ordinary conversation. With large audiences and in formal speaking situations, gestures are larger and more dramatic. In the classroom, the situation is often fairly formal and the audience relatively small, so gestures are ordinarily bigger than they would be in casual conversation but not as exaggerated as they would be in a large auditorium.

Another way to learn appropriate gestures is to practice a speech in front of friends who are willing to make constructive comments. Constructive criticism is one of the benefits your speech teacher and fellow students can give you. For example, actresses and actors spend hours rehearsing lines and gestures so that they will look spontaneous on stage. You may have to appear before many audiences before you learn to speak and move naturally. After much practice, you will learn which arm, head, and hand movements seem to help and which hinder your message. You can learn, through practice, to gesture naturally in a way that reinforces your message instead of detracting from it.

Use Bodily Movement for Purpose

The fourth nonverbal aspect of delivery is **movement,** or what you do with your entire body during a speech presentation. Do you lean forward as you speak, demonstrating to the audience how serious you are about communicating your message? Do you move out from behind the lectern to show that you want to get closer to the audience? Do you move during transitions in your speech to signal physically to the audience that you are moving to a new location in your speech? These are examples of purposeful movement in a public speech. Movement without purpose is discouraged. You should not move just to work off your own anxiety like a caged lion.

Always try to face the audience even when you are moving. For instance, even when you need to write information on the board, you can avoid turning your back by putting your notes on the board before class or by putting your visual material on posters. You can learn a lot about movement by watching your classmates and professors when they speak. You can learn what works for others and for you through observation and practice.

Think of physical movement as another way for you to signal a change in emphasis or direction in your speech. In the same way that a new paragraph signals a directional change in writing, moving from one side of the podium to the other can signal a change in your speech. All of the movements mentioned so far have been movements with a purpose. Purposeful movement can reduce your anxiety and hold audience attention. Speakers have "nervous energy" that can be worked off with movement. On the other hand, you should avoid channeling your anxiety into purposeless movement—movement unrelated to the content. Examples of purposeless movement are rocking back and forth or side to side, or the "caged lion" movement in which a speaker circles the front of the room like a lion in a zoo.

The environment in which you give your speech helps determine which movements are appropriate. The presence of a podium or lectern affects the formality of a speech. When a podium is present, the speaker is expected to use it, and the result is a higher level of formality than would otherwise be the case. The podium or lectern suggests a speaker-superior relationship with the audience, whereas the absence of a podium suggests more of an equal relationship with the audience. You should ask your professor's opinion about the use of the podium or lectern.

The distance between the speaker and the audience is also significant. A great distance suggests speaker superiority or great respect. That is why pulpits in most churches loom high and away from the congregation. A speaker often has a choice about how much to move toward or away from the audience. In the classroom, a speaker who clings to the far wall may appear to be exhibiting fear. Drawing close suggests intimacy or power. Large people can appear threatening or aggressive if they approach the audience too closely, and small people behind large podiums tend to disappear from sight. You need to decide what distances make you and your listeners most comfortable and make you as a speaker most effective.

Consider Your Unique Physical Appearance

How you look can make a difference in public speaking. You can do little or nothing about some aspects of your **physical appearance** or how you look. You might be unusually tall, short, wide, or good looking, but you can't change those characteristics for a public speech. Neither can you change racial characteristics, scars, or the wheelchair in which you sit, but the audience may still observe and make judgments.

Almost anyone who has a noticeable difference from others can be faced with discrimination. Unusually short people report discrimination in employment opportunities and suffer from anxieties about social stigmas such as the tendency to equate size with age (Moneymaker 1989). Short males suffer discrimination ("Heightism: Short guys finish last," 1996; Eiholzer, Haverkamp, and Voss 1999). Young adults exhibit hostile stereotypes toward obese individuals (Harris and Furukawa 1986). Functionally disabled people experience social discrimination from a dominant majority that is similar to that experienced by minority individuals (Hahn 1988). Often people who look different are avoided, ignored, or sometimes even ridiculed.

In the public speaking classroom, a person who is different in appearance for any reason can choose to ignore his or her uniqueness or address the difference directly. For example, a woman in a wheelchair introduced herself to her classmates with a different perspective. She said she did not want them to think of her as "handicapped" because in nearly all ways she was not—any more than most of them were limited in some way. She referred to her classmates as "temporarily able-bodied" because they never knew when they might end up as she had from an automobile accident. By directly facing the issue her classmates wondered about, she gave them permission to listen to her and talk with her without anxiety.

Even so-called normal people must consider the relationship between appearance and audience response. Christine Craft was one of the early successful anchorwomen on television. After years of successful reporting, her employer told her: "The people of Kansas City don't like watching you anchor the news because you are too old, too unattractive, and you are not sufficiently deferential to men." Originally hired because they loved her "looks," she quickly found repeated attention to her "squarish jaw and somewhat uneven eyes" (Craft 1988). Being a woman is another factor you cannot control, but gender does make a difference in how an audience perceives you.

In an article entitled "Personal Appearance: Is Attractiveness a Factor in Organizational Survival and Success?" Nykodym and Simonetti (1987) questioned 662 managers and found that appearance ranked 8th out of 20 survival and success factors. They also found that internal promotions tended to go to "individuals who have an acceptable corporate image" (p. 70). Schindler and Holbrook (1993) found a "critical-period phenomenon": men formed a lifelong preference for women's styles that were popular when the men were in their early twenties. Women's preferences and even men's preferences for other men's styles were not so specific. Appearance makes a difference on the job, and the age and gender of audience members makes a difference in what styles are preferred.

Finally, Stuart and Fuller (1991) in an article in the *Journal of Business Research* found that male sales associates dressed in different attire were perceived quite differently. Nearly 400 purchasing agents were asked to judge photographs of a model dressed as a salesperson. The result: the salespeople in traditional outfits were perceived as better, more ambitious, self-assured, and optimistic. Furthermore, the traditionally dressed male was seen as representing a larger, more ethical company with more products, better credit, and better service. Apparently, the purchasing agents made a lot of judgments about the salespersons based on their clothing.

Just so you do not get the impression that clothing choices are an overwhelming factor, consider the study of young people (average age 17) who applied for seasonal employment at an amusement park. Eight interviewers interviewed 517 applicants and judged them on personal style, bodily movement, and speech characteristics. Speech characteristics like articulation and proper pauses proved more important than personal appearance (Parsons and Liden 1984). On the other hand, when 165 subjects viewed simulated interviews and judged the credibility of casually and conservatively dressed sources, the results showed that women between 18 and 34 years of age gave high ratings of competence, character, and dynamism regardless of attire but women 35 years old and older gave the lowest ratings on competence, character, and dynamism to casually dressed interviewees, especially female sources. Men of all ages judged all sources similarly. Thus younger women proved nonjudgmental, but older women proved very judgmental, especially against female sources (Engstrom 1996).

Your clothing and accessories make a difference in how people perceive you, but big differences can appear between a classroom speech and a speech in another setting. Following are some suggestions for choosing appropriate attire for the classroom setting.

1. Wear clothing that is normative for your audience, unless you are wearing clothing that makes some point about your speech. An international student speaking about native dress could wear clothing unique to her country, for example.

2. Avoid wearing clothing or jewelry that is likely to distract your audience from your message: too many holes in the denims in the wrong places, too much neckline, or too many rings in too many places.

3. Wear clothing and accessories that contribute to your credibility, not that lower your standing in the eyes of the audience.

Public speaking outside the classroom is clearly more complicated because you have to dress for the topic, the audience, and the occasion. Violate audience expectations and they will tend to respond negatively. Wear a wild Hawaiian shirt for an Upper Midwest audience, and they will consider you odd. When in doubt, ask the people who invited you to speak how you should dress.

✔ **Reality Check 11.2** ✔
The Importance of Appearance

Paul, A. M. (1997, Nov./Dec.). Judging by appearances. *Psychology Today, 30,* 20. This article concerns how defendants' representation of themselves can sway juries. The article adds that jury consultants advise clients on attire, speech, and gestures. Appearance in the courtroom is so important that a business has emerged for trained professionals who do jury consulting.

Mulford, M., Orbell, J., and Shatto, C. (1998, May). Physical attractiveness, opportunity, and success in everyday exchange. *The American Journal of Sociology,* 103(6), 1565–92. This scholarly article on the attractiveness of the physically attractive demonstrates once again that people prefer to relate to physically attractive individuals. An interesting sideline is that men who see themselves as attractive are likely to cooperate with other men, but women who see themselves as attractive are less cooperative than other women.

Perlini, A. H., Bertolissi, S., and Lind, D. L. (1999, June). The effect of women's age and physical appearance on evaluations of attractiveness and social desirability. *The Journal of Social Psychology,* **139(3),** 343–54. In this Canadian study of cultural expectations of beauty, 160 younger and older subjects rated the attractiveness and personality traits of four target women. The results: judges young and old downrated the social desirability of the younger unattractive female; younger judges saw younger and older females as equal in social desirability; and older male judges rated older attractive targets as less socially desirable than younger attractive targets. In short, old white men were more judgmental about the attractiveness of older women than were the younger judges.

How Can You Improve Your Delivery?

A student confessed that he had disobeyed instructions. Told to write a brief outline from which to deliver a speech, the student, instead, was afraid

to speak in front of the class without every word written out. He practiced the
speech by reading the entire manuscript word for word. After rehearsing the
speech many times, he wrote the entire speech
using a tiny font so the speech would appear to
be delivered from a brief outline on small
sheets. However, as he began his speech, he
found that he could not read the tiny print on
his small sheets, so he delivered the whole
speech without using any written cues. All of
the practice had helped him; the small font
manuscript had not.

To help you improve your own delivery,
you might want to follow these steps, which
many students find useful:

1. Start with a detailed working outline
   that includes the introduction, the
   body, and the conclusion. Remember
   to include all main points and supporting materials.

2. Distill the working outline into a
   speaking outline that simply includes
   reminders of what you intend to
   include in your speech.

*Practice your speech in the room where
you will deliver it.*

3. Practice your speech alone first, pref-
   erably in front of a mirror, so you will notice how much or how
   little you use your notes. Ideally, 80 to 90 percent or more of your
   speech should be delivered without looking at notes.

4. Practice your speech in front of your roommate, your spouse,
   your kids, or your colleagues. Try again to maintain eye contact
   as much as possible. After the speech, ask your observers to
   explain your message—and seek their advice for improving the
   speech.

5. Practice your speech with minimal notes in an empty classroom
   or a similar place that allows you to become accustomed to its
   size and the situation. Focus on some of the more sophisticated
   aspects of delivery, such as facial expression, vocal variety, gestures, and movement.

6. Use past critiques from your instructor or classmates to provide
   direction for improvement on delivery.

7. If possible, watch a videotape of your own performance for feedback. If practice does not make perfect, at least it will make you
   confident. You will become so familiar with the content of your
   speech that you will focus more on communicating your message to your audience.

A common error among beginning speakers is that they finish composing
their speech late the night before delivery, leaving no time for practice. The
most beautifully composed speech can be a delivery disaster, so protect your-

self by leaving time for three to five practice sessions. Then you will be self-assured, and your delivery will show that confidence.

Effective delivery has many advantages. Research indicates that effective delivery, the appropriate use of voice and body in public speaking, contributes to the credibility of the speaker (Bettinghaus 1961). Indeed, student audiences characterize the poorest speakers by their voices and the physical aspects of delivery (Henrikson 1944). Poor speakers are judged to be fidgety, nervous, and monotonous. They also maintain little eye contact and show little animation or facial expression (Gilkinson and Knower 1941; Prisbell 1985; Manusov 1991). Good delivery also tends to increase the audience's capacity to handle complex information (Vohs 1964). Thus, your credibility and ability to convey complex information may be affected by the vocal and physical aspects of delivery.

To put this chapter on delivery in perspective, remember that eye contact, facial expression, gestures, and movement are important, but content may be even more important. The same researcher who found that poor speakers are identified by their voices and the physical aspects of their delivery also found that the best speakers are identified by the content of their speeches (Henrikson 1944). Two other researchers found that an audience's evaluation of a speaker is based more on the content of the speech than on vocal characteristics, such as intonation, pitch, and rate (Hard and Brown 1974). Still another pair of researchers found that a well-composed speech can mask poor delivery (Gundersen and Hopper 1976). Finally, one researcher reviewed studies on informative speaking and reported that although some research indicates that audiences who have listened to good speakers have significantly greater immediate recall, other findings show that the differences are slight. His conclusion was that the influence of delivery on comprehension is overrated (Petrie 1963).

What are you to do in the face of the reports that good delivery influences audience comprehension positively but also that the influence of delivery on comprehension is overrated? What are you to do when one study reports that poor vocal characteristics reveal a poor speaker and another states that good content can mask poor delivery? Until more evidence is available, the safest position for you as a public speaking student is to regard both delivery and content as important. What you say and how you say your message are both important—and probably in that order.

Summary

This chapter on delivery began with a discussion of what constitutes effective delivery. This section was followed by a consideration of the four methods of delivery: extemporaneous, manuscript, memorized, and impromptu. The method of delivery that most speech professors prefer for classroom instruction is the extemporaneous mode, which allows for minimal use of notes but invites spontaneity and maximum focus on message and audience.

Next, you reviewed the vocal aspects of delivery: rate, pause, duration, rhythm, pitch, volume, enunciation, and fluency. These vocal characteristics need to be orchestrated by the speaker into a symphony of sound and movement attractive to the audience. Monotony and unintended verbal blunders, such as the dreaded vocalized pause, are the enemies of effective delivery.

Nonverbal aspects of delivery, the fourth section in this chapter, examined eye contact, facial expression, gestures, movement, and physical appearance. The keys to delivery are naturalness, sincerity, and sensitive responsiveness to the audience. You learn to look and move in ways that you find comfortable and the audience finds inviting.

We concluded with some ideas about perfecting your delivery. Starting with a script of your speech or preferably a sentence outline, with practice you move toward fewer and fewer notes and more and more attention to your audience. The key word is practice. Too much practice can turn your extemporaneous speech into a memorized one, but too little can turn your well-composed speech into a comedy of errors. Allowing time to practice your speech is about as difficult as finding a topic in a reasonable amount of time, but those who practice usually receive the best evaluations.

Communication Narrative 11.1

Madeline Rockingham was basically a shy person who did not feel comfortable speaking in front of groups. Unfortunately, her immediate superior asked her to take the lead in presenting her company's services to a client. The trouble was that Madeline saw herself as the most unlikely spokesperson for her company. In high school, she flourished in the reading club, not the drama club. Even in band she was 7th chair clarinet, not first chair. In college, she had avoided public speaking out of sheer fear. The only reason her supervisor asked her to present this service to the client was because she knew more about the service than anyone else in the company. At the moment, she wished that she did not know so much.

Always a carefully prepared person, Madeline assembled her information, narrowed the material down to what she thought the client wanted, and then wrote a detailed outline of the contents. Once she had on paper what she wanted to say, she felt better. The difficulty for her was determining how to deliver the speech, how to say the words loud enough and in the correct way. She worried that her knees would shake, that she would look wet with sweat, and that she would possibly just faint.

Madeline practiced the speech at home, first in front of her dog then in front of the landlady. She even practiced the speech once in front of a full-length mirror, but she found that she distracted herself because she did not like how she looked. Mainly she worried about the presentation day, which was coming very soon.

Only a dozen people were in the room that day, a crowded meeting room with windows on one side and a few unwatered palms with half-dead fronds. Half the people represented the client; the remainder of the spectators were from Madeline's own firm—mostly people above her in the hierarchy. When she started her speech, she knew she was looking too much at her notes, but she was too nervous to just speak without looking at her cue cards. When she focused the listener's attention on the visual aids—the company's service mission, the main points of the proposed contract, and the number and titles of the people committed to this one client—she felt relief because they were not looking at her. When she completed her formal part of the presentation she was very disappointed in her speech. Neither the prospective clients nor her bosses looked very pleased.

If Madeline was not thrilled by her performance during the speech, she felt much better about the question-and-answer session that followed. She was

> brilliant. The prospective clients were asking her tough questions about costs, commitment, and timeliness of service—all of which she answered with accuracy and authority. Madeline even noticed that her supervisor and the company vice-president exchanged reassuring glances when she provided a very competent answer to a particularly difficult question.
>
> Madeline knew that she had saved the day with the Q and A. She also knew that she had to improve her delivery during her public speeches in the future. Success in the business world is a series of discoveries: You discover what you do well and what you do poorly. You repeat what you do well and improve upon what you do poorly. Madeline almost looked forward to her next opportunity to show what she could do for a prospective client.

Vocabulary

addition An articulation problem that occurs when an extra sound is added.

articulation The physiological process of creating the sounds of a word.

deletion An articulation problem that occurs when a sound is dropped or left out of a word.

duration The amount of time devoted to the parts of a speech (e.g., introduction, evidence, main points) and the dwelling on words for effect.

enunciation A vocal aspect of delivery that involves the pronunciation and articulation of words; pronouncing correctly and producing the sounds clearly so that the language is understandable.

extemporaneous mode A method of speech delivery in which the speaker delivers a speech from an outline or from brief notes.

eye contact A nonverbal aspect of delivery that involves the speaker's looking directly at audience members to monitor their responses to the message; in public speaking, eye contact is an asset because it permits the speaker to adapt to audience responses and to assess the effects of the message.

facial expression A nonverbal aspect of delivery that involves the use of eyes, eyebrows, and mouth to express feelings about the message, audience, and occasion; smiles, frowns, grimaces, and winces can help a speaker communicate feelings.

fluency A vocal aspect of delivery that involves the smooth flow of words and the absence of vocalized pauses.

gestures A bodily aspect of delivery that involves the movement of head, hands, and arms to indicate emphasis, commitment, and other feelings about the topic, audience, and occasion.

impromptu mode A method of speech delivery in which the speaker has no advanced preparation.

malapropism Mistaking one word for another.

manuscript mode A method of speech delivery in which the speaker writes out the complete speech in advance and then uses that manuscript to deliver the speech.

memorized mode A method of speech delivery in which the speaker commits the entire manuscript of the speech to memory, by either rote or repetition; appropriate in situations where the same speech is given over and over to different audiences.

movement A nonverbal aspect of delivery that refers to a speaker's locomotion in front of an audience; can be used to signal the development and organization of the message.

nodders Individuals who overtly indicate whether your message is coming across or not.

pause An intentional silence used to draw attention to the words before or after the interlude; a break in the flow of words for effect.

physical appearance The way we look, including our display of material things such as clothing and accessories.

pitch A vocal aspect of delivery that refers to the highness or lowness, upward and downward inflections of the voice.

project To increase your volume so that all may hear the speech.

pronunciation The production of the sounds of a word.

rate A vocal aspect of delivery that refers to the speed of delivery, the number of words spoken per minute; normal rates range from 125 to 190 words per minute.

rhetorical question A question for which you expect no oral answer.

rhythm The tempo of a speech, which varies by part (e.g., introductions are often slower and more deliberate) and by the pacing of the words and sentences.

substitution An articulation problem that occurs when one sound is replaced with another.

transposition An articulation problem that occurs when two sounds are reversed.

vocalized pause A nonfluency in delivery characterized by such sounds as "Uhhh," "Ahhh," or "Mmmm," or the repetitious use of such expressions as "O.K.," "like," or "for sure" to fill silence with sound; often used by speakers who are nervous or inarticulate.

volume A vocal characteristic of delivery that refers to the loudness or softness of the voice; public speakers often project or speak louder than normal so that distant listeners can hear the message; beginning speakers frequently forget to project enough volume.

Application Exercises

Selecting a Method of Delivery

1. Examine each of the following topics, audiences, and situations and indicate which method of delivery would be most appropriate by placing the appropriate letter in each blank on the left. Instead of turning to "correct answers" for these items, you should discuss them with your classmates or teacher and defend your choice based on the message, the audience, and the situation.

   A = Manuscript Method   **B = Extemporaneous Method**

   C = Impromptu Method   **D = Memorized Method**

   ____1. You have to answer questions from the class at the conclusion of your speech.

❖ ❖ ❖ ❖

____2. You have to describe the student government's new statement of policy on student rights to a group of high-level administrators in the college.

____3. You have to deliver the same speech about student life at your college three times a week for sixteen weeks to incoming first-year students.

____4. You have to give parents a "walking tour" of the campus, including information about the buildings, the history of the college, and the background of significant places on campus.

____5. You have to go door-to-door, demonstrating and explaining a vacuum cleaner and its attachments that you are selling to individuals, couples, and even groups of roommates.

Bodily Aspects of Delivery

2. Observe a talented public speaker—a visiting lecturer, a political speaker, a sales manager—and study that person's gestures, facial expressions, eye contact, and movement. Then answer the following questions.

1. Do the speaker's gestures reinforce the important points in the speech?

2. Does the speaker's facial expression reflect the message and show concern for the audience and the topic?

3. Does the speaker maintain eye contact with the audience, respond to the audience's reactions, and keep himself or herself from becoming immersed in the manuscript, outline, or notes?

4. Does the speaker's movement reflect the organization of the speech and the important points in it?

5. Are the speaker's gestures, facial expressions, and movements consistent with the occasion, the personality of the speaker, and the message being communicated?

6. Do the speaker's clothing and other adornments reinforce, rather than distract from, the message?

Evaluating Your Delivery

3. For your next speech, have a classmate, friend, or relative observe and evaluate your speech for delivery skills. Have your critic use this scale to fill in the blanks on the left.

1 = Excellent   2 = Good   3 = Average   4 = Fair   5 = Weak

Vocal Aspects of Delivery

❖ ❖ ❖ ❖

____ Pitch: highness and lowness of voice, upward and downward inflections

____ Rate: words per minute, appropriate variation of rate for the difficulty of content

____ Pause: intentional silence designed to aid understanding at appropriate places

____ Volume: loud enough to hear, variation with the content

____ Enunciation: correct pronunciation and articulation

____ Fluency: smoothness of delivery; lack of vocalized pauses; good pacing, rhythm, and cadence without being so smooth as to sound artificial, contrived, or glib

Nonverbal Aspects of Delivery

____ Gestures: natural movement of the head, hands, arms, and torso consistent with the speaker, topic, and situation

____ Facial expression and smiling behavior: consistent with message, used to relate to the audience, appropriate for audience and situation

____ Eye contact: natural, steady without staring, includes entire audience, and is responsive to audience feedback

____ Movement: purposeful, used to indicate organization, natural, without anxiety, use at podium and distance from audience

____ Physical appearance: appropriate for the occasion, speaker, topic, and audience

References

Beebe, S. A. (1974). Eye contact: A nonverbal determinant of speaker credibility. *Speech Teacher, 23,* 21–25.

Bettinghaus, E. (1961). The operation of congruity in an oral communication situation. *Speech Monographs, 28,* 131–142.

Burgoon, J. K., Birk, T., and Pfau, M. (1990). Nonverbal behaviors, persuasion, and credibility. *Human Communication Research, 17,* 140–170.

Cobin, M. (1962). Response to eye-contact. *Quarterly Journal of Speech, 48,* 415–418.

Craft, C. (1988). *Too Old, Too Ugly, and Not Deferential to Men.* Rocklin, CA: Prima Publishing and Communications.

Diehl, C. F., White, R. C., and Burk, K. W. (1959). Rate and communication. *Speech Monographs, 26,* 229–231.

Eiholzer, U., Haverkamp, F., and Voss, L. D. (Eds). (1999). *Growth, Stature, and Psychosocial Well-Being.* Seattle: Hogrefe & Huber Publishers.

Ekman, P. (1969). Pan-cultural elements in facial displays of emotion. *Science, 164,* 86–88.

Ekman, P., and Friesen, W. V. (1967). Head and body cues in the judgment of emotion: A reformulation. *Perceptual and Motor Skills, 24,* 711–724.

Emerson, R. W. (1860). Power. In *The Conduct of Life, Nature, and Other Essays*. New York: Dutton.

Engstrom, E. (1996, October). Audience's perceptions of sources' credibility in a television interview setting. *Perceptual and Motor Skills*, 83, 579–588.

Gilkinson, H., and Knower, F. H. (1941). Individual differences among students of speech as revealed by psychological tests—I. *Journal of Educational Psychology*, 32, 161–175.

Gosselin, P., and Simard, J. (1999, June). Children's knowledge of facial expressions of emotions: Distinguishing fear and surprise. *The Journal of Genetic Psychology*, 160(2), 181–193.

Grigg, R. (1988). *The Tao of Relationships*. New York: Bantam Books.

Gundersen, D. F., and Hopper, R. (1976). Relationships between speech delivery and speech effectiveness. *Speech Monographs*, 43, 158–165.

Hahn, H. (1988, Spring). The politics of physical differences: Disability and discrimination. *Journal of Social Issues*, 44, 39–47.

Hard, R. J., and Brown, B. L. (1974). Interpersonal information conveyed by the content and vocal aspects of speech. *Speech Monographs*, 41, 371–380.

Harden, M. (1999, January 13). Making the grate. *The Columbus Dispatch*, 1D.

Harris, N. B., and Furukawa, C. (1986, Spring). Attitudes toward obesity in an elderly sample. *Journal of Obesity and Weight Regulation*, 5(1), 5–15.

Hayworth, D. (1942). A search for facts on the teaching of public speaking. *Quarterly Journal of Speech*, 28, 247–254.

Heightism: Short guys finish last. (1996). *The Economist*, 337, 19–20.

Henrikson, E. H. (1944). An analysis of the characteristics of some 'good' and 'poor' speakers. *Speech Monographs*, 11, 120–124.

Hildebrandt, H. W., and Stevens, W. (1963). Manuscript and extemporaneous delivery in communicating information. *Speech Monographs*, 30, 369–372.

Kendon, A. (1983). *Gesture and speech: How they interact*. Sage Annual Reviews of Communication Research, Vol. II. J. M. Wiemann and R. P. Harrison (Eds.). Beverly Hills, CA: Sage Publications.

Kramer, E. J. J., and Lewis, T. R. (1951). Comparison of visual and non-visual listening. *Journal of Communication*, 1, 16–20.

Lesly, P. (1988, May–June). Managing the human climate. *PR Reporter*. Exeter, NH: PR Publishing Co., Inc.

Manusov, V. (1991). Perceiving nonverbal messages: Effects of immediacy and encoded intent on receiver judgments. *Western Journal of Speech Communication*, 55, 235–253.

Miller, N. (1976). Speed of speech and persuasion. *Journal of Personality and Social Psychology*, 34, 615–624.

Moneymaker, J. M. (1989). The social significance of short stature: A study of the problems of dwarfs and midgets. *Loss, Grief and Care*, 3, 183–189.

Mulford, M., Orbell, J., and Shatto, C. (1998, May). Physical attractiveness, opportunity, and success in everyday exchange. *The American Journal of Sociology*, 103(6), 1565–1592.

Napieralski, L. P., Brooks, C. I., and Droney, J. M. (1995, June). The effect of duration of eye contact on American college students' attributions of state, trait, and test anxiety. *The Journal of Social Psychology*, 135, 273–280.

Nykodym, N., and Simonetti, J. L. (1987). Personal appearance: Is attractiveness a factor in organizational survival and success? *Journal of Employment Counseling*, 24, 69–78.

Parsons, C. K., and Liden, R. C. (1984, November). Interviewer perceptions of applicant qualifications: A multivariate field study of demographic characteristics and nonverbal cues. *Journal of Applied Psychology*, 69(4), 557–568.

Paul, A. M. (1997, November/December). Judging by appearances. *Psychology Today*, 30, 20.

Pearson, J. C., West, R. L., and Turner, L. H. (1995). *Gender and Communication*. Dubuque, IA: Wm. C. Brown Publishers.

Perlini, A. H., Bertolissi, S., and Lind, D. L. (1999, June). The effect of women's age and physical appearance on evaluations of attractiveness and social desirability. *The Journal of Social Psychology,* 139(3), 343–354.

Petrie, C. R., Jr., (1963). Informative speaking: A summary and bibliography of related research. *Speech Monographs,* 30, 81.

Philodemus. (1920). Rhetorica. In *Transactions of the Connecticut Academy of Arts and Sciences* (Trans. By H. M. Hubbell), 23, 243–382.

Prisbell, M. (1985). Assertiveness, shyness and nonverbal communicative behavior. *Communication Research Reports,* 2, 120–127.

Richmond, V. P., McCroskey, J. C., and Payne, S. K. (1987). *Nonverbal Behavior in Interpersonal Relations.* Englewood Cliffs, NJ: Prentice-Hall, Inc.

Rosenthal, R. (1974). Body talk and tone of voice: The language without words. *Psychology Today,* 8, 64–68.

Schindler, R. M., and Holbrook, N. B. (1993, November–December). Critical periods in the development of men's and women's tastes in personal appearance. *Psychology and Marketing,* 10(6), 549–564.

Socrates, Xenophon. (1974). Memorabilia III. In *Nonverbal Communication: Readings with Commentary,* Shirley Weitz (Ed.). New York: Oxford University Press.

Stuart, E. W., and Fuller, B. K. (1991, November). Clothing as communication in two business-to-business sales settings. *Journal of Business Research,* 23(3), 269–290.

Taylor, L. (1996, August 30). Next time you don't get the job, grab a mirror and practise [sic] eye contact, and do stay rooted to the spot. *New Statesman,* 125, 55.

Vohs, J. L. (1964). An empirical approach to the concept of attention. *Speech Monographs,* 31, 355–360.

Walter, O. M., and Scott, R. L. (1969). *Thinking and Speaking.* New York: Macmillan.

Weinberg, M. K., Tronick, E. Z., and Cohn, J. F. (1999, January). Gender differences in emotional expressivity and self-regulation during early infancy. *Developmental Psychology,* 35(1), 175–188.

Weitz, S. (Ed.) (1974). *Nonverbal Communication: Readings with Commentary.* New York: Oxford University Press.

Chapter 12

Presentational Aids

pixel, n.: A mischievous, magical spirit associated with screen displays. The computer industry has frequently borrowed from mythology: Witness the sprites in computer graphics, the demons in artificial intelligence, and the trolls in the marketing department.

—Jeff Meyer

Question Outline

I. Why should you use presentational aids?

II. What factors affect the use of presentational aids?

III. How can you relate your visual aids to your topic, situation, and audience?

IV. What types of presentational aids are available for the public speaker?

V. Why should public speakers consider computer-generated graphics?

Abdul Hamid had a problem with his public speech. As an international student, he wanted Americans to understand the nation he left when he was 10 years old. Because his English was not the best, he did not think his descriptions would be understood. How could he get Americans to understand the beauty of his homeland and the richness of Muslim traditions? To have them understand the customs of a nation they probably could not locate on a map would be difficult.

Abdul's solution was presentational aids. A local travel agent had a poster, a colorful photo of the open market, that he could hang in front of the classroom *as he gave his speech. He could wear traditional clothing during the speech, and he had a dozen good slides that he could show the class as he explained, as best he could, what they showed about his country. He had to reserve the slide projector, to find an extension cord, to write note cards for each slide, and to explain in English what each slide revealed about his country.*

Abdul received his highest grade on his informative speech—and the most positive comments from his classmates. The students were much more interested in him and his country after the speech, and they seemed to appreciate learning about other parts of the world. Not only did his fellow students inquire about his country, they also asked him after class about his religion, the food, and the way people met and married in his country.

Ours is a visual world. The average student has spent more hours in front of a television than in the classroom. With the publication of *USA Today* and the advent of new color technology, newspapers have become more colorful and pictorial than ever before. Digital and video cameras are a hot item, with families recording every important event, and many unimportant ones, with their own cameras. In this highly visual world, the importance of *showing* what you are talking about has developed into a fine art.

You will be able to speak with more confidence when you learn how to use presentational aids to communicate your message to an audience. This chapter will help you learn the possibilities and the problems with the most commonly used presentational aids.

Why Use Presentational Aids?

Presentational aids are important for at least five reasons.

1. They *reinforce the message* you provide to the audience.
2. They *clarify your message.*
3. They may make your message *more interesting* to an audience.
4. They make your speech *more memorable.*
5. They *reduce speech anxiety.*

Often, presentational aids add these benefits to your speech and are, at the same time, economical. They take effort to produce, but they do not add much time to your speech.

Presentational Aids Reinforce Your Message

Presentational aids can help reinforce your message. Bess Pittman (1999) reinforced her message as she began the body of her speech with an enlarged photograph she had obtained from a local insurance company. The presence of flashlights and car lights indicated that the picture had been taken at night. The picture showed shoes. The shoes were spread across the road and in the ditch as if boxes of them had fallen off a truck. They were the shoes of teenagers. Thirteen high school seniors had died in a head-on, two-car crash near the city limits. The impact of the two speeding cars had knocked the shoes off most of the victims and had blasted them across the road and into the ditch. Bess was discussing the unusually high number of car accidents among our youth. Her photo showed no mangled wreckage, no blood, and no bodies. The shoes told the story.

Presentational Aids Clarify Your Message

Presentational aids can also clarify a message. They are often clearer than words alone. A public speaker trying to show how our financial situation has changed over a five-year period could use hundreds of words and many minutes explaining the effects of inflation, but a bar graph could show it more clearly in a couple of minutes.

Neal Resnick (1999) began his speech with a poster with eight names: Mordechai, Rachel, Sarah, Joe, Miriam, Max, Etta, and Julie. Above each name was a colored geometric figure. As Neal spoke of the six relatives he lost in the Holocaust, he removed the colored cover from the pictures of the relatives who never reappeared after the war. Only two were left by the time the speech was finished. An American soldier from Chicago spoke Czech, met Neal's grandfather, and helped him move to Cleveland after the war. The names were easier to forget than the faces, and the serial revelation of his relatives' pictures clarified Neal's message in a way that the words alone would have struggled to do.

Presentational Aids Make Your Speech More Interesting

Another benefit of using presentational aids is that pictures, graphs, charts, maps, and other presentational aids are often more interesting to an audience than just using words. Jill Janu (1999) surprised her classmates when she started her speech by undressing. Underneath her outer garments (she did not strip), she exhibited a totally black outfit. Her speech was "what to wear to a rave." She had big pants, a tank top, comfortable shoes, and a sweat shirt tied to her waist. Jill already was well adorned with rings and things, but during this speech she added a water bottle, "pass-a-fire," glow stick, and a whistle. The speech explained the function of the clothing and the accessories. She used herself as her visual aid, and made the speech considerably more interesting than it otherwise might have been.

Presentational Aids Make Your Speech Memorable

An additional reason to incorporate presentational aids into your speech is that audiences find visualization memorable. We learn much of what we know through sight. According to Zayas-Baya (1977–1978) in the *International Journal of Instructional Media*, we learn 83 percent of all we know through sight. The effect of our other senses on memory is equally dramatic. The same author reports that we are likely to remember:

10 percent of what we read	50 percent of what we see and hear
20 percent of what we hear	80 percent of what we say
30 percent of what we see	90 percent of what we say and do

A speech that appeals to the senses through words, images, and actions is most likely to be remembered.

The speaker who says, "Repeat after me: 'I will begin my diet tomorrow'" is urging listeners to do more than passively receive her message. By encouraging the audience to SAY the message, they are more likely to remember the message. Similarly, the speaker who has us folding origami as we receive instruction is increasing our comprehension and our memory by having us DO the message. The speaker who instructs us in ballroom dancing by having us do a few steps as we count out loud is greatly increasing our memory of the event by having us SAY and DO the dance.

Presentational Aids Reduce Your Anxiety

Finally, the use of presentational aids may actually result in lowered levels of speech anxiety. Maybe having the audience look at the visual aids instead of staring at the speaker is an anxiety reducer. Perhaps speakers feel more confident as they focus on their presentational aids rather than on their own nervousness. Presentational aids serve to reinforce the message, which encourages the speaker to feel more assured. Presentational aids also allow the speaker to look away from the audience, which can relieve the speaker of tension. Whatever the specific factors, visual aids appear to lower speech anxiety. Joe Ayres (1991), at Washington State University, demonstrated that people who were generally apprehensive about speaking but used presentational aids reported less anxiety than those who were generally apprehensive but did not use presentational aids.

Seeing is an important component of learning and retaining information. That is exactly what you are trying to do with presentational aids—help the audience see what you are talking about, concisely, clearly, interestingly, and memorably.

Some experimental studies support the use of presentational aids. In one study, university students were exposed to a series of words and/or pictures and were tested on their ability to recall what they had seen. When the students were exposed to two stimuli at a time (i.e., sound plus pictures or printed words plus line drawings), they remembered better than they did with just one stimulus (Gadzella and Whitehead 1975). Another study demonstrated that two-dimensional objects, simple figures against a background, are better remembered when they move than when they stand still (Bogard 1974).

A third study used male and female subjects from junior high to college age and tested them for audio and visual cues. The experimenters determined that these audiences are more influenced by what they see than by what they hear (DePaulo 1978). For the public speaker, the message is clear: presentational aids reinforce your message and will probably be the part of your speech that the audience remembers.

Factors Affecting the Use of Presentational Aids

Following are six questions to ask yourself before using presentational aids:

1. What is the composition of my audience?
2. What is the occasion?
3. What is the setting?
4. What is the message?
5. What is the cost?
6. What are the rules?

Your answers to these questions will help you decide if, what kind of, and how many presentational aids are appropriate for your speech.

Who Is Your Audience?

This question considers the audience members' ages, education, status, and reason for attending your speech. In other words, the question considers audience analysis. The younger your audience, the more necessary presentational aids become. Preschool and elementary children are captivated by visual aids. That is why elementary teachers need to learn how to use them.

People who have had little formal education may be more dependent on graphic illustrations, whereas highly educated people are more accustomed to interpreting what they hear. Regardless of educational level, some materials, such as statistics, mathematical formulas, and weather maps, are very difficult to comprehend without accompanying visuals.

High-status people need to be treated carefully lest they feel that the speaker is "talking down" to them with a visual presentation, but boards of directors, developers, and fund-raisers find that architects, lawyers, and investors often use visual displays to influence their decisions.

If an audience must learn something from a speaker, then presentational aids usually come into play. Thus, informative speeches to most groups invite the use of visuals for clarification and understanding. If the audience is expecting to be entertained, then the need for aids may be less imperative. Nonetheless, even in a special-occasion speech, visual aids may be helpful. The grand openings of buildings, bridges, and roadways are usually accompanied by blueprints, plans, and elevations of the new structures.

What Is the Occasion?

Ceremonial occasions often call for decoration—political bunting, ribbons, flags—but not often for presentational aids. Similarly, rituals such as funerals, baptisms, or bar mitzvahs call more for religious symbols than for presentational aids. Even evangelists and most visiting lecturers depend more on words than on visuals. However, some occasions cry out for presentational aids.

Instruction is an occasion that practically demands presentational aids, whether the venue is elementary school, high school, college, or a place of business. Where the purpose is pedagogical and the idea is to impart knowledge to a group, the need for presentational aids is high.

Persuasive situations, too, invite presentational aids. When the military tries to make a case for more funding, Congress is treated to graphs, charts, pictures, and even the very objects of defense. When a speaker is trying to convince an audience to stop drinking, start exercising, and continue eating appropriately, that speaker usually tries to persuade the audience with facts and figures presented visually. In short, the kinds of speeches that predominate in the classroom—informative and persuasive speeches—are the ones that need visual reinforcement if the audience is to understand and remember the message.

What Is the Setting?

The place where the speech is to occur helps determine if, and what kind of, presentational aids should be used. The size and shape of the room can forbid their use—or make them appropriate. Huge rooms demand specialized equipment: large screens, projectors, amplifiers, and lights. Small rooms—such as classrooms—are appropriate for a wide variety of presentational aids.

Classrooms, lecture halls, or conference rooms are usually designed for visual display; they often come equipped with viewing screens, chalkboards, and places to hang posters. At the same time, you should not assume that all classrooms have all, or any, of these. A church sanctuary, lounge, or private office may be ill equipped for visual presentations. You will need to decide what is possible to do in the particular setting in which your speech is to occur.

The setting should not be seen as an absolute limitation. One speech communication professor tells of a student who said his visual aid was too large for the classroom. The student had designed a mini-car with award-winning mileage. Larger than a midget racer, the mini-car required a site out-of-doors. The teacher made an exception by permitting the speech to be delivered outside on the building patio, with the audience attending. After an inspiring speech about the mini-car, the speaker jumped into his self-designed auto and drove off. Speakers can—with permission—alter the setting for their presentational aid. Students should exercise caution and gain instructor permission in advance, however. Some instructors may feel that visual aids that overwhelm the speaker or take too much attention away from the speaker—like an automobile, horse, dog, or motorcycle—are inappropriate.

What Is Your Message?

Some messages are so simple or so compelling that presentational aids are superfluous, but most messages have parts that are difficult to comprehend without some visual assistance. The complexity of the material is the main variable that determines the appropriateness of presentational aids: the more complex or difficult the message is to understand verbally, the more necessary presentational aids become. Some speech professionals feel that any speech can be made more memorable and interesting with presentational aids—no matter how simple the topic. Even spelling out your main points on a poster may enhance a simple speech.

Most quotations, narrations, and examples do not demand visual reinforcement; most messages about economic changes over time, statistical trends, series of dates, financial reports, sales records, and weather predictions do demand visual reinforcement. To determine when presentational aids will be most helpful, exercise the interpersonal skill of empathy: what parts of your speech will be better understood by the audience if they are presented visually or on audio tape?

What Will Presentational Aids Cost?

Poster board is cheap, film is more expensive, and videotape or quadraphonic sound in the classroom could be prohibitively expensive. Expense has to do with both time and money: few students have the time to make slides, films, or videos. Fortunately, the chalkboard, flipcharts, posters, physical objects, and handouts—the most common presentational aids—are neither very expensive nor very time-consuming. You have to consider how much time and money you can afford to spend on your public speech. You should also keep in mind that expensive, professionally produced aids are not necessarily more effective than homemade ones.

What Rules Should You Follow?

When you are pondering the use of presentational aids, you should consider their safety and legality. Students often ask teachers about using drugs, drug paraphernalia, alcohol, guns, and fire in the classroom. Teachers tell of students pulling out a gun when talking about banning handguns or about a student who brought a flaming wastebasket into the room to talk about the effectiveness of various fire extinguishers.

You should use your imagination and creativity when you plan your speech, but you need to consider also the safety and legality of your presentational aids. Guns are illegal on nearly every campus, and liquor is illegal on most. If you have any doubt about the safety or legality of something you plan for your speech, check first with your teacher.

Now that you know some of the broad questions to ask about your presentational aids, you are ready to consider the types available for your use in a public speech.

What Are the Types of Presentational Aids?

Think of presentational aids in categories. You can begin with the kinds of visual aids used the most—graphics—and move through display boards and equipment to persons and things—which are used less often in public speeches.

What Are Graphics?

Graphics include photographs; pie, line, and bar graphs; rank order listings; charts and tables; drawings; and maps. All of these presentational aids are in the public speaker's repertoire.

Photographs. Photographs are useful in a public speech if they are large enough for the audience to see. A student from the Philippines gave a speech about her native land accompanied by large travel posters borrowed from a travel agency. The large pictures of the beaches, the city of Manila, and the countryside reinforced what she told the audience about her country.

Avoid passing snapshots or small pictures because as they look at the snapshots, the audience will not be listening to your speech. Instead, use large pictures, like the student who showed a large satellite photograph of the region, with circles drawn to indicate how far various AM, FM, and TV signals would carry. Any picture that needs to be passed is too small and distracting for use in a public speech.

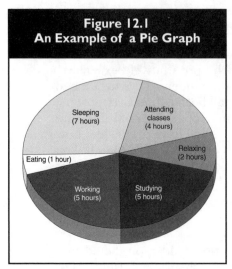

**Figure 12.1
An Example of a Pie Graph**

Graphs. Graphs are of three types—pie, line, and bar. A **pie graph** is a graph that looks like a pie cut in slices. The entire pie equals 100 percent and each slice equals a smaller percentage. Pie charts are easy to misread because people tend to underestimate the relative area of circles (MacDonald-Ross 1977). Although some people have difficulty determining percentages by looking at a pie graph, your pie graph will serve you well if everyone can see the form, if your pie is divided into fewer than six slices, and if the parts are clearly labeled. The pie graph in Figure 12.1 illustrates how time is spent by students on average during a school day. Writing in the hours is necessary because some pieces of the pie—like sleeping and studying—appear almost identical but are actually two hours different.

The second type of graph is the line graph. The **line graph** draws a line according to a vertical and a horizontal value such as average income on the vertical scale and the years listed serially on the horizontal scale. The advantage of a line graph is that the depiction can be exact. The disadvantage is that audiences often have difficulty reading and interpreting the vertical and horizontal information. They can see the lines but they do not have the slightest notion of what they mean. The speaker usually has to help an audience interpret a line graph. The line graph in Figure 12.2 shows the median (middle

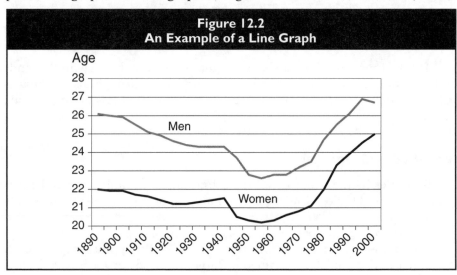

**Figure 12.2
An Example of a Line Graph**

number on a distribution) age at first marriage of men and women for more than a century. With age on the vertical scale and year on the horizontal scale, the graphic shows that both men and women are older when they marry than they were in the past.

The third type of graph is the **bar graph.** The bar graph is like a thermometer that shows how far some item measures on a scale. The advantage of the bar graphs is that they are easy to read and comprehend; the disadvantage is that bar graphs are an inexact measure. Audiences seem to have an easy time understanding the meaning of bar graphs, so their use in public speeches is encouraged. For a traditional bar graph, see Figure 12.3, which shows the racial composition of college students in 1995 and projecting to 2015.

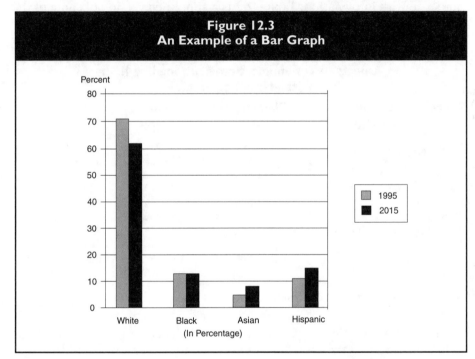

Figure 12.3
An Example of a Bar Graph

Regardless of the type of graph you use in your speech, the pie, line, or bar graph needs to be large enough for the audience to see everything on the visual aid, including any print that explains the pie, the lines, or the bars.

Rank Order Listings. A **rank order list** is a series of items from best to worst according to some stated or unstated criteria. One example would be a list that ranks the maintenance records of vehicles by origin of the manufacturer:

1.   Vehicles made by Japanese firms

2.   Vehicles made by European firms

3.   Vehicles made by American firms

Listings can be informative, but in a speech you would want to include the criteria used to select the rank ordering along with the list itself.

Charts and Tables. A **chart** is a presentational aid that summarizes information, lists steps, or otherwise displays information difficult to convey orally. For example, you might want your audience to know the emergency numbers to call in your area for police, fire, rape crisis, or abuse. A chart is an easier way to display that information than to announce the numbers. Also, the audience is more likely to write the information correctly if they see the numbers instead of merely hearing them. Similarly, a chart showing the names and prices of personal computers is easier to comprehend in print.

A **table** is a presentational aid that usually consists of columns of numbers. A table is particularly useful because columns of numbers are nearly impossible to communicate orally.

When composing a chart or table, be careful not to overload it with too much information. Table 12.1 is an example of a chart that overwhelms the audience with information. Table 12.2 is a simplified version of some of the same information, reduced in scope and written in a more digestible form.

Table 12.1
Aspects of Communication Mentioned by Name In Standards Requirements

Aspects of Speech/ Oral Communication	Elementary School	Middle School	High School
Speaking Skills	43 (95%)	43 (95%)	42 (93%)
Listening Skills	44 (97%)	42 (93%)	41 (91%)
Media Literacy	32 (71%)	31 (68%)	33 (73%)
Visual Literacy	33 (73%)	32 (71%)	34 (75%)
Persuasion	21 (46%)	25 (55%)	27 (60%)
Debate	9 (20%)	12 (26%)	18 (40%)
Technology and Communication	29 (64%)	33 (73%)	32 (71%)
Other	group dynamics art and music	group dynamics art and music	oral interpretation group dynamics

Note: Based on responses of 45 states.

Instead of explaining every number to audience members, you should help them interpret the data. For example, with Table 12.2 you could say that over 90 percent of the surveys indicated that speaking and listening skills were mentioned in their state standards and three-fourths of the surveys mentioned media and visual literacy in their state standards. Omit the items with small percentages since the audience is unlikely to be interested in them and is unlikely to remember them.

Table 12.2
Simplified Table for Oral Presentation

Aspects of Communication Mentioned in State Standards for High Schools

Speaking Skills	mentioned by over 90% of high schools
Listening Skills	mentioned by over 90% of high schools
Media Literacy	mentioned by 75% of high schools
Visual Literacy	mentioned by 75% of high schools

Table 12.1 and 12.2 adapted from Table 1 in Hall, Morreale, and Gaudino (1999, April). A survey of the status of oral communication in the K–12 public education system in the United States. *Communication Education*, 48(2),139–148.

If you use charts and tables, you will want to ensure that the audience can read them. What size print should you use? Osborn and Osborn (2003) suggest that the speaker should use three-inch-high letters for titles, two-inch-high letters for subtitles, and one-and-one-half-inch-high letters for other text. Their advice seems highly appropriate in most normal-sized classrooms. If you are speaking in a larger room, you may wish to create presentational aids with larger print. Letter heights are always dependent on distance.

Drawings. Public speakers can use illustrations prepared by themselves or others. A talented artist presented her speech on the various species of ducks. Each species was illustrated by a large colored drawing. She did not say that she had drawn them herself until the question-and-answer session. Nonetheless, her classmates were suitably impressed with her speech and her artistry.

The main things to remember about drawings and illustrations are that they must be relevant to the message, they must add something to the speech that cannot be provided by language alone, and they must be large enough for all to see (see Figure 12.4).

Maps. Some informative speeches tell an audience about locations that are difficult to specify without a map. Some informative speeches encourage students to write to legislators, but the audience does not know who the legislator is without the name and a legislative map. As long as your map is large and the lines are clear, it can be useful in your public speech. (See Figure 12.5).

You have now seen the appropriate use of photographs; pie, line, and bar graphs; rank order listings; charts and tables; drawings; and maps. In order to review all that you have learned about the kinds of presentational aids and the types of graphics, you are invited to use the checklist at the end of this chapter.

**Figure 12.4
An Example of a Drawing**

WHY YOU SHOULD EAT BREAKFAST
1. Energy and efficiency gains
2. Attitude improvement
3. Scholastic improvement
4. Weight reduction
5. Pure aesthetic pleasure

**Figure 12.5
Map Showing Places Where AIDS Epidemic was Particularly Prevalent**

On the Web

You may be required to use PowerPoint in your speech. If you want to learn more about this tool for giving public speeches, participating in video-conferencing, and enhancing other communication situations, you can go to *http://www.presentations.com*. This website for *Presentations* magazine includes an article entitled, "Learning to live with PowerPoint (and maybe even love it a little)."

❖ ❖ ❖ ❖   ## What Are Display Boards?

Three kinds of **display boards** are commonly used by public speakers: chalkboards or slickboards, posters, and flip charts. Let us examine them systematically and consider the possibilities of each.

Chalkboards or slickboards. In most classrooms, the chalkboard is the most available presentational aid. The chalkboard is a place to state your name and the title of your speech, to keep the audience's attention on the main points of your speech, to spell difficult words, and to exhibit simple drawings. The advantage is that you can use a chalkboard or slickboard spontaneously if you wish; the disadvantage is that to use them effectively, you must turn your back on your audience.

The main difficulty faced by speakers who try to write on the board is that their writing cannot be read. If you expect your audience to be able to read what you write, you have to write legibly:

1. Use print instead of cursive writing.

2. Use bold block letters.

3. Use chalk that shows up well on the board (white or yellow on green- or blackboards).

4. Use lettering that is 2 inches high and 1/4 inch wide for every 25 feet of viewing distance.

Another useful suggestion is to use a pointer or laser when talking about items on the board so you do not have to turn your back on the audience.

Slickboards, common in business conference rooms, are like blackboards except that they have a slick white or light-colored surface that accepts water markers of many colors.

Both slickboards and chalkboards are good for diagrams, definitions, outlines of main points, brief reviews, a line or two of poetry, and mathematical problems or formulas. Both can make your speech seem too much like a classroom lecture instead of an extemporaneous speech.

Avoid writing on the board during your speech by writing your message before class. If you do not want your classmates to see your written message until you speak, then cover the words with a sheet of newspaper. If you have any doubts about your teacher's attitude concerning the use of the board, check with the teacher.

Posters. Posters overcome many of the disadvantages of the presentational aids listed so far. Because they must be prepared ahead of time, they can be designed for easy viewing. Because they are made of heavy, high-grade paper, a black magic marker can produce a highly visible message. Because they are

Display boards on an easel allow for a series of visuals while the speaker faces the audience. (Photo: SMART Technologies Inc.)

prewritten, you need not turn your back on the audience when the poster is being discussed.

A student delivering a speech on child abuse used posters to highlight her message. She had three main points and three posters, each displaying a true-or-false question. She placed the three posters on the chalk tray and introduced the speech by asking her audience to answer the questions.

Most abused children come from poor families.	True	False
Most children are abused by their own mothers.	True	False
Most people now in prison were abused as children.	True	False

The listeners were uncertain of the correct answers, but the questions aroused their curiosity. The speaker used each of the questions as a main point in the speech. The posters eliminated the speaker's need for notes because they were on the posters.

The following suggestions for using posters might help you use them effectively:

1. Keep your message simple. The audience should be able to quickly grasp what you are illustrating. Consider using only key words and a relatively small number of points.

2. Make sure the poster and the print are large enough and positioned for everyone to see (remember, the teacher usually sits in the back of the room).

3. Use clips or masking tape to keep the poster up while you are referring to it, or ask a classmate to hold it for you. Avoid the embarrassment of having to pick up your poster off the floor, or having it curl off the wall.

Look at the poster in Figure 12.6 for an idea.

Whether you choose to use chalkboards, slickboards, or posters, remember that their purpose is to reinforce your message, not to be used for their own sake.

Flip charts. A **flip chart** is a large pad of paper, usually on a stand, that allows the speaker to flip the sheets over or tear them off as they are used. Colored pens may be used on this medium as long as the ink does not soak through to the next sheet.

Flip charts are frequently used in business presentations to give structure to, define, explain, or gather ideas. In a brainstorming situation, for example, the ideas can be listed on the page, torn off, and stuck to the wall or board with masking tape for later review or evaluation.

A flip chart can have some material already printed on the pages, but the advantage of the flip chart is that it allows spontaneity. The flip chart shares some of the disad-

Figure 12.6
Poster Showing Calories Burned in Different Activities

Item	CAL./HR.
Skiing Downhill	530
Skiing x/country	625
Tennis–singles	380
Tennis–doubles	270
Ice skating	390
Mountain climbing	650
Bicycle riding	500
Walking	260
Jogging	450
Horse riding	360
Dancing (continuous)	225
Sitting	75

vantages of the chalk- or slickboard in that the speaker usually has to turn his or her back to the audience in order to write, and the speaker must write legibly in block print large enough for all in the room to see. Lettering must be at least 3 inches high and the width of the broad edge of a marker.

Another advantage of flip charts is that they are portable and relatively inexpensive. Like a chalkboard, they can be used for definitions, difficult words, and simple drawings to illustrate or reinforce your message. Next we will look at some presentational aids that demand specialized equipment.

What Are Computer-Generated Graphics?

Many students today have their own personal computers or they have access to computers. If this statement is true for you, you may want to consider the possible presentational aids that you can make on a computer. Consider, too, some of the sophisticated new software packages that have been especially designed to create graphs, charts, and other presentational aids. You may wish to make handouts, illustrations, transparencies, and slides from materials created on the video screen. While others may use the computer for "desktop publishing," you can use it for "desktop presentations."

Even if you do not have strong artistic talent, you will be able to make professional-looking presentational aids. In general, computer-generated materials are more accurate and may be neater than those you can create by hand. In addition, some computer programs can create dramatic or eye-catching graphics that are more impressive than those drawn by hand.

An example is Microsoft PowerPoint,[1] a highly versatile program which can supplement a speech as long as the PowerPoint does not become the speech. PowerPoint can be used by itself as a "slide show," operated either on a timed sequence or manually. The computer can show your visual creations just as a slide projector does, except the audience sees the graphics on the video screen.

If you use a computer to generate your presentational aids, you may want to consider how large your print should be. Printers generally have a wide array of font sizes. Some of the more common sizes are 10 point, 12 point, 14 point, 18 point, 24 point, and 36 point. Each of these is successively larger. These different sizes of print are illustrated in Figure 12.7.

Osborn and Osborn (2003) provide precise suggestions for you if you create your presentational aids on the computer using these font sizes. Their recommendations follow.

	Transparencies	Slides	Handouts
Title	36 pt	24 pt	18 pt
Subtitle	24 pt	18 pt	14 pt
Other text	18 pt	14 pt	12 pt (p. 250)

What Is Display Equipment?

This section on display equipment begins with a warning. Do not use display equipment unless you know what you are doing. Display equipment includes films and videotapes, slides, audio amplification and recording

**Figure 12.7
Type Sizes**

10 point

12 point

14 point

18 point

24 point

36 point

equipment, and opaque and overhead projectors. Let us look at each in turn for their possibilities in your public speaking.

Films and videotapes. Films and videotapes can be great for demonstrating, illustrating, and clarifying. One student used a film very persuasively in a speech on violence in football. The varsity football-playing speaker showed three minutes of punt returns using his own voice to explain the action. He showed how football players can disable an opponent who does not call for a safe catch. He said the coaches taught the players to hurt opponents with fists, face masks, and helmets. The brief film supported his topic: violence in football.

Videotape is easier to edit and simpler for the amateur to produce, but video should be used sparingly for support. Your class is about public speaking, not video editing and production. Both video and film have disadvantages. One is that, in inexperienced hands, the content and the aesthetics may be poor. A second is that both film and video presentations require a darkened room, which takes all the attention away from the speaker. Gestures, attire, and facial expressions are lost in the darkness. Film and video presentations also require equipment—which may or may not work—so the speaker has to be ready to deliver the speech in another mode in case of failure.

Videos are becoming increasingly popular with speakers. The equipment necessary to use videos includes a videotape and a VCR with a large monitor. The mechanics of effective use include the following:

1. Show your video in below-normal light but not in complete darkness.

2. Adjust the volume, contrast, and position before the presentation.

3. Center the monitor in the front of the room for optimal viewing (maximum viewing distance is twelve times the diagonal width of the monitor, or 19 feet for a 19-inch diagonally measured screen).

4. Practice with your equipment before your presentation.

5. Cue your videotape to where you wish it to begin. Be careful—some machines begin playing the tape when they are inserted, which could throw you off. Other machines begin rewinding if the pause button is depressed for more than a couple of seconds.

Try to make your videotaped presentation as natural as possible by treating the video as an integral part of your speech. Avoid a big buildup on the one hand or making excuses for your video on the other. Also, be prepared to substitute your own material in case of mechanical failure. When machines fail, you will still be expected to succeed.

You may wish to consult your instructor before you decide to investigate the possibility of using film or videotape. Your speech will probably be relatively short, which will lessen the likelihood of being able to use such presentational aids. Generally, films or videotapes provide examples of your main points. If your speech is only five to seven minutes long, for example, an appropriate length for an example may only be thirty seconds or less. Few films or videos can be shown in such a short period of time. In addition, equipment may not be available for you, or equipment may malfunction during your presentation. You should be able to present your speech even if the equipment becomes unavailable or malfunctions. A presentational aid is an aid and not a substitute for information. Finally, some instructors prefer that students do not take on the additional burdens associated with such presentational aids in their first speech class.

Slides. Slides are another valuable presentational aid. A rather tough-looking fellow who always wore a black leather jacket, jack boots, and lots of chrome studs delivered an impressive speech using slides. A biker who was always surly toward his classmates, the speaker surprised them by giving a speech on motorcycle safety. His classmates thought this guy probably never wore a helmet, but he encouraged that habit in his talk. He showed six slides, each of a badly battered, vividly colored helmet. Each slide of a dented helmet was accompanied by a story about its owner. They were the helmets of friends who had survived serious accidents because they had worn them. Another surprise was that this rough-and-tumble guy taught motorcycle safety to teenagers on his own time.

Slides are much easier to produce than video and film. As long as they do not become the speech—as long as they supplement, illustrate, and reinforce—they are an asset in a presentation. The disadvantages are the same as those cited for film and videotape: equipment can fail and this equipment requires semi-darkness. A burned-out projector bulb or an upside-down slide can ruin an otherwise effective presentation.

Some suggestions for the effective use of slides follow:

1. Limit yourself to one basic idea per slide and keep the message or picture short and simple.

2. Arrange your information with more width than height. A slide is one-third wider than it is high.

3. Check for visibility of the screen and slides in the room where the audience will do the viewing.

4. Check your slides to see if they work in the projector before you use the equipment in class.

5. If possible, use a remote slide changer, so you do not have to stay by the machine.

6. Practice with your visual aids in the same place where your speech will be delivered. You can avoid the problem faced by the student who practiced at home only to discover that the only electrical outlet in the classroom was out of order.

Slides and film can add dramatic impact and involvement to your speech, but think twice before using them if you are inexperienced. Also, whenever you use mechanical devices in your presentation, you should have a backup plan in case your devices fail. The best public speakers are ready for anything—including a fast change of plans.

Audio. **Audio aids** are presentational aids that you can hear. Audio can include both the projection of the natural voice with a microphone or the use of audio tape to play voice or music.

A microphone is rarely used in classroom speeches, but the device is often used in speeches where the audience is larger than 25, when the speech is delivered outside, or where the room is too large for unaided speaking.

Microphones are of two basic types. One type is attached to the lectern or podium. Another type is cordless so the speaker has freedom of movement. Both require that the speaker stay relatively close to the microphone itself to be heard.

If you have never used a microphone before, practice with one before you give your speech. One reason for this is that you are likely to be startled by the sound of your own voice. Just as your voice does not sound the same to you when recorded on tape, your voice will not sound like your own when amplified. Being startled by the sound of your own voice can be distracting when you are trying to concentrate on your speech.

Slides can help the audience understand your information. (Photo: SMART Technologies Inc.)

Another reason to practice before delivering a speech is to learn the appropriate distance to stay from the microphone. Broadcasters call it "popping the mike" when a speaker stands so close that plosive sounds, such as words beginning with k, p, and t, blow too much air into the instrument. If you stay a distance of 12 inches away, you are unlikely to "pop" the microphone. On the other hand, you have to speak toward the microphone because averting your head can cause your voice to fade or disappear.

Audio recorders are another form of audio equipment that are useful presentational aids. In a speech about types of music, a few short excerpts can best illustrate what you mean in an informative speech differentiating among different musical formats. One of the effective uses of audio occurred when a student who was a deputy secured the tape of the sheriff questioning a suspected drug pusher. The part of the tape used began at the point where the young pusher's story fell apart, and he started to implicate himself and others. The 90-second tape was a dramatic illustration of what can happen to drug pushers when they are caught. The confession was enough to make the audience members glad they were not suspects.

The mechanical aspects of using tape recorders in a public speech include the following:

1. Set the volume before the presentation so that all can hear.

2. Cue your tape so the sound will start exactly where you wish.

3. Have the machine turned on and warmed up before you speak.

4. Practice several times to ensure that you can cue the tape smoothly.

You might want to have someone else take care of turning the machine off and on, but if you exercise this option, practice the speech and the use of the recorder with that person until you establish complete trust in each other.

Some practical suggestions concerning the recorder's use during your speech include the following:

1. Avoid saying anything while the tape is playing: a "voice-over" is inappropriate in this case.

2. Integrate the taped portion into your speech so that the tape becomes a natural extension of your talk.

3. Avoid any big buildup or excuses for the content of the tape or the quality of the recording.

If you observe these mechanical and delivery suggestions, you can make an audio recording an important supplement to your speech.

Overhead and opaque projectors. An **overhead projector** is a machine that shines light through an acetate (clear plastic) sheet. Any images or letters drawn on the acetate with magic marker or grease pencil will be projected and enlarged on a wall or movie screen. The advantage of this device is that you can face the audience while you speak. The lights immediately over the screen should be dim, but otherwise the room can be bathed in normal light so the audience can see the speaker. The lettering or images can be prepared ahead of time (an excellent idea) or drawn spontaneously during the speech (less desirable).

For the cost of a poster, you can produce your own transparencies for an overhead projector. Use an enlarging copy machine to bring printed material up to a minimum of 3/16 of an inch letter height and then run the master through a copy machine to produce the transparency. These transparencies can be produced even more easily with a laser printer using 18-point type or a larger font. You can even incorporate line drawings or photocopied materials into the master.

Some suggestions for using the overhead projector include the following:

1. Express one idea on each transparency. Otherwise, the screen becomes too crowded with verbiage and too complex for easy understanding.

2. Compose letters at least 3/16 of an inch tall; these letters will be considerably larger when projected.

3. Place most of your message toward the top and center of the transparency. Information close to the bottom or sides of the transparency tends to get cut off the screen.

4. Place your transparencies in hard paper frames and number them for ease of handling, or the sheets may not separate for you during your speech.

5. Be sure that you know how to place the transparencies on the projector correctly. A transparency that looks correct from your vantage point might be upside-down or backward from the audience's viewpoint.

6. Practice using the overhead projector while you rehearse your speech until use of the transparencies becomes natural.

A disadvantage of the overhead projector is that lights must be dimmed for better viewing. When changing materials, you must either turn on the lights or subject yourself to blinding light when the projector bay is opened.

Some helpful hints about delivery when using an overhead projector include the following:

1. You might have to talk a bit louder to compensate for the sound of the machine's fan. Older machines tend to be noisier than newer models.

2. Point with a pencil, light, or laser instead of your finger to eliminate any unwanted shadows.

3. Make sure you have your transparencies numbered on your working outline and on the transparency frames so that you use them in correct order during the speech.

4. Finally, you would be well advised to bring an extra bulb and more than one marker.

Follow these suggestions and your use of the overhead projector can be an asset to your speech.

Two creative ways to use transparencies are the reveal method and the overlay method. The reveal method blocks out parts of the information on the transparency, which is then revealed as the speaker proceeds (Figure 12.8).

The overlay method allows you to use one transparency to make one point and a second transparency placed over the first to make another point.

❖ ❖ ❖ ❖   In Figure 12.9, the speaker first shows a line drawing in one color and then places the second over the first to illustrate the different aspects of a van.

The **opaque projector** is an instrument that can project the image of small objects or the top surface of thick items, such as a magazine. Many of the suggestions for use of the overhead projector apply to the opaque projector as well. Older models of both have noisy fans requiring voice projection. They both use screens and lights that can result in the keystone effect. Finally, both require a practice session or two to ensure smooth and uninterrupted use. In addition, opaque projectors often generate considerable heat, which can melt the finish on some photographs.

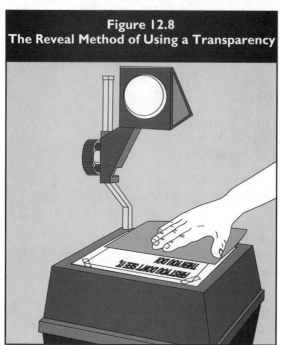

Figure 12.8
The Reveal Method of Using a Transparency

What Is the Display of Persons and Things?

Another type of presentational aid used in public speaking is displays—using living models, objects, handouts, and even yourself.

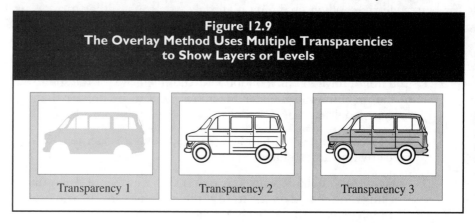

Figure 12.9
The Overlay Method Uses Multiple Transparencies
to Show Layers or Levels

Transparency 1   Transparency 2   Transparency 3

Living models. W. C. Fields, an early film star, once warned about performing on the same stage with a small child or an animal: they tend to steal the show from the performer. Speakers should be aware of the same danger when they consider using persons or things as presentational aids: human "helpers" can catch the smell of grease paint and steal the show from you.

Charles Roberts, a communication professor from Eastern Tennessee State University, tells of a gentleman who gave a demonstration speech on body painting. When he completed his speech, few could remember his main points, but they certainly remembered the man in the demonstration, who stood there for ten minutes in his bikini briefs.

A living model is a person used in your speech to illustrate an important point. A woman explaining the fine points of ballet found she could not speak and dance simultaneously, so she asked another ballet artist to show the audience what she was talking about as she described the moves. A person speaking about pumping iron, playing an instrument, or practicing first aid or lifesaving might similarly find a living model useful in a public speech.

Celebrating Diversity

Historically, Germany and Russia were linked and a number of Germans lived within the borders of Russia. Catherine the Great issued two manifestos inviting Germans to move to Russia. The first invitation on December 4, 1762, was met with some enthusiasm, but on July 22, 1763, Catherine added thousands of people to Russia with promises of transportation, land, and religious and political autonomy. More than a century later, in 1872, Alexander II revoked the privileges that the Germans in Russia had enjoyed. The Germans from Russia began to emigrate to the United States. The first people to arrive settled in the upper Midwest—the Dakotas, Nebraska, Kansas, and Illinois. As more immigrants arrived, they moved into the western part of the nation.

Because of Catherine's promises of German autonomy in Russia, most Germans from Russia continued to speak their own language and practice their own cultural and religious rituals. When they moved to the United States, they formed themselves into communities and continued many of these practices. However, the negative feeling toward Germany during the first and second world wars encouraged many people to adopt the English language and culture (*http://www.ahsgr.org/german_russia_info.htm*).

Imagine that you were going to give a speech on the Germans from Russia. What kinds of visual aids could you use? How would you begin the research process?

Some suggestions for the use of living models include the following:

1. Selecting a person whom you know to assist you in the speech usually works better than asking for a volunteer from an unsuspecting audience.

2. Except when the living model is demonstrating something, the person should sit down or otherwise move out of the audience's line of vision so the focus shifts to the speaker.

3. The model who performs should be introduced, since the individual's credibility will affect your own in the speech that you share.

4. Living models should be dressed appropriately for the topic, audience, and situation.

One student speech included a thirty-second display of a living model. The speaker was a varsity football player. The class thought he was a pretty large specimen at 6 feet 2 inches and 220 pounds. The speech discussed how football was changing and that giants were being recruited into the game. At that point, in walked a first-year football player who was 6 feet 11 inches and well over 300 pounds. He stood in front of the room for thirty seconds while he was introduced and then went back into the hall. The speaker had made his point with a living model.

Animals are a special risk. Not only do most universities prohibit any animals except seeing eye dogs, but animals are likely to embarrass the person who uses them as presentational aids. One student begged to bring his well-trained dog to class to demonstrate obedience training. The teacher got permission, and the dog performed admirably—until it decided to wet the floor right in the middle of the speech. The dog did not know any better. The owner should have.

Physical objects. Another presentational aid is the use of physical objects in a public speech. An architecture student who is talking about house design might use miniature models large enough for the audience to see. An art student might show a few pieces of wood sculpture to show how wood can be hewn into marvelous shapes. A physics student might demonstrate some laws of gravity and momentum by showing an audience how a pendulum swings.

Some suggestions about the use of physical objects include the following:

1. Select an object that can be seen by everyone.

2. Avoid passing an object through the audience, since that is a distraction from yourself and your speech.

3. Make the object an integral and natural part of your speech through your own practiced familiarity.

4. Address the audience instead of talking at, or to, the object being discussed.

5. Do not use too many objects—such as all of the parts of a camera. Too many parts can be distracting, time-consuming, and can make you anxious.

When you consider using an object in your speech, be aware that the most common problems with physical objects is that they can be too small, too complicated, or too dangerous for classroom use. A student who tried to give a speech on contact lenses found, to his dismay, that no one past the second row could see what he was showing. A student who tried to show all of the parts of a small engine became hopelessly confusing to her audience as she came to her 50th small part. Similarly, students who come to class with fireworks, chemicals, or weapons will find that they are either breaking a community or college ordinance or are so disturbing to the audience that the speech is ineffective.

Handouts. Before using any handouts, inquire about your professor's attitude toward them. Some speech communication teachers have a very negative attitude about handouts because they see them as a constant distraction, not only during the speaker's presentation but also for the speakers who follow.

Handouts, if allowed, can be a useful supplement and can reinforce or show what the speaker means. Perhaps a person speaking about the danger signs of diabetes could depend on the audience to take notes, but a way to ensure that the audience has a record of the danger signs is to distribute them on a handout at the end of the speech. Maybe an audience could remember all of the radio stations, their call letters, and their positions on the FM band, but a more definite way is to distribute a chart for future reference.

The distribution of handouts creates problems that you can cleverly avoid. What you want to avoid is wasting your speaking time by passing out papers; having long rows of people passing, dropping, and rattling papers; having audience members fight over too few copies; and producing the equivalent of "The Wave" as the papers ripple across the room. Some of the ways to avoid these problems include the following:

1. Count out the handouts by row ahead of time.

2. Enlist in advance the help of others so handouts can be distributed quickly.

3. Have the audience pick up the handouts after class.

4. Make sure everyone has a handout.

Some suggestions for the effective use of handouts include the following:

1. Make your handouts simple so they do not have to be studied for understanding.

2. Type or print your handouts so they are readable.

3. Try to keep your handout to a single page so it is easy and quick to distribute.

4. Be certain that having your information in print is the most effective way to communicate that information to your audience.

5. Provide the handouts just before you are going to refer to them, if you hand them out during the speech. If you plan on distributing them after the speech, have them ready as people leave the room.

By following these suggestions, you can make sure that a handout is an effective means of communication.

Yourself. You can be a presentational aid. The way you look, the way you dress, and the way you behave in front of the audience are part of your presentation. You are an important part of your message.

You do not have to dress up for every presentation unless that is an expectation in your class. Instead, dress in a manner appropriate to the topic and the audience. A person delivering a speech on how to interview for a job can reinforce the point by dressing the way a person should dress for an interview. A speaker demonstrating how to dissect a frog ought to wear lab clothes. A speaker talking about fashion should look like an authority on that subject.

You can use yourself and other objects as a presentational aid. (Photo: Mark C. Ide)

A slovenly appearance is telling the audience how you feel about yourself and about the audience. People who give public speeches often dress in a way that shows respect for the audience. Consider carefully how you fare as a presentational aid in your own public speech.

Summary

As a final step in critically evaluating your own use of visual aids and their use by others, ask yourself the following questions:

1. Have you used presentational aids to supplement and reinforce important points in your speech? Presentational aids should not be used for their own sake; instead, they should always be used for clarity, illustration, or explanation.

2. Have you been careful not to let your presentational aids dominate your speech so much that they have become the speech? Do not be so infatuated with your living model, your charts and graphs, and your objects that they become your speech.

3. Have you prepared your presentational aids as much as possible in advance of the speech so you do not have to be absorbed in their use when you give your speech? Most presentational aids, especially the printed, taped, and projected ones, should be ready before you give the speech.

4. Have you made your presentational aids big, loud, and central enough for everyone to see or hear? A presentational aid can detract from your speech if it becomes a deterrent to effective communication.

5. Have you displayed your presentational aids where the audience can see them? Most presentational aids cannot be simply set on a desk or lectern. You may need tape or tacks to display poster boards and other presentational aids. Also, do not block the audience's view of your presentational aids by standing in front of them.

6. Have you explained your presentational aid so the audience knows its message and its purpose? Presentational aids rarely explain themselves, so the speaker is expected to reveal their role in the speech.

7. Have you avoided passing your presentational aid through the audience? Passing handouts may be permissible, but objects and pictures will detract from your speech if distributed during the presentation.

8. Have you displayed your presentational aids only when you are discussing them? Presentational aids that are on display before they are mentioned or after they are needed may distract the audience. You do not want to compete with an interesting visual or an unusual object.

9. Have you practiced with your equipment, living model, and other presentational aids so that they are smoothly integrated into your speech?

10. Have you, during your speech, avoided talking to your presentational aid, and focused instead on the audience? Sometimes when speakers are nervous, they tend to look at their presentational aids rather than at their audience.

11. Have you spent a reasonable amount of time preparing your presentational aids? Too little preparation can result in chaos; too much can keep you from other important aspects of your public speech.

12. Have you spent enough time practicing with your presentational aids? If you spend too little time practicing with your presentational aids, you may be awkward in your presentation.

Armed with the information in this chapter, you are ready to use presentational aids in an intelligent and effective manner. You will find, as others have, that practice in using presentational aids will help you speak with confidence.

Communication Narrative 12.1
A Tale of Two Professors

Professor Harold "Colonel" Hardcastle has been teaching civil engineering for 25 years. His method of instruction reflects his years in the Army Reserve where he was in the armored division driving a tank. Although he never saw a real battle, he often wore military-type clothing and still wore his hair short. He taught by stating the mission first: "Today, we are going to learn how to design a bridge. . . ." The students called Dr. Hardcastle "Professor Overhead" because every day, without fail, Hardcastle would arrive with over 50 transparencies to show his class. He would darken the room, launch his first transparency—the one with the mission statement—and do a "voice over" during the next fifty transparencies. Some students claimed, half kidding, that they could not recognize Hardcastle because they had never seen him in the light.

Professor Samuel Krowl, or "Sam" as his students called him, was the Jerry Springer of the college lecturers. His admiring large classes gave him an audience suitable for his ego. He was an excellent speaker, but he also sprinkled his lecture on American history with film clips from the CNN archives, the History Channel on cable, and even online materials downloaded from websites. As if all the razzle-dazzle on the big screen were not enough, Sam came to class one day dressed as Thomas Jefferson and did the entire lecture as if he were Jefferson himself. His classes were a media bonanza—never a dull moment, always visually interesting, and forever active.

Now that you have met Professors Hardcastle and Krowl, critique their use of presentational aids in their classes. According to this chapter on presentational aids, what are they doing correctly and what could they do better? How would you teach their courses differently?

❖ ❖ ❖ ❖   ## Vocabulary

audio aids Presentational aids that you can hear.

bar graph A presentational aid like a graphic thermometer that shows how some item measures on a scale.

chart A presentational aid that summarizes information, lists steps, or otherwise displays information difficult to convey orally.

display boards Presentational aids such as chalkboards or slickboards, posters, and flip charts.

flip chart A presentational aid consisting of a large pad of paper, usually on a stand, that allows the speaker to flip the sheets over or tear them off as they are used.

graphics Presentational aids including photographs; pie, line, and bar graphs; rank order listings; charts and tables; drawings; and maps.

line graph A visual presentation with a line drawn according to vertical and horizontal values.

opaque projector An instrument that can project the image of small objects or the top surface of thick items.

overhead projector A machine that shines light through an acetate (clear plastic) sheet, projecting an image onto a wall or movie screen.

pie graph A visual presentation that looks like a pie cut in pieces. The entire pie equals 100 percent and each slice equals a smaller percentage.

rank order list A series of items from best to worst according to some stated or unstated criteria.

table A presentational aid that consists of columns of numbers.

Application Exercises

Proper Topics for Presentational Aids

Exercise 1: Either individually or in a small group, compose a list of 10 topics that require audio or visual presentational aids. For example, a speech on the topic of "Comparative Shopping for Certificates of Deposit" demands interest rate figures, time periods, and figures from various banking or lending institutions.

Proper Presentational Aids for Topics

Exercise 2: After completing Application Exercise 1, you will have a list of 10 topics. Examine the topics carefully and list for each the presentational aids that would be most appropriate for that topic. For example, on the topic of comparing certificates of deposit, you could present a chart showing local rates from five banks and a slide showing how the yields change depending on how often interest is determined.

——**Note**——

1. Microsoft's PowerPoint is a registered trademark of Microsoft Corporation.

References

Ayres, J. (1991, June–December). Using visual aids to reduce speech anxiety. *Communication Research Reports*, 8, 73–79.

Bogard, D. A. (1974, April). Visual perception of static and dynamic two-dimensional objects. *Perceptual and Motor Skills*, 38, 395–398.

DePaulo, B. M. (1978, March). Decoding discrepant nonverbal cues. *Journal of Personality and Social Psychology*, 36, 313–323.

Gadzella, B. M., and Whitehead, D. A. (1975, February). Effects of auditory and visual modalities in recall of words. *Perceptual and Motor Skills*, 40, 255–260.

Hall, B. I., Morreale, S. P., and Gaudino, J. L. (1999, April). A survey of the status of oral communication in the K–12 public education system in the United States. *Communication Education*, 48(2), 139–148.

Janu, J. (1999). What to wear. An unpublished speech delivered in Interpersonal Communication 103, Public Speaking, Ohio University, Athens, Ohio, in Paul Nelson's class.

MacDonald-Ross, M. (1977, Winter). How numbers are shown: A review of research on the presentation of quantitative data in texts. *AV Communication Review*, 25, 359–409.

Osborn, M., and Osborn, S. (2003). *Public Speaking* (5th ed.). Boston: Houghton Mifflin Company.

Pittman, B. (1999). Accidents kill our youth. An unpublished speech delivered in Interpersonal Communication 103, Public Speaking, Ohio University, Athens, Ohio, in Paul Nelson's class.

Poor sports (1999, September). *Consumer Reports*, 54–55, 59.

Pressley, S. A. (1999, August 31). FSU's party line: 'We're NOT no. 1.' *The Washington Post*, A3.

Resnick, N. (1999). How my family got to Cleveland. An unpublished speech delivered in Interpersonal Communication 103, Public Speaking, Ohio University, Athens, Ohio, in Paul Nelson's class.

Zayas-Baya, E. P. (1977–1978). Instructional media in the total language picture. *International Journal of Instructional Media*, 5, 145–150.

Chapter 13

Informative Speaking

We believe that an informed citizenry will act for life and not for death.

—Albert Einstein

Question Outline

I. What are four purposes of informative speaking?

II. Can you name two rhetorical principles of informative speaking?

III. How do learning styles relate to informative speaking?

IV. Which principles of learning can be applied to the informative speech?

V. How should you organize your informative speech?

VI. Can you identify four types of informative speeches?

VII. What ethical choices do you make in informative speaking?

Angelique Valdez, a single mother of three young children and a sophomore, is older than many other students. Her day at school can best be described as hectic. On this particular morning, she has an 8:00 class, which means she must be up at 6:00 a.m. to bathe, dress, and prepare breakfast for the kids. At 7:30 she is at the day-care center, where she has to tell the teacher that a friend will pick up her youngest daughter at 1:30 so her child can keep an appointment with the doctor.

Angelique arrives at the classroom just five minutes before the bell. She is lucky to be a little early because she has to ask the professor about the length of the term paper and whether or not the paper is to be double-spaced.

On her way to the next class, she sees her friend Diane, another busy stu-dent-mother, and arranges to meet her for lunch at the Oasis, a gathering place for nontraditional students. At noon Diane asks Angelique what she should do about her 2-year-old, who cried much of the night. If it is an ear infection, she asks, does she have to go to the doctor or will an over-the-counter drug do the trick? Angelique recommends the free clinic and in turn asks Diane about where she can get information for her speech, which is due next week.

We will not continue to follow Angelique throughout her day because the point is already well made: Angelique, like all of us, provides and receives information many times each day. The only difference between our everyday conversations and the informative speech, the subject of this chapter, is that the speech is longer, better organized, better researched, and delivered to more people. The similarities between the preceding conversations and the informative speech are more numerous:

1. You tell people about things they want to know, need to know, or can use;

2. You adapt your knowledge to increase their understanding; and

3. You define, explain, and give examples that help them apply the knowledge to their situation.

You know many things. You know how to play games, repair items, drive a car, read a book, or write an essay. Parents, teachers, coaches, employers, and friends have helped you increase your knowledge. In many cases, the vehicle for learning probably has been the informative speech. A physical education instructor may have taught you how to bowl, dance, and partici-pate in team sports. Other teachers taught you how to read, write, and take examinations. Employers may have taught you how to serve a customer or sell a product.

As you learn more in college and in life you may find yourself communi-cating your knowledge to your children, employees, or fellow workers. The purpose of this chapter is to examine the primary means of communicating information to other people: the informative speech. You will discover the purposes of informative speaking, the rhetorical principles for communicat-ing information, and the principles of learning that are especially important for communicating information to an audience. At the end of this chapter, you will find a checklist for the informative speech and assignments that apply what you learn in this chapter. Once you have completed those exer-cises, you will know enough about informative speaking to increase your con-fidence as a public speaker.

Two Rhetorical Principles of Informative Speaking

1. Relate Yourself to the Topic   Y $\longrightarrow$ T
2. Relate Your Topic to Your Audience   T $\longrightarrow$ A

Two Rhetorical Principles of Informative Speaking   ❖ ❖ ❖ ❖

Two **rhetorical principles** are (a) *to relate the speaker to the topic* and (b) *to relate the topic to the audience*. Related to any public speech, they require special emphasis in informative speaking because they are so often overlooked. These two principles focus on the relationship between the speaker and the topic and the audience and the topic.

Relate the Speaker to the Topic

The first rhetorical principle states that you, the informative speaker, must show the audience the relationship between yourself and the topic. What are your qualifications for speaking on it? How did you happen to choose this topic? Why should the audience pay particular attention to you on this subject? Audiences tend to respond favorably to high-credibility sources because of their dynamism, expertise, trustworthiness, and common ground. This credibility is unrelated to understanding: an audience apparently learns as much from a low-credibility source as from a high-credibility source. However, audience members are more likely to apply what they comprehend if they respect the speaker as a source.

Consider this hypothetical example. Suppose a husky male athlete gives an informative speech to your class on macramé, an activity that helps him relax. Would the men in the class comprehend the information as well if a female art major were to deliver the same information? Research says that the comprehension would be the same: they would learn about macramé equally well from a high- or low-credibility source (Andersen and Clevenger 1963). However, would the men in the class be more likely to actually try macramé themselves if the male athlete suggested it? The athlete and art major would be equally successful at teaching macramé, but the athlete would be more likely to secure a behavioral response from the men in the audience. Here is an example of how one student related the topic to himself:

> You heard the teacher call my name: Gary Klineschmidt. This is a German name. My grandparents came from Germany and the small community in which I live—New Ulm—is still predominantly German with a full allotment of Klopsteins, Kindermanns, Koenigs, and Klineschmidts. Many German customs are still practiced today in my home and in my hometown. Today I want to tell you about one German custom that has been adopted by many Americans and two German customs that are practiced primarily by people of German descent.

The speaker established a relationship between himself and his topic by stating explicitly the origins of his authority to speak on German customs.

The informative speaker relates the topic to himself/herself and to the audience. (Photo: Randall Reeder)

The point is that you must relate the topic to yourself, so that the audience will respect and apply the information you communicate. Are you giving a speech on street gangs? Let the audience know if you once belonged to one. Are you giving a speech on skydiving? Tell the audience how many times you have dropped. Are you giving a speech on hospital costs? Tell the audience the cost of your last hospital stay.

Relate the Topic to the Audience

A second rhetorical principle of informative speaking is to relate the topic to the audience early in the speech. This tactic is a wise one for ensuring audience interest and understanding. Again, you must be explicit. To assume that the audience members understand the connection between themselves and the topic may not be enough. Instead, to be direct is best: specifically tell listeners how the topic relates to them. Remember, too, that many topics may be very difficult to justify to an audience. An informative speech on taxes is lost on an audience that pays none. An informative speech on raising thoroughbred horses is lost on an urban audience. Therefore, the informative speaker is encouraged to scrutinize audience analysis information to discover indications of audience interest in a topic.

This example demonstrates the rhetorical principle of relating the topic to the audience:

> Over half of you indicated on the audience analysis form that you participate in team sports. We have two football players, two varsity tennis players, one gymnast, three hockey players, and four persons in men's and women's basketball. Because you already possess the necessary dexterity and coordination for this sport, you are going to find out today about curling.

This speaker carefully detailed the many ways in which the topic was appropriate for the particular audience. When you deliver your informative speech, remember to relate the topic to yourself and your audience.

What Are Four Purposes of Informative Speaking?

An **informative speech** can be defined as a speech that increases an audience's knowledge about a subject, one that helps the audience learn more about an issue or idea. Four purposes of informative speaking are (1) to create information hunger, (2) to help the audience understand the information, (3) to help the audience remember the information, and (4) to help the audience apply that information.

Create Information Hunger

The first purpose of informative speaking is to generate a desire for information—to create **information hunger.** Audiences, like students, are not always receptive to new information. You have observed teachers who were skilled at inspiring your interest in poetry, advanced algebra, chemistry, or physical education. You will have an opportunity to demonstrate whether you are skilled at communicating information to an audience of classmates.

If you read this chapter carefully, you should become an effective informative speaker. The first step is to arouse the audience's interest in your topic.

What are some strategies for creating information hunger? Among the many possibilities are these: arouse audience curiosity, pose a puzzling question for which your speech is an answer, and provide an explanation for an issue that has confused people.

On the Web

Find an informative speech on the web. One example is Bertrand Russell's speech, "Why I Am Not a Christian: An Examination of the God-Idea and Christianity" (found at *http://www.positiveatheism.org/hist/russell0.htm*). Does the speaker relate himself or herself to the topic? Is the topic related to the audience? How is information hunger created?

Arouse audience curiosity. A useful strategy for creating information hunger is to arouse audience curiosity about your topic. One student began his informative speech by telling his audience that the information he was about to reveal could be worth $100 per hour. The speech did turn out to be informative because he told them how to start a business. He had started his own business and was earning $100 per hour while going to college full-time.

Romona Anderson, using a different strategy to induce information hunger, began her speech by asking :

> Have you read your "Mountain Dew" bottle? Your "Diet Pepsi" bottle? Your "Classic Coke" can? If you take the time to read your bottle or can you will find an interesting message, sometimes in distinctive red print. That message says: "phenylketonurics: Contains Phenylalanine." Is this a message to aliens who dwell among us? Have you ever personally met a "phenylketonuric?" Today you are going to find out what this label means and why you should read the warning. My speech is entitled "The Phenylketonurics Among Us." (Anderson 1999, p. 1)

The speaker aroused the audience's curiosity about this mysterious word and its cryptic message. Another student stimulated audience inquiry with his question: "Did you know that catechins, a class of flavonoids, can prevent cell damage by inhibiting free radicals?" His speech explained the words and demonstrated that drinking green tea is healthy for you. Arousing curiosity is just one possible strategy for launching an informative speech.

Pose a puzzling question. Arnold Krusmark (1999) opened his speech with this query: "Have you ever wondered why the other lane of traffic always looks faster?" As he discovered, many other people in his audience had been caught in traffic, many of them had switched lanes believing that the other lane was faster, but none of them had given much thought to the truth concerning which lane is faster. The speaker had studies using computer simulations of traffic conditions that demonstrated that more often than not our notion that the other lane is faster is a mere illusion. The speaker had the sources to support his answer to a puzzling question. You can start an informative speech by thinking of other puzzling questions that emerge in everyday life: What is Hanukkah? What is Kwaanza? What is Ramadan? What is the difference between whole life and term insurance? How often should I change the oil?

Explain a confusing issue. A number of conflicts occurred around the year 2000 that received considerable news coverage without much understanding of the issues: lots of smoke and fire but little light. One example is the long-smoldering Middle East issue (Hockstader 1999). How many people really understand the West Bank issue, the Palestinian autonomy issue, or the Jewish settlement issue? A conflict in Bosnia followed by another in Kosovo pitted "ethnic Albanians" against Serbs in a federation of provinces that few Americans could locate on a map. Many saw the carnage on the news; few understood why the "ethnic cleansing" was occurring; and some never did figure out that the euphemism "ethnic cleansing" meant destruction of an entire group of people for religious and ethnic reasons. Such day-to-day mysteries invite an informative speech.

At any given time, no shortage of confusing issues exists. Who is fighting whom is just one opening for an informative speech. Others abound. Why are businesses close to a campus more expensive than businesses farther away? Why are you required to take some courses but not others? What evidence supports gun control? Can you help your audience understand the abortion issue? Still a confusing topic after many years, the abortion issue spawned two articles by famous writers only one week apart. Robert J. Samuelson (1999), the economist and columnist for Newsweek, argued that abortion may reduce crime, and George F. Will (1999), the somewhat prickly columnist for the same news magazine, wrote that a pro-choice Princeton professor "is the abortion-rights movement's worst nightmare" (p. 80). If you can locate confusion—easily uncovered in issues like abortion, gun control, and immigration policies—you have found yourself the topic for an informative speech. Remember, however, that you are trying to explain an issue—to bring light, not smoke. Your purpose in the informative speech is elucidation, not advocacy.

Help the Audience Understand the Information

The second general purpose of informative speaking is to increase the ways in which the audience can respond to the world.

The kind of knowledge we possess affects our perception of the world. A poet can look at a boulevard full of trees and write about her vision in a way that conveys nature's beauty to others. A botanist can determine the species of the trees, whether their leaves are pinnate or palmate, and whether they are healthy, rare, or unusual. A chemist can note that the sulfur dioxide in the air is affecting the trees and know how long they can withstand the ravages of pollution. A knowledgeable person may be able to respond to the trees in all of these ways. Acquiring more information provides us with a wider variety of ways to respond to the world around us.

The informative speaker's goal is to increase the audience's understanding of the topic. Whether the audience is interested in the topic before you speak about it is less important than the interest you arouse during your speech (Petrie 1963). The effective informative speaker analyzes an audience to find out how much the individuals already know about a subject, so she does not bore the informed or overwhelm the ignorant. The effective speaker

narrows the topic so that she can discuss an appropriate amount of material ❖ ❖ ❖ ❖
in the allotted time. Finally, the effective speaker applies her own knowledge
to the task to simplify and clarify the topic.

How can you encourage the audience to understand your topic? You can
apply the following ideas to your own informative speeches:

1. Remember that audiences understand main ideas and generalizations better than specific facts and details (Petrie 1963). Make
   certain that you state explicitly, or even repeat, the main ideas
   and generalizations in your own informative speech. Limit your
   speech to two to five main points.

2. Remember that audiences are more likely to understand simple
   words and concrete ideas than complex words and abstract ideas
   (Ernest 1968). Review the content of your informative speech to
   discover simpler, more concrete ways of stating the same ideas.

3. Remember that early remarks about how the speech will meet
   the audience's needs can create anticipation and increase the
   chances that the audience will listen and understand (Petrie
   1963). In your introduction, be very explicit about how the topic
   is related to the audience members. Unless your speech is related
   to their needs, they may choose not to listen.

4. Remember that audience members' overt participation
   increases their understanding. You can learn by listening and
   you can learn by doing, but you learn the most—and so will your
   audience—by both listening and doing (Zayas-Baya 1977–1978).
   Determine how to encourage your listeners' involvement in your
   speech by having them raise hands, stand up, answer a question,
   comment in a critique, or state an opinion.

If you will remember and apply these four suggestions in your informative
speech, you will probably increase the audience's understanding of your
topic.

Help the Audience Remember the Information

The third general purpose of informative speaking is to help the audience
remember important points in your speech. How can you get listeners to
retain important information?

One method is to reveal to the audience members specifically what you
want them to learn from your speech. A speaker can tell you about World War
I and let you guess what is important until you flounder and eventually forget
everything you heard. However, the audience retains information better if the
speaker announces at the outset, "I want you to remember the main causes of
World War I, the terms of the armistice, and the immediate results of those
terms." Similarly a student speaker may say, "After this speech, I will ask several of you to tell me two of the many causes for blindness that I will discuss in
my speech." Audiences tend to remember more about an informative speech
if the speaker tells them specifically at the outset what they should remember
from the speech.

A second method of encouraging an audience to remember (and one also closely tied to arousing audience interest) is to indicate clearly in the informative speech which ideas are **main ideas,** generalizations to be remembered, and which are **subordinate ideas,** details to support the generalizations. Careful examination of students' textbooks and notebooks shows that in preparing for examinations, students highlight important points with a highlighter pen. You can use the same method in preparing your informative speech. Highlight the important parts and convey their importance by telling the audience, "You will want to remember this point . . .," "My second main point is . . .," or "The critical thing to remember in doing this is. . . ."

A third method that encourages an audience to retain important information includes repeating an idea two or three times during the speech. Audiences expect important parts of the speech to receive more than temporary attention. They expect important points to be repeated. An early study demonstrated that if you repeat important matters either infrequently (only one time) or too often (four repetitions or more), your audience will be less likely to recall your information (Ehrensberger 1945). While excessive repetition can be distracting, a second or third restatement can help the audience understand. You can and should follow the old adage: "tell 'em what you are going to tell 'em; tell 'em; and then tell 'em what you told 'em." Research supports the idea that the old adage is a kind of recipe for the introduction, body, and conclusion of a speech. The audience usually expects a summary ending in which the listeners are reminded of the main points with a review (Baird 1974).

A fourth method of encouraging retention is the nonverbal practice of pausing or using a physical gesture to indicate the importance of the information (Ehrensberger 1945). Just as repetition signals an audience that the thought was important, a dramatic pause or silence just before an important statement is also effective. Similarly, your own energy level signals importance, so using bodily movement, gesture, or facial expression can grab audience attention and underline a statement's importance.

Most of the research on retention has been conducted with middle-class, white audiences. If you are speaking to a more diverse audience, you may want to accept these conclusions cautiously. Some audiences appear to appreciate and learn more from several repetitions. Others may expect a great deal of vocal volume, a factor which in most audiences is unrelated to helping people remember (Ehrensberger 1945).

How can you ensure that your audience will retain the information that you provide them? In the classroom, listen to your instructors' and classmates' informative speeches and try to determine what these speakers do to inspire you to remember the information. In other settings where you are likely to speak, similarly observe the successful informative speakers you encounter. Then see if you can apply the same techniques in your own informative speeches.

Invite the Audience to Apply That Information

The fourth general purpose of informative speaking is to encourage the audience to use or apply the information during the speech or as soon afterward as possible. An effective speaker determines methods of encouraging the audience to use information quickly. Sometimes the speaker can even determine ways that the audience can use the information during the speech.

Komiko Tanaka, who was delivering an informative speech on the Japanese art of origami, for example, had everyone in class fold paper in the form of a bird with moveable wings. Another student speaker had each classmate taste synthetic foods made with chemicals. Amanda Agogino invited everyone to try one dance step to music. These speakers were encouraging the audience to apply the information from their speeches to ensure that they retained the information.

Why should the informative speaker encourage the audience to use the information as quickly as possible? One reason is that *information applied immediately is remembered longer.* A second reason is that *an action tried once under supervision is more likely to be tried again.* An important purpose of informative speaking is to evoke behavioral change in the audience. To think of informative speeches as simply putting an idea into people's heads, of increasing the amount they know about a topic, is easy. However, the speaker has no concrete indication that increased information has been imparted except by observing the audience's behavior.

Therefore, the informative speaker seeks a **behavioral response** from the audience, an overt indication of understanding through action. What behavioral response should the informative speaker seek? Many kinds are possible. You can provoke behavioral response by inviting the audience to talk to others about the topic, to actually apply the information (for example, trying a dance step), or to answer questions orally or in writing. If the audience cannot answer a question on the topic before your speech but can do so afterward, you have effected a behavioral response in your audience.

The four general purposes of informative speaking, then, are to create a desire for information in the audience, to increase audience understanding of the topic, to encourage the audience to remember the information, and to invite the audience to apply the information as quickly as possible. Next we will examine learning styles and five learning principles that relate to informative speaking.

Learning Styles and Informative Speaking

Informative speaking is instructional. Informative speaking teaches an audience more about a subject. People do not learn or even think alike (e.g., Gadzella and Masten 1998). The discoveries about learning styles spawned a Knowing Styles Inventory (Knight, Elfenbein, and Martin 1997), studies of temperament-related learning styles (Horton and Oakland (1997), examinations of gender and learning styles (Philbin, Meier, and Huffman 1995), and even books on "brainstyles" (Miller 1997), cognitive styles and learning strategies (Rayner and Rayner 1998), and individual differences in learning and instruction (Jonassen and Grabowski 1993).

All you need to remember so far in this material is that researchers are certain that people vary considerably on how they receive information and ideas and how they process that information in their minds. The effective informative speaker needs to know that you do not just tell an audience some information and hope for the best; instead, you try to account for individual differences and different learning styles when you create your speech. The very important first step for the informative speaking is being aware that audience members are going to have diverse learning styles.

Children and adults learn differently. One distinction concerning learning styles is that adults in college learn differently than do children. Knowles' (1970) theory of **andragogy** or adult learning and Kolb's (1993) Learning Styles Inventory generated a number of assumptions about adult learning, including the following, outlined by Cantor (1992) and Cranton (1992):

- adults are autonomous and self-directed
- adults are goal oriented
- adults are relevancy oriented, and
- adults are practical problem solvers (Blackmore 1996)

Celebrating Diversity

Imagine that you are going to deliver a speech to residents of an assisted care home. The people in the facility range in age from 75 to 101. They are mostly women and most have graduated from college. You have been asked to deliver an informative speech that will be of interest to the residents. While 140 people live in the building, you are told that about 90 to 100 will probably attend your talk. You are given 45 minutes to give your talk and to answer questions from the audience. What topics will you consider? How can you relate these topics to yourself and to your audience? How will you create information hunger? How will you help the audience understand, remember, and apply the information you provide? Can you use humor and wit? Will presentational aids be helpful? After you have made some of these decisions, talk with a family friend who is actually in assisted care. How well does she believe you would have done if you had delivered the speech?

Unlike children, who are dependent on adults and guided by them, college students and other adult learners see themselves as independent and as guiding themselves. Also, they are goal oriented, driven by goals such as earning a degree, securing a job or job advancement, receiving certification, and advancing toward graduate or professional education. College students are attracted to what they regard as relevant to their pursuit of goals, so they dislike information and ideas that seem unrelated to their goals. Finally, adult learners are drawn toward information and ideas that allow them to solve practical problems.

Adult motivations differ from child motivations. A second distinction between young children and adult learners is what motivates the adult learner. Cantor summarizes the motivations by saying that adult learners try

- to make or maintain social relationships
- to meet external expectations
- to better serve others
- to advance professionally
- to seek stimulation or escape
- to pursue pure interest (Cantor 1992, in Blackmore 1996)

Unlike children, adults are more concerned about how information and ideas relate to their relationships with mates, partners, employers, co-workers, and the complex web of relationships they have or will establish. They are much more concerned than children about meeting the expectations of supervisors and employers who may want them to upgrade their skills and knowledge. On the other hand, adult learners may be attracted to some information and ideas that simply stimulate them ("I wanted the astronomy course because I always wanted to know more about the universe") or that provide escape ("I took the film course because I thought I would enjoy it"). Adults have more interests and they pursue those interests.

Males and females exhibit different learning styles. Several researchers (Bodi 1988; Cranton 1992; McNeer 1991) believe that they have found a pattern in how young men move through a developmental sequence as they mature in their thinking. For example, when male students begin college, they perceive the world as binary, two-valued, black and white, right or wrong. At first, they think one right answer exists for any question. They see that a variety of opinions exist but "feel that authorities that describe diversity [of opinions] are poorly qualified or just 'exercising students' so students will be forced to find the 'right answer' themselves" (Blackmore 1996). As the male student matures, he still believes that a multitude of opinions is temporary, that the "right answer" simply has not yet been found. Still later, the male student believes that multiple opinions may be present and legitimate, but he would prefer to know that "right answer." Finally, he moves to a different level in which he sees that people have a right to their own opinions and he begins to see his own position in a world of different opinions whose legitimacy he accepts (Blackmore 1996).

Women's way of knowing is not described as a developmental sequence; instead, the following describes how college women depict their own manner of acquiring knowledge (Belenky et al. 1986). Female students feel that they are subject to external authorities before which they find themselves with little to say. They see themselves as receivers but not creators of knowledge. They believe that truth and knowledge are discovered privately, subjectively and intuitively though they are "interested in learning and applying objective procedures for obtaining and communicating knowledge" (Blackmore 1996).

Keep in mind that these depictions of the way men develop their way of knowing and the way women feel about acquiring knowledge are always changing. They may not describe you or the men and women with whom you associate. The generalizations are not frozen in time but are a dynamic, ever-changing mosaic, which must be reassessed frequently and with different populations.

People reflect different learning styles and multiple intelligences. You now know some of the theory behind learning styles and some of the conclusions about them, so you can better understand some specific features of learning styles that can directly affect your informative speeches. Although researchers classify learning styles in many ways, one of the easiest to understand is that of Gardner's **Multiple Intelligences,** or multiple ways of knowing and learning, which identify seven styles of learning (Winters 1995; Wang 1996). The seven styles of learning reveal the person who

1. plays with words (verbal/linguistic)
2. plays with questions (logical/mathematical)

3. plays with images (visual/spatial)

4. plays with music (music/rhythmic)

5. plays with moving (body/kinesthetic)

6. plays with socialization (interpersonal)

7. plays alone (intrapersonal) (Blackmore 1996)

You may use more than one style of learning, but most people prefer one or a few. Our learning styles often lead us to courses and professions that play to our learning-style strengths. Hence, the verbal/linguist person majors in English or a foreign language. The logical/mathematical person majors in computer science; the visual/spatial, in photography or art. The music/rhythmic learner plays in the orchestra; the body/kinesthetic learner majors in dance or theatre; the interpersonal prefers the social sciences and jobs in sales and law; and the intrapersonal person might choose a major that relates more to machines and equipment than to people (technical theater, software developer, or accountant).

In your informative speech, the variety of learning styles resident in your audience requires that you think of more than one way to present your information:

- Certainly the verbal/linguistic audience members are likely to respond favorably to a lecture-style format, but perhaps with interaction such as is achieved in a question and answer period.

- A logical/mathematical person likes puzzles to solve, logical organization and formulas, and "right answers." Your informative speech can pose a case study for them to solve.

- The visual/spatial person may be partial to models, diagrams, graphs, charts, and pictures, anything that allows them to see how your idea looks.

- The music/rhythmic audience member responds to sound, music, and rhythm, so pleasing sounds from good word choice, pleasing rhythms from parallel construction, and good voice qualities would help.

- The body/kinesthetic audience member likes demonstration, movement, and action like having everyone practice a first aid procedure, lifting a few weights, or demonstrating a ballet move.

- The interpersonal audience member will listen to messages that will enhance social interaction and may appreciate opportunities to interact with the speaker or other audience members during or after the formal presentation.

- Finally, the intrapersonal audience member will not wish to be called upon during or after the speech, will respond favorably to messages that allow personal thought without interpersonal interaction, and will appreciate most the messages that allow autonomy.

The audience's varied learning styles invite the effective speaker to vary the teaching strategies in the speech.

Sometimes you can assess your own class's learning styles by knowing their majors, by observing their choice of topics, and by noting their manner of presentation. In any case, using a variety of verbal, nonverbal, image, spatial, and even bodily strategies in your informative speech will reach a wider audience than adhering strictly to a lecture-style approach. At least this section on learning styles should invite you to think more creatively about all of the different ways that you can present your information so your speech will be appealing to more audience members with different learning styles.

Kolb's Learning Styles Inventory (LSI)

Based on theories by Dewey, Piaget, and Lewin, Kolb (1979) developed a **Learning Styles Inventory** (1993) to explore an individual's learning strengths and weaknesses. The LSI looks for a relative emphasis on one of four learning modes:

Concrete Experience (CE) is learning by feeling;

Reflective Observation (RO) is learning by watching;

Abstract Conceptualization (AC) is learning by thinking; and

Active Experimentation (AE) is learning by doing.

Kolb also labeled four learning styles:

The **Accommodator** (CE and AE) who learns best from hands-on experience;

The **Diverger** (CE and RO) who learns best by viewing a situation from multiple points of view but who prefers observation over action;

The **Converger** (AC and AE) who learns by finding practical uses for ideas (they do well on conventional examinations) and by defining and solving issues; and

The **Assimilator** (AC and RO) who learns by merging much information into efficient, orderly form with more interest in logical soundness than in practical value. (Cook 1997)

Five Principles of Learning

Informative speaking is a type of teaching. Listening to informative speeches is a type of learning. If you expect an audience to understand your informative speech and apply the knowledge learned, you must treat the speech as a phenomenon in which teaching and learning occur. Because you, as an informative speaker, are inviting the audience to learn, you can apply these five **principles of learning** to your speech: building on the known, using humor and wit, using presentational aids, organizing your information, and rewarding your listeners.

❖ ❖ ❖ ❖   ## Build on the Known

One principle of learning is that *people tend to build on what they already know, and they accept ideas that are consistent with what they already know.* An informative speech, by definition, is an attempt to "add to" what the audience already knows. If the audience is to accept the new information, the new material must be related to information and ideas that they already hold.

Let us say that you are going to give an informative speech on the topic of depression ("Beating . . . Depression," 1999). What do most people in your audience know about the subject? Do they know the possible causes of depression? Do they know the difference between "feeling down" or "feeling blue" and clinical depression? Do they know the symptoms of depression? Do they know the profiles of the most likely victims? Are the most likely victims old, young, chronically ill, female, new mothers, or postmenopausal? Your mission is to start with what the audience knows and then to build on that knowledge with new information presented so the material will be attractive to a variety of learning styles.

Use Humor and Wit

A second principle of learning to observe in informative speaking is to *use humor and wit*. **Humor** is the ability to perceive and express that which is amusing or comical, while **wit** is the ability to perceive and express humorously the relationship or similarity between seemingly incongruous or disparate things. Any of us can find topics about which we know more than our classmates. They may be our religion, hobbies, travels, political position, eating habits, or major in college. However, the aim in informative speaking is to make the information palatable to the audience and to present the material in such a way that the audience finds the information attractive. Notice that the principle does not dictate that you must be funny. The principle says "use humor and wit." Wisdom is the information that you know about the topic. Wit and humor are the clever ways you make the information attractive to the audience. Wit and humor are the packaging of the content.

One pre-med student, for example, decided to give a speech on chiropractors, even though he was clearly prejudiced against them. He decided to handle his prejudice with wit rather than anger or bitterness. He entitled his speech "Chiropractors: About Quacks and Backs." Another student used wit in her speech about parenting. She was unmarried and well known by her classmates. The audience could hardly hide its shock when she stated in the introduction to her speech, "I did not think anything of parenting until I had my son." Her "son" turned out to be an uncooked hen's egg. She was taking a course on the family, in which she was required to care for her "son," the egg, for one week. When she went out on a date, she had to find a "babysitter" to care for the egg. She had to protect the egg from breaking as she went from class to class, take the egg to meals, and tuck the egg in at night. The introduction of her "son," the egg, added wit to the wisdom of her informative speech on parenting.

Often language choices help add vigor to your presentation. Darris Snelling (1999), who was delivering a potentially boring speech on "TV and Your Child," enlivened his speech with witty language. He began this way:

Within six years almost everybody in this room will be married with a young one in the crib and another on the way. Do you want your youngster to start babbling with the words sex, violence, and crime or do you want him to say Mommy, Daddy, and pepperoni, like most normal kids? (p. 1)

The speaker hit the audience with the unexpected. The words were witty, and they made his speech more interesting to the audience.

Use Presentational Aids

A third principle of learning is to *communicate your message in more than one way because members of the audience have different learning styles.* Verbal/linguistic individuals learn best by listening or reading. Accommodators learn best when they do what the speaker is explaining. Visual/spatial individuals learn best by seeing. Effective informative speakers recognize that different people have varied learning styles. Therefore, such speakers try to communicate their messages in a variety of ways to meet diverse learning styles.

A student giving an informative speech about life insurance used a chart to explain to his audience the main differences among whole life, universal life, and term insurance. Because much of his explanation depended on the use of statistics to indicate costs, savings, and loan value, he and the audience found the chart necessary for the informative speech.

You, too, can find a variety of methods of communicating your message to an audience that learns in diverse ways. Some material in an informative speech is simply too detailed and complex to present orally. You might be able to get more of the message across by presenting these complex materials in a handout to the audience at the conclusion of your speech. Other complex data may be easier to understand through a graph, a picture, an object, a model, or a person. Consider using every means necessary to get your informative message to the audience.

Organize Your Information

A fourth principle of learning is to *organize your information for easier understanding.* Organization of a speech is more than outlining. Outlining is simply creating the skeleton of a speech. In an informative speech, consider other organizational possibilities. How often should you repeat your main point? Where is the best place to repeat it? How can you try to create a proper setting for learning to take place? Where in the speech should you reveal what you expect the audience to remember? Do you place your most important information early or late in the speech?

No solid answers exist to these questions, but research does hint at some likely outcomes (Ehrensberger 1945):

1. *How often should you repeat main points?* Two repetitions have little impact, and positive effects fade with four or more. The best answer seems to be to repeat main ideas three times.

2. *Where do you create a setting for learning?* The earlier you create an atmosphere for learning, the better. Make clear to audience members early in the speech exactly what you want them to learn from your presentation.

3. *Where should important information be placed?* Audiences remember information placed early and late in the speech, so avoid placing your most important material in the middle of your presentation. **Primacy** or placing the best argument early in the speech seems to work better in speeches on controversial issues, on topics that the audience cares little about, and on topics highly familiar to the audience. **Recency** or placing your best argument late in your speech seems to work best when audience members care about the issue, when the issue is moderately unfamiliar, and when the topic is not terribly interesting (Janis and Feshbach 1953).

4. *Should you present one side of the issue, both, or many?* A speaker who intends to inform an audience about an issue needs to avoid advocating one side or another. The ethical informative speech would attempt either to cover the issue comprehensively (both or many sides) or to at least reveal to the audience that other, equally plausible, positions exist.

5. *How do you indicate orally which parts of your speech are main points and which are subordinate or supporting?* In writing, subordination is easy to indicate by levels of headings, but people listening to a speech cannot necessarily visualize the structure of your speech, which is why the effective informative speaker indicates early in the speech what is going to be covered. This forecast sets up the audience's expectations; they will know what you are going to talk about and for approximately how long. Similarly, as you proceed through your speech, you may wish to signal your progress by indicating where you are in your organization

Presentational aids help people who play with images and movement (Gardner's Multiple Intelligences) or reflective observers who learn by watching (Kolb's Divergers and Assimilators). (Photo: Mark C. Ide)

through transitions. Among organizational indicators are the following:

- "My second point is . . ."

- "Now that I have carefully explained the problem, I will turn to my solution."

- "This story about what happened to me in the service will illustrate my point about obeying orders."

In each case, the speaker is signaling whether the next item is a main or subordinate point in the informative speech.

Organizational Tips

1. Limit your information to three to five main points—or fewer.

2. Repeat information three times or fewer.

3. Tell the audience early what you want them to learn.

4. Place your most important information early or late in the body, but not in the middle.

5. Inform the audience about various positions on an issue.

6. Indicate clearly your main points.

Reward Your Listeners

A fifth principle of learning is that *audiences are more likely to respond to information that is rewarding for them.* **Reward** in this context means a psychological or physical reinforcement to increase an audience's response to information given in a speech. One of the audience's concerns about an informative speech is "What's in it for me?" The effective informative speaker answers this question not only in the introduction, where the need for the information is formally explained, but also throughout the speech. By the time a speaker is in the middle of the presentation, the audience may have forgotten much of the earlier motivating information presented, so the speaker continually needs to remind the audience how the information meets its needs.

A student speaker, talking to his audience about major first-aid methods, made this statement in his informative speech:

> Imagine being home from school for the weekend, having a nice, relaxing visit with your family. Suddenly your father clutches his chest and crumples to the floor. What would you do to help him?

The student reminded the audience throughout the speech how each first-aid technique could be applied to victims with heart attacks, serious bleeding, and poisoning. The benefit for the audience was in knowing what to do in each case. Another student began her speech by saying the following:

> Did you realize that, at this very moment, each and every one of you could be and probably is suffering from America's most widespread ailment? It is not a sexually transmitted disease, cancer, or heart disease, but a problem that is commonly ignored by most Americans—the problem of being overweight.

As the speaker proceeded through her information on low-calorie and low-carbohydrate diets, she kept reassuring the audience members that they could overcome the problem in part by knowing which foods to eat and which to avoid. The audience benefited by learning the names of foods that could help or hinder health.

Rewards come in many forms. In the preceding examples, the reinforcement was in the form of readily usable information that the audience could apply. A speaker can use other, more psychological forms of reward. "Do you want to be among the ignorant who do not know what a 'value added tax' is?" The speaker who confidentially tells you about value added tax is doing you a service because you will no longer be ignorant. A student from Chicago found that most of her classmates thought first of muggings when someone mentioned Chicago in conversation. She devoted her informative speech to the positive aspects of living in that city. The result was that the students in the audience had many more positive associations with Chicago, including the fact that one of their fellow students, who looked not at all like a mugger, was from Chicago, and she thought that city was a good place to live.

Skills for the Informative Speaker

Informative speaking employs a number of skills that help make a speech effective. In informative speaking, four of those skills are defining, describing, explaining, and demonstrating. Let us explore for a moment how these skills work in an informative speech.

Defining in an Informative Speech

Defining is revealing the speaker's intended meaning of a term. Why make an issue out of definitions when the concept is so simple? One reason is that speakers often forget to define the terms they use in a speech. You are listening to a medically oriented speech in which the speaker has mentioned something called "a plah-see-bow" about five times without telling you what a *placebo* is. You hear a female student talk about "hormone replacement therapy," but you never find out from her what those words mean. One reason for this section on defining is so you will not forget to define the terms you use in your speech.

A second reason for discussing defining as a skill in informative speaking is that the way you define a term can start a fight or establish peace. Much of the battle over abortion rights is centered on how the Supreme Court defined the beginning of life, when a mass of cells becomes a person, and when and who can stop the development of a fetus. Recently a man in Maryland buried his young daughter without reporting her death to her mother or to the authorities. People who read about the case thought that surely he would be charged with a crime because of the mystery surrounding how she died; because he never notified a coroner, police officer, or even a relative; and because he buried her in an unauthorized area. The man was never charged with anything because under Maryland law nothing he did was *illegal*. To be a crime, an act must be "against the law," but archaic laws in Maryland did not require notification of death, did allow a family member to bury another family member, and allowed burial outside a cemetery. Because of the definitions, the man went free.

Three ways to define a word are to reveal its **denotation** or dictionary-type of definition; its **connotation** or meaning in a particular situation, often with emotional loading; and its **etymological meaning** or defining by revealing the origins of a word. The word *patois* (a French word pronounced Paa-TWAA) is the language spoken by many black inhabitants of the Island of Jamaica in the Caribbean. That would be the word's dictionary meaning. The connotative meaning of *patois* is a bit more complicated because few white people can speak this language, which has been mastered by so many black people in Jamaica. Connotatively, patois suggests a private language limited

---

Technical Tip 13.1
Finding Information for the Informative Speech

Specialized Sources of Information

ProfNet This source invites online requests for information which are answered by experts from around the world. The experts are professors, researchers, corporate managers and workers, and government employees. The address: *http://www1.profnet.com.*

Censored News This source stretches back to 1989 with stories that the mainstream media kept out of the news. Some stories about important issues are refused for various reasons by the establishment press. If you use materials from this source, you need to tell the audience where you found the information since one of the reasons the article may not have been published is that the article or the reporter was irresponsible. *http://www.projectcensored.org.*

Freedom Forum Dedicated to free speech and free press, this forum started by Gannett is nonpartisan but highly informative about news coverage, access to information, and the freedom to criticize without fear of retribution. *http://www.freedomforum.org.*

Ecola Newsstand A site to use for searching for information. The site brings indexes for newspapers, computer publications, and magazines (including electronic newspapers and magazines). Search for the publication by name on this site if you wish. *http://www.ecola.com.*

---

pretty much to black people who grew up in Jamaica. Consequently, *patois* is a rare language that does not even extend to the other Caribbean islands and that is more of a spoken than a written tongue since even its spelling is not standardized. The etymology is also interesting. *Patois* developed in Jamaica when black people from different tribes worked for white masters whose language they could not understand. For them to understand each other, the slaves put together their own West African languages along with some English words to develop a language of their own that was widely understood by them but not their white employers. Put together the denotative, connotative, and etymological meanings and you have a more complete understanding of the word *patois.*

Perhaps you still think that defining is a little-used skill in informative speaking. If so, consider how important the definition of terms is in determining what you mean by *child abuse* (spanking? open hand? who is a child?), *privacy* (your email? your medical records? your use of psychotropic drugs?), *pro-life* (killing the unborn? killing convicted felons?), or even poor grades (Ds and Fs? anything below a B?).

Actually you can define words or concepts by using methods beyond denotation, connotation, and etymology. You can compare and contrast, provide an example, or provide synonyms (similar meanings) or antonyms (opposite meanings). Whatever method you use, the important point is to remember to help your audience by defining your terms.

Describing in an Informative Speech

Describing is when you evoke the meanings of a person, a place, an object, or an experience by telling about its size, weight, color, texture, smell, and/or your feelings. Describing relies on your abilities to use precise, accurate, specific, and concrete language to demonstrate a diverse vocabulary.

How can you tell what your life as a single parent is like without describing some incidents from your life? How can you reveal what life is like as a Latino in an Anglo world without describing some of your personal experiences? Similarly, describing works well in revealing why you like a particular neighborhood, live in a specific kind of dwelling, and buy a particular kind of car. One doctoral student wrote her dissertation about "bag ladies" by living as one for a few months; a professor in Illinois has become an expert on gangs by living with them for months at a time. Both of these researchers found that the only way to really capture life as a bag lady or life in a gang was to become a participant-observer in their culture. Only that experience allowed them to describe accurately.

Mark DuPont (1979), in a public speaking class at Iowa State University, told his classmates about his hometown of Phoenix, Arizona, with the descriptive words in Figure 13.1.

Figure 13.1
Describing in an Informative Speech

Transition

The heat cannot be escaped. As the sun beats mercilessly on the endless lines of automobiles, waves of shimmering heat drift from the blistering pavement, creating an atmosphere of an oven and making the minutes drag into eternity. The wide avenues only increase the sense of oppression and crowding as lane after lane clogs with rumbling cars and trucks. Drivers who have escaped the heat of the sun in their airconditioned cars fall prey to the heat of frustration as they do battle with stoplights and autos that have expired in the August sun. Valiant pedestrians wade through the heat, pausing only to wipe from their foreheads the sweat that stings their eyes and blurs their vision. It is the afternoon rush hour at its peak, Phoenix, Arizona, at its fiercest. The crawl of automobiles seems without end as thousands of people seek out their homes in the sweltering desert city.

Gradually, almost imperceptibly, the river of traffic begins its descent past the 100-degree mark; the streets become quieter and more spacious. The mountains enveloping the city begin to glow as their grays and browns awaken into brilliant reds and oranges. The haze, which has blanketed the valley throughout the day, begins to clear. The lines of buildings become sharper, their colors newer and brighter. The shadows of peaceful palm trees lengthen, inviting the city to rest. The fiery reds and oranges of the mountains give way to serene blues and purples. The water of hundreds of backyard swimming pools, which have been turbulent with the afternoon frolicking of overheated children and adults alike, calms and mirrors the pink and lavender dusk sky. The fading sunlight yields to the lights of homes and streets as the Valley of the Sun becomes a lake of twinkling lanterns reflecting the sea of stars above. The inferno is gone, forgotten. The rising swell of crickets and cicadas lulls the desert inhabitants into relaxation and contentment. The desert floor gives up its heat, cooling the feet of those who walk on it. The heat of anger and hatred for the valley dissipates, and in the hearts of the people who have braved another summer day in Arizona, there is only the warmth of love for their desert home.

Explaining in an Informative Speech

❖ ❖ ❖ ❖

Explaining in an informative speech reveals how something works, why something occurred, or how something should be evaluated. You may explain a social, political, or economic issue; you may describe an historical event; you may discuss a variety of theories, principles, or laws; or you may offer a critical appraisal of art, literature, music, drama, film, or speeches. A wide collection of topics may be included in this category.

Do you or your classmates understand *postmodernism, the New World order, lyric opera, NASCAR, Chateau Malmaison Moulis wine, titanium chronograph watches,* or a *shahtoosh "ring shawl"?* The informative speaker takes lesser-known words and concepts and renders them understandable to the audience through explanation, as in Figure 13.2.

Figure 13.2
Explaining in an Informative Speech

OEM and Non-OEM: Only Your Body Shop Knows for Sure

Until my daughter wrecked her Honda Civic, I had never thought about what happens at the body shop. In fact, a chance remark alerted me to the problem. When I stopped by the body shop after two weeks to see when the vehicle would be repaired, the person behind the desk said, "This one's going to take a while. Your insurer is recommending non-OEM parts." Probably he was not supposed to make that statement because the repair of that one relatively inexpensive car became a nightmare that revealed the cracks in our insurance/auto repair system.

OEM is an acronym for "original equipment manufacturer." A body shop that completely repairs a Honda with OEM parts is using Honda-made parts to replace the damaged portions of your vehicle. The body shop's other choices are to use salvage, that is, parts borrowed from wrecked vehicles or, more likely, to use non-OEM parts or imitations. The imitation parts could be as good as OEM parts, but they could also be misshapen, inferior in quality, and likely to peel and rust quickly. According to the February 1999 *Consumer Reports*, imitation door shells can be installed without the guard beams, with weak welds on guard beams, or with guard beams made with weaker steel. Similarly, knock-off hoods sometimes come without the crumple initiators that keep sheet metal from crashing straight through the windshield. Imitation bumpers can compromise your headlights, radiator, and even your airbags.

The OEM versus Imitation Parts controversy is more complicated than a quick look would indicate. Insurance companies want to reduce costs, and imitation parts cost less. My daughter's Honda cost $4000 to repair; the entire car was worth less than that amount. So do I want my insurance company to insist on genuine "original equipment manufacturer" parts for all of the several hundred bits and pieces that had to be replaced? Also, insurance companies are sometimes compromised by dishonest body shops that use imitation parts but charge the insurance company for original equipment. An imitation Honda hood costs $100 less than an OEM Honda hood according to the *Consumer Reports* article entitled "Cheap Parts Can Cost You A Bundle" (1999). Finally, nobody really knows whether imitation parts are safe. The National Highway Safety Administration and the Insurance Institute for Highway Safety test the safety of new vehicles but not replacement parts. Nobody checks to see if the hood that sliced through your windshield was an original or ☞

a cheap imitation, and maybe neither you nor your insurance company knows either.

You know more than you did before about car repair, the insurance industry, the use of OEM parts, the upside and downside of imitation, knock-off replacement parts, and the risks assumed by the customer when having a car repaired. My daughter's Honda? That newly renovated piece of junk spent two months in the body shop because, as a low-level manager explained, "the after-market [imitation] parts didn't fit." Switching to OEM parts cost the insurance company twice the original estimate, raised the annual insurance premium by over $500 for five years (the accident was her fault), and doubled the amount of time to repair the car. Welcome to the world of insurance and car repair!

Demonstrating in an Informative Speech

Demonstrating is showing the audience an object, a person, or a place; showing the audience how something works; showing the audience how to do something; or showing the audience why something occurs. In other words, demonstrating may be similar to the explaining or the describing, but the focus of demonstrating is on the visualization of your topic. For example, a student who was informing her classmates about the virtues of some cellular phones over others used five cellular telephones as models. To help her classmates see the features on these relatively small objects, she used an instrument called an Elmo, which magnified each phone on the screen in front of the classroom. Seeing the models helped the class understand the features. Describing can accompany demonstrating.

As you attempt to decide on a topic, you should consider demonstrating those ideas, concepts, or processes that are too complex to be understood through words alone. Similarly, consider the wide variety of items and materials that can be used to demonstrate your topic. You may wish to learn more about presentational aids, such as chalkboards, posters, movies, slides, opaque and overhead projections, living models and physical objects, handouts, and you (as a visual aid). Which items will be most useful for your topic? Do not rely on those aids that are the simplest to construct or the most obvious; instead, use those items that best illustrate your topic.

Some examples of speeches that invite a demonstration are:

- a speech by a varsity wrestler on various take-downs,

- a speech by an art major on painting with oils,

- a speech by a fashion major on fall fashions,

- a speech by a woman on how to fillet a fish,

- a speech by an advertising major showing us the best ads for the year, and

- a speech by a library science major showing us how to find more and better information on the Internet.

All of these topics, and some topics that you discover on your own, will lend themselves to demonstration.

Ethics and Informative Speaking

Can you make inappropriate ethical choices when you present information to others? Yes, tainted information is a common problem with people who are less than honest. A charlatan feeds people incorrect information, blatant lies: your home is infested with termites, your roof won't last another year, and the lead in your paint will give your kids brain damage.

What are some guidelines for positive ethical choices in an informative speech?

1. **Be sure of the quality of your information.**
   - Is the information accurate, verifiable, consistent, and placed in context?
   - Have you avoided implying that you have information that you lack?
   - Have you avoided making up facts or distorting information?

2. **Exercise caution when using the words of others.**
   - Have you accurately quoted the sources you have cited?
   - Have you paraphrased accurately if you have summarized the words of others?
   - Did you cite the sources that are responsible for your material?
   - Have you avoided plagiarism?
   - Have you kept all quotations in proper context?

3. **Be careful not to mislead your audience.**
   - Have you told the audience of your association with groups whose work or purpose may be relevant to the topic?
   - Have you been honest?
   - Did you present all of the relevant information?
   - Did you tell your audience that your examples were hypothetical or real?
   - Have you used appropriate language to clarify words or concepts that the audience does not understand?

4. **Be sure the audience needs the information.**
   - Are you providing the audience with new information?
   - Are you allowing the audience free choice?
   - Can your audience make reasoned choices about the importance and accuracy of the information you are providing?

5. **Be sure that the information you are providing is in the best interests of the audience members.**
   - Are you providing information that helps rather than hurts the audience?
   - Are you providing information that advances rather than inhibits our culture and society?

Ethical choices affect your source credibility. If your audience finds that you bend the truth, twist the evidence, and shape information for selfish purposes, then the audience may find you less credible in the speeches that remain.

> ## ✔ Reality Check 13.1 ✔
> ## Contentious Issues More Complicated Than They First Appear
>
> How old is the gun control issue? Did it began in earnest with crazed adolescents killing school children or is the issue as old as the Constitution? As with all contentious issues, events spark new vigor into old controversies; time passes and passions cool; and even the patient find that some issues never seem to be settled or solved. Gun control is just one such issue. As usual, this issue is accompanied by considerable political posturing and torrents of words, but this issue, like some other thorny issues, is nourished by the blood of our own children, our fellow workers, and victims selected for their ethnicity or life style.
>
> To illustrate how complicated an issue can become, *Harper's Magazine* (1999)—a left-tilting publication—embraced what gun advocates have been saying all along: that the Constitution "holds that Americans have a right to bear arms whether they are serving in an official state militia or not" (p. 58). The author adds:
>
> > The truth about the Second Amendment is something that liberals cannot bear to admit:
> >
> > The right wing is right. The amendment does confer an individual right to bear arms,
> >
> > And its very presence makes effective gun control in this country all but impossible.
>
> In the article entitled "Your Constitution is Killing You: A Reconsideration of the Right to Bear Arms," Daniel Lazare reveals the historical complications of interpreting the briefly stated Second Amendment to the Constitution. He points out that we have almost as many guns as people, that we add 5 to 7 million guns per year, and that polls show that two Americans favor stricter gun controls to every one American who does not. You can read the article to find out the author's recommended solution, but the point of this reality check is that information is rarely neutral, persistent issues are ordinarily very complicated, and the ethical speaker tries in earnest to be honest about the multiple sides of complex issues. "To provide information honestly" should be the goal of the informative speaker, especially the speaker who tries to explain complex issues.

If you provide accurate information placed in an appropriate context, you are making ethical choices. Cite the sources you are using to avoid plagiarism. Be accurate in direct quotations and in the intent of the writer if you have summarized someone's words. Do not mislead your audience by omission or commission. Consider the audience's need for the information you are providing—do not give them information they already have or provide them with information about which they cannot exercise free choice. Finally, be sure that the information that you are providing encourages the improvement of self and society.

NCA Credo for Communication Ethics

One of the principles from the NCA Credo is relevant to this chapter:
* We advocate sharing information, opinions, and feelings when facing significant choices while also respecting privacy and confidentiality.

Summary

In this chapter, you learned two rhetorical principles in informative speaking. The first principle is that the speaker should explicitly state the relationship between himself or herself and the topic. The second is that the speaker needs to link the audience to the topic. These principles can be observed by describing your qualifications to discuss the topic and by demonstrating how the audience will find this information useful.

Next, you learned that the purposes of informative speeches are to generate information hunger, to help the audience understand the information, to help the audience remember the information, and to invite the audience to apply the information from the speech.

Among the important points concerning the purposes of informative speaking, you learned that audiences comprehend generalizations and main ideas better than details; audiences comprehend simple words and concrete ideas better than big words and abstractions; a sense of anticipation can encourage listening and understanding; and audience participation increases comprehension.

Informative speeches need to be adapted to the audience's learning styles. You learned that children and adults learn differently, that adult's motivations are different from children's motivations, and that males and females have different learning styles. You looked briefly at Gardner's concept of Multiple Intelligences with its seven styles of learning and at Kolb's Learning Styles Inventory (LSI), which classified four learning modes and names for four learning styles: accommodaters, divergers, convergers, and assimilators.

You learned five principles of learning related to the informative speech. The principles are (1) build on the known, (2) use humor and wit, (3) use presentational aids, (4) organize your information, and (5) reward your listeners.

Four methods of organizing the informative speech seem to be especially useful to the informative speaker. They are the time-sequence, the spatial relations, the cause-effect, and the topical sequence patterns.

Finally, you learned about four special skills useful in informative speaking: defining, describing, explaining, and demonstrating. Defining explains the meaning of a word or a few words. Describing relies on your ability to offer precise, accurate, and concrete language; to demonstrate a sufficient vocabulary; to use appropriate words; and to offer definitions. Explaining reveals how something works, why it occurred, or how it should be evaluated. The speech of demonstration includes objects, processes, or procedures observed by the audience. Figure 13.3 is a checklist that you can use to assess your own informational speech and the speeches delivered by others.

Vocabulary

abstract conceptualization (AC) A term in the Learning Styles Inventory signifying learning by thinking.

accommodator (CE and AE) A person whose preferred learning style blends concrete experience with learning by doing.

active experimentation (AE) A term in the Learning Styles Inventory signifying learning by doing.

Figure 13.3
A Checklist for the Informative Speech

____1. Have you created a desire for information?

____2. Have you related the topic to your audience, its modes of learning, and learning styles?

____3. Have you revealed your relationship to the topic?

____4. Have you used wit and humor when appropriate?

____5. Have you helped your audience understand your information?

____6. Have you helped your audience remember information?

____7. Can the audience apply the information?

____8. Have you built new information on old information?

____9. Have you used presentational aids or demonstration when needed?

___10. Have you organized your message effectively and ethically?

Communication Narrative 13.1
The Need to Know

Maybe Svetlana was trying to curry favor with her boss, Mr. Alsizer, but she knew that inviting him to the meeting of middle managers was the right thing to do. After all, her boss was the one who decided her annual raise or maybe even an end-of-the-year bonus for increasing the company's productivity. She was quite sure that inviting him to speak to the twenty people who worked under her would be a smart move. Nobody else seemed to have thought of this strategy for attracting Mr. Alsizer's attention. When she issued the invitation through the assistant to the president, she suggested that Alsizer speak to her staff about the proposed managed-care policy that was being prepared for the next fiscal year.

When Mr. Alsizer appeared in the meeting room, flanked by his administrative assistant who was carrying a large pile of transparencies, the room was completely full. Most of the staff had never heard Alsizer speak except at ceremonial events. Svetlana had informed everyone that Alsizer was going to present and answer questions about the new health policy. Before he even opened his mouth, the administrative assistant lowered the lights, turned on an overhead projector, and pushed a button to lower a screen behind the projector.

Svetlana realized almost immediately that she had made a serious mistake. Alsizer had apparently not talked with any other groups about the proposed health policy. He was reading information off the overheads in a manner that suggested he did not know what he was talking about. Furthermore, the information was too detailed. Every transparency was a heavy block of print, full of divisions, sections, subsections, and footnotes. Each transparency took a full two to three minutes to read in the darkened room. Svetlana saw to her horror that half the heads in the room were nodding, and Cecil Schwartz, full from lunch, had his head on the table and was snoring lightly.

Alsizer had said not a word about why Svetlana's staff should listen to his report. He could have told them that almost 2 percent of next year's raise pool had evaporated into the health care costs. He could have told them that the frequent visits to the emergency room instead of going to appointments with a primary care physician were quadrupling the costs of medical care. Every employee's child seemed to be taking an expensive battery of tests for learning disabilities, and the "mental health" costs were an uncontrolled flood of bills.

Buried in all the details on Alsizer's transparencies was important information about diminished raise pools, uncontrolled medical expenses, and unbridled mental health expenditures. All of that information was in the report somewhere, but Svetlana's staff never knew this information because their minds were numbed by the presentation.

When the lights came on, Svetlana's employees looked like startled marmots. They jerked to attention when Alsizer's administrative assistant abruptly turned on the overhead lights, they rubbed their red-rimmed eyes as if they were just emerging from their pillows, and many of them stretched their arms and arched their backs like a lackluster aerobics class. Nobody asked even one question. The entire room was so thankful that Alsizer had completed his presentation that they applauded his departure as he and his administrative assistant whisked out of the room with their pile of transparencies in hand. Svetlana worried that Alsizer realized the lack of questions signaled disinterest, that he had heard Cecil snore, or saw the rest of them nodding. Perhaps her idea of inviting the boss to give a speech to her staff was not such a great idea after all.

andragogy A term that refers to adult learning as opposed to child learning; used in adult education disciplines.

assimilator (AC and RO) A person whose preferred learning style blends abstract conceptualization with reflective observation.

behavioral response An objective of a speech to inform which is met when the audience shows an overt indication of understanding through action.

conclusion Restates the main points, provides incentive for understanding and remembering, and reveals how the audience can apply the newly learned knowledge.

concrete experience (CE) A term in the Learning Styles Inventory to signify learning by feeling.

connotation The meaning of a word in a particular situation, often with emotional loading.

converger (AC and AE) A person whose preferred learning style blends abstract conceptualization with active experimentation.

defining Revealing the intended meaning of a term.

demonstrating Showing the audience an object, person, or place; showing the audience how something works; showing the audience how to do something; or showing the audience why something occurs.

denotation A dictionary-type of meaning.

describing When the speaker evokes the meanings of a person, place, object, or experience by revealing size, weight, color, texture, smell, and/or feelings.

diverger (CE and RO) A person whose preferred learning style blends concrete experience with learning by watching.

etymological meaning Defining by revealing the origins of a word.

explaining Reveals how something works, why something occurred, or how something should be evaluated.

humor The ability to perceive and express that which is amusing or comical.

informative speech A speech that increases an audience's knowledge about a subject; a speech that helps the audience learn more about an issue or idea.

information hunger The speaker generates a desire in the audience for information.

learning styles inventory (LSI) Kolb's method of exploring an individual's learning strengths and weaknesses; includes four learning modes.

main ideas Generalizations to be remembered in an informative speech.

multiple intelligences Gardner's term for multiple ways of knowing and learning.

primacy Placing your best argument early in the speech organization.

principles of learning Principles governing audience understanding by building on the known, using humor or wit, using presentational aids, organizing information, and rewarding listeners.

recency Placing your best argument late in the speech organization.

reflective observation (RO) A term in the Learning Styles Inventory to signify learning by watching.

reward A psychological or physical reinforcement to increase an audience's response to information given in a speech.

rhetorical principles Two principles of public speaking that focus on the relationship between the speaker and the topic, and on the relationship between the audience and the topic.

subordinate ideas Details that support the generalizations in an informative speech.

wit The ability to perceive and express humorously the relationship or similarity between seemingly incongruous or disparate things.

Application Exercises

1. Think of three topics about which you could give a three-minute speech to inform. List the topics in the blanks at the left. In the blanks at the right, explain how you relate to the topic in ways that might increase your credibility with the audience.

Topics   **Your Relationship to Topic**

a._____   _____

                                  _____

b._____   _____

                                  _____

c._____   _____

                                  _____

2. In the topic blank below, name one topic that you did not use in the previous exercise and explain in the blanks following how you would relate that to your own class in an informative speech.

Topic:_____

The audience's relationship to topic:

_____

_____

_____

3. Write down a topic for an informative speech that you have not used in previous application exercises. Explain in the spaces provided how you could apply each of the principles of learning to that topic.

Topic: _____

One way that I could relate this topic to what the audience already knows is by

_____

One way that I could relate wit to wisdom in an informative speech on this topic is by

_____

One way that I could use several channels to get my message across on this topic is by

_____

One way that I could organize my speech to help the audience learn my information is by

_____

One way that I could provide reinforcement to my audience for listening to my informative speech on this topic is by

_____

References

Andersen, K., and Clevenger, T. (1963). A summary of experimental research in ethos. *Speech Monographs,* 30, 59–78.

Anderson, R. (1999). The phenylketonurics among us. An unpublished speech delivered in Interpersonal Communication 101, Public Speaking, Ohio University, Athens, Ohio, in Paul Nelson's class.

Baird, J. E. (1974). The effects of speech summaries upon audience comprehension of expository speeches of varying quality and complexity. *Central States Speech Journal,* 25, 124–125.

Beating the blues: Dealing with depression (1999, Fall). *Inova Health Source,* 9.

Belenky, M. F., Clinchy, B. M., Goldberger, N. R., and Tarule, J. M. (1986). *Women's Way of Knowing: The Development of Self-Voice and Mind.* New York: Basic Books.

Blackmore, J. (1996, August 11). *Pedagogy: Learning Styles. http://www.cyg.net/~jblackmo/diglib/styl.html.* 1/10/99.

Bodi, S. (1988). Critical thinking and bibliographic instruction: The relationship. *Journal of Academic Librarianship,* 14(3), 150–153.

Cantor, J. A. (1992). *Delivering Instruction to Adult Learners.* Toronto: Wall & Emerson.

Cheap parts can cost you a bundle: Auto insurers are pushing shoddy collision-repair parts, and consumers may not know it (1999, February). *Consumer Reports,* 12–19.

Cook, M. J. (1997). *An Exploratory Study of Learning Styles as a Predictor of College Academic Adjustment. http://www.matthewjcook.com/research/learnstyle.pdf,* 9/10/99.

Cranton, P. (1992). *Working with Adult Learners.* Toronto: Wall & Emerson.

DuPont, M. (1979). Transition. An unpublished speech delivered in the honors section of Public Speaking, Iowa State University, Ames, Iowa, in Paul Nelson's class.

Ehrensberger, R. (1945). An experimental study of the relative effectiveness of certain forms of emphasis in public speaking. *Speech Monographs,* 12, 94–111.

Ernest, C. (1968). Listening comprehension as a function of type of material and rate of presentation. *Speech Monographs,* 35, 119–127.

Gadzella, B. M., and Masten, W. G. (1998, December). Relation between measures of critical thinking and learning styles. *Psychological Reports,* 83(3), 1248–1250.

Hockstader, L. (1999, August 19). Plotting a future on West Bank: Palestinians wait impatiently for transfer of land. *The Washington Post,* A15.

Horton, C. B., and Oakland, T. (1997, Spring). Temperament-based learning styles as moderators of academic achievement. *Adolescence,* 32, 131–141.

Janis, I., and Feshbach, S. (1953). Effects of fear-arousing communication. *Journal of Abnormal and Social Psychology,* 48, 78–92.

Jonassen, D. H., and Grabowski, B. L. (1993). *Handbook of Individual Differences, Learning, and Instruction.* Hillsdale, NJ: Lawrence Erlbaum Associates.

Knight, K. H., Elfenbein, M. H., and Martin, M. B. (1997, September). Relationship of connected and separate knowing to the learning styles of Kolb, formal reasoning, and intelligence. *Sex Roles,* 37, 401–414.

Knowles, M. S. (1970). *The Modern Practice of Adult Education: Andragogy vs. Pedagogy.* New York: Association Press.

Kolb, D. A. (1993). *LSI-IIa: Self Scoring Inventory and Interpretation booklet.* Boston: McBer & Company.

Kolb, D. A., Rubin, I. M., and McIntyre, J. M. (Eds.). (1979). *Organizational Psychology: A Book of Readings.* Englewood Cliffs, NJ: Prentice-Hall, Inc.

Krusmark, A. (1999). The Other Lane Is Always Faster: The Story of an Optical Illusion. An unpublished speech delivered in Interpersonal Communication 101, Public Speaking, Ohio University, Athens, Ohio, in Paul Nelson's class.

Lazare, D. (1999, October). Your Constitution is killing you: A reconsideration of the right to bear arms. *Harper's Magazine,* 57–65.

Litzinger, M. E., and Osif, B. (1993). Accommodating diverse learning styles: Designing instruction for electronic information sources. In L. Shirato (Ed.), *What Is Good Instruction Now? Library Instruction for the 90s.* Ann Arbor, MI: Pierian Press.

McNeer, E. J. (1991). Learning theories and library instruction. *Journal of Academic Librarianship,* 17(5), 294–297.

Miller, M. (1997). *Brainstyles: Change Your Life Without Changing Who You Are.* New York: Simon & Schuster.

Petrie, C. R. (1963). Informative speaking: A summary and bibliography of related research. *Speech Monographs,* 30, 79–91.

Philbin, M., Meier, E., and Huffman, S. (1995, April). A survey of gender and learning styles. *Sex Roles,* 32, 485–494.

Rayner, R. R., and Rayner, S. R. (1998). *Cognitive Styles and Learning Strategies: Understanding Style Differences in Learning and Behavior.* London: David Fulton Publisher.

Samuelson, R. J. (1999, September 6). What do we care about truth? *Newsweek,* 76.

Sizer, T. R., and Sizer, N. F. (1999, September 6). "Tests are an easy way out: Two educators urge parents to look beyond the numbers." *Newsweek,* 50–51.

Snelling, D. (1999). TV and your child. An unpublished speech delivered in Interpersonal Communication 103, Public Speaking, Ohio University, Athens, Ohio, in Paul Nelson's class.

Wang, P-C. (1996). *Gardner's Multiple Intelligences.* Penn State Educational Systems Design Home Page: Penn State University. *http://www.ed.psu.edu/insys/ESD/Key/Keyschool/key1.htm.*

Will, G. F. (1999, September 13). Life and death at Princeton. *Newsweek,* 80.

Winters, E. (1995). *Seven Styles of Learning: The Part they Play When Developing Interactivity. http://www.bena.com/ewinters/styles.html,* 9/10/99.

Zayas-Baya, E. P. (1977–78). Instructional media in the total language picture. *International Journal of Instructional Media,* 5, 145–150.

Chapter 14

Persuasive and Presentational Speaking

Persuasion is often more effectual than force.
—Aesop

Question Outline

I. What is persuasive speaking?

II. How does persuasive speaking compare with informative speaking?

III. Why is persuasive speaking important?

IV. What are three purposes of persuasive speaking?

V. How does persuasive speaking affect beliefs, attitudes, and values?

VI. What are some of the principles of persuasion?

VII. What are three types of persuasive speeches?

VIII. How ethical is your persuasive speech?

Gabriella Rajna had a big day ahead. Her boss, the CEO of Tidewater Supplies, Inc., had asked her to make a presentation to the company's most profitable customer. That customer, Modern Motels of America, brought in over 30 percent of Tidewater Supplies' annual earnings. Gabriella's job was to convince the CEO and six vice-presidents from Modern Motels to continue using Tidewater

Supplies for their linens, soap, shampoo, and cleaning supplies. The presentation would take place in their new high-rise office building in Atlanta.

Gabriella knew that at least three competitors had approached Modern Motels of America about changing accounts. She knew also that Modern Motels was not dissatisfied with Tidewater Supplies. However, like any business, Modern Motels was interested in securing the same service and supplies at a lower price if possible. She had no way of knowing the competition's bids, but her boss had given her the authority to bargain down to a certain point. If Gabriella bargained higher than that figure and still gained the bid, she would receive a healthy bonus. If she had to drop to the minimum, she would receive no bonus and no cheers from her boss or her colleagues because Tidewater would make little profit at that bottom-line figure. Gabriella Rajna knew that she had to give the most important persuasive speech of her life.

This chapter will reveal what Gabriella Rajna needed to know for her persuasive presentation. You will learn:

- how to distinguish informative speaking from persuasive speaking,
- why persuasive speaking is important,
- three purposes of persuasive speaking,
- some principles of persuasion,
- three types of persuasive speeches, and
- some ethical considerations.

When you have completed this chapter, you will understand better what persuasive speaking is and what results to expect from persuasive speaking.

What Is Persuasive Speaking?

Persuasive speaking is a message to influence audience members' choices by shaping, reinforcing, or changing their responses toward an idea, issue, concept, or product. Sometimes the influence occurs immediately after the speech and sometimes it occurs far later (Kumkale and Albarracin 2004). Persuasion may be more effective when multiple messages are received, as in a campaign.

Let us compare informative and persuasive speaking. Perhaps no speech is completely informative or completely persuasive, but Figure 14.1 might help highlight the characteristics of the two kinds of speeches.

Why Is Persuasive Speaking an Important Topic?

You are a consumer of persuasive messages each day. Persuasive messages bombard you. As often as not, when the phone rings, your pager goes off, you access the Internet, or the doorbell chimes, you are confronted with someone who wants something of you. Television and radio programs are punctuated every few minutes by advertisements. Magazines and newspapers are filled with flashy ads designed to sell you something. Many websites

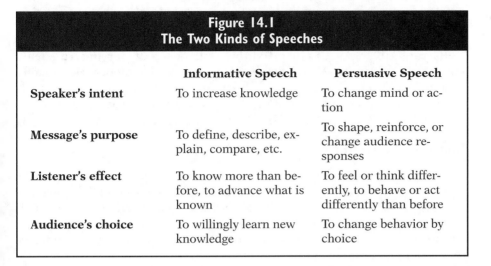

Figure 14.1
The Two Kinds of Speeches

	Informative Speech	Persuasive Speech
Speaker's intent	To increase knowledge	To change mind or action
Message's purpose	To define, describe, explain, compare, etc.	To shape, reinforce, or change audience responses
Listener's effect	To know more than before, to advance what is known	To feel or think differently, to behave or act differently than before
Audience's choice	To willingly learn new knowledge	To change behavior by choice

are surrounded by ads for products and services. The mall and the supermarket are designed to sell products and services to you.

Today, more than ever, the media, the Internet, and other people compete for your attention, your money, your time, your vote, or your membership. Large corporations that are busy merging with each other have swallowed up small, family-owned businesses. In the U.S. economic food chain, big banks eat little banks and the big banks merge to become even bigger banks. These large entities compete for popularity and profit. As a consumer and citizen, you have become the target of their persuasive campaigns.

You also serve as the producer of persuasive messages. Whether you are selling a product, soliciting votes, marketing services, canvassing for donations, seeking a job, or simply attempting to convince someone that they should believe as you do, you are engaged in persuasive speaking. Whether you have had training in persuasive speaking or not, you are familiar with the subject, which is as prevalent as the air around us.

At the same time, your happiness and success may largely depend on your persuasive skills. If you cannot sell the product you have been given, you may lose important income. If you cannot successfully gain employment, you may live in poverty. The inability to encourage others to vote for the party of your choice or to hold particular political views may lead you into disappointment and discouragement.

Your satisfaction in both private and public spheres is dependent, in great part, on your ability to be both a competent consumer and a producer of persuasive messages. You do not want to be tricked by others. You want to be able to understand why you feel compelled to respond to certain messages while you disregard others.

You also want to learn to be an effective and ethical persuader. The success of your personal life and the achievements in your professional life rely not on luck but on your developed ability to convince others that you are a credible individual who understands social influence. Persuasive appeals are expected in a democracy and in commerce. This chapter helps you to understand and to practice persuasive speaking.

Three Purposes of Persuasive Speaking

Gerald Miller (1980) portrayed three **purposes of persuasive speaking**—to shape, reinforce, and change responses in an audience. Historically, shaping has been associated with learning, reinforcing has been largely ignored, and changing has been the main focus of persuasive speaking.

Shaping Audience Responses

Shaping responses means that the persuasive speaker tries to move the audience toward a predetermined goal. A parent shapes a child's behavior to encourage the child to walk: sitting up draws cheers, standing up brings encouragement, and the first step is a photo opportunity. Similarly the persuasive speaker shapes responses in the audience by moving the audience toward a predetermined goal.

For instance, imagine that you want the audience to have a more positive attitude toward the disposal of nuclear waste from power plants. Most people do not want a nuclear waste dump in their state much less in their backyard, so the persuasive speaker must shape the audience's responses by first demonstrating the marvelous potential of nuclear energy to generate the power necessary for our lifestyle. Next the speaker might shape the audience by asking them to explore alternatives to nuclear power, most of which are even more expensive or too dirty to contemplate. Shaping, then, is moving an audience closer and closer to the speaker's solution by presenting ideas in small, appealing doses.

Reinforcing Audience Responses

Reinforcing responses is a second purpose of persuasive speaking. Reinforcing means rewarding the audience for sustaining present beliefs, attitudes, and values. Wallace Fotheringham (1966) called this concept "continuance," which means that you want your audience to continue a behavior. Examples of reinforcing or continuance are:

- Political speakers try to keep audiences loyal to a certain party and a particular candidate;

- Religious speakers try to encourage faithfulness to a certain doctrine and to a particular faith;

- Educators try to persuade students that knowing how to read, write, and speak, as well as having a wide knowledge about many subjects, is the mark of an educated person;

- All politicians are trying to persuade people to continue voting, believing, and gaining education as in the past; and

- Business people try to persuade the marketers to advertise, the sales associates to increase sales, and the design people to attract customers' attention to the product.

Encouraging people to keep doing something is big business in America.

Changing Audience Responses ❖ ❖ ❖ ❖

A third purpose of persuasive speaking is **changing responses,** altering an audience's behavior toward a product, a concept, or an idea (Miller 1980). Often the professional speaker pursuing this purpose persuades the audience to:

- start or stop a behavior,
- start exercising,
- stop smoking,
- start studying,
- stop eating unhealthy foods, or
- start drinking fruit juice instead of alcohol (Fotheringham 1966).

Changing audience responses is a challenging assignment. People tend to behave the way they have in the past, but the persuasive speaker who adopts this purpose is asking the audience to behave differently. Changes that alter well-established habits are difficult to achieve for most people.

What Is Being Influenced?

A public speaker needs to keep in mind the goal of persuasion. What are you trying to shape, reinforce, or change in an audience? Usually what you are trying to influence are the audience's feelings, beliefs, attitudes, and values for the purpose of securing behavioral change.

Feelings

Feelings are our affective states or dispositions, our emotional responses. When you cry at a romantic movie, laugh at a comedian, or become angry at the referee's call at a game, you are expressing your emotions and showing your feelings. Sometimes you may change your feelings about a particular topic even though you do not express yourself quite so obviously. You have affective responses to your spouse, partner, roommates, or children as well.

Sometimes persuasive speakers are interested in changing the feelings of others. Hart (1998) studied people's letters to the editor, the press (ads, print, and broadcasts), and politicians (speeches, debates) and found that "politicians are largely responsible for the nation's reservoir of political hope" (p. 115). Politicians communicate positive feelings more so than do the press or the people. Zullow (1994) demonstrated that economic optimism rises nationally every four years with the advent of presidential

Persuasion shapes, reinforces, and changes audience responses. (Photo: Amy Peng/*Daily Bruin*)

campaigns. When politicians speak, they hope to create hopefulness and optimism in the audience.

When a motivational speaker talks about the positive attributes of successful people, she is attempting to engender feelings of excitement and enthusiasm in the audience. The religious leader, the poet, the storyteller, and the entertainer all attempt to influence their audience's feelings.

Beliefs

Beliefs are things you believe to be true even in the absence of proof. You may have once believed in Santa Claus; you believed in him though you couldn't prove his existence. You may believe that the cat that crossed your path this morning will bring bad luck; that including your birth day, month, and year in your lotto guess will bring you good luck; or that your astrological sign predicts your future. On a more serious note, you may believe that your physician can cure most any physical ill that you have, that prescription drugs can kill most any ailment that might occur, or that the safety features on your vehicle can keep you from getting killed. You probably have a relatively large number of beliefs of various kinds.

Rokeach (1973) envisioned five levels of beliefs. The persuasive speaker needs to distinguish the beliefs that are least challenged and perhaps most believed from those that are easiest to change. If you know the levels of belief of your audience on the topic of your speech, then you can better predict what persuasive appeals are most challenging and which are easiest to achieve.

- First-level beliefs are **primitive beliefs with unanimous consensus** which are based on direct experience and which are widely believed. Not only do we hold these beliefs because they are consistent with our senses, but the people around us believe the same thing. Examples would be beliefs such as night is dark, day is light, a dropped object will fall, objects accelerating straight at each other will crash, and a sharp object can pierce the skin.

- Second-level beliefs are **primitive beliefs with zero consensus** which are unverified personal beliefs about which we lack external confirmation. Examples would be your belief that you are too fat even though nobody else seems to think so and the belief that you are destined to be great even though you dreamed up that notion yourself. Both kinds of primitive beliefs are difficult to change because they are at the core of your belief system.

- Third-level beliefs consist of **authority beliefs** that we embrace because people we respect have told us to believe them. Examples are parental lessons on telling the truth, being considerate of others, or being respectful toward the person who decides your pay. Other examples of authority beliefs are following instructions, obeying the police, doing what the teacher says, and doing what your boss asks you to do.

- Fourth-level beliefs consist of **derived beliefs** that are beliefs that we learn indirectly from sources we trust. Examples are beliefs that we learn from reading a text, listening to the news, or in conversations with others. Authority beliefs are more difficult to change than are derived beliefs, but both are easier to change than primitive beliefs.

- Fifth-level beliefs and the easiest level to change are **inconsequential beliefs** which are beliefs linked to taste, fashion, or impulse. You might always buy the least expensive toothpaste because you do not have brand loyalty; you might move easily from one perfume to another; or you might not care too much what kind of shoes you buy as long as they fit. These inconsequential beliefs are relatively easy to change.

Attitudes

Attitudes, according to Eagley and Chaiken (1993), are "a psychological tendency that is expressed by evaluating a particular entity with some degree of favor or disfavor" (p. 1). Your attitudes invite you to respond in a favorable or unfavorable way; they constitute a kind of intention to act in a certain way about certain things (Fishbein and Ajzen 1975). If you dislike studying, you may indicate that negative attitude by avoiding studying, talking with friends, playing video games, watching TV, or taking long showers. You *learn* your attitudes about study, work, relatives, and other people. They lead you to dislike smokers, like people with dimples, despise the Internal Revenue Service, or like flying airplanes.

In persuasive speaking, your goal might be to alter audience attitudes. You might want them to favor assisted suicide, embrace tax reform, enjoy mathematics, or support big business. Some attitudes—your attitude toward organized religion, toward other ethnic groups, or toward a stepparent—are difficult to change. Others—liking foreign cars, disliking aspirin, or favoring a certain politician—might be easier to change.

In persuasive speaking, beliefs can be problematic because claims about your beliefs are unverifiable, unprovable. You can tell an audience about your beliefs. You can even say what your beliefs do for you. Ethically you have to accept the personal nature of beliefs and accept the idea that other people's beliefs are equally important to them. Beliefs are not true or false, nor are they facts that can be verified. They exist, they influence our behavior, and they can be changed through persuasion, but not by proving that one set of beliefs is true or false. Be cautious about attacking the beliefs of others because they are often deeply felt and resistant to change. They are not, however, as resistant to change as values.

Values

Values are learned social principles, goals, or standards found acceptable or even desirable by the people we live with, the groups to which we belong, and the institutions we respect. Values include the abstractions we embrace: honesty, courage, loyalty, friendship, freedom, trustworthiness, and patriotism. Values tend to be the basis from which beliefs and attitudes spring. For example, our value of freedom may inspire a belief that government should never interfere with our right of expression or an attitude against rules like not talking during the film in a movie theater.

In persuasive speaking, values might be the stated or unstated basis of many issues. Pro-life advocates have a belief in the sanctity of life, which is based on a value that says life is so precious that no human should tamper with procreation, the survival of the species. Values rarely change abruptly, and often are held for a lifetime. The persuasive speaker is more likely to chip

❖ ❖ ❖ ❖   away at the edges of audience attitudes than to alter the fundamental values by which the audience lives.

Behavior

Behavior is our observable action. The persuasive speaker sometimes wants to change unobservable feelings, attitudes, values, and beliefs. At other times you will want to change the actual behavior of your audience. The behavioral change may be obvious: vote for a certain candidate, buy a certain product, go to a certain place, or try a certain exercise. Sometimes the behavioral change is less obvious: read more about modern warfare, listen to a talk about taxation, or tell people about socialized medicine.

Sometimes the behavioral change is almost imperceptible. For example, an audience member becomes slightly less conservative and votes for a bond issue in the secrecy of the voting booth; an audience member answers questions from a pollster just a little differently than she would have before she heard your speech; or an audience member earns somewhat better grades because of your motivational speech about study habits. In all of these cases, behavioral change took place as a result of a speech (see Figure 14.2).

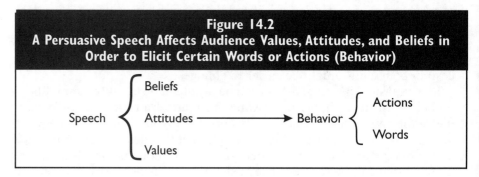

Figure 14.2
A Persuasive Speech Affects Audience Values, Attitudes, and Beliefs in Order to Elicit Certain Words or Actions (Behavior)

The public speaker often meddles in the cognitive domain, in the minds of the audience, tinkering with this belief, that attitude, or this value. However, we never know if that tinkering had any effect except through the audience's behavior. What audience members say and do, their behavior, tells us what they must think.

Elaboration likelihood theory. To unite what you have just learned about beliefs, attitudes, values, and behavior, you can turn to Petty and Cacioppo's (1986) **elaboration likelihood theory.** This theory of information processing states that we respond to information cognitively, affectively, and behaviorally. That is, we can know and understand the information in our mind (cognitive); we can feel or respond emotionally to the information (affective); or we can behave in a certain way in response to the information. The persuader is interested in what a person thinks and feels about information because both affect what the receiver will do.

Petty and Cacioppo think that people want to embrace correct attitudes; that they will change attitudes based on what they perceive to be correct; and that their attitudes can be subject to bias. You might be a courteous driver because you firmly believe that everyone should be courteous, and your attitude will be easiest to sustain when nearly everyone acts courteously. On the other hand, you might have a bias against rude sports car drivers so you do not let the guy in the screaming yellow roadster squeeze in between your car and the one in front of you.

Two important concepts are central to this theory. One is how much thinking (elaboration) you do about a decision, and the other is your personal involvement with the decision. A decision about which toothpaste to buy may be a "thoughtless" decision for you because you are personally "uninvolved" with the decision. You do not think much about the decision and you do not see the decision affecting your self-concept. On the other hand, you might care a great deal about what car you buy. You might think about the decision, read the car ads, and talk with friends about the matter. In other words, you exhibit high involvement and considerable thinking and elaboration. All of this central processing signals reasoning, scrutiny, and evaluation—none of which you did concerning the toothpaste decision which was peripheral to your concerns.

Most difficult for a persuader to change are issues over which an audience member has thought deeply, an issue over which agreement is wide and deep, and an issue over which considerable scrutiny, reasoning, and evaluation has occurred. Much advertising aims to change beliefs and behaviors that are relatively inconsequential: buy this cologne instead of that one, this lipstick instead of that one, and this soft drink instead of that one. What is difficult for a persuader is securing change in core values, heavily elaborated attitudes, and deeply held beliefs. The effective persuader chooses strategies that take into account the audience's current thinking about an issue or idea.

Principles of Persuasion

How can the successful public speaker be persuasive? A number of principles are instructive. In this section we identify five principles of persuasion. We will learn that consistency, small changes, benefits, fulfilling needs, and gradual approaches all are effective ways to persuade others.

Consistency Persuades

The first principle of persuasion is that **consistency persuades,** that audiences are more likely to change their behavior if the suggested change is consistent with their present beliefs, attitudes, and values. People who have given money for a cause (a behavior) are the likely contributors to that and other related causes in the future. People who like competition (a value) are the most likely candidates to enter into another competition. People who want to segregate old people in communities of their own (a belief) are the most likely to promote bond issues that provide separate housing for the aged. Finally, people who dislike immigrants (an attitude) are likely to discourage immigrants from moving into their neighborhood.

Fortunately for public speakers, people tend to be relatively consistent. They will do in the future what they did in the past. The public speaker uses this notion of consistency by linking persuasive proposals to those old consistencies. Following are some examples of appeals based on consistency. The members of this audience were among the first in their neighborhoods to buy the latest software, the newest computer system, and the most recent video hardware. The persuasive speaker says:

> Now you can be among the first to own a newly configured sound system that will please like no other system ever devised. I know that you are basically conservative individuals who do not spend money without deep thought and careful scrutiny. That is why you will find this new sound system so appealing. The system is expensive but will outlast every appliance in your house; it is small but more powerful than any previous system; and it is new but designed to bring to you with great clarity all the music that you like to hear.

The public speaker shapes, reinforces, and changes by showing how the promoted activity is consistent with the audience's past behavior.

Small Changes Persuade

The second principle of persuasion is that **small changes persuade,** that audiences are more likely to alter their behavior if the suggested change will require small rather than large changes in their behavior. A common error of beginning persuaders is that they ask for too much change too soon for too little reason. Audiences are reluctant to change, and any changes they do make are likely to be small ones. Nonetheless, the successful persuasive speaker determines small changes that are consistent with the persuasive purpose that an audience would be willing to accept.

What if you, as a persuader, are faced with an audience of overweight Americans who are loath to exercise and resistant to reduced eating? Your temptation might be to ask for too much too soon: quit eating so much and start losing weight. The message would likely fall on unreceptive ears, because the appeal is both inconsistent with present behavior and asking for too much change too soon. You could limit your persuasive message by encouraging the audience to give up specific foods, or a specific food that is part of their problem. However, an even better example of a small change consistent with the audience's present behavior would be to have listeners switch from ice cream to low-fat frozen yogurt. An audience that would reject a weight-loss program might be more willing simply to switch from one form of food to another, because that change would be minimally upsetting to its present life patterns.

Are there any qualifications or limitations on this second principle of persuasion? One factor that needs to be considered in deciding how much to ask of an audience is **commitment level,** or an intensity of belief that makes one intolerant of opinions that differ. Studies in social judgment show that highly committed persons, people who believe most intensely or strongly about an issue, are highly resistant to any positions on the issue except their own or ones very close to it. To such an audience, reinforcement would be welcome, shaping would be a challenge, and change would be very difficult. On the other hand, audience members who do not feel strongly about an issue are susceptible to larger changes than are those who already have established positions to which they are committed.

Consider these examples of the principle. A speaker addressing a religious rally of persons who prohibit drinking, dancing, and smoking can get warm acceptance for a persuasive message that reinforces or rewards those ideas. The same message to the same audience would be greeted with cautious skepticism with a speech attempting to shape any responses different from those already established. And the same message to the same audience would be met with outright rejection when requesting changes in behavior that run counter to those already embraced. On the other hand, a heterogeneous audience of persons uncommitted on the issue of regular exercise would be susceptible to considerable response shaping, and an audience of the already committed would receive reinforcement and would at least consider adopting some small changes in behavior. The successful persuader is skilled at discerning which small changes, consistent with the persuasive purpose, can be asked of an audience.

Benefits Persuade

The third principle of persuasion is that audiences are more likely to change their behavior if the suggested change will benefit them more than it will cost them. **Cost-benefit analysis,** for example, is considered every time we buy something: "Do I want this new jacket even though it means I must spend $150 plus tax? The benefits are that I will be warm and will look nice. The cost is that I will not be able to get my shoes resoled or buy a new watch." The persuader frequently demonstrates to the audience that the benefits are worth the cost.

A student who sold vacuum cleaners told of a fellow sales representative who wore white gloves and a surgical mask when he looked at the customers' old vacuum cleaner. By the time he had inspected the brush and changed the bag, he was filthy. He would then demonstrate that the old vacuum threw dust all over the house as it dragged across the carpet. By the end of his sales pitch, the sales representative was convincing the customer that the old vacuum was not only ineffective but also increased the amount of dirt flying around the house. The cost of the new vacuum would, according to this salesperson, be worth the benefit of owning a cleaning machine that picked up dirt instead of spreading it around. Remember that you need to reveal to your audience the benefits that make your proposal worth the cost.

How can you use cost-benefit analysis in your classroom speech? Consider the costs to the audience of doing as you ask. What are the costs in money, time, commitment, energy, skill, or talent? Consider one of the most common requests in student speeches: write to your representative or senator. Many student speakers make that request without considering the probability that nobody in class has ever written to a senator or representative. Even if the speaker includes an address, the letter writing will take commitment, time, and even a little money. Few students are willing to pay those costs. On the other hand, if the speaker comes to class with a letter already composed and simply asks for signatures from the class, then the cost is a few seconds of time, and the speaker is more likely to gain audience cooperation. Whenever you deliver a persuasive speech, consider the costs and how you can reduce them so the audience will feel the costs are worth the proposed benefits.

❖ ❖ ❖ ❖   ## Fulfilling Needs Persuades

The fourth principle of persuasion is that audiences are more likely to change their behavior if the change meets their needs. Abraham Maslow created an often-quoted **hierarchy of needs** (Maslow 1943). Maslow's pyramid makes sense (see Figure 14.3). As a human being, you do need all of the items in the hierarchy, though many people never get very far above the second level from the bottom, and few people think they have achieved complete self-fulfillment.

You can use Maslow's hierarchy in your public speeches. Are you in a place where the air and water are so bad that they threaten public health? If so, speeches on those issues are about the basic physiological needs. Do the people in your audience have decent places to live? If not, then speeches about space and psychological health are appropriate. Is everyone in your audience happy with his or her relationships? If not, then speeches about approval and acceptance have appeal.

You can analyze your audience for specific needs. Do they need money? Jobs? Day care? Do they need help in dealing with government bureaucracies? Do they need better living conditions? Do they need to learn how to study, how to handle children, or how to live with spouses? Check out your own audience and determine what they need because a speech that meets the audience's needs is likely to be successful.

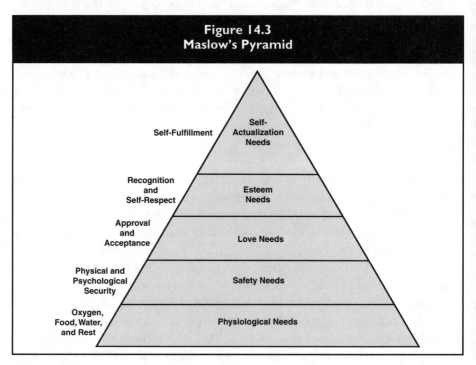

Figure 14.3
Maslow's Pyramid

Gradual Approaches Persuade

Gradual approaches work best when the audience is likely to be unreceptive to your message. With friendly audiences, you can ask them to do what you already know they are likely to accept and then simply give them reinforcement and a good rationale for doing so. However, many persuasive speeches ask for audience changes that listeners may not wholeheartedly endorse just because you say they should.

Do not ask a hostile audience for too much too soon. Persuading a reluctant audience is a kind of seduction in which the audience is more likely to cooperate after courtship than after an abrupt proposition. Start with common ground to show the audience that you share its basic humanity. Move from arguments and evidence that listeners will find quite acceptable to that which they find more difficult to accept. Avoid pushing an opposed audience too hard toward acceptance or you will get a **boomerang effect,** in which the audience will like you and your proposal even less after your presentation.

A Democratic governor faced a highly Republican audience of radio and television owners and managers. The governor disarmed his potentially hostile audience by beginning with a story about how he sent his young son to school that morning. The story was amusing but, more important, the tale showed that the governor—like most of the people in the audience—had the same kinds of things going on in his life that they had in their own. This common ground set the stage for the rest of the speech, in which he gently pushed the audience toward his position on the issues.

Similarly, in a persuasive speech do not start by saying, "I want you to donate your eyes to the eye bank." Instead, start gently with "safe" information about how many people have been saved from blindness by cornea transplants. Mention that the local Lion's Club sponsors the program. Reveal how many other people in the community, students in particular, have signed donor cards to allow their eyes to be used to help another person. Only after this careful courtship do you reveal that you have cards for them to sign if they have compassion for their fellow human beings. The behavioral change—the signing of a donor card—is the end result of a gradual approach.

Remember, as you prepare your persuasive speech, that audiences are more likely to change their behavior if the suggested change is consistent with their present beliefs, attitudes, and values. They are more likely to change if your proposal requires small rather than large changes in their lives. They are more likely to change if your proposal benefits the audience more than the proposal costs them. They are more likely to accept change if the proposal meets their needs. And they are more likely to accept change if the proposal is a culmination of acceptable ideas. With these principles to apply in your persuasive speeches, you can move to the matter of content in the persuasive speech.

On the Web

The American Rhetoric website (*http://www.americanrhetoric.com/ rhetoricofterrorism.htm*) includes 114 active links to speeches surrounding the terrorism of September 11, 2001. Select one or two of them and identify the principles of persuasion that you learned about above.

Types of Persuasive Speeches

The three types of persuasive speeches that we will examine in this chapter are the speech to inspire, the speech to convince, and the speech to actuate.

❖ ❖ ❖ ❖   ## The Speech to Inspire

The **speech to inspire** is a persuasive speech, although we often do not think about inspirational messages as persuasive. The purpose of this speech is to influence listeners' feelings or motivations. Speeches of inspiration are often used for ceremonial events. They occur in churches, mosques, synagogues, and temples; at graduations and rallies; and on holidays or at special events. An example of a speech to inspire was provided by Patricia Harris, who was the first African American woman to serve in a United States president's cabinet, both as Secretary of Housing and Urban Development and as Secretary of Health, Education, and Welfare. Harris was also the first African American woman to serve her nation as ambassador and to lead an American law school. In a speech to the National Women's Political Caucus Convention, she said, in part,

> I want to hear the Speaker of the House addressed as Madam Speaker and I want to listen as she introduces Madam President to the Congress assembled for the State of the Union. I want Madam President to look down from the podium at the women of the Supreme Court who will be indicative of the significant number of women judges throughout the Federal and State judicial systems. (1979)

Since her speech over 20 years ago, two women have ascended to become Associate Justices of the Supreme Court of the United States; the Speaker of the House continues to be a male; and so far no woman has been elected President of the United States.

You also can deliver a speech to inspire. Can you inspire your fellow students to join some cause in which you believe? Can you inspire them to be more spiritual, less materialistic, more focused on learning, or less focused on smoking and drinking? Many topics lend themselves to inspirational talk, and many needed changes require inspiration to fulfill the change. For examples of such speaking watch real or TV ministers, see politicians during the campaign season, or observe individuals who believe strongly in saving the environment, stopping nuclear tests, or exploring the universe.

Technical Tip 14.1
Speeches on the Net

To find many persuasive speeches on the Internet, find on your university's service the publication entitled *Vital Speeches*. Most college libraries also carry the published version of this periodical. Two speeches to start with are the following:

Byron, W. J. (1999, July 1). Old ethical principles: The new corporate culture. *Vital Speeches*, 65(18), 558–562.

This speech by a Jesuit priest who is also a Distinguished Professor of Management at the McDonough School of Business at Georgetown University in Washington, D.C., was delivered at the annual luncheon of the Duquesne University NMA Students Association in Pittsburgh, Pennsylvania on April 21, 1999.

Gilmartin, R. V. (1999, January 15). Innovation, ethics and core values: Keys to global success. *Vital Speeches*, 65(7), 209–214. This speech by the CEO of Merck and Co., a major drug company, was delivered to the Harvard Magazine Conference Board in New York City on October 20, 1998.

The Speech to Convince

The **speech to convince** is a persuasive speech given with the intent of influencing listeners' beliefs or attitudes. You may wish to convince the audience that Rush Limbaugh is a reasonable man, that gender equality is beneficial to both women and men (Condit 1998), that culturally correct language is a reasonable goal of a multicultural society, that our current health care plan is superior to alternatives that have been suggested, or that our nation's children are at risk.

The speech to convince attempts only to encourage listeners to believe a different position on an issue. They are not required to act. In a speech to convince, you do not ask your audience to do anything, but rather to rethink their beliefs and attitudes. An example of a speech to convince is presented in Figure 14.4. Only the opening words of the speech are included so you can capture the idea of the speech to convince. The student speaker, Douglas Burch, was a Special Forces veteran who knew about weapons but who wished to convince the audience that the focus on eliminating guns might not solve the problem.

Figure 14.4
The Speech to Convince: Changing Minds in the Audience

The Witch Hunt
By Douglas Burch (1999)

I had difficulty trying to decide on a speech to convince until I was motivated by Vanessa's speech entitled "Guns." So I decided to refute "Guns" with my speech entitled "The Witch Hunt" because I think the focus on ridding society of guns is not going to solve the problem.

Exactly how am I qualified to speak on a topic related to guns and violence? Most of you know that I served in the United States Army for eight years. During that time I was trained to operate and to perform maintenance on a wide variety of weapons; for example: the M-14, the M-16, the M-60, the AK-47, the AR-15, 9 mm pistols, Light Anti-Tank Weapons (LAW), and explosive devices. I know what these weapons can do to an individual and to the objects they try to hide behind.

Unfortunately, guns and the violence associated with them have crept into our homes, schools, and places of business. This problem affects all of us! Today, I would like to share information with you that will challenge you to think differently. I want to make you aware of research studies that are being performed on violent crimes committed by America's youth. Finally, I want to demonstrate to you that we need to concentrate on the violence, and not the guns most commonly associated with violence.

The Speech to Actuate

The **speech to actuate** is a persuasive speech given for the purpose of influencing listeners' behaviors or actions. The foundation of the speech of action is the changing of listeners' beliefs and attitudes, but it goes further to request action. You may wish to ask listeners to join an organization, to volunteer their time at local social service agencies, to eat a low-fat diet, to practice safe sex, or to vote for a particular candidate.

In the speech to actuate, the speaker seeks an overt behavioral effect, some evidence of response. In the speech introduction featured in Figure 14.5, the student speaker from Ohio University is telling his audience to consider taking a vacation in Minnesota. The speaker is not simply seeking cognitive change, a change of mind; instead, he is seeking a change of mind followed by an action—taking a vacation in Minnesota. Remember, this excerpt is only the introductory portion of the speech, provided here to show you a speech to actuate.

Figure 14.5
The Speech to Actuate: Moving an Audience to Action

A Better Vacation
By Kyle Messaros (1999)

How many of you are sick of the same boring vacation every year? A vacation in which mom, dad, and the kids all pile into the family minivan and drive countless hours to the beach only to get sunburned, get sand in their shoes, and pay outrageous amounts of money for just about anything. Well, if this story sounds like your family, then I may have a solution for you. Instead of driving south for your next vacation, how about heading north for something a little different? I am talking about a vacation spot that most of you have never even considered, and that is Minnesota.

Now for most of you women, I know exactly what is going through your mind: I HATE CAMPING! Well, that may be true, but even in the deep wilderness of Minnesota you can find civilization. Honestly, most people wouldn't want to spend a week living in a tent with no electricity, running water, or even an indoor bathroom. Well, how about a fully loaded cabin with air conditioning, sauna, and a view like no other? If any of that grabs your attention, then Minnesota might just be the place for your family. I am by no means trying to persuade you to believe that Minnesota is the best vacation spot in the world; I just want to enlighten you on a vacation spot that is little known and incredibly relaxing.

Celebrating Diversity

The Japanese American Citizens League (JACL) is "a membership organization whose mission is to secure and maintain the human and civil rights of Americans of Japanese ancestry and others victimized by injustice." The group hosts a website at *http://www.jacl.org/*. The following material was posted in February 2004. Try to determine the principles of persuasion the group uses in urging readers to take action.

Mr. President—is there a double-standard at play here?

I urge you to repudiate Rep. Coble's endorsement of the internment of Japanese Americans.

Millions of Americans' concerns continued to be ignored!!!

On radio station WKZL-FM, Representative Coble endorsed the internment of Japanese Americans by saying: "We were at war. They [Japanese Americans] were an endangered species. For many of the Japanese Americans, it wasn't safe for them to be on the street. Some probably were intent on doing harm to us, just as some of the Arab Americans are probably intent on doing harm to us."

❖ ❖ ❖ ❖

Rep. Moran was removed from his leadership position, as was Senator Lott, for their offensive and insensitive remarks—so why hasn't Rep. Coble been asked to step down or otherwise repudiated by the House Republican leadership or the White House? Is there a double-standard at play here?!?!?!

Please call, fax, or email the White House to urge them to repudiate Rep. Howard Coble's (R-NC) position and seek his resignation as chairman of the Judiciary Subcommittee on Crime, Terrorism and Homeland Security because he lacks the objectivity, sensitivity and respect for the Constitution to continue in this leadership role, as evidenced by the comments he made on February 4, 2003.

It is imperative that the White House, Speaker Hastert and the Republican leadership are made aware of millions of Americans' concerns over Representative Coble's dangerous view of history and his cavalier attitude toward discrimination based on race and ethnicity. JACL urges you to contact the White House and Speaker Hastert to voice your opinion.
PLEASE TAKE ACTION NOW!

Directly quoted from
http://capwiz.com/jacl/issues/alert/?alertid=1997601&type=PR (February, 2004)

Ethics and Persuasive Speaking

Persuasive speaking offers ample opportunities for ethical mischief. Certainly persuasive speaking can be used for positive purposes: stop smoking, start exercising, stop charging your expenditures, and avoid sexually transmitted diseases. However, persuasive speaking can also result in a vacuum cleaner you do not need, insurance you never wanted, a pile of ignored CDs at $24.99 plus shipping and handling, and exercise equipment that you never use. Distinguishing between ethical and unethical persuasive appeals is a challenging task for which the following guidelines apply:

1. *Be careful whom you trust.* The best-looking, smooth-talking individual can be a pathological deceiver, whereas an unattractive, inarticulate person can have your best interests in mind. When buying or selling, dating or mating, you should look at past behavior and the testimony of others who have had more experience with the person with whom you are dealing. In short, source credibility should always be an issue (Pornpitakpan 2004).

Because persuasion can influence many, the speaker has a special responsibility to speak ethically. (Photo: Jesse Porter/*Daily Bruin*)

2. *Analyze and evaluate messages for reasonableness, truth, and benefit to you and the community.* Our social norms discourage acceptance of messages purely for emotional reasons: "I bought the $3000 ring because it looked pretty," "I married her because of her cute little dimple," etc. However, messages that are framed with the emotional overtones that are matched with the emotional state of the audience members are more likely to persuade (DeSteno et al. 2004).

   Nonetheless, our social norms encourage us to accept messages because they meet our standards of reason, because we find them to be true, or because the message seems to benefit others or us more than it will harm us. Be especially observant of language choices used by the persuader—even subtle changes in language can persuade (Walton 2001).

3. *You and your messages will be more persuasive if you have a long, positive history* ("The thing you get to lose once is your reputation"); *if your past invites others to trust you and your word; and if others tend to benefit from your messages as much or more than you do* (that is, they do not seek compliance for selfish purposes). A nationally known evangelist was caught for a second time with a prostitute. Will the money keep flowing to a person who cannot be trusted to stay on the straight and narrow himself? Are you building a history that will help you or harm you when you attempt to persuade others? Similarly, when you share similar values with an audience, you are more likely to be persuasive (Gordon and Miller 2004).

NCA Credo for Communication Ethics

One of the principles included in the NCA Credo is relevant here:
- We accept responsibility for the short- and long-term consequences of our own communication and expect the same of others.

Summary

This chapter began with a definition of persuasive speaking that indicated the persuader intends to change the audience's behavior through reinforcing, shaping, and changing the audience's responses to an idea, issue, concept, or product. Persuasive speaking is important to you because you provide and consume persuasive messages constantly. Persuasive speaking has three purposes: (1) shaping audience responses, (2) reinforcing audience responses, and (3) changing audience responses. Typically, persuasive speakers are attempting to influence the audience's feelings, beliefs, attitudes, and/or values.

We considered five principles of persuasion. First, we observed that consistency persuades. Second, we noted that small changes persuade. Third, we stated that benefits persuade. Fourth, we asserted that fulfilling needs persuades. Finally, we contended that gradual approaches persuade.

We identified three types of persuasive speeches. The speech to inspire is given to influence listeners' feelings. The speech to convince is intended to influence listeners' beliefs or attitudes. The speech to actuate is given to influence listeners' behaviors or actions.

The following checklist provides another means of reviewing the main points of this chapter.

A Checklist for the Persuasive Speech

___ 1. Have you determined if your intent is to shape, reinforce, or change your audience's responses?

___ 2. Have you shown how the change you are suggesting for the audience is consistent with their past behavior?

___ 3. Have you kept your requested changes gradual so that the audience does not perceive your request as too much to ask?

___ 4. Have you demonstrated for the audience the benefits received if they do as you request?

___ 5. Have you shown the audience ways that your request will fulfill their needs?

___ 6. Have you approached your suggested change gradually so the audience does not perceive that you are asking for change without sufficient preparation?

___ 7. Did you determine if your purpose is to inspire, convince, or actuate?

___ 8. Do you believe your audience will know what you want them to feel, think, or do after you have finished talking?

Finally, you should consider the ethical aspects of persuasive speaking by carefully regarding the credibility of the source; by analyzing and evaluating the message for truth, reasonableness, and benefit; and by bolstering your own credibility by building a history of trust and goodwill.

Vocabulary

attitudes "A psychological tendency that is expressed by evaluating a particular entity with some degree of favor or disfavor" (Eagley and Chaiken 1993).

authority beliefs Beliefs that we embrace because we were told to believe them by people we respect.

behavior Observable actions.

beliefs Things you believe to be true without certainty or proof that they are true.

boomerang effect A phenomenon in which the audience likes you and your position on the issue less after the speech than they did before your presentation.

changing responses Altering an audience's behavior toward a product, a concept, or an idea.

Communication Narrative 14.1
Saving the Poor from Fires

Harold Glick sold fire alarm systems, lots of them. In fact, he had increased his personal wealth substantially since he switched from selling textbooks to reluctant professors and started selling fire alarms to the poor. His strategy was simple. He would go to a neighborhood where people had jobs but were forced to live in shabby apartments, overly used condos, and dowdy duplexes. He would gather a crowd on the corner or on a vacant lot with a brief fire display. A candle in a pan with a handful of explosive dust would usually bring people around Harold's little table. On the table was a beautiful leather case closed and resting on its side. Harold started by displaying enlarged newspaper headlines and articles, each about a fire in which property was destroyed and lives snuffed out. He also showed an enlarged photo of a man in a bathrobe desperately hanging onto his wife's waist as she tugged toward their home with flames belching out the windows. She was trying to save her baby, says Harold, as he somberly put away the picture. Then he reminded them of the kind of homes in this neighborhood and asked if any of them had ever seen that little spark that occurs when you switch on a light in the dark. Many raised their hands. Harold pointed out that most old houses had piles of dirt and dust—combustible dust—in the walls and that the little spark could easily start a fire that could go undetected until everyone was in bed. At this point Harold opened the pretty little case. Inside were six very shiny, chrome-like bowls, each with a small mechanism inside. These, Harold announced, were fire alarms, the best ever made. Each contained a temperature sensitive metal trigger that would set off an alarm that would wake everyone in the house. Harold triggered one of his little air horns and nearly broke eardrums in his audience. All people had to do to get these safety devices for their own homes was to pay Harold $35.00 down and $15 per month for 9 months. He had contracts ready to sign and allowed each buyer to take one "bowl" home until the entire ensemble was paid in full. Harold had paid around a buck a bowl or six dollars for the fire alarms. The leather case had cost $80.00 but the customers did not get the leather case. Harold was a happy salesperson.

commitment level Intensity of belief that makes one intolerant of opinions that differ.

consistency persuades The concept that audiences are more likely to be persuaded by messages that grow out of their current beliefs, attitudes, and values.

cost-benefit analysis The idea that an audience is more likely to be persuaded if costs in time, money, and effort are lower than the expected benefits or advantages.

derived beliefs Beliefs that we learn indirectly from sources we trust.

elaboration likelihood theory This theory states that we respond to information cognitively, affectively, and behaviorally.

feelings Affective states or dispositions; emotional responses.

gradual approaches Approaching an unreceptive audience with slow change.

hierarchy of needs A rank-ordered list of physical and psychological requirements for a healthy mind and body.

inconsequential beliefs Beliefs linked to taste, fashion, or impulse.

persuasive speaking A message delivered to an audience by a speaker who intends to influence audience members' choices by shaping, reinforcing, or changing their responses toward an idea, issue, concept, or product.

primitive beliefs with unanimous consensus Widely believed beliefs that are based on direct experience.

primitive beliefs with zero consensus Unverified personal beliefs about which we lack external confirmation.

purposes of persuasive speaking The shaping, reinforcing, or changing of an audience's responses toward an idea, an issue, a concept, or a product.

reinforcing responses Rewarding the audience for sustaining present beliefs, attitudes, and values.

shaping responses Moving the audience toward a predetermined goal.

small changes persuade The principle of persuasion that says audiences are more likely to alter their behavior if the suggested change will require small rather than large changes in their behavior.

speech to actuate A persuasive speech given for the purpose of influencing listeners' behaviors or actions.

speech to convince A persuasive speech given for the purpose of influencing listeners' beliefs or attitudes.

speech to inspire A persuasive speech given for the purpose of influencing listeners' feelings and motivation.

values Learned social principles, goals, or standards found acceptable or even desirable by the people we live with, the groups to which we belong, and the institutions we respect.

Application Exercises

A. Persuasive speeches often appeal to an audience's unmet needs. Since needs vary according to the community, college, class, and individual, you can make yourself more sensitive to audience needs by ranking the five unmet needs that you believe are important to your audience.

   1._____

   2._____

   3._____

   4._____

   5._____

B. After reading the section on principles of persuasion, you should be able to identify cases in which they are correctly used. Examine the following cases and indicate which of the following principles is being observed:

   C = *Consistency persuades*

   S = *Small changes persuade*

   B = *Benefits persuade*

   N = *Fulfilling needs persuades*

G = *Gradual approaches persuade*

1. To save my audience members considerable time and effort, I am going to provide them with a form letter that they can sign and send to the administration.

2. Because I know that most of my classmates are short of cash, I am going to tell them how to make some quick money with on-campus jobs.

3. I plan to wait until the end of the speech to tell the audience members that the organization I want them to join will require two hours of driving per week.

4. My audience of international students already believes in the values of learning public speaking, so I think the listeners will respond favorably to my recommendation for a course in voice and articulation.

5. I would like my audience to cut up all their credit cards, but since they are unlikely to do so I am instead going to ask that they try for a zero balance each month to avoid interest and fees.

Answers

1. B, 2. N, 3. G, 4. C, 5. S

References

Alstadt, D. (1999). Little, plastic, harmful. An unpublished speech delivered in Interpersonal Communication 103, Public Speaking, Ohio University, Athens, Ohio, in Paul Nelson's class. The published outline is adapted from one submitted by Alstadt.

Burch, D. (1999). The witch hunt. An unpublished speech delivered in Interpersonal Communication 103, Public Speaking, Ohio University, Athens, Ohio, in Paul Nelson's class.

Burgoon, J. K., Birk, T., and Pfau, M. (1990). Nonverbal behaviors, persuasion, and credibility. *Human Communication Research*, 17, 140–170.

Condit, C. M. (1998). Gender diversity: A theory of communication for the postmodern era. In J. Trent (Ed.), *Communication: Views from the Helm for the 21st Century* (pp. 177–183). Boston, MA: Allyn & Bacon.

DeSteno, D., Petty, R. E., Rucker, D. D., Wegener, D. T., and Braverman, J. (2004). Discrete emotions and persuasion: The role of emotion-induced expectancies. *Journal of Personality and Social Psychology*, 86, 43–57.

Eagley, A. H., and Chaiken, S. (1993). *The psychology of attitudes*. New York: Harcourt Brace Jovanovich.

Fishbein, M., and Ajzen, I. (1975). *Belief, attitude, intention, and behavior: An introduction to theory and research*. Reading, MA: Addison-Wesley.

Fotheringham, W. (1966). *Perspectives on Persuasion*. Boston, MA: Allyn & Bacon.

Gordon, A., and Miller, J. L. (2004). Values and persuasion during the first Bush-Gore presidential debate. *Political Communication*, 21, 71–93.

Harris, P. R. (1979, June 14). A speech delivered for the National Women's Political Caucus Convention, Cincinnati, Ohio.

Hart, R. P. (1998). Rhetoric, hope, and American politics. In J. Trent (Ed.), *Communication: Views from the Helm for the 21st Century* (pp. 113–121). Boston: Allyn & Bacon.

Kumkale, G. T., and Albarracin, D. (2004). The sleeper effect in persuasion: a meta-analytic review. *Psychological Bulletin,* 130, 143–173.

Maslow, A. H. (1943). A theory of human motivation. *Psychological Review,* 50, 370–396.

Messaros, K. (1999). A better vacation. An unpublished speech delivered in Interpersonal Communication 103, Public Speaking, Ohio University, Athens, Ohio, in Paul Nelson's class.

Miller, G. R. (1980). On being persuaded: Some basic distinctions. In M. E. Roloff and G. R. Miller (Eds.), *Persuasion: New Directions in Theory and Research* (pp. 16–26). Beverly Hills, CA: Sage Publications.

Petty, R. E., and Cacioppo, J. T. (1986). *Communication and Persuasion: Central and Peripheral Routes to Attitude Change.* New York: Springer-Verlag.

Pornpitakpan, C. (2004). The persuasiveness of source credibility: A critical review of five decades of evidence. *Journal of Applied Social Psychology,* 34, 243–282.

Rokeach, M. (1973). *The Nature of Human Values.* New York: Free Press.

Wallace, S. (1995). Heaven. An unpublished speech delivered in the English and Communications Division of Seneca College, Toronto, Canada, in David Turnbull's class.

Walton, D. (2001). Persuasive definitions and public policy arguments. *Argumentation and Advocacy,* 37, 117–134.

Zullow, H. (1994). American exceptionalism and the quadrennial peak in optimism. In A. Miller and B. Gronbeck (Eds.) *Presidential Campaigns and American Self-Images* (pp. 214–230). Boulder, CO: Westview.

❖ ❖ ❖ ❖

Chapter 15

Speeches for Special Occasions

With Wendy H. Papa and Michael J. Papa, *Ohio University*

Wit makes its own welcome, and levels all distinctions. No dignity, no learning, no force of character, can make any stand against good wit.
—Ralph Waldo Emerson

Question Outline

I. What six guidelines should you follow in preparing a speech of introduction? Why should you coordinate your remarks with those of the speaker?

II. What are the four major traits of a speech of welcome? How do the speech of welcome and the speech of introduction differ?

III. Identify three major characteristics of a good speech of presentation. What is the basic premise of such a speech?

IV. What is the purpose of an acceptance speech? Why can a speech of acceptance fail miserably and be painful for the audience?

V. What is the fundamental purpose of a speech of tribute? In preparing the speech of tribute, what five guidelines should you consider?

VI. Define the purpose of a eulogy. Differentiate between the two organizational patterns eulogies typically follow.

VII. What is the role of humor in after-dinner speaking? Why would a highly technical topic usually be unsuitable for an after-dinner speech?

Carolyn Hartfelter attended a banquet honoring a local health care administrator with a humanitarian award.

Just before the banquet began, the master of ceremonies learned that Carolyn's husband, the pastor, who was supposed to offer the invocation, could not attend. They needed someone to fill in, and the master of ceremonies turned to Carolyn. "Would you be kind enough to offer grace?"

Would she? More to the point, could she? Could she come up with an appropriate grace for a mixed gathering of individuals? A gathering that included Catholics, Jews, Protestants, Hindus, and others?

Fortunately, this was not the first time Carolyn had been called upon to speak before an audience. She was aware that every time she made use of any form of oral communication, the situation would be "special," with its own unique attributes and requirements. Therefore, Carolyn was able to offer an invocation that honored human dignity and showed respect for people of all backgrounds.

Special occasions for speechmaking occur frequently. Weddings, funerals, graduations, award ceremonies, and retirement parties represent some of the special occasions in which speech making is expected. For example, you may be asked to give a toast to the bride and groom at a close friend's wedding, a eulogy at a deceased relative's funeral, a brief speech introducing the main speaker at a meeting, an acceptance speech to thank an association for an award, an inspirational speech to lift the morale of fellow employees, or an entertaining speech at a community service banquet. These kinds of speeches are important because they help to make the occasion special by offering the audience a unique and insightful perspective on the event.

Special occasion speaking occurs frequently. (Photo: Mark Ide)

Speeches for special occasions are similar to other types of speeches in that all public presentations call for some information and for some persuasion. However, speeches for special occasions are distinguished by the unique situations in which they are presented and by how speakers address each distinctive situation. In this chapter, we will discuss the most common special occasions that may require public speaking and the kinds of speeches appropriate for such events.

The Speech of Introduction

Introducing a speaker to an audience is similar to introducing one friend to another. You want the two parties to feel friendly toward one another, as well as to be interested enough in each other so both parties look forward to learning more about their new acquaintance. The **speech of introduction** has a general objective—to create among audience members a desire to listen to the person you are introducing. In essence, your goal is to "sell" that individual to the audience. The specific purpose of the speech of introduction is to inform the audience of the qualifications of the speaker, so that the speaker's views will be received with respect, and to provide a link between the speaker and the audience regarding the nature and tone of the occasion.

Guidelines for Giving a Speech of Introduction

A good speech of introduction should be pleasing to hear and should ease the task confronting the main speaker. Typically, this type of speech provides some information about the speaker and about the topic—in that order. Some guidelines for giving speeches of introduction are:

1. *Discuss with the speaker ahead of time what kind of introduction he or she prefers.* Some speakers will have an introduction written out and send it to you prior to the speaking engagement. You should use this document as the basis for your remarks, but avoid reading it word for word. Alternatively, the speaker may provide you with a lengthy resume or list of achievements that you can use to write your introduction. Remember, however, that introductory speeches should be limited to two or three minutes so as to not distract from the main speaker's presentation. Thus, your goal is to identify those aspects of the main speaker's professional background that would be most appropriate for the audience and the occasion. Introductory speakers should not talk at such length that they create the impression that they are principal speakers. Rather, the attention should be focused on the primary speaking guest. Don't forget, the speaker you are introducing is the main attraction.

2. *Pronounce the speaker's name correctly.* A clearly audible pronunciation of the speaker's name, so that all will understand it, is extremely important. Verify the pronunciation of the speaker's name in advance. If the speaker's name is particularly difficult to pronounce, practice saying it beforehand so that you articulate it comfortably during the introduction. Mention the speaker's name several times so that the audience will remember it. Finally, make sure you use the name the speaker prefers. Many professional married women, for example, keep their maiden names. Contact the speaker in advance and inquire as to what he or she prefers to be called.

3. *Provide information about the speaker.* Who is this individual? What is his or her title, educational background, and professional experience? What types of accomplishments or experiences has the speaker had that qualify him or her to speak on this particular occasion? Also, be sure that you have accumulated relevant information about the speaker and that you have mastered it sufficiently to accurately communicate it to the audience.

4. *Refrain from exaggeration.* Avoid using excessive or extravagant praise, since such an introduction may serve to embarrass the speaker. Overcomplimenting puts immense pressure on the speaker. If you exaggerate the speaker's expertise or credentials, you establish unreasonable expectations among the listeners that are difficult for the speaker to meet. For example, if you tell an audience that a speaker will hold them captivated and mesmerized or have them rolling in the aisles with laughter, such predictions can be disastrous. No speaker can live up to these expectations; thus, an audience is bound to be disappointed. Your goal in the speech of introduction is to say enough to excite the audience about hearing the speaker discuss his or her topic, and to motivate the speaker to address the audience.

5. *Provide information about the topic.* Some speakers will request that you address the importance of their subject during the speech of introduction; other speakers would rather discuss the significance of their topic during their presentations. Prior to preparing a speech of introduction, discuss with the speaker what you intend to say regarding the topic, and then make certain to get his or her consent about your planned statements. This demonstrates respect and consideration for the speaker and helps to promote the success of the speaker's presentation.

6. *Establish a welcoming climate.* Above all else, remember your intention is to make this particular audience want to hear this speaker discuss this topic. Assess the formality of the occasion and adapt your comments appropriately. Create a warm reception by conveying your enthusiasm for the speaker, and make sure your speech of introduction leaves the speaker feeling comfortable with the task at hand. Finally, tell the audience what it wants to hear. Present information about the speaker that is interesting and relevant to the members of the audience. This type of speech should also be delivered extemporaneously, creating a climate of enthusiasm and sincerity.

Virgil M. Hancher, president of the University of Iowa, delivered the following introduction of Eleanor Roosevelt to the Adult Education Forum in Des Moines, Iowa, on March 14, 1949.

It is probable that few persons in this or any age have touched life at as many points as has Mrs. Roosevelt. She has been the witness of both tragedy and triumph, and has faced each with wisdom and equanimity.

The political party of which her illustrious husband was so long the head has won five consecutive national elections. If one cause more than another can be assigned for that unique record, it is that that party and its leaders convinced large segments of our people that the problems which concerned them in their personal lives were of concern to the party. I venture the prophecy that when the history of our era is written, historians will agree that no one had more to do with the creation of this attitude than had Mrs. Roosevelt.

But her interests transcend our national boundaries, and she has made her contribution to international affairs. We live in fearful and anxious times. To an extraordinary degree our hopes for peace lie in the success of the United Nations. As one of the delegates of the United States to the United

Nations, Mrs. Roosevelt has carried into that organization the broad human-itarian interests so characteristic of her efforts within the nation. With her have gone hopes, and in her efforts we wish her every success.

Ladies and gentlemen, I have the privilege and honor of presenting to you Mrs. Franklin D. Roosevelt, who will speak on the subject "The Success and Failures of the United Nations" (Hancher 1953).

The preceding example supports the guidelines discussed above for speeches of introduction. The information about the speaker was not exaggerated but was accurate, supportive, and helped establish Mrs. Roosevelt's credibility. President Hancher provided sufficient information about the topic to create audience interest in her planned address. Finally, the introduction established an enthusiastic and sincere climate, creating a warm reception for Eleanor Roosevelt.

The Speech of Welcome

The **speech of welcome** is analogous to the speech of introduction; yet, the speech of welcome centers predominately on the audience rather than on any particular guest speaker. A speech of welcome could serve as a common greeting to an audience that will hear a series of speakers. It should refer to the occasion and to the status or achievements of those being welcomed. Welcome speeches may be given at a reception for a single individual, such as a military hero, a state representative, or a new employee of an organization. A speech of welcome may also be given to the members of an organization, such as the Lions Club or The International Communication Association. Sometimes social groups such as college fraternities or sororities hold welcoming receptions for returning members, with speeches included in the program. The welcoming speech is especially audience-centered with the focus on the listeners, guest speakers, and any special interest groups in the audience, such as media representatives.

Guidelines for giving a speech of welcome. The speech of welcome delivered on special occasions is comparable to the warm and friendly welcome with which you might greet a guest in your home. The speech should be genuine and forthright. The speech of welcome may exhibit the following pattern:

1. A congenial welcome on behalf of the group you represent.

2. An acknowledgment of the individual or individuals being welcomed.

3. An announcement about the occasion, its objective, focus, and important features.

4. A cordial and straightforward repetition of welcome (Griffith, Nelson, and Stasheff 1960).

The Speech of Inspiration

Often, the speech of welcome takes the form of an inspirational speech. The goal of the **speech of inspiration** is to build confidence and stimulate positive self-esteem in the listeners. Inspirational speeches motivate people to feel enthusiastic, inspired, and encouraged. People often give inspirational speeches at annual "kick-off" meetings, such as when a manager gives an enthusiastic "you-can-do-it" speech to get employees fired up to work to the best of their abilities. Or a coach can give his or her players a preseason "pep talk" to instill confidence and a winning attitude. The primary purpose of the inspirational speech is to stir emotions; thus, the speaker must communicate passion and excitement. A college dean presents, as an inspirational welcome speech, the following hypothetical example to a class of entering graduate students. The purpose of the speech is to inspire them to prepare for an exciting academic year.

Welcome to Springfield, Illinois, the University of Springfield, and the College of Education. One of the reasons I most enjoy being dean of the college is that every fall I get to introduce a new group of individuals to our college and our community!

My goal this morning is to provide you with a sense of our organizational culture. First of all, I would suggest that you are entering an environment that values team research and joint projects. For example, you will find many graduate students working with faculty members on research projects throughout the year. I believe this is an excellent way for new scholars to learn the process of doing research, and it increases the likelihood that you will graduate with several research projects completed.

Second, we value a balance between content areas and approaches to learning. Thus, we offer a comprehensive program including counselor education, curriculum, and supervision; elementary, secondary, and higher education; and educational administration. Because we believe that all of these areas are significant to your intellectual growth and understanding of different academic environments, we require a course in each area. We also require an educational foundations course and an introductory research course. Finally, we believe in a balance between theory and practice, so we offer a blend of theoretical courses, research methods, and applied course work to build your study program.

Third, we believe that past history provides us with inspiration to continue our successes. The College of Education has a rich history with one of the oldest Ph.D. programs at the University of Springfield, and the first undergraduate major in secondary education in the state of Illinois. Two years ago we celebrated the 100th anniversary of the College of Education. We are also fortunate to have a number of distinguished retired faculty who teach for us on a part-time basis and provide us with a sense of our history on a regular basis.

The reputation of our program will continue into the future primarily because of the quality of our faculty. When I think of the recognition they have received within the university, and among their peers in the field of education, I know why our reputation remains strong today. This faculty has received numerous teaching awards, research grants, and recognition for their professional accomplishments. For example, five of our faculty have been recognized as outstanding researchers by professional organizations, and four have received the prestigious University of Springfield Teaching Award. Our faculty have written dozens of textbooks, and regularly publish their research in the top professional journals in the field of education.

Our returning graduate students have also sustained our tradition of excellence by being selected as outstanding teaching assistants by Springfield students for three consecutive years. And, of course, we also look to each new graduate student to sustain our tradition of excellence. We only admit 10 percent of the students who apply to our graduate program, so you are among the best students in the country. In short, you have a very strong group of individuals with whom to work, and we are delighted to have you join us for one or more years of academic study. I look forward to meeting each of you personally in the coming months.

The preceding speech of welcome effectively accomplishes the speaker's goals. The new graduate students are sincerely welcomed to the College of Education by the dean and they are acknowledged for their special talents and abilities in the field of education. The dean describes aspects of the college's culture and history, with particular emphasis on the accomplishments of the faculty and returning graduate students. By identifying the educational and professional opportunities available to the new graduate students, the dean effectively motivates them to start the new academic year.

The Speech of Farewell

This type of speech occurs more frequently than you might presume. **Speeches of farewell** generally fall into one of two classifications. What differentiates the two types of speeches is whether the retiree or departing individual is speaking or is being spoken about. When a person retires or leaves an organization to join another, or when a revered individual leaves the community where he or she has resided, public recognition of the individual's achievements, successes, and kindness may be voiced in speeches appropriate to the given occasion. Alternatively, the individual who is leaving may use the opportunity to give a farewell address in which he or she expresses appreciation for the thoughtfulness and generosity provided by co-workers or neighbors. In such a farewell address, the speaker can challenge audience members to carry on the customs, practices, and long-range goals that characterize the organization, business, or community.

Guidelines for giving a speech of farewell. A farewell speech should be clear and concise. What you say and the manner in which you say it should be suitable to the special occasion. The farewell speech may include the following:

1. A sincere and appreciative tribute to those individuals who are leaving (or remaining behind).

2. An announcement about the special occasion and its importance, referring to the gratification gained from your relationship with those leaving (or remaining behind).

3. Best wishes for the future successes and happiness of those leaving (or remaining behind) (Griffith, Nelson, and Stasheff 1960).

Abraham Lincoln delivered a superb example of a speech of farewell from the rear platform of a train about to depart his hometown of Springfield, Illinois. The speech was addressed to the townspeople of Springfield, as Lincoln was departing for Washington, D.C., to assume the presidency:

My friends: No one, not in my situation, can appreciate my feeling of sadness at this parting. To this place, and the kindness of these people, I owe everything. Here I have lived a quarter of a century, and have passed from a young to an old man. Here my children have been born, and one is buried. I now leave, not knowing when or whether ever I may return, with a task before me greater than that which rested upon Washington. Without the assistance of that divine Being who ever attended him, I cannot succeed.

With that assistance, I cannot fail. Trusting in Him, who can go with me and remain with you, and be everywhere, or good, let us confidently hope that all will yet be well.

To His care commending you, as I hope in your prayers you will commend me, I bid you an affectionate farewell (Peterson 1954).

In his farewell address, President Lincoln gave an honest and grateful tribute to the townspeople of Springfield, Illinois. He addressed the special occasion and its significance in the history of our nation. Finally, the President provided a sense of hope for the future of the United States of America.

The Speech of Presentation

Speeches of presentation are given when an individual is receiving a gift or an award. The basic premise of a speech of presentation is to honor the person to whom the award is being presented and to acknowledge the recipient's achievements. The speech of presentation should identify the individual or organization making the presentation, the nature of the contributed gift or award, and the purpose for its being given. It is unnecessary to address everything the award recipient has ever accomplished in his or her life; rather, focus on achievements and contributions relevant to the award, and address these accomplishments in a manner that will make them relevant to the audience as well as the special occasion.

Guidelines for giving a speech of presentation. When delivering a speech of presentation, the speaker may utilize the following procedures:

1. *Keep opening comments brief.* Often, the speaker includes an appropriate story about the award recipient, either serious or humorous. Then, the speaker identifies the reasons for the presentation, and a few words describing the organization represented by the speaker.

2. *Present, in chronological order, the achievements of the award recipient and the reasons for presenting the award to this individual.* The speaker should include complimentary anecdotes and stories. These are especially worthwhile if they are familiar to the audience. Then, the speaker explains the gift or award and its dedication to the recipient.

3. *Present the gift.* Prior to actually presenting the gift, it is standard procedure to call the recipient to the platform so that it may be handed directly to the individual. Emphasize what the gift represents. Always remember, the gift is not as significant as the sentiment behind it. Always notify the person beforehand so that he or she will be ready to accept the gift and express appropriate appreciation. A handshake usually concludes the presentation with an expression of congratulations and wishes for continued success (Martin, Robinson, and Tomlinson 1963).

A model of a speech of presentation (or award presentation) was delivered by Sue DeWine, Director of the School of Interpersonal Communication, at Ohio University. The speech was delivered on April 29, 1994, during the University's Communication Week celebration. Here is the speech she presented:

> I am indeed privileged to present the School of Interpersonal Communication's highest award this evening, the Andersch Award. This is a very special presentation because of the unique person for whom the award is named and because of the outstanding record of the person receiving it this evening.
>
> Elizabeth Andersch was the first female professor of the School of Dramatic Arts and Speech at Ohio University, joining the faculty in 1943. Upon her retirement she moved to Florida where she died in 1974. She served the university with distinction and was best known as a superior teacher, advisor, and friend of students. The best measure of the personal impact and the professional contributions of a lifetime of service are found in the memories of friends, students, and colleagues. As one remembered her, "Betty Andersch was a free and liberated woman before Betty Friedan and Gloria Steinem invented the movement. She had the poise, grace, and humaneness never to allow that liberated spirit to degrade either herself or those she touched. She didn't have to tell you she was a liberated soul; you knew it because of the freedom she granted you."
>
> Betty Andersch came from a family of strong independent women. Betty earned a Ph.D. at a time when few women were achieving such excellence in education, and her sister received a medical degree in 1934 and became the first woman to head a medical lab in the state of Michigan. Betty's mother was the first policewoman in Grand Rapids, Michigan, and her grandmother ran a manufacturing company at the turn of the century. Because of the outstanding achievements this award represents, it gives me great pleasure to present it to another individual who has achieved recognition as an outstanding scholar and mentor of the field of communication.
>
> Jesse Delia is the Dean of the College of Arts and Sciences at the University of Illinois where he had previously served as chair and faculty member in the communication department. He is well known for his research and contributions to the discipline and is frequently called upon by his colleagues to provide direction for the field. Would Jesse Delia please come forward.
>
> (Sue DeWine reads the inscription on the Andersch Award, to Jesse Delia, which honors him as a distinguished theorist, influential researcher, outstanding educator, caring mentor, perceptive leader, and skilled administrator.)
>
> We are pleased to recognize you as this year's Andersch Award winner. Congratulations (DeWine 1994)!
>
> (DeWine and Delia shake hands.)

The preceding speech effectively meets the requirements for an award presentation. The life of Elizabeth Andersch is briefly described so the audience can gain an appreciation of her contributions and understand why an award was named in her honor. Then, the achievements of the award recipient (Jesse Delia) are described in a way that links him to what the award represents. Finally, Delia is offered sincere congratulations by the speaker, who then shakes his hand.

The Speech of Acceptance

An acceptance speech usually follows an award presentation. The purpose of the **speech of acceptance** is to offer gratitude for a gift or an award. When giving such a speech, the award recipient should thank the individual or organization presenting the award, as well as recognize the people who helped the recipient achieve it.

The speech of acceptance can fail miserably, which can be painful for audience members to witness. We are all too familiar with annual award programs on television (e.g., Academy Awards, Emmy Awards, Tony Awards) in which the recipients drone on endlessly by thanking hundreds of people who have contributed to their career success. By way of nomination, most people know in advance that they may be praised or awarded. These individuals should prepare a few words. Although this speech should appear impromptu, it is more important that the speech appear sincere and credible. An unprepared speaker who rambles on communicates insincerity and confusion to most audiences.

Another important consideration that many speakers overlook is the emotional response they will feel at the moment they are recognized for their achievements and the audience begins to applaud. It is easy for the award recipient to be emotionally moved, making it strenuous to speak. Once the audience finishes applauding, the speaker needs to collect his or her thoughts with respect to the preplanned speech.

Guidelines for giving a speech of acceptance. The following organizational structure works effectively for a speech of acceptance:

1. *Start with a sincere opening comment.* Share your personal feelings about receiving such an honor or gift. Also, since the speech is a reply, it must be adapted to what was said in the speech of presentation.

2. *Express your gratitude and acknowledge the audience.* The body of the speech of acceptance should include an expression of gratitude and acknowledgment of the audience members' integrity as professional colleagues. Next, recognize individuals who have assisted you personally in your career and give them adequate credit for whatever achievement is being celebrated. If a few individuals made your recognition possible, identify them by name; if a number of people did, refer to the most significant contributors who aided in your attainment of this honor.

3. *End with a heartfelt thanks.* Thank the organization giving you the award and acknowledge the importance and value of the work they are doing. Finally, give a closing "thank you" with an appropriate exit.

The following edited version of an earlier speech would be appropriate to present at a retirement dinner. When a person retires, a party or dinner is often given in his or her honor. Friends and colleagues give speeches, and gifts are given; then, the audience usually expects the recipient to say a few words in response. The speech presented below serves as an example of the sort of comments that could be made by a person being honored upon her or his retirement from the teaching profession.

> You know, I was watching closely as these people came up to speak [about me] tonight. Most of them I have known for almost all of my adult life. I [had] a difficult time listening to those speeches. They paint a picture of a life spent in education, and they were flattering in the extreme. For all those kind words, I am grateful and I thank you. From my heart, for all that love, I thank you.

Yes, I have a life of thirty-five years in education to look back on, and I know that the memories from those years will remain with me in the days ahead. Of course, not all of the times were good ones, but neither were they all bad. Rather, they were like all of life, a mixture of hills and valleys, ups and downs, that make up a span of years. Yet, as I look back even now, the unpleasant fades into the background, and that which was good and worthwhile remains vivid and clear.

And there was so much that was fine. I have seen students grow and mature; I have seen our school system grow and develop; I have seen education itself grow into a powerful and dynamic profession. That I was a part of it all, however small, gives me the greatest of pleasures, and I am thankful that I was allowed to be there.

Now I am stepping aside, but I am not stepping down. Education has been my life, and I fully intend to keep abreast of all that is happening. I also fully intend to visit from time to time just to keep in touch and, of course, to see to it that all of you keep on your toes.

And, while I do look forward to my retirement and to finally having the time to pursue some personal interests and, most importantly, to be able to spend more time with Arlene, my wife of thirty-seven years, whom I love dearly—while I do look forward to all of this, I know that I shall also miss my daily contact with all of you, my colleagues and my friends.

Because, and I make no mistake about it, if some of the things that have been said about me this evening are true, it is because I have, in my professional life, been fortunate enough to be surrounded by some of the finest educators this country has produced; people whose dedication and drive and expertise could not help but rub off on me. I have learned from them, and, for that tutoring, I shall be eternally grateful.

For all that has been said this evening and for all that has been done, you have my deep thanks; for all the toil and care and concern that I have witnessed you give for the good of the children of this land, you have my respect; and for all that you have been, are tonight, and will be tomorrow, you have my love.

Thank you for everything, and good evening (Mamchak and Mamchak 1992).

The preceding example meets the guidelines discussed earlier for speeches of acceptance. The recipient shares his feelings about being recognized by his colleagues for his career accomplishments. He then provides an overview of what he considered most important about his career, and he thanks the audience members for their gracious comments about his work. Finally, he wishes the audience members a good evening and he returns to his seat.

Celebrating Diversity

The website *http://www.americanrhetoric.com/speeches/marychurchterellcolored.htm* includes a speech by Mary Church Terrell entitled, "What It Means to Be Colored in the Capital of the United States" which was delivered on October 10, 1906, to the United Women's Club in Washington, D.C. Read this special occasion speech and comment on the use of language to paint vivid pictures. How did the speaker maintain audience interest?

The Speech of Tribute

A **speech of tribute** honors or celebrates a person, a group, an institution, or an event. Sometimes tributes are paid to an individual. At other times, tributes honor an entire group or class of people such as teachers, soldiers, or mothers. For example, at a groundbreaking ceremony for the construction of a new library, the mayor of the city may give a speech honoring the individual for whom the building will be named. On Memorial Day, the leader of a veterans' organization might deliver a speech of tribute to commemorate soldiers who died defending the interests of the United States.

A speech of tribute honors a person, group, or event. (Photo: Jesse Porter/*Daily Bruin*)

Guidelines for giving a speech of tribute. The fundamental purpose of a speech of tribute is not merely to inform your audience, but to inspire them. The speaker should stimulate and heighten audience members' adoration for the person, group, institution, or event being honored. In preparing the speech of tribute, Detz (1984) offers five guidelines that speakers should consider.

1. *Be generous with the praise.* Without question, the speech of tribute should be thoroughly positive. It is inappropriate to identify faults or rehash old conflicts. All commentary should be commendable and respectable.

2. *Be specific.* Never give a speech of tribute that is "canned." The remarks should be so specific that they could not be said about anyone else or for any other occasion.

3. *Be personal.* Make your speech of tribute reveal a real human being who is personable and vulnerable.

When Senator Ted Kennedy gave a memorial tribute to his brother John, he said of the late President, "He took issues seriously but never himself too seriously. Indeed, his family would not let him. After his election, when we were all at dinner one night. Dad looked at him and then turned to Mother and said with a smile, 'He may be President, but he still comes home and swipes my socks.' "

4. *Be sincere.* If you must pay tribute to a person you've never met or for an occasion at which you were not present, do not pretend to be a close friend or feign your presence at the occasion. Simply get information about the person or the important event and share this information in a genuine, honest manner.

5. *Be inspirational.* The speech of tribute should stir sentiments, causing people to feel joy, hope, or excitement. The speaker should attempt to uplift the audience. We find speeches of tribute meaningful and inspiring, as they generate a deep sense of respect for the person or event being honored.

In a memorial tribute to Martin Luther King, Jr., given at Harvard University, the Reverend Peter Gomes said, "We remember Martin Luther King, Jr., not because of his success, but because of our failures; not because of the work he has done, but because of the work we must do" (Detz 1984).

On June 6, 1994, the 50th Anniversary of D-Day, Great Britain's Queen Elizabeth delivered a speech of tribute at Arromanches, France.

> Monsieur le Marie, thank you for the welcome which you and the citizens of Arromanches have extended to Prince Philip, to me and to all our countrymen. I am glad that the Government of France is represented here by Madame Simone Veil. By the courage which she and a multitude like her displayed in the Nazi concentration camps, she represents perfectly why we are here today—to remember and to give thanks for deliverance.
>
> This town and this beach must hold a unique place in the memories of those of you who were here in June 1944. I am proud to see so many veterans of Operation Overlord, one of the most remarkable amphibious operations ever accomplished. You and the widows of those who fought will be remembering the deeds that were done that day, the comrades and husbands who never returned, and those who did come home but sadly are no longer with us.
>
> D-Day was indeed the beginning of the end. The months of planning at home, of preparation by the French Resistance, all conducted in the utmost secrecy, culminated here in Normandy that day, beginning the Liberation first of France and finally of Europe.
>
> Many of you will have in your minds vivid pictures—some perhaps all too vivid—of that epic day, and of the heroism and endurance shown by our own troops and by our Allies. Those of us who were far away can only imagine what it was like, and stand back in admiration of those who planned and fought for the establishment of that hard won bridgehead.
>
> It was you, and your comrades and Allies fighting on other fronts, who delivered Europe from that yoke of organized barbarism from which the men and women of following generations have been mercifully free. They should remember that they owe that freedom to those who fought and defeated Nazism. Next year we shall commemorate the fiftieth anniversary of the end of the Second World War. Old adversaries are now reconciled. But the Europe which we know today could not exist had not the tide of war been turned here in Normandy fifty years ago.
>
> Veterans of the Normandy campaign, you deserve your nation's thanks. May we, your fellow countrymen, be worthy of what you did for us (Queen Elizabeth 1994).

The speech presented by Queen Elizabeth was quite effective in offering tribute to those who participated in the planning and execution of the D-Day invasion. She was generous in her praise and she offered specific observations about the events that transpired on the beaches of Normandy in 1944. She personalized the speech by explaining her personal feelings about those who fought nobly on that momentous day. Finally, her presentation was inspirational in that it generated a sense of deep respect and admiration for those who played a role in the D-Day invasion.

The Eulogy

A speech to pay public honor and praise the dead is called a **eulogy.** Funerals are the most common occasions for such speeches; however, eulogies can also be delivered at memorial services that are independent of the funeral. Eulogies should be sincere and consist of an explicit presentation of

---

✔ Reality Check 15.1 ✔
A Letter to the Editor About Communication Courses

Kunkel and Dennis (2003) provide an interesting perspective in a recent article on Death Studies. Their article is entitled, "Grief Consolation in Eulogy Rhetoric: An Integrative Framework." They observe that rhetoric honoring the deceased is viewed as the primary, or exclusive, goal of a eulogy. They note that in uncertain times, such as those days following September 11, 2001, another important function of a eulogy is comforting the survivors.

---

the deceased person's achievements, justifying the praise that is given to him or her.

Eulogies typically follow one of two organizational patterns: chronological or topical. The chronological pattern too often fades into a rudimentary recital of the year-by-year course of the subject's life: parentage, childhood, education, and so on. This is an uninspiring approach that should be avoided. However, the chronological method can be used to good effect if the eulogist divides the individual's life into periods such as preparation, achievement, and recognition, thereby developing each major period of the subject's life into a well-rounded unit. The topical method is more flexible. This method allows a wider range of selectivity regarding the subject matter.

Guidelines for giving a eulogy. Topical eulogies concern themselves with such questions as the following:

1. Why was the subject a great human being?

2. What did this individual accomplish?

3. What unusual difficulties did this person overcome?

4. What admirable qualities did this individual possess?

5. To what agencies or sources did the subject owe his or her success?

6. What dramatic or interesting life incidents best reveal this person's personality and character?

7. What did the honoree's contemporaries think of him or her?

8. What benefits do we reap from this specific individual's labors?

9. What lessons can we learn from this special person's manner of living?

10. What should be our final judgment of this human being (Oliver and Cortright 1961)?

In some instances, a eulogy—particularly for a famous person—commemorates certain unique qualities that represent the person. In such a case, the speaker uses the memorial service to present a eulogy that revitalizes and strengthens the audience's devotion to certain ideals, as well as compels them to think about problems facing humanity in general. The following excerpts eulogize the former first lady of the United States, Jacqueline Kennedy Onassis. This eulogy was delivered by Edward Kennedy, United States Senator from Massachusetts, at Jacqueline Kennedy Onassis' funeral mass at St. Ignatius of Loyola Roman Catholic Church in New York City, on May 23, 1994.

> No one else looked like her, spoke like her, wrote like her, or was so original in the way she did things. No one we knew ever had a better sense of self.
>
> And then, during those four endless days in 1963, she held us together as a family and a country. In large part because of her, we could grieve and then go on. She lifted us up, and in the doubt and darkness, she gave her fellow citizens back their pride as Americans. She was then thirty-four years old.
>
> Afterward, as the eternal flame she lit flickered in the autumn of Arlington Cemetery, Jackie went on to do what she most wanted—raise Caroline and John, and warm her family's life and that of all the Kennedys.
>
> Her two children turned out to be extraordinary, honest, unspoiled and with a character equal to hers. And she did it in the most trying of circumstances. They are her two miracles. Her love for Caroline and John was deep and unqualified. She reveled in their accomplishments, she hurt with their sorrows, and she felt sheer joy and delight in spending time with them. At the mere mention of one of their names, Jackie's eyes would shine brighter and her smile would grow bigger.
>
> She never wanted public notice—in part, I think, because it brought back painful memories of an unbearable sorrow, endured in the glare of a million lights.
>
> In all the years since then, her genuineness and depth of character continued to shine through the privacy, and reach people everywhere. Jackie was too young to be a widow in 1963, and too young to die now (Kennedy 1994).

Senator Kennedy's touching tribute to Jacqueline Kennedy Onassis provides us with an excellent example of a eulogy. The audience was provided with a clear picture of the life of this former first lady, and why she was considered a great human being by so many. Her accomplishments, despite difficult and extraordinary circumstances, were clearly and persuasively documented by Senator Kennedy. The eulogy presented by Senator Kennedy provided the audience with the image of a loving mother who valued her privacy, yet, through her public actions, touched the lives of millions.

The Entertaining Speech

The entertaining speech should be fun, humorous, and uncomplicated to listen to. The entertaining speech should not be a lecture or a sermon.

The entertaining speech serves a variety of purposes, but it is most often referred to as an **after-dinner speech** because it is usually given after a luncheon or dinner. Club meetings, class reunions, graduation dinners, athletic banquets, and similar gatherings of friends, colleagues, and associates provide occasions for the after-dinner speech. People who have just con-

The speech to entertain is humorous and uncomplicated.
(Photo: Randall Reeder)

sumed a generous meal want to relax and let their food settle. They don't want to listen to any upsetting or distressful information, and they don't want to be intellectually challenged. The after-dinner speaker's only goal is to entertain the audience.

An entertaining speech can involve humor—often in the form of anecdotes, wit, exaggerated descriptions, puns, irony, satire, play on words, and jokes. Be cautious, however, as the entertaining speech is more than a series of unrelated one-liners. Comedy is a demanding and uncertain business. Remember, ". . . a little humor is like a little salt. It adds spice and zest. Too much kills the taste. Listeners like serious ideas sprinkled with a dash of wit" (Griffith, Nelson, and Stasheff 1960).

An entertaining speech does not have to be humorous to be impressive. As an after-dinner speaker, you may entertain an audience with a well-told story about the calamities that transpired on your first job interview or a dramatic account of your recent trip to Bangladesh. Although these speeches may not elicit hysterical laughter from the audience, they could be profoundly entertaining.

On the Web

Looking for quotations for your special occasion speech? Try *http://www.quotationspage.com*. Do you need some inspiration for adding humor to your speech? The website *http://www.less-stress.com/jokes/* includes dozens of jokes.

Guidelines for giving an entertaining speech. Although entertaining your audience is your primary purpose for an after-dinner speech, this does not preclude the speaker from integrating some persuasive, informative, or inspirational ingredients. Whether the after-dinner speech is serious, light, or a combination of both, the following rules are of value:

1. *Be good-humored.* For after-dinner speaking, the tone of good humor is fundamental. The speech should be consistent with the spirit of friendly good fellowship that brought the diners together.

2. *Be brief.* After a heavy dinner, the audience's attention span may be limited. Frequently, several speeches are to be given; therefore, make your speech brief and be prepared to condense it even more if you find your audience is getting restless.

3. *Be positive.* Take an affirmative approach toward your subject. Be straightforward and confident. Assume that your audience will support what you have to say. Keep in mind, audience analysis is essential and your perspective on the subject should be reasonable and comply with the opinions and experiences of your audience.

4. *Be clear and simple in your presentation.* Your ideas will need to be understood easily, in order to be understood at all. Use interesting illustrations, facts, and statistics but translate your sup-

portive evidence into vivid, meaningful language (Oliver and Cortright 1961).

By organizing your speech with the suggestions above, you not only provide your audience with entertainment, but you also help them remember your theme or central idea. The following after-dinner speech was written by Amie Niekamp, an undergraduate student at Ohio University. The speech was given at the annual celebration of Communication Day for the School of Interpersonal Communication, Ohio University.

Ladies and gentlemen, I . . . have jumped out of an airplane. On purpose.

It was last summer. I had been planning to go skydiving for quite some time and finally, on Labor Day weekend, I made the trip.

The place was . . . on a farm.

Okay, cool, no big deal. This way it would be gritty, and rugged. An airport setting would be too sterile, too . . . safe.

Anyway, despite the rural setting I was still very excited. Then I met our jumpmaster. I was expecting a big, wild, almost crazed man, with long bleached hair, and an aura of danger. In reality our jumpmaster was a short, balding man in a John Deere hat. I was hoping for Patrick Swayze and I got Buck Henry.

Then I had to sit through six hours of deathly dull training class. This involved a number of boring videos and demonstrations using specially dressed G. I. Joe dolls, which was misleading because none of the actual equipment had the COBRA emblem on it, and of course none of us had special kung-fu grip.

Finally we got to go out and meet some of the "regulars." They were middle-aged men with big guts and mustaches. They were wearing Achey Breaky Heart t-shirts. This wasn't *Point Break,* this was *Hee Haw.*

At this point I had to ask myself why was I doing this? Why would anyone do this? Why do so many people do this? The United States Parachute Association, a group of people with way too much time on their hands, reported a 20 percent increase in jumpers between 1985 and 1989. There have been similar, although less dramatic, increases in other high-risk sports such as hang gliding, bungee jumping, and rock climbing. For those of us whose idea of a high-risk sport is lawn darts, the obvious question is "what the hell is wrong with these people?"

Well, one possibility is that people are becoming increasingly dissatisfied with their lives and feel they need something dramatic to turn things around. Basically, people's lives aren't as exciting as they think they should be, so they've started jumping out of planes.

So, first we're going to understand what makes people think their lives need to be dramatic and why they feel they're not. Then we'll find out why high-risk sports have become a popular attempt to bridge this gap. And finally I'll let everyone off the hook with excuses why we don't have to immediately go out and try to kill ourselves to feel fulfilled. Then we'll adjourn for cookies and punch.

The June 1993 *Journal of Consumer Research* suggests that more and more people are turning to high-risk sports because their lives don't live up to the dramatic worldview presented by today's mass media. The idea that the mass media has some kind of mysterious influence on our actions is a pretty common one in our society. Critics continue to insist that violent films lead to aggression, sexually explicit films lead to discrimination against women, and John Hughes films lead to excessive retching. But Marshall McLuhan suggested that we are being influenced in a much more subtle way. In his book, *Understanding Media,* he taught that the medium is the message. We aren't so much influenced by the events that take place as by the dramatic framework within which the overt storyline unfolds. We begin to see the world through the terms of a movie or television show.

I have to admit to being personally guilty of this. I've often thought that my life would be ten times more exciting if it just had a soundtrack. That spooky music would let me know when my life is being threatened by some psycho killer, or you know . . . there's a cat in the trash! And whenever I'd hear that funky jazz beat, waka-chicka-wow, it would be a pretty safe bet that someone was going to have sex. On the playground I didn't play cowboys and Indians or war, I played *Thundercats*. And the game of doctor was replaced by . . . *The Love Boat*.

I always got to be Gopher.

Waka-chicka-wow.

The problem is, most of our lives can't live up to the ideal that the mass media puts forth. Random stuff always happens, issues aren't always resolved, and often we seem to have no control over the outcome of our own lives. The winter 1981 edition of *Symbolic Interaction* states that the increasing specialization in our industries has caused most individuals to feel as if they're being pushed through life by unidentifiable forces that rob them of their true individual choice . . . "Bring out the Gimp." Few people see the outcome of their effort and begin to feel as if they're working in a vacuum, which would suck. In the 1870s Karl Marx insisted that capitalism itself is dehumanizing and reduces individuals to an appendage of the machine. Over a century later, Richard Marx insisted that wherever you go, whatever you do, I will be right here waiting for you.

Anyway, a large percentage of the population are dissatisfied with their lives because they're not as dramatic as the ideal. So what makes people think that high-risk sports are the answer? Well, it all goes back to the media. Figures, huh? Shows like *MTV Sports* and movies like *Point Break*, *Terminal Velocity*, and *Drop Zone* romanticize skydiving and give the audience a leisure alternative they probably hadn't considered before.

The amazing thing is, however, in several cases high-risk sports are capable of bridging the dramatic versus reality gap, at least in a short-term way. According to the January 1990 *American Journal of Sociology*, a reference I was only allowed to check out for one day because it's in such high demand, participants in almost all high-risk sports report feeling a sense of "self realization." The climactic moment, be it free fall, climbing a mountain, or . . . waka-chicka-wow, brings on a sense of "hyper-reality." Participants describe the experience as being much more real than the events of their day-to-day life. Personally, I have to agree. As mundane as all the preparations were, the actual moment when I fell out of the airplane was thrilling beyond description. For one euphoric moment I was Keanu Reeves!

I guess you could draw some kind of Zen parallel here. I mean, Keanu did recently star in *Little Buddha*. But come on, Keanu Reeves as Buddha? That's like Joey Lawrence as Moses. Moses leads the Israelites across the desert and to freedom . . . on a very special *Blossom*.

(In best Joey Lawrence voice) "Woh!"

But the question remains, did skydiving somehow improve my life? Well . . . no. I mean sure, I can always impress people at parties—"Speaking of Tupperware, I once jumped out of an airplane"—but it hasn't made me content, it hasn't made me happier, it hasn't kept me from crying myself to sleep at night.

Basically, it's a distraction. An expensive, dangerous, adrenaline-pumping, kick-ass, mind-altering, sensory-overloading distraction, causing you to scream at the top of your lungs as you plummet madly towards the ground at life threatening speeds until you see THE FACE OF GOD HIMSELF! . . . but a distraction nonetheless.

If we're dissatisfied with our lives, it's better to find out what's causing the dissatisfaction than to rely on some alternative sport we heard about from

Dan Cortess to turn things around. Dan Cortess, "I love this speech!" There may be major discrepancies between what our lives are and what we think they should be, but there are ways of bridging that gap without actually jumping off the bridge. If we're considering something as frightening as a high-risk sport, we might as well sit down and consider some of the frightening life options we haven't been brave enough to take seriously. If we want to pursue a different, possibly more fulfilling, job, maybe we should rethink our occupation. If we want to finally make some kind of a concrete, lasting commitment in a relationship, maybe we should get married. If we want to order that spray paint stuff that makes it look like we have a full head of hair, maybe we should jump out of an airplane. I hate to admit it but there are no easy answers to improving our lives, and facing that fact can be scarier than any high-risk sport. There's nothing wrong with escapism, and I'd recommend skydiving to anyone, but we can't replace our reality with an endorphin-induced hyper-reality or even an idealized media reality. We have to be honest with ourselves and find real world solutions. Go ahead, kick out Puck! He's inconsiderate, and he smells bad.

If I hadn't been so set on my skydiving training living up to some kind of Hollywood stereotype, maybe I could have appreciated it for the unique experience it was. There were some genuinely insightful moments. At one point we were rigged up in simulated chute harnesses that cut painfully into the inner thigh, and hung from the ceiling. As I hung there an exhilarating two, three feet off the ground I realized for the first time why traditionally on stage Peter Pan is played by a woman. Maybe if I hadn't been caught up in living out some mass media fantasy, instead of being disappointed by an airport on a farm, I could have been impressed by its rural *Hee Haw* charm. (To the tune of that annoying old *Hee Haw* song) "We skydived together and I thought I found true love. But your chute was faulty and THPTT you were gone" (Niekamp 1995)!

The preceding example of an after-dinner speech effectively meets the guidelines discussed earlier. This is a good-humored presentation that deals with a subject appropriate for an audience of college students, parents, and professors. This speech meets the brevity criterion, as it can be presented in approximately six minutes. The ideas and images presented in the speech are clear and simple; they do not require a great deal of specialized knowledge for audience members to understand. Regarding the criterion of positiveness, the speaker offered sound advice by exhorting his listeners to focus on their own behavior and actions rather than laughing at others' shortcomings.

Summary

In this chapter, we have provided an overview of the different types of speeches that can be presented on special occasions. In providing this overview, guidelines were offered to assist the speaker in preparing different types of speeches. Also, representative examples of various special occasion presentations were presented. For all of these special occasions, the speaker needs to keep a few important points in mind. First, what are the demands or requirements associated with the specific situation in which you have been called to speak? In order to address this question, you should consider the guidelines discussed in this chapter, as well as talk with those people who are planning the events that call for your specific presentation. Second, remember to be brief in your comments, especially if your presentation is one among several to be given at a particular event. Third, prepare your presentation adequately so you do not make errors in pronunciation and so you can deliver your speech in an extemporaneous style. Following these simple suggestions should help you to prepare and deliver a speech that is appropriate to your particular occasion as well as one that is well received by the audience.

Communication Narrative 15.1
Expect the Unexpected

Corey belonged to a service club that had a different speaker every week. Following a light lunch, the president of the club would have the person who invited the speaker introduce him or her. What caught Corey off-guard was the day the speaker showed up but the person who invited her did not. As soon as the president noticed that he had no one to introduce the guest, he whispered in Corey's ear, "You know her. Fran's not here. You introduce her." Corey felt his mouth go dry, looked at his lunch without interest, and started to sweat. Finally he worked up enough courage to go talk with the woman he barely knew.

Fortunately, Corey had taken a speech course in college, and he remembered a few suggestions about introducing someone. He had some diplomatic skills. He walked up to the guest, reminded her that they knew each other, mentioned that Fran was absent, and convincingly said he would be happy to introduce her. He quickly wrote down her name, her job title, and her employer. He then asked her about her education, her current position, previous employment, and what she liked best about her job. Armed with this information, Corey returned to his seat to finish eating before he had to introduce the guest. He was no longer sweating, and his hunger had returned. He knew what he was going to say.

Vocabulary

after-dinner speech An entertaining speech that may be presented in a variety of situations, but is frequently given after a luncheon or dinner.

eulogy A speech to pay public honor and praise to a deceased person.

special occasion A distinctive time, event, ceremony, or celebration which has a particular function, purpose, or application.

speech of acceptance A speech to offer gratitude for a gift or an award.

speech of farewell A commemorative speech that falls into one of two categories: a speech of appreciation given by the departing individual, or a speech of public recognition given by someone about a revered individual who is departing.

speech of inspiration A speech given to build the confidence and stimulate the positive self-esteem of the listeners.

speech of introduction A speech to inform the audience of the qualifications of the upcoming speaker, so that the speaker's views will be received with respect, and to provide a link between the speaker and the audience regarding the nature and tone of the occasion.

speech of presentation A speech given when an individual is receiving a gift or an award.

speech of tribute A speech to honor or celebrate a person, a group, an institution, or an event.

speech of welcome A speech that is analogous to the speech of introduction; yet the speech of welcome centers predominately on the audience rather than on the speaker.

Application Exercises

1. Choose a classmate for a speech partner. Introduce your partner to the class following the guidelines for a speech of introduction.

2. In groups of three or four, brainstorm a list of 10 living individuals who, in your opinion, are most deserving of speeches of eulogy. Each group chooses one individual to eulogize and, as a group, prepares and delivers a five-minute eulogy explaining the merits of the individual named.

3. As a class, draw up a list of five important historic events and discuss the unique characteristics of these occasions. Prepare and deliver a five-minute speech of tribute on one of the selected events.

4. Assume the Congress is about to be organized for a new session. Give a five-minute speech nominating your choice for Speaker of the House. Or, assume that the United Nations is to begin a new session, and present a speech for your nominee as President of the General Assembly.

Application Assignments

1. Watch several speeches of presentation and acceptance on a television program such as the Academy Awards, Grammy Awards, Emmy Awards, or Tony Awards. Which speakers did you find most competent? Least competent? Were any speakers poorly prepared? How did their lack of preparation affect their sincerity and credibility? Were any speakers emotionally moved? What impact did this have on the speech and the audience?

2. Examine the eulogy given by Senator Edward Kennedy at Jacqueline Kennedy Onassis' funeral mass. Evaluate the speech with regard to the guidelines for the eulogy as presented in the chapter.

References

Detz, J. (1984). *How to write and give a speech.* New York: St. Martin's Press.

DeWine, S. (1994, April). *Speech of presentation: Dr. Jesse Delia,* presented at the annual celebration of Communication Day for the School of Interpersonal Communication, Ohio University. Courtesy of Sue DeWine, Ohio University, 1994.

Griffith, F., Nelson, C., and Stasheff, E. (1960). *Your Speech.* New York: Harcourt, Brace, and World, Inc.

Hancher, V. M. (1953). In G. R. Lyie and K. Guinagh (Eds.). *I am happy to present: A book of introductions.* New York: The H. W. Wilson Company.

Kennedy, E. (1994, May). Farewell to a first lady. *USA Today,* 3A. Reprinted with the permission of Senator Edward M. Kennedy.

Mamchak, P. S., and Mamchak, S. R. (1992). *School administrator's public speaking portfolio with model speeches and anecdotes.* West Nyack, NY: Parker Publishing Company, Inc. Reprinted by permission of Parker Publishing/A Division of Simon & Schuster.

Martin, R. C., Robinson, K. F., and Tomlinson, R. C. (1963). *Practical speech for modern business.* New York: Appleton-Century-Crofts, Inc.

Niekamp, A. (1995, April). Speech presented at the annual celebration of Communication Day at Ohio University.

Oliver, R. T., and Cortright, R. L. (1961). *Effective speech* (4th ed.) New York: Holt, Rinehart, and Winston.

Peterson, H. (1954). *A treasury of the world's great speeches.* New York: Simon & Schuster.

Queen Elizabeth, Queen of England. (1994, June). 50th anniversary of D-Day. *Vital Speeches of the Day,* 60(18), 547–548.

Chapter 16

Speech Criticism

If our democracy is to flourish, it must have criticism; if our government is to function, it must have dissent.
—Henry Commager

Question Outline

I. What is the value of criticism in our society?

II. Who was responsible for founding speech criticism?

III. What is the difference between acting as a coach and acting as a critic in evaluating speeches?

IV. What kinds of potential biases might you find in speech evaluations?

V. What are some underlying causes of biased speech evaluation?

VI. What important questions should you ask before and after evaluating speeches?

VII. How does speech evaluation in the classroom differ from that outside the classroom?

VIII. How can speeches be evaluated outside the classroom?

At *a public speaking workshop, twenty women who were health professionals saw two videotapes of student speeches: one by a male student, the other by a female student. The workshop teacher wanted the women's observations before they received instruction on speech criticism.*

The workshop participants said of the male speaker, "good organization," "used lots of gestures and examples," and "seemed to really know what he was talking about." Of the female speaker the participants said, "must have been a bad hair day," "she seemed cold and distant," and "I wish she would have smiled more."

The workshop teacher wisely noted, "Everyone comes to the public speaking situation with standards and with biases." Like the workshop, this chapter is designed to help you understand evaluation, to show you how to minimize bias, and to establish standards of appraisal.

In order to help you become a better critical thinker and evaluator, this chapter will provide guidelines for criticism of others' speeches and presentations. Since you will not be in a basic speech classroom for the rest of your life, this chapter will also offer suggestions for you to use when you evaluate speeches outside the classroom, particularly in political settings. More importantly, this chapter will emphasize the importance of criticism and critical thinking for those of you who want to be active, involved members of a society that is growing, changing, and diversifying.

The Value of Criticism

In contemporary life, you are exposed to more and more information all the time. In order to criticize speeches effectively, you must learn how to think critically about and respond critically to the world. Critical thought and response are important for the following reasons:

1. Critical thought and response allow you to sift through the information you receive on a daily, even minute-by-minute, basis to determine what is important, useful, *and* trustworthy to include in your bases of knowledge.

2. Critical thought invites us to maintain standards of evaluation while at the same time to appreciate the creative ways that people think, know, and speak.

Now that you are aware of the importance of criticism, think about the tradition of criticism, as it exists in the study of speech communication. Your understanding of criticism needs to be grounded in your knowledge of the past and applied to present and future public speaking performances.

A Brief History of Criticism

Criticism has been an important part of many disciplines of study, such as art, music, literature, and now even popular culture. **Criticism** is the practice of applying standards to an object, a person, a place, a trend, an idea, or a movement. The item or idea under critique is evaluated for its success, worth, or value in light of the critical standards. The object of the criticism is sometimes referred to as a *text* or an **artifact,** depending on whether it is written or made physically tangible in a form other than writing.

Critical efforts in the discipline of speech communication are often referred to under the label of *rhetorical criticism.* This designation comes from the definition offered centuries ago by the Greek philosopher Aristotle, who defined *rhetoric* as "the faculty of observing in any given case the available means of persuasion" (*The Rhetoric and Poetics of Aristotle* 1954). In other words, Aristotle recommended that scholars study how successful speakers communicate their persuasive messages. Furthermore, he instructed scholars to study how such messages could be improved.

Aristotle divided the process of preparing a speech into five parts or stages (often referred to as the canons of classical rhetoric). Rhetorical scholars Patricia Bizzell and Bruce Hertzberg identified these stages:

In order to criticize a speech, you must listen to it completely. (Photo: Roxbury Publishing Co.)

1. *Invention,* or the search for persuasive ways to present information and formulate arguments.

2. *Arrangement,* the organization of the parts of a speech to ensure that all the means of persuasion are present and properly disposed.

3. *Style,* the use of correct, appropriate, and striking language throughout the speech.

4. *Memory,* the use of mnemonics[1] and practice.

5. *Delivery,* presenting the speech with effective gestures and vocal modulation.

If these appear familiar, this is not surprising; Bizzell and Hertzberg (1990) observed that this five-stage process "remains a cornerstone of the study of rhetoric" (pp. 3–4)—and, in many cases, of speech criticism. So began a tradition of criticism that has lasted to our present day.

In recent history, however, some scholars have argued that the critical standards established in ancient Greece and in the centuries since are not necessarily appropriate or useful in contemporary life and reflect the biases of those times rather than encourage us to confront and eliminate bias. Another problem with the tradition of formal criticism is that it is time consuming, especially if you object to the speech's message and have to reflect before you can frame your arguments.

In the rush to save time, reject old critical standards, and create new ones, however, the purpose for which rhetorical criticism was established might be lost. After all, when many people hear the word criticism—even prefaced by the adjective constructive—they cringe, waiting for the worst to happen. That was not Aristotle's purpose at all. In fact, he and others hoped to use criticism to educate the new landowners of ancient Greece—former peasants who needed such skills to argue their cases in court. As one scholar has claimed, the purpose was to "help truth and justice maintain their natural superiority" (Hudson 1961). That is a purpose that can certainly be fulfilled in even the most informal critical and evaluative interactions. To honor that noble purpose as you carry out speech criticism in the classroom and in everyday life, you need to understand the difference between functioning as a coach and acting as a critic.

On the Web

Do you want to learn more about classical criticism, feminist criticism, and Burkian criticism? Information is available at this website: *http://www.ksu.edu/sctd/sp_comm/resources*.

Coach or Critic—What's the Difference?

The distinction between being a coach and being a critic is one you must understand if you are to be an effective critic. When most of us are taught to "critique" someone, we often focus on the negative. This process of "tearing down" others' work has gone on for centuries in Western culture under the mistaken assumption that the more you can pick apart someone's work, the more insightful and learned you are.

One solution to the problem of negative criticism might be to think of yourself as a coach rather than a critic. A coach does not tear down players day after day, nor does a coach focus only on what players have done "wrong." Instead, a good coach offers suggestions for improvement to help players succeed, recognizes the strengths and abilities already in place, and provides individually oriented instruction to help each player live up to his or her potential. Also, a good coach knows that he or she cannot force anyone to follow suggestions; it is up to the players to evaluate their trust in the coach and their willingness to work. Most importantly, a coach always explains *why* players would benefit from listening to, and following, his or her suggestions.

If you can function as a coach in providing criticism and evaluation, you will likely receive a more receptive response to your comments. Your peers are also more inclined to treat you with the respect you have shown them. You do not assume control of anyone else's performance; you simply do the best you can in providing feedback and suggestions. Best of all, you focus on the behavior in need of work, rather than attacking the person who is speaking.

These suggestions probably sound very reasonable. Unfortunately, negativity can be so deeply ingrained and so subtle that you might have a hard time even recognizing when you are being negative. Next, this chapter will describe some of the biases and prejudice that enter into speech criticism, explain the effects of such biases, and explore why these biases occur.

Biases in Evaluating Speeches

Perhaps there are some saints among us who harbor no bias against other human beings, but most people have biases, and this section briefly explores some of them.

Kinds of Biases That Occur in Evaluating Speeches

Numerous studies have demonstrated that when people of varied ethnic, socioeconomic, and gender identities are evaluated as public speakers, those who do not belong to "dominant" groups are discriminated against (Bjork and Trapp 1994; Bruschke and Johnson 1994; Hart and Williams 1995; Pearson 1979). Generally, these studies indicate that white males are most often evaluated as the most powerful and effective speakers. Women, students with disabilities, and students of color are often given less favorable evaluations not only from instructors, but also from their peers.

This is an example of bias in speech criticism. **Bias** is an inclination or a prejudice that keeps us from evaluating or judging impartially. The problems of bias in speech criticism are twofold. First, biased criticisms hurt speakers who genuinely want to participate but are poorly evaluated because of who they *are*. Second, biased criticisms keep speakers who are rated positively because of who they are from being evaluated fairly and honestly on what they *do*. Discussing issues such as these is an important step in increasing our understanding and ability to evaluate speeches fairly and effectively, and to provide useful criticism for other speakers.

✔ Reality Check 16.1 ✔

Samuel McCormick (2003), in an insightful article in the *Quarterly Journal of Speech*, illustrates the importance of speech criticism on ordinary talk. In the past, rhetorical scholars provided criticism of only well-known or famous speeches.

You might believe that this type of bias is confined only to either informal or classroom criticisms and interactions, such as the one described in the opening story about the public speaking workshop. The problem of bias is evident in the following exchange between former member of Congress Clare Boothe Luce and columnist William F. Buckley, which took place on the nationally broadcast television program "Firing Line":

Buckley: [Following his introduction of Clare Boothe Luce] I should like to begin by asking her [Luce] whether she finds implicit condescension in the rhetorical formulations with which men tend to introduce her.

Luce: Bill, I thank you for that warm and extraordinarily friendly introduction. You'll be pleased to know that in the entire introduction, which was flattering, to say the least, there was only one masculine put-down. This is a high level of achievement for a man introducing a woman.

You spoke of her [woman's] inability, on occasions, to hold her tongue. Now, had you been speaking of a man who spoke out and made enemies for himself in the process, whether he was speaking out stupidly or rightly . . . you would have said, "He is blunt. He makes enemies by what he says. He is overly candid." You might have used many phrases. But the phrase "hold her tongue" is a phrase that men frequently use about children and women. . . . It comes out of man's desire, highly successful, through the centuries to master women. (Miller and Swift 1977)

Comments about the nature and behavior of women, students with disabilities, or students of color are not the only sources of bias in speech evaluations, however. If these were the sole sources of bias, it would be much easier to correct the problem. You might not realize that you could also be demonstrating bias if you were to write comments such as "You need to use more statistics," "I didn't think your organization was laid out in a very logical manner," or "You need to make more eye contact with your audience."

For starters, the bias toward the use of statistics as proof is a very Western cultural preference. More and more often, questions are being asked about the value of using numbers as a form of "proof"; articles in both *Time* and *Newsweek* magazines offered examples of just how wrong published statistics can be. The author of one such article noted, "The numbers are presented as though they carry all the weight of scientific truth. Don't believe it" (Toufexis 1993).

Members of other cultures often prefer to focus on *pathos,* or the use of personal, sometimes emotional appeals, as a form of proof, rather than relying on published numerical data (Garrett 1993a, 1993b; Jensen 1992). Stories and analogies, as well as emphasis on silence rather than speaking, are typical of communicative and public speaking strategies used in other cultures (Cooke, Klopf, and Ishii 1991; Hecht, Ribeau, and Alberts 1989). Some Native American and African cultures, for instance, have a long performance tradition of telling stories as a way of making arguments (Gates 1990). Comments about the "logic" of a speech's organization might be an example of Western or European-American bias. Many speakers in Western cultures follow a "linear" form of logic, such as the syllogism, in which a major premise ("All professors have experience") is combined with a minor premise ("My teacher is a professor") to reach a conclusion ("My teacher has experience"). However, this is certainly not the only way of organizing messages in public communication. Some cultures follow what has been called a "spiral" type of logic, in which pieces of information are drawn from many sources and then evaluated together in order to reach a conclusion. This is often used in cultures such as Japan, where people are highly skilled at drawing inferences from nonverbal cues as well as from spoken or written messages (Ting-Toomey 1985). In such cultures, it is not considered respectful to establish continuous eye contact, since that can be a sign of hostility or resentment. The pattern of argument and speech construction might not be the same as the linear model, but is it logical? Ask any woman who has been accused of operating on "illogical feminine intuition" and you will receive your answer. Rejecting a speech solely on the basis of its failure to meet your expectations of logical organization is not always good criticism. In some cases, as communication professor and forensics coach Kevin Dean (1992) has argued, the most effective speech might be the one that "defines a place of commonality between [the speaker] and audience . . . instead of merely finding buttons to push to elicit audience reaction."

How Biases Affect Us as Speakers and Evaluators

Think for a moment about the consequences of these biases. If you are a member of a group that is consistently devalued as public speakers, you know the implications for your own progress in and enthusiasm for public speaking. There is little incentive to continue an activity in which you can never succeed based on your own unique ability. If you are not a member of one of these groups, think about how you suffer when these voices are silenced.

As an evaluator, you run the risk of appearing to be prejudiced if you cannot recognize and remove these biases. Your comments will never be taken fully to heart, nor will they result in significant change in speakers' performances. Also, you might never be able to improve your own performance to the fullest because you will not understand why others fail to respond to your messages.

Why Biases Occur

Why evaluators are biased in their criticisms of speakers is difficult to answer. We can, however, identify at least a few of the factors that might contribute to biased evaluation:

- *Fear.* We often fear that which we do not understand. This is true when we encounter people from other cultures who communicate in a manner that seems foreign, even when they speak the same language we do.

- *Time.* Writing or delivering thoughtful, instructive criticism is not only a time-consuming task, but it might well be something that takes a lifetime to perfect.

- *Lack of knowledge.* Already, in reading this chapter, you are more knowledgeable about criticism than some people will ever be. Only in the past few years has there been a call for criticism to be reinstituted as a part of educational planning.

- *Power.* Bias can also be due to the perception that evaluating another person harshly somehow increases your power by making you look stronger, or that evaluating someone else favorably gives you more power because that person will then owe you something. In either case, you might stand to gain more power by providing an ethical, reasonable, and useful criticism than by "playing games" with critiques.

Whatever the factors are that contribute to bias in criticism and evaluation, you can now recognize such biases and can guess why they are present. The following sections will take you on the next step in the journey—educating yourself to be a better critic and evaluator.

Celebrating Diversity

On April 12, 1999, Elie Wiesel delivered a speech, "The Perils of Indifference" in Washington, D.C. Wiesel's speech was powerful because of his credibility as a survivor of the Holocaust. Read the speech (or listen to it) at *http:// www.americanrhetoric.com/speeches/ewieselperilsofindifference.html.* Provide a critique of the speech using the information that is contained in this chapter.

Training Yourself to Be a Better Evaluator

In evaluating speeches, as in many aspects of life, you become better through practice. Simply thinking about speeches as you see them in the classroom, however, does little to improve your critical ability. One method for becoming a better evaluator is *writing down comments* as they come to mind while you watch other students' presentations. After class, look at the comments you wrote. Practice giving the comments orally as well, since you might be tempted to "soften" valid criticisms when speaking face-to-face with someone. Do you see any evidence of bias in your comments? Are there any people from certain backgrounds that you evaluate more favorably or more negatively than others?

Another method is *practicing evaluating speeches in small groups*. Several researchers suggest that more useful and satisfying evaluations are constructed by groups of students working together (Jones 1988). This will be easier if you practice by evaluating a videotaped speech of a speaker outside the class before you begin evaluating other students' speeches (Rollman 1990). Even if this is not a part of your course, you can meet with classmates on your own time to discuss presentations and compare your evaluation to that of others.

A third method is *beginning your comments with the word I*. Don't write in the passive voice, such as "Most people usually do X in a speech" or "Generally, good speakers do X"; these imply that you have access to some universal information that the speaker might or might not know about. Also, general and universal comments seem to indicate that there is a magically "correct" form for speakers to follow in all cultures. That is not true.

A fourth method is *focusing on behavior*. What did the speaker do that you thought was effective? What should the speaker *do* differently next time? Comments such as "Good energy" or "Need more enthusiasm" don't give a presenter anything specific to work with. Also, criticisms of the speaker's appearance or dress don't have a great deal to do with improving the behaviors and skills of effective public speaking; therefore, such comments should not take up the greater part of your evaluation.

A fifth method is *making the best use of **thought speed***. Listening expert Ralph Nichols estimated that if thought were measured in words per minute, most of us would probably be able to think at the rate of about 500 words per minute. He compared that rate to the speed at which most Americans speak—about 125 words per minute—and called the gap between these two rates "thought speed" (Nichols 1957). Nichols argued that rather than using our thought speed to daydream, as most of us do, we could become better listeners and evaluators by putting it to more productive use. Specifically, he claimed that we should:

- Anticipate what's coming from the speaker, mentally asking yourself, "What is this person going to say or do next?"

- Sum up what you have already heard, asking yourself, "What points has the speaker already covered?"

- Continually evaluate the supporting information the speaker is providing. Instead of merely observing that a speaker is using facts, statistics, stories, or illustrations, think to yourself, "Are these the best sources of information the speaker could have used? How relevant are they to the claims being made? What do these sources of information mean to me?"

- Pay attention to the nonverbal cues the speaker is providing. Look for a "goodness of fit"—that is, evaluate whether or not what the speaker is *doing* appears congruent or supportive of what the speaker is *saying*.

You might be surprised at just how active your mind can be if you are able to capitalize on thought speed, as Nichols suggested. There are also added benefits. Not only will you be a better evaluator, but you might also become a better notetaker in your courses. In addition, the time you spend listening to speeches will fly by.

A sixth and final method is *preparing yourself mentally before beginning an evaluation.* Remember the difference between coaching and criticizing. Think about your own physical and emotional well being. Are you tired? Cranky? Resentful? If so, you need to put those emotions aside for the time being so that you will do the best job possible. Former Chicago Bears coach Mike Ditka had hip replacement surgery that left him in great pain during his years in professional football, but it never stopped him from being focused on the perfor-

When called upon to critique a speech, a person needs a variety of skills. (Photo: Michael Jennings/*Daily Bruin*)

mance of his team and on individual players, offering all the guidance he could give. Your responsibility as a peer evaluator is to do just that—give all you have in terms of feedback and advice. To ensure that you have done your job, you can also use the accompanying checklist of questions to quiz yourself before and after you evaluate speeches and presentations.

Using these methods and the checklist questions is a start toward giving more effective criticism. Some of these issues will also be relevant for your lifelong experiences in evaluating speeches and presentations outside the classroom.

Questions to Ask When Evaluating Speeches in the Classroom

Before Evaluating a Speech

- Have I put aside all physical and mental distractions to focus on the speaker and the message?

- Do I have any history with this speaker that might unfairly bias my evaluation?

- Am I hoping to gain something from the way I evaluate this speaker?

- Have I already begun forming expectations based on the speaker's appearance?

- Am I willing to be receptive to strategies of communication that are different from my own?

> ### After Evaluating a Speech
>
> - Did I evaluate the speaker's performance independently of my opinion about the topic?
> - Did my comments begin with I, indicating that I focused on my personal responses and reactions to the speaker?
> - Did I write comments that were focused on specific behaviors rather than on feelings or perceptions?
> - Did I provide positive comments, as well as suggestions for improvement?[2]
> - Is my evaluation clearly written and understandable?
> - Was I enlightened by the speech and speaker? Did I learn something new?
> - Did I reject the speaker's claims because he or she did not provide statistics as a form of proof?
> - Did I make the best use of my thought speed?

Evaluating Within and Outside the Classroom— Critical Differences

One of the critical differences you will encounter in evaluating presentations as you begin to move away from the classroom and into the world of work and career is the difference of **setting.** Many speakers in the professional world do not use podiums or notes. Some do not use extensive citations of information. Some use styles of presentation that appear confusing. For instance, imagine yourself at a nominating convention held by a major American political party during a presidential election year. The speeches probably would not present both sides of the issues. They also might not give sources of information for the claims being made. They would be full of emotional appeals, would not invite audience questions or comments, and would have little or no regard for time constraints. Nonetheless, these could all be very successful speeches *within that particular setting*, because the purpose of these speeches is to unify the political party, to get the attendees emotionally involved and excited, and to promote one candidate to receive the party's nomination.

Another crucial difference is in the **genre,** or type, of speech being presented. Special occasion speeches, for instance, have traditional expectations and rules. A eulogy is normally focused on praise of a person's life and accomplishments. An **epideictic speech** either praises or blames a famous historical event or figure. Commencement addresses usually refer to the past and conclude with a look to the future. After-dinner speaking is usually based on personal experience and is focused on containing a mildly serious message within a largely humorous speech. Before you can evaluate speeches outside the classroom, then, you also must be familiar with the cultural expectations associated with the genre of speech being delivered.

A third difference between evaluating speeches outside the classroom and evaluating speeches in class is the **medium,** or channel, through which the speech is translated. In evaluating speeches in the classroom, you have the advantage of seeing the speaker face-to-face, so that you can observe all the speaker's verbal and nonverbal behavior. Far fewer speeches outside the classroom are delivered in face-to-face interactions. More often, they are mediated by an alternative delivery system of communication. We might see presidential press conferences on television, read the texts of famous speeches in *Vital Speeches* or on electronic bulletin boards, or see excerpts published in the *New York Times*. These alternate forms of delivery have their advantages and disadvantages. For instance, when we see the text of a speech, we can better evaluate its structure of arguments and the use of supporting information. We cannot, however, discern how persuasive or appropriate the speaker's delivery style was for the occasion. Seeing a speech on television allows us to record it on videotape and review it for more thorough analysis. This format does not, however, give much of a sense of the audience's reaction to the speech itself. In evaluating speeches outside the classroom, then, remember the crucial factors of setting, genre, and medium in order to provide criticism that is both insightful and appropriate.

Questions to Ask in Evaluating Speeches Outside the Classroom

- Is the speaker discussing a topic appropriate to this audience?
- Do I find any of the speaker's statements offensive to me or to others in the audience?
- Has the speaker raised a variety of supporting information?
- Am I able to determine the speaker's main points and subpoints without difficulty?
- Would I take the opportunity to hear this speaker again?
- Does the speaker provide a balanced discussion of the issues?
- Is the speaker's style appropriate for this setting?
- Does the speaker fulfill my expectations for performance at his or her level of experience and knowledge?
- Does the speaker invite questions from the audience?
- Does the speaker answer audience questions fairly, completely, and respectfully?

Guidelines for Evaluating Speeches Outside the Classroom

Four excellent maxims for critical analysis were offered by communication scholars William L. Nothstine, Carole Blair, and Gary A. Copeland in their book on criticism, *Critical Questions* (1994). They suggested that people interested in any kind of critical work, particularly when it involves rhetorical (persuasive) or media analysis, should consider the following principles:

Maxim #1: Criticism requires understanding and pursuing one's own interests.

Maxim #2: Criticism is written to and for an audience.

Maxim #3: Criticism is both served and confined by theory and method.

Maxim #4: Criticism rarely travels a straight line to its end.

Nothstine, Blair, and Copeland claimed that criticism requires understanding and pursuing one's own interests. This means that you must acknowledge what you bring to evaluating a speech. Rather than trying to provide broad, vague criticism of a speech on its universal merits, focus on *I* statements and on what the speech does or does not mean to *you*.

Second, the authors noted that criticism is written to and for an audience. As you have discovered, you often need to put yourself in the speaker's place to write useful criticism. However, if you are evaluating speeches outside the classroom, you have to imagine yourself in the speaker's place *at the speaker's level of experience*. After all, if you listen to a political speech given by the president of the United States and evaluate it based on how you as a college student would perform in the same situation, you would undoubtedly give the speaker glowing reviews. Realistically, however, it is more constructive to evaluate the speech based on how you would perform in that situation *at the speaker's expected level of experience and expertise*.

Speech criticism begins with one's own interests (Photo: Roxbury Publishing Co.)

Third, Nothstine, Blair, and Copeland suggested that criticism is both served and confined by theory and method. This means that you benefit from reading textbooks that offer suggestions for critical thinking and evaluation, just as you benefit from listening to your instructors' classroom presentations and even your parents' lectures. The process of critical thinking, however, does not stop here. If you evaluate public speakers based solely on your parents' opinions and political viewpoints, or on the opinions of your college roommates, you are being *confined* by other people's thoughts and views. To be a truly effective evaluator, you need to read, think, and speak out independently. Will you still be influenced by others' views? Of course. We are all social beings. However, that influence can become problematic when it limits—or worse yet, eliminates—independent investigation and thinking.

Finally, these scholars observed that criticism rarely travels a straight line to its end. As you continue your education, you should also continue to expand your universe of information—the knowledge base that forms the foundation of your critical responses. One of the difficulties in doing this is that you run the risk of falling prey to "information overload." As you become more and more knowledgeable about criticism, you will have to find out by trial and error which standards are most appropriate for you, and which are most true to your own system of beliefs, attitudes, and values. For many of us, this is a lifelong process; yet, as the Greek philosopher Socrates observed and as many scholars believe, "the unexamined life is not worth living."

Summary

We often have negative connotations of the word criticism—a negativity also expressed by British statesman Benjamin Disraeli when he commented, "How much easier it is to be critical than to be correct." In this chapter, you have learned that in our ever changing—and sometimes overwhelming—world, we need to rethink these associations and rediscover the value of critical thought and discussion, accepting the challenge to (1) sort out information to determine its value and (2) establish critical standards that do not restrict our appreciation of diversity.

Another challenge is to overcome the biases that can enter into the critical process. Whatever the causes of these biases, and in whatever way they manifest, you can be better prepared not only as an evaluator but also as a public speaker to confront and defeat them.

Significant differences can exist in setting, genre, and medium between the classroom and other speech contexts. You can use the chapter guidelines and lists of questions in evaluating speeches.

Perhaps the most important, and certainly the most delightful, result of working to become a more observant critical thinker and evaluator is the improvement you will see in your own performance as a public speaker. Providing helpful coaching suggestions rather than negative critic's commentary to others is an important step toward being able to coach yourself into better speaking. It also aids us in recognizing that, as former President John F. Kennedy noted, "Civility is not a sign of weakness."

Communication Narrative 16.1
Message Analysis

Political season had arrived with a seemly endless series of TV ads, speeches, news stories, and articles about the candidates. The negative ads about votes, military service, policy decisions, and warfare were enough to convince anyone that we should vote for no one. Because his friends loved to argue about politics, Irwin felt frustrated that he did not really know what to say about candidates. Should he just talk about how they look? Should he just comment on how awkwardly or smoothly they spoke? He was uncertain how to show his friends that he too knew about politicians.

Irwin's communication course came to his rescue. He learned about speech delivery: facial expression, gestures, and eye contact. He learned about how a politician earns the right to speak on a topic. He learned that arguments demand evidence and evidence invites believability. Most of all, he learned that politicians need to be able to defend their positions on issues. He even learned that much of the message is what is not said, what the politician refuses to talk about.

Now Irwin loves to get into political discussions. He can more than hold his own in analyzing political messages. He has even found that his newly acquired analytical skills make him feel more intelligent.

Vocabulary

artifact A physically tangible object of criticism.

bias An inclination or a prejudice that keeps us from evaluating or judging impartially.

criticism The practice of applying standards to an object, a person, a place, a trend, an idea, or a movement in order to evaluate its worth and effectiveness.

epideictic speech A speech designed to commemorate a famous historical event or person, usually by assigning either praise or blame.

genre The type of speech being delivered, such as a eulogy, a persuasive speech, an informative speech, an after-dinner speech, a commencement address, or an epideictic speech.

medium The communication channel through which a speech is delivered, such as face-to-face, mass mediated (television and radio), transcription (text), or electronic transmission.

setting The physical and social environment in which a speech or presentation is given.

thought speed The gap between how rapidly we can think (about 500 words per minute) and how rapidly most people speak (about 125 words per minute).

Application Exercises

1. Break into small groups. Discuss what the members of your group believe an effective presentation should be. Just brainstorm at first, without evaluating or ranking which suggestions are "best." After everyone is finished, discuss your ideas. Decide as a group what standards you will use in evaluating speeches for this class. Be sure that you decide this by consensus—unanimous vote—and that you allow all members of the group to express their opinions.

2. In small groups, have each member take out a sheet of paper. Draw a line down the center of the paper and head one column "Coach," the other "Critic." Watch a videotape or in-class presentation and write comments as both coach and critic. After you are finished, read your lists aloud to each other. Discuss the differences between the lists; consider how you would feel as a speaker if your evaluations came solely from everyone's "Critic" list.

3. Use the evaluation form below to respond to a classroom speech.

Sample Speech Evaluation Form

Use the following scale to indicate your reactions to the presentation. Circle the number that best reflects your response to each statement. Please read the items carefully, as some are reverse-coded. Evaluation items are to be rated as follows:

1 = Strongly agree
2 = Somewhat agree
3 = Somewhat disagree
4 = Strongly disagree

Interest

1. I had little interest in this presentation.	1 2 3 4
2. I found this presentation of great interest to me.	1 2 3 4
3. I thought the speaker was interesting to the audience.	1 2 3 4
4. I have no further interest in this topic.	1 2 3 4

Information

1. I do not think the speaker had enough information. 1 2 3 4
2. I think the speaker used varied sources. 1 2 3 4
3. I believe the speaker needed different information. 1 2 3 4
4. I think I am now well informed about the topic. 1 2 3 4

Insight

1. I learned something from the speaker's presentation. 1 2 3 4
2. I did not receive any additional insights. 1 2 3 4
3. I have suggestions for the speaker's progress. 1 2 3 4
4. I have suggestions for the development of this topic. 1 2 3 4

In the space below, act as a coach for this speaker. Provide at least three suggestions for specific changes in behavior this speaker can make to become a more effective presenter.

1. _____

   _____

2. _____

   _____

3. _____

   _____

Application Assignments

1. Go to your university or public library and look up the "Great Speeches on Tape" series. Choose one of the many speeches available and watch it. You might need to watch the speech several times to do a thorough evaluation. Imagine yourself as a speechwriting consultant to this speaker and write a list of coaching guidelines that could have made this speech more effective. In order to do this, you will need to consider the setting and purpose of the speech, the mannerisms and style of the speaker, the nature and beliefs of the audience, and the time frame within which the speech had to be given. The publication *Vital Speeches* can serve as a source of background information to help you with this assignment; also, on-line databases such as *Newsbank* and *ERIC* can provide information about articles mentioning the particular speech at the time it was given.

2. During local political campaigns in your area, go and watch a public press conference or political campaign speech. Take notes on the speaker's performance. Compare this performance to the campaign literature distributed by the candidate, such as direct mail appeals and flyers. Do you see any differences in messages between the oral and written formats? Any similarities? To what would you attribute these differences or similarities? As a political

consultant, could you offer any suggestions for how this candidate should improve his or her oral and written communication?

3. Write a short personal essay on an experience you or someone you know has had as a public speaker. You might reflect on speeches given in other classes; at your fraternity, sorority, or campus organization meetings; or in local political campaigns. Discuss whether the experience was positive or negative, as well as the kinds of responses received. Reflect on the performance. Should anything have been done differently? If so, what elements of the performance could have been improved, and why? Did the people evaluating the performance act as coaches or critics? Should they have acted differently? What suggestions would you offer them?

—Notes—

1. Mnemonics are "word tricks" that help you memorize information. For instance, a piano student with a poor memory might remember the lines of the treble clef by reciting "Every Good Boy Does Fine"—E, G, B, D, F.
2. A note of caution must be offered here. Some public speaking texts suggest that you always begin and end a critique with positive statements to provide reinforcement. This might not necessarily be the most effective strategy for criticism. Dr. Suzette Haden Elgin, an expert in applied psycholinguistics and gender research, has suggested that if male speakers are given positive reinforcement first, they conclude that nothing further needs correction and often fail to listen to the rest of the critique. Perhaps the most effective speech criticism, then, should begin with suggestions for correction and then move to including positive reinforcement for the elements that were successful. For more detail, you can read Dr. Elgin's book *Genderspeak: Men, Women, and the Gentle Art of Verbal Self-Defense* (New York: John Wiley & Sons, 1993).

References

Adier, J., Gegax, T. T., and Hager, M. (1994, July 25). The numbers game. *Newsweek*, pp. 56–58.

Bizzell, P., and Hertzberg, B. (1990). *Rhetorical tradition: Readings from classical times to the present.* Boston: St. Martin's Press.

Bjork, R., and Trapp, R. (1994). Sexual harassment in intercollegiate debate: Introduction. *Argumentation and Advocacy*, 31, 34–35.

Bruschke, J., and Johnson, A. (1994). An analysis of differences in success rates of male and female debaters. *Argumentation and Advocacy*, 30, 162–173.

Cooke, P. A., Klopf, D., and Ishii, S. (1991). Perceptions of world view among Japanese and American university students: A cross-cultural comparison. *Communication Research Reports*, 8, 81–88.

Dean, K. W. (1992). Putting public back into speaking: A challenge for forensics. *Argumentation and Advocacy*, 28, 192–199.

Garrett, M. M. (1993a). Wit, power, and oppositional groups: A case study of 'pure talk.' *Quarterly Journal of Speech*, 79, 303–318.

Garrett, M. M. (1993b). Classical Chinese conceptions of argumentation and persuasion. *Argumentation and Advocacy*, 29, 105–115.

Gates, H. L., Jr., (1990). The signifying monkey and the language of signifyin(g): Rhetorical difference and the orders of meaning. In P. Bizzell and B. Hertzberg (eds.), B. *The rhetorical tradition* (pp. 1193–1223). Boston: Bedford Books.

Gleick, J. (1994, May 30). The doctor's plot. *The New Republic*, pp. 31–32.

Hart, R. D., and Williams, D. E. (1995). Able-bodied instructors and students with physical disabilities: A relationship handicapped by communication. *Communication Education,* 44, 140–154.

Hecht, M. L., Ribeau, S., and Alberts, J. (1989). An Afro-American perspective on interethnic communication. *Communication Monographs,* 56, 385–410.

Hudson, H. H. (1961). The field of rhetoric. In R. F. Howes (Ed.). *Historical studies of rhetoric and rhetoricians.* Ithaca, NY: Cornell University Press.

Jensen, J. V. (1992). Values and practices in Asian argumentation. *Argumentation and Advocacy,* 28, 153–166.

Jones, K. T. (1988, November). Toward a new method of classroom speech evaluation: The small group. Paper presented at the Speech Communication Association, New Orleans, LA.

Miller, C., and Swift, K. (1977). *Words and women: New language in new times.* Garden City, NY: Anchor Books.

Nichols, R. G. (1957, July). Listening is a ten-part skill. *Nation's Business,* 45, 56–58.

Nothstine, W. L., Blair, C., and Copeland, G. A. (1994). Invention in media and rhetorical criticism: A general orientation (pp. 10–12). In *Critical questions: Invention, creativity, and the criticism of discourse and media* (pp. 10–12). New York: St. Martin's Press.

Pearson, J. C. (1979, May). The influence of sex and sexism on the criticism of classroom speeches. Paper presented at the International Communication Association, Philadelphia, PA.

The Rhetoric and Poetics of Aristotle. (1954). W. R. Roberts, (Trans.) and F. Solmsen (Ed.). In P. Bizzel and B. Hertzberg (Eds.). (1990). *The Rhetorical Tradition* (p. 153). Boston: Bedford Books.

Rollman, S. A. (1990, November). Leading class discussions which evaluate students' oral performance. Paper presented at the Speech Communication Association, Chicago, IL.

Ting-Toomey, S. (1985). Toward a theory of conflict and culture. In W. Gudykunst, L. Stewart, and S. Ting-Toomey (Eds.). *Communication, Culture, and Organizational Processes* (pp. 71–86). Beverly Hills: Sage.

Toufexis, A. (1993, August 26). Damned lies and statistics. *Time,* pp. 28–29.

❖ ❖ ❖ ❖

Chapter 17

Dynamics of Small Group Discussion

With Gloria J. Galanes, *Southwest Missouri State University*

Never doubt that a small group of thoughtful, committed people can change the world; indeed it's the only thing that ever has!

—Margaret Mead

Question Outline

I. What is small group communication, and why is it important to understand?

II. What are the two main types of groups?

III. What are some of the elements that help determine a group's culture?

IV. How do gender and race affect small group communication?

V. How do roles and norms develop in a group?

VI. What are three elements that create a group's climate?

Jonetta Johnson wanted to join an African American sorority where she could share experiences with other African American women, give and receive academic support, and participate in service projects focusing on African Americans in her community. The problem was that no such African American sorority existed on her campus. Jonetta invited five of her friends to discuss the *problem, and together they made plans to establish a local chapter of a national African American sorority. First, the women listed all the things that needed to be done to make their dream a reality. They would have to determine whether there were enough women interested to justify proceeding. If so, they would need to write a mission statement, set goals, establish membership criteria, secure approval from campus officials to begin organizing, and contact several national sororities to determine which would best fit their vision. Eventually, they would have do such things as write and pass bylaws, plan rush activities, and decide what to do about housing. Although there were many items on the list, Jonetta didn't feel overwhelmed—she felt excited that so many friends shared her dream. As a group, they would make it happen!*[1]

Understanding Small Group Communication

Although Jonetta's particular experience may not be one you share, you too will find yourself working in groups at some point, if you haven't already. Small groups are essential and unavoidable in modern life, and their importance is growing, in both public and private life. Working together in groups provides certain advantages to working alone. Groups have more information available to work with than individuals do, and several people can accomplish more than one person can. Group members can think of more suggestions, ideas, and alternatives than one person working alone. Also, group members can correct each other's misinformation, flaws in reasoning, and incorrect assumptions. Members are usually more loyal to solutions and decisions reached in groups, and more willing to implement them.

However, whether these advantages are realized or not depends on how well members understand the process of small group communication. Effective participation in small groups does not happen by chance. To help a group achieve its highest potential, you must know how groups operate, especially how *your* behavior affects a group. This chapter introduces you to concepts important for understanding communication in small groups so that your participation in groups will be as effective and rewarding as possible.

Why You Should Learn About Small Groups

Small groups are basic building blocks of our society, especially of organizational life. Families, work groups, support groups, church circles, and study groups are all examples of the ways in which our society is built upon groups. In modern organizations, the higher up you go, the more time you will spend working in groups. For example, one report estimated that executives spend about *half* of their time in business meetings (Cole 1989).

Small groups are important to us for five reasons. These reasons clarify why you will want to learn how to communicate effectively in a small group. First, humans need groups; membership in groups meets needs that we cannot meet for ourselves. William Schutz, a psychologist who studied group interaction, said that humans have needs for inclusion, affection, and control (Schutz 1958). Inclusion suggests that people need to belong to, or be included in, groups with others. As humans, we derive much of our identity, our beliefs about who we are, from the groups to which we belong. Starting with our immediate families and including such important groups as our church, mosque, or synagogue; interest groups; work groups; groups that meet for primarily social reasons—all of these help us define who we are. Affection, another essential need, means that we humans need to love and be loved, to know that we are important to others who value us as unique human beings. Finally, we have a need for power or control over our environment. We are better able to exercise such control if we work together in groups. One person alone cannot build a school, or a bridge, or a new business. However, by working together in groups we *can* accomplish these and other complex tasks. We need others to meet our needs.

✔ Reality Check 17.1 ✔
Oral Communication in the Workplace

What communication skills are important in the workplace? Ann Darling and Deanna Dannals (2003) provided a research report entitled, "Practicing engineers talk about the importance of talk: A report of the role of oral communication in the workplace," in *Communication Education*. They found that practicing engineers felt that small group communication was more likely to occur in the workplace than was public speaking or making presentations.

Second, groups are everywhere. You won't be able to escape working in them. For a moment, list all of the groups to which you currently belong, including informal groups such as study groups or your "lunch bunch." Students typically list between eight and ten groups, but sometimes list as many as twenty or more, and never fewer than two. In corporate America, reliance on groups is even more prevalent and is expected to increase. Although American companies were slow to respond to calls for participatory management, many have discovered how helpful groups can be and have installed groups at *all* levels. For example, General Motors' successes in the 1980s, and more recently with the Saturn subsidiary, can be attributed in part to the involvement of groups at every point in the design, manufacture, and marketing of GM cars (Stroud 1988). No matter what your occupational level, you are likely to find yourself in at least one, but probably several, work groups.

The third reason is related to the second. Because group work is expected to increase in the future, particularly in business and industry, knowing how groups function and the ability to operate effectively in them will be highly valued skills. If you expect to advance in the America of the future, you will have to know how to work in a group. In a recent national survey of 750 leading American companies, 71.4 percent of the respondents mentioned "ability to work in teams" as an essential skill for MBA graduates—more important by far than knowledge of quantitative and statistical techniques (DuBois 1992). William Ouchi (1981), who developed the concept of Theory Z management, said that how well Americans counter Japanese competition will depend on how well we manage our work groups. So, if you plan to advance in your career, or if you just want to get anything done, you must learn how to participate as a member of a team.

Fourth, being an effective group or team member cannot be left to chance. Just because you are placed on a team doesn't mean you know how to

❖ ❖ ❖ ❖   work effectively in that team. As helpful as groups can be to any organization, they often fail because group leaders have not thought through exactly what they want the groups to accomplish, or because group members have not been trained in how to behave appropriately as part of a team (Drucker 1992). Effective participation in a group cannot be taken for granted. Group members need training to understand the dynamics of small group interaction, which is much more complex than dyadic (two-person) interaction.

Group work is essential in business settings. (Photo: Roxbury Publishing Co.)

Finally, groups can be an important way for Americans to participate in the democratic process, and thus have the potential to help us achieve our ideals as a society. Because we can accomplish so much more in groups than we can as individuals, group participation can be an important vehicle through which we participate in creating and governing our society. A lone voice "crying in the wilderness" may have little effect, but a group of people working hard for a cause they believe in can make great changes. For example, in Springfield, Missouri, a recent controversy developed over where to locate a Materials Recovery Facility (MRF) to handle disposal of solid wastes. A task force assembled by the city council recommended construction of the MRF in a relatively undeveloped area north of Springfield. Residents near the proposed site objected, formed a neighborhood coalition to organize opposition to the MRF, distributed petitions, lobbied legislators, and conducted a public relations campaign to stop the MRF. Partly as a result of the coalition's efforts, the MRF proposal has been put on hold indefinitely. Every one of these entities—the city council, the task force, and the neighborhood coalition opposing the MRF—was composed of citizens exercising their right to participate in the democratic process. Every one was a small group trying to control its environment. This human need to contribute to something larger than ourselves cannot be underestimated:

> The basic ingredient cementing social cohesion is not the satisfaction of basic needs, but rather the availability for contribution. What best binds individuals to groups may not be so much the pressure to obtain necessities as the opportunities to give of oneself to something beyond merely self-interested acquisition. (Larkin 1986, p. 37)

People who give money, energy, and other resources live healthier, happier, more fulfilled lives and describe their lives as more meaningful than those who do not (Lawson 1991). Groups facilitate giving because they enable people to participate directly in something greater than self. What better way to do this than through a group?

> ### On the Web
>
> Blogs (Better Listings on Google) have become very popular in a relatively short time. If you do not have a blog, you can create one by going to several different sites, such as Blogger.com or blogspot.com. If you would like to see someone else's blog, go to *http://www.instapundit.com* or *http://www.gawker.com*.
>
> Blogs, also known as web logs, are useful for finding information, for receiving breaking news, and for communicating with others. In what ways are blogs a form of small group communication? In what ways are they not? Could a blog help a small group facilitate a face-to-face discussion?

What Is Small Group Communication?

We define **small group communication** as the interaction of a small group of people to achieve an interdependent goal (Brilhart and Galanes 2001). The various elements of this definition imply several things. First, *small* implies that each member of the group perceives and is aware of the other members of the group and reacts to each as an individual. Thus, *small* refers to members' mutual awareness of each other as individuals, not to absolute size. To illustrate this idea of mutual awareness, a class of twenty-five students may seem large on the first day of school, but may come to seem like a small group by the end of the term. Typically, small groups contain at least three people but may have as many as fifteen (rarely more) members. We arbitrarily eliminate the dyad (two people) because small groups are fundamentally different from dyads. For example, if one member leaves a dyad, the dyad falls apart. However, members often leave small groups, sometimes to be replaced by new members, and the group itself continues. Coalitions may form in small groups, but are not possible in dyads. Clearly, small groups are different from dyads.

Members of a small group *interact* in such a way that each can influence and be influenced by the others. This interaction occurs through communication, which is usually face-to-face, but other channels of communication, such as over a computer network, can qualify. The substance that creates a group and the glue that holds it together is the verbal and nonverbal communication that occurs among members. Even group members who communicate by electronic mail often convey nonverbal signals by using punctuation, such as exclamation points for emphasis or question marks for questions. In a small group, members continually send and receive signals from each other. This constant sending and receiving is relatively spontaneous and impromptu rather than prepared, as for a speech. The work of the group is accomplished through this communicative activity.

Finally, *interdependence* implies that one member cannot achieve the group's goal without the other members achieving it also. For example, it is impossible for one basketball player on a team to win a game while the other members lose. They *all* win or lose together. The success of one member is dependent on the success of all the members. This suggests that cooperation among members must exist. Even though members may disagree, at times vehemently, they must be seeking a joint outcome that will be satisfactory to all.

❖ ❖ ❖ ❖   ## The Role of Communication in the Small Group

The definition of small group communication just presented establishes *communication* as the essential process within a small group. Communication creates a group in the first place, shapes each group in unique ways, and maintains a group. In a way, a group is never fully created, but is always in the process of being created. This concept is known as **structuration,** the process of forming and maintaining a small group through verbal and nonverbal communication that establishes the norms and rules governing members' behaviors. The theory of structuration, developed by Poole, Siebold, and McPhee (1985), is quite complex. However, the main point is this: The *communication among members* is what creates group rules and operating procedures in the first place, and once they are established, communication tends to keep the rules and procedures in place.

As with other forms of human communication, small group communication involves sending verbal and nonverbal signals that are perceived, interpreted, and responded to by other people. Group members pay attention to each other and coordinate their behavior in order to accomplish the group's assignment. Perfect understanding between the person sending the signal and those receiving it is never possible; in a group, members strive to have enough understanding that the group's purpose can be achieved.

Small group communication differs from dyadic interpersonal communication and from public communication in several important ways:

1. *Complexity.* Communication among small group members is more complex than dyadic communication. It is hard enough for one person to tune in to the communicative signals of just one other person, and this process is complicated tremendously by the addition of even one additional person. Add several others, as in the typical five- to eight-person small group, and the process can lead to information overload. For example, in a dyad, one interpersonal relationship is possible, but in a three-person group, three unique relationships are possible. In a five-person group, ten such relationships may exist.

2. *Purpose for communicating.* Humans communicate for many reasons, including for self-expression, persuading, and informing. In dyadic encounters, much communication occurs for the purpose of self-expression. Persuading and informing are important purposes for public communication. While all of these are motives for communication in groups, another important purpose for communicating in groups is to get things done, to accomplish tasks. Members must coordinate their efforts through communication to reach goals. While this can also be a purpose for dyadic communication or for public speaking, it is often a defining purpose for small group communication.

3. *Formality.* Small group communication is more spontaneous and casual than public speaking, which is more formal and pre-planned. In this regard, it is similar to dyadic communication. A public speaker has likely prepared a speech in advance by deciding what topics to address in what order, what evidence to pres-

ent, what arguments to make, and how best to make them. Some shifting to accommodate the unique needs of the audience may occur, but a speech is generally a preplanned event. In small group communication, however, most remarks are made spontaneously. Although group members may decide in advance what topics they want to bring up or mentally rehearse what they want to say about them, usually they do not plan the exact wording. In addition, it is not possible to predict exactly how others in the group will respond. Thus, in contrast to public speaking, it is less possible to foresee the outcome of a small group discussion.

4. *Interchange of speaker/listener roles.* During public communication, the roles of the speaker and the audience members are relatively fixed; the speaker speaks, and the audience listens. Even if the audience interrupts or there is a question-and-answer section following the speech, the speaker generally controls the flow of the discussion. In small group communication, the roles of primary sender and primary receiver alternate frequently. For example, Mohammed makes a suggestion to his fellow group members. His remarks will be short in comparison to most speeches. After he finishes (or maybe even before he's done), Sativa responds verbally and Mohammed becomes the receiver. The roles of sender/receiver shift quickly among members.

5. *Immediacy of feedback.* The example described above implies that in small groups, feedback is immediate, whereas in public speaking situations, feedback is often delayed. A public speaker receives nonverbal feedback from an audience and may sense their approval, disagreement, and so forth, but usually a speaker does not know specific reactions and the reasons behind them. Unless audience members choose to communicate with a speaker immediately after a speech or write a letter wherein they share their reactions, a public speaker may never know exactly what others think. In groups, a speaker often knows what the others think. To return to the previous example, Mohammed gives his suggestion, and Sativa, frowning, says, "I don't think that's going to work at all." Tomas, with a puzzled expression, asks Mohammed to clarify a couple of points, which Mohammed does. Mary Beth leans forward to gain the group's attention and says, "I think Mohammed's idea will work well with two minor changes," and proceeds to modify Mohammed's suggestion to accommodate Sativa's disagreement. Each of these members has given immediate feedback, verbal and nonverbal, to the others.

6. *Creation of outcomes.* Because of the several reasons discussed so far, the speaker is largely responsible for creating the speech and determining its outcome. In a small group, the previous example illustrates that the group members themselves are mutually, equally responsible for creating the group's outcomes. The final outcome is a result of what Mohammed, Sativa, Tomas, and Mary Beth said and did during their group discussion. Thus,

as with dyadic communication, all participants have an equal share and an equal responsibility for what happens.

How Should We Communicate in Groups?

If each of us, as a group member, is responsible for the outcomes of the groups to which we belong, what can we do to help achieve productive outcomes? The ability to speak fluently and with polish is not essential, but the ability to speak clearly is. Just as you should organize your remarks when you give a speech, you will help fellow group members understand you better by organizing your comments during small group discussions.

1. *Relate your statements to preceding remarks.* Public speakers do not always have the opportunity to respond to remarks by others, but small group members do. Your statement should not appear to come out of the blue. Make it clear that your remark is relevant to the topic under discussion by linking it to the immediately preceding remark.

2. *Use conventional word arrangement.* When you speak, you should use conventional sentences so people can understand you better. You have more latitude with written English, where punctuation helps readers follow the thought and readers have time to think about what you write.

3. *Speak concisely.* Don't be long-winded. During a speech, the audience expects the speaker to monopolize the floor, but during a small group discussion, every member wants and deserves a turn.

4. *State one point at a time.* Sometimes this rule is violated appropriately, such as when one group member presents a report to the rest of the group. However, during give-and-take discussion, stating one idea at a time makes it easier for the group to discuss a topic effectively and for other members to respond directly to each topic.

Types of Small Groups

There are two major classifications of groups, depending on the reason the group was formed and the major human needs that it meets. **Primary groups,** such as the family, are usually long-term, and exist to meet our needs for affection (love, esteem). Other examples of primary groups may include your roommates, friends you socialize with regularly, co-workers who regularly share coffee breaks, and other groups principally designed for friendship. Even though primary groups exist mainly to provide love, affection, attention, and support for their members, such groups also have to solve problems and make decisions, although that is not their main goal. The tasks they perform are less important than their primary purpose of providing affection. Primary groups are the main sources of our identity. They also provide personal attention and support for the members, who may chat about a variety of topics, let off steam, and generally enjoy each other. Conversation in primary groups is usually informal and can appear very disorganized. It is often an end in itself rather than the means to an end.

Secondary groups are formed for the purpose of completing tasks, such as solving problems or making decisions. Although secondary groups sometimes meet members' needs for inclusion or affection, their main purpose is to enable members to exercise power and control over their environment and others. In secondary groups, communication is the means to a task-related end. These groups enable people to accomplish more as part of the group than they could as individuals, and they are the backbone of American business, educational, and governmental accomplishment. The various groups involved in the MRF controversy described earlier are examples of secondary groups. Learning how to interact in secondary groups is essential, because so many decisions reached in secondary groups affect our lives, and, unfortunately, all of us have had to suffer the consequences of poor decisions reached in such groups.

You are likely to find yourself involved in many different kinds of secondary groups. For example, most organizations get work done through **committees,** which are small groups that have been given an assignment by either an individual or an organization. Assignments given to committees can range from gathering information and reporting it to formulating policies to carrying out a plan. Typical committees have six to ten members, but sometimes committees can be quite large, up to twenty-five people or even more. Many organizations are actually composed of layers of committees. For instance, the sorority described at the beginning of the chapter eventually developed an executive committee, consisting of the officers who established the sorority's agenda and oversaw the work of the other committees; a membership committee, whose responsibility was to recruit and retain new members; a fund-raising committee; and a service committee, whose members looked for worthwhile service projects for the sorority. Because the sorority was small, one member often belonged to at least two committees. This interlocking committee structure is typical of modern organizations.

In many business organizations, secondary groups such as quality control circles and self-managed work teams have very important functions. A **quality control circle,** sometimes shortened to quality circle, is a small group of employees who meet regularly on company time to recommend improvements to products or to the way work is done. Quality circles were originally developed after World War II by American and Japanese collaboration (Ruch 1984). They took hold readily in Japan, which has a small-group-oriented culture. Japanese industry made extensive use of quality circles to improve the quality of Japanese goods. As a result, a Japanese label represents high quality. Quality circles were slower to be adopted in America, where managers feared they would reduce managers' power, and labor union members feared that they were a ploy to increase production without compensating workers (Lawler and Mohrman 1985). However, in recent years many U.S. companies have used quality circles to improve worker safety, create new products, save production costs, improve current products, and improve the quality of the work environment.

Self-managed work teams, also called *autonomous work groups,* are groups of workers who are given the freedom to manage their own work. For example, an automobile assembly team may be responsible for assembling a car from start to finish, as is done at the Volvo and Saturn plants. Workers are free to select their own team leaders and sometimes to hire and fire their own members. They determine who will do what job, and in what order the work will be completed. Members of self-managed work teams are often cross-trained so that each member can perform several tasks competently. This arrangement gives the team tremendous flexibility to use workers' skills most efficiently. Members of both self-managed work teams and quality control circles are usually more committed to their jobs, believe they are able to use more of their abilities and skills on the job, and believe their work is more personally rewarding than workers who do not belong to such teams.

As you probably can tell, there are no pure primary or secondary groups. Members of primary groups such as families engage in work, make decisions, and must cooperate to complete tasks. Members of secondary groups forge strong personal bonds and provide each other with affection and recognition. In fact, some of the best secondary groups are those with strong primary characteristics, where members feel appreciated and valued. Thus, both primary and secondary groups meet many needs in addition to the ones for which they were initially formed.

Communication and the Development of Group Culture

Culture refers to the patterns of values, beliefs, symbols (including language), norms, and behaviors shared by an identifiable group of individuals. Any group of people with a shared identity may be perceived as belonging to the same culture. For example, a cultural grouping can refer to ethnicity (African American, Latino, German), a professional grouping (college students, communication professors, lawyers, physical therapists), an interest grouping (bowlers, bridge players), or even gender. A grouping that is part of a larger culture but sees itself as distinct from that larger group is termed a **co-culture.** For example, all of the professors at your institution can be considered a cultural grouping of college professors, and the female professors might perceive themselves as a co-culture within that grouping.

Just as large groupings develop cultures, small groups develop their individual cultures as well. Each small group is unique. No two groups develop exactly the same patterns of behavior, norms, and roles—in other words, group culture. In this next section, information is presented about how each group develops its unique group culture, or "personality." Many elements combine to create a group's culture, but the one factor common to all is communication, or what members say and do in the group. Among the elements that contribute to a group's culture are the culture or co-culture from which members come, norms and rules that guide the group's interactions, the roles members enact, the communication networks that form, and the extent to which trust, cohesiveness, and supportiveness are present in the group.

Dimensions of Cultures and Co-Cultures

Cultural rules and behaviors are learned. Cultures and co-cultures often develop specialized or observable communication rules that stem from several broad dimensions on which cultures differ. If you understand and appre-

Celebrating Diversity

Each of us is a unique blend of gender, nationalities, histories, etc. Consider with a small group of people the way you communicate as a result of these features for you. For example, some people in Miami are expressive, jovial, and wear brightly colored clothes. Some people in Nebraska are reserved, polite, and regularly wear dark clothing. Women are frequently more expressive than men. People from the Scandinavian countries are generally quieter than people from Latin America.

Spend some time in the group talking about yourself and have one person record the conclusions. Next, compare the similarities and differences among you. Why do you believe that you are so similar or so different? How do these similarities and differences affect your communication?

ciate such differences, perhaps you can prevent misunderstandings in groups to which you belong. Five such cultural dimensions are worldview, individualism versus collectivism, power distance, uncertainty avoidance, and low versus high context communication.

Worldview encompasses what we believe about the nature of the world around us and our relationship to it. For example, in some cultures, people "go with the flow" because they believe that what happens to them is the result of fate, not their own efforts. In contrast, people in other cultures emphasize change and progress, which they believe depends solely on the efforts of people. Groups from each of these worldview extremes develop cultures markedly different from each other.

Some cultures value individual goals whereas others value group goals. Gudykunst and Ting-Toomey (1988) note that in **individualistic cultures** the development of the individual is more important than development of the group, while in **collectivist cultures** individuals are expected to conform to the group. Communication rules in these cultures will differ. For example, conformity is valued in collectivist cultures, but competition and dissent are more esteemed in individualistic cultures.

Power distance refers to whether status differences among individuals are minimized or maximized (Hofstede 1980). In low power-distance cultures, such as Australia, Israel, and New Zealand, equality is prized, but in high power-distance cultures, such as the Philippines, Mexico, and India, a rigid, hierarchical status system is preferred. In small groups, differences in power distance affect the type of leadership, roles, and norms members prefer. For example, members from high power-distance cultures expect a controlling group leader to whom they will defer and whom they will address by title ("Mr. Chavez"). In contrast, members from low power-distance cultures will treat the leader as an equal and are more likely to use first names.

Uncertainty avoidance refers to how comfortable people are with ambiguity and uncertainty (Hofstede 1980). In high uncertainty-avoidance cultures (e.g., Greece and Japan), ambiguity and unpredictability make people anxious; people prefer clear (even rigid) rules that tell them exactly how to behave. In contrast, people in low uncertainty-avoidance cultures (e.g., Great Britain) have a high tolerance for ambiguity, are more willing to take risks, and have flexible rules about how to behave. Lustig and Koester (1993) suggest that when low and high uncertainty-avoidance individuals are in the same group, they may threaten or frighten each other. High uncertainty-avoidance people perceive low uncertainty-avoidance people as too unconventional, but low uncertainty-avoidance people think high uncertainty-avoidance people are too structured.

Finally, cultures differ on the level of importance they assign to the context or situation when trying to establish meaning (Hall 1976). In a culture with **low-context communication,** such as the United States, the primary meaning of a message is conveyed by the words used. In **high-context communication,** certain features of the situation provide most of the meaning. In other words, in a high-context culture, what is not said may be more important in determining meaning than what is said. In low-context cultures, direct, clear, and unambiguous statements are valued, and the same statement made in a classroom, a dentist's office, or to a close friend means about the same thing, regardless of the situation. In contrast, in high-context cultures such as China, Japan, and Korea, ambiguity is preferred, with several shades of meaning possible, in part because this helps people save face. To understand fully what someone means, you must be able to read subtle cues in the context.

The dimensions discussed above affect the communication rules under which group members operate. Other factors that affect communication rules are members' gender and ethnicity.

Gender and Ethnicity As Co-Cultures

Gender and ethnicity are considered co-cultures. Behaviors appropriate to genders and the various ethnic groups are learned. With little conscious effort we learn to become a female or a male, an African American or a European American, in the same way we learn to become a salesclerk or a Protestant (Ruben 1988). Research findings describing some effects of ethnicity are described below (Pearson, West, and Turner 1995). This information merely scratches the surface, and is presented mainly to heighten your awareness of how much of our behavior is culturally transmitted.

Sex refers to the biological characteristics with which we are born, whereas **gender** refers to learned characteristics associated with masculinity and femininity. Each culture or co-culture establishes "rules" for what is appropriate behavior for males and females. However, these gender rules have changed so much and so fast that past findings may not apply today, and they may not apply to you in particular.

Research about interpersonal communication suggests that males and females have different goals and rules for communicating. Lea Stewart and her colleagues (1990) suggest that male behavior signifies power and status, whereas female behavior conveys subordination. Women display more signs of immediacy (liking) and men more signs of potency (power). Women ask questions to keep a conversation going, but men ask questions for information. Maltz and Borker (1982) note that men and women seem to have different rules about what constitutes friendly conversation, about how to conduct such conversation, and what certain behaviors mean. For women, backchannel responses (i.e., saying things such as "Mm-hmm" and "I hear you" while another is talking) seem to mean "I'm paying attention to you, keep talking," but for men they seem to mean "I agree with you" or "I follow you so far." A male speaker receiving "Mm-hmms" from a woman is likely to believe she agrees with him, but a woman speaker receiving only occasional "Mm-hmms" from a man is likely to believe he is not listening.

In an early summary of research on male-female behavior in small groups, John E. Baird reported that women paid more attention to the relationships among group members, while men were more instrumental, or task-focused (Baird 1986). Recent research suggests differences, also. For example, Lynn Smith-Lovin and Charles Brody (1989) found that women interrupt men and women equally, but men interrupt women more often than they interrupt other men. In all-male groups, men interrupt to support each other, but the more women in the group, the less likely this is to occur. Men seem to consider sex to be a status variable, whereas women do not. Anthony Verdi and Susan Wheelan (1992) suggest that male-female differences are exaggerated. They found that all-male and all-female groups behaved similarly to each other, but mixed-sex groups behaved differently; size seemed to be a more important factor than sex. Although early findings showed that men talked more than women, Edward Mabry (1989) found that women dominated group interaction and that men showed subtle forms of resistance to a dominant presence of women, and Georgia Duerst-Lahti (1990) found that women talked more often, but for shorter periods.

Even though men and women behave similarly, their behavior is perceived differently. For instance, when women speak more tentatively in mixed-sex dyads, they are less influential with other women, but more influential with men (Carii 1990). In a study of trained and untrained mediators, trained males and females behaved the same, but untrained females were more controlling than untrained males. However, the men, trained or not, were *perceived* as more controlling (Burrell, Donohue, and Allen 1988).

Ethnicity is another important factor that affects communication rules and contributes to the development of group culture. Many people have had serious, even lethal, misunderstandings about what a particular communication behavior, performed by someone from another ethnic group, means. This section focuses on some of the communication differences between African Americans and European Americans because misunderstandings between these two cultural groupings have been particularly volatile.

African Americans and European Americans express themselves differently both verbally and nonverbally. Anita Foeman and Gary Pressley (1987) note that African American culture in the United States is an oral culture, with verbal inventiveness and playfulness highly valued. African Americans use the backchannel to indicate interest and involvement in a discussion. Congregation members in African American churches freely call "Amen," "Go ahead," or "That's right," to the minister as they would in a dialogue; such responses are less frequent in most European American churches. During a conflict, an African American manager is more likely to confront the other individual directly, whereas a non-African American manager is more likely to approach the problem indirectly. Consequently, some African Americans perceive European Americans as underreactive, and some European Americans see African Americans as overreactive. Degree of expressiveness differs, also. African Americans are both verbally and physically expressive (e.g., gesturing often), whereas most European Americans focus on verbal responses.

The African American culture is more collective than the European American culture of the United States. According to Foeman and Pressley, African Americans strongly identify with other African Americans *as a group*.

This communal structure helps offset the discrimination and prejudice many African Americans still receive in this culture.

This discussion of how ethnicity and gender affect group culture is not exhaustive. It is designed to increase your awareness that we carry our cultural learning with us, and that our individual cultural rules affect the joint culture we create in small groups. It is also important to remember that both gender roles and cultural rules are learned, and thus subject to change.

Development of Group Norms

The first time members meet as a group, they begin to establish the **norms,** or informal rules, that will eventually guide the members' behaviors. George Homans calls a norm ". . . an idea in the minds of the members of a group, an idea that can be put in the form of a statement specifying what the members . . . should do, ought to do, are expected to do, under given circumstances" (1950, p. 23). At first, the full range of human behavior is available to members. For example, they may greet each other formally by using titles (Ms., Dr., Professor, and so forth) or they may speak informally and use first names. The initial pattern of behavior tends to set the tone for subsequent meetings and to establish the general norms that members will follow. Notice that it is the communication among members that establishes the norms.

Most norms are established tacitly instead of directly. For example, if Sue comes late to a meeting and no one seems bothered, other members may get the message that coming on time to meetings is not necessary. By not saying anything to Sue, the group, without actually thinking about it or formally "deciding" it, has begun to establish a norm that members need not be on time.

The norms in any particular group tend to mirror the norms of the general culture or co-culture in which the group exists. For example, compare a small group of your college friends with a small group of your grandparents' friends. You and your friends use different kinds of language, dress differently, and act differently from the way your grandparents interact with their friends. Differences in age, class, status, physical condition, and so forth between these two co-cultures produce slightly different norms in groups formed from these co-cultures. As Susan Shimanoff stated:

> When group members come together for the first time, they bring with them past experiences and expectations regarding cultural and social rules and rules for specific groups they assume may be similar to this new group; it is out of these experiences and expectations as well as its unique interaction . . . that a particular group formulates its rules. (1992, p. 255)

Norms often develop rapidly, without members consciously realizing what is occurring. They can be inferred by observing what members say and do. For example, behaviors that are repeated regularly (e.g., members always sit in the same seats or always start their meeting with chit-chat irrelevant to the meeting's purpose) provide evidence of a norm operating. In addition, behaviors that are punished (e.g., one group member chastises another by saying, "It's about time you got here," or members look away and seem embarrassed when another member shares highly personal information) often indicate that a norm has been violated.

Members should pay attention to group norms to ensure that the norms are appropriate for what the group must accomplish. For example, sometimes an "overpoliteness" norm becomes established at a group's first meeting because members suppress disagreements or speak tentatively and ambiguously in an effort to be considerate. Later in a group's life, however, this behavior may be inappropriate because members need to challenge each other's thinking and express their opinions clearly. If the "overpoliteness" norm is entrenched, the group may never get around to doing its necessary critical thinking. Members should monitor norms to ensure that they are helpful, not harmful, to the group.

Development of Role Structure

A **role** is a part within a larger, interlocking structure of parts. For example, plays and movies contain interlocking roles, each of which is a different character in the cast. Each character's role must fit within the play or movie structure. The same is true for groups, but whereas in a movie the actor learns lines that are highly scripted, in a small group the "actor" (the group member) creates the role spontaneously, in concert with the other members. Just as an actor plays different roles in different scripts, like Anthony Hopkins as a sadistic murderer in *Silence of the Lambs,* a stiff-upper-lipped servant in *Remains of the Day,* and author C. S. Lewis in *Shadowlands,* individuals enact many diverse roles in the numerous groups to which they belong. For example, your role might be daughter or son, husband or wife in your main primary group; in a group of your best friends you may be the good listener or the comedian; and in yet another group you may be the club treasurer or committee chair. You may be a leader in one group and play a supporting role in another. Whatever someone's role in a given group, that role results from an interplay involving that member's personality, abilities, and communication skills, the talents of the other members, and the needs of the group as a whole.

Roles emerge through the group's interactions. (Photo: Randall Reeder)

Types of Roles

There are two major types of group roles, formal and informal. A **formal role,** sometimes called a *positional role,* is an assigned role based on an individual's position or title within a group. For example, Indira may be her service club's treasurer. As treasurer, she is expected to perform certain duties, such as paying the club's bills, balancing the checkbook, and making regular reports to the club about its financial status. These duties may even be specified in a job description or job manual for the position of treasurer. In addition to the duties mandated for certain positions, we also expect the person in the particular position to behave in certain ways. For example, what do you think Indira's fellow group members expect of her in addition to her assigned duties? Very likely they expect her to be well-organized and to present her report in a clear and concise way without wandering into topics irrelevant to the treasury.

An **informal role,** sometimes called a *behavioral role,* refers to a role that is developed spontaneously within a group. Informal roles strongly reflect members' personality characteristics, habits, and typical ways of interacting within a group. For example, Rich jokes around during fraternity meetings. He refuses to take anything seriously, cracks jokes that interrupt others, and calls members who work hard for the fraternity "overachievers." Rich's constant failure to take the group's job seriously has earned him the informal role of playboy in his group. In contrast, Jeff, one of the "overachievers," constantly reminds members about upcoming deadlines. His fraternity brothers have started calling him the group's timekeeper.

Role Emergence

Informal roles emerge by trial and error through the group's interaction, and are determined largely by the relative performance skills of the rest of the members. For example, well-organized Tamara, who likes structure and order, knows exactly how the group can accomplish its tasks and may try to structure the group's work: "I suggest we first make a list of all the things we need to do to finish our project." If no one else competes for the organizer role, and if the others think Tamara's structuring behavior is helpful to the group, they will reinforce and reward her statements and actions: "OK, Tamara, that sounds like a good idea." This reinforcement, in turn, encourages Tamara to perform more of those structuring behaviors. On the other hand, members may perceive Tamara's attempts to structure the group as pushiness or bossiness and may discourage her: "What's the rush, Tamara, we have lots of time," or "Who died and made you queen, Tamara?" They may collectively support another member as the group's organizer. If Tamara is not supported as the group's organizer, she will search for some other way to be valuable to, and valued by, the group. For instance, she may help to clarify the proposals of the other members ("In other words, are you saying that . . .?") or become the group's critical evaluator ("I think there are two major flaws with that proposal."). This example illustrates a major principle of small group communication: *The role of each group member is worked out by the interaction between the member and the rest of the group* and continues to evolve as the group evolves. Every member needs to have a role that makes a meaningful contribution to the group. If one role doesn't work in a given group, the member will usually try to find another way to participate.

Categories of Behavioral Functions

From these examples, you should be able to see that any particular role comprises a set of behaviors that perform some function for the group. For formal roles, the set of behaviors is often specified in writing; for informal roles, the member performs the set of behaviors so regularly that others begin to expect it. Jeff's fraternity relies heavily on his timekeeping "duties" and would be lost (at least temporarily) if he didn't perform them.

When you observe the particular roles people perform in groups, ask yourself what function is performed by the behaviors that person regularly displays. It is the function, not the behavior itself, that determines someone's role. For instance, Rich's joking would have a positive function if he joked occasionally to relieve tension during an argument, but his constant and inappropriate joking performs the negative function of pulling the group off task. A member's behavior must be interpreted in the context of what else is happening in the group.

A number of classification schemes describe typical functions that behaviors serve in groups. One common scheme classifies behaviors by whether they perform task, maintenance, or self-centered functions. **Task functions** are directly relevant to the group's task and affect the group's output. Their purpose is to focus group members productively on their assignment. **Maintenance functions** focus on the interpersonal relationships among members; they are aimed at supporting cooperative and harmonious relationships. Both task and maintenance functions are considered essential to effective group communication. On the other hand, **self-centered functions** serve the needs of the individual at the expense of the group. The person performing a self-centered behavior implies, "I don't care what the group needs or wants. I want . . ." Self-centered functions manipulate other members for selfish goals that compete with group goals. Examples of statements that perform task, maintenance, and self-centered functions are shown below. For each specific function, a sample statement illustrating the function is provided. The list is not exhaustive; many more functions could be listed.

Task Functions and Statements

Initiating and orienting:	"Let's make a list of what we still need to do."
Information giving:	"Last year, the committee spent $150 on publicity."
Information seeking:	"John, how many campus muggings were reported last year?"
Opinion giving:	"I don't think the cost of parking stickers is the worst parking problem students have."
Clarifying:	"Martina, are you saying that you couldn't support a proposal that increased student fees?"
Elaborating:	"Another thing that Toby's proposal would let us do is . . ."
Evaluating:	"One problem I see with Cindy's idea is . . ."
Summarizing:	"So we've decided that we'll add two sections to the report, and Terrell and Candy will write them."
Coordinating:	"If Carol interviews the mayor by Monday, then Jim and I can prepare a response by Tuesday's meeting."
Consensus testing:	"We seem to be agreed that we prefer the second option."
Recording:	"I think we decided that at our last meeting. Let me check the minutes."

Maintenance (Relationship-Oriented) Functions and Statements

Establishing norms:	"It doesn't help to call each other names. Let's stick to the issues."
Gatekeeping:	"Pat, you look like you want to say something about the proposal."
Supporting:	"I think Tara's point is well made, and we should look at it more closely."
Harmonizing:	"Jared and Sally, I think there are areas where you are in agreement, and I would like to suggest a compromise that might work for you both."
Tension-relieving:	"We're getting tired and cranky. Let's take a 10-minute break."
Dramatizing:	"That reminds me of a story about what happened last year when . . ."
Showing solidarity:	"We've really done good work here!" or "We're all in this together!"

Self-Centered Functions and Statements

Withdrawing:	"Do whatever you want, I don't care," or not speaking at all.
Blocking:	"I don't care if we've already voted, I want to discuss it again!"
Status and recognition seeking:	"I have a lot more expertise than the rest of you, and I think we should do it the way I know works."

These behavioral functions combine to create a member's informal role, which is a comprehensive, generalized picture of how a particular member typically acts in a group.

Networks of Communication

As the role structure develops in a group, so does the **communication network,** which refers to the pattern of message flow (who actually speaks to whom in discussions). The frequency and direction of communication both creates the group's network and maintains it. If Toshio calls the group's first meeting to order, the others may expect him to call all their meetings to order. If Andrea speaks frequently, she may find others looking (literally) to her for some comment on each new issue. Quiet members may find themselves increasingly ignored. The type of network created in a group has an important bearing on group member productivity, cohesiveness, and satisfaction.

Ideally, a small group of peers has an all-channel network, in which all participants are free to comment on a one-to-one basis with all others and with the group as a whole. Members do not need clearance from a central gate-keeping authority to speak; they can contribute while ideas are fresh in their minds without having to wait for someone's O.K.

❖ ❖ ❖ ❖

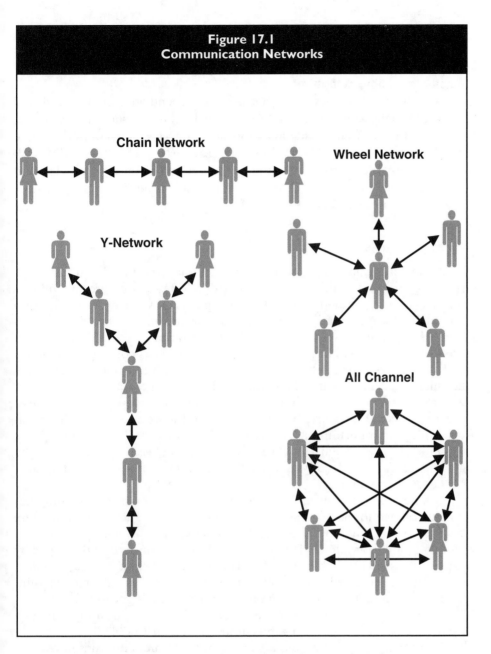

Figure 17.1
Communication Networks

In both the chain and Y networks, each member speaks only to one or two other members. Such networks are typical of hierarchical organizations with strict chains of command. For instance, the president may speak only to the vice-presidents, who speak to the division chiefs, who speak to the department managers, but department managers almost never speak directly to the president. Everyone must follow formal channels.

A wheel network is one where all comments are directed toward one central person (usually the designated leader) who alone has authority to speak to the other members. Sometimes designated leaders inadvertently create wheel networks when they get into the habit of commenting after each person's remarks or constantly restate what the other members say. The person in the center of the wheel can become overloaded with information, which may result in a severe bottleneck for the group. For certain types of tasks, the wheel can be faster than other networks. In the wheel and Y networks, the central members may be satisfied with the communication, but peripheral members usually are not.

Which is the best network? That seems to depend on the type of task and the time available to the group. Centralized networks such as the wheel, chain, and Y are often quicker and more accurate, especially for fairly simple problems, although members are usually less satisfied. The decentralized all-channel network seems to take more time but may in fact be quicker and more accurate for complex problems. It generally produces higher member satisfaction, as well (Shaw 1964).

Group Fantasy

So far, information about the contribution of members' cultural patterns, norms, roles, and networks to the development of a group's uniqueness has been presented. One of the most powerful ways by which a group establishes its individuality is through fantasy. Technically, **fantasy** refers to "the creative and imaginative shared interpretation of events that fulfill a group's psychological or rhetorical need to make sense of their experience and to anticipate their future" (Bormann 1986). Fantasy, in this sense, does not mean fictitious or unreal. It means that during certain periods of the group's interaction, rather than sticking to the group's immediate business, the members tell stories, relate past events, and share anecdotes. These fantasies play an important part in creating the group's unique identity. While the talk of group members during fantasy may seem tangential to the group's real task, it actually may meet important psychological and rhetorical needs of the members.

A fantasy is introduced whenever a group member says something not directly related to the present task of the group. Often, fantasies stop there, but sometimes, other members pick up the story line and elaborate on it in a kind of group storytelling. This is called a **fantasy chain,** first described by Robert Bales (1970). During a fantasy chain, members talk faster and louder, and seem more excited than usual. Fantasy chains may last from half a minute to half an hour, ending when one member gets the group back on task. This group storytelling can be creative and fun; more importantly, it plays a central role in creating the group's culture (Peterson 1987).

The content of a fantasy is called a **fantasy theme.** Fantasies have obvious, or manifest, themes and latent, or below-the-surface, themes that reveal the culture, values, and norms of the group. Often, fantasies have heroes and villains, plot lines, and a well-developed ethical structure that gives moral or psychological guidance to a group. To interpret the latent meaning of a fantasy, Bales suggests looking for a sudden insight rather than trying to analyze the fantasy systematically.

This discussion of group fantasy has been necessarily abstract, but the following example should clarify the concept. In the short fantasy chain below, taken from an actual student group meeting, members of the group are working on their major project for the semester. Mary is taking notes for the group when Louisa comments on her inch-long fingernails.

	Discussion	**Commentary**
Louisa:	Mary, I don't know how you can write anything with those fingernails! Don't they get in your way?	Louisa starts the fantasy chain; commenting about Mary's nails is clearly "off task" behavior.
Mary:	(Laughs) You like those? I had to figure out new ways to do things, but I like them!	
Grady:	Gee, Mary those are dragon lady claws! I'll be staying out of your way!	Grady picks up the chain.
Manny:	That's right, man, that's one lady I don't want to cross!	Manny adds his part.
Mary:	(Still laughing) Oh, you don't have to worry, I'd only use them if you *really* made me mad! (She makes a cat-like swiping motion at Manny and hisses like a cat.)	Mary's comment and behavior captures the playful nature of the fantasy.
Louisa:	That's right, Manny, you better not get on her evil side! You better do everything this lady asks you to do!	Louisa lightly touches on a possible meaning this fantasy may have for the group.
Grady:	You've got fair warning, man. Say "Yes, Ma'am" when she gives you an assignment.	Grady's remark echoes Louisa's comment that Mary is a force to be listened to in the group.

In this segment, Louisa starts out by making an irrelevant comment about Mary's fingernails. After Mary's comment, Grady introduces the "danger" element and Mary participates in expanding the image of herself as a dangerous lady. When the guys talk about not crossing her, she assures them that they don't have to worry—unless they make her *really* angry. Louisa suggests what might make Mary angry (not doing what Mary wants), and Grady brings the group back to the task by mentioning the "assignment" for the project. What function has this fantasy served? The manifest theme of the fantasy is "Mary's long fingernails will be dangerous if she's angry." However, fantasy chains are relevant to the *present* group. In this sequence, the connection between someone not doing an assignment and Mary being angry (and therefore "dangerous") is not a big stretch. The group seems to be establishing some standards for itself ("We will complete assignments") and some penalties for noncompletion ("Mary will be *really* mad!"). This fantasy says something about members' expectations and also, very likely, about Mary's informal role in the group. It helps build up the emerging culture of the group indirectly rather than directly, and humorously rather than seriously.

Group Climate

Another important element that helps shape a group's culture is the **group climate,** which is the emotional tone or atmosphere members create within the group. For example, you have probably attended a group meeting where you could cut the tension with a knife. That atmosphere of tension describes the group's climate. Three factors that contribute heavily to group climate are trust, cohesiveness, and supportiveness.

Trust

Trust means that members believe they can rely on each other. If Joe says he'll have the membership report finished in time for the meeting, other members believe him. When Lorene disagrees with a suggestion, other members know that she's trying to improve the group's output, not trying to back-stab another member. When members trust each other, the group process can work in an ideal way. All members are free to attend to the group's task instead of trying to defend themselves.

Two types of trust are relevant to small group communication. Trust regarding the task means members can count on each other to get things done. A common source of conflict for many groups is having a member who doesn't contribute a fair share of the work, so the others have to pick up the slack. That makes members angry and the climate tense. Interpersonal trust means that members believe the others are operating with the best interests of the group in mind and not from **hidden agendas,** secret motives that place individual needs and wants ahead of the group. When a trusted member disagrees with your suggestion, you usually feel free to explore the problem and are motivated to improve your idea. However, when a member you *don't* trust does the same thing, you may become defensive because you don't believe his or her motive is to help the group. This generally poisons good feelings in the group, tearing the group apart. Not being able to trust other group members is one of the most serious problems that even effective groups face (Larson and LaFasto 1989).

Cohesiveness

Cohesiveness refers to the attachment members feel toward each other and the group. When a group is cohesive, members feel a strong sense of belonging to the group, value their relationships with each other, and consider the group attractive. Cohesive groups look and sound different from noncohesive groups. In cohesive groups, members sit close together and conform to the group's norms. They respond directly to each other and say positive things to and about each other. Cohesive groups seem to converge in using a dominant sensory metaphor (Owen 1985). For example, at first, various members indicate their understanding by saying, "I see," "I hear you," or "I grasp that." Each of these metaphors for "I understand" concentrates on a different sense—sight, sound, touch. In cohesive groups, members tend to use the same sensory metaphor. For instance, if the visual metaphor is "chosen," members convey understanding with "I see," "I've got the picture," and "I've spotted a flaw." This happens below the level of conscious awareness

and indicates that members have influenced each other in subtle but significant ways.

Interestingly, there is more open disagreement in highly cohesive groups,
probably because members trust each other enough to disagree openly on
issues, facts, and ideas. Highly cohesive groups display more characteristics
of primary groups (such as affection and inclusion) than less cohesive groups
(Barker 1991). They have higher rates of interaction. Members are more satisfied with the group and its products. In addition, cohesive groups exert
greater control over member behaviors (Nixon 1979). Cohesive groups cope
more effectively with unusual problems and work better as a team to meet
emergencies. Usually, cohesive groups produce more than noncohesive
groups, but if there is a group norm that supports low production, they may
produce less. One study found that there is an optimum level of cohesiveness
beyond which performance decreases (Kelly and Duran 1985). Whether or
not a cohesive group is productive also depends upon whether members
accept their task. When the members support an organization's goals and are
motivated and enthused about completing the task, they are productive
(Greene 1989). However, highly cohesive groups that are socially oriented
rather than task oriented may end up accomplishing nothing (Wood 1989).

Although there may be problems with highly cohesive groups that are
socially oriented, cohesive groups are very satisfying to their members. In
general, cohesiveness is desirable.

Supportiveness

A **supportive climate** is created when members care about each other
and treat each other with respect (Gibb 1961). Members who are supportive
foster trust and create cohesiveness. In a supportive climate, members feel
safe to express themselves because they believe the others value their opinions. On the other hand, when members judge and attack each other, they create a **defensive climate** in which members feel they must defend themselves
from verbal or psychological attacks. In this case, members spend so much
energy defending themselves that little energy is available for productive and
creative group work. Thus, a defensive climate robs the group of valuable
ideas, energy, and enthusiasm.

Supportive and defensive climates are each created communicatively, by
what members say to each other and how they say it. Examples of defensive
and supportive comments are included below.

Defensive Behaviors and Statements

Evaluation:	Judging another person: "That's a completely ridiculous idea!"
Control:	Dominating or insisting on your own way: "I've decided what we need to do."
Strategy:	Manipulating: "Don't you think you should try it my way?"
Neutrality:	Not caring about how others feel: "It doesn't matter to me what you all decide."
Superiority:	Pulling rank, maximizing status differences: "As group leader, I think we should . . ."
Certainty:	Being a "know-it-all": "You guys are completely off base. I know exactly how to handle this."

Supportive Behaviors and Statements

Description: Describing your own feelings without making those of others wrong: "I prefer the first option because . . ."

Problem orientation: Searching for the best solution without predetermining what that should be: "We want to produce the best results and that may mean some extra time from all of us."

Spontaneity: Reacting honestly and openly: "Wow, that sounds like a great idea!"

Empathy: Showing you care about the other members: "Jan, originally you were skeptical. How comfortable will you be if the group favors that option?"

Equality: Minimizing status differences by treating members as equals: "I don't have all the answers. What do the rest of you think?"

Provisionalism: Expressing opinions tentatively and being open to others' suggestions: "Maybe we should try a different approach . . ."

Being an Ethical Group Member

The term **ethics** refers to the "rules or standards for right conduct or practice . . ." (Random House Dictionary 1987). The unique nature of small groups requires attention to special ethical concerns regarding the treatment of speech, of people, and of information.

The field of communication strongly supports the value of free speech (Arnett 1990), which is directly relevant to small group communication. Many secondary groups are formed because several heads perform better than one, but that advantage will not be realized if group members are unwilling or afraid to speak freely in the group. An important ethical principle for small groups is that group members should be willing to share their unique perspectives and should refrain from saying or doing things that prevent others from speaking freely. Members who are trustworthy and supportive are behaving ethically.

Second, group members must be honest and truthful. In a small group, they should not intentionally deceive one another or manufacture information or evidence to persuade other members to adopt their point of view.

Third, group members must be thorough and unbiased when they evaluate information. Many decisions made in groups, from where to locate an MRF to whether or not it is safe to launch a space shuttle in cold weather, affect people's lives. Such decisions will be only as good as the information on which they are based and the reasoning members use to assess the information. Group members must consider *all* relevant information in an openminded, unbiased way by employing the best critical thinking skills they can; otherwise, tragedies can result.

Finally, group members must behave with integrity. Integrity implies that members are willing to place the good of the group ahead of their own individual goals. Some individuals cannot be team players because they are utterly unable or unwilling to merge their personal agendas with those of the group. Groups are better off without such individuals, who make lousy team members. If you make a commitment to join a group, be the kind of team member who will benefit rather than harm the group. If you cannot in good conscience give a group your support, it is better for you to leave the group than to pretend to support it while sabotaging it.

Summary

In this chapter, you learned how important small groups are to contemporary life and why you should understand the process of small group communication. Groups are important to us because they help us meet needs we cannot meet alone. Groups are everywhere, and their importance is increasing. Groups can help us participate in the democratic process, but we must learn how to communicate effectively in them. Group communication is more complex and typically more task oriented than dyadic communication. Compared to public speaking, group communication is less formal, the speaker/listener roles alternate frequently, feedback is immediate, and all members are jointly responsible for the group's outcomes. Primary groups meet our needs for affection, and secondary groups, such as committees, quality circles, and self-managed work teams, meet our needs for control.

Each group has a unique culture. Contributing to that culture are elements such as the broader culture or co-culture (e.g., gender and ethnicity) to which members belong, the norms and roles members develop, the networks created, the fantasies shared by members, and the group climate. Cultural dimensions affecting a group include worldview, whether a culture emphasizes individualism or collectivism, whether status differences are emphasized or not, how important the situation is in conveying meaning, and the extent to which uncertainty is tolerated. Members' genders and ethnicities affect the group's culture, also. Males and females appear to have different rules for communicating. Males communicate to establish status and show more signs of power, whereas females attempt to establish connection and show more signs of liking. Recent findings do not support earlier findings that men are more task-oriented and women more expressive. Differences seem to exist in how members of various ethnic groups communicate. African Americans are more verbally playful and physically expressive than European Americans, and seem to use the backchannel more often. However, gender and ethnic differences are learned behaviors, and thus subject to change.

Norms and roles are created through interaction among members. Formal roles are associated with specific titles or positions, such as chair or secretary, but informal roles emerge through interaction between a member and the rest of the group. Informal roles are based on members' behaviors and the functions they perform, including task, maintenance, and self-centered functions. Networks are created by members' patterns of interaction; generally, all-channel networks are more productive and satisfying to members than other networks. Group culture also depends on the imaginative shared stories that members mutually create. Finally, culture is affected by group climate—the emotional atmosphere in a group—in particular, whether members can trust each other, are cohesive, and support each other.

This chapter concluded with a discussion of the ethical behavior of group members. Valuable team members are willing to speak in the group and to refrain from doing things that prevent others from speaking freely, are honest, are unbiased and thorough when they evaluate information, and always behave with integrity. Members who are unable to support the actions of a group should leave the group rather than fake support.

Communication Narrative 17.1
Lapse in Leadership Ethics

"Freeloader," "Hitch hiker," "lazy loafer"—all of these labels described Vera, a woman who just could not get her act together. She earned all of these names at work because every time she was asked to serve on a committee, you could be certain that she would do none of the work.

Her fellow sales associates got tired of carrying Vera on every task, so they decided to quit covering for her. When the sales manager asked the sales associates to plan the annual roll-out of new fashions, the sales associates all selected Vera as their leader. Of course Vera, the irresponsible person she was, did nothing as leader of the group. She knew that the others would be too worried about failure to just let the project fail. But this time was different. Everyone, including the bosses, knew that Vera was the designated leader.

On roll-out day the bosses were all seated in a row waiting for the models to appear with the new fashions. Unfortunately, nobody had contacted the models, and even the runway was not set up. Mr. Erols, the top boss, was furious. He blamed the middle managers who blamed the sales associates who blamed Vera. Her name was mud. Nobody would talk to her. And she got a new job on the loading dock where the design apparel was a blue overall with her name stitched on the front.

Vocabulary

co-culture A smaller group that is part of, but sees itself as distinct from, a larger group.

cohesiveness The attachment members feel toward each other and the group.

collectivist culture A culture that believes development of the group is more important than development of the individual.

committees Task-oriented small groups that have been given an assignment by a person or organization.

communication network The pattern of message flow, or who talks to whom.

culture Patterns of values, beliefs, symbols, norms, and behaviors shared by a group of people.

defensive climate An atmosphere of tension in which members feel they have to defend themselves from psychological or verbal attacks.

ethics Standards for right or appropriate conduct.

fantasy Remarks in a group that do not pertain to the here-and-now of the group, but represent creative and imaginative interpretations.

fantasy chain Fantasies to which all (or most) group members contribute to create a kind of group storytelling.

fantasy theme The content, obvious or hidden, of the fantasy.

formal role A part in the group that is based on a member's assigned position or title, such as *leader* or *secretary*.

gender Characteristics of femininity and masculinity that are learned.

group climate The emotional tone or atmosphere that exists within the group.

hidden agendas Secret motives that place individual needs and wants ahead of the group.

high-context communication A culture wherein features of the situation or context, rather than the words used, convey most of the meaning.

individualistic culture A culture that believes development of the individual is more important than development of the group.

informal role A part in the group that is based on a member's individual skills, abilities, and behaviors and how these interact with the abilities and behaviors of the other members.

low-context communication A culture wherein the words rather than the context convey most of the meaning.

maintenance functions Behaviors in a group that focus on improving (maintaining) harmonious interpersonal relationships among members.

norms Informal rules for interaction that are learned.

power distance Whether status differences are minimized or maximized by a culture.

primary group A group whose main purpose is to meet our needs for inclusion and affection, such as a family.

quality control circle A small group of employees who meet on company time to recommend improvements in products and work procedures.

role A particular position in a group that is part of an interlocking structure of other parts.

secondary group A group whose main purpose is completing a task, such as a committee.

self-centered functions Behaviors that serve the individual's needs at the expense of the group.

self-managed work team A group of workers who have freedom to manage their own work, including deciding which member will perform which job in what order.

sex Biological characteristics with which people are born.

small group communication The interaction of a group of people, small enough to be perceptually aware of each other, to achieve an interdependent goal.

structuration The communicative process whereby a group is created and maintained.

supportive climate An atmosphere of openness created by members' mutual respect and caring.

task functions Behaviors in a group that are directly relevant to helping the group complete its assignment.

uncertainty avoidance The extent to which a culture is comfortable with ambiguity or prefers clear rules for communicative behavior.

worldview What a culture believes about the world and humans' relationship to the world.

Application Exercises

1. For the next week, keep a list of every group in which you interact, describe the type of group, and explain what needs are met by each group.

2. Families can be considered co-cultures. Form groups of five or six. Members should share what the communication norms are in their families. It is easier to focus on norms for a specific family activity, such as "dinner in my family" or "celebrating holidays in my family." For example, does each family member have "his" or "her" seat? Is the atmosphere formal or informal? How are guests treated? After each person has shared family norms, members should discuss similarities and especially differences. How do family norms carry over into other situations?

3. Observe either a live or videotaped small group discussion and determine each person's role by describing each person's behavioral functions. List all the behavioral functions described in the chapter along the left side of your paper, and list the members' names across the top, as in the example below:

	Jun	Toyomi	Angela	Shyler
Initiating	——	——	——	——
Information Giving	——	——	——	——
Information Seeking	——	——	——	——
Opinion Giving	——	——	——	——

(and so forth)

Each time someone makes a comment, put a mark in that member's column in the appropriate space. At the end of the observation period, tally all the marks and draw a pie chart for each person showing how that person's remarks were distributed. Based on each person's comments, come up with a role title or name that you think captures the person's contributions to the discussion.

4. Consider the most and least cohesive groups you have ever observed. List as many characteristics as you can recall of each one. In small groups or as a class, develop general principles that are associated with cohesiveness.

Application Assignment

Locate a film that involves significant group activity. *The Breakfast Club* is an ideal film for this assignment. Form groups of five to six students. Watch the film (it is available on video), and select one or more of the following as a topic for a written report:

1. Describe how the group formed initially and how the verbal and nonverbal communication created and maintained the group.

2. Describe the various cultures or co-cultures represented by the group members, how the communication rules in these cultures affected the members' communication within the group, and how the cultures contributed to misunderstandings among members.

3. Describe the norms in the group and explain how you know they are norms.

4. Describe each member's behavioral role in the group, how that member's role developed, and what specific behaviors comprise the role.

5. Describe any fantasies you observe, including who started the fantasy, which members contributed, what the manifest and latent themes were, and what function you think the fantasy served.

6. Describe the climate within the group and how it changed. Include the specific behaviors that helped create the climate, and explain how you think they affected the climate.

—Note—

1. This narrative is based on the actual experiences of an African American undergraduate student at a mid-sized midwestern university. She and her friends formed a Nu Epsilon chapter of Sigma Gamma Rho Sorority, Incorporated. The name of the student has been changed, but she has signed a release allowing us to share her story.

References

Arnett, R. C. (1990, Summer). The practical philosophy of communication ethics and free speech as the foundation for speech communication. *Communication Quarterly, 38*, 208–217.

Baird, J. E. (1986). Sex differences in group communication: A review of relevant research. *Quarterly Journal of Speech, 62*, 179–192.

Bales, R. F. (1970). *Personality and interpersonal behavior.* New York: Holt Rinehart and Winston, Inc.

Barker, D. B. (1991, February). The behavioral analysis of interpersonal intimacy in group development. *Small Group Research, 22*, 76–91.

Bormann, E. G. (1986). Symbolic convergence theory and communication in group decision making. In *Communication and Group Decision Making* (p. 221). In R. Y. Hirokawa and M. S. Poole (Eds.). Newbury Park, CA: Sage Publications.

Brilhart, J. K., and Galanes, G. J. (2001). *Effective group discussion* (10th ed.). Dubuque, IA: Brown & Benchmark.

Burrell, N. A., Donohue, W. A., and Allen, M. (1988). Gender-based perceptual biases in mediation. *Communication Research,* 15, 447–469.

Carii, L. L. (1990). Gender, language, and influence. *Journal of Personality and Social Psychology,* 59, 941–951.

Cole, D. (1989, May). Meetings that make sense. *Psychology Today,* 23, 14.

Drucker, P. (1992). *Managing for the future: The 1990s and beyond.* New York: Truman Talley Books/Dutton.

DuBois, C. C. (1992, September–October). Portrait of the ideal MBA. *The Penn Stater,* p. 31.

Duerst-Lahti, G. (1990, August). But women play the game too: Communication control and influence in administrative decision making. *Administration and Society,* 22, 182–205.

Foeman, A. K., and Pressley, G. (1987). Ethnic culture and corporate culture: Using black styles in organization. *Communication Quarterly,* 35, 293–307.

Gibb, J. R. (1961). Defensive communication. *Journal of Communication,* 11, 141–148.

Greene, C. N. (1989). Cohesion and productivity in work groups. *Small Group Behavior,* 20, 70–86.

Gudykunst, W. B., and Ting-Toomey, S. (1988). *Culture and Interpersonal Communication.* Newbury Park, CA: Sage Publications.

Hall, E. T. (1976). *Beyond Culture.* New York: Doubleday.

Hofstede, G. (1980). *Culture's Consequences: International Differences in Work-Related Values.* Beverly Hills, CA: Sage Publications.

Homans, G. C. (1950). *The human group.* New York: Harcourt Brace Jovanovich.

Kelly, L., and Duran, R. L. (1985). Interaction and performance in small groups: A descriptive report. *International Journal of Small Group Research,* 1, 182–192.

Larkin, T. J. (1986). Humanistic principles for organization management. *Central States Speech Journal,* 37, 37.

Larson, C. E., and LaFasto, F. M. J. (1989). *TeamWork: What Must Go Right/What Can Go Wrong.* Newbury Park, CA: Sage Publications.

Lawler, E., and Mohrman, S. (1985, January–February). Quality circles after the fad. *Harvard Business Review,* pp. 65–71.

Lawson, D. M. (1991). *Give to Live: How Giving Can Change Your Life.* LaJolla, CA: ALTI Publishing.

Lustig, M. W., and Koester, J. (1993). *Intercultural Competence: Interpersonal Communication Across Cultures.* New York: HarperCollins Publishers.

Mabry, E. A. (1989). Some theoretical implications of female and male interaction in unstructured small groups. *Small Group Behavior,* 20, 536–550.

Maltz, D. N., and Borker, R. A. (1982). A cultural approach to male-female miscommunication. In J. J. Gumperz (Ed.). *Language and Social Identity* (pp. 195–216). Cambridge: Cambridge University Press).

Nixon, H. L. (1979). *The small group.* Englewood Cliffs, NJ: Prentice-Hall.

Ouchi, W. (1981). *Theory Z: How American Business Can Meet the Japanese Challenge.* Reading, MA: Addison-Wesley.

Owen, W. F. (1985). Metaphor analysis of cohesiveness in small discussion groups. *Small Group Behavior,* 16, 415–426.

Pearson, J. C., West, R. L., and Turner, L. H. (1995). *Gender and Communication* (3rd ed.). Dubuque, IA: Wm. C. Brown Publishers.

Peterson, E. E. (1987). The stories of pregnancy: On interpretation of small-group cultures. *Communication Quarterly,* 35, 39–47.

Poole, M. S., Siebold, D. R., and McPhee, R. D. (1985). Group decision-making as a structurational process. *Quarterly Journal of Speech,* 71, 74–102.

The Random House Dictionary of the English Language (2nd ed.) (1987). New York: Random House.

Ruben, B. D. (1988). *Communication and Human Behavior* (2nd ed.). New York: Macmillan Publishing Company.

Ruch, W. V. (1984). *Corporate Communications: A Comparison of Japanese and American Practices.* Westport, CT: Quorum Books.

Schutz, W. (1958). *FIRO: A Three-Dimensional Theory of Interpersonal Behavior.* New York: Rinehart.

Shaw, M. (1964). Communication networks. In L. Berkowitz (Ed.). *Advances in Experimental Social Psychology,* vol. 1, (pp. 111–147). New York: Academic Press.

Shimanoff, S. B. (1992). Coordinating group interaction via communication rules. In R. S. Cathcart and L. A. Samovar (Eds.) *Small Group Communication: A Reader* (6th ed.) (p. 255). Dubuque, IA: Wm. C. Brown Publishers.

Smith-Lovin, L., and Brody, C. (1989, June). Interruptions in group discussions: The effects of gender and group composition. *American Sociological Review,* 54, 424–435.

Stewart, L. P., Stewart, A. D., Friedley, S. A., and Cooper, P. J. (1990). *Communication Between the Sexes: Sex Differences and Sex Role Stereotypes* (2nd ed.). Scottsdale, AZ: Gorsuch Scarisbrick, Publishers.

Stroud, L. (1988, November 15). No CEO is an island. *American Way,* pp. 94–97, 140–141.

Verdi, A. F., and Wheelan, S. A. (1992, August). Developmental patterns in same-sex and mixed-sex groups. *Small Group Research,* 23, 356–378.

Wood, C. J. (1989). Challenging the assumptions underlying the use of participatory decision-making strategies: A longitudinal case study. *Small Group Behavior,* 20, 428–448.

❖ ❖ ❖ ❖

Index